corporate responsibility

corporate responsibility

a critical introduction

MICHAEL BLOWFIELD &

ALAN MURRAY

OXFORD
UNIVERSITY PRESS

Great Clarendon Street, Oxford OX2 6DP

Oxford University Press is a department of the University of Oxford.
It furthers the University's objective of excellence in research, scholarship,
and education by publishing worldwide in

Oxford New York

Auckland Cape Town Dar es Salaam Hong Kong Karachi
Kuala Lumpur Madrid Melbourne Mexico City Nairobi
New Delhi Shanghai Taipei Toronto

With offices in

Argentina Austria Brazil Chile Czech Republic France Greece
Guatemala Hungary Italy Japan Poland Portugal Singapore
South Korea Switzerland Thailand Turkey Ukraine Vietnam

Oxford is a registered trade mark of Oxford University Press
in the UK and in certain other countries

Published in the United States
by Oxford University Press Inc., New York

British Library Cataloguing in Publication Data

Data available

Library of Congress Cataloging in Publication Data

Blowfield, Mick.
Corporate responsibility: a critical introduction / Michael Blowfield & Alan Murray.
    p. cm
ISBN-13: 978–0–19–920909–5
1. Social responsibility of business. I. Murray, Alan. II. Title.
HD60.B59 2008
658.4'08–dc22
2007050160

Typeset by Graphicraft Limited, Hong Kong
Printed in Italy by Legoprint S.p.A.
on acid-free paper by Ashford Colour Press Ltd., Gosport, Hampshire

ISBN 978–0–19–920909–5

10 9 8 7 6 5 4 3 2 1

■ PREFACE

The subject of 'corporate responsibility' is at a stage at which it needs a text that introduces the key ideas and practices in the field, and places them in wider contexts. Neurologists talk of 'proprioception'—the body's sense of its own position in relation to the surrounding world—under which a deficit can result in a person leaning at an angle, but thinking he or she is standing straight. Corporate responsibility, at times, suffers from a proprioception deficit, under which its reality can be skewed by people's enthusiasm, ignorance, or scepticism. Our introduction to corporate responsibility is, therefore, critical in that it presents different perspectives on both theory and practice.

The book is intended for students and tutors of corporate responsibility at both undergraduate and graduate levels, although it is also relevant to other disciplines that are concerned with the role of business in modern society. The text provides a strong framework for studying corporate responsibility, which links a wealth of theoretical analysis with more practitioner-oriented materials. Its 14 chapters are divided into three broad themes: the origins and meaning of corporate responsibility; how it is being managed and implemented; its impact to date and likely future directions. Under these themes, we examine such topics as: the social and historical context of corporate responsibility, and its business case; key areas of management practice, including stakeholder engagement, partnership, ethical supply chains, social auditing, and corporate governance; the role of responsible investment, as well as that of government and civil society.

Michael Blowfield
Alan Murray

■ ACKNOWLEDGEMENTS

This book reflects our experiences as academics, practitioners, and consultants working in the field of corporate responsibility for companies, civil societies, and government organizations. I am grateful to the many friends and colleagues who have knowingly, or unknowingly, contributed to that experience. It would be unfair to single out anyone in particular, but this in no way diminishes my accumulated gratitude over the years, and I trust that those involved will understand why the only people mentioned by name are John MacLean, Catherine, Ieuan, Lucy, and Terry.

MEB

I would like to acknowledge the work of the Centre for Social and Environmental Accounting Research at the University of St Andrews—particularly the efforts of Rob and Sue Gray, and all of the researchers who have attended the annual summer schools over the last decade or so, whose scholarship and rigour has helped to develop and inform my views and opinions. I would also like to acknowledge the love of Kathryn, Rosie, Ellie, and Florence in supporting me in this endeavour.

AM

We would like to express our sincere thanks to Kimberly Ochs, who wrote the chapter on socially responsible investment and who brought to that chapter a depth of knowledge that neither of us could have offered. We are also grateful to the anonymous reviewers whose comments have added immensely to the text, and to the Center for Corporate Citizenship at Boston College, CANOPUS, and the Ethical Trading Initiative, each of which has granted permission to use some of their materials.

■ CONTENTS

■ LIST OF FIGURES

■ LIST OF BOXES

■ LIST OF CASE STUDIES

■ LIST OF ABBREVIATIONS

ACCA	Association of Chartered Certified Accountants
BAU	business-as-usual
BCCI	Bank of Credit and Commerce International
BITC	Business in the Community
BSE	bovine spongiform encephalopathy
BSR	Business for Social Responsibility
CCAB	Consultative Committee of Accountancy Bodies
CEO	chief executive officer
CERES	Coalition for Environmentally Responsible Economies
CFA	chartered financial analyst
CPI	University of Cambridge Programme for Industry
CSEAR	Centre for Social and Environmental Accounting Research
CSP	corporate social performance
CSR	corporate social responsibility
EAI	Enhanced Analytics Initiative
EBITDA	earnings before interest, taxes, depreciation, and amortization
EIL	Environmental Impairment Liability Centre for Competence
EIRIS	Ethical Investment Research Service
EPA	Environmental Protection Agency
EPZ	export processing zone
ESG	environmental, social, and governance
ETF	Exchange Traded Fund
ETI	Ethical Trading Initiative
EU	European Union
EurepGAP	European Retailers Group Guidelines on Good Agricultural Practice
EuroSIF	European Sustainable and Responsible Investment Forum
FDI	foreign direct investment
FLA	Fair Labor Association
FRC	Financial Reporting Council
FSC	Forest Stewardship Council
GAAP	Generally Accepted Accounting Principles
GEMI	Global Environmental Management Initiative
GRI	Global Reporting Initiative
IBLF	International Business Leaders' Forum
ILO	International Labour Organization
IMF	infant milk formula
IPCC	United Nations Intergovernmental Panel on Climate Change
ISC	Institutional Shareholders' Committee
ISO	International Organization for Standardization

LEAF	Linking Environment and Farming
LSE	London Stock Exchange
MDG	Millennium Development Goal
MFA	Multi-fibre Agreement
MIC	methyl isocyanate
MIMCO	Mattel Independent Monitoring Council for Global Manufacturing Principles
MSC	Marine Stewardship Council
NGO	non-government organization
NPV	Net present value
OECD	Organisation for Economic Co-operation and Development
OFR	Operating and Financial Review
ONS	Office for National Statistics
PETA	People for the Ethical Treatment of Animals
PPP	public–private sector partnership
PRI	United Nations Principles for Responsible Investing
RAN	Rainforest Action Network
ROSPA	Roundtable on Sustainable Palm Oil
SAI	Social Accountability International
SCP	sustainable consumption and production
SIF	Social Investment Forum
SME	small and medium-sized enterprise
SRI	socially responsible investing/investment
SSE	social stock exchange
UN	United Nations
UNCED	United Nations Conference on Environment and Development
UNEP	United Nations Environment Programme
UNFCC	United Nations Framework Convention on Climate Change
UNGC	United Nations Global Compact
UNRISD	United Nations Research Institute for Social Development
VBLI	Vietnam Business Links Initiative
WBCSD	Word Business Council for Sustainable Development
WCED	World Commission on Economic Development
WEF	World Economic Forum
WMO	World Meteorological Organization
WRAP	Worldwide Responsible Apparel Production
WRI	World Resources Institute
WTO	World Trade Organization

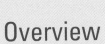

Introduction

Overview

This chapter introduces the book to its users. In particular, we explain:

- the significance of a new introduction to corporate responsibility;
- differences between the discipline and the practice of corporate responsibility;
- how the book is structured;
- the content of the book and the Online Resource Centre.

The right time to examine corporate responsibility

The price of greatness is responsibility.

(Winston Churchill)

Action springs not from thought, but from a readiness for responsibility.

(Dietrich Bonheoffer)

To gain a good reputation, endeavour to be what you desire to appear.

(Socrates)

A colleague once said that to alienate your audience, begin with a quote from Socrates—but central to this book has been our ignoring good advice whenever possible. That advice has included that corporate responsibility is a fad and thus has no place in business schools or elsewhere in higher education; that it is a pseudo-discipline, lacking analytical rigour, and therefore should simply be absorbed into other disciplines, rather than be treated as a subject in its own right; that it is too new and fragile, yet too crucial to the future of the modern corporation, to risk its being damaged by a discussion of its weaknesses instead of only praising its strengths.

It is certainly true that cynics, detractors, and cheerleaders are all participants in the corporate responsibility debate, but, over time, each group has had to add more nuance and sophistication to its arguments. In many ways, the fact that there is now a multifaceted debate suggests that a critical overview of corporate responsibility is neither a distraction nor an irrelevance, but an essential step in the maturation of the field.

There is the risk, however, that in such a swiftly moving field, this book will seem outdated as soon as it is published, that this initiative or that publication will not be included, and that too much attention will be paid to 'old news'. Such comments are especially pertinent in a book that intends to provide a critical overview of the field, because supporters of corporate responsibility as a movement have frequently rebuffed criticisms by saying they will be addressed the next time around. Linking the text edition with the Online Resource Centre helps us to overcome this. But, more importantly, we believe that corporate responsibility is now at a stage at which changes and developments are occurring within the context of a stable orthodoxy that is able to explain both existing and future initiatives or innovations. This book builds on that orthodoxy to provide a framework for discussing corporate responsibility and, although in the later chapters we discuss the kind of shifts that might challenge this orthodoxy, there is little indication that the framework we have used will become irrelevant in the foreseeable future.

Ways of examining corporate responsibility—field, discipline, and practice

There is no single definition of corporate responsibility and, in Chapter 1, we discuss the array of issues to which people can refer when they use the term. But before we consider such matters as whether 'corporate responsibility' is different to 'corporate citizenship', the distinctions between 'corporate responsibility' and 'business ethics', or how 'eco-efficiency' relates to animal rights, it is useful to consider the quite different starting points that inform any discussion about the field.

Corporate responsibility is often used as if it were a subject or an actor, in sentences such as '*corporate responsibility benefits disadvantaged workers in developing countries*', or '*corporate responsibility is a distraction for corporate managers*'. Often, this is shorthand for the array of issues or approaches bundled together beneath a 'corporate responsibility' umbrella and it can mask important distinctions. For some, corporate responsibility is an academic discipline, i.e. a coherent body of knowledge addressing a central theme. Its focus is the relationship between business and wider society, and how that can be managed. This discipline is informing business practice, and also the debate about corporate and public governance, giving it an importance outside business management. Within the discipline, there are particular subject areas, such as management practice, governance and accountability, ethics, and strategy, and these significantly influence what is emphasized in a particular discussion.

Corporate responsibility can also be presented as a management approach: a technical, instrumental response to the business environment. Thus, for example, one finds guidelines, consultancy services, and case studies of best practice on managing social issues in supply chains, conducting environmental and human rights impact assessments, and compiling corporate responsibility reports. Although these approaches are sometimes studied by academics from the corporate responsibility discipline and there is a degree of overlap with the subject area of corporate responsibility as management practice, when corporate responsibility is discussed as a management approach, its content and focus are quite different to those that emerge when the field is addressed as an academic discipline. Corporate responsibility as management approach is dominated by practitioners, and there can be tension between these practitioners and the academics: the former focusing on the application of ideas; the latter on the rigour of academic enquiry.

In this book, we treat corporate responsibility as a field that includes both the academic and practitioner perspectives. The emphasis changes according to what we are discussing: for example, our examination of the historical origins of corporate responsibility is inevitably theoretical, drawing on the insights of various academic disciplines (Chapter 2), while in describing how standards are used to manage corporate responsibility, we pay more attention to practice. Irrespective of whether we are dealing with theory or practice, however, our aim is to apply objective analysis that not only sets out an array of perspectives, but also provides a critical commentary on those perspectives. Thus, for example, we not only explain corporate responsibility theory, but also place it in its historical context; similarly, we do not only describe stakeholder partnerships, but also explore the underlying concept of the stakeholder, and the strengths and weaknesses of the partnership approach.

In offering this critical perspective, we draw on different disciplines. Likewise, although corporate responsibility is especially relevant for students of management, we recognize that other disciplines are interested in the field, including, for example, those involved in international development, political economy, sociology, and others who want to understand the role of business in contemporary society. Therefore, in discussing corporate responsibility, we have tried to make our examination relevant beyond the business world.

Structure

The book is divided into three broad themes, as follows.

1 The meaning and origins of corporate responsibility (Chapters 1–3).

2 Managing and implementing corporate responsibility (Chapters 4–11).

3 The impact, critics, and future of corporate responsibility (Chapters 12–14).

Part 1—The meaning and origins of corporate responsibility

In the first part of the text, we present a framework for understanding what is meant by 'corporate responsibility' and the scope of the issues involved (Chapter 1). We offer a historical overview of corporate responsibility, going back to the early days of capitalism and examining how notions of responsibility have changed from the early Industrial Revolution, to the mid-twentieth-century welfare state and New Deal, to the more recent era of globalization (Chapter 2). Indeed, globalization is so significant to both the theory and practice of corporate responsibility that it warrants a chapter of its own (Chapter 3).

Part 2—Managing and implementing corporate responsibility

In the second part of the text, we introduce the main approaches to managing corporate responsibility, and the variables that affect what companies and industries do (Chapter 4). The business case for corporate responsibility is discussed, including the evidence that corporate responsibility affects business performance, and we consider the significance of a focus on business performance indicators to the way in which corporate responsibility is practised (Chapter 5).

We provide a detailed discussion of the theory and practice behind two important aspects of corporate responsibility management—stakeholders and standards (Chapter 6). The use of social auditing, verification, reporting, and new models of accountability is examined (Chapter 7), as is the relevance of changing notions of corporate governance in a corporate responsibility context (Chapter 8).

Reflecting the importance of environmental issues in contemporary corporate responsibility, we discuss sustainable development as an approach to private sector management (Chapter 9). We also explore how partnerships with stakeholders from different sectors are used as a management approach (Chapter 10) and how responsible investment has emerged as a means whereby investors can exert influence on the non-financial performance of companies (Chapter 11).

Part 3—The impact, critics, and future of corporate responsibility

The tangible consequences of corporate responsibility for both society and business are examined from a variety of angles (Chapter 12), and, based partly on what is known about the impact of corporate responsibility, we present different critiques of the field, including economic, political, and social perspectives (Chapter 13). The final chapter discusses emerging trends and the different directions that corporate responsibility might take in the future (Chapter 14).

Using the book and related resources

This book and the resources on the Online Resource Centre provide a comprehensive introduction to corporate responsibility for students and teachers. The book has been written so that it can be used either as the core reference for courses on corporate responsibility, or as a source of materials on particular dimensions of the field for individual modules. Chapters are self-contained and can be used as a teaching resource in any order that the user may wish. The book can also be used as a standalone reader for anyone looking for an introduction to the field and chapters are cross-referenced accordingly.

The chapters share the following common structure and format:

1 narrative discussion of the chapter's subject, broken into sections;
2 figures, boxes, and tables;
3 five case studies, focusing on real-world corporate responsibility experiences, and accompanied by questions on issues raised;
4 a summary of the chapter's contents;
5 an annotated list of key further reading;
6 discussion points, relating to important issues raised in the chapter, for use as class exercises and/or as individual or group assignments.

The following additional aids are at the rear of the book:

1 an appendix featuring key newsletter, journal and web resources cited in the book;
2 a glossary of key terms;
3 a bibliography of all references used in the book;
4 an index of authors and sources cited in the book;
5 an index of topics and themes.

Online Resource Centre (ORC)

Supplementary resources for each chapter are available on the accompanying Online Resource Centre. The ORC features separate areas for students and tutors, and contains the following elements.

1 **Student area**
   - Additional references to publications, other websites, and other resources.
   - Links to corporate responsibility organizations.
   - Information on important new legislation and guidelines affecting the field.
   - Suggested films that deal with issues relevant to corporate responsibility managers.

2 Tutor area

- Additional and more extensive company case studies.
- Suggested essay and discussion questions for use in the classroom or for assignments.

Please note that while some materials will be downloadable from the Online Resource Centre, for copyright reasons, the ORC may feature only links to where other web-based materials can be found.

The Online Resource Centre can be accessed at **http://www.oxfordtextbooks.co.uk/ orc/blowfield_murray/**

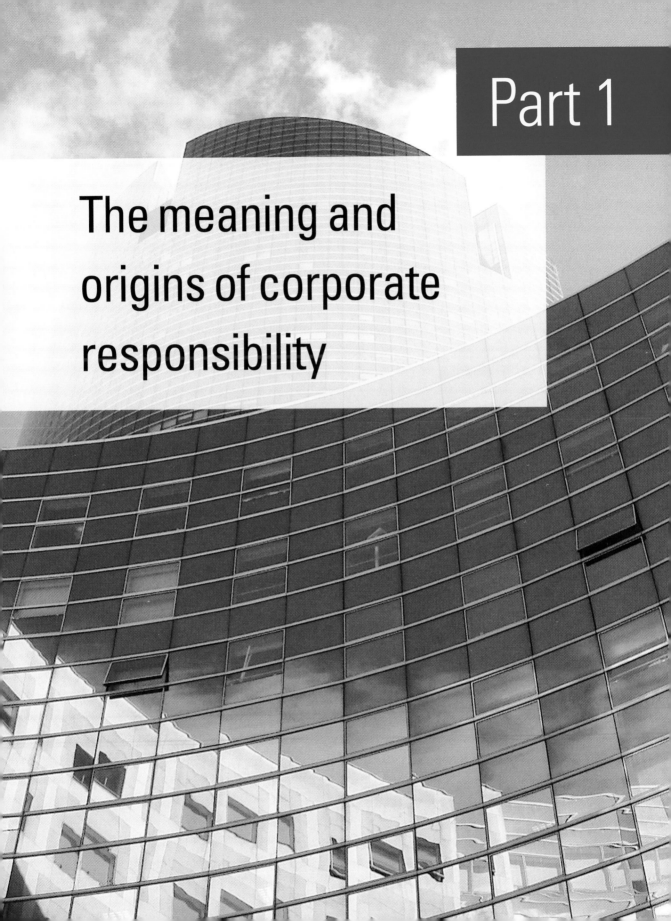

Part 1

The meaning and origins of corporate responsibility

1

Introducing corporate responsibility

Chapter overview

In this chapter, we introduce the idea of corporate responsibility: its concerns, its meanings, and why it has become a significant part of the business agenda. In particular, we will:

- set out the context within which contemporary corporate responsibility has flourished;

- examine the different definitions of corporate responsibility and what they have in common;

- discuss the values that companies are being asked to uphold;

- explore the elements of business' relationship with wider society;

- provide a typology of the main issues with which contemporary corporate responsibility is wrestling.

Main topics

■ **Key terms**

Business and society

Business ethics

Corporate governance

Corruption

Rights

Sustainability

■ **Online resources**

- Additional case studies about the approaches of individual companies to corporate responsibility

- Exercises and discussion topics for students

- Case studies on specific corporate responsibility issues, such as corruption and sustainability

- Links to other web-based resources

Why corporate responsibility?

Eighty-one per cent of executives said, in a 2005 poll, that corporate responsibility is essential to their business. They disagree about what exactly 'corporate responsibility' means, but the majority believe that business should serve as a steward in society, and that it has a duty to investors, employees, consumers, communities, and the environment.[1] These views were shared by executives from small, medium, and large-sized enterprises, and reflect a trend that sees more and more companies publicly reporting on their social and environmental performance.

We live in a world in which the richest 20 per cent of people possess 86 per cent of gross national product, in which one country accounts for 23 per cent of worldwide energy consumption, and in which the USA and Europe account for 65 per cent of annual wealth creation.[2] We live in a world in which prosperity is measured in terms of economic growth, made possible through greater productivity and production. With the drive for growth comes greater demand for natural resources and the quest for lower cost production in what was once called the Third World. Great store is put into the new economy of ideas, creativity, and innovation, within which a prerequisite for being competitive is being able to participate in a virtual global network, and which brings with it new patterns of employment, social interaction, and investment, as well as new threats to national and personal security.

This shifting world brings prosperity for some and change for many. New economic powerhouses are emerging, although the distribution of wealth within, and between, countries is often highly unequal. The capacity not only to manufacture, but also to research and develop, is being dispersed more widely around the world, even if the vast majority of patents still originate in a handful of established industrial economies, such as Japan, the USA, and Germany. Out of this, different levels of conflict arise, such as those between the affluent and the poor, between short-run gains and long-term success, between senior managers and the rest of a company's stakeholders, and between the interests of companies and nations.[3]

In the midst of this world, business is being ascribed roles and a significance that had never previously been imagined. The private sector creates wealth, generates employment, utilizes natural resources, and attracts investment at unprecedented levels. Consumption plays a pivotal role in our social lives and in our personal identities. Brands have a significance that is not dissimilar to that of religion and ideology in previous eras. Companies play important roles in public policy, not least in countries where the standard of governance is low, or in situations in which international governance mechanisms are inadequate.

In today's world, widespread business failure is unthinkable, because we seem increasingly less able to imagine an alternative to the free enterprise economy. Yet individual companies do find themselves under social, as well as competitive, pressure. They are subjected to new levels of transparency, whether in terms of the demands that the largest stock markets make for greater disclosure and changes to corporate governance, or in terms of public outcry on issues as diverse as environmental pollution, consumer rights, child labour, corruption, and support for military regimes. Adverse disclosure threatens shareholder confidence, brand reputation, production stability, employee trust, and other corporate assets, both tangible and intangible.

What is more, the conditions that leave companies open to charges of irresponsibility, when looked at differently, can become business opportunities. Public opinion is becoming less tolerant of corporate excess and malfeasance, but there are also increasing expectations that business will come up with solutions to some of the twenty-first century's main social and environmental challenges, such as water accessibility, global warming, and affordable health care. These are the twin hemispheres that corporate responsibility is charged to embrace: on the one hand, it must deal with what Baker (2005) calls 'capitalism's Achilles heel', within which capital, poverty, and inequality are intertwined; on the other, it must promote capitalism as a solution to the key social and environmental issues of the age.

Definitions of corporate responsibility

The above is the context within which corporate responsibility has come to the fore—but what does the term itself actually mean? There never has been a straightforward answer to this, and growing interest in the field—whether from companies, governments, the general public, or civil society organizations—has only served to extend the array of definitions.

Long before there was a name for corporate responsibility, there were ideas about what it meant for business to make a positive contribution to the rest of society. Carnegie, Cadbury, and Lever were among the many individuals who utilized company assets to improve the conditions of nineteenth-century workers. Throughout the twentieth century, companies such as Norsk Hydro would take responsibility for social conditions in their, often isolated, company towns; many logging, mining, plantation, and oil operations throughout the world set up housing schools, clinics, and other social amenities. Just as importantly, many more were criticized for failing to take on such responsibilities.[4]

The positive and the negative impacts that business had on society generated public, political, and academic debate. While it was quite clear that business sought a profit from providing goods and services in response to society's demands, it was much less obvious what constraints should be put on its activities and who should impose them. Was all profit legitimate? Was all profit legitimate, provided that the company stayed within the law? What was a fair distribution of the wealth business created between shareholders, employees, and wider society? Should companies give part of their wealth back to the communities within which they operated? Could markets be relied upon to set a fair price, whether for labour, products, or natural resources? Could governments reliably decide what was in the public interest?

Questions such as these gave rise to different notions of corporate responsibility. The field called 'corporate social responsibility' (CSR) began with a focus on the role of business leaders: particularly, on how they managed their companies with a view to society and how they gave back to their local communities. In the 1950s, the focus of CSR shifted to the behaviour of companies rather than that of individuals. This generated a fair degree of academic debate about what companies should be responsible for; it also spawned the concepts of 'corporate social responsiveness' and then 'corporate social performance', which, in the 1980s, put less stress on the philosophical meaning of responsibility and more on the role of the organization in acting responsibly.

Other terms were also introduced. 'Corporate sustainability', for example, was used in the 1990s to emphasize how environmental concerns were increasingly an area in which companies were expected to exhibit responsibility. More recently still, 'corporate citizenship' (originally used to refer to the types of corporate philanthropy common in the USA) has been used as a development of CSR that emphasizes the role of business as a citizen in global society and its function in delivering the citizenship rights of individuals.[5]

Changes in the focus of corporate responsibility inevitably affect the way it is defined. For Davis (1973), corporate responsibility begins where the law ends. In other words, it is about what companies do with regards to making a positive contribution to society above

Box 1.1 Definitions of corporate responsibility

A responsible company is one that listens to its stakeholders and responds with honesty to their concerns.

Starbucks, CSR Report, 2004

CSR commits us to operate in a socially responsible way everywhere we do business, fairly balancing the needs and concerns of our various stakeholders—all those who impact, are impacted by, or have a legitimate interest in the Company's actions and performance.

Chiquita, **www.chiquita.com**, accessed 24 March 2004

CSR [is] the proposition that companies are responsible not only for maximising profits, but also for recognising the needs of such stakeholders as employees, customers, demographic groups and even the regions they serve.

PricewaterhouseCoopers, **www.pwcglobal.com**, accessed 24 March 2004

CSR is the continuing commitment by business to behave ethically and contribute to economic development while improving the quality of life of the workforce and their families as well as of the local community and society at large.

Lord Holme, former executive director of Rio Tinto, and Philip Watts, former chair of Royal Dutch Shell

CSR requires companies to acknowledge that they should be publicly accountable not only for their financial performance but also for their social and environmental record. . . . CSR encompasses the extent to which companies should promote human rights, democracy, community improvement and sustainable development objectives throughout the world.

Confederation of British Industry, 2001

[CSR is] a concept whereby companies integrate social and environmental concerns in their business operations and in their interactions with their stakeholders on a voluntary basis.

European Commission, Directorate General for Employment and Social Affairs

CSR is the commitment of business to contribute to sustainable economic development, working with employees, their families, the local community and society at large to improve their quality of life, in ways that are both good for business and good for [international] development.

World Bank, **www.worldbank.org/privatesector**, accessed 24 March 2004

and beyond that which constitutes their legal obligations. This simple parameter gets to the heart of much of the debate about corporate responsibility in recent years, i.e. the desirability and effectiveness of market-based solutions to social and environmental challenges, and, in particular, their voluntary and self-regulatory nature.

The different definitions of corporate responsibility shown in Box 1.1 share in common the belief that companies have a responsibility for the public good—but they emphasize different elements of this. The definitions used by Starbucks and Chiquita, for example, highlight that responsibility is gauged by how companies listen and respond to stakeholders' concerns. PricewaterhouseCoopers' definition sets out the kinds of stakeholder groups to whom companies are responsible (although the exact scope of 'stakeholder' varies from region to region—for example, between Europe and the USA). It also stresses that responsibility involves balancing profit maximization and stakeholders' needs. Those definitions provided by Holme and Watts, and the Confederation of British Industry, shed light on what some of the responsibilities to these stakeholders are, while that of the European Commission stresses that actions under the corporate responsibility umbrella are voluntary in nature. Finally, the World Bank introduces the additional element of companies' responsibilities for development in poor nations.

Alongside these definitions, there are others that describe responsibility in terms of the values that companies should strive to uphold, such as honesty, fairness, and integrity, and these are often set out in standards or codes of practice (see Box 1.2). There are also those that define corporate responsibility in terms of its commercial benefits. Windsor

Box 1.2 Published standards of corporate responsibility

The following is a selection of standards, guidelines, and declarations that set out some of the rights that companies are being asked to uphold.

Agenda 21
A far-reaching plan of action for governments, companies, and civil society to address human impacts on society.
www.un.org/esa/sustdev/documents/agenda21

Beijing Declaration
An international United Nations declaration on the rights of women.
www.un.org/womenwatch/daw/beijing/platform

CERES principles
A ten-point code of corporate environmental conduct, for use as an environmental mission statement or ethic.
www.ceres.org/coalitionandcompanies

Convention on Biological Diversity
Principles for the conservation of biological diversity, including sustainable use, sharing of benefits, and access to genetic resources.
www.biodiv.org/convention

Global Reporting Initiative
A framework for reporting on social, environmental, and economic performance.
www.globalreporting.org

Organisation for Economic Co-operation and Development (OECD) guidelines for multinational enterprises
Government recommendations on responsible business conduct.
www.oecd.org

Principles for Responsible Investment
Principles on environmental, social, and corporate governance issues pertaining to investors.
www.unpri.org/principles

Social Accountability 8000
Workplace standard against which to assure worker rights and welfare.
www.sa-intl.org

Wolfsberg Anti-Money Laundering Principles
Principles for private banks to counter money laundering.
www.wolfsberg-principles.com

(2001) says that the degree and types of responsibility that individual companies have are a factor of the wealth and power of the company, so that a multinational corporation will have different responsibilities to those of a small or medium-sized enterprise. Equally, separate industries have distinctive social and environmental impacts, so that, for example, good performance in cosmetics will look quite different from that in transportation. Indeed, according to Werther and Chandler (2006), there are so many variables that it is impossible to prescribe what mix of responsibilities any company faces: companies should not look for universal definitions, but should instead build their strategies around the perspectives of their stakeholders (even though that term is itself subject to multiple interpretations—see Chapter 6).

CASE STUDY 1.1

Explorers discover 147 species of corporate responsibility

'*Explorers discover at least 147 species of CSR*': so was headed an article in *Ethical Performance* about a 2005 Ashridge Business School study of corporate responsibility activities. Based on research in Denmark, the study identified seven main areas of corporate responsibility activity, which were then divided into 31 classes of activity, as follows.

Area 1 Leadership, vision, and values
(a) Defining and setting the corporate purpose, values, and vision
(b) Translating this into policies and procedures
(c) Putting it into practice, including empowering and embedding
(d) Ethical leadership and championing

Area 2 Marketplace activities
(a) Responsible customer relations, including marketing and advertising
(b) Product responsibility
(c) Using corporate responsibility product labelling
(d) Ethical competition
(e) Making markets work for all

Area 3 Workforce activities
(a) Employee communication and representation
(b) Ensuring employability and skills development
(c) Diversity and equality
(d) Responsible/fair remuneration
(e) Work–life balance
(f) Health, safety, and well-being
(g) Responsible restructuring

Area 4 Supply chain activities
(a) Being a fair customer
(b) Driving social and environmental standards through the supply chain
(c) Promoting social and economic inclusion via the supply chain

Area 5 Stakeholder engagement
(a) Mapping key stakeholders and their main concerns
(b) Stakeholder consultation

(c) Responding to and managing stakeholders

(d) Transparent reporting and communication

Area 6 Community activities

(a) Financial donations

(b) Volunteering employee time

(c) Giving gifts in kind

(d) Being a good neighbour

Area 7 Environmental activities

(a) Resource and energy use

(b) Pollution and waste management

(c) Environmental product responsibility

(d) Transport planning

(Ethical Performance, 2006c; Ashridge Centre for Business and Society, 2005)

Questions

It is sometimes argued that companies are expected to take on too many different types of responsibility and that there are too many corporate responsibility initiatives.

1 Should companies be allowed to choose which issues to address?

2 Which of the above activity areas do you think are most important for companies to tackle?

3 How can companies set about prioritizing the areas of activity in which they should get involved?

A framework for understanding corporate responsibility

There is a vast variety of corporate responsibility activities presently being practised by companies, as Case Study 1.1 demonstrates. Given this array, it is not surprising that no single definition is sufficient to capture the range of issues, policies, processes, and initiatives covered in this book. Yet different definitions contain elements that help us to understand what is meant by corporate responsibility. As we will explore in the coming chapters, the notion of stakeholders, the recognition of particular issues, and the role of values are all important elements of corporate responsibility today. Likewise, the tensions that arise because of competing interests, priorities, and values affect what corporate responsibility means in practice.

Rather than try to adopt and defend a particular definition, in this book, we use corporate responsibility as an umbrella term that captures the various ways in which business' relationship with society is being defined, managed, and acted upon. We identify areas of common ground and difference, and we summarize areas of agreement and disagreement, but we do not pretend that there is a unifying vision of corporate responsibility. To help to make sense of the multitude of definitions, however, in this chapter, we set out three ways of thinking about corporate responsibility. The first is the idea that companies, like people, have values that guide their interactions with other society members. The second is to consider corporate responsibility in terms of business' role in society and the different types of business–society interaction. The third is to categorize the specific areas in which business is now expected to take action. We tackle these different ways of thinking in the following sections.

Values-driven business

When they talk about corporate responsibility, many executives stress the importance of their companies' values. Sam Palmisano, IBM CEO, describes his company's values as innovation that matters for the world as well as the company, trust and personal responsibility in all relationships, and dedication to client success.[6] Nestlé's core values include favouring long-term development over short-term profit, entering into long-term commitments and relationships, being fair and honest, and showing respect for diverse cultures. According to Waddock (2001), at the core of what she calls '*corporate citizenship*' are:

1 a company's adoption of policies, procedures, and processes that are based on integrity (i.e. honesty to oneself and to others), and which allow it to build values-based practices; and

2 a company's capacity to perceive and evaluate the long-term consequences of its behaviour, and its willingness to make short-term sacrifices to realize long-term gains.

Others flesh out what those policies, procedures, and processes might embrace (e.g. transparency, empowering stakeholders, managing a triple bottom line of economic, social, and environmental value added, etc.), offering different political and philosophical frameworks for understanding what ethical constructs should be included (e.g. human liberty, social justice, communitarianism, a duty of care).[7]

There is debate about who decides the values to which business should adhere: companies themselves or the societies within which they operate. For those who see corporate responsibility as a choice that business makes, companies face three competing cases that will ultimately determine their corporate responsibility strategy: the moral case (obligations that the company has to society); the rational case (taking proactive steps that will minimize the restrictions society imposes on business); the economic case (adding financial value to the company by preserving its legitimacy with its stakeholders).[8] For others, however, companies do not choose to practise corporate responsibility; rather, it is an integral part of the free enterprise system, and the issues and problems at the heart of corporate responsibility are:

> a natural consequence of the industrialized quest for profits [and] represent the raw edge of business values rubbing against the social values of human communities and the ecosystems that sustain those communities.
>
> (Frederick, 2006, p 59)

Underlying these different vantage points is a common acceptance that a legal construct such as a corporation can have values, and that notions of ethics, justice, responsibility, and obligation rooted in human experience can be meaningfully adapted to guide corporate behaviour. As we discuss in Chapter 2, these are debatable assumptions, and an important question is whether corporate responsibility practice today makes companies sufficiently accountable for adhering to society's values in the same way that people are held to account, or whether it, de facto, allows companies to pick and choose those things for which they want to be responsible in a way that would seem preposterous if the choices were to be made by individuals.

Business ethics

Not surprisingly, this pushes us in the direction of the field of 'business ethics', which refers to ethical systems applied in the context of profit-oriented organizations. There are valid reasons for arguing that business ethics provides the overarching framework within which corporate responsibility is situated, and hence should not be presented as an aspect of corporate responsibility. If we were concerned only with a theory of corporate responsibility, we would not necessarily disagree with that, but our interest is something broader, that embraces theory, management practice, and the societal context within which business exists. Just as neither politics nor religion can be entirely explained by reference to theoretical principles, neither can corporate responsibility.

Business ethics is, in part, concerned with the behaviour of individuals as members of the company and wider society, but it is also increasingly concerned with the values of business as a whole and how a company integrates values, such as honesty, trust, integrity, respect, and fairness, into its policies, practices, and decision making. This can involve ensuring that employees abide by the law and are not left in a position in which, in order to achieve one set of targets (e.g. earnings), they are necessarily encouraged to bend or break the law. It can also involve going beyond legal requirements and adhering to company, industry, or professional codes of conduct, such as those that have long been adopted in the medical, military, and legal professions.

It might be argued that, before business management can be considered a mature profession, it too needs to develop comprehensive and relevant codes of ethics. Certainly, there is now resurgence in interest in business ethics, both in companies and business schools, as a result of the corporate corruption scandals of the late 1990s and early 2000s. The changing nature of business also presents new ethical challenges in order to resolve issues arising from operating globally and within multiple cultural norms, from new industries such as biotechnology and information technology, and from increasing public scrutiny of business behaviour. Some companies and industries have invested in internal mechanisms to manage the ethical dimensions of their operations, such as the medical company Baxter International's overarching set of bioethics principles, and defence and aircraft manufacturer Raytheon's appointment of a corporate director for ethics compliance and ethics officers in its major business segments.

There are, however, two readily identifiable difficulties with how companies currently implement business ethics. First, there are many examples of even companies with strong ethical policies and processes being found in breach of the law. This was the case with Boeing, which, despite its extensive ethical guidelines on procurement, corruption, and marketing, used confidential materials stolen from rival Lockheed Martin to win nearly

$2bn-worth of defence procurement contracts with the US government in 1998, an action that later led the company to be suspended from bidding for defence contracts.[9]

The second difficulty is that company codes and guidelines, as Davies (1997) points out, mostly take the form of usable algorithms that are intended to guide managers through ethically contentious situations, rather than help them to develop a coherent ethical theory that will inform overall business practice. Consequently, ethics is often described as something that is necessary to achieve business imperatives such as profitability, growth, and shareholder value, rather than as something that is at the heart of business behaviour and a prime determinant of what that behaviour should be, especially if there is conflict between business and moral imperatives.

This may seem odd given that much of business ethics seeks to apply ethical theory to the business context. Thus, we find a variety of texts seeking to adapt the ideas of Aristotle, Kant, Mill, Locke, Heidegger, and others to the needs of business.[10] In Chapter 2, we examine how ethical theory relates to corporate responsibility, but it may be that this kind of approach is too divorced from the world in which business is conducted and that, rather than understand philosophy, we should consider the context that frames ethical decisions.

For example, in what has been characterized as part of a distinct European school of business ethics, Crane and Matten (2004) focus on three core themes that influence the ethical dimension to business behaviour—globalization, sustainability, and citizenship—and, in doing so, refer as much to sociology, political economy, and international relations as they do to philosophy. They highlight, for example, how the Rhenish model of capitalism, found in Italy, Germany, Spain, France, and elsewhere, creates different expectations and challenges to those of the Anglo-Saxon model that is typical of the UK and USA (see Case Study 1.2). They also describe how factors such as age, gender, national identity and culture, level of education, personal integrity, and moral imagination all affect individuals' ethical decisions. And they make clear that the concerns of business ethics are affected by the role, capacity, and responsibilities of government and other social institutions.

CASE STUDY 1.2

Comparison of corporate governance regimes in Europe and North America

Two significantly different models of corporate governance have dominated the successful capitalist economies of Europe and North America: the Anglo-Saxon model that is typical of the USA and UK, and the Rhenish model found, for example, in Germany, Italy, Spain, and France. The former is characterized by a dispersed ownership structure, frequent changes in ownership, and an emphasis on shareholders as the key stakeholder. The latter, by contrast, is typified by concentrated, interlocking patterns of ownership, involving the corporation, banks, and other financial institutions—something that helps to account for relatively rare changes in ownership, and also helps to explain why both owners and employees have rights as stakeholders. The goals of ownership also differ with the Anglo-Saxon model stressing shareholder value and short-term profits, while the Rhenish model concentrates more on sales, market share, headcount, and long-term ownership.

Some argue that the Rhenish model is inherently more responsible and accounts for why corporate responsibility is less pronounced in German firms, for example, as a distinct form of management practice. Yet the nature of ownership and the practice of co-determination, i.e. decision making involving management, investors, and workers—what Germans call *Mitbestimmung*—has been blamed for making companies less competitive. Although by no means a stampede, companies such as Allianz, Porsche, and BASF have switched from legal forms associated with the Rhenish model to the European Company (SE) form, which requires smaller supervisory boards with fewer requirements about stakeholder representation.

(Crane and Matten, 2004, based on Coffee, 2000; Wiesmann and Simensen, 2007)

Questions

The Anglo-Saxon and Rhenish models of capitalism have a number of distinguishing differences.

1 Which of these differences have the greatest relevance for corporate responsibility?
2 What problems might arise if Anglo-Saxon based ideas of corporate responsibility were to be applied in the Rhenish context?
3 What pressures might weaken the Rhenish model in the future?

Business and society

For some, values are an unsatisfactory way of thinking about corporate responsibility, because they encourage the idea that responsibility is an end state, or a goal to be strived for, rather than a way of thinking about the role of business. According to Jonkers:

> [Corporate responsibility] is a 'sensitising concept': a term that draws attention to a complex range of issues and elements that are all related to the position and function of the business enterprise in contemporary society.

(2005, p 20)

There is a long tradition of business and society as an area of academic study and public policy, but its primary concern has been how to regulate and motivate business so as to contribute more to the public good. Thus, for example, governments have passed legislation on issues from working hours, to maternity leave and the minimum wage, so as to enhance workers' well-being; economists such as Mises, Keynes, and Galbraith have debated the merits of government intervention in the marketplace as a way of capturing the power of business for the common good. Business and government are depicted as having separate concerns: the former, to do with creating wealth; the latter, to do with social cohesion and security, which has often required intervening in the world of business through both regulation and redistribution.

Since the 1950s, it has become clear that this idea of separate sectors with discrete responsibilities is misleading and, moreover, that different societies around the world have very specific, and often complex, expectations of the role that business should play, which go well beyond paying taxes and abiding by the law. These became apparent in the flurry of literature about CSR in the 1960s and 1970s, which provided the theoretical context for contemporary corporate responsibility (see Chapter 2). In 1979, Carroll offered what is perhaps the most widely cited framework for understanding the different aspects of social responsibility that had emerged. He identified four types of responsibility, as follows.

1 **Economic responsibility**
   This refers to the fundamental responsibility of business to produce goods and services that society wants, and which it sells at a profit.

2 **Legal responsibility**
   This refers to the obligation of business to fulfil its economic mission within the confines of the law.

3 **Ethical responsibility**
   This refers to the ethical responsibilities of companies that go beyond legal compliance.

4 **Discretionary responsibilities**
   This refers to voluntary responsibilities, such as philanthropy, which a company can assume even if there are no clear-cut societal expectations.

These are ways in which business manages its relationship with wider society. They embrace the notion of the company as a values-based organization by including the ethical and discretionary responsibilities within which such values might be most apparent. But they go beyond the idea that corporate responsibility is purely voluntary by emphasizing the significance of legal responsibility. Moreover, they make clear that companies have obligations—not just options—even when there is no legal compulsion. This is the meaning of economic responsibility, whereby responsibility is defined not only in terms of making a profit for shareholders, but also in terms of producing goods and services that society wants.

A recurring criticism of corporate responsibility is that trying to engineer the benefits of business in this way is wrong-headed. This is partly because, under the free enterprise system, creating jobs, shareholder value, and goods and services—and doing this in a law-abiding, ethical manner—are all inherent ways in which business contributes to society. But it is also connected to the perceived problem of a company having multiple objective functions, so that it ends up having no clear accountability or definition of good performance.[11] As we will see in other chapters of this book, there are various objections to this view. But the idea that companies have a purpose other than simply to make money —that, at the very least, they should consider not only profitability, but also the way in which profits are made—is central to understanding corporate responsibility in terms of business' relationship to society.

There are now more sophisticated frameworks for comprehending corporate responsibility than that of Carroll (1979), as we explore in Chapter 4, and some of these put much greater emphasis on the process of managing the relationship with wider society. Interestingly, although Carroll came to deny that his was a hierarchical framework under which some types of responsibility were more important than others, many of these subsequent theories have perpetuated and expanded on the idea that there are qualitatively different tiers of responsibility. This, in turn, has encouraged the idea that companies undergo different evolutionary stages within which their responsibilities and the nature of their relationship with other elements of society discernibly change.

Demonstrating that these transitions are beneficial either to business or society is an important part of the debate about corporate responsibility, as we explore in Chapters 5 and 12. One indicator of progress that is widely cited is the way in which the company engages with its stakeholders, i.e. those entities upon which the company impacts or by which it is affected. Companies' relationships with certain stakeholders, such as employees and customers, have long been an object of management interest and, in some jurisdictions, obligations to different types of stakeholder are set out in law. But, in the latter part of the twentieth century, management theory emphasized the primacy of shareholders to the point at which responsibility to other stakeholders was portrayed as a dereliction of executives' duty. In that process, all other responsibilities were made subservient to a very narrow interpretation of economic responsibility. A feature of modern corporate responsibility is not only that broader notions of responsibility have become more appreciated, but also that stakeholders have come to be recognized as an important way in which sets of responsibilities are identified and granted legitimacy. Paying attention to stakeholders has affected business decisions, from investing in apartheid South Africa to procurement of timber and recycling mobile phones, and, as we discuss in Chapters 6 and 10, stakeholders are a major element of corporate responsibility management.

One consequence of involving a wider array of stakeholders in thinking about the role of business in society is that it has drawn attention to the importance of long-term corporate performance. Just as an important test for a values-based approach to corporate responsibility is how successful it is in getting business to take actions that are not in its financial self-interest, so the test of a business-and-society-based model is whether it leads companies to use their power and resources for the long-term benefit of society, even if there are short-term costs to the company. In its 2005 *Citizenship Report*, multinational conglomerate GE stressed that good citizenship has a more positive and enduring purpose than tackling the ills of the moment: it is about delivering high performance with high integrity over a sustained period of time, so as to create benefits for the long-term health of society and the enterprise. Commentators on business and society have pointed to a number of situations in which private enterprise is most at odds with society's interests, such as when monopolies replace competitive markets, or when companies get so powerful that they unduly influence public policy. These threats exist today, but to these has been added a situation in which the short-term interests of investors prevent companies from taking a long-term view of either the enterprise's, or society's, well-being.

It is interesting to note that economist Milton Friedman, who made probably the most forceful statement that companies are responsible only to shareholders (see Case Study 1.3), introduced his theory of corporate responsibility at a time when investors were more inclined to hold shares for the longer term. Nowadays, notably in the Anglo-Saxon model that has become the norm against which other business systems are examined, many of his unspoken assumptions about what underpins the business–society relationship no longer hold, because investors look for higher and speedier returns, employees are more mobile, and senior managers are rewarded for pushing up the price of shares and increasing productivity, regardless of the human cost.

It is these types of change that some feel corporate responsibility should redress, either by putting limits on what is acceptable behaviour in the short run, or by encouraging companies to pay more attention to long-term performance. As one group of managers within the World Business Council for Sustainable Development has concluded, corporate responsibility (specifically sustainability) becomes a logical element of profit maximization as soon as one insists that shareholder value equates with long-term shareholder value.[12] The reality for many companies, however, is that they have to straddle the demands of both the short and the long terms. In the words of an oil industry CEO who had to contend with pressure from both the financial markets and civil society:

> On the one hand, you've got Wall Street squeezing you harder and harder for shorter and shorter term performance. On the other hand, you have a broader constituent base that wants more than financial results . . . Most CEOs will tell you, 'This is damn hard work'.[13]

CASE STUDY 1.3

What responsibilities do companies have?

The only social responsibility a law-abiding business has is to maximize profits for its shareholders.

This, in short, is economist Milton Friedman's theory of free market corporate responsibility. It is a controversial viewpoint among corporate responsibility theorists, but even among liberal economists and libertarian entrepreneurs, it has been interpreted in different ways. For example, John Mackey, CEO of US retailer Whole Foods and a self-proclaimed libertarian, has said: 'The enlightened corporation should try to create value for all of its constituencies.' In a dialogue with Friedman, he argued that shareholders are one group with an interest in the company and that they want the firm to maximize profits. But others, such as customers, employees, suppliers, and the community, have different expectations. According to Mackey, it is too narrow to say that shareholder interests are paramount: the entrepreneur defines the company's purpose and if he says from the outset that part of that purpose is, for example, to give a stated percentage of net profits to philanthropy, then subsequent investors have no right to dispute that—they know what they are buying into.

In response, Friedman says: '[The] doctrine of social responsibility is frequently a cloak for actions that are justified on other grounds.' The point here is that such seemingly socially responsible actions have a sound business rationale (e.g. by supporting programmes in local communities). But once companies go further than this, not only are they misusing what belongs to investors, they are going beyond the bounds of their special competence.

In a separate discussion, Fred Smith, of free market think tank the Competitive Enterprise Institute, has argued that 'the modern firm solves one (but only one) of the major problems of mankind—the creation of wealth'. The problem is that corporate responsibility takes managers' minds off wealth creation and forces them to spend too much time on others who are 'antagonistic to economic and technological change'. He supports Friedman's view that maximizing profits is a private end, but argues that it is a means to achieve the highest social goals. A system based on private property and free markets enables people to cooperate freely in their economic activities and to assure that resources are allocated to their most valued use.

(*Rethinking the Social Responsibility of Business*, www.reason.org, accessed 17 May 2006; *Wall Street Journal*, 2005)

Questions

The three people here share similar ideological perspectives, but have not always reached the same conclusions about corporate responsibility.

1 How convincing is Mackey's argument that profits are not the purpose, but a means to realizing social and environmental ends?

2 Is Smith right to say that corporate responsibility advocates are opposed to economic and technological progress?

3 Is Friedman agreeing with corporate responsibility advocates in saying that there is a business rationale for many philanthropic acts?

A taxonomy of business responsibilities

Values or business–society perspectives of corporate responsibility essentially ask: '*Why should a company be responsible?*' A more direct approach is to ask what it is that companies are being held responsible for. Although the answer is a broad and seemingly disjointed array of issues, this type of taxonomy appeals to many practitioners who are concerned less with underlying rationales and more with technical problem solving.

There are various ways of categorizing the main issues that fall under the corporate responsibility heading today and, in the following pages, we provide an overview of the most prominent of these (see Box 1.3). Whether this taxonomy is comprehensive enough to include all of the issues for which business might be held responsible is a topic for debate to which we return in later chapters. Nonetheless, the list, as it stands, is a challenging one and relates to many aspects of business that companies might have been reluctant to consider in the past. We have already provided a brief overview of 'Business ethics' (see p 18), so we will turn now to legal compliance.

Box 1.3 Prominent areas of corporate responsibility activity today

Business ethics
Legal compliance
Philanthropy and community investment
Environmental management
Sustainability
Animal rights
Human rights
Worker rights and welfare
Market relations
Corruption
Corporate governance

Legal compliance

Perhaps the most fundamental responsibility that a company has towards society is to obey the law. No matter how innovative or exciting corporate responsibility may sometimes appear, the fact remains that, in most of the world, the basic expectation is that companies make a profit and stay within the law. But not all companies are law-abiding, just as they are not always profitable; any definition of responsibility that ignores legal compliance is inherently flawed. Local, national, and international law sets out the rules by which corporations play, and, over time, has prescribed what companies can and can not do with regards to areas such as employment, environmental protection, corruption, human rights, and product safety. One only needs to think of pornography, arms sales, and narcotics to realize how the law defines what is legitimate business activity; one need only consider corporate law to appreciate how it spells out the purpose of the company.

There are, however, strong reasons for saying that corporate responsibility is more than legal compliance. Corporate philanthropy is, for the most part, discretionary, but many companies feel compelled to give back to society in this way (see below). Ever since the nineteenth century, some companies have sought to do more than meet statutory obligations, sometimes to pre-empt tough legislation and sometimes because it is seen as socially beneficial. Since the 1980s, there has also been renewed awareness that, in a global economy, legal institutions rooted in the nation state are inadequate to regulate multinational companies. Moreover, there are many instances in which governments have promised a weak regulatory environment in order to attract inward investment, leaving companies open to charges of exploiting workers, communities, and the environment.

The degree to which voluntary initiatives and self-regulation can address such issues is central to many contemporary debates about corporate responsibility. But, even if it is true that governments find it harder to regulate business than in the past, it is a mistake to ignore the very real power that legislation has. The Alien Torts Claims Act 1789, for example, despite being a US law, has been used to make companies legally accountable for their behaviour overseas and laws modelled on the US Foreign Corrupt Practices Act 1977 are starting to find their way onto statute books in other countries. There is also a complex body of international law for issues such as labour rights, slavery, economic rights, and the environment, which, despite being incomplete, unwieldy, and poorly enforced, nonetheless offers the basis for regulating business in the coming years.

Philanthropy and community investment

As noted, for some, corporate responsibility is what lies beyond the law and an important area of discretionary responsibility has been the idea of 'giving back' to society through philanthropic donations. Business leaders such as Carnegie, Rowntree, and Ford gave back large amounts of their individual wealth to establish foundations or to invest in favoured projects. Companies such as Hitachi, ExxonMobil, and Tata, often encouraged by tax regimes, gave as much as 5 per cent of their pre-tax income to the arts, community development, education, and other valued causes. Even though it no longer defines corporate responsibility, philanthropy remains important, as the multi-billion-dollar endowments by Bill Gates and Warren Buffet show. In the USA, where 2,600 companies have charitable foundations, corporate giving rose 14 per cent in 2005 to $8.4bn, equivalent to $685 per employee.[14] That same year, the UK's 500 largest business donors contributed £1.07bn in cash and kind, a rise of 15 per cent.[15]

In the 1990s, companies increasingly began to take a more strategic view of philanthropy, seeking out causes that were aligned with their business goals. For example, AT&T's foundation used its funding of education projects to win the ear of government policy advisers and this gave it an inside track in subsequent policy making about the information superhighway.[16] Companies such as Taiwan's King Car Food, and Japan's Sony and Toyota, have shown this to be a worldwide trend[17] and the US Conference Board (2006) reckons nearly half of companies align their community investment programmes with business objectives. Moreover, some even claim that philanthropists may potentially contribute more to eliminating world poverty than do the leading industrial nations.[18]

This has led some companies to adopt cause-related or affinity marketing, under which companies invest in social causes that complement their brands.[19] But companies are wary of criticism that anything they do to give back is perceived as a public relations exercise and have sought to emphasize the win–win nature of investing in communities, while also taking a more critical view of staff volunteering and product gifting. Company-backed initiatives, such as the Partnership for Quality Medical Product Donation and the London Benchmarking Group, have helped focus attention on what constitutes good practice and the impact that philanthropy can have.

Environmental management

The environmental dimension to business is nothing new: industries such as agriculture have always recognized the importance of managing nature to achieve commercial ends. Pioneers of environmental thinking such as Steiner, Morris, and Huxley recognized the impact of business on the need for environmental management. Nonetheless, the environment—by which we mean the natural conditions under which any entity lives or develops—has often been treated as something to be exploited by business, with pollution, contamination, and resource depletion regarded as the necessary price of economic prosperity.

Since the 1960s, however—especially, but not exclusively, in advanced industrial economies—society has increasingly questioned the cost of growth to the environment. Exposés such as Carson's *Silent Spring* (1962), a study of the environmental impact of chemical pesticides, and the emergence of a new kind of citizen activism around environmental issues led to tough legislation and the creation of special government agencies. Throughout the 1970s, Western governments produced an enormous body of command-and-control regulation to limit the environmental impact of business. For companies, however, there always seemed to be a trade-off between environmental and financial performance, and, for most, it was a distraction from, rather than a component of, good management. Environmental issues such as pollutants, emissions, and waste were typically dealt with as 'end of the pipe' problems (i.e. involving costly remediation or litigation), rather than as something that might be tackled upstream, as part of core strategy.[20]

In the 1980s, the effectiveness of command-and-control regulatory solutions started to be questioned, and both companies and regulators began to accept that preventing pollution could be a more effective way forward than simply punishing it. Environmental issues found their way into marketing strategies, and industries focused on environmental technologies and services emerged. In the 1990s, environmental management standards such as BS 7750, the EU Eco-Management and Audit System (EMAS), and the ISO 14000 series provided new ways for companies to understand and manage their environmental impacts. Companies began to realize that, in certain situations, improved environmental performance could have a positive impact on the financial bottom line. In what came to be called the 'greening revolution', the business–environment relationship became, for some companies, less a costly problem than a strategic opportunity.[21]

The greening revolution was accompanied by a shift in government attitude, notably in Europe, where the legal responsibility of producers for their products began to cover more of the product life cycle, so that factors such as disposal and recycling had to be considered in product design, manufacturing, and marketing. 'Cradle to grave' thinking has become part of designer philosophy in industries ranging from electrical goods, to footwear, to automotives. Major chemical companies have invested heavily in developing more environmentally beneficial substitutes for harmful materials. At the same time, new industries, such as biotechnology, have presented new environmental challenges (e.g. the perceived environmental consequences of genetically modified organisms) and established industries, such as energy, have generated new debates by investing in renewable energy at the same time as they remain dependent on environmentally damaging carbon-based fuels.

Sustainability

With its emphasis on financial and environmental benefits, the greening revolution marked a significant step forward in corporate responsibility and one that most corporate responsibility theorists failed to predict. The term 'eco-efficiency' has become widely used, highlighting that there need not be a trade-off between business and environmental performance. As McDonough and Braungart (2002) point out, however, there is a significant difference between being eco-efficient and being eco-effective: it is the distinction between being *less bad* and consciously striving to do *more good*. If the greening revolution helped companies to think about making their products less harmful, eco-effectiveness (what has been called 'beyond greening') requires companies to rethink their technologies, their products, and their whole vision of the contribution that business makes to society.

The importance of beyond greening has grown as sustainability has become a major public concern. Sustainability—the ability to sustain a high quality of life for current and future generations—requires companies to rethink what they produce and how they do so. It also involves society rethinking what it wants from commercial enterprise:

a question that is capturing widespread attention, as the potentially catastrophic consequences of global climate change become more widely believed.

Although 'sustainability' is still used in some corporate responsibility literature to refer to a much narrower eco-efficiency agenda, in its fullest sense, it refers to something that cannot be captured only by reference to an environmental or a business rationale.[22] The triple bottom line was developed to address this by encouraging companies to think in terms of adding economic, social, and environmental value.[23] This provides the framework for some companies' sustainability reports, but merging these three dimensions of value in a way that shows the company's relationship to sustainable development has proved difficult and there is a marked tendency to treat each topic in isolation.

There are other ways of conceptualizing sustainability. For example, Hawken et al. (1999) have adapted the Natural Step—a framework for understanding sustainable ecological systems—to the business context. Hart (2005) argues that there are three interdependent economies—the money economy of the industrialized world, the traditional economy of poorer countries, and nature's economy (the natural systems and resources that support the other economies)—of which business needs to be aware, but each of which has to be approached through different strategies. Such frameworks are themselves a response to questions about whether capitalism is itself sustainable, and we delve deeper into sustainability and its business case in Chapters 5 and 9.

CASE STUDY 1.4

Green is green—a business case for the environment

People sometimes say that corporate responsibility means being irresponsible with other people's money: using a company's assets to solve problems that business should not have to solve; distracting management from creating shareholder wealth. But business leaders are becoming more outspoken, arguing that the most pressing problems facing society need business involvement, and that, what's more, there may be money to be made in realizing this fact.

Take, for example, Diavik Diamond Mines Inc in Canada, which used to haul equipment and supplies for its mines on an ice highway that straddled rivers, lakes, and tundra. Now, owing to climate change, the ice never gets thick enough to support trucks and the company has to pay millions of extra dollars to airlift its materials. In Mali, rising temperatures and a shorter rainy season have prompted researchers to find alternatives to staple foods, and, until they come up with an answer, the country's economy is in jeopardy. Industries from oil and gas, to cruise lines and power supply, are wrestling with the consequences of a warming earth, finding ways to adapt to it, and of reducing the effects.

Some companies, notably in the USA, have notoriously been linked to public relations and political campaigns that seem to deny that global warming exists. The Competitive Enterprise Institute, for example, says that it receives funding from ExxonMobil and the American Petroleum Institute to advocate against the roles of oil and coal in climate change. Yet there seems increasingly less sympathy for deniers and growing support for finding solutions. Reinsurance companies were among the first to warn businesses that they needed to have global warming policies in place or face being considered too high an insurance risk.

Investors are increasingly aware of the opportunities that green investment represents and now it is not only about where *not* to put your money (e.g. avoiding investing in environmentally destructive dam projects), but also about where *to* put that money (e.g. investing in green technologies and in major environmental challenges). The fact that carbon-based fuels are linked both to climate change and a dependence on unstable political regimes has proved a double spur to investment in renewable energy, from solar panels and ethanol, to hydrogen and nuclear power.

At the company level, Nike and Wal-Mart claim that organic cotton is no more costly than its conventional alternative and are among the many businesses that have found cost savings in rethinking their relationship to the environment. B&Q, the DIY store, distinguished itself in a competitive marketplace by its early-mover support of sustainable forest management and other environmental issues. But a passion for the environment is no guarantee of popularity or business success: Ford motor company renovated its River Rouge plant as a model of green engineering, but lost any market advantage because the opening of the plant coincided with the launch of one of the most fuel-hungry vehicles in the world. And therein lies the challenge of the new green business model: whether alternative energy, less harmful practices, and new technology will be enough to offset the global environmental consequences of a billion-plus new consumers in countries such as India and China all demanding more, while the old consumers of the West seem unwilling to settle for less.

(Adapted from Adler, 2006; Carey, 2006; Veitch, 2006)

Questions

There has been increasing coverage of companies identifying business opportunities relating to environmental challenges.

1 Does the fact that a company is driven by a business case to 'think green' make its claim to be a responsible corporation more or less credible?

2 In addition to energy, what are some of the other areas in which green products might reap returns for investors?

3 Which companies do you think are leaders, and which are laggards, in terms of addressing environmental challenges?

Animal rights

With the current focus on social and environmental concerns, it tends to be forgotten that animal rights was a stimulus of corporate responsibility in the 1980s. Before that, animal rights were dealt with in more conventional ways. In the UK, Ruth Harrison's 1964 book, *Animal Machines*, drew public attention to what she called 'factory farming', and a world of industrial farm buildings, dense stocking, and mechanized feeding and watering. In 1965, the UK government, as a result, convened the Brambell Committee, which made what were to become influential recommendations on mandatory animal husbandry standards and statutory provisions. But Harrison's book also catalysed public concern about the treatment of animals. Animal rights' activists targeted factory farming, but also spread to include animal testing, hunting, and the very idea of using animal products, notably fur. Typically, business has been on the receiving end of these campaigns through boycotts, protests, shareholder activism, and attacks on company facilities. The highly publicized campaign against Huntingdon Life Sciences, where most recently activists have tried to 'name and shame' shareholders, is but one example of such campaigning.

Some companies have, however, responded positively to animal rights concerns. Organic animal husbandry standards include stringent animal welfare requirements and form the backbone of new markets responding not only to public concern about livestock, but to recurring public health scares connected to aspects of intensive farming, such as *E. coli* and BSE ('mad cow disease'). People for the Ethical Treatment of Animals (PETA) runs a number of highly visible campaigns targeting particular companies and, among other things, has succeeded in getting fast-food chains such as McDonald's to establish animal welfare committees involving outside experts. Perhaps most famous of all is The Body Shop, which, as a global chain of beauty stores, prohibited the use of animal testing in its own products and used its position to redefine what were acceptable practices for the cosmetic industry as a whole.

Human rights

Since 1945, in the aftermath of the atrocities inflicted during World War II, the notion of a universal set of human rights shared by all people has gained strength. These are typically portrayed as fundamental principles allowing individuals the freedom to lead a dignified life, free from fear or want, and free to express independent beliefs.[24] The 1948 Universal Declaration of Human Rights is the most widely used codification of human rights and includes the rights to life, recognition before the law, freedom of thought, conscience and religion, and freedom from torture, slavery, and imprisonment for debt or through retroactively applied legislation.

The Universal Declaration puts the onus on individuals and organs of society to uphold these rights and, in recent years, business has been singled out as one of the key social institutions that has responsibilities beyond its conventional fiduciary obligations. Thus, for example, when workers at factories in Vietnam suffer beatings and sexual harassment, or children in India are enslaved by debt bondage, or forced labour is used for the benefit of multinational firms in China and Burma, or companies fail to speak out about oppressive government actions in Nigeria, all of these well-documented acts are interpreted as business failing to uphold human rights. The notion of companies as organs of society has been vague, but the idea of their being explicit subjects of international human rights law began to be tackled in the United Nations' (UN) 2002 draft Norms on the Responsibilities of Transnational Companies and Other Business Enterprises with regard to Human Rights. Moreover, aspects of these rights have found their way into numerous voluntary codes of conduct, such as the Global Sullivan Principles that were initially targeted at businesses operating in apartheid South Africa, the MacBride Principles that were aimed at ending workplace discrimination in Northern Ireland, and the OECD Guidelines for Multinational Enterprise. They are also explicitly mentioned in standards of labour practice that multinational companies employ in their supply chains, such as SA8000 and the ETI Base Code.

The scope of universal human rights agreements has expanded since the Universal Declaration. The UN's International Covenant on Economic, Social and Cultural Rights focused on fair wages, the rights to work and education, to freedom of association and collective bargaining, and to workplace health and safety. Its International Covenant on Civil and Political Rights emphasized the rights to life, to peaceful assembly, freedom from torture and cruel or degrading treatment, freedom from arbitrary arrest and detention, and ethnic and minority rights. As corporate responsibility has evolved, some industries, such as apparel, electronics, and retail, have focused more on economic, social, and cultural rights, while others, such as mining, oil and natural gas, and logging, have found themselves more involved in issues of civil and political rights. Thus, for example, as we see in the next section, companies such as Tesco, Gap Inc, or Hewlett Packard have paid most attention to fair wages, working conditions, and other worker rights and welfare issues, whereas those such as BP, B&Q, and Rio Tinto have had to address issues such as the behaviour of security forces, indigenous people's rights, and the management of civil protest.

Workers' rights and welfare

Although workers' rights were accepted as part of international rights from the outset, they were less widely promoted than were some other dimensions. Partly, this was because, in industrial economies, worker legal protections were already strong and newly independent nations typically provided strong guarantees in their constitutions. It was also because, in the Cold War era politics, worker rights were seen as a Soviet Bloc issue, while economic and cultural rights were seen as Western Bloc priorities. While workers' rights never vanished entirely because of the continued presence of organizations such as the International Labour Organization (ILO) and the international trade union movement, it was only with the rapid flow of stories of worker exploitation in newly globalized supply chains in the early 1990s that a broader momentum of concern became discernible.

The conditions in Indonesian factories producing for Nike, Reebok, and Adidas described in Case Study 1.5 came to be seen as the norm, not the exception. Some said that companies could not be held responsible for their suppliers; some said that this was the job of the ILO; some said that exploitation was the price paid for economic progress. But the stark reality of high-priced jeans and sports shoes, and low-waged, abused workers fuelled public protests that companies could not ignore, not least in the main consumer markets. Consequently, companies such as Levi Strauss began to produce, or sign up to, codes of conduct that covered various aspects of worker rights and welfare. Non-government organizations and trade unions cajoled companies into joining collaborative initiatives to encourage higher standards, and local organizations, such as Coverco in Guatemala and the ABRINQ Foundation formed by the domestic toy industry in Brazil, emerged to improve factory monitoring. While there are differences from code to code, typically, the most respected codes today address issues that broadly mirror the concerns of the ILO's Declaration on Fundamental Principles and Rights at Work about forced labour, freedom of association, child labour, and discrimination; in practice, however, there is still a marked tendency for issues such as child labour, or health and safety, to be dealt with more rigorously than freedom of association and working hours.

CASE STUDY 1.5

Labour rights and wrongs—producing apparel for export in Indonesia

In 1991, Indonesia was a booming location for producing garments and sports shoes for major Western brands such as Nike, Calvin Klein, and Puma. But the largely female workforce was poorly paid, with over 72 per cent receiving less than the already paltry legal minimum wage. Although it was bribes to local officials (that were as high as 30 per cent of production costs) rather than wages (calculated at as little as 2 per cent of production costs) that ate into corporate profits, local managers said they were powerless to treat workers better.

Compulsory overtime, leading to 14-hour shifts, was a regular feature of workers' lives, yet some women were happy for the extra hours in order to survive. Workers described how they could not afford to go to hospital after workplace accidents, and a survey of factories producing shoes for Nike revealed that the basic wage for an experienced employee was less than half the Indonesian government's estimate of what it cost to meet a person's basic physical needs. On top of this, retired military personnel were a regular sight guarding the factories, while workplace accidents were so common that a nurse said he had lost count of how many fingers had been amputated.

Representatives of Western brands denied that they had any say in how the factories were managed, although journalists witnessed at first hand production supervisors from companies such as Nike turning up at the factories on a daily basis and giving orders to local management. Claims that it was untenable to raise wages rang hollow as media and academic reports argued that the cost of paying a living wage and cutting back working hours would add a mere 13 cents to the retail price of a $100 pair of trainers. Increasingly, companies found themselves challenged by the Western media to justify their actions as, gradually, worker rights found their way onto corporate and political agendas.

(INGI, 1991a,b; Ballinger, 1992)

Questions

One of the most significant changes in corporate responsibility in recent years has been the acceptance by major companies of their responsibility for working conditions in their suppliers' factories.

1 Why do you think these companies denied this kind of responsibility in the early 1990s?

2 For what types of workers' rights should they take responsibility?

3 Why were these companies made responsible, rather than local governments and international agencies such as the ILO?

Market relations

In the 1950s and 1960s, faith-based and other organizations responded to their members' concerns about unequal distribution of the wealth created by trade by establishing alternative trade organizations. Oxfam Trading, Traidcraft, and others invested in building the capacity of producers in poor countries, and sold their handicrafts and other products in Western markets. Later, beginning in the Netherlands, fairtrade labelling organizations were formed, guaranteeing to the consumer that certified producers and traders, in commodities such as coffee, tea, and cocoa, met specified fairtrade standards that include

Box 1.4 Comparing the features of ethical sourcing and fairtrade

Ethical sourcing	Fairtrade
Primary focus is conditions of production	Primary focus is terms of trading
Works within existing trading chains	Offers an alternative trading chain, especially producer organization (cooperatives), worker shareholdings (on plantations), and alternative buying relationships
Current standards mostly applicable to commercial producers (although guidelines for smallholders may be introduced soon)	Mostly targeted at small producers (although some fair-trade commodities are also sourced from plantations)
Does not directly support institution or capacity building	Actively facilitates capacity building and promotes active partnership between producers and buyers
Guarantees living wage for workers	Except on plantations, does not address workers' wages
Does not guarantee prices to producers	Guarantees a minimum farm-gate price equal to the cost of production
Guarantees core labour standards	Assumes that smallholders depend on family labour and therefore does not always insist on core labour standards
Does not require producers to adopt social development programmes	Provides funding for social development by producer groups

a minimum price to growers that exceeds the cost of production, and payment of a social development premium.

Fairtrade is often confused with initiatives to protect workers' rights such as ethical sourcing (see Box 1.4). Certainly, as fairtrade has expanded beyond small producers to include plantations, the movement has become more explicit about workers' rights. What distinguishes fairtrade, however, is that it is market-focused, engineering trading relations so that the weakest elements of the trading chain, such as small growers, prosper. It acknowledges the need for profitability, but is also founded on the assumption that markets do not distribute benefits fairly and have negative social consequences.

The same principle of harnessing the power of the markets for the benefit of the poor is found in initiatives popularized under the headings 'bottom of the pyramid' and 'corporate social opportunity'.[25] A well-known example of this is the microfinance model, originally developed in Bangladesh, but now found throughout the world. Microfinance provides poor people with financial capital without the need for collateral, helping them to avoid astronomically high usury charges and providing them with a safe place to keep their money. Initially, it was promoted by non-government and aid organizations, but more recently, major banks such as Citigroup and Deutsche Bank have started to offer microfinance services. A variety of models have evolved, such as the pioneering Grameen Bank, BRI in Indonesia with 30 million savers, and ProCredit with banks throughout Eastern Europe.

Outside finance, companies such as Unilever and Procter & Gamble target basic soap, micronutrients, and other products at low-income consumers.[26] Companies have found that by investing in poor communities, they can increase their sales, improve their work-force, develop new products, and increase the range of services for otherwise underserved markets.[27] As we will see in later chapters, there are questions as to whether the rhetoric matches the reality when it comes to this type of market engineering, but the market relations aspect of corporate responsibility is one that is attracting increasing attention, not least because it more readily allows debates about corporate responsibility to be framed in terms of opportunities rather than problems. The language of corporate responsibility is also evident, for example, in the debate about obesity, as a result of which food and bev-erage firms such as Cadbury-Schweppes and PepsiCo are starting to review their product lines and marketing strategies, or in the debate about the impact of major retail chains on local businesses.

Corruption

Business has long been criticized from different parts of the ideological spectrum for using bribery and corruption to influence policy, win contracts, and otherwise distort both the functioning of free markets and the political process. Transparency International, an international non-government organization that lobbies against corrupt practices, defines corruption as the abuse of entrusted power for private gain. Although often portrayed as a victimless crime, corruption has been associated with low wages, unsafe counterfeit products, and hazardous living and working conditions. It is also blamed for undermin-ing democracy and sound governance, stifling private sector growth, and encouraging inefficient business management (because winning contracts comes down to influence rather than competency).

Industries such as mining, construction, and defence have been especially criticized for paying commissions to win business, not least in countries with limited transparency and accountability. This is only partially accurate, because the influence of business on gov-ernment remains a hot topic in many advanced democracies and industries from bank-ing, to pharmaceuticals, to football, have all been implicated in corruption scandals. Nonetheless, the traditional targets have been at the forefront of corporate responsibility initiatives in this area, including the Extractive Industries Transparency Initiative, which compares company payments with government revenues from oil, gas, and mining, and the Business and Corruption project on the role that business can play. Combating cor-ruption has also been added to the principles of the United Nations' Global Compact, but, despite these developments, some still downplay its importance, either because it is held to be culturally acceptable in some parts of the world, or because of fears that, by getting too strict with certain governments, companies will lose business to less scrupulous competitors.

Corporate governance

Corruption and malfeasance within companies is one reason why some see corporate governance—the way in which rights and responsibilities are shared between different corporate actors—as an essential part of corporate responsibility. The fact that Enron had been praised for its leadership in corporate responsibility just before it collapsed because of failed governance made it very clear that ignoring the latter can seriously undermine the credibility of the former. At the same time, governance—and, in particular, how it prescribes the fiduciary duties of corporate officers—is recognized as posing particular challenges for corporate responsibility, not least how companies can meet obligations to shareholders while fulfilling the expectations of other stakeholders.

Both Harvard University's Kennedy School and the environmental non-governmental organization (NGO), CERES, for example, have, in different ways, put governance to the fore of their work on corporate responsibility. Many companies are, however, reluctant to tackle some of the inconsistencies that have been highlighted. For example, political lobbying remains an important activity for many companies, even though it can leave them open to accusations that they are working against the public good while simultaneously claiming to promote it. The disparity between executive remuneration packages and those of the vast majority of employees regularly attracts media and academic scrutiny, reflecting wider concerns about the rich–poor divide around the world. Yet governance reform has made little impact in this area.

This is not to say that there has been no progress with governance in areas of interest to corporate responsibility. There is more racial and gender diversity on the boards and amongst senior management teams of leading multinational companies than in the past, thanks, in part, to investor concerns, tougher equal opportunities legislation and government enquiries such as the Higgs Report in the UK. Although there is nothing like equality, the reasons for disparity are much less likely to be connected with overt prejudice than they were in the past, and are more likely to be to do with education, wealth, and other systemic factors. Corporate responsibility has also found its way, although with mixed results, onto governance reform initiatives such as the UK Company Law Review, and the Australian government's Corporations and Markets Advisory Committee enquiry into directors' duties, corporate responsibility, and reporting. Central to such initiatives is a debate about directors' duties to those other than shareholders and the idea of enlightened shareholder value.

More generally, companies such as Walt Disney, IBM, and Intel include corporate governance as part of their corporate responsibility reports, while pressure groups such as the Interfaith Center on Corporate Responsibility see aspects of governance, such as executive compensation, the independence and inclusivity of boards of directors, and transparency and accountability to shareholders and other stakeholders, as important parts of the corporate responsibility agenda. Transparency and disclosure are recurring themes in debates about good governance and corporate responsibility more broadly. But while some argue that good corporate governance is an indicator of efficiency, ultimately, the degree of transparency depends on legal and stock market requirements. As the number of privately held companies, or the number of multinationals from emerging economies, grows, it will be interesting to see how the relationship between corporate governance and corporate responsibility develops.

SUMMARY

Corporate responsibility is the newest 'old' thing in business management. What we mean by 'corporate responsibility' is constantly changing as society itself evolves, affecting our expectations of business and the way in which its relationship with society is handled. The discussion about what corporate responsibility means can be entered into from several gateways. We can think of the company as an entity with its own values, or at least as a vessel that has to accommodate the competing values and moral principles of different people. We can also think of it as a member of society that has to uphold certain duties and obligations in order to be a good citizen. Alternatively, we can treat it as something that is compelled to react to a wide range of disparate issues reflecting the concerns of the contemporary world.

Each gateway has its advantages and disadvantages from an analytical standpoint, but it would be a mistake to conclude that corporate responsibility is diminished because there is no universal definition or overarching theory. Instead, what these different perspectives reveal are a multitude of ways in which business impacts upon, and is affected by, the rest of society and hence a multiplicity of reasons why companies might want to manage that relationship. They will do this differently, depending on such variables as the type of company, the moment in history, the nature of the industry, and the geopolitical context. Similar variables will also determine the benefits of addressing the relationship. But the constant and central concern of corporate responsibility is how the relationship between business and wider society is defined and acted upon, whether by business as a whole, through collective action, or by single corporate actors.

DISCUSSION POINTS

1 We have set out three ways of thinking about corporate responsibility: company values, the business–society relationship, and a taxonomy of issues.
   * Which of these do you find most useful as a way of starting to think about the meaning of 'corporate responsibility'?
   * Which of these do you think would resonate most with business managers?
   * Do you think the type and size of a company and its industry affect how it approaches corporate responsibility?

2 Many companies interpret corporate responsibility as 'giving back to their communities' through philanthropy and community affairs.
   * Why do you think 'giving back' is increasingly less acceptable as a definition of corporate responsibility?
   * When some executives say their companies do not give back to communities because they have 'already given', what do they mean?
   * Why do you think there is a stronger tradition of corporate philanthropy in the USA than in Europe?

3 The range of issues that companies are expected to tackle is broad and complex, as we have seen.
   - If you were working for a large retail company, which three sets of issues would you prioritize?
   - For which issues would you not want to take responsibility?
   - What do you think the ideal corporate responsibility statement would look like?

4 When people talk about 'company values' and 'business ethics', they imply that there are differences between those of companies and those of individuals.
   - What do you think are the unique values of the free enterprise company?
   - Do you think that people are required to park their values outside the company door?
   - What are some examples of how companies have grown more, or less, ethical in the last fifty years?

5 Surveys of executives and the public repeatedly show that business is distrusted as a member of society.
   - Why do you think there is a high degree of distrust?
   - Is corporate responsibility a good way to restore business' reputation?
   - How would you factor distrust into a company's business plan?

FURTHER READING

VISIT THE WEBSITE for links to useful sources of further information

- Andriof, G and McIntosh, M (eds), 2001, *Perspectives on Corporate Citizenship*, London: Greenleaf Publishing.
  An informative overview of different approaches to corporate responsibility.

- Barrett, R, 1998, *Liberating the Corporate Soul: Building a Visionary Organization*, Boston, MA: Butterworth-Heinemann.
  An interesting approach to blending and aligning personal and organizational values.

- Carroll, AB, 2000, 'A commentary and an overview of key questions on corporate social performance measurement', *Business and Society*, 39(4), pp 466–78.
  Useful summary of academic work on the relationship between financial and social performance.

- Crane, A and Matten, D, 2004, *Business Ethics*, Oxford: Oxford University Press.
  Comprehensive introduction to business ethics, with an interesting focus on the company as a member of society.

- Davis, I, 2005, 'Ian Davis on business and society', *The Economist*, 26 May, online at **www.economist.com**.
  Provocative take on the need to rethink the role of business, from the head of McKinsey's management consultancy.

- Frederick, WC, 2006, *Corporation Be Good!: The Story of Corporate Social Responsibility*, Indianapolis, IN: Dog Ear Publishing.
  Several decades of corporate responsibility thinking collected together by an often overlooked US academic.

- Grayson, D and Hodges, A, 2004, *Corporate Social Opportunity: Seven Steps to Make Corporate Social Responsibility Work for Your Business*, Sheffield: Greenleaf Publishing.
  Discussion of why corporate responsibility should be seen as a business opportunity rather than as a business risk.

- Hawken, P, Lovins, AB and Lovins, LH, 1999, *Natural Capitalism: Creating the Next Industrial Revolution*, Boston, MA: Little, Brown and Co.

  Seminal work on how business can contribute to sustainable development.

- Jenkins, RO, Pearson, R and Seyfang, G (eds), 2002, *Corporate Responsibility and Labour Rights: Codes of Conduct in the Global Economy*, London: Earthscan.

  Good collection of articles on issues to do with voluntary codes of labour conduct in supply chains.

- Nelson, J and Zadek, S, 2000, *Partnership Alchemy: New Social Partnerships in Europe*, Copenhagen: The Copenhagen Centre.

  Early, but still useful, introduction to mainstream corporate responsibility thinking about partnerships.

- Prahalad, CK, 2005, *The Fortune at the Bottom of the Pyramid*, Upper Saddle River, NJ: Wharton School Publishing.

  Influential book on why, and how, business should treat poor, underserved markets seriously.

- Roddick, A, 2000, *Business as Unusual*, London: Thorsons.

  The Body Shop founder's take on her own experiences of creating a successful company rooted in ethical principles.

- Sullivan, R, 2003, *Business and Human Rights: Dilemmas and Solutions*, Sheffield: Greenleaf Publishing.

  Important overview of the relationship between business and international human rights issues.

ENDNOTES

1. CCC, 2005c.

2. Mattar, 2001.

3. Starbuck, 2005.

4. May et al., 2007.

5. For overviews of CSR, see Carroll, 1999; Birch, 2001; Basu and Palazzo, 2005. For a discussion of corporate social responsiveness and performance, see Wartick and Cochran, 1985. Bennett et al., 1999, contains essays on the progress of corporate sustainability. Wood and Logsdon, 2001, 2002 and Moon et al., 2005, provide different viewpoints on corporate citizenship.

6. Hemp and Stewart, 2004.

7. See, e.g., Birch, 2001; Woods and Logsdon, 2001; Dion, 2001.

8. Werther and Chandler, 2006.

9. Anderson, 2003; 2005.

10. See, e.g., Sorell and Hendry, 1994; Chryssides and Kaler, 1993; Donaldson and Dunfee, 1999; Ladkin, 2006.

11. Jensen and Meckling, 1976. For a fuller discussion, see Chapter 8.

12. WBCSD, 2006.

13. Blowfield and Googins, 2007, p 22.

14. See CECP, 2006—accessed 5 June 2006.

15. www.cafonline.org—accessed 5 June 2006.

16. Smith, 1994.

[17] See, e.g., www.alibaba.com (for King Car Food Industrial Ltd); www.sony.net; www.toyota.co.jp—all accessed 27 November 2006.

[18] Jefferey Sachs, quoted in Boulton and Lamont, 2007.

[19] Bloom and Canning, 2006.

[20] Hart, 2005.

[21] Freeman et al., 2000; Schaltegger et al., 2003.

[22] Renn, 1995, cited in Schaltegger et al., 2003.

[23] Elkington, 1998.

[24] Sullivan, 2003.

[25] Prahalad, 2005; Grayson and Hodges, 2004.

[26] www.pg.com; www.unilever.com—accessed 11 July 2006.

[27] Weiser et al., 2006.

2

The origins of corporate responsibility

Chapter overview

In this chapter, we set out the theoretical and historical origins of modern-day corporate responsibility. In particular, we will:

- plot the evolution of the modern corporation and its relevance for the business–society relationship;

- examine the significance of the Industrial Revolution to corporate responsibility;

- explore how religion influenced early ideas of corporate philanthropy;

- discuss how ideas of corporate responsibility altered in the aftermath of two World Wars and the Great Depression in the twentieth century;

- introduce the concept of globalization and its implications for contemporary corporate responsibility;

- discuss the strands of social theory that influence how people think about business and corporate responsibility;

- trace the development of theories of corporate responsibility.

Main topics

■ Key terms

Capitalism

Corporate philanthropy

Environmental ethics

Ethical theory

Globalization

Industrial Revolution

Liberal economics

Licence to operate

Limited liability

New Deal

Social contract

Welfare state

■ Online resources

- Additional material on business as a member of society

- Exercises and discussion topics for students

- Case studies on corporate responsibility issues from different periods of history

- Links to other web-based resources

Introduction

In 1909, Lord Cadbury found himself in court because the company bearing his name had been buying cocoa produced by slaves in Africa.[1] In 2000, the company again found itself accused of the same offence. These events (see Case Study 2.1) show that issues such as slavery do not go away. But they are also evidence that, throughout history, society has judged business from a moral perspective.

In this chapter, we examine how society has consistently held expectations of business that go beyond the narrow sphere of wealth creation. We approach this in two ways. First, we explore how the relationship of business with society has been acted out during different historical periods; second, we use that historical context to unravel various theories of how business relates to society.

What the following sections reveal is that private enterprise has always been the subject of public scrutiny. What we mean by 'corporate responsibility' today has been influenced enormously by our economic systems, the evolution of the modern corporation, and the emergence of theories of corporate responsibility itself. This chapter is a discussion of that heritage.

The *Cadbury* case is a useful starting point for putting corporate responsibility in context. The issues in 1909 were, in many ways, the same as those today. First, companies were then and are now felt by many to have a duty to uphold certain human rights, even when there is no legal liability. Second, companies that purchase commodities or manufactured goods are held to have influence over, and responsibility for, the behaviour of their producers. These principles were apparent in the 1909 court case and are central to areas of modern corporate responsibility, such as ethical trade.

Echoes of the Cadbury experience can be heard throughout this chapter as we explore the origins of corporate responsibility. The company's experiences are not unique: stick a pin anywhere in the timeline of corporate evolution and the issues of what a company should be responsible for, who decides, and where accountability lies are recurring themes. Responses can vary, as do the levels of trust in corporations (see Figure 2.1), but

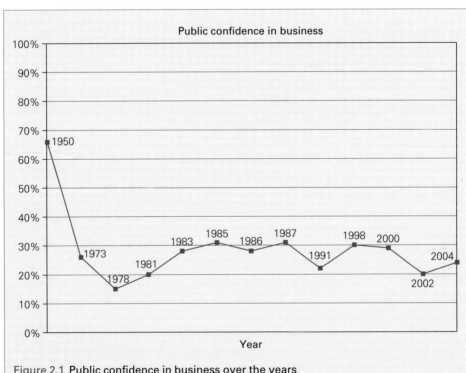

Figure 2.1 Public confidence in business over the years
Source: Based on data from Frederick (2006)

what this chapter shows is that the issues of corporate responsibility and the role of commercial endeavour in society are constants throughout human history.

CASE STUDY 2.1

Chocolate and slavery—a century of corporate responsibility

In 1909, the *London Evening Standard* accused the confectionary company Cadbury's of knowingly profiting from the widespread use of slaves on cocoa plantations in the Portuguese colony of Sao Tomé. The public was shocked: the company was not only one of the most famous brands in the British Empire, but also an exemplar of compassionate capitalism founded in the Quaker religious tradition.

Cadbury's sued the *Evening Standard* for libel. But over the course of the trial, Lord Cadbury, head of the firm and a figurehead of virtuous capitalism, was forced to admit that he not only knew slaves were being used, but actually regarded it as essential to his company's prosperity.

A century later, in 2000, the company found itself once again accused of buying slave-farmed cocoa beans from West Africa in a media assault by the full spectrum of the British press, from the *Daily Mirror* to the *Financial Times*. Acting with others in the industry, Cadbury's (now Cadbury Schweppes) denied the allegations. In contrast with the 1909 case, this time the industry condemned the use of slavery outright, but to no avail, because it was unable to prove that it really knew what was happening on cocoa farms. The fact that human rights advocates seemed to know little more did not matter: these groups held the moral high ground and the industry could do nothing to displace them. Once again, the company lost in the court of public opinion.

(Du Cann, 1993; www.antislavery.org)

Questions

The events of 1909 and 2000 had few major commercial ramifications for Cadbury's and the company is a long-time member of the Fortune Global 500 list of leading businesses. In fact, Cadbury Schweppes won the 2004 UK 'Most Admired Company' award presented by Nottingham Business School.

1 Did the company overreact by stopping its sourcing of 'slave-produced' cocoa?

2 Why did the company feel the need to act at all?

3 Is it not the role of government to regulate how industries are run and to prevent these practices from recurring?

Three eras of responsibility

The Cadbury experience straddles three historical periods, during which the nature of business' relationship with society has changed significantly:

1 the Industrial Revolution;

2 the mid-twentieth-century welfare state;

3 globalization.

Each period has raised new issues about what business should be responsible for, but, as we will see, many of the issues remain relevant from one era to the next.

The Industrial Revolution

Throughout much of Europe, the biggest change in human demographics and human working life came with the Industrial Revolution, as the poor from the countryside headed towards the cities in search of work. In the UK, the first industrial power, between 1801 and 1871, the proportion of the population engaged in manufacturing increased from one fifth to nearly two-thirds.[2]

But this massive increase in urban living brought with it problems of overcrowding and disease. Children were employed in sweeping chimneys, domestic service, and manufacturing, as depicted in the popular novels of Dickens and Kingsley. Factories and mines were responsible for a large number of injuries and fatalities. Slave labour on the African and American continents produced many of the raw materials that industrialization required. In some industries, women became important components of the workforce, not out of choice, but due to poverty.

Industrialization provoked civil unrest. From the late 1770s, there were numerous popular, frequently violent, protests aimed at resisting industrialization or improving the lives of those affected by it. Information about human exploitation spurred various reform movements, such as Wilberforce's anti-slavery society, while the UK's first Factory Acts were passed in 1819 and laws to control conditions in mines were passed in 1842.

In addition to government intervention, it was around this time that writers such as Carlyle and Arnold began to suggest how heads of industry might behave, marking the start of the era of Victorian philanthropy. Robert Owen had already set up his mills at New Lanark and was an instigator of the early Factory Acts. He strove to establish a new model of industrial development in Scotland and the USA, based on the belief that a man's character was formed by his surroundings, and the conditions under which he worked and lived. This vision was developed later in the century by the likes of Cadbury and Rowntree, who established villages at Bourneville and New Earswick respectively, within which their workers could live in supportive communities with open spaces, shops, and schools in easy reach.

Perhaps the most famous philanthropist from this era was the Scottish-born Andrew Carnegie, who made his fortune manufacturing the steel needed to develop America's railway network. When he sold up, he embarked on a philanthropic quest that saw him donate some $350m to charitable and other philanthropic causes, including the building of libraries, the establishment of educational trusts, and contributions towards creating such iconic buildings as the Carnegie Hall in New York and the Peace Palace in The Hague.

Each industrial economy has its own history of industrialization, and we only have to look at the different timelines of the abolition of slavery in the UK, the USA, and Belgium, for example, to see that change happened at different speeds and in different ways. More importantly for contemporary corporate responsibility, however, the social and environmental consequences of early industrialization in countries such as the UK remain relevant today, especially in countries such as China, which is now witnessing a massive influx of rural people into urban areas, and where economic growth can appear to be at the expense of human and environmental well-being.

The evolution and rise of the modern corporation

The first Industrial Revolution in Europe and the USA was part technological invention, part institutional innovation, and we should not overlook the importance of the latter, in particular the emergence of the 'limited liability company' and changes in the meaning of 'incorporation'. Today, the meaning of 'business' is either taken for granted, or the subject of typically polarized debates about whether it is a good or a bad thing. But in capitalism's early days, the advantages and disadvantages of different types of company were widely debated. A major factor that allowed the modern corporation to emerge was the legal construct known as 'limited liability': the system by which shareholders in a company are not liable for its debts beyond the nominal value of their shares. The economist, Adam Smith, disliked this idea and favoured partnerships over corporations, because he felt that separating the owner from direct control of the company opens the way for professional managers to pursue their own self-interest.[3] But, despite the fact that the limited liability company is only one of several forms of commercial enterprise, it has nonetheless come to dominate the modern business world.

Limited liability encourages entrepreneurship, but has also been singled out as the root cause of problems in the business–society relationship. It has made possible the emergence of multinational corporations, the power of which Korten (1995) views as a threat to society and Henderson (2004) sees as an asset. It also creates the tension between shareholders and corporate officials that is central to arguments about where a company's responsibilities lie. For some, such as Friedman (1962), and Laffer and Miles (1982), the primacy given to shareholder interests is the genius of capitalism; for others, such as Mitchell (2001) and Ellsworth (2002), it is the reason why managers focus on short-term results and therefore restricts their freedom to serve the interests of others in society. Thus, limited liability is central to the roles that companies play in creating jobs, paying taxes, and generating wealth, but also to aspects of corporate behaviour such as downsizing, bankruptcy, and who has claim to the company's assets. We discuss these issues in other chapters, not least in the context of the socially responsible investment movement, which seeks to change the investor–company relationship (Chapter 11).

CASE STUDY 2.2

Corporate free speech—*Nike Inc v Marc Kasky*

In April 1998, Marc Kasky, a student, filed a suit in California against the sports company Nike, alleging it had made false claims in a PR campaign about working conditions in its suppliers' factories. The case hinged not on whether the claims that Nike had made in press releases and similar documents were true or false, but on whether they constituted free expression or commercial speech. Commercial speech is not protected under the free speech provisions of the US Constitution because it can materially affect consumer and investor decisions. But Nike argued that the comments about working conditions were essentially a contribution to public debate—not commercial speech—and that, consequently, the company should not be held liable for factual inaccuracies.

The case was settled before going to full trial. The Council of Public Relations Firms, the industry body that numbers prominent corporate responsibility consultancies among its members, said that, if a company's First Amendment rights were not affirmed, it would likely have *'a chilling effect on businesses across America'*.[4] Anti-corporate groups, such as CorpWatch, felt that the outcome offered leverage to activists monitoring corporations, because companies knew that there was still the risk of similar lawsuits. Within the corporate responsibility field, there were mixed feelings, with some arguing it would stifle open reporting about social and environmental performance and others saying it would raise the standard of non-financial reporting.

(www.business-ethics.com; www.firstamendmentcenter.org; www.prfirms.org)

Questions

The *Nike v Kasky* case raises an important issue for corporate responsibility. On the one hand, there are many who fear business' power and influence when it steps into the public policy arena; on the other, many expect companies to take on more responsibilities than they have in the past.

1 Is it reasonable or feasible to expect companies to stay out of public policy debates if society wants them to act like responsible citizens?
2 Should putting limits on how companies participate in such debates (e.g. through lobbying, political contributions, etc.) be part of the field of corporate responsibility?
3 Should other countries draw similar distinctions with regards to freedom of expression and commercial communications?

The mid-twentieth-century welfare state

Between World Wars

Charitable giving by Carnegie and others did not ameliorate concerns about the growing strength of corporations. In the USA especially, the nature of incorporation underwent major reforms that removed limits on company size, for how long they could exist, and what they could own. From the mid-nineteenth century onwards, the idea that companies shared certain rights comparable to those of citizens began to be established and, as Case Study 2.2 shows, some now believe that this extends to rights such as free speech. By the early twentieth century, there was a huge increase in the number of mergers and corporations came to be seen by some as huge, impersonal monoliths that were beginning to exert political pressure as never before, leading to public calls for greater regulation and supervision (see Case Study 2.3).

It is difficult to generalize, because of the differences in national experience, but the period before World War I, during which global free trade flourished, was largely one in which corporate power grew and private self-interest was promoted as serving the public good. This triumphalism died after the war, and momentum increased for greater equality and a rethinking of the social order following the leadership failures that had left eight million dead on battlefields around the world. The International Labour Organization, founded in 1919 as part of the League of Nations, brought together government, business, and trade unions, and explicitly recognized the dangers of an unjust political or economic order. Business leaders were forced to consider the impact their activities were having on wider society and, by the end of the war, a number of leading companies were engaged in what became known as 'New Capitalism'.[5] This movement was founded on the idea that the company should voluntarily take steps to portray itself and its activities as beneficial to society at large.

But New Capitalism gained limited traction, partly because of the greater struggle between managers and organized labour that was a feature of the post-war period, and also because economic growth (particularly increases in share value in some countries) encouraged a belief that markets could be the ultimate guarantors of the public good. The principles of New Capitalism came more to the fore, however, following the Great Depression, when corporate greed was blamed as one of the possible causes of the 1929 Wall Street Crash that left millions destitute in the USA, with ramifications across the world's economy.

But voluntary constraints on business behaviour did not prevent government intervention. In 1934, US President Franklin D Roosevelt initiated the 'New Deal', a series of measures that were, in part, designed to limit the power of corporations. If the 1920s' view of corporate managers is encapsulated in the phrase of Sloan, '*The business of business is business*', Roosevelt's view can be seen in the quote: '*We consider too much the good luck of the early bird, and not enough the bad luck of the early worm.*' Despite the vehement opposition of some industry leaders, the provisions of the New Deal remained until the early 1970s, when oil shortages forced the US government to rethink economic policy.

CASE STUDY 2.3

Monster business—the ideas of Thomas Quinn

Thomas Quinn's views of the modern corporation are interesting for three reasons:

- he was a business insider—a star executive at General Electric, who established the firm's refrigerator division;
- he wrote during the Great Depression, a time at which trust in business was at an all-time low;
- his concerns about business still resonate in discussions about corporate responsibility today.

Quinn believed that companies evolve from small enterprising firms to large ones, then into giant corporations, and finally into what he termed '*monster businesses*'. These not only stifle competition, but also affect social and political institutions, and even pose a menace to the democratic way of life.

His examples of how this happens find echoes in corporate responsibility discussions today. For example, he pointed to big-banker trustees who control voting at the dominant corporations, representing what he called '*the highest degree of concentrated economic power in our history*'. Reflecting recent criticisms about board responsibility, he claimed that directors were responsible for setting '*wholly arbitrary, self-serving judgments, compensation and recognition awards*'.

He also blamed corporate officials for paying themselves excessive salaries, bonuses, pensions, and stock options, and what he called the '*anti-social, dollar-directed groups*', such as the confederations of industry and chambers of commerce, that supported the political interests of executives and investors.

Significant parts of Quinn's analysis have been proved wrong (e.g. that big business causes inflation) and his hyperbolic style detracts from his message—but some of his observations remain insightful and predate much of corporate responsibility theory.

(Quinn, 1962; Blowfield, 2005c)

Questions

Quinn's commentary on business was based on what he saw happen in the 1920s and 1930s.

1 Does the fact that parts of what Quinn observed still resonate today suggest that 'the problem' of big business is nothing new and is something that society adequately controls through conventional political processes?

2 Is there something different about 'the threat' of big business today that did not apply in Quinn's time?

3 Is it accurate to think about irresponsibility as solely an issue for big business?

Post World War II

After World War II, the principles of the New Deal influenced the type of welfare state that was to define Western European public policy over the coming decades. In the UK, the post-war Labour government put in place a system of welfare safety nets. It also acted on its belief in state-owned industry by nationalizing major industries such as coal, railways, steel, gas distribution, and power generation. The idea that business best served the public good if it was state-controlled took hold in much of Western Europe and, of course, in the Eastern Bloc of Communist countries, in which private enterprise was outlawed. It also characterized the role of business in newly independent countries such as Indonesia and India.

In West Germany and Italy, new models of governance were put in place to ensure that workers, as well as shareholders, had a say in how companies were run. In the USA, a seemingly spontaneous interplay between business and society emerged, similar to what chaos theory would later term 'complex adaptive systems', but which, at the time, was seen as a debate over how much of its power business would cede to wider society.[6]

These different approaches to managing the role of business in society all marked a significant change in thinking from that of the days when it was assumed that business best benefited others by being left largely to its own devices. The welfare state was primarily concerned with a more equitable distribution of the benefits of economic prosperity. Distribution was the responsibility of government and the primary role of business was to create jobs, obey the law, and pay taxes. The concerns of the welfare state, however, such as health care, living wages, and education, influence what we think of as 'corporate responsibility' today. Equally, national governments' renewed interest in human rights in the aftermath of the war gave rise to such agreements as the United Nations' Universal Declaration of Human Rights, which is now referenced in important corporate responsibility initiatives.

But post-war prosperity brought with it new social concerns. In the early 1950s in both the UK and USA, smog claimed the lives of many citizens, with serious instances in London, New York, and Los Angeles. Pollution became a political issue, resulting in the passing of the US Air Pollution Control Act in 1955 and the UK Clean Air Act in 1956. A year later, scientists working with the Scripps Oceanographic Institute were surprised to discover rising carbon dioxide levels in the world's oceans.

In 1962, Carson's *Silent Spring* was published, detailing the effect of man-made pesticides, and, throughout the decade, scientific discovery into the effects of leaded petroleum, water pollution, and chemical seepage served to make increasing numbers of people aware of the connection between environmental degradation and corporate activity. In the following decades, regular instances of corporate malfeasance, such as the Love Canal, Bhopal, Chernobyl, and the *Exxon Valdez*, served to reinforce this connection.

Non-government environmental groups, such as Greenpeace (founded in 1971), began advocating for change outside the mainstream political process. In terms of organization and strategy, they set the agenda for a much broader range of rights-focused activists, such as those protecting the interests of workers, indigenous people, animals, children, bonded labour, etc.—the advocacy groups that play an important in contemporary corporate responsibility.

The women's rights movement also became more visible in the 1970s and, among other things, raised issues of equality in the workplace. One aspect of this was equal treatment in terms of remuneration and working conditions, and another was equality of opportunity. The movement worldwide has had an enormous impact in a relatively short space of time, most notably in the area of legislation (e.g. maternity rights, equal pay). In terms of corporate responsibility, the women's rights movement established the basic principle that companies shall not discriminate against women. Similar principles have been applied in relation to age, ethnicity, race, disability, and sexual orientation, and, in the USA especially, racial discrimination has been a significant part of the corporate responsibility agenda.

Globalization

The third era during which a marked shift in the nature of corporate responsibility can be witnessed is the contemporary era of globalization. Indeed, so important is globalization to corporate responsibility that we devote the next chapter to a detailed discussion of what it means, and how it relates to current ideas and practices. All that we will emphasize for now is that not everything about globalization is unique: indeed, as we discuss in Chapter 3, it can be difficult to describe what it is that makes globalization a distinct phenomenon. What is discernible are a number of policy shifts that have allowed international trade to flourish to a degree not seen since World War I and which have ultimately stimulated new thinking about the business–society relationship.

Historically, these shifts have common roots in the Bretton Woods' Summit, at which, towards the end of World War II, policymakers set about establishing three major institutions that would ensure that the economic collapse that led to war did not reoccur. Two of these—the International Bank for Reconstruction and Development (commonly called the World Bank) and the International Monetary Fund—have long been champions of free trade, but, arguably, their younger sibling, the World Trade Organization (established in 1995), is the most relevant to corporate responsibility because it governs international trade relations, prescribing much of what its member States can and cannot do in this area.

Free trade was seen as essential to global peace and prosperity, but the post-war decades saw only grudging steps away from protectionism. The economic prosperity that Western Europe and North America enjoyed in the 1950s and 1960s was, however, threatened by the 'stagflation' of the 1970s when, contrary to mainstream economic theory, relatively high unemployment (stagnation) was accompanied by a rise in prices (inflation). This was blamed on regulatory constraints and the power of the labour movement, as well as on taxation systems that stifled investment.[7] Most famously, Margaret Thatcher and Ronald Reagan enacted policies supporting more private enterprise, less labour power, freer markets, government control of currencies, and more incentives for private investment. These types of economic and social policy came to define good government in many countries and institutions such as the World Bank, and were reflected in what came to be called the 'Washington Consensus': the set of policies that countries around the world had to adopt if they were to receive assistance from the major international financial institutions.

The term applies to a package of policies that were widely adopted by borrower countries in Latin America, Africa, and Southeast Asia and which created the conditions for overseas companies to set up factories, or to source from suppliers, in countries that hitherto had adopted policies of protectionism and import substitution. They were also accompanied by neoliberal ideas promoting the minimal state, ending income redistribution and reducing welfare provision, and were eventually stripped down to what Krugman (undated) calls the Victorian economic values of free markets and sound money.

The impact of the Washington Consensus on the course of globalization has been enormous, creating an environment in which foreign investment, global trade, and the removal of tariff barriers are all part of mainstream policy, compared with only four decades ago, when private enterprise was barely recognized as being a partner in economic development. Although, in recent years, it has been roundly criticized by anti-globalization activists, economists, and even the World Bank,[8] many of the elements of the Consensus remain part of orthodox economic policy and, in what Rodrik calls the '*augmented consensus*', it has been expanded to include issues such as corporate governance, combating corruption, transparency, and poverty reduction.[9]

Corporate responsibility theory in historical context

Alongside the historical context, it is important to understand how social and economic theory has evolved over the same period, because this defines how we think about corporate responsibility today. As we will see, the whole meaning of 'corporate responsibility' can alter depending on what lens we use to understand the world in which we live. This is readily apparent in the following section on the world's different economic systems.

Business before and beyond capitalism

Many think of capitalism as the only economic system and, certainly, many may not consider how different types of economy affect the way in which we think commerce should contribute to society. Yet there are many different types of economic system, and understanding something about non-capitalist economies helps both to show how capitalism shapes the way in which we think about the business–society relationship and to highlight that even today religious and political ideologies influence economic behaviour.

Trade is a basic human activity, but it is not always about making money. The idea that trade is synonymous with profit is very culturally specific. In the highlands of Papua, for example, the purpose of trade is to extend one's network of social relationships and wealth is less important than creating alliances.[10] Contrast this with capitalist society, in which often what we value most is the accumulation of wealth and in which, unless things go wrong, we feel we have no further obligation to the trading partner.[11]

Clashes rooted in the different assumptions of economic systems are highly relevant to many modern enterprises. One of the main reasons why international logging, oil, and mining companies operating in regions such as Papua, for example, have faced persistent opposition from local populations is because they fail to understand community expectations: witness, for example, BP's Tangguh natural gas project.[12]

Different types of economy also affect other aspects of economic life. We may take it for granted that someone wants to work for a wage. Yet even today, in parts of Africa, for example, working for someone can be part of a complex social system under which the worker may receive little in the way of money, but may instead learn important skills and may even establish rights to inherit property from his 'employer'.[13] Understanding this type of relationship is important: both in recognizing that the commoditized labour typical of modern business (i.e. people 'selling' their labour for a wage) is not universal and in helping companies better to address slavery, child labour, and other exploitative practices that may arise along their supply chains.

The influence of political and religious beliefs

1 **Politics**
Within modern economies, different types of political system still affect the form that business takes. Gilpin and Gilpin (1987), for example, set out three ideologies of political economy:
(a) the liberal model of the USA, the European Union, etc., that is based on notions of individual equality and liberty;
(b) the nationalist/mercantile model, within which economic activities are subordinated to the goals of the state (e.g. as in Nazi Germany or imperial Japan);
(c) the Marxist model, under which investment and enterprise is controlled by the state, as still found in Cuba and, to some degree, in China.
It is easy to forget that, for much of the twentieth century, there were lively debates about which political systems were most productive and that it is only relatively recently, with what Fukuyama (1989) called '*the end of history*' and the emergence of liberal democracy as the dominant political system, that interest in this aspect of political economy has, at least for the time being, subsided.

2 **Religion**
Religion also affects economic behaviour and what is considered ethical. For believers, the 'morally right' thing to do is generally synonymous with the notion of what God might have commanded and, conversely, the 'morally wrong' choice is what God might have forbidden. There have been some attempts to examine corporate responsibility from a religious perspective and religious ideas are today influencing faith-based

companies in parts of the USA.[14] In many cultures, religion is connected with trade. According to Evers and Schrader (1994), traders have traditionally occupied a unique position in society: on the one hand, they are expected to represent the community's interests when dealing with other communities; on the other, they risk being ostracized for exhibiting the same behaviour within the community. This 'traders' dilemma' may account for why traders often pursue separate religions, such as the Jains in India, the Jewish traders of medieval Europe, and the Chinese Christian churches in Indonesia.

Hostility to trade has certainly led to racial stereotyping and violent outbursts in many parts of the world. It has also, as in the spread of Islam throughout Asia by Arab traders, led to significant cultural and religious change. Moreover, as economic theory evolved, it became possible to argue that a certain type of economy, as well as religion, was morally superior. Nowhere was this to become more apparent than in the American idea of manifest economic, political, and religious destiny.

Religion was depicted by Weber as playing an important role in the shaping of economic systems and he argued that the values of Protestantism, in particular, explain why capitalism took hold in some societies rather than in others.[15] It is certainly true that many successful Victorian enterprises sprang from relatively small Quaker and Calvinist communities, which emphasized the connection between work and religious belief.

Economics and society

The examples so far all show how commercial activity is affected by the world around it. In modern capitalist societies, it is common to look at society through the lens of economics and economic well-being is a major factor in our lives. But does it make sense to think of society as synonymous with the economy? Can the economy be trusted to produce a just, sustainable society, or do markets need to be tamed by other institutions? Do we believe that economic reasoning can establish the responsibilities of companies, or does there need to be a broader perspective?

Such questions require us to think about the nature of the economy. Today, we tend to think of economics as a distinct discipline, but this was not always the case. It was Marshall and Pigou, his successor, who, in the nineteenth century, did much to establish economics as a discipline in its own right: as an enquiry into flows in goods and services.[16] Perhaps the most far-reaching consequence of this shift is how it has made the market a central reference point in how we view the world. Certainly, how we look at markets in terms of their contribution to the public good is an important factor when thinking about corporate responsibility. If we believe, as pure classical economists do, that the good of society is served by letting the market function without external intervention, then major areas of corporate responsibility should be rejected as unwarranted interference (e.g. attempts to set a fair wage, to limit overtime, or set environmental legislation). But if we are uncertain about markets acting as the main arbiter of the public good, corporate responsibility offers the promise of rectifying their deficiencies.

What underlies questions about the role of markets is how we see the relationship between the economy and society. Contrasting views of this relationship are apparent in the works of Polanyi, Veblen, and Hayek. Economic anthropologist Polanyi (1944) argued that classical economics had become too focused on the '*formal economics*' of Marshall and that what matters more is '*substantive economics*', i.e. the instituted process of interaction between man and his natural and social environment. For Polanyi, the significance of capitalism's emergence in the nineteenth century is that it '*disembedded*' economic behaviour from society and led to the economy being seen in terms of markets, rather than in terms of actors, and their actions and values.

'Institutional economics' also refutes the notion that all economic issues can be described and resolved in terms of individual interactions with the market. Veblen (1904), its founder, argued that continually changing customs and institutions, not only economic rationality, affected people's economic decision making and the importance of these other factors increases the less perfect competition is present in the market. This idea has been taken further by New Institutional theorists such as Coase (1937), who treats the role of institutions and the imperfect nature of competition as central to any understanding of business.

Hayek (1944; 1960), the liberal economist, accepted the importance of social institutions, but argued that it is one thing to say that man created the institutions of society, such as the law and moral codes, but another to say these can be altered to satisfy man's desires or wishes.[17] He likened institutions such as the market to a footpath across a field, worn away over time by people pursuing selfish motives while producing something that appears collaborative and planned. For Hayek, the problem is not that the capitalist economy is unalterable, but that, in changing it, we might unwittingly destroy the complex overall order that we are hoping to improve.

Such theories provide more than only a context for understanding modern enterprise: they tell us something about how some of the basic issues addressed in corporate responsibility, such as fairness, sustainability, and well-being, are viewed within theories of capitalist society. These differing views are worth considering in the corporate responsibility context because, although corporate responsibility is not overtly wedded to any particular political ideology, it does assume that conscious human intervention is necessary to improve the business–society relationship. Why this is the case becomes more apparent when we examine the capitalist economic system in greater depth below.

Capitalism—the backdrop to corporate responsibility

Capitalism is the dominant economic system in today's world. Even though there are other systems, what we think of as 'business' is essentially a capitalist business model and what we think of as 'corporate responsibility' is framed in important ways by the principles, norms, and values of that model. Therefore, any attempt to understand corporate responsibility divorced from an understanding of capitalism will make it difficult to grasp why certain courses of action have been taken and others not, why certain things are valued and others considered unimportant, and why particular behaviours are taken for granted that, in other systems, would seem strange, if not abhorrent. Although, as we will see, there are different interpretations of what capitalism is, could, and should be, the various theories have much in common that sets them apart from the alternative systems that we discussed in the opening section of this chapter: for example, the notion of profit; markets as the main determinants of price and utility; the commoditization of things (goods, labour, land, etc.); the concept of private property.

Liberal theories of capitalism

The characteristics of capitalism are most clearly seen by comparing the liberal (or classical) perspective and the critique provided by socialist (or Marxist) theory. The difference between liberal and socialist views of capitalism is less in their underlying analysis of capitalist economics than in what they saw as its consequences. The founder of liberal economics was Adam Smith (1776), who argued that what made the individual enterprise competitive (i.e. division of labour and availability of capital) also made nations competitive. The idea that the specialization promoted by the division of labour leads to greater productivity informed early thinking about free trade, under which nations are predicted to benefit from producing goods for which they have a competitive advantage. It is nations with free competitive markets, Smith argued, that are best able to allocate resources and that ultimately grow wealthier, because they allow people to pursue their own self-interest.

Ricardo (1817) developed many of Smith's ideas, and his law of comparative goods (i.e. that trade exists between countries only when there are differences in cost) has probably had more influence on arguments for economic globalization and free trade than has Smith's belief that trade happens because of the benefits of specialization.[18] What both Smith and Ricardo believed, however, was that the capitalist economic system tends towards an equilibrium between buyers and sellers of goods, and labour and capital, and that there should be little government intervention in what came to be known as the 'laissez faire' system. How much intervention and under what circumstances it should occur has become a major theme of both economic theory and government policy since Smith wrote in the late eighteenth century. Left unfettered, liberal economists claim, competitive markets will both check the power and profits of business, and induce firms to allocate resources effectively enough so that the economy always returns to full employment. This tradition of seeing market forces as the most efficient determinant of utility is still very much evident in contemporary politics, although some have pointed out that even Smith did not believe in unconstrained self-interest, as is apparent in his argument that the self-interest of business people should be shaped by moral forces in the community, so that it does not degenerate into greed and selfishness.[19]

Socialist critique of capitalism

Smith and Ricardo's theories of labour value were fundamental to the ideas of Karl Marx (1865), but he differed from them in highlighting labour as the basic determinant of a product's value. He distinguished between a worker's '*exchange value*' (the price paid to raise, feed, clothe, and educate a worker) and that worker's '*use value*' (the value of the worker's labour to the capitalist, as reflected in the final product's market price). For Marx, the capitalist's profit was the difference between exchange value and use value, which he called '*surplus value*'.

At the heart of Marx's critique of capitalism is that markets are unfair to workers, who are unable to capture a fair price for their labour and who repeatedly suffer, because of the

periodic depressions and economic fluctuations that Marx saw as characteristic of capitalism. Clearly, this is in contrast with the liberal notion of market equilibrium, under
which imbalances between supply and demand are typically temporary or the result of
external interference.

Relevance today

Liberal and socialist perspectives on capitalism framed much of the debate about economic policy in the nineteenth and twentieth centuries, and continue to have a significant influence on how we think about the route to economic prosperity and justice, even
if, since the collapse of Communism in the Eastern Bloc, Marx's ideas, in particular, have
typically been derided.

   In the Western world, much of twentieth-century policy sought to create a middle
ground between laissez faire and socialism. Keynes, and later Galbraith, significantly influenced government policies that sought to mediate between society and markets following
the economic crises of the 1920s.[20] Elsewhere, the very different policies of Nazi Germany
and Nehru's India also sought to harness the power of the private sector for the public
good. In the latter part of the twentieth century, economists, such as Friedman (1962),
and philosophers, such as Oakenshott, argued for a return to a purer form of market capitalism. Public policy has also been significantly affected by recognition of other factors
that influence economic life, such as gender, race, and forms of identity other than social
class. Yet the policies of most liberal democratic governments boil down to questions about
the strengths and weaknesses of markets that stem from insights into liberal economics.
Moreover, such questions are central to corporate responsibility, and add significantly to
our understanding of corporate responsibility's origins and its current concerns.

Theories of corporate responsibility

Evolution of corporate responsibility theory

As explained in Chapter 1, there is no unifying corporate responsibility theory, but the
various social and economic theories outlined so far all, in some way, help to explain the
role of business in society and to frame society's expectations regarding the private sector.
The theories of corporate responsibility that have emerged since Berle and Means' work
in 1932 reflect, and are rooted in, the wider world of the social and environmental sciences, even if this is not always made explicit. Therefore, corporate responsibility theory
should not be treated as if it were an alternative to mainstream social theory, but rather
as an examination of if and of how such theory is put into practice.

   Before corporate responsibility had a name, theology was already informing the
thinking of entrepreneurs ('Business before and beyond capitalism', p 50), but what distinguishes much of contemporary corporate responsibility from corporate philanthropy
is that today's corporations are becoming involved in implementing policies and programmes that, rather than only giving back to the community, affect core management
practices. What is more, these programmes are not necessarily legally required. The use of

a company's assets for purposes that do not maximize shareholder value makes corporate responsibility a target for some liberal economists (see Chapters 1 and 13) and raises questions about the fiduciary duty of managers (Chapter 8). As we will see, corporate responsibility theory provides various answers to such criticisms, but informing mainstream corporate responsibility thinking is the implicit belief—contradicting pure liberal economic theory—that markets are imperfect and that, therefore, the behaviour of business needs additional controls, yet also—in contrast to socialist analysis—that private enterprise is not inherently exploitative and can be managed in such a way as to contribute to the general good of society.

It is worth noting that what amounts to an expression of ideology within corporate responsibility theory is rarely, if ever, made explicit, much less analysed. In the following pages, we trace the evolution of corporate responsibility theory as a distinct field and the most important texts seldom employ larger political or similar frameworks. The exception is ethical theory, which, in the form of business ethics, has played an important role in corporate responsibility debates, although as we touch on later ('Ethical theory', p 61), the adoption of philosophical frameworks can sometimes appear to be a co-option of these ideas for narrow business ends. We focus on the period between 1930s and the early 1990s, because, before that, the business–society relationship was not treated as a separate area of enquiry and because the 1990s mark the point at which interest in corporate responsibility accelerated more rapidly than can be dealt within a single chapter (see Figure 2.2). What this section shows, however, is that many of the ideas and arguments that are at the heart of corporate responsibility are not new. We have separated these out as follows:

1 the responsible enterprise;
2 the extent of corporate responsibilities.

The responsible enterprise

One thing that distinguishes corporate responsibility today from earlier ideas is that the focus is on the company rather than on the individual entrepreneur. Corporate philanthropists were among the early practitioners of corporate responsibility and the first theories of corporate responsibility were similarly focused on the duties of individual business leaders. For Davis, the power that business leaders held brought with it certain moral obligations. His frequently cited 'Iron Law of Responsibility' says that the social responsibilities of business leaders need to be commensurate with their social power.[21]

Davis (1973) was, however, also one of the first corporate responsibility theorists to argue that social responsibility was more than the acts of individuals; that corporate responsibility should refer to the company as an institution. The shift in focus from the individual to the company led to a new discussion of responsibilities. Some saw corporate responsibility as a way of utilizing company resources towards broad social ends rather than to serve only narrow private interests.[22] In addition to linking responsibility to power, Davis himself held that the social responsibility of business demanded that companies should be open to public input and scrutiny; that social costs and benefits

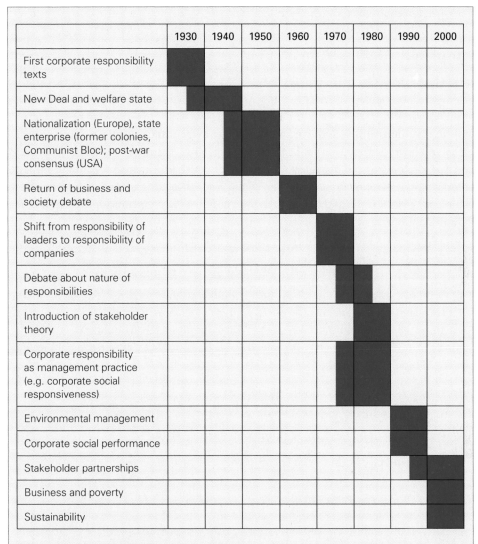

Figure 2.2 Timeline of corporate responsibility

should be factored into their business decisions and also priced into products, and that, where it has the necessary competencies, the company as a citizen should be involved in social affairs.[23] He also noted that there might be long-term economic gain from behaving responsibly.

Davis' views spurred thinking about how companies could demonstrate their contribution to social goals such as economic justice, stability, and freedom,[24] and the ways in which this can be accomplished. Three questions that cut across recent corporate responsibility theory are as follows.

1 How can business be responsible?

2 For what is it responsible?

3 To whom is it responsible?

It is to these questions that we now turn.

How can business be responsible?

Identifying the enterprise as the focus of corporate responsibility led theorists to question when and how companies should exhibit responsibility. Manne and Wallich (1972) said that corporate responsibility refers to actions for which the company is under no legal compulsion. If corporate responsibility begins where the law ends, however, what does this mean? Manne claimed that true corporate responsibility expenditure, as well as being voluntary, was that which:

1 generates marginal returns less than those available from alternative courses of action;

2 is an actual corporate expenditure, not a conduit for individual largesse.[25]

This raises two interesting questions: first, should corporate responsibility be limited to what companies do to generate a profit; second, should companies be denied moral credit for actions taken for commercial reasons? The Committee for Economic Development, comprising US corporate leaders, identified three concentric circles of responsibility that blurred Manne's distinctions:

1 creating products, jobs, economic growth;

2 sensitivity to changing social values;

3 emerging responsibilities such as poverty and urban blight.[26]

These circles embrace both core business activity and how the company manages its relationship with society more widely, but, again, the emphasis is on voluntary actions and in no case is the company required to be accountable for failing to carry out these responsibilities.

Debates about voluntary versus mandatory approaches to corporate responsibility continue to this day. They are further complicated because companies may feel they have to take particular actions even without legal compulsion (e.g. because of civil society pressure—see Chapter 10). We explore these issues elsewhere and so, for now, limit ourselves to flagging voluntarism as a recurring theme in this book.

For what is business responsible?

Defining corporate responsibility as voluntary action does little to explain for what business should take responsibility. In Chapter 1, we set out various perspectives on this, including Carroll's (1979) multidimensional model of corporate responsibility, which has proved one of the most widely referenced frameworks because it makes clear important principles and spheres of responsibility (i.e. economic, legal, ethical, and discretionary responsibilities—see Figure 2.3). Its strength is that it draws together different types of responsibility that had tended to be treated as mutually exclusive or otherwise problematic.

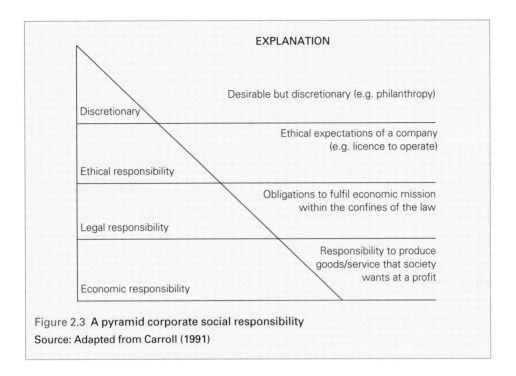

EXPLANATION

Desirable but discretionary (e.g. philanthropy)

Discretionary

Ethical expectations of a company
(e.g. licence to operate)

Ethical responsibility

Obligations to fulfil economic mission
within the confines of the law

Legal responsibility

Responsibility to produce
goods/service that society
wants at a profit

Economic responsibility

Figure 2.3 **A pyramid corporate social responsibility**
Source: Adapted from Carroll (1991)

It does this by identifying separate categories and any action that falls under one category or another can be considered part of corporate responsibility. But this, in itself, can cause problems: for example, does a company accept responsibility for any issue that fits into one of the categories? If not, how does it prioritize its response? Equally, how does the company go about deciding what is ethical, or what discretionary actions it should take?[27] Consequently, at least as important as what companies are responsible for is how those responsibilities are defined; a question to which we now turn, with reference, first, to the notion of legitimacy and, second, to ethical theory.

To whom is business responsible?

It may seem self-evident that business is responsible to those that the law says it is. But the array of responsibilities set out in Chapter 1, plus the fact that legal compliance is only one type of responsibility, make it clear that many voices have a say in defining what companies are responsible for. The idea that business has responsibility to a variety of stakeholders has been an important element of corporate responsibility theory, at least since Preston and Post's 1975 book on how host environments affect corporate behaviour. As we explore in Chapters 6 and 10, stakeholder theory suggests a way of explaining with whom and why corporations should engage. It is based on the notion that many people (and groups of people) have a stake in any corporation and that, in order for a company to achieve its objectives effectively, it must consider them all, not only the shareholders to whom corporations have long discharged accountability.

Stakeholder theory promises a way in which companies can learn what is needed to establish and maintain what Donaldson and Dunfee (1999) term a *'licence to operate'*, i.e. the idea that business requires the approval of others in society in order to function effectively. It provides a potentially stronger rationale than Carroll's framework for choosing certain courses of action by implying that a company should do whatever is necessary to maintain its legitimacy, but that it is under no obligation to go further than that.

The licence to operate is central to legitimacy theory and posits that an organization can only continue to exist if its core values are aligned with the core values of the society in which it operates. The fate of accounting firm Arthur Andersen, in the wake of the Enron scandal, brought this into stark relief when the company's integrity was so badly damaged that it went out of business. Legitimacy theory offers a method of managing stakeholders in the face of various threats, through, for example, educating them about the company's intentions, changing their perceptions of events, diverting their attention, and altering their expectations.[28] Such strategies are evident in the actions taken by Shell in response to Brent Spar, or the treatment of the Ogoni people in Nigeria (see Case Study 2.4).

Important though theories such as those described above are in their own right, one of their major contributions is that they have made management practice part of corporate responsibility enquiry. Early corporate responsibility theory was primarily concerned with the normative behaviour of companies, but, since the 1970s, there has been at least equal emphasis given to corporate responsibility as management practice.[29] For example, Ackerman and Bauer's (1976) theory of 'corporate social responsiveness' put the emphasis on what companies *can* do to respond to societal expectations (i.e. capacity), in contrast to more theoretical ideas of what they *should* do. Social responsiveness shunned the idea of philosophy in favour of a managerial approach and, in many ways, helped corporate responsibility to get out of academia and into day-to-day business. By the 1990s, managerial approaches to corporate responsibility were evolving rapidly and measurement had become an integral part of this, summed up in MacGillivray and Zadek's phrase: *'If you want it to count, count it.'*[30]

We take a closer look at corporate responsibility as management practice in Chapter 4 and later chapters. But we would not pretend that responsiveness to society is an unproblematic way of resolving what business should take responsibility for; on the contrary, as later discussions of stakeholder theory reveal (Chapter 6), it can leave companies without clear moral guidance of the kind promised by ethical theory. Therefore, we finish this chapter by looking at ethical theory in the corporate responsibility context.

CASE STUDY 2.4

Royal Dutch Shell Group

In the development of the 'global company', the energy sector has probably led the way by virtue of its need to search for reserves worldwide. Shell is a major sector player and has a massive impact on the economies of the 135 countries it operates in.

In the 1990s, two Shell subsidiaries were caught up in events that undermined the company's reputation, causing it to alter long-held approaches to business practice and find new strategies to regain lost trust. In Nigeria, where the company had been extracting oil in the Niger River Delta since 1956, local populations were increasingly agitated by what they saw as the high social and environmental costs, and slender rewards, of oil production.

The Ogoni People, in particular, under the leadership of Ken Sara-Wiwa, staged public protests that were met with extreme force by the Nigerian government forces, leading to the deaths of demonstrators and accusations that Shell was complicit in the killings. Sara-Wiwa was eventually arrested and executed for allegedly killing pro-government tribal leaders. His death provoked international outcry and, despite assertions by Shell that it was not in any way involved, the impression lingered that it had a case to answer.

A continent away, Shell was also facing criticism for wanting to scrap its Brent Spar oil storage platform in the deep Atlantic: something that environmental groups saw as a dangerous precedent. Greenpeace mobilized a number of popular campaigns to raise awareness among the public. In the UK and Germany, people began picketing Shell petrol stations and mounting anti-Shell campaigns, and the firm Pensions Investments Research Consultants (PIRC) warned investors of the possible negative fallout.

Despite denials by Shell of its involvement in the Sara-Wiwa affair and the subsequent findings that Brent Spar was not carrying toxic waste, the company was under pressure to respond to the concerns being expressed by many stakeholder groups, including its shareholders. It employed the consultancy company, SustainAbility, to review its policies on reporting and it was not long before the company was rebranded with the slogan 'People, Planet, Profits', echoing the 'triple bottom line' philosophy of the consultancy's founder, John Elkington.

(Mirvis, 2000; **www.pirc.co.uk**—accessed 30 July 2005)

Questions

Shell's experience shows how, historically, companies have tended to develop strong relations with government.

1 In what ways can a commercial organization put pressure on a sovereign government to act on its behalf?
2 How can corporations guard against allegations of complicity in government actions against indigenous peoples?
3 How can companies reconcile increasing production with sustainable development?

Ethical theory

Ethics holds a contentious position in corporate responsibility theory and vice versa. There are those who see corporate responsibility as a subset of business ethics—an attempt to resolve how the values identified through ethical enquiry can be applied through management practice. Equally, business ethics might be regarded as a branch of corporate responsibility that never quite fulfilled its promise because, for whatever reason, it was never adequately incorporated into management practice. It is not our intention to discuss the relationship of corporate responsibility and business ethics; rather, we will show that, as with theories of economics, politics, culture, and religion, ethical theory helps to explain the expectations that society has of business. It should also be noted, however, that there are those who argue that appeals to universal theories of ethics are outdated and that, following Habermas' notion of 'consensus ethics' (see Chapter 4), the outcome of legitimate stakeholder dialogue is, by definition, ethical.

Natural rights and the social contract

To understand the origins of corporate responsibility, it is important to consider the ethical traditions that have emerged within capitalist society. Ancient Greek philosophers considered whether or not there is some way of presenting a theory of natural law, i.e. a series of logical considerations based on nature. Aristotle suggested just such a theory and his theory of virtue continues to inform important theories of social justice, such as Sen's capability approach, while also being implicit in recent thinking about corporations as citizens.[31]

Enlightenment ethics introduced ownership and the accumulation of private property as central ethical issues. Donaldson's work on the licence to operate builds upon social contract theorists such as Locke, Hobbes, and Rousseau, who held that the governing and the governed entered into a social contract. The issues they raised about natural rights and the proper functions of government have had enormous influence in the shaping of modern democracy.

For Locke, the rights that need to be upheld by government as part of the social contract are those he regarded as the natural rights of life, freedom, and property. These are still among the fundamental rights in Western democracies, treated as inalienable entitlements to be respected and protected at all times.[32] But what was self-evident to Locke proved more problematic to other ethicists. When he made the case for the right to private property, he brought to the forefront of Western ethics questions relevant to any corporate responsibility debate, such as how can we behave morally while protecting what is legally ours? How do we best look after the rights of those who have no capital? And why, in any case, should only those with capital make these decisions? In corporate responsibility, not only is it far from clear what rights business should uphold, but, if social contract theory is its base, then companies may be under little obligation to engage with society except in respect of upholding the values of life, liberty, and property.[33] Since the eighteenth century, there have been two main strands of ethical theory in the Western world—consequentialism and non-consequentialism—that demand more of moral actors in setting out the logical basis for deciding what is a moral act.

Consequentialism

'Consequentialism' refers to theories of ethics that assess right and wrong in terms of the consequences of actions. It most famously includes the utilitarian theories of Bentham and Mill, but also embraces the moral philosophy of Adam Smith, as well as that of Hobbes and Hume.

Many notions about the business–society relationship reflect utilitarianism. The term refers to the capacity of actions to achieve beneficial outcomes. In a utilitarian theory of justice, actions are neither good nor bad in themselves, but only in terms of what they bring about, captured in Bentham's (1789) view that 'good' acts are those that bring the greatest happiness to the largest number of people. A good act is, therefore, one that maximizes utility and minimizes disutility, not in individual terms, but a total sum of utility that will result in a surplus of pleasure over pain. Thus, in the context of corporate responsibility, it is the aggregate benefit of a company's actions that matters, rather than any disbenefit to particular individuals or entities.

Non-consequentialism

Utilitarianism is often criticized for its apparent claim that individual rights can be subverted to the greater good of society and that, therefore, people are to be treated as a means to an end. For example, applying utilitarianism in the context of corporate responsibility makes it possible to justify the laying off of large numbers of employees and reducing the wages of workers, provided that these acts maximize the total happiness of the majority of those affected by the company. Those who expect corporate responsibility to be about active citizenship and doing more than paying taxes, obeying the law, and engaging in philanthropy would certainly hope to see more active engagement with society than this.[34]

Non-consequentialist philosophers, such as Kant and Rawls, reject the apparent claim that the good of the majority can be used to justify considerable harm to others. They hold that, for an action to be ethical, it must have a motive beyond self-interest and mutual advantage, and that justice is something contained within an action itself, not in its consequences.[35] As Rawls (1971) puts it: '[Non-consequentialist] *justice denies that the loss of freedom for some is made right by a greater good shared by others.*'

Rawls' alternative theory of distributive social justice has been particularly influential in Western democracies in recent years. It is no less part of a liberal tradition than utilitarianism, but emphasizes equality of resources (the means of realizing a good life) rather than gains in utility as indicating a fair distribution of benefits. The potentially negative results of power and self-interest are at the forefront of Rawls' theory of justice, and he argued that what is fair or just can only be determined if, in defining fairness or justice, people are removed from any personal consequences of their decisions.[36]

From theory to practice

Utilitarianism was a significant influence in shaping the European welfare state, with its focus on social safety nets, and it is evident in areas of corporate responsibility, such as labour standards, that define outcomes intended to benefit the majority of workers. In many ways, however, the history of political thought since the 1970s—the period during which contemporary corporate responsibility took shape—is captured in the opposing views of Rawls and Nozick, his fellow liberal philosopher.

Rawls (1971) argued for a strong role for government as the primary way of ensuring fair distribution. He believed that an unequal distribution of wealth and income is acceptable only if those at the bottom are better off than they would be under any other distribution. Nozick (1974) argued that Rawls was wrong about distributive justice, because he looked at outcomes (the patterns of distribution over time) rather than at whether the transactions that led to these outcomes were just. For Nozick, any distribution of wealth or other things ('*holdings*'), no matter how unequal, is just if—and only if—it is the result of a just distribution through legitimate means. Under his '*entitlement theory of justice*', the distribution of holdings in a society is just if all are entitled to what they have.

In other words, Rawls and Nozick present justifications for quite different roles for government. This is highly relevant to corporate responsibility, within which there are important debates about the regulation of companies and the role of business in administering justice. As we saw when discussing the historical context ('Corporate responsibility theory in historical context', p 50), part of the liberal tradition has treated companies as citizens and thus, *pace* Nozick, has argued for limited government interference.[37] From this perspective, corporate responsibility can be seen either as an unwarranted intrusion into the rights of corporate citizens, or as a way of reducing government interference by offering a voluntary means of preventing companies intruding on the entitlements of others. Equally, building on the Rawlsian tradition, corporate responsibility can be viewed as a way of harnessing the resources of business to achieve social justice, or as an arena in which issues of justice arising from the relationship of business with society can be thought through.

Environmental ethics

One other area of ethical theory that has had a significant influence on corporate behaviour is environmental ethics, which expanded the scope of what we think of as being worth moral consideration beyond that which relates to human beings. It is also highly evident in aspects of corporate responsibility, such as sustainability and animal rights. The underlying theories of environmental ethics can still be classified as part of consequentialist, non-consequentialist, or other ethical traditions and there are several different schools (e.g. bioregionalism, sentientism, ecofeminism). But recurring concerns include the rights of non-human species and ecosystems, the rights of future generations, and the issues of equity and justice.[38]

Environmental ethics has also allowed sustainability to be seen as an ethical issue, something that demands that we extend ideas of moral consideration in terms of space and time. This expanded sense of responsibility is evident in recent corporate responsibility thinking and, for many in business, part of the challenge of being a responsible company is wrestling with Dower's dilemma of how we shift from being citizens with local souls to ones with global souls.[39]

CASE STUDY 2.5

Is a product a right? The case of pharmaceuticals

The pharmaceutical industry, along with other segments of the health sector, is popular among ethical investors because of the social good that its products bring. On top of this, the industry has long donated drugs to poor countries, to treat tropical diseases such as elephantiasis, river blindness, and leprosy.

This reputation was put in jeopardy, however, when, in 1998, a consortium of drug companies filed a suit against the South African government, naming Nelson Mandela as a defendant. The case revolved around the companies' attempt to block the distribution of generic drugs used in treating HIV/AIDS; drugs that 39 major companies had patented, but which were 98 per cent cheaper in their generic form. The industry said it was simply protecting its intellectual property rights, but it came under repeated assault for price fixing and for denying the poor access to medicine.

In the same year, a Canadian drug maker applied to manufacture a generic form of the popular anti-depressant, Paxil. With its original patent about to expire, GlaxoSmithKline (GSK), the drug's original inventor, filed four patent infringement lawsuits that effectively stopped the generic drug entering the US market.

The drug industry dropped the case in South Africa in 2001 and GSK was among the companies that proceeded to sell HIV/AIDS treatments at heavily discounted prices in developing countries. Jean-Pierre Garnier, GSK CEO, famously stated that he did not want to head a company that catered only to the rich and said that the company's primary objective must always be public health.

The Paxil case, however, continued and 46 US states accused the company of filing frivolous patent infringement lawsuits that drove up the cost of medicine for the poor. Again, the company was accused of denying access to the most needy in order to maximize its profits. GSK settled the suit with a $14m payment to the states in 2006, but admitted no wrongdoing.

(Adapted from Smith, 2003a; Barmann, 2006)

Questions

The pharmaceutical industry has asserted its right to protect its intellectual property, while its critics claim that the right of people to have access to certain drugs is more important.

1 Are these two rights incompatible?

2 Is GlaxoSmithKline justified in making drugs available on a not-for-profit basis in Africa, but not in the USA?

3 Is the industry responding to a business case or a moral case by providing patented drugs to the African market?

SUMMARY

Corporate responsibility did not spring out of nowhere. What we think of as the responsibilities of business and how these get acted upon reflect some of the main debates about social justice going far back in time. Nowhere is this more apparent than in theories about how private enterprise impacts upon economic well-being and how the economy itself relates to society. In this chapter, we have discussed how different types of economy affect what we mean by 'justice' and 'well-being'. We have also compared different theories of how business and free markets can best contribute to the good of society in capitalist societies. What emerges is a set of questions on issues such as the relationship between private self-interest and the public good, and how the rewards of enterprise are distributed—things that lie at the heart of contemporary corporate responsibility.

Tackling these questions has occupied politicians, academics, company managers, and community leaders since the earliest days of capitalism. We have explored how corporate responsibility theory developed as one way of finding answers about what business should be responsible for and to whom. We have also examined the way in which different approaches to thinking about responsibility can lead to quite different conclusions about what companies should be responsible for.

The origins of corporate responsibility are not, however, only to be found in theory. The evolution of modern business, and, in particular, the emergence of limited liability and the corporation, have all affected business' relationship with society and expectations about companies' responsibilities. Equally, the specific aspects of business activity that society addresses have, paradoxically, both changed and remained constant over time. What the exploration of aspects of corporate responsibility over three eras does show, however, is how the role of business in resolving these issues has changed. In fact, the unintended consequence of the market liberalization that was central to economic globalization is that business is being expected, as never before, to take action to rectify perceived weaknesses in markets on issues such as social justice and sustainability. It is how globalization has affected corporate responsibility to which we turn in the next chapter.

DISCUSSION POINTS

1 George Soros, American financial speculator, stock investor, philanthropist, and political activist, has said: '*We can have a market economy, but we cannot have a market society.*'[40]
   • What distinction is he making between 'economy' and 'society'?
   • Does corporate responsibility help the market economy to become a market society?
   • Describe how a company from the former Eastern Bloc might use corporate responsibility to establish its licence to operate in the European Union.

2 There are expectations across the political spectrum that big business has the power and responsibility to benefit society. There are also fears across the spectrum that big business is a 'monster'.
   • Does 'big business' have different responsibilities to those of other types of business?
   • How does limited liability influence how companies view their relationships with society?
   • Find examples, at the national and provincial levels, of ways in which company law makes companies responsible to stakeholders other than shareholders.

3 In trying to define business' responsibilities, there are various schools of ethics to which we can turn.
   • Which ethical theories have influenced aspects of corporate responsibility (e.g. labour codes, stakeholder engagement, licence to operate)?
   • From a moral perspective, what strengths and weaknesses do current approaches to deciding and prioritizing responsibilities have?
   • Take an example of a business decision (e.g. closing a factory) and describe how the outcomes would be different if management were to adopt a Rawlsian, rather than a utilitarian, perspective.

4 A number of theories have been suggested to explain why companies engage in corporate responsibility practices.
   • What is the role of theory in helping us to understand practice?
   • Can you suggest any other theories for corporate responsibility policies being undertaken?
   • Contrast the ways in which areas of corporate responsibility might differ between a large corporation and a small to medium-sized enterprise.

5 A number of companies publicize the amounts they make in donations to philanthropic causes. Indeed, it is one of the measures used by some rating agencies when scoring corporate responsibility points.

- To what extent does philanthropic donation act as a measure of corporate responsibility?
- What arguments can you put forward against using this criterion as a measure of corporate responsibility?
- Using other companies as benchmarks, present a case to the board for adopting a particular philanthropic strategy.

FURTHER READING

VISIT THE WEBSITE
for links to useful sources of further information

Historical context

- Bakan, J, 2004, *The Corporation: The Pathological Pursuit of Profit and Power*, New York, NY: Free Press.
  Readable and provocative critique of the dominance of corporations.

- Bronte, C, 1849, *Shirley*, London: Smith, Elder.
  Novel set against the backdrop of unrest and protest during the early Industrial Revolution.

- Dilorenzo, TJ, 2004, *How Capitalism Saved America: The Untold History of Our Country, from the Pilgrims to the Present*, New York, NY: Crown Forum.
  A popular history of how capitalism has benefited the USA.

- Nace, T, 2003, *Gangs of America: The Rise of Corporate Power and the Disabling of Democracy*, San Francisco, CA: Berrett-Koehler.
  Lively account of the dangers of modern business by one-time entrepreneur.

- Thompson, EP, 1963, *The Making of the English Working Class*, London: Victor Gollancz.
  Comprehensive study of workers, working conditions, and worker protest in nineteenth-century England.

Theoretical context

- Carroll, AB, 1999, 'Corporate social responsibility: evolution of a definitional construct', *Business and Society*, 38(3), pp 268–95.
  Widely cited overview of corporate responsibility theory.

- Drucker, PF, 1946, *Concept of the Corporation*, New York, NY: The John Day Company.
  Early work by leading management thinker on the nature of the corporation.

- Kelly, M, 2001, *The Divine Right of Capital: Dethroning the Corporate Aristocracy*, San Francisco, CA: Berrett-Koehler.
  Insightful and contentious discussion of the nature and role of business.

- Marx, K, 1865, *Value, Price, and Profit: An Introduction to the Theory of Capitalism*, abridged by P Zarembka, 2000, Amsterdam and New York, NY: JAI/Elsevier Science, online at ourworld.compuserve.com.
  Marx's own attempt to make basic Marxist theory accessible—the first 'Marx for Dummies'?

- Polanyi, K, 1944, *The Great Transformation*, New York, NY: Farrar and Rinehart.
  Influential analysis of economics and the economy as a social construct.

ENDNOTES

1 Du Cann, 1993.

2 Kennedy, 1987; Evans, 1983.

3 Carney, 1998, p 662.

4 CPRF, 2003—accessed 4 July 2005.

5 McQuaid, 1977.

6 Frederick, 2006.

7 Englander and Kaufman, 2004.

8 See, e.g., World Bank, 2005; Maxwell, 2005; Stiglitz, 2002.

9 Cited in Maxwell, 2005.

10 Koch, 1974.

11 Gregory, 1982.

12 The company's perspective on what it hoped would be a model of business–community collaboration can be found at www.bp.com—accessed 5 July 2005. A more critical perspective can be found in the pages of www.westpapuanews.com.

13 See, e.g., Okali, 1983; Hill, 1970.

14 Jones, 1995; Hebrew Union College–Jewish Institute Of Religion, 1980; Kaminsky, 1995.

15 Weber et al., 1992.

16 Bagehot and Marshall, 1885.

17 Cited in Butler, 1985.

18 Buchanan and Yoon, 2002.

19 Hutton, 1995; Smith, 1759.

20 Galbraith, 1952; Felix, 1995.

21 Cited in Carroll, 1999, p 271.

22 Frederick, 1960, cited in Carroll, 1999, p 271.

23 Birch, 2003, pp 7–8.

24 See the discussion of the work on corporate social performance by Anshen and Johnson in Birch, 2003.

25 Cited in Carroll, 1999, p 276.

26 Cited in Carroll, 1999, p 278.

27 Carroll is not unaware of these types of question and revisited his model in Schwartz and Carroll, 2003.

28 Lindblom, 1994.

29 Tinker, 1985; see also: Sethi, 1975; Wartick and Cochran, 1985.

30 MacGillivray and Zadek, 1995; see also Gray, 1996.

31 Nussbaum and Sen, 1993.

32 Crane and Matten, 2004, p 89.

33 Moon et al., 2005.

34 Moon et al., 2005.

35 Sorell and Hendry, 1994, p 34.

[36] A good overview of non-consequentialist ethics in the business context is contained in Sorell and Hendry, 1994.

[37] We use the term 'liberal' here in its historical sense, as evident in concepts such as liberal economics and liberal free trade. In the USA, in particular, 'liberal' is often used to distinguish social democratic political theory from conservative or republican theory.

[38] For overviews of different schools of environmental ethics, see Wijnberg, 2000; Attfield, 1999; Light and Smith, 1997; Welford, 1995.

[39] Cited in Attfield, 1999.

[40] Soros, undated.

3

Globalization and international development

Chapter overview

In this chapter, we explore the importance of globalization for corporate responsibility, not least, its relevance to international development and poverty alleviation. In particular, we will:

- examine why globalization is so important for corporate responsibility;

- discuss the different meanings of globalization and how these affect the way in which we view its merits;

- identify the main areas in which globalization has had an impact;

- explore how globalization affects poor nations in the developing world;

- discuss the ways in which globalization has altered trade, production, and investment, and how these changes relate to corporate responsibility;

- consider how globalization influences governance and the implications of this for corporate responsibility;

- provide an overview of the major government and civil society responses to globalization;

- explore corporate responsibility as a business response to the challenges of globalization, identifying what it addresses and examining why some feel it is inadequate.

Main topics

■ **Key terms**

Civil society

Deterritorialization

Global commons

Global governance

Globalization

International development

Liberal economics

Self-regulation

■ **Online resources**

- Suggested additional material on business and globalization

- Exercises and discussion topics for students

- Case studies on corporate responsibility in specific countries

- Links to other web-based resources

Globalization and corporate responsibility

In Chapter 2, we saw how the relationship of business with society has altered during different historical periods. Globalization is often portrayed as a new era, bringing changes that are as momentous as those of the Industrial Revolution. It is certainly an era during which business' place in society is being transformed and, for that reason alone, it is important that we understand its meaning and consequences.

But we can go further than this. Writers such as Wood et al. (2006), Pedersen and Huniche (2006), and Crane and Matten (2004) tie corporate responsibility to the social, political, and environmental challenges of globalization. In fact, to some degree, its success may influence the direction of globalization overall.[1] This is because globalization is associated, on the one hand, with a limited set of global governance mechanisms and weakened national governments, and on the other, with unprecedented private sector wealth, power, and impact. Corporate responsibility has thus become an important means for addressing what Stiglitz (2002) sees as the fundamental problem with contemporary globalization—a system of global governance without global government.

We will explore corporate responsibility's role in globalization and especially its suitability for addressing the main challenges later in the chapter, but before we do so, we need to be clear what it is that we mean by 'globalization' and to explore its consequences.

The meaning of 'globalization'

There are many ways to view globalization, but it can help to think of ice cream. Growing up in the UK, we remember summers consuming Walls ice creams, and it was a shock to go to France and Spain to find that there were brands called Miko and Frigo, with very different ideas about what an ice cream should be. Travel to far-off Indonesia and one did not find any ice cream brands, only locally produced, garishly coloured lollies, sold from homemade insulated boxes. Today, Walls, Miko, and Frigo are all part of Unilever; they all market identically tasting, identically packaged Magnums and Cornettos; the products are developed at a single Unilever laboratory and a single website (www.icehot.com) offers identical marketing for 26 different countries. In Indonesia, sellers wearing uniforms featuring the Walls/Heartbrand logo now sell the same products from specially adapted tricycles.

How this came about is the result of many innovations and events, and what one considers most significant about globalization often depends on one's individual perspective. For example, for globalization critics such as Naomi Klein (1999), it is part of the colonization by brands—what she calls '*McDonaldization*'—and a wider process as part of which Western norms and values wipe out diversity and local cultures. For globalization's supporters, such as Friedman (2005), it is evidence that the earth is getting flat, i.e. that technological innovation and investment, especially in the areas of communications and data management, allow vital aspects of economic activity, such as design, investment, or marketing, to take place anywhere that is hooked into global networks.

According to Hoogvelt (2001), we cannot divorce globalization from the growing disparities between rich and poor nations. There are also those, such as Rosenberg (2000) or Ferguson (2003), who see nothing new in globalization. Rather, ice cream is part of the story of increasing global trade and the expansion of consumer markets that is essential to capitalism, or the re-emergence of a model of free trade and market liberalization that is perhaps as old as capitalism itself, and was certainly a worldwide phenomenon from the 1870s until World War I.

The term 'globalization' is used in two main ways.

1 **Globalization as economic liberalism**
   Globalization is considered to be a process by which to achieve sustainable economic growth by creating a global market built on free trade. We discussed liberal economic theory in the last chapter, and liberal globalization is essentially the realization of the economic relations explained by Smith, Ricardo, or Marx, and the socio-economic system described by Mises and Hayek.

2 Globalization as 'deterritorialization'[2]

Globalization is not considered to be a process, but rather a social condition. Economics is one part of that condition, along with politics, culture, ethics, ecology, and all of the other facets that affect human life. But what separates globalization today from any previous historical period is that a combination of technological innovation, policy shifts, power relations, and values has meant that physical space and time have become much less important determinants of economic and social activity, and of social identity. Alluding to Fukuyama's (1989) idea that globalization marks the end of history, Virilio (2000) concludes that globalization is really the end of geography.

The main features of liberal globalization have been covered in Chapter 2 and there is no need to repeat them here. As we discuss below, the consequences of liberal globalization, and debates about its strengths and weaknesses, resemble those of liberal economics as a whole. In fact, in terms of market interconnectedness and openness, globalization is often portrayed as an inevitable outcome of implementing liberal economic policies.

It is, however, worth spending time to understand a little more about globalization as deterritorialization. One way in which many people experience deterritorialization is in the way in which they can live a social life without stepping away from their computers: messaging friends in Thailand, engaging with the blogosphere, and online gaming with people they may never meet or of whom they may never know the 'real' identities. In our business lives, we witness many symptoms of globalization, such as the offshoring of jobs, rapid growth in international trade, and international capital flows.

Deterritorialization theorists say that all of this reflects more fundamental changes in our social condition:

1 new or intensified social networks, leading to the creation of new social orders that transcend traditional political, cultural, economic, and geographical boundaries;

2 stretched and expanded social relations, activities, and interdependencies, leading to the emergence of powerful organizations that are not linked to a specific place (e.g. global corporations, international non-government organizations, and international crime syndicates and terrorists);

3 intensified and accelerated interaction between these networks and organizations, so that what happens in one area can be shaped by events anywhere in the world;

4 a growing consciousness of our interconnectedness and interdependence, so that people do not simply observe globalization—it is something that is shaping who we are and how we act in the world.[3]

Case Study 3.1 shows the consequences of these four phenomena and how they have at once allowed an industry to prosper, but subjected it to unprecedented public scrutiny. It also shows some of the ways in which globalization is interpreted as both beneficial and damaging. It is to the merits and criticisms of globalization that we now turn.

CASE STUDY 3.1

Globalization and the rose

Non-existent before 1990, the Kenya cut flower industry is now one of that country's major economic success stories, exporting over $100m of produce to Europe annually. It is also portrayed as an example of the success and failure of globalization: an industry that has captured significant export earnings, and introduced new technologies and investment to one of the world's poorest nations, but an industry that is blamed for damaging the environment, exploiting women, endangering workers, and damaging local communities.

In part, the industry grew out of Washington Consensus policy reforms that made it easier to invest in Kenya and export to Europe. The industry is also, however, a result of technological innovations that accelerated the impact of these policies. The removal of barriers to trade and investment created the opportunity for European entrepreneurs to establish flower farms around Lake Nayvasha to serve the European market. But equally, getting freshly cut flowers to European supermarkets was only made possible by improvements in transport and storage technology, and by a downward trend in transportation costs.

The same industry is, however, also an example of what has been called the 'dark side' of globalization. Environmental experts claim that the water levels of Lake Nayvasha have gone down and that local towns suffer water shortages. There are questions about the environmental cost of air freighting flowers from one continent to another. The influx of migrant workers has taxed the infrastructure of local towns, while on-farm accommodation is sometimes overcrowded and unsanitary. Wages are low by European standards, and the mostly casual workforce can work long hours during peak periods, such as in the run-up to Valentine's Day, and then be left without employment when demand slackens off.

Complaints about the industry have attracted attention from the European media, international NGOs and unions, development agencies, and, not least, the major retailers that have made Kenya Europe's number one source of imported flowers. The industry has adopted a code of labour and environmental practice, and has collaborated with European-based companies, NGOs, and trade unions on a two-year programme to improve working conditions. Despite being an economic success story, by 2005, the industry was being widely portrayed (in the title of one television documentary) as *Costing the Earth*.

(ETI, 2005b; Dolan and Opondo, 2005; O'Reilly, 2005)

Questions

The Kenya flower industry exemplifies how an economic success story can be tarnished by perceptions of its social and environmental impacts.

1 Do you think that the initial arguments that any such impacts were more than outweighed by the jobs created, the export earnings, the technology transfer, and other economic benefits are valid?

2 Do you feel that Kenya's producers were justified in seeing European protests as protectionism?

3 Should retailers have the right to set social and environmental standards for their suppliers?

Globalization—a tale of the glass half full

Few would deny that globalization is problematic. Even the many politicians—from Clinton to Blair, Yeltsin to Berlusconi—who have acted as its cheerleaders have referred to the unavoidable pain and the need to have faith that it is ultimately for the good. Some of that good we experience today. Since 1990, the volume of international trade has increased enormously (for example, averaging 6 per cent annual growth for manufacturing). This has created jobs in many countries, allowed new industries to grow, encouraged the transfer of technology, increased the flow of capital, and, for the well-educated at least, has allowed people to pursue opportunities across the world. It has also meant that, because of international competitiveness, prices have remained stable or have fallen, and this has been an important factor behind low inflation in advanced economies.

Moreover, growth has not been confined to the major industrialized countries, as shown by the phenomenal expansion of the Chinese and Indian economies. And while China and India account for a disproportionate amount of foreign direct investment, other developing countries have entered the global economy as suppliers of everything from flip flops to flowers and, increasingly, as consumer markets themselves. What is good for business is meant to be good for society as a whole, and many have benefited from new opportunities, new technology, and the cultural shifts that phenomena such as urbanization have brought. Whether because of class, educational opportunity, or entrepreneurship, many people have seen their life expectations expand by virtue of the new types of skilled employment that have been created. The most fortunate have been able to pursue opportunities in stable, prosperous economies as multinational companies increasingly embark on a global war for talent.

Economists and politicians agree that in a capitalist or free enterprise system, economic growth is essential to long-term prosperity, and international free trade is held to be vital for sustainable growth and equity. Therefore, for many policymakers and politicians, globalization is nothing short of essential for global prosperity, demanding the removal of government-imposed trade and investment barriers, increased integration of markets across national boundaries, and the spread of market-oriented policies around the world.[4] These elements were characteristics of the first era of liberal globalization that started in the nineteenth century, the end of which is blamed on a revival of government controls and the closing down of economic interdependence, which ultimately ushered in decades of conflict and instability in the twentieth century. For Martin Wolf, the significance of liberal globalization is not only that it fosters economic growth: *'Liberalism is . . . far more than a purely economic creed. It is the bedrock of democracy at home and peaceful relations abroad.'*[5] As Friedman (2005) has observed, no two countries with McDonald's franchises have ever gone to war.

Wolf's belief, therefore, goes further than those who say globalization is simply about economics. In the traditions of Adam Smith and Hayek, he treats the rights to freedom and property, democratic government, the rule of law, and a supportive values system as being as important as liberalizing markets. Although individual elements may develop at different speeds, ultimately this is the full package that globalization both depends upon and promises. The benefits of globalization, therefore, are not simply economic growth, but the particular cultural, political, and ethical model associated with the liberal demo-cracies of Europe, North America, and other 'Western' societies. All of this leads Wolf to conclude that, for all of globalization's shortcomings, *'the world needs more globalization, not less'*.[6]

Globalization—a tale of the glass half empty

Champions of globalization, such as Bhagwati (2004) and Henderson (2004), find it frus-trating that so much time is spent dissecting its deficiencies. If we spend more time here on criticisms of globalization than its strengths, it is because corporate responsibility is, to some degree, a response to the excesses, rather than the successes, of globalization. Many of these criticisms are of the liberal economics model rather than of globalization as a social condition. In fact, some of the disagreement about globalization's success stems from whether one is talking about economics or something wider.

We focus on three main areas of globalization criticism, as follows:

1 wealth, poverty, and equity;

2 global commons, climate change, and sustainability;

3 universalization of norms, values, and culture.

Wealth, poverty, and equity

In 2002, Joseph Stiglitz provided a wake-up call to those who felt that criticism of global-ization was misguided. It was one thing for what Wolf labels *'antiglobalization.com'* to protest about injustice, poverty, and environmental degradation; it was quite another when a one-time chief economist of the World Bank appeared to be joining their ranks. Yet Stiglitz's conclusion was that, for millions, globalization is a failure: *'Many have actu-ally been made worse off, as they have seen their jobs destroyed and their lives become more insecure.'*[7]

The Washington Consensus policies outlined in Chapter 2 are at the heart of Stiglitz's criticism. They have created the conditions for overseas companies to set up factories, or source from suppliers, in countries that hitherto had adopted policies of protectionism and import substitution. They have also encouraged governments to promote market solutions to the challenges of welfare and equity, rather than earlier policies of govern-ment intervention. Figures from the World Bank's 2006 *World Development Report* show the difficulty of determining whether these policies have been successful. More poor people are going to school than ever before, and although life expectancy in parts of the world is worsening (after improving from 1960–1980), this is largely attributable to the HIV/AIDS pandemic in Africa and a rise in mortality rates in transition economies. At the same time, global income inequality is starting to decline both between and within countries. Yet this is almost entirely due to economic growth in China and India since the 1980s, and, if these countries are excluded, inequalities between rich and poor countries continue to rise.

Concerned by the lack of clear evidence, O'Rourke and Williamson (1999) examined the first wave of liberal globalization in the nineteenth century to see if this offered clues about what we might expect in the future. They found that the benefits were unevenly distributed both within and between countries. Moreover, they concluded that the reason that the era had ended was not because of World War I, but because of a political backlash in response to globalization's *real or perceived* distributional effects.

This same inconclusiveness and the sense of distributional injustice, whether real or perceived, is central to many of today's responses to globalization. For some, the strengths and weaknesses of the liberal model are those of capitalism. Hardt and Negri (2000), for example—building on Wallerstein's (1978) systems theory—argue that globalization needs to be understood as a '*grid of power*', informed by the ways in which capitalism copes with the overproduction, high labour costs, and devaluation that blocks the capitalist process once markets become saturated.

For Stiglitz (2002), however, the issue is not the intractable logic of capitalism, but the way in which globalization is implemented and how rich countries use their power to their advantage in institutions such as the World Bank, the International Monetary Fund, and the World Trade Organization. He and Wolf are in agreement that there needs to be change, but they disagree on how much change is necessary and desirable. For Wolf (2004), the big fear is too much government intervention, leading to a return to tariff barriers, nationalism, and state control. For Stiglitz, the countries that have benefited most from globalization are those, such as China and India, in which governments have challenged the notion of self-regulating markets and taken charge of their own destiny.

Globalization affects developing economies and the developed world, in which formerly major industries such as steel have shrunk, if not vanished, and the number of manufacturing jobs has declined. The offshoring of certain types of blue-collar job is now being followed by that of white-collar jobs, such as data processing, computer programming, and research and development. There is public anxiety as to whether new jobs— and especially well-paying jobs—will be created in their place.[8] As predicted by early globalization theorists such as Beck et al. (1994), the nature of employment is changing. Repeatedly, surveys in the richest countries point to longer working days, stress, job insecurity, and difficulties in balancing working lives with personal lives as causes of public concern. As important as traditional divisions between skilled and unskilled, white collar and blue collar, are the distinctions between those of classes in secure employment and underclasses, such as illegal migrants and 'guest workers', without secure employment. This is not to say, however, that being a migrant is itself a disadvantage: on the contrary, according to Bauman (1998), mobility is a coveted value, because it allows people to follow opportunities. The person who cannot move is threatened by downsizing, mechanization, offshoring, and outsourcing, whereas mobility is a form of wealth, because it means the individual is not bound to a particular locality.[9] This is as true of the millions of rural migrants flocking to China's cities as it is of workers from Eastern Europe trying to enter the UK or Ireland.

Labour in developing countries has become a priority issue within corporate responsibility. Mostly, the focus is on wages, child labour, working hours, forced labour, discrimination, housing, freedom of association, and occupational health and safety. From stitching footballs to farming cocoa, industries have found themselves embroiled in debates about when child labour is acceptable, while others have argued over whether a worker has the right to exploit her own labour by working over sixty hours a week. Furthermore, it is often pointed out that seemingly poor conditions may be better than those that individuals experienced before and that what globalization provides is not wealth, but the opportunity for future advancement.

It has long been observed that women experience poverty in different ways to men and some authors argue that globalization impacts upon women in particular ways. For example, in some cases, it can worsen their position by limiting them to low-paid casual work, while in others, it can create opportunities that allow them to escape oppressive cultural norms.[10] Also, certain types of worker and producer are less able to take advantage of the most rewarding opportunities. For example, smallholder farmers and home-workers can find themselves forced out of global supply chains, or having to accept low incomes because of the structure of trading relations.[11] Equally, domestic producers can find it difficult to compete with imports, especially if, as with some crops from Europe and North America, the imports are subsidized.

But the impact of globalization is not only on jobs, incomes, and trading opportunities. One reason for not thinking only in economic terms is that, for many, a major impact of globalization is on their right to choose a way of life. At the same time that liberal advocates talk about freedom, convergence has created new opportunities for slavery and international crime. As we discuss in the section on 'Universalization of norms, values, and culture' (p 79), it poses a threat to indigenous peoples and from cigarettes, to infant formula, to credit cards, it has increased people's exposure to aggressive marketing that has damaged people's lives.

We should, however, also remember that people who experience negative consequences of globalization are not simply passive victims, nor is any progress they make necessarily attributable to the success of capitalism. Improvements in working conditions are often the result of workers' protest and struggle, as the rising number of strikes at Chinese factories in recent years bears witness.[12] As many trade union activists have pointed out, workers should not think that equity is bestowed, but rather that it is something won.

Global commons, climate change, and sustainability

In any discussion of globalization's impacts, it can be difficult to separate out those things that would not have happened but for globalization from those for which the speed and intensity characteristic of globalization has exacerbated what were existing problems. This is certainly true in relation to the natural environment. The pollution and squalor that one sees around Jakarta or Shenzhen today is not substantially different to that which was experienced, because of industrialization, in Sheffield or in the Rhine in the early twentieth century. Likewise, population growth that puts pressure on natural resources because of demands for housing, energy, and food existed without globalization, and is only exacerbated by it in so far as innovation and trade deliver better diets, health care, security, etc.

There are, however, ways in which globalization affects the environment other than by increasing demand. With the demand for energy to fuel economic growth has come ever-more-rapid growth in carbon emissions, which now approach 7,000 million tonnes per year compared with less than 1,500 million in the 1950s.[13] These, in turn, are a major factor in global warming and, in this sense, we can draw a more direct link between globalization and the environment—something we explore in more detail in Chapter 12. We should also not ignore the contribution that the act of international trade makes to how we use energy. For example, the more flexible production systems that are typical of the current era of globalization have depended on innovations and improvements in storage and transportation that aid the transferability of commodities. Although energy-per-unit usage for this is declining, total usage is increasing, not least because of lower transportation costs that, many have argued, are a result of business being allowed to externalize its environmental impacts onto society in general.

Perhaps the clearest way in which globalization per se affects the environment, however, is in the way in which we think about, and respond to, concepts such as the global commons and sustainability. On the one hand, the sense of global competition evident in the political and business arenas has led certain politicians—most notably in the USA and Australia—to abandon multilateral agreements, such as the Kyoto Protocol, and subordinate environmental concerns to economic imperatives. On the other hand, globalization has probably added to our understanding and awareness of major environmental issues. At one level, it gives us rapid access to stories and pictures about land clearance in the Amazon or forest fires in Borneo. At another level, it can be said to create the ways of thinking and constructing the world that allow people who were once separated geographically to understand global interdependence, and hence the significance of a lost species in New Guinea or a tsunami in the Bay of Bengal.

Universalization of norms, values, and culture

We have already mentioned that globalization is often portrayed in terms of how it affects society and culture, and, in particular, how some see it as spreading the values, ethics, and institutions of the West. MacLean (1999) argues that a key feature of globalization that distinguishes it from its historical antecedents is that it fosters, legitimizes, and universalizes a transcending form of knowledge, especially in respect to political, economic, ethical, and social ideas. For Wolf (2004), this is one of its benefits; for Klein (1999), it is one of its dangers. Whatever stance one takes, the idea that globalization can alter the world in this way is a powerful one.

There are many empirical studies of how particular industries and companies have affected local populations, especially those of indigenous peoples who, by definition, live in non-capitalist societies. Logging, mining, oil and gas drilling and pipelines, and industrial agriculture have all been in the spotlight for the ways in which they affect indigenous people's land, livelihoods, and lifestyles.[14] The impact is not necessarily as simple as appropriating resources or putting people out of work. It can also involve changes in basic social institutions so that, for example, communal land becomes privately owned, or diverse economic livelihoods are replaced with daily waged labour.[15]

Such examples can be seen as evidence of more fundamental assertions of power. In addition to understanding how organizations and individuals operate in the new networks and alliances that globalization is producing, various authors have argued that we need to understand the underlying biases that favour particular norms and values,[16] and how the technologies and techniques that we use to analyse, control, and regulate globalization extend or limit the possibilities for change as much as the actions of any actor.

As the discussion of partnerships in Chapter 10 reveals, this distinction between overt actors and underlying agency has a significant impact on corporate responsibility, and helps to explain some of its successes and failures. It also helps to explain why corporate responsibility is sometimes accused of spreading particular values, or of failing to accommodate others' world views.[17] In terms of understanding the meaning of globalization, it alerts us to the fact that even seemingly neutral views can be charged with norms, values, and meanings that legitimate and advance specific interests. Indeed, building on Gramsci's political theory, Levy and Newell (2005) argue that the moral and intellectual leadership role exhibited by business in areas such as corporate responsibility is a contemporary example of how, throughout history, powerful forces rule through consensus and hegemony.

CASE STUDY 3.2

One nation, different values in China

In 2006, search engine companies Yahoo! and Google found themselves in the public spotlight for seemingly censoring the data that their Chinese users could see and handing over information that led to the imprisonment of users. Google's senior corporate responsibility executive defended the company as making an imperfect decision in an imperfect situation. Others pointed out the similarities with Star TV's dropping of the BBC from its Chinese network, again at the government's request.

But many companies are seemingly involved in double standards in China. Retailers employing social and environmental standards for imports to Europe and North America feel under little pressure to adopt the same ones in China, where consumers are more concerned with safety and quality issues than with labour or the environment. Government still feels that the nation's prosperity and stability depends on a vast pool of disenfranchised labour, and is worried by attempts to improve labour standards and organize workers. Moreover, officials and factory owners, sensitive to hints of imperialism, feel that corporate responsibility is a foreign concept that is insensitive to the Chinese context.

Some multinationals justify their very presence in China on the basis of their potential to be a force for good and see corporate responsibility in this light. Yet the double standards leave retailers open to accusations that what they want most of all is cheap produce and access to the potentially vast Chinese middle class.

(Lort-Phillips, 2006; CCC, 2005a)

Questions

Western companies selling into the Chinese market say that the country does not yet have the same ethical concerns and that it is more important for the companies to be present than absent.

1 What do you think are the moral arguments for such companies staying in China?

2 Is it acceptable that they vary their values from country to country?

3 Do you think companies are trying to spread universal values and is it appropriate for them to do so?

Globalization, global poverty, and international development

An interesting upshot of globalization's impact on how we view the world is that it has stimulated new interest in the condition of poor countries. This is a direct result of the networks and alliances mentioned earlier, which make it much easier to communicate that experience rapidly and vividly across vast geographical, but miniscule virtual, distances. These communications have become more important because many see a direct connection between those conditions and their own. For example, the outcry about conditions in factories producing for Nike in the early 1990s was, in part, because Western consumers felt, in some way, responsible for those conditions.[18]

There is considerable evidence that poor nations are disadvantaged and the widely used statistics are alarming. To take the example of foreign debt, the interest that African countries have had to pay to service their debts to the West each year is, by some estimates, about what it would cost to curb the AIDS pandemic, one of the major reasons that African economies are shrinking.[19] Poverty and underdevelopment existed long before the contemporary interest in globalization, but there are certainly examples in which policies intended to foster liberal globalization have disadvantaged developing nations. For example, the agreements on trade-related intellectual property rights (TRIPS) that were introduced as part of the Uruguay Round of trade negotiations resulted in the enforcement of patents for certain medicines, driving out generic manufacturers and making many drugs unaffordable in poor countries. Equally, there have been attempts to patent medicinal plants and the indigenous knowledge of developing country communities, creating the impression that the rich world—often exemplified by major corporations—is using globalization to exploit the poor.

Nonetheless, it is quite possible to argue that poverty has nothing to do with geography and that what causes poverty in Ghana is the same as that which causes it in Marseille or Burnley, i.e. factors such as class, education, health, gender, race, etc. But, for the time being, it is important to note that international development poses particular questions for globalization, ones to which we return to later in this chapter ('Corporate responsibility as a response to globalization', p 87).

Major consequences of globalization

So far, we have discussed what is meant by 'globalization' and offered different perspectives on how it alters society. We now examine how it affects two crucial elements of society in particular: the practice of business and the process of governance.

Global capital, production, and trade

For business, the most important outcome of globalization has been the enormous increases in international trade and investment. In the last half of the twentieth century, the value of world trade soared from $57bn to $6 trillion. This has gone hand in hand with the liberalization of financial transactions, whereby a combination of technological advances and policies to remove credit controls, deregulate interest rates, and privatize banking has created much greater investment opportunities. Today, global business-to-business transactions are worth about $6 trillion and the world's financial markets are becoming more like networks in cyberspace that can relay billions of trades almost instantaneously.[20]

A consequence of greater global investment opportunities and the technology to conduct fast, low-cost transactions is that speculative investment has increased, the turnover in shares has accelerated, and the investment horizon of the investor has become shorter. Short-termism was blamed for the economic crises in South-East Asia and Argentina in the 1980s and 1990s, when 'hot money' flooded countries that had adopted the Washington Consensus, causing rapid growth, and then fled almost overnight, leading to collapsed currencies, political upheaval, and public anger and distrust that lingers until today.

Global investment has also led to industry consolidation and increased foreign ownership, not least of formerly state-owned companies. What unites many globalization sceptics is what is viewed as an unhealthy growth in corporate power and alarm at facts such as that a third of world trade occurs between multinational corporations, or that five companies control the global market for consumer durables.[21] At times, the growing presence of multinationals has been highly contentious, not least in the case of the utilities sector (see Case Study 3.3). It has also provoked fears about security and other national imperatives, as seen, for example, in the last few years during which a Chinese company bid for US oil and gas producer Unocal, and a Dubai company obtained the lease to manage several US container terminals.

Freeing up of capital and trade created the conditions necessary for shifting certain aspects of production to new locations. As countries, such as Malaysia, Indonesia, and, later, China, removed barriers to foreign investment, companies from developed economies rushed to them, either to invest directly or to source from new vendors. Today, we take for granted that goods and services, from training shoes to banking, can be delivered from around the world, but it is important not to overstate the degree to which poorer countries have succeeded in attracting capital and accessing markets.[22] For all of the focus on multinational firms in India and China, the bulk of investment remains within developed economies and there are still significant barriers in some industries for developing countries to access wealthy markets.[23] Moreover, investment in developing countries is often centred on export processing zones (EPZs) offering financial incentives to investors, and even labour and environmental regulations and enforcement policies which are different to those that are available elsewhere in the country. Such zones create jobs that, in turn, result in workers remitting savings back to other regions. But they also exhibit features of enclave economies, in which the bulk of the wealth created is enjoyed elsewhere, and the revenues generated locally may not be enough to support the kinds of enforcement and social investment that offset negative impacts.

Claims about the wealth of corporations being on a par with that of many governments may be exaggerated,[24] and corporate responsibility is full of examples demonstrating that wealth and power are not always synonymous. Nonetheless, the behaviour of multinational companies on a global stage is an important part of corporate responsibility's story and, as we examine later in the chapter ('Corporate responsibility as a response to globalization', p 87), set important parameters for what corporate responsibility addresses and how.

Water—privatizing basic rights or giving access to basic needs?

Water is essential to life, yet the amount of accessible water per person worldwide is falling. This is why water is a global issue, with the private sector at its centre. Over 150 years after John Snow discovered the link between water and cholera, 1.1 billion people are still without access to clean water and 2.4 billion lack proper sanitary provision.

The global water crisis is more about management than true scarcity. The current supply of fresh water is a small percentage of our planet's total water, yet it would be more than enough for the world population's current needs if it were more evenly distributed. Unfortunately, that is not the case. According to the UN Environmental Programme, demand for water will soon exceed availability by 56 per cent and two-thirds of the world's population will face water stress. Major investments in infrastructure and management are needed to amend this problem: challenges that the private sector would seem well suited to tackle.

Yet private sector interventions have met considerable resistance in some regions. Privatization of water utilities in Europe encouraged organizations, such as the World Bank, to promote private sector involvement to reach 2.4 billion new consumers by 2015 in order to meet the Millennium Development Goals. The major water companies were, however, accused of privatizing water sources, and have repeatedly been under the media spotlight for cutting off poor consumers and favouring rich customers. In Bolivia, Argentina, and the Philippines, major utilities companies terminated government contracts.

At the heart of the protests is that, for many, water is not simply a human need, but a human right. Some feel that by calling water a 'need', it opens the door to privatization and provision on a for-profit basis, whereas declaring water to be a 'right' might be used to prevent companies from buying up water sources. There are some signs that a middle ground may be reached and that the private sector should be considered neither panacea nor pariah. Talking to fellow business leaders, George Kuper, President of the Council of Great Lakes Industry, said business had a key role to play in making water accessible, but that it had no need to own the resource.

(FAO, 2003; Gleick, 1999; UN, 2003)

Questions

The privatization of water has provoked debate about what we mean by basic rights and basic needs.

1 Is the distinction between water as a human need and a human right valid?

2 What are the implications of this distinction for business?

3 Is it accurate to see access to water as a 'management problem', as politicians and business leaders have tended to?

The changing nature of governance and enforcement

Globalization is also closely connected to changes in how society is governed. In part, this is because liberal globalization depends on the slew of policy changes described earlier. At the same time, deterritorialization creates a new space that cannot be readily governed by existing governance structures, such as national governments, or even the international mechanisms housed within the United Nations. For example, a national government can legislate on toxic emissions, but once those emissions affect the global commons, a multi-national solution is required.

There are a few long-established institutions with an international regulatory mandate —notably the International Labour Organization (ILO), which, since the end of World War I, has brought national governments, the business community, and international trade unions together to set and enforce international labour standards. There are also national laws applying to actions overseas, such as the US Alien Tort Claims Act 1789, which has been used to hold US companies to account for human rights violations around the world. More noticeable since the 1970s, however, has been a trend away from seeing government as the sole, or even primary, solution to both regulation and social welfare.

This trend may have reached its peak on 11 September 2001,[25] but for anyone born before the 1970s, the changes in the roles and expectations of government have already been enormous. They continue to be at the heart of debates about how society responds to globalization and attitudes towards corporate responsibility across Europe.[26]

There are four main interpretations of what has happened.

1 **National government has seen its power eroded by globalization**

   As a condition of joining the global market, national governments surrender much of their power to create policy autonomously and poor countries, in particular, have had policies forced upon them. Some of those policies have undermined state sovereignty, not only in areas of macroeconomic policy, but also in areas such as taxation, social welfare, and human development. Even in rich countries, governments not only no longer try and control exchange rates, but they are also afraid to raise corporate taxes or to raise the minimum wage, for fear of driving business overseas.

2 **There is a governance vacuum at the global level**

   There is no clear responsibility or accountability for issues such as human rights and poverty, for which the forces of economic globalization may have unacceptable consequences that cannot be resolved by market forces. Equally, there are new challenges, such as the management of the global commons, that cannot be solved through conventional governance mechanisms. As Bell puts it: '*The nation-state is becoming too small for the big problems of life, and too big for the small problems of life.*'[27] Yet there are many examples in which national governments have exerted enormous influence on the governance of globalization. For example, the World Trade Organization (see Box 3.1) is a direct result of national government negotiation and agreement, and has been criticized for being too influenced by the interests of the wealthiest economies (e.g. its slowness in tackling agriculture subsidies).[28] As Braithwaite and Drahos (2000) observe, what we are witnessing may not be deregulation but '*re-regulation*', with state rollback in some areas, such as capital and trade, and a strengthening of regulation to protect other rights.

3 **Government has deliberately chosen where and where not to exert influence**

   Migration, for example, is an issue relating to which governments have been accused of hypocrisy, because, while they have removed barriers to trade and investment, they

Box 3.1 New models of international governance—the World Trade Organization

Establishment of the World Trade Organization in 1995 was one of the most important steps in creating a new model of international governance. Part international negotiating forum, part court of arbitration, it has the power to affect trade rules and to resolve disputes, and its role is to focus on trade. Globalization sceptics point out that, while globalization raises issues about social and environmental justice, the one major international body to come out of globalization so far is an organization that focused entirely on liberalizing trade. But the WTO's defenders argue that it is not, and should not be, a world court and point, for example, to the International Labour Organization as the competent body for addressing labour rights issues.

(Jones and Pollit, 2004)

Box 3.2 Millennium Development Goals

Goal 1   Eradicate extreme poverty and hunger

Goal 2   Achieve universal primary education

Goal 3   Promote gender equality and empower women

Goal 4   Reduce child mortality

Goal 5   Improve maternal health

Goal 6   Combat HIV/AIDS, malaria, and other diseases

Goal 7   Ensure environmental sustainability

Goal 8   Develop a global partnership for development

(Based on United Nations Millennium Project)

have put up barriers to allowing most people to pursue job opportunities through international migration. This has generated criticism from liberal economists and from globalization's opponents. For the former, the conclusion is largely that governments should truly step aside; for the latter, it is evidence of the need for different approaches to governance.

4 Governments still maintain power

As Ward (2003) emphasizes, it is important not to dismiss the regulatory role of government. National laws, such as the US Foreign Corrupt Practices Act 1977 and Alien Tort Claims Act 1789, can affect the behaviour of multinational companies around the world. Bilateral trade agreements, for example, are one way in which the poor in developing nations can benefit from global trade and, in some instances, these agreements have created favourable environments for corporate responsibility.[29] Multilateral institutions have created the UN Global Compact, the UN Millennium Development Goals (see Box 3.2), the Organisation for Economic Cooperation and Development's guidelines for multinational enterprises, the ILO's tripartite declaration of principles concerning multinational enterprises and social policy, and the ILO's Declaration on Fundamental Principles and Rights at Work.

Another feature of governance in this era of globalization is that it is no longer the dominant preserve of government. There is a growing element of self-regulation by business and, in particular, of business being used by government as the initial enforcer (e.g. in the UK, supermarkets are liable for enforcing food safety standards in their supply chains). There is also widespread outsourcing of the policing of business behaviour, building on approaches originating in financial auditing, and quasi-independent bodies, notably the International Organization for Standardization (ISO), have had a significant impact on environmental management and are developing systems for corporate responsibility more broadly.

Civil society organizations are increasingly involved in both 'street regulation', through campaigns, watchdog activities, and 'naming and shaming' of particular companies, and participation in new regulatory systems, such as international standards and multi-stakeholder partnerships.[30] These different views of public governance are all relevant to the relationship between notions of corporate responsibility and globalization, and the changing nature of governance is especially important in the corporate responsibility context, as we discuss in the next section.

CASE STUDY 3.4

The Multi-fibre Agreement

The Multi-fibre Agreement (MFA), which had governed garment and textile imports to the EU and USA since 1974, ended in 2005. Quotas that had helped developing countries to export while sheltering them from global competition were ended, allowing buying companies to consolidate their supply base and raising fears that China would dominate the industry. It was predicted that the end of the MFA would bring job losses in poor countries without China's advantages and, at the same time, jeopardize major brands' reputations while fomenting scepticism about companies' corporate responsibility agendas. Some predicted a 'great garment massacre', with nearly half of world's 250,000 garment factories vanishing.

Early signs were that the impact would be large. Within months, the 'bra wars' began, as European and US governments insisted that Chinese manufacturers limit their imports as per China's WTO accession agreement. At the same time, concerned that countries such as Bangladesh, Cambodia, and Lesotho would see their apparel industries collapse, an alliance of public institutions, labour and civil society organizations, and businesses was formed. Known as the MFA Forum, its purpose was to better understand and respond to the implications of the end of the MFA, particularly for workers and communities.

(Abrami, 2003; www.ethicaltrade.org; O'Reilly, 2005)

Questions

The phasing out of the MFA was part of the process of global trade liberalization, but it also reveals a range of responses from different sectors.

1 To what fears were the US and European governments responding when they restricted imports and do you think that corporate responsibility addresses this type of fear?

2 What negative impacts do you think the MFA Forum was trying to understand?

3 Why do you think a multi-organizational response was chosen to address them?

Corporate responsibility as a response to globalization

Understanding the phenomenon of globalization is a necessary part of comprehending the context within which contemporary corporate responsibility has emerged. Ruggie (2003) treats it as a manifestation of Polanyi's notion of the embedded economy (see Chapter 2): an attempt to contain and share the social adjustment costs that open markets inevitably produce. Criticisms of business—and of big business, in particular—as reaping the benefits of globalization without taking responsibility for its negative consequences have become an important driver of corporate responsibility as a whole. Moreover, specific initiatives, such as codes of labour practice or participation in the environmental agenda that first emerged out of the 1992 Rio Earth Summit, address the perceived mismatch of regulatory scope and actual economic structure that is a consequence of expanding global trade.

This does not mean that the issues that corporate responsibility addresses are necessarily the consequences of globalization. For example, slavery, deforestation, child labour, and over-fishing all took place before globalization. In some cases (e.g. slavery), it may not even be the case that what is happening is worse than that which occurred in the past.[31] But globalization exaggerates and exacerbates by making things quicker, larger, and more visible than before, and this has increased the pressure on companies to act responsibly. For some, corporate responsibility is about making the benefits of globalization accessible to more people, either by limiting the need for government intervention,[32] or by making new resources available for human development. It can also be seen as a reflection of the growing interdependence of government and business, under which the former looks to the latter to create wealth in order to retain power, while the latter looks to the former to develop human capital and maintain stability.[33] What is more, reflecting the general widespread growth in self-regulation and voluntary agreements by business, corporate responsibility can be regarded as an element of a new system of global governance that sits alongside the democratic model of national government that is promoted by the most powerful countries.[34]

CASE STUDY 3.5

Making poverty accessible

In June and July 2005, the media markets of the world's richest countries ran hot with news about Africa. An original film on BBC1; celebrities everywhere seen wearing the signature white wristband; a mass rally in Edinburgh; major bands playing stages in cities across the Western world: these were the manifestations of the Make Poverty History campaign, designed to force political leaders at the G8 Summit to do something about Africa's problems.

The campaign showed both the power of shrewd marketing and the kind of single-issue focus that typifies much of modern 'political' activity. It brought together a powerful, short-term coalition that readily captured media and public attention. But it went beyond most such campaigns: the politicians, the business leaders, the rich, and the famous that Bono and Bob Geldof were able to bring on board showed, according to Madeline Bunting, '*how a political and corporate world is hungrily casting around for new sources of legitimacy to bolster its positions*'.

In all of this, Africans themselves were noticeably absent, except as passive faces in photos and on screens, as if the rich world were conversing with itself while Africa waited at the door. After years of struggling to overcome public indifference to the complex problems of Africa since the heyday of Live Aid and Comic Relief, however, modern marketing and addressing an impatient consumer culture in its own terms appeared to have spurred the public to pressurize politicians to take action.

(Bunting, 2005; Orr, 2005)

Questions

Make Poverty History was, in many ways, a response to the same kind of public understanding of globalization that influences corporate responsibility.

1 What are the benefits of high-profile campaigns such as this for people working in corporate responsibility?

2 Are there trade-offs in making the story of globalization accessible in this way?

3 Is the charge of 'absent Africans'—with its connotations of paternalism by the rich towards the poor—something that can be levelled at corporate responsibility?

How corporate responsibility addresses the challenges of globalization

Some of contemporary corporate responsibility's earliest initiatives were related to globalization. The Rio Earth Summit, for example, brought together different sectors of society to address global environmental challenges. It succeeded in sending the message that business could and should act, and indirectly encouraged business and environmental groups to work together on initiatives such as sustainable forest management. It also lit a flame in the oil industry that influenced Shell's early corporate responsibility reporting and eventually led to BP rebranding itself as Beyond Petroleum, as its CEO, John Browne, began to speak out on the importance of business addressing greenhouse gases and other threats to the environment.[35]

In a different way, early initiatives intended to rethink the nature of working lives were a response to the ways in which globalization had influenced the workplace. Business in the Community in the UK was started as a response to urban decay and industrial decline during the 1980s, and the lack of government action. The Prince of Wales Business Leaders' Forum was a tentative step to encourage UK business executives to think about their role in the world. At that stage, these organizations were still firmly rooted in traditions of giving back to communities through, for instance, philanthropy, community investment, and volunteering.

At the same time, the fairtrade movement was establishing itself as a way of dealing with what were seen as inequitable trading relations with poor producers in developing countries. Trade union and NGO campaigns raised public awareness about labour conditions in the apparel and sporting goods industries, which had been early movers in globalizing production. This, in turn, led to a number of companies, primarily in the UK and USA, adopting codes of labour practice and partnering with civil society organizations to implement them. This interest spilled over into parts of agriculture, which was already becoming more global, and which, in Europe, was increasingly interested in improved environmental management and product safety.

Other industries that were, perhaps, more removed from globalization were nonetheless feeling the consequences of rapid information exchange and the power of civil society alliances. Mining companies in Papua, or oil companies in Burma, came under the spotlight because of allegations about human rights, environmental damage, and corruption. Such criticisms, in turn, raised questions about the funding of major private sector projects, such as the Chad–Cameroon oil pipeline; public and private sector finance bodies, such as the Commonwealth Development Corporation, the International Finance Corporation, and Citigroup began to pay more attention to non-financial aspects of their investments. This eventually led, in 2003, to the Equator Principles—a framework promoting environmental and social responsibility in project financing. As we explore in Chapter 10, similar industry partnerships have emerged to address other aspects of corporate responsibility.

Towards the end of the 1990s, developing countries became a particular focus area within corporate responsibility, and today there are many, both within and outside the business community, who, to a degree, judge corporate responsibility's credibility based on its contribution to international development.[36] Initially, there was a strong sense that developing countries needed to be protected from certain forms of exploitation. As well as particular codes of conduct, new partnerships emerged, including those bringing together business, civil society, and government, such as the Extractive Industries Transparency Initiative and the Ethical Trading Initiative in the UK, or Kenya's Horticultural Ethical Business Initiative, and the Agricultural Ethics Assurance Association of Zimbabwe.

In 1999, the UN announced its Global Compact to bring companies together with UN agencies, labour organizations, and civil society, to promote responsible corporate practices and to help business be part of the solution to the challenges of globalization. Publications from the World Economic Forum (2006) and the World Business Council for Sustainable Development (2006) make clear that the UN's Millennium Development Goals have also provided a catalyst for some in business to focus on particular development-oriented activities.[37] WEF's Centre for Public–Private Partnership has also stressed that meeting these goals cannot be done by governments, business, or civil society alone. Its mission highlights that, in addition to business' role in upholding and advancing principles on human rights, labour, environmental, and anti-corruption practices in countries with weak regulatory capacity, business competencies can improve the effectiveness of development programmes (e.g. technology development, providing essential goods and services, and managing large-scale operations).

The Prince of Wales Business Leaders' Forum renamed itself the International Business Leaders' Forum (IBLF) in 2001 and, in the same year, adopted the interface between business, globalization, and poverty as a central theme in its report. Since then, IBLF has called for the corporate responsibility world to stop seeing developing countries as a place in which companies are a threat and to treat corporate responsibility in the developing country context as being about opportunities. The same sentiment lies behind Business Action for Africa, a coalition of 35 multinational companies aiming to support the expansion of small and medium-sized enterprises, invest in prevention and treatment of HIV, and fight corruption. Such initiatives emphasize that poverty reduction can only be achieved by strengthening of the private sector and the efficient operation of market economies. They also reflect a conviction, in some quarters, that these goals require intervention by business coalitions rather than by individual companies.[38]

There is also growing interest in business models that combine profits with poverty alleviation, which Prahalad (2005) refers to as *'the fortune at the bottom of the pyramid'*. Companies in financial services, such as GE, have started to develop products for poorer consumers; Citigroup has adopted the microfinance model that was pioneered by NGOs and aid agencies in Bangladesh to finance small entrepreneurs ignored by commercial banks;[39] companies, such as Abbott Laboratories, have extended volunteering to make skilled personnel available to build developing country infrastructure.

The above examples are revealing at several levels. First, they are evidence that business is not comfortable relying on the market and other sectors of society to address some of the consequences of globalization. Second, in addition to any regulatory requirements, companies are responding by giving back to communities: by using voluntary standards, by involvement in partnering between companies and sectors, and by developing new products and business models. Third, after a long period during which business was positioned as the problem, it is now increasingly being positioned as the solution, particularly to challenges associated with poverty and inequity.

Unmet challenges

Corporate responsibility faces three main areas of criticism relating to how it addresses the challenges and impacts of globalization. The first of these—not least from within the business community itself—is that business can, and should, do more to find new solutions to meet the challenges that globalization presents. There is general consensus that governments cannot meet these challenges alone: hence the formation of alliances with non-state actors, such as the private sector, are essential.[40] But private sector involvement needs to be responsible and values-driven, and it is here that the overlap between development and corporate responsibility becomes apparent.[41]

This criticism takes different forms: for example, it underpins the calls for action from Business Action for Africa and WEF's Centre for Public–Private Partnership. It takes a different shape in the concept that Wood et al. (2006) call *'global business citizenship'*, which seeks to develop a new framework for corporate responsibility within which its boundaries are not prescribed by the competitive pressures of globalization. And it appears again in authors, such as Hart (2005), who recognize business as part of the solution to creating a sustainable environment, but push it to go beyond the business case-related thinking of the triple bottom line. What is common to all of them, however, is the acceptance of business as a crucial actor, not simply because it does harm, but because it has unique resources, scope, and competencies that need to be harnessed for society's good. As Wettstein (2005) notes, if multinational companies are as powerful as they are portrayed, perhaps they should not be allowed to stay out of political debate or to ignore global problems, but rather should be thought of as quasi-governmental institutions with an inherent responsibility for global well-being. The challenge, therefore, is to get business to use its resources in alternative ways.

The second criticism is more accusatory. It acknowledges that business has tried to address society's concerns through certification schemes, adoption of global framework agreements, standard setting and monitoring, and dialogues with other sectors and its critics, but deems all of these approaches to voluntary regulation inadequate. Utting's (2005b) analysis concludes that too many companies have not participated; there has been limited penetration of corporate responsibility ideas across the corporate structure; compliance procedures are often weak; initiatives, such as codes of conduct, are often top-down and technocratic, and while focusing on particular named issues, they do not examine the impact of corporate responsibility, especially in developing countries. There are some signs of change,[42] but Vogel (2005) concludes that, ultimately, corporate responsibility demonstrates the limitations of self-regulation and the need for government to assert its regulatory role, or, as Utting argues, a more robust approach to '*articulated regulation*', under which different regulatory approaches and agents would come together in ways that are complementary, mutually reinforcing, and synergistic.

The final criticism of corporate responsibility as a response to globalization builds on these arguments over self-regulation and centres on corporate responsibility's capacity to alter perceptions of corporate self-interest. It holds that many of globalization's short-comings are exacerbated, or at least overlooked, by companies pursuing their narrow self-interest. For example, lay-offs and plant closures make sense in terms of global competitiveness, but can be devastating for individuals and communities. Similarly, lobbying for lower corporate tax rates can appear concordant with executives' fiduciary duties, but depriving government of revenues can lead to cuts in public services. Indeed, as Visser (2006) has argued in an African context, accepted corporate responsibility frameworks, such as Carroll's pyramid, can appear simplistic and static when applied in developing countries, and may not recognize that conflicts and contradictions should be anticipated as the norm, rather than treated as the shocking exception.

One strand of this critique holds that companies do not try to understand the consequences of their behaviour and focus only on those issues that they feel will affect their reputation, or that will serve their self-interest in other ways (e.g. investing in maintaining a healthy, educated workforce and protecting their image).[43] Thus, for example, European retailers committed to ethical sourcing were slow to recognize the different tiers of their supply chains, and the specific social and environmental challenges at each level.[44] Moreover, the logic of efficient supply chain management made the entry level for small producers too high and even forced some out of export markets.

There are indications that companies committed to corporate responsibility are becoming more sensitive to these issues. For example, the Multi-fibre Alliance that came out of a stakeholder meeting at Nike head offices in 2004 brought together NGOs, business, and trade unions to consider the social consequences of the ending of the Multi-fibre Agreement (see Case Study 3.4). The collaboration between Unilever and Oxfam to examine ways the behaviour of a multinational affects poverty in Indonesia is also an example of how partnerships are beginning to wrestle with the complexity of international development.[45] While this was an extension of Unilever's strategy to consider the overall societal positioning of selected brands (something that led, for example, to the innovative rebranding of Dove beauty products), it is unclear, as yet, how this increased understanding will affect business behaviour. A critical dimension to this will be how far companies can align around a corporate responsibility sensibility so that they are not, for example, claiming improved environmental practices, while at the same time aggressively marketing high-risk products to ill-educated consumers,[46] or not promoting better labour conditions, while using just-in-time contracting that can exacerbate labour exploitation.

The second strand of the same critique argues that aspects of trading and other contractual relationships are inherently unfair and biased towards the interests of the most powerful companies, but mainstream corporate responsibility has done little to address this. For example, as Oxfam's Make Trade Fair campaign asks, to what extent will corporate responsibility push for fairness in trading relations, both between countries and within specific supply chains?[47] And as Jenkins (2005) has noted, there are many areas that might be important for long-term development in which business seems to be silent or hostile (e.g. corporate taxation and tort reform), and corporate responsibility has done little to influence corporate investment in countries with the least foreign direct investment.

Finally, it is argued that the mindset and tools of corporate responsibility are so deeply embedded in the normative frameworks of business that corporate responsibility ends up taking for granted, reproducing, and legitimising, rather than providing an alternative to, the values and priorities associated with free enterprise. We saw earlier how some believe that globalization universalizes certain values; it has been argued that corporate responsibility is one way in which this is done, not only by what is included or excluded from standards of acceptable social and environmental performance, but by the way in which those tools are used.[48] At the very least, current approaches, such as ethical sourcing, have been observed to ignore the priorities of workers, and to fail to consider the broader impacts of initiatives on other producers and neighbouring communities;[49] as case studies from Newell (2005) and Fig (2005) have shown, initiatives driven from the bottom up run the risk of being ignored or discounted by corporate responsibility. Such case studies reveal how important voices are missing from corporate responsibility partnerships and other initiatives that claim to engage with stakeholders, but often end up doing so on a selective basis.

SUMMARY

Globalization is a specific historical era that is redefining the role of business in the world. The human and environmental consequences of globalization are causing us to rethink corporate responsibility. Yet there are competing definitions of globalization and these, in turn, affect what we think the responsibilities of business are, and how we believe companies should approach them.

There are various definitions, but the two strongest are globalization as economic liberalization and globalization as deterritorialization. The former emphasizes globalization as an economic phenomenon that fosters the convergence of the world's economies in a global market. The latter considers globalization to be a social condition that can only be partially explained with reference to economics. The unique feature of this condition is the way in which physical space and time have become much less important determinants of economic and social activity, and of social identity.

The meaning that we give to 'globalization' affects how we look at its impacts. For some, these impacts are synonymous with 'liberalism', whether we mean by that the benefits of free trade, comparative advantage, and enlightened self-interest, or the exploitation of workers, social inequality, and the externalization of industry's ecological costs. Others may not deny these impacts, but instead highlight that what is distinctive about globalization is how it affects social networks, generates new types of organization, and creates the need for new approaches to governance. These different views are highly evident in debates about corporate responsibility. Some treat it as either a hindrance or a palliative to economic liberalization; others see it as related to the new organizations and alliances that globalization has spawned, and as part of the response to the challenges of global governance.

Neither of these definitions of globalization particularly applies to developing nations, but poverty and its consequences have become closely associated with globalization. Liberalization, as implemented to date, has brought mixed benefits for poor nations, but technological innovation and related advances in transparency have made it easier to draw attention to, and rally around, stories of globalization gone awry. The image of wealthy multinational firms seemingly indifferent to, or taking advantage of, poor countries has proved particularly resonant, as, to some extent, has been the idea of poor nations as missed opportunities for free enterprise. Today, important companies and organizations see poverty and international development as critical missions for corporate responsibility.

DISCUSSION POINTS

1 If we compare the issues raised in the sections on globalization as 'A tale of a glass half empty' (p 76) and on 'Corporate responsibility as a response to globalization' (p 87), there are clearly gaps between the consequences of globalization and the concerns of corporate responsibility.
   - What are the main aspects of globalization that corporate responsibility does not address?
   - What are the reasons for these gaps?
   - Which of these gaps will corporate responsibility attempt to bridge in the future and why?

2 Liberal globalization theorists, such as Wolf and Henderson, take umbrage with companies and others that support corporate responsibility.
   - What are the main reasons for their hostility?
   - Do you think there are shifts within corporate responsibility thinking that address their concerns?
   - Referring to examples such as Unilever's work with Oxfam in Indonesia and theorists such as Stiglitz and Porritt, how would you refute Wolf and Henderson's arguments to a business audience?

3 Corporate responsibility has been variously described as a 'response' to globalization and as its 'reflection'.
   - What distinction is being made here?
   - Do companies' policies and programmes appear to reflect one of these views more than the other?
   - Selecting the ideological framework of a particular political party, how would you make the case that corporate responsibility complements its policy objectives?

4 International development and poverty are increasingly emphasized as something that corporate responsibility must tackle.
- Why are the social and environmental issues associated with international development important for business?
- For which aspects of underdevelopment and poverty can business be blamed?
- What are the opportunities and threats for corporate responsibility if it is seen primarily as an approach to the alleviation of global poverty?

5 Since the 1990s, worries about the global environment have been an important driver of corporate responsibility, although some believe that social issues are now more prominent.
- What environmental challenges are most clearly associated with globalization?
- To what extent can, and should, business seek to tackle the major global environmental challenges?
- Over fifteen years after the Rio Earth Summit, what are the main overall achievements of the environmental initiatives in which business has been involved?

VISIT THE WEBSITE for links to useful sources of further information

FURTHER READING

- Allen, T and Thomas, A (eds), 2000, *Poverty and Development into the 21st Century*, revised edn, Oxford: Open University in association with Oxford University Press.
  Introduction to the theories and ideas of international development.

- Mcmichael, P, 2004, *Development and Social Change: A Global Perspective*, 3rd edn, Thousand Oaks, CA: Pine Forge Press.
  How globalization is affecting social processes worldwide.

- Narlikar, A, 2005, *The World Trade Organization: A Very Short Introduction*, Oxford: Oxford University Press.
  Useful handbook for understanding what the WTO is and is not.

- Porritt, J, 2005, *Capitalism: As if the World Matters*, London: Earthscan.
  An alternative view of capitalism's future from an important sustainability thinker and activist.

- Steger, MB, 2003, *Globalization: A Very Short Introduction*, Oxford: Oxford University Press.
  Accessible overview of theories of globalization.

- Stiglitz, JE, 2005, *Fair Trade For All: How Trade Can Promote Development*, Oxford: Oxford University Press.
  Influential economist's view on the shortcomings of liberal economic globalization.

- Wolf, M, 2004, *Why Globalization Works*, New Haven, CT: Yale University Press.
  Feisty response to globalization's critics.

ENDNOTES

[1] See, e.g., Demirag, 2005; Blowfield, 2005a.

[2] The term comes from Scholte, 2000, but a similar conceptualization of globalization has been set out by many theorists (e.g. Gray, Mittelman, Held) and has evolved from early work on inter-dependence, such as Giddens, 1990, and Robertson, 1992.

[3] Steger, 2003.

[4] Henderson, 2001; Lindsey, 2002.

[5] Wolf, 2004, p 36.

[6] Wolf, 2004, p 320.

[7] Stiglitz, 2002, p 248.

[8] Johnston, 2003; Johnson, 2004.

[9] Schirato and Webb, 2003, pp 96–7.

[10] Kabeer, 2000; Coleman, 2002.

[11] Frynas, 2000; Freeman, 2003.

[12] See, e.g., Kurtenbach, 2005; Cody, 2004.

[13] Marland et al., 2003.

[14] Caufield, 1996.

[15] See, e.g., Blowfield, 2004.

[16] For example, Germain, 1999; MacLean, 1999; Levy and Newell, 2005, build on theories of power from writers such as Lukes, Gramsci, and Foucault to examine how exertions of power are not necessarily overt or attributable to recognizable actors.

[17] Blowfield and Frynas, 2005.

[18] Ballinger and Olsson, 1997.

[19] Steger, 2003, p 43.

[20] Steger, 2003; Waters, 2001.

[21] Bendell, 2004a.

[22] World Bank, 2005.

[23] Wolf, 2004.

[24] This is Wolf's position: he says that corporate wealth has been exaggerated by dubious arithmetic. The merits of different claims about the power and influence of multinational companies is examined in Chandler and Mazlish, 2005.

[25] Ring et al., 2005.

[26] McMurtry, 2002.

[27] Cited in Waters, 2001, p 123.

[28] See, e.g., Stiglitz, 2002; Wolf, 2004; Oxfam, 2005.

[29] Elliott and Freeman, 2003. Abrami, 2003, discusses the US–Cambodia bilateral textile agreement, which was lauded for increasing market access to the USA to improvements in workers' rights.

[30] Utting, 2005b.

[31] For an overview of modern slavery, see Bales, 2004.

[32] Block and Barnett, 2005.

[33] Stopford et al., 1991.

[34] Blowfield, 2005a.

[35] Browne, 2004.

[36] Blowfield, 2005b.

[37] For a summary of partnerships, see Fox and Prescott, 2004.

[38] Fourie and Eloff, 2005.

[39] Maitland, 2005; Prahalad, 2005.

[40] See, e.g., UN, 2005; World Bank, 2005.

[41] Fox and Prescott, 2004.

[42] See, e.g., the shift from policing suppliers to engaging suppliers and workers in labour monitoring (CCC, 2005a; ETI, 2005a).

[43] Maitland, 2005.

[44] Zadek, 2004.

[45] Clay, 2005.

[46] Christian Aid, 2004, and Utting, 2005b, provide examples of this kind of non-alignment.

[47] Materials on Make Trade Fair are available at www.oxfam.org.

[48] Blowfield, 2004.

[49] DFID, 2002.

Part 2

Managing and implementing corporate responsibility

4

How corporate responsibility is managed

Chapter overview

In this chapter, we begin to examine the way in which corporate responsibility is being managed within companies, comparing the experiences of different countries, industries, and regions, and also identifying the common lessons. In particular, we will:

- discuss the different goals that companies are trying to achieve;

- identify the types and levels of corporate responsibility that companies exhibit;

- examine the shared lessons and common elements of corporate responsibility management;

- explore how corporate responsibility is managed inside companies;

- look at the role that service providers play in corporate responsibility management;

- explore how companies influence the corporate responsibility practices of their suppliers and customers;

- consider how corporate responsibility practices differ between industries;

- discuss corporate responsibility management for small and medium-sized businesses.

Main topics

■ Key terms

Change management

Defensive corporate responsibility

Integrated business strategy

Offensive corporate responsibility

Small and medium-sized enterprises

■ Online resources

- Suggested additional material on corporate responsibility for small and medium-sized enterprises

- Exercises and discussion topics for students

- Company-specific case studies about corporate responsibility management

- Links to other web-based resources

What is the company trying to achieve?

Corporate responsibility management is mostly depicted in terms of organizational change and transformation. For this reason, its analysis typically distinguishes between:

1 the purpose and results (the why and the what);

2 the principles and processes (the how);

3 leadership (the who).

The next sections broadly follow these distinctions and, therefore, we begin with a discussion of the way in which companies decide whether to adopt corporate responsibility.

The most basic questions that any company thinking about corporate responsibility must answer are as follows.

1 What is our purpose in doing this—i.e. what Holliday et al. (2002) call the '*corporate magnetic north*'?

2 What do we need to do to achieve it?

The wide range of definitions, approaches, and issues related to corporate responsibility mean that these basic questions do not necessarily have simple answers (see Chapter 1). Should a company focus on things that affect its financial bottom line? If so, what exactly are those things on which it should focus? Threats to the company's reputation; risks to the supply of materials; attempts to undermine the share price; harms to the company's ability to recruit or retain top quality personnel; acts that expose the firm to costly law-suits: all of these are things that can affect financial performance and require that significant attention be given to corporate responsibility. But should the company define its corporate responsibility more in terms of addressing social issues, such as access to education, support for the arts, or reducing inequality? Must it try to do both and, if so, is there a point at which the company's social mission overwhelms the conventional business purpose?

Immediately, we see what one survey of corporate responsibility approaches concludes is the distinction between operational responsibilities and citizenship responsibilities.[1] Companies are not limited to focusing on one set of responsibilities to the exclusion of the other, but the resource implications of any decision mean that even the largest corporation has to choose what to prioritize. Yet the same survey also makes clear that it is not only the company that decides what responsibilities to act upon. Consumers, for example, have their own priorities and may reward or punish a company in the marketplace if its values do not concord with their own. Until recently, many companies prioritized their citizenship responsibilities through, for example, corporate philanthropy and community investment, but now consumers are ambivalent about firms' performance in these areas, while demanding that business lives up to operational responsibilities, such as product quality, environmental protection, fair treatment of employees, and ethical supply chains.

Defining the company's corporate responsibility purpose is further complicated by the fact that perceptions of responsibility differ from country to country. For example, in Germany, it is a priority that companies provide secure employment; in South Africa, it is a priority that companies improve health, education, and other elements of social welfare; in Australia, the emphasis is on environmental protection. These priorities shift and often reflect recent local crises, so that in Argentina, for example, the main expectation that people have of business is job creation, because of the unemployment and financial loss caused by the recent economic collapse. In China, the main expectation is for safe, high-quality products, because of recent incidents of fire and serious injury caused by shoddy electrical goods.

Other factors and actors also influence the purpose of corporate responsibility. For example, the European Commission has defined corporate responsibility in a way that is intended to reflect what it calls the unique European social model, under which employers and other stakeholders, such as trade unions, function together to shape society and the economy. Reflecting the ideal that companies should not focus solely on profit, but also on the welfare of the workforce, consumers, and the environment, the model sets out the purpose of corporate responsibility in terms of the benefits to workers, customers, communities, and wider society. Acknowledging the importance of different types of company across Europe, it requires that corporate responsibility be relevant to small and medium-sized enterprises. Reflecting the need to establish European competitive advantage in the global economy, it also requires that corporate responsibility find ways of demonstrating that responsible business attracts investment and builds a skilled workforce.[2]

Similarly, an industry or a multi-industry collaboration can influence a company's corporate responsibility purpose. For example, the US Business Roundtable's SEE Change initiative, comprising companies such as Alcoa, Coca Cola, Dow Chemicals, and Xerox, aims to combine the traditional business goals of higher profits and lower costs with strong corporate commitments to environmental stewardship. Not only does the initiative suggest areas in which member companies should take action (e.g. eco-efficiency and demonstrating the business impacts of sustainable investment), it also goes some way to defining how corporate responsibility is to be managed by, for example, requiring companies to report their progress against individually determined timelines and goals.

The increase in the range of organizations, individuals, and sectors of society that seek to influence business behaviour is one trend that needs to be understood in terms of thinking about a company's corporate responsibility purpose; how companies consider other trends is also an influencing factor. For example, what significance does the company attach to changing patterns of demand for (and often shrinking supplies of) natural resources, or the influence of climate change? How will the growing number of tangible and intangible financial factors that might affect the way business is valued and its success measured influence the way in which the company is managed, and in what it invests? Or does the company need to respond to the growing role of international institutions, and the to continued acceleration in the speed of policy and behavioural change caused by the global media?[3] Each of these trends has relevance for corporate responsibility, whether in terms of the need to change energy use, or to invest in new building technology because of the natural resource situation, or the financial case for investing in innovative technologies to solve social problems, or the challenges of participating in new models of global governance.

Basic distinctions in corporate responsibility purpose

One way of thinking about what the company aims to achieve from corporate responsibility is to distinguish between what Kramer and Kania (2006) call 'defensive' and 'offensive' corporate responsibility. In their view, most companies view corporate responsibility in terms of vulnerability, i.e. as an external risk that needs to be managed with minimal investment. Thus, for example, a non-government organization will raise an issue and the company will seek to find the least costly way to defuse attention, through actions such as lobbying, public relations, and advertising. The defensive approach can also be used, as others have pointed out, to maintain the company's reputation and to avoid legal liabilities, and is generally employed when companies are seeking to resolve problems of their own making.

In contrast, the offensive approach can involve companies offering themselves as the solution even if they had no part in creating the problem. It requires companies to exploit their full capabilities to find and implement solutions, and requires the company to do four key things.

1 Pick the right issue—one that is important, timely, and that leverages the company's core competencies.
2 Establish concrete goals and report on progress, both inside the company and externally.
3 Deploy the company's key assets in addressing the issue, including, for example, its products and services, the relevant skills of its employees, industry expertise, and its infrastructure.
4 Work in partnership with other sectors.

BP is a widely cited example of a company deciding to adopt an offensive approach, because the company chose the single issue of global warming, confronted it squarely before others in its industry did so, publicly announced quantitative targets and deadlines, and provided objectively verified reports of its progress.

As Nike's approach to corporate responsibility demonstrates, defensive and offensive approaches are not mutually exclusive, but the two bring different results. For example, a defensive approach allows the company to make short-term gains when it has to respond to specific charges (e.g. child labour in supplier factories), but the gains flatten out as the company meets its critics' expectations. Meanwhile, a company might see little tangible benefit from initial social investments, but, as these become more focused, they can have a significant impact in differentiating the company from its peers.[4] Put simply, as Kramer and Kania conclude:

> offensive [corporate responsibility] can distinguish a company's reputation but cannot protect it; defensive [corporate responsibility] can protect a reputation but cannot distinguish it.
>
> (2006, p 25)

Others have offered similar frameworks for examining what a company is trying to achieve with corporate responsibility. For example, Martin (2002) distinguishes between acts that are instrumental, because they maintain or enhance shareholder value, and those that are done for their own sake, which are therefore regarded as having an intrinsic value. In what he calls the '*virtue matrix*', he divides instrumental acts between those that are done because they conform to norms and customs, and those that are necessitated by legal compliance. He divides intrinsically valuable acts between those that create social and shareholder value, and those that benefit society, but not shareholders.

This kind of distinction reflects one made in wider management theory between 'denominator managers' and 'numerator managers', under which the former are focused on achieving results through efficiencies and lower costs, while the latter are focused on high impact and are looking for the next point on the curve of innovation as a way to gain competitive advantage.[5] Advocates of corporate responsibility largely favour the more innovative, forward-looking agendas that are implied in the concepts of numerator managers, intrinsic virtue, and offensive corporate responsibility. These people see corporate responsibility, to paraphrase Paul Tebo of DuPont, as the right to operate and grow, because products that make lives better and reach more people equate with expanded markets and new customers.[6] But for many companies, as we will see, the denominator/instrumental/defensive approach to corporate responsibility better defines what they want to achieve. Moreover, Waddock (2007) has argued that the defensive–offensive distinction is not comprehensive enough. She accepts that corporate responsibility can be a defensive response to crises and scandals, or a way in which to harness the power of business to meet societal needs. But she adds a third distinction, under which the company's corporate responsibility purpose is to respond to concerns in society that arise from the very success of the company's strategy. This arises when public expectations about business' behaviour are neither the result of particular abuses, such as forced labour or oil spills, nor linked to demands that companies fill societal needs. Rather, the expectations (or criticisms) are directly related to the consequences of business implementing a system within which success is equated with:

1 continual growth and expansion;

2 a focus on efficiency and externalizing costs wherever possible;

3 corporate control or influence over resources, markets, customer preferences, and employees.

This accounts for a set of expectations that do not comfortably fit within the two-approach model, but which, as noted earlier, clearly inform public perceptions of responsibility, such as job security, workforce prosperity, and aspects of environmental stewardship.

Stages of corporate responsibility

Several theorists use the analogy of a journey when explaining how companies define, and then develop, their corporate responsibility goals. This is a convenient way of exploring why companies' policies, processes, and programmes change, and also of discussing to what companies should aspire. The idea of responsibility as a journey was used by Post and Altman (1992) to describe the evolution of environmental management, and is the subject of numerous case studies of corporate transformation that set out the steps and missteps taken by individual companies.[7] Clarkson (1995), building on others, developed the RDAP framework that separated the 'Reactive', 'Defensive', 'Accommodative', and 'Proactive' stages of corporate responsibility. Zadek (2000) identified four types of corporate responsibility (defence of reputation, cost–benefit orientation, the strategic business case, and the 'new economy' case, in which corporate responsibility is seen as part of new approaches to learning, innovation, and risk management). More recently, he has developed this idea to analyse the experience of Nike in moving from being what he calls a '*stubborn resister*' to the idea it was responsible for the consequences of its products, into what he regards as an active citizen and what Nike itself describes as a stage at which sustainability is a core attribute of Nike product innovation.[8]

Mirvis and Googins (2006) warn that there is no single developmental pathway, but believe that there is a natural progression. Their model builds on ideas of behavioural

	Stages				
	Stage 1 Elementary	Stage 2 Engaged	Stage 3 Innovative	Stage 4 Integrated	Stage 5 Transforming
Citizenship concept	Jobs; profits; taxes	Philanthropy; environmental protection	Stakeholder management	Sustainability/ triple bottom line	Change the game
Strategic intent	Legal compliance	Maintain licence to operate	Make business case	Integration of value and values	Create new markets/social change
Leadership	Minimal	Supportive	On top of the issues	Ahead of the curve	Visionary
Structure	Marginal	Functional ownership	Cross-functional coordination	Organizational alignment	Integrated into mainstream
Issues management	Defensive	Reactive	Responsive	Proactive	Defines the issues
Stakeholder relationships	Unilateral	Interactive	Mutual influence	Alliances and partnerships	Multi-organizational
Transparency	Enough to protect flanks	Public relations	Public reporting	Assurance	Full disclosure

Dimensions (row axis label)

Figure 4.1 Stages of corporate responsibility
Source: Adapted from Mirvis and Googins (2006)

psychology and posits that companies, like individuals, exhibit distinct patterns of behaviour at different stages of development, their activities becoming more complex and sophisticated as they mature. We can tell the level of maturity by the company's actions in seven areas of management (see Figure 4.1).

1 How corporate responsibility is defined and the comprehensiveness of the definition (what they call the '*citizenship concept*').

2 The purpose of the company's corporate responsibility ('*strategic intent*').

3 The support given by company managers ('*leadership*').

4 The day-to-day management of corporate responsibility within the firm ('*structure*').

5 Responses to social, environmental, and other relevant issues ('*issues management*')

6 Managing the relationship with key constituencies within and outside the company ('*stakeholder relationships*').

7 Openness, transparency, and disclosure about different aspects of corporate responsibility performance ('*transparency*').

Thus, for instance, a company at the '*elementary*' stage might define corporate responsibility in terms of the creation of profits and jobs, and payment of corporate taxes (its citizenship concept), it might see its corporate responsibility purpose as complying with the law (strategic intent), and it might adopt a defensive approach to issues management. By contrast, a company at the '*engaged*' stage might in addition conceptualize corporate responsibility in terms of philanthropy or environmental protection, see its purpose as maintaining a licence to operate, and begin to develop policies that allow it to predict what issues it will need to manage. Meanwhile, a company at the '*integrated*' stage might be thinking in terms of the triple bottom line, be using corporate responsibility as a way to inform its product development, and have in place management systems that allow it to predict societal trends (see Figure 4.1 and Case Study 4.1).

Both Zadek and Mirvis and Googins agree that companies have yet to reach the most developed stage of corporate responsibility (what they respectively call the '*new economy*' and '*transforming*' stages) and, as the overview of corporate responsibility's critics in Chapter 13 shows, there are good reasons for doubting whether companies, especially large corporations, can ever have the kind of game-changing purpose envisioned for them. Furthermore, in reality, the stages are not distinct silos, and individual companies may find themselves exhibiting features of one stage in some areas and features of another stage in others. Nonetheless, as a whole, the stages provide a framework for understanding the different purposes that companies are pursuing. Equally, as we turn consider in the next section, they reveal some of the key dimensions to corporate responsibility management.

CASE STUDY 4.1

Stages of corporate responsibility

According to Mirvis and Googins (2006), there are five stages of corporate responsibility, each with their own characteristics. We can identify which stage a company is at by looking at its citizenship concept, strategic intent, leadership, structure, management of issues, stakeholder relations, and transparency (see Figure 4.1).

Stage 1 Elementary

The company's corporate responsibility activities are episodic, with little senior management support, and largely focused on legal compliance.

Stage 2 Engaged

Top management is more aware of society's expectations, there are corporate responsibility policies, and there are attempts to use corporate responsibility in public relations.

Stage 3 Innovative

The company broadens its corporate responsibility agenda, and is much more involved in owning and stewarding it. Senior management is clearly on top of the issues and there is a supportive organizational structure. The business case is a significant driver of corporate responsibility management.

Stage 4 Integrated

There is much more internal collaboration and corporate responsibility—typically defined in terms of social and environmental performance—is driven into the lines of business. In the words of Nike's Hannah Jones: '*Our corporate responsibility team no longer is simply working with the business. More than ever, we're part of the business.*' Senior management is not simply on top of the agenda, but championing it.

Stage 5 Transforming

Values clearly influence business decisions, as is the case at the UK's Cooperative Bank, which reports on the business opportunities it has declined for ethical reasons. Corporate responsibility comes to mean not only social and environmental performance, but also, more importantly, changing the nature of the role of business in society. The CEO, and the company as a whole, takes on an external leadership role (e.g. building cross-sector, cross-industry cooperation) and the company fully discloses what it is doing, not doing, and aspiring to do.

(Mirvis and Googins, 2006; www.nike.com—accessed 1 August 2006;
www.co-operativebank.co.uk—accessed 1 August 2006)

Questions

The five stages are a framework for understanding where companies stand in their management of corporate responsibility.

1 Bearing in mind that the separation between stages is not rigid and that some companies might have progressed further in certain areas than others, what companies would you classify as being at Stages 1 and 2?

2 What companies would you put at Stages 3 and 4?

3 Which companies do you think have reached, or are soon likely to reach, Stage 5? (See Figure 4.2 on p 124 for further guidance.)

Qualities of good corporate responsibility management

Following the three critical areas of business transformation mentioned earlier, we move now from the company's purpose in managing corporate responsibility to a discussion of its implementation. There are an increasing number of books about how to manage corporate responsibility, aimed largely at existing managers. Peters' *Waltzing with the Raptors* (1999) was one of the first of these, promising a practical roadmap to protecting a company's reputation and, since then, further titles have concentrated on particular advantages of corporate responsibility (e.g. risk management, the business case, enhanced strategy), and/or the needs of particular business functions (e.g. corporate responsibility for PR professionals).

A glance at the contents of these books reveals the central elements of corporate responsibility management today. For example, the *Guide to Best Practices in Corporate Social Responsibility*,[9] a book targeted at mid-level PR managers, features chapters on communicating corporate responsibility, building an integrated corporate responsibility strategy, demonstrating its value to senior management, working with stakeholders, managing

crises, corporate responsibility reporting, and measuring corporate responsibility performance. Such books reveal a managerial orthodoxy that embraces much of corporate
responsibility today. This orthodoxy comprises:

1 particular tools and approaches—the ingredients of good corporate responsibility
management;

2 advice on execution—the qualities of that management.

We discuss these two dimensions below and also take a more in-depth look at some of the
ingredients in the next three chapters.

One of the things that distinguishes corporate responsibility today from that of the past
is that it is becoming an identifiable area of management expertise. As we discuss later in
this chapter, in 'Structuring the corporate responsibility function' (p 112), this expertise
is housed in a variety of organizational structures, but there is also a large amount of general advice that is presented as best practice, which draws on analysis of diverse corporate
experiences and case studies. This ranges from identifying broad areas to which the company should pay attention (e.g. integrating strategies into the corporate culture; adhering
to declared values and standards; communicating what the company is doing, including
both achievements and challenges),[10] to more specific steps. Some of the most common
advice that can be offered to a company once its purpose is clear is set out in Box 4.1.

Box 4.1 Common advice on introducing corporate responsibility into management

- Get started—don't take too long before getting under way with the first activities.
- Pay attention to terminology—for example, a term such as 'sustainable growth' may have
  more resonance with company managers than 'sustainability', 'sustainable development', or
  'social responsibility', because the latter terms can be interpreted as discarding the idea of
  economic growth with which managers are most familiar.
- Be frank and transparent—this is the best way to get staff attention and winning their attention makes it easier to change the corporate ethos.
- Instil a company ethic of education and learning around issues of responsibility.
- Find useful partners and corporate responsibility champions across the company.
- Get to know the communities within which the company exists, including understanding its
  norms, values, cultures, traditions, and, of course, applicable laws.
- Establish dialogues and debates with stakeholders from different sectors and sections of
  society, and make these transparent and honest, not least in terms of agreeing realistic
  expectations.
- Form 'smart partnerships' with stakeholders to achieve genuine corporate responsibility
  goals, rather than only public relations imperatives.
- Measure and account for what the company does in areas of corporate responsibility.
- Report to the public and key constituencies on what the company is doing and make these
  reports accessible to all who have an interest.

(Adapted from CCC, 2005a; Olsen, 2004; Holliday et al., 2002;
SustainAbility/UNEP, 2001; Peters, 1999)

Box 4.2 The business case for corporate responsibility at BT

Enhance customer satisfaction

Grow customer loyalty

Enhance corporate/brand reputation

Increase employee motivation

Sales tenders

Cost savings

Source: adapted from www.btplc.com

Much of this advice relates to the initial stages of adopting corporate responsibility and, as, we discuss in Chapter 6 in relation to stakeholder engagement, for example, some aspects of corporate responsibility management ultimately involve many layers of skill and complexity. This is also true of making the business case for corporate responsibility, which some consultants and theorists stress needs to be established as early as possible within the company. The business case constructed by telecommunications company, BT, is an example of this complexity (see Box 4.2). The business case is so central to contemporary corporate responsibility theory and practice that we address it in detail in Chapter 5. But even though some recent research among company managers suggests that cost–benefit analysis is a less important influence on corporate responsibility practices in some companies than is widely believed,[11] specific steps in making the business case have become part of corporate responsibility management practice, as follows.[12]

1 Communicating the importance of the business case across the company.

2 Joining key inter-firm initiatives, designed to develop and test the business case.

3 Building an understanding of how performance in different aspects of corporate responsibility might affect measures of business success.

4 Inventorizing tangible evidence of areas in which corporate responsibility has, or could have, an impact on business success.

5 Adopting the systems and language of mainstream business in managing corporate responsibility, so that it becomes more readily identifiable as part of business practice.

6 Disclosing headline level results that demonstrate the business benefits both internally and externally.

7 Engaging investors and financial analysts to raise their awareness of the business case for corporate responsibility.

8 Ensuring that the business case is continually evolving.

9 Lobbying for policy changes within the company that will make the business case stronger.

Case Study 4.2 gives examples of how these kinds of advice play out within companies, but the business case alone may be insufficient to drive corporate responsibility forward within the company, and some emphasize both the roles of individuals as champions and leaders, and the creation of systems. Hemingway and Maclagan (2004) argue that the commercial imperative is only part of effective corporate responsibility management and that it should also be linked to the personal values of individual managers. They point out that individual discretion allows personnel to introduce their values into corporate responsibility policies, whether through officially sanctioned actions, the unintended consequences of an individual resolving a problem by drawing on personal beliefs, or an individual's entrepreneurship in bringing values into the workplace.

CASE STUDY 4.2

Putting management in place

The challenges that companies face when putting in place corporate responsibility management systems depend on the industry and the characteristics of the company. Consider, for example, the reinsurance company, Swiss Re. As an industry leader, it was well aware that major losses due to natural disasters, and shifting social and political environments around the world, were having an effect on its business. It knew, too, that managing these increasingly important liabilities put new demands on the company's knowledge capacities and capabilities. So the company built new structures to facilitate knowledge transfer, including its Environmental Impairment Liability Centre for Competence (EIL).

EIL allows Swiss Re to develop new products that are focused on environmental liability, and the company has developed tools to allow client managers, claims managers, and underwriters to understand environmental risks, and to make appropriate decisions. The company sponsors knowledge centres for itself, its clients, and others, such as the Centre for Global Dialogue, which the company advertises as '*a forum to deal with global risk issues and to facilitate new insight into future risk markets*'. The decentralized nature of the company means, however, that there also need to be group-wide knowledge networks that bring together expertise from across the company to exchange and generate knowledge. A number of these have been set up, such as the Environmental Risk and Underwriting network, the company's main resource for information pertinent to environmentally related claims handling, underwriting, risk management, and product development. With nearly a hundred members across the company, it falls under the Environmental Steering Committee, which is chaired by a member of the company's board.

Knowledge networks are a small—but important—part of the way in which the company integrates corporate responsibility into its business. It has also developed products and services to manage social and environmental risks, including its Flood Risk Assessment Tool, and its new mortality tables. It is also mandated to manage the UN Commission for Europe's Energy Efficiency Fund and has created a Greenhouse Gas Risk Solutions unit to develop financial products to help to reduce CO_2 emissions.

(Innovest, 2005; Holliday et al., 2002; www.swissre.com—accessed 22 August 2006)

Questions

Swiss Re has regularly been cited as an example of a company that has integrated corporate responsibility issues into its mainstream management practices.

1 To what extent are Swiss Re's networks an example of corporate responsibility management rather than of conventional knowledge management?

2 What is the value of these management systems to the company as whole?

3 Are there other industries that might learn from Swiss Re's experience of how to build management systems?

Leaders—or, perhaps more accurately, 'initiators'—can come from almost any part of the company and a key ingredient is what Arnold and Hartman (2003) call '*moral imagination*'. For example, at BAT, some of the early enthusiasm for corporate responsibility is said to have come from middle managers in corporate affairs, while at The Body Shop and Timberland, it stemmed from the moral imagination of CEOs from the outset. Regardless of how it begins, however, there comes a stage at which senior management needs to give legitimacy to the corporate responsibility agenda, so that it gets valued across the company. Part of this legitimization is the creation of relevant systems to develop policies, processes, indicators, and targets, so that the full range of corporate responsibility-related activities are managed.

In corporate responsibility literature, there is much more discussion of the aims of these systems (e.g. that they be inclusive, responsive, and engaged with stakeholders),[13] than there is of what they look like in practice. There are some general recommendations, based on different company experiences, such as the need to have board-level accountability and senior management roles, including dedicated corporate responsibility positions, and to introduce corporate responsibility thinking into company-wide decision making (e.g. rethinking the processes for designing products, hiring practices, and employee rewards). But even when companies accept these ideas as good practice, they can look very different in execution from company to company. For example, at IKEA, the head of corporate responsibility reports directly to the CEO, while at Novozymes, although there is a Sustainability Development Centre, the company's lines of business and geographical entities have full responsibility for day-to-day management of corporate responsibility within their operations.[14]

We examine the structuring of the corporate responsibility function in more detail in the next section, but it is typical for systems to evolve and change as the company becomes more familiar with corporate responsibility as a management area. Part of this is the creation of corporate responsibility capacity, and comparative research of company practices shows that systems can include capacity building both within the company (e.g. to understand corporate responsibility issues, or to engage with stakeholders) and among stakeholders themselves, so that they can interact more effectively with firms.[15] For example, through its Leadership Development initiative, 3M has taken the idea of ethics programmes a step further than many companies by having executives give examples of where opportunities for business advantage did not concord with the company's values, and then debating and undertaking role play based on how others would react in that situation. Companies, such as Levi Strauss and Nike, are investing in building the capacity of suppliers to manage their human resources more effectively, so as to avert the need for abusive labour practices.[16]

Although the above ideas of how to manage corporate responsibility reflect received wisdom, they should not be treated as infallible truths. Research with managers from several leading companies has shown that following received wisdom can assist the corporate responsibility effort, but can, at the same time, lay potential traps.[17] For example, making the business case can help to explain why a company should take corporate responsibility seriously and legitimate the topic inside the business—but managers' experiences also show that it can cause companies or individuals to promise more than they can actually deliver or demonstrate, given the available data. In the long run, this makes it more difficult to make a compelling non-financial case. Moreover, the business case tends to be demonstrated using lagging indicators that only explain what happened in the past and do not necessarily help in deciding about future investments. We return to these 'half-truths' surrounding corporate responsibility management wisdom later in the chapter, in 'Corporate responsibility as strategy' (p 114).

Structuring the corporate responsibility function

One area in which more detailed information about the actual management of corporate responsibility is starting to emerge is the structuring of corporate responsibility management within companies. Some of this information takes the form of consultancy advice to individual firms and is not in the public domain, but what is available (both officially and unofficially) provides one of the more detailed pictures of actual corporate responsibility management practice.

A relatively early management guide on this topic identified what it considered nine essential steps for designing a corporate responsibility structure,[18] as follows.

1 Understanding the drivers of corporate responsibility within the firm.

2 Identifying the key corporate responsibility issues.

3 Identifying and evaluating stakeholders.

4 Identifying functions within the company that support corporate responsibility efforts.

5 Analysing company systems, culture, and impending changes.

6 Evaluating structural options.

7 Developing a staff plan.

8 Creating a structure for cross-functional interaction.

9 Assessing the process and framework for budget and resource allocation.

At first glance, this can appear to be an unwieldy list of actions, but the steps can be divided between four main areas of activity:

1 understanding the drivers (Step 1);

2 mapping what is already happening inside and outside the company (Steps 2, 3, and 4);

3 coming to grips with existing systems (Step 5);

4 designing a specific corporate responsibility management structure (Steps 6, 7, 8, and 9).

Nobody knows how often this type of methodical approach is followed in real life, but it does highlight aspects of corporate responsibility structuring that have engendered debate within companies. These include the importance, or otherwise, of cross-functional interaction within the firm, decisions about resource allocation, staffing the corporate responsibility function, and, perhaps most significantly, deciding what is the most appropriate structure for a specific company. What has emerged is an array of structures. For example, at Pfizer, there is a long-standing tradition of the full board of directors making major decisions rather than specific committees and, as a result, while some firms have brought specialists in at the non-executive director level, the company has sought to diversify the full board with corporate responsibility expertise. Another approach is to place formal responsibility for corporate responsibility issues in the hands of existing executives: for example, at Novartis, the heads of legal affairs and human resources have formal responsibility for corporate responsibility issues inside the executive committee. Corporate responsibility can also be placed in other parts of the organization: at General Motors, it is under the Public Policy Center; at IBM, it comes under the executive vice president for innovation and technology; at Groupe Danone, the head of sustainable development and social responsibility reports to the company general secretary; at Telefónica, a standalone department was created, reporting to the head of corporate communications.

A 2005 survey of 254 managers and directors, who saw corporate responsibility as part of their role, found they had 23 job titles.[19] Another survey of 580 company structures worldwide found that, in 30 per cent of cases, corporate responsibility was managed by an existing department, such as communications or HR, without staff who have corporate responsibility as their primary function.[20] Ten per cent of companies had set up non-departmental working committees to manage corporate responsibility and 4 per cent had outsourced corporate responsibility activities to an external consultancy. In the majority of companies (56 per cent), however, there were designated corporate responsibility personnel of some kind. The majority of these were either part of a standalone corporate responsibility department or team in the corporate centre (22 per cent), or part of another department, such as corporate communications (24 per cent). The remaining companies had several teams dispersed across the organization, either as standalone entities (9 per cent), or as part of a number of different departments (10 per cent).

These statistics tell us something about how far companies have moved towards the kind of idealized structure and systems that are depicted as corporate responsibility best practice. The fact that only 10 per cent of companies have dedicated corporate responsibility managers in the regions or business lines suggests that there is a long way to go before the ideal of embedding corporate responsibility into business operations is realized. This is in marked contrast to the areas of knowledge management and quality management, in which specialists are less likely to be located in the corporate centre and more likely to be found in teams dispersed across the business.

But before one puts too negative an interpretation on this situation, it must be asked how perfect is the idealized structure to begin with. Sutcliffe (2005) argues, based on interviews with managers and external commentators, that the right location for the corporate responsibility function depends on the company, the nature of its industry, and its internal culture. For example, at Marks and Spencer, there was a strong belief that corporate responsibility needed to be housed with corporate governance, because of its control over the board's sub-committees. But this view changed when the head of corporate responsibility came to believe that a process-driven approach of the kind associated with governance was less effective than the ability to communicate with different stakeholders and, consequently, corporate responsibility was housed in corporate affairs.

There are strong arguments for structuring corporate responsibility in numerous ways. Some argue that it needs to be at the locus of internal power, so that corporate responsibility factors influence business decisions (e.g. housing it where prices and deadlines are negotiated with suppliers rather than in public affairs). Some believe it should be at the nodes where key business areas connect, so as to build cross-functional influence. There is a widely felt sentiment that as important as a knowledge of corporate responsibility is an understanding of what affects company performance (e.g. operations, investors, sourcing) and, related to that, there is a desire among many external commentators that corporate responsibility issues be dealt with in the operational functions to which they belong (e.g. employee issues to be addressed by HR; sourcing issues by buying; customer issues by sales and marketing). As already noted, however, this kind of integrated corporate responsibility function is a long way from being realized in most firms.

Alongside the question of where to situate the corporate responsibility function lies that of how to resource it. Early movers in the field, such as The Body Shop, tended to establish separate, well-resourced corporate responsibility departments that were a statement of serious commitment. Now, it is less certain how large a corporate responsibility department should be, or even if there should be such a thing. In a company such as GlaxoSmithKline, a small team is said to have made significant progress, because it gained the attention and commitment of multiple departments, encouraging them to deploy their own resources and to incorporate corporate responsibility into their own practices. In other companies, such as Gap Inc, relatively large teams have been created because of the challenges faced.

Corporate responsibility as strategy

Out of the extensive literature intended to show what constitutes good corporate responsibility management, there are several common elements that seem to be determinants of performance excellence. As already discussed, these include having a clear purpose and knowing what one wants from corporate responsibility, putting in place a well-defined strategy, building effective relations with one's main constituencies, and creating adequate systems and processes. There is another recurring theme that we have yet to discuss: having an integrated strategy that makes corporate responsibility part of the corporate DNA.[21]

As early as 1973, Andrews recognized that:

> the overriding master problem . . . impeding the further progress of corporate responsibility is the difficulty of making credible and effective, throughout a large organization, the social component of a corporate strategy originating in the moral convictions and values of the chief executive.
>
> (p 57)

Although few would now agree that corporate responsibility is simply a reflection of a CEO's convictions, the central point remains valid, and there is now widespread agreement with Andrews' subsequent point that a company's social policy should be as much a function of strategic planning as is its choice of products and marketing, or its establishment of profit and growth objectives. As already noted, there is a widely held belief among corporate responsibility thinkers that companies should develop management approaches that establish corporate responsibility as a core driver of business performance, thereby fully aligning it with the firm's strategic operations.

This kind of belief is reflected in the definitions of the more evolved forms of corporate responsibility that we described earlier ('Stages of corporate responsibility', p 104), but there is often frustration among theorists that current corporate responsibility scorecards, standards, reports, and other widely used management tools fail to support strategic alignment or planning.[22] Subsequently, there is a stark contrast between conventional business management excellence and corporate responsibility management excellence. The former involves building a strategy that creates competitive advantage and then reinforcing that strategy with high-quality operational processes that lead to best quality and productivity. In top companies, strategy, operations, research and development, and other dimensions of the business are aligned and integrated. By contrast, corporate responsibility often creates programmes to tackle specific issues, and then puts in place systems to enforce and sustain what it considers to be ethical practices, finally producing a report reviewing its commitments and practices. In other words, there is a strong tendency to define excellence as the production of a report about programmes and systems, begging the question: is there any other area of business management in which this would be considered acceptable, let alone 'excellent'?

By contrast, the strategic integration of corporate responsibility means that corporate responsibility is seen as a business driver. It involves corporate responsibility creating value within the company and the company creating value for wider society. An example of this type of integration is when GE began to see spiralling health costs and difficulties in accessing health care both as social problems and a business opportunity. It responded by investing in products that were tailored to the needs of specific markets around the world, instead of focusing purely on the best technology accessible only to the wealthy.[23] Moreover, as the quote in Case Study 4.3 shows, serving emerging markets through this kind of approach has become central to the company's strategy for growth.

The GE case is an example of a strategy for offensive corporate responsibility, but strategic integration can also be applied to more defensive objectives. For example, it is already common for companies to use corporate responsibility as part of a strategy to protect their reputations, as was the case when leading IT companies, such as IBM, HP, and Dell, established the Electronics Industry Code of Conduct as a common approach to monitoring the corporate responsibility issues in their suppliers' operations. Similarly, Fedex is applying integrated thinking in its collaboration with the Alliance for Environmental Innovation, which aims to develop trucks that are 50 per cent more fuel-efficient and less harmful to the environment than those it currently operates.

The examples above might imply that integrating corporate responsibility into business strategy is another way of making the business case for improved social and environmental performance. But true integration requires that there be processes to ensure that corporate responsibility imperatives are considered on their own merits in strategic planning, regardless of the financial implications. What proponents of integration claim is that the distinction between business imperative and responsibility imperative will become irrelevant, pointing for comparison to quality management, for which poor quality came to be seen as symptomatic of unproductive systems, just as waste, emissions, and environmental impacts are seen today. In this way, corporate responsibility ceases to be a contained entity, and becomes an inseparable part of a larger complex and changing system that, as Van Tulder (2006) says, needs to influence different levels (at which it will take different forms) and functions such as marketing, quality control, financial management, and research and development.

CASE STUDY 4.3

Integrating corporate responsibility as a business driver

Edison once said, '*Vision without execution is hallucination*'. Yet much of the information on managing corporate responsibility deals with aims, expectations, and general principles, and not with the detail of its implementation. Part of what is missing is the connection between the why, the what, and the how of transformation management, i.e. the rationale, the expected results, and the way in which these will be achieved.

GE, which owns businesses in industries as diverse as aviation, film and television, transportation, energy, and healthcare, is trying to make this connection. In developing its 'ecomagination' initiative, managers consulted across the company and with what were sometimes hostile external groups, and came up with a list of social and environmental issues in relation to which it could employ its assets to bring about change. They then created a business plan that committed company resources to, set output targets for, and not least promised to double company revenues to $2,000m by 2010 by developing products offering environmental advantage to customers.

The same kind of integration is depicted in the company's 2005 *Citizenship Report* (p 42):

> In 2004, GE's revenues from the developing world reached $21 billion, a 37% increase. We now expect to get as much as 60% of our future revenue growth from emerging markets including China, Russia, Eastern Europe, India, and the Middle East. In these markets, GE can provide much-needed infrastructure. We will deliver vital systems for water, power, healthcare, and transportation to improve the quality of life and access to opportunity in these countries . . . By providing critical infrastructure needs, GE has the opportunity to lay a foundation for sustainable growth.

(Stewart and Immelt, 2006; GE, 2005)

Questions

Under long-time CEO Jack Welch, GE was widely admired by investors, but repeatedly criticized for its environmental performance.

1 What will GE have to demonstrate to its stakeholders to prove that its business strategy is successful?

2 Are the reasons that GE gives for integrating corporate responsibility convincing from a shareholder's perspective?

3 Given the conglomerate's diverse businesses, do you think its commitment to corporate responsibility invites pressure to alter the types of industry in which it is invested?

Challenges

Following the above advice on management to the letter would not be a complete solution to the corporate responsibility challenge. As we will discuss later in this chapter, managing supply chains, confronting industry-specific issues, and taking into account differences in company size all affect corporate responsibility management. Yet, even without these factors, there are challenges that need to be addressed. We mentioned earlier ('Qualities of good corporate responsibility management', p 107) that some of the received wisdom about good management practice should not be treated as wholly accurate and, as Case Study 4.4 explores, a challenge for managers is understanding the limitations of sound advice.

CASE STUDY 4.4

Half-truths of corporate responsibility

Corporate responsibility has quickly accrued a large body of conventional wisdom. But a 2004 project involving eight large companies found that some of these 'truths' may only be 'half-truths.'

Conventional wisdom	Why it's true	Why it's a half-truth
'Make the business case for corporate responsibility'	It connects corporate responsibility to the main business agenda and opens the door to more strategic discussions	It can be overstated, less than convincing, and mask the real value of corporate responsibility to the company
'Adopt an external standard'	It lends credibility and legitimacy, as well as providing a structure for measuring performance	It can lead to an overwhelming amount of data, and may not help the company to develop its specific corporate responsibility vision and programmes
'Get buy-in from the top'	It ensures that corporate responsibility is a priority and is essential in securing resources	Waiting for executive endorsement can delay progress and inhibit activities for which approval may not be necessary
'Produce a social/ environmental report'	It drives accountability and provides a public record of the company's performance	It can be a time-consuming and bureaucratic exercise that distracts from more meaningful progress, and can even be a substitute for actual corporate responsibility activity
'Build on existing policies and systems'	It increases the comfort level and reduces resistance, allowing corporate responsibility to progress more quickly	In the long run, it can dampen innovation and energy

(Adapted from CCC, 2005b)

Questions

There are various areas in which conventional wisdom about corporate responsibility management might be questioned.

1 What do you think the 'truth' and the 'half-truth' might be surrounding the recommendation that a company designate an owner of corporate responsibility?

2 What are some other areas of conventional wisdom that might be questionable?

3 Are stakeholders outside the company likely to accept the arguments about why producing a social/environmental report or adopting an external standard might hinder the organization's progress in corporate responsibility?

Management capacity and outside expertise

Managers themselves are sometimes described as a challenge, especially in terms of presenting obstacles within companies to pushing ahead with corporate responsibility. Olsen (2004) is among those who highlight middle management (what is sometimes called the 'clay layer') as an area in which corporate responsibility efforts can flounder. It is difficult to treat this as a general rule, however, because, in many companies, middle managers have been the initiators of corporate responsibility, not least because of what Chris Tuppen, corporate responsibility head at BT, sees as their passion.[24]

One way in which to boost a company's corporate responsibility capability and capacity is to turn to outside consultants. Large management consultancy firms, such as PricewaterhouseCoopers, KPMG, and McKinsey, offer corporate responsibility-related services and, in many instances, have personnel located in offices around the world. Environmental management firms such as ERM and CH2M Hill have also branched out to offer broader corporate responsibility services, such as social impact assessments, as have industry consultants such as Cambridge Energy Research Associates and Emerging Market Economics. Verification companies such as SGS and BVQI have developed corporate responsibility products, and specialist corporate responsibility auditing companies have also emerged such as Verité and Global Social Compliance.

Some companies obtain corporate responsibility advice through being part of membership organizations, such as Business for Social Responsibility, CSR Europe, and the International Business Leaders Forum. There are also initiatives of which companies can be a part, such as Accountability and the Ethical Trading Initiative, within which business can build its knowledge of specific aspects of corporate responsibility.

A growing number of universities, especially business schools, offer executive education and other advice on corporate responsibility management. There is also a large number of boutique consultancies offering specialist corporate responsibility services, ranging from general management consultancy, to monitoring, to verification of corporate responsibility reports. A few of these, such as SustainAbility, have established a reputation as thought leaders; others, such as the Corporate Citizenship Company and Impactt Ltd, not only offer consultancy, but also make some of their knowledge publicly available through magazines and reports.[25]

Altogether, it is now possible to get corporate responsibility advice from any number of perspectives, including those of public relations, the law, international development, and cause-related marketing. While many organizations offer high-quality services, corporate responsibility is still a relatively new field, and not only is there a high turnover in service providers, but even the best will admit that, in some areas, they are still figuring out what does and does not work.

The corporate responsibility mindset

Perhaps more challenging than building capacity is creating what has been called the 'corporate responsibility mindset'. While vision statements, programmes, and systems are important, they do not necessarily capture (and, in some cases, may even hinder) what some see as the need to change from traditional paradigms and concepts to a position at which companies think not in terms of command and control, but rather in terms of being part of a web of dynamic relations.[26] For some, corporate responsibility's value is that it provides the framework for rethinking the role of the company and how it relates to society, and that it therefore is nothing less than a transformational endeavour for business as a whole. But at the very least, a change in mindset is required as part of approaching corporate responsibility as an integral part of business strategy ('Corporate responsibility as strategy', p 114).

Even companies with well-respected programmes addressing particular aspects of corporate responsibility, such as ethical sourcing or environmental management, may not have a corporate responsibility mindset. Indeed, there is some evidence to suggest that companies that have strong reputations built on a particular issue face greater difficulties in thinking more broadly about corporate responsibility. Research has identified two tests of whether a company is developing such a mindset. The first mirrors our earlier discussion of integration and asks how far corporate responsibility is factored into business decisions. The second concerns how comfortable the company becomes in managing uncertainty, because—unlike quality management and product design, which are based on universal standards—some see corporate responsibility as being about managing the uncertainty that comes from diversity, flux, and the unknown.[27]

Nowhere is this shift from a simplified model of control to a more complex one dealing with apparent chaos more evident than when one looks at business in a global context. From a management perspective, an important part of this is how a company manages relations with the web of customers and suppliers that are not only essential for business success, but also for the company's management of corporate responsibility. It is to this aspect that we now turn.

Influencing suppliers and customers

One of the major changes in company behaviour over the past few years has been companies' acceptance of responsibility for the social and environmental performance of the companies with which they do business. Previously, companies did not readily take responsibility for what happened beyond the boundaries of their own offices and facilities. The nineteenth-century case in the UK, in which public pressure forced the East India

Company to abandon slave-grown sugar from the West Indies, was a rarity, and it had often taken decades of legislative reform to get companies to take responsibility for the safety and quality of their products.

The attitude to suppliers' behaviour thirty years ago was based on a corporate culture that viewed what happened beyond the company's boundaries as something hostile from which it needed protection. But with the drive towards global markets and the removal of barriers to trade and investment, boundaries have become blurry, permeable, and difficult to discern, creating a situation in which it is difficult to say which stakeholders (and hence which responsibilities) are internal or external.[28] Companies are less vertically integrated and, instead, are part of value chains within which the company owns some functions and others are outsourced. Some companies are, however, seen as having greater power within these chains than others, and social and environmental groups have been effective in making the case that such companies have a duty to use their influence to affect the behaviour of others.

All manner of unethical practices resulting from power imbalances have been documented in value chains, such as restricting opportunities to bid for contracts, asking for information from suppliers on competitors, overestimating demand to gain volume discounts, and bribery. But for reasons that are rarely discussed in the corporate responsibility literature, these issues are not normally considered part of corporate responsibility. Rather, corporate responsibility management within the value chain is more typically concerned with social and environmental rights. For example, animal rights group PETA used the power of McDonald's in its 'unhappy meal' campaign to get meat suppliers to stop using growth-promoting antibiotics; the chocolate industry was held to public account for the use of child labour by cocoa suppliers in West Africa; European supermarkets have been used by consumers to reduce the use of genetically modified crops.

The buyer–supplier relationship is not the only part of the value chain that raises corporate responsibility concerns. For example, the social impact of offshoring is not confined to working conditions in the country receiving investment; it also includes the loss of jobs in another country, and the company's responsibility for reskilling, job development, and redeployment of its native workforce. But it is the conditions in which multinational companies choose to invest, or from which they choose to source, rather than those in which they disinvest that companies have so far tended to try and manage.

The array of companies that have been threatened with legal action demonstrates that managing the behaviour of others is a challenge for various industries. Unocal, Gap Inc, Calvin Klein, ExxonMobil, Rio Tinto, Fresh Delmonte, and ChevronTexaco are among the companies that have been brought to task because of the behaviour of suppliers or subcontractors.[29] Jewellery retailers, DIY stores, and computer brands are among the many industries that have put in place systems for managing corporate responsibility in their supply chain, and which have endorsed initiatives such as the Kimberley Process Certification Scheme for conflict diamonds, the Forest Stewardship Council, and the Electronic Industry Code of Conduct.

Typically, these management systems comprise some kind of code of practice that sets out the principles and criteria with which a supplier needs to comply. They may also include monitoring mechanisms, and some kind of audit that is conducted by the company and/or a contracted external party. Some systems have complaints and remediation mechanisms through which workers, communities, and other parties can raise, and have resolved, alleged violations of the code of conduct. Reebok, for example, was one of the first companies to instigate such a system, including in Indonesian workers' pay packets a stamped complaints form that could be returned anonymously to the US head office. Some companies also look to local organizations to assist with monitoring, complaints, and remediation in an attempt to provide objectivity and to protect workers from managerial pressure.

Many companies today have compliance teams that are responsible for ensuring the social and environmental performance of suppliers. They can be separate from line operations, based on the assumption that this will give them greater integrity, or embedded within the main business, based on the assumption that this will give them greater internal influence. To take but one example, adidas has suppliers in 17 countries across Asia. Some of these factories produce almost exclusively for adidas, especially in the sports shoe business, while some contract with multiple buyers, a situation that is typical for garments. Its leverage is therefore greater among sports shoe suppliers, but the company's Standards of Engagement apply to all of its suppliers and began because of controversy over child labour used in making footballs. The Standards encompass labour, safety, health, and environmental issues, and are the joint responsibility of the social and environmental affairs department, country managers, and the director of apparel operations. Factory owners participate in auditing, adidas-run training programmes, supplier summits, and costing negotiations that can be influenced by compliance with the standards. The Fair Labor Association verifies supplier performance, and adidas produces an annual social and environmental report.[30]

We discuss standards and their implementation in more detail in Chapter 6, but various issues have been raised by critics about transparency, the independence of auditors, and the role of civil society organizations and governments in enforcement. Organizations involved in improving corporate responsibility among suppliers have pointed out that large companies exert pressure on their suppliers to cut costs and will switch suppliers in pursuit of lower prices, all of which can serve to worsen working conditions.[31] Even companies with a sincere commitment to upholding social and environmental standards in the value chain can find that the issues are complex, and it is difficult to find out what is the best solution in a myriad of national, cultural, and ecological contexts. For example, a buying company that is only one of several customers for a supplier can find it difficult to instigate change if it cannot persuade other companies to become involved.[32] Moreover, the supply base for major companies in industries such as retailing are vast and few companies know where all of their goods come from. A major challenge for supply chain managers today is getting beyond the first production tier, such as the factories that assemble sports shoes, to find out conditions at other levels of production, such as the factories that make shoelaces or homeworkers who do some of the stitching.

There are, however, examples of companies collaborating together to address institutional or endemic causes of poor social and environmental conditions. For example, when the Multi-fibre Agreement ended, threatening to draw the Bangladesh garment industry into a race to the bottom with China over low wages (see Chapter 3), local manufacturers entered into an agreement with companies such as Asda, KarstadtQuelle, H&M, Marks and Spencer, and Wal-Mart, whereby buying companies promised to maintain their orders and prices in return for improvements in labour standards, productivity, and quality.[33] Similar deals were also proposed with Lesotho and Sri Lanka.

This kind of partnership is significant, because it is increasingly clear that a focus on codes of conduct and auditing alone does not improve standards, especially if suppliers are resistant, or buyers' commercial practices undermine their ethical agendas.[34] But these partnerships can create their own management challenges: for example, the strength that partnerships bring in terms of capacity and leverage is often won at the expense of narrowing their focus onto a single issue, leading to a situation in which labour issues may have been given more attention than environmental ones, or even than other aspects of human rights. (We explore partnerships in detail in Chapter 10.)

CASE STUDY 4.5

Expanding impact through partnerships—the Vietnam Business Links Initiative (VBLI)

There is much talk that companies should move from seeing corporate responsibility as a defensive strategy to one that is proactive, under which reputations are not only protected, but also enhanced by the contributions that firms make to society. Yet while there are strong moral and business imperatives for ridding value chains of poor labour practices, there can be less incentive to take proactive action in the countries from which major brands source.

The International Business Leaders' Forum's Vietnam Business Links Initiative involved companies in looking beyond the conditions in their suppliers' factories, towards raising the standards of workers as a whole. Building on a study by the Pentland Group (owners of the Speedo, LaCoste, Mitre, and other brands) that highlighted hazardous working conditions, VBLI brought together competitors, such as Nike and adidas, in pursuit of a system-wide objective, i.e. the raising of health, safety, and environment standards in all factories. What is more, the factories in most need of assistance were not those supplying these companies, but those without contracts with multinationals.

The companies justified their funding and effort, in part, because it would increase the pool of potential suppliers in the country and, additionally, because participation by government agencies meant that the companies could strengthen important local relationships. From taking responsibility for those in their own value chain, the companies had moved to assuming a system-wide responsibility.

(Arnold and Hartman, 2003; www.iblf.org—accessed 1 August 2006)

Questions

VBLI demonstrates how, in as short a space of time as a decade, some companies have changed from denying any responsibility for suppliers to imposing social and environmental conditions and to assuming broader obligations.

1 Are companies right to invest in programmes that do not relate to their immediate supply base?

2 How can such partnerships improve corporate responsibility management in the value chain?

3 Is participation in such partnerships a reliable indicator that a company is at an advanced stage of managing corporate responsibility?

Variations in management between industries

The issues that corporate responsibility addresses, and therefore the approach to managing them, vary, to some degree, by industry. The comparison of issues in selected industries in Figure 4.2, for example, shows that what matters to Construction is quite different to the priorities of Financial Services, which is in turn different from that which matters to the chemical industry. A comparison between other industries would reveal similar differences. For example, the diamond industry has focused on workplace health and safety, workers' rights, and, above all, the place of origin of its primary commodity, because diamond mining has been used to fund destabilizing and destructive conflicts in Africa. In contrast, the law firm Freshfields decided that the key issues for the legal profession were prejudice against women in career opportunities, energy efficiency and increasing the use of renewable energy in offices, reducing the volume of materials used, transportation (e.g. the number of air journeys), and volunteering staff time.

Nonetheless, there are common themes in what different industries are seeking to manage. Issues can be divided between:

1 major societal challenges (e.g. energy conservation, protecting biodiversity, climate change, and terrorism);

2 business-to-business practices, such as social or environmental exploitation in the supply chain;

3 the consequences of product use (e.g. vehicle emissions, how to dispose of products, obesity);

4 the consequences of production (e.g. workplace health and safety, the environmental footprint of production facilities, the impact of facilities on communities);

5 the development, marketing, and accessibility of products (e.g. financial services for poor communities, access to basic needs such as water, products for underserved markets).

Although there may be significant differences between industries in how they tackle these themes, the existence of common management concerns suggests that there are opportunities for inter-industry learning on effective management approaches.

Various initiatives have been developed to help companies to tackle industry-specific issues with the greatest resonance. The Global Environmental Management Initiative (GEMI), for example, is an alliance of forty companies developing management approaches for improved environmental performance; the Sustainable Agriculture Initiative Platform comprises food and agriculture companies working on sustainable agriculture production; Responsible Care is an initiative established by the chemical industry to set voluntary standards and related management mechanisms.

Corporate responsibility in small and medium-sized companies

There are other variants that affect how corporate responsibility gets managed. In Chapter 6, we discuss in depth how corporate responsibility management differs between

Issue	Automotive	Chemicals	Construction	Financial services	Food	Mining	Utilities
Climate strategy/energy efficiency	■	■					■
Resource conservation and efficiency			■	■			
Natural resource depletion						■	■
Biodiversity						■	■
Privatization of natural resources							■
Impact of climate change on business lines (e.g. on borrowers, insurance, and financial markets)				■			
Money laundering				■			
Security of energy supplies	■						
Responsibility for social and environmental issues in the value chain	■	■					
Use of genetically modified organisms in agriculture					■		
Sustainable production (e.g. organic farming; integrated pest management)					■		
Due diligence in lending				■			
Sustainable building design and materials			■				
Vehicle emissions	■						
Impact of chemicals on the environment		■					
Public exposure to chemicals		■					
Product end-of-life	■						
Human living environment (e.g. the role of products in the urban environment)	■						
Consumer obesity and nutrition					■		
Customer safety	■				■		
Social/community impact of production		■	■			■	■
Social and environmental impact of large projects				■		■	
Environmental footprint of facilities				■			■
Workers' rights and working conditions					■		
Workplace health and safety		■	■		■		
Human rights and indigenous rights						■	
Impact of project financing				■			
Project development and closure						■	
Accessibility of services to the poor; underserved markets				■			■
Access to clean water							■
Socially responsible investment, lending, and marketing				■			
Product labeling and packaging					■		

Figure 4.2 Comparison of priority issues between industries

Sources: Adapted from Steger (2004) and Van Tulder (2006)

countries and continents; another factor is size of company. The relationship between corporate responsibility, and small and medium-sized enterprises (SMEs), in particular, has attracted attention and various perspectives have been presented on such businesses. We discuss four of these now.

The first perspective is SME as a danger: SMEs are considered to have the poorest standards of social and environmental performance, and, in so far as they are part of the value chain of large companies, they present a risk to those corporations' reputations. In many people's minds, the companies in Africa, China, and elsewhere that sell products to Western retailers are SMEs. In reality, this is far from the truth: flower farms in Kenya or Colombia can employ thousands of workers and may be part of multinational operations themselves; the garment factories in Taiwan, China, and Vietnam are often part of large Asian corporations that are major business success stories in their own right. Therefore, the arguments often heard on behalf of producers in poor countries that imposing strict corporate responsibility standards will hamper the growth of local businesses and that they cannot afford to invest in better wages or environmental management needs to be treated cautiously. Moreover, it might equally be argued that large companies with low social and environmental standards are themselves having a negative effect on local SMEs, because they are gaining a competitive advantage by externalizing costs.

Nonetheless, some genuine SMEs clearly do have social and environmental standards that are unacceptable to their customers. Many of these are buried within the supply chain and, as noted earlier, may not even be known to the buying company. Those that find themselves in the spotlight claim that not only can they not afford to improve conditions, but also that they are unable to make the investment in the kinds of management systems that their customers demand to ensure chains of custody and due diligence. The validity of such claims is uncertain, and some research suggests that the costs are relatively small for well-managed SMEs and only become significant if the company already has serious management inefficiencies.[35] What can cause more disgruntlement is that investment in these systems may be no guarantee of future contracts: for example, one Kenyan SME invested heavily in new systems to improve labour conditions, only to find its contract terminated by retailer J Sainsbury for 'business reasons'.[36]

Connected with examples such as this, the second perspective views the SME as a victim. SMEs can be forced out of lucrative export contracts if overseas customers suspect they represent a high corporate responsibility risk, and if social and environmental performance is too difficult to monitor among a dispersed supply base. It can also be the case that SMEs wanting to enter international markets find that social and environmental conditions seem too difficult to manage, and therefore amount to a non-tariff barrier to trade. In addition, SMEs can be seen as victims in that they have a very different relationship with society than that of larger companies and this, in turn, creates alternative expectations of responsibility. For example, in Ghana, small pineapple farmers producing for European markets are expected locally to create opportunities for family members, to train youths so that eventually they can establish their own farms, and to invest in local community amenities. But European importers do not value these responsibilities and instead want attention paid to higher wages, reduced working hours, and preventing child labour, all of which present problems for the small farmer.[37]

The third perspective is that corporate responsibility should not be a concern for SMEs, at least not beyond their meeting the requirements of customers, fulfilling the expectations of local communities, and complying with the law. Each of these dimensions is part of conventional management and does not require separate consideration under a corporate responsibility heading. Corporate responsibility itself, it is claimed, is about the distribution of rights on a global stage and this is not an arena in which SMEs can actively participate or have influence.[38]

The fourth perspective is to see SMEs as an important channel for delivering corporate responsibility. This is increasingly apparent in emerging models of corporate responsibility for the developing world (see Chapter 3), although it is also relevant in developed nations, where small businesses often account for the bulk of jobs created and taxes paid. Moreover, some SMEs believe that they have a unique relationship with local communities and that they are being socially responsible by being successful in the context of the local economy.[39]

While there are these different perspectives on corporate responsibility and the SME, attention is only now turned to how SMEs can actually develop this area of management competency. Consequently, it is not surprising if corporate responsibility is seen by many SMEs as an unwelcome burden. The experiences of the fairtrade movement in building up the competency of small enterprises, especially cooperatives, and creating niche markets in which SMEs can thrive may be relevant to corporate responsibility more widely in the coming years. Furthermore, resources such as Cardiff University's Centre for Business Relationships, Accountability, Sustainability and Society (BRASS), Business in the Community's small business channel website, or the Carbon Trust's materials to assist SMEs reduce energy usage, help such companies to manage corporate responsibility. The GRI has produced a handbook for SMEs, and the European Commission and the Danish Commerce and Companies Agency are among those who have hosted events to discuss the particular challenges of corporate responsibility for SMEs. But the experience by governments and others in building SME capacity shows that focusing on corporate responsibility alone without also investing in building basic business capability will not turn corporate responsibility into an area of advantage for SMEs.[40]

SUMMARY

Managing corporate responsibility in companies is often described as a form of change management. As with other types of corporate transformation, corporate responsibility management activity is divided between: identifying the purpose and intended results; establishing the principles and processes to achieve the end goal; allocating responsibility for its execution.

The purpose and intended results differ according to the level of corporate responsibility at which the company finds itself. There are important distinctions to be made between defensive approaches to corporate responsibility, which are focused on reducing risks, protecting the company's reputation, and ensuring that it stays within the law, and offensive approaches, which employ corporate assets in finding solutions to societal problems. These approaches can be broken down further into evolutionary levels of responsibility, beginning with a focus on creating jobs, paying taxes, and abiding by the law, and eventually reaching a stage at which values are clearly at the heart of business decisions, the company is transparent about what it is doing, not doing, and hoping to do, and sees part of its role as standing out as a leader in tackling societal issues.

There is a multitude of advice on management practices that will help companies to realize their corporate responsibility goals. There is a strong consensus that good practice involves consulting internally and externally to decide the purpose, engaging with those upon whom the company impacts or by whom it is influenced as part of the management process, and communicating what the company is trying to achieve and the progress it is making. It is also widely held that companies should integrate corporate responsibility into their business strategy. Although there are examples of companies making progress in this area, corporate responsibility is often something apart from, and in conflict with, conventional business imperatives. Different organizational structures have been proposed and tested to deal with this—but companies should not expect to find an off-the-peg model.

Structure, organizational culture and mindsets, leadership, and building capacity are just some of the management challenges that companies face. Another set of challenges emerges when companies take responsibility for the behaviour of their suppliers and others in their value chains. This requires the development of additional management styles and approaches, as companies committed to corporate responsibility seek out ways of improving others' performance, not least by exerting their own power as customers.

Some aspects of responsibility vary significantly from industry to industry, so that the priorities and issues that extractive companies need to manage, for example, are different to those of financial services. Differences in management also occur because of the size of the company, with small and medium-sized enterprises facing their own distinct corporate responsibility challenges.

DISCUSSION POINTS

1 Corporate responsibility is often presented as an evolutionary journey, during which companies progress from a primitive form of corporate responsibility to increasingly more advanced forms.
   - Does it help managers to think of corporate responsibility in this way?
   - Are the criteria used to measure progression adequate and appropriate?
   - What are the weaknesses of evolutionary corporate responsibility as a theory?

2 The structure of corporate responsibility functions is often seen as an indication of how well corporate responsibility is embedded into the company and of how serious the company is about realizing its corporate responsibility vision.
   - Do you think structure is an important indicator of a company's attitude to corporate responsibility?
   - What ways of structuring corporate responsibility do you think will be most effective?
   - How would you structure the corporate responsibility function in a sports shoe or apparel company?

3 Integration of corporate responsibility into mainstream business strategy is a widely touted ambition among both theorists and practitioners.
   - What arguments might managers make to persuade a company of the advantages of the integration of corporate responsibility?
   - If integration does not happen more widely than at present, how will this affect future developments in corporate responsibility?
   - What examples are there of companies successfully integrating corporate responsibility into business management decisions?

4   One of the debates in the corporate responsibility field is whether or not corporate responsibility should be a discrete management competency or something in which all managers should be trained.

- What are the advantages and disadvantages of having corporate responsibility as a separate management discipline, similar to that of human resources, corporate law, finance, etc.?
- What message does it send when, as happened at Nike, a company promotes a labour rights specialist to be head of overall operations for Asia?
- How will a growth in corporate responsibility awareness affect the composition of senior management teams and company boards in future?

5   Some believe that SMEs are a special case in terms of corporate responsibility management.

- Should SMEs be held to different standards than other types of company?
- Do large companies have particular responsibilities to SMEs?
- Putting yourself in the position of a SME manager with a contract to supply a major European supermarket change, how would you go about determining the corporate responsibility priorities of your company?

VISIT THE WEBSITE
for links to useful sources of further information

FURTHER READING

- Ethical Trading Initiative, 2006, *Ethical Trade: A Comprehensive Guide for Companies*, 2nd edn, London: Ethical Trading Initiative.

  Manager-oriented handbook on the different facets of monitoring labour practices in global supply chains.

- Hennigfeld, J, Pohl, M and Tolhurst, N (eds), 2006, *The ICCA Handbook on Corporate Social Responsibility*, Chichester: John Wiley and Sons.

  Collection of papers on the meaning and management of corporate responsibility, targeted at corporate managers.

- Jackson, IA and Nelson, J, 2004, *Profits with Principles: Seven Strategies for Delivering Value with Values*, New York, NY: Currency/Doubleday.

  Empirically derived guidance on adopting and embedding corporate responsibility into management practice.

- Werther, WB and Chandler, D, 2006, *Strategic Corporate Social Responsibility: Stakeholders in a Global Environment*, Thousand Oaks, CA: Sage.

  Aspects of the business case for stakeholder engagement and other corporate responsibility management practices.

- Zadek, S, 2004, 'The path to corporate responsibility (best practice)', *Harvard Business Review*, 82(12), pp 125–33.

  Evolutionary model of corporate responsibility, based on the experience of Nike.

ENDNOTES

1   Maitland, 2006.

2   European Commission, 2002.

3   PWC, 2006.

[4] Cited in Kramer and Kania, 2006.

[5] See the work of Porter, and of Hamel and Prahalad, described in Holliday et al., 2002, p 27.

[6] Holliday et al., 2002, p 27.

[7] See, e.g., Schwartz and Gibb, 1999; Holliday et al., 2002, pp 142–9; Jackson and Nelson, 2004; Werther and Chandler, 2006.

[8] Zadek, 2004; www.nike.com/nikebiz—accessed August 1 2006.

[9] *PR News*, 2006.

[10] PWC, 2006.

[11] CCC, 2005a.

[12] Adapted from *PR News*, 2006; SustainAbility and UNEP, 2001.

[13] BSR, 2002.

[14] Melcrum, 2005.

[15] CCC, 2005a.

[16] CCC, 2005a.

[17] CCC, 2005b.

[18] BSR, 2002.

[19] CCC, 2005c.

[20] Melcrum, 2005.

[21] PWC, 2006.

[22] This section draws on Holliday et al., 2002; Olsen, 2004; Werther and Chandler, 2006. The authors are also very grateful to Steve Rochlin at AccountAbility for his ideas on this topic.

[23] Stewart and Immelt, 2006.

[24] Sutcliffe, 2006.

[25] A more comprehensive list of corporate responsibility service providers can be found on the Online Resource Centre.

[26] Olsen, 2004.

[27] CCC, 2005b, pp 26–7.

[28] Phillips and Caldwell, 2005.

[29] Phillips and Caldwell, 2005.

[30] Arnold and Hartman, 2003; Henriques and Richardson, 2004.

[31] ETI, 2003; Hale and Shaw, 2001.

[32] ETI, 2003.

[33] *Ethical Corporation*, 2006.

[34] Jamison and Murdoch, 2004; World Bank, 2003.

[35] Collinson, 2001.

[36] Dolan and Humphrey, 2004.

[37] ETI, 2005b; Blowfield, 2000a.

[38] This argument is implicit in Matten and Crane, 2005.

[39] Jenkins, 1999.

[40] Nelson and Tallontire, 2002; Deloitte, undated.

5

The business case for corporate responsibility

Chapter overview

In this chapter, we explore the different aspects of the business case for corporate responsibility. In particular, we will:

- examine what is meant by a 'business case';

- consider why the business case is important;

- establish the areas of business performance that are linked to corporate responsibility;

- examine evidence that there is a business case;

- assess how strong the evidence is of positive or negative business benefits;

- consider how the business case is evolving.

Main topics

■ Key terms

Eco-efficiency

Reputation management

Risk management

Sustainable development

■ Online resources

- Additional case studies of the business case for specific companies

- Exercises and discussion topics for students

- Further debates about the strengths and weaknesses of the business case

- Links to other web-based resources

Importance of the business case

Pick up any book on corporate responsibility, browse the session themes of conferences, or look at companies' social or environmental reports, and you will soon discern how important the business case has become to contemporary corporate responsibility. For business managers, government officials, academics, consultants, to name but a few, making the business case has become the Holy Grail. There is a simple reason for this: demonstrating a positive correlation between corporate responsibility and business performance (especially financial performance) is seen as giving social and environmental issues legitimacy in the world of mainstream business. In this way, it greatly increases the likelihood that corporate responsibility practices will be adopted. Consequently, information, such as that 91 per cent of executives believe that corporate responsibility creates shareholder value, or that 80 per cent say that non-financial indicators are essential to characterize future financial performance, is widely cited as proof positive of corporate responsibility's importance, not as the nice thing to do, but as part of good management practice.[1]

Making the business case has grown in importance as the focus of corporate responsibility has moved from philanthropy and generally giving a proportion of revenues back to society, to the function of corporate responsibility in core business activities. Showing how corporate responsibility relates to business performance is intended to help managers to understand why they should be paying attention and to what they should be attending. It is also meant to help companies to explain the importance of social and environmental performance to investors, and vice versa. Meanwhile, away from the company-specific level, it provides a basis for corporate responsibility's advocates to demonstrate to mainstream management theorists and liberal economists that corporate responsibility can add to shareholder value, or at least will not damage it.[2]

There are, then, good reasons why the business case has become so important to corporate responsibility. But the *gravitas* that it has accrued gives rise to two further questions that are the main topics of this chapter: what evidence is there of a business case, and how does its presence or absence affect corporate responsibility now and how will it affect it in the future? Neither question is easy to answer—not least, because of the methodological challenges facing any measurement of the business case ('How reliable is the evidence?', p 144)—and, as we discuss towards the end of the chapter, there is good reason to consider what the consequences are for corporate responsibility if the business case continues to be brought to the fore.

Examples of the benefits to business

When BP met its target of reducing greenhouse gas emissions at twice the rate specified in the Kyoto Protocol nine years ahead of schedule, the reductions were the equivalent of 9.6 million tonnes and the company achieved operational savings of $250m. When Ford improved energy efficiency at its North American manufacturing facilities by 18 per cent and cut water use by 5 bn gallons, it saved millions of dollars. Dow Chemical has developed technology that allows it to make a 60 per cent saving in the energy used to prepare aluminium cans for filling. DuPont, which tops *Business Week*'s 2005 list of 'Green Companies', has saved $2bn by reducing energy consumption and aims to generate 25 per cent of its revenue using renewable resources by 2010. The Asahi Kasei Group felt no negative financial effects when it made changes to the way in which it produces polycarbonate that resulted in the elimination of hydrochloric acid as a by-product. When 3M pre-empted new government regulations by abandoning the use of solvent-based coatings in favour of water-soluble ones, it benefited commercially from having an early mover advantage, and operationally from reductions in downtime, product loss, and waste related to the new technology. Philips Electronics' Marathon light bulbs, a line of eco-friendly, energy-saving fluorescent bulbs, have achieved 12 per cent annual growth in a typically flat market. Gap Inc has found that purchasing decisions that negatively impact working conditions also undermine quality, on-time delivery, and cost.[3] Wal-Mart favours suppliers that share its commitment to less packaging, and the use of recycled and non-toxic materials, while major DIY and furniture stories, such as Home Depot, Ikea, and B&Q, have made sourcing from sustainably managed resources part of their buying policy.

Different industries; different countries; different dimensions of corporate responsibility: all suggesting that a link can be made between social and environmental performance, and business performance. According to the investment group, Innovest, 85 per cent of studies show a positive correlation between environmental governance and financial performance.[4] According to UK-based telecommunications company BT, the benefits of corporate responsibility to a company's reputation, and the money that can be saved through efficient environmental planning and the identification of new market opportunities, *'often amount to a convincing financial reason for why business should engage with such issues'*.[5] According to one former executive, strategies built around the triple bottom line can yield a 46 per cent increase in profit over five years, fully costed.[6]

Porter and Van der Linde (1995) describe how the Dutch flower industry responded to an increasingly tough regulatory regime, which was concerned about the environmental problems of intensive cultivation (e.g. contamination of soil and groundwater), by developing a closed-loop system that reduced the industry's environmental impact at the same time as it brought various financial benefits related to less plant infestation and lower usage, or wastage, of fertilizer, pesticides, and water. Recent studies are providing other examples of the business case within other industries (e.g. aviation, financial services, and pharmaceuticals), at least from an environmental perspective.[7]

The business case can also be thought through from an issues perspective. For example, industries as diverse as agribusiness, chemicals, pharmaceuticals, and the automotive industry may recognize the business costs related to water sustainability, such as increases in water prices and treatment costs, growth in worker absenteeism related to water-borne illnesses, the disruption to business caused by conflicts over water rights, and threats to a company's reputation if it is subjected to civil society criticism about its water management.[8] It is not difficult to find similar company- or issue-focused examples of the business case and a number of corporate responsibility organizations have produced management-oriented tools that provide evidence of the business case, coach managers on how to build such a case, and help them to quantify it.[9]

CASE STUDY 5.1

Fonebak—building a multi-million-pound business out of recycling

There are over 1.28 billion mobile phone users across the world and over 342 million users in Europe alone. UK consumers get rid of their mobile phones on average every 18 months, leaving behind the lithium ion, platinum, gold, silver, copper and plastics that make up every phone. Established in 2002, Fonebak recycles and reuses mobile phones for phone operators, retailers, and corporations. Individuals can drop off their phones at major stores or send them direct to the company, which donates part of the value to nominated charities. The materials are removed and recycled from broken or obsolete phones, while serviceable phones are refurbished for use in developing countries. It has over a thousand clients representing all network operators in the UK and many major networks, retailers, manufacturers and charities across Europe, and had generated £60.4m in revenues as of mid-2006.

(www.fonebak.com; england.shelter.org.uk)

Questions

Fonebak is not only an example of recycling and reuse, but also of how a business case for corporate responsibility can be made to an industry.

1 Why are major phone networks and retailers collaborating with Fonebak (e.g. by putting recycling bins in their stores)?

2 Is Fonebak a genuine business or an example of social entrepreneurship?

3 Does the existence of trade-back facilities encourage more frequent trade-in of phones and is this inconsistent with Fonebak's goals?

What is meant by the 'business case'

Examples such as those above have generated considerable excitement about the business case, but they also highlight some of the problems in making that case. They refer not only to a variety of measures of business performance, but also to different aspects of corporate responsibility. At times, the measures are those of performance (e.g. shareholder value, access to capital), but they can also be to do with drivers (e.g. maintaining reputation, innovation, licence to operate). It is not immediately clear which dimensions of corporate responsibility have the strongest or weakest links to business performance. It is also not always apparent what type of relationship exists between corporate responsibility and business performance, i.e. whether the one causes the other and under what circumstances.

Preston and O'Bannon (1997) divide the business case into three types of relationship:

1 that within which corporate responsibility relates to financial performance;

2 that within which financial performance relates to corporate responsibility;

3 that within which corporate responsibility and financial performance are synergistic.

In all three types, the relationship can be positive, neutral, or negative, so that according to Friedman (1962), for example, there is a negative relationship between corporate responsibility and financial performance, because the former misuses company assets (see Chapter 2). According to Cornell and Shapiro (1987), there is a positive relationship, because meeting the needs of stakeholders other than shareholders enhances financial performance. Case studies and other analyses exist for each type of relationship: for example, Waddock and Graves (1997) study how the strength of performance affects the amount that a company invests in corporate responsibility and some of the most recent work discussed towards the end of this chapter emphasizes synergistic relationships. Moreover, as we discuss later, financial performance is only one aspect of business performance. Nonetheless, most effort has been spent on examining how corporate responsibility helps or hinders financial performance,[10] and, as we will see, much of the discussion about the efficiency of the business case revolves around the way in which monetary values are assigned to actions that may, or may not, have had a financial motivation, at least to begin with.

Dimensions of corporate responsibility

To make sense of the business–corporate responsibility relationship, we need to know what we mean when we refer to both 'corporate responsibility' and 'business performance'. A recurring problem mentioned in overviews of studies related to the business case is that it is hard to draw firm conclusions because of the differences in the way in which 'corporate responsibility' or 'business performance' are defined.[11] Much of the literature, especially that originating in the USA, concentrates on the relationship between what is called 'corporate social performance' (CSP) and 'financial performance', within which CSP is typically a measure of the overall contribution that companies make to society.[12] In Europe, recent literature has focused more specifically on company activities that contribute to society beyond products, employment, returns on investment, and legal compliance. The specific elements of corporate responsibility that receive attention include:

1 the influence of *ethics, values, and principles* on a company's actions, as evident, for example, in business principles, decisions, and legal actions;

2 a company's *accountability and transparency* for its corporate responsibility performance, as evident, for example, in its reporting and management systems;

3 a company's overall commitment and performance in social, economic, and environmental areas (i.e. the *triple bottom line*);

4 a company's record on *eco-efficiency*, evident, for example, in its minimization of adverse environmental impacts associated with product processes;

5 the *environmental product focus* of a company, as seen, for example, in its redesign of products to reduce their environmental impact (e.g. cradle-to-grave product stewardship);

6 the use of a company's resources to support the *social and economic development* of communities;

7 a company's respect for, and protection of, *human rights*;

8 efforts by a company to foster a high-quality *work environment*, including health and safety issues, but also those such as work–life balance;

9 involvement of the company's *business stakeholders* (e.g. suppliers, partners, contractors, shareholders) in implementing its corporate responsibility strategy;

10 the quantity and quality of a company's engagement with *external stakeholders* (e.g. civil society organizations, government) in relation to corporate responsibility.[13]

There are other dimensions of corporate responsibility that might be included (e.g. animal rights, internal stakeholders such as employees, and the factoring of social issues into management processes, or 'socio-efficiency'), but the above list covers those dimensions for which most information seems to be available. The emphasis on environmental issues is noticeable, reflecting the fact that, although corporate responsibility increasingly embraces social, as well as environmental, performance, much of the work on the business case has focused on sustainability, or sustainable development (see Chapter 9).

Measures of business performance

The next step is to understand what the measures of business performance are on which corporate responsibility might have an impact. These measures relate to the various conditions that management attends to so as to enhance company prosperity. In the literature, ten measures are commonly mentioned.[14]

1 **Shareholder value**
   Changes in a company's stock price and dividend.

2 **Revenue**
   Changes in a company's revenues due to pricing, market share, new markets, etc.

3 **Operational efficiency**
   A company's cost-effectiveness in turning inputs into productive outputs.

4 **Access to capital**
   A company's access to equity and debt capital.

5 **Customer attraction**
   A company's ability to attract and retain customers.

6 **Brand value and reputation**
   The value assigned to a company and its brands due to their reputation.

7 **Human capital**
   The knowledge and skills of a company's employees, resulting from the ability to attract, develop, and retain a workforce.

8 **Risk management**
   Exposure of a company's assets to short- and long-term risks.

9 **Innovation**
   A company's ability to maintain its competitive advantage through better products, services, and business models.

10 **Licence to operate**
    A company's ability to maintain a level of acceptance among its stakeholders that allows it to operate effectively.

Again, there may be other measures that one might use, or that might be made more explicit. For example, the importance of trust in reducing transaction costs in the modern value chain is probably not sufficiently apparent in this model, and, as we discuss later, the consequences of corporate responsibility for business regulation are more important and complex than they appear here. Nonetheless, using these ten measures of business performance, along with the aforementioned ten dimensions of corporate responsibility, provides a matrix for assessing the business case (see 'Evidence of a business case', p 138).

Factors affecting the business case

Before we look at the evidence for a relationship between business and corporate responsibility performance, it is important to understand some of the variables that come into play. First, different audiences interpret the business case in specific ways. For example, business managers may want information that will help to convince their superiors or colleagues, while shareholders will want to know if corporate responsibility pays; governments will want information that will test if corporate responsibility is a viable basis for delivering social and environmental benefits.[15] Each audience requires information that meets its needs, or, at the very least, an analysis that fits its customary frameworks. For example, a criticism of information on the business case for sustainable development is that it is not presented in the language of managers or shareholders.[16]

Second, the business case differs from industry to industry. For a mining company, such as Placer Dome, corporate responsibility might result in preferred access in future gold-mining projects, whereas for Royal Ahold, the supermarket company, it might help the company to relate better to consumers in fiercely competitive mature markets.[17] A criticism of studies to date is that the industry-specific nature of the business case is not normally recognized.[18]

Third, the business case partly depends on how corporate responsibility is viewed within a company and on how developed that company's approach to corporate responsibility is. For example, in the late 1990s, a company such as Premier Oil would have seen corporate responsibility as a way to offset criticism for its investment in Burma, while BP or Shell, despite being in the same industry, were thinking less about reputation and more about how corporate responsibility related to their long-term strategies.[19]

Finally, studies tend to overlook how the local, national, or regional contexts affect the business case.[20] For example, there might be quite different arguments to be made for eco-efficiency in a country with a tough regulatory regime and a strong utilities infrastructure, compared with that in a country in which environmental regulations are weak, but the cost of energy or clean water is relatively high. Just as corporate responsibility can look different from country to country (see Chapter 3), so, too, can the business case.

CASE STUDY 5.2

How government can create the business case

The business case is not simply a question of economics; it also depends on the environment within which business operates. Some of the technologies we take for granted originally became viable because of government actions. The catalytic converter is an excellent example of how legislation created a market for an environmental product, and of how major automotive manufacturers overcame their resistance and worked with suppliers to reduce vehicle emissions, even as vehicle use grew.

The market for catalytic converters was a direct consequence of vehicle emissions controls introduced in 1970, notably, amendments to the US Federal Clean Air Act 1963 and the Californian Zero Emission Vehicle Mandate. The legislation was passed even though the technology to achieve the targets they set out was barely proven and not commercialized, and the automakers lobbied aggressively that it would harm their industry. But the strong stance of the Californian government and of the newly established US Environmental Protection Agency (EPA) forced automakers to enter into forward commitment procurement agreements with potential catalytic converter suppliers, towards working together to develop the technology that would meet demands for a 90 per cent reduction in carbon dioxide and nitrous oxide.

Engine modifications alone would have been unlikely to meet these much tougher standards, however, and so a real commercial opportunity emerged for companies such as Johnson Matthey, which had relevant experience from working with other industries, to work with the automakers. These companies were encouraged by the EPA's insistence that vehicle manufacturers prove they were making a determined effort to meet the targets and, in 1972, EPA held the first of several public hearings to assess progress. Despite the automakers' initial reluctance, catalytic converters have become the norm and emissions from cars are now lower than they were in the 1960s, despite the increase in total car mileage. In terms of government action, the key learnings are that government is able to motivate private industry to deliver better technology for environmental gain at no particular cost to the public purse over the long term.

(www.managementtoday.co.uk; www.environmental-expert.com—accessed 20 March 2007)

Questions

1 What were the main government actions that encouraged automakers to adopt catalytic converters?

2 Why do you think automakers were resistant?

3 Are there other examples in which government has created a new market in this way?

Evidence of a business case

In 2001, SustainAbility, the consultancy company, in association with the UN Environmental Programme, reviewed multiple reports, case studies, and academic analyses pertaining to the business case for sustainable development, and issued a report that remains one of the only attempts to correlate specific dimensions of corporate responsibility with measures of business performance. A similar study (that additionally involved the International Finance Corporation) focused on emerging markets and was published in 2002.[21] Subsequent studies, such as the IMD management school's work on the business case for sustainability, have added new insights, but also show that the key findings from 2001 and 2002 remain valid. In addition, the business case has been made central to claims for the efficacy of corporate responsibility by influential management thinkers (e.g. Porter and Kramer 2002, 2006).

Positive relationships

The findings of the SustainAbility reports, summarized in Figure 5.1, show that there are 21 areas in which there is strong evidence that corporate responsibility positively affects business performance, although in emerging and developing economies, this figure drops to seven.[22] The most demonstrable contribution is in the area of eco-efficiency, in which changes in the use of raw materials, recycling and reuse, reductions in emissions, and other new practices have had tangible benefits in terms of shareholder value, operational efficiency, access to capital, reputation, risk management, and innovation. Eco-efficiency has become so prevalent in industries such as chemicals, energy, and electrical goods that it is barely thought of as 'corporate responsibility', and may even be dismissed by those opposed to corporate responsibility as nothing more than rational profit maximization, i.e. common sense management practice. But it is relatively recently that pollution has come to be seen not as the inevitable by-product of economic prosperity, but as a form of

Dimensions of corporate responsibility

Columns: Ethics; values, principles | Accountability and transparency | Adoption of triple bottom line | Eco-efficiency | Environmental products | Social development | Human rights | Working conditions | Business stakeholders | Non-business stakeholders

Business measures:

- Shareholder value
- Revenue
- Operational efficiency
- Access to capital
- Customer attraction
- Brand value and reputation
- Human capital
- Risk management
- Innovation
- Licence to operate

Key:

▮	Strong positive impact of corporate responsibility on business performance
▯	Some positive impact of corporate responsibility on business performance
▨	Neutral or negative impact of corporate responsibility on business performance

Figure 5.1 Areas of correlation between corporate responsibility and business performance

Source: Analysis of data in SustainAbility et al. (2001, 2002)

economic waste,[23] and this change has occurred because of, not despite, the kind of transformation associated with corporate responsibility (see also Chapter 9).

There is also strong evidence that other dimensions of corporate responsibility are linked to better business performance, including: protection of human rights; high-quality working conditions; relationships with external stakeholders; transparency and accountability around corporate responsibility performance. What also stands out is that, whereas eco-efficiency delivers a wide variety of benefits, these other dimensions affect a much narrower selection of business performance measures. By far the greatest impact is on brand value and reputation, for which there is evidence of a strong positive impact from six different dimensions of corporate responsibility, although in emerging and developing economies revenue and operational efficiency are also important. The next most frequent area of impact is risk management, for which dimensions such as eco-efficiency, the development of environmental products, protection of human rights, and a commitment to values and principles all have a strong positive impact. In other words, corporate responsibility is most likely to have a strong positive impact on intangible, rather than tangible, aspects of business performance.

This is an important part of the debate about the business case. Even though reputation and brand cannot be quantified with the same precision as can cash flow or earnings before interest, taxes, depreciation, and amortization (EBITDA), they have significant economic value. In companies such as Coca Cola, 96 per cent of the company's value is intangible.[24] Corporate responsibility theorists have picked up on arguments that business success today has less to do with tangible assets, such as production facilities and financial capital, than it has to do with intangibles, and that perhaps as little as 20 per cent of a company's market value is captured by its conventional accounting system.[25] They argue that corporate responsibility provides a way of capturing and recognizing this less quantifiable value, and that the more companies that begin to adopt non-financial reporting, the more apparent the business case for corporate responsibility will become.

Risk management and licence to operate are, likewise, areas to which it is difficult to assign a monetary value (for example, it is easier to see the cost–benefit of a lawsuit won or lost than of the lawsuit that was avoided because of good stakeholder engagement), but for which there is evidence that corporate responsibility is having a strong impact. There are, however, areas of corporate responsibility that do impact financial performance measures: for example, high-quality working conditions and policies favouring a good work–life balance have been shown to contribute to revenues, operational efficiency, and human capital, because they help companies to attract and retain employees. Similarly, although not strongly evident in the SustainAbility study, companies such as New Balance, GE, and Toyota are making significant investments in products with environmentally beneficial impacts, because they believe that these will be growth areas in the future.

As SustainAbility's analysis readily recognizes, however, and as subsequent authors such as Margolis and Walsh (2003) and Salzmann et al. (2005) underline, in assessing the business case, we are often using data that are difficult to compare, drawn from a mixture of case studies and quantitative surveys, covering different industries and countries, and often focused on different dimensions of both corporate responsibility and business performance. This partly accounts for why there is so little of what can be considered 'hard' evidence. In the SustainAbility study, 65 per cent of the data sources were categorized as providing weak evidence and, as Figure 5.2 shows, there is only hard evidence to support claims of a strong positive impact in eleven of nineteen instances. In the majority of cases, there is some evidence of a moderate positive impact (that denoted by white squares in Figure 5.1), but because this is a conclusion that is based, for the most part, on weak evidence, it does not really constitute a strong case in favour of corporate responsibility.

Business measures	Dimensions of corporate responsibility									
	Ethics; values; principles	Accountability and transparency	Adoption of triple bottom line	Eco-efficiency	Environmental products	Social development	Human rights	Working conditions	Business stakeholders	Non-business stakeholders
Shareholder value				■						
Revenue								■		
Operational efficiency				■		▨		■		
Access to capital				■						
Customer attraction										
Brand value and reputation	■						■			
Human capital								■		
Risk management	■			■						
Innovation			▨		■			▨		
Licence to operate										

Key:

■	Strong evidence for positive impact on business performance
☐	Weak evidence for any positive or negative impact on business performance
▨	Strong evidence for neutral or negative impact on business performance

Figure 5.2 **Areas in which there is strong evidence of a correlation between corporate responsibility and business performance**
Source: Analysis of data in SustainAbility et al. (2001, 2002)

The data do, however, help to identify the dimensions of corporate responsibility for which there is most evidence of a positive relationship to business performance. Using the same data set as above, but applying a simple weighting system based on the relative strength of the data source, we find that the most significant corporate responsibility dimensions are eco-efficiency, working conditions, and environmental products.[26] The areas of business performance for which there is most evidence that corporate responsibility has an impact are brand value, reputation management, and human capital (Boxes 5.1

Box 5.1 Dimensions of corporate responsibility for which there is most evidence of an impact on business performance (lowest score = highest ranking)

Ranking	Dimension	Weighted score
1	Eco-efficiency	25
2	Working conditions	38
3	Environmental products	39
4	Adoption of triple bottom line	42
5	Accountability and transparency	43

Box 5.2 Measures of business performance for which there is most evidence of an effect by corporate responsibility (lowest score = highest ranking)

Ranking	Measure	Weighted score
1	Brand value and reputation	31
2	Risk management	36
3	Human capital	37
4	Revenue	41
5	Shareholder value	44

and 5.2). This concurs with anecdotal evidence and case studies that argue that the business case is increasingly considered in terms of brand reputation, the creation of brand image, building customer loyalty and lifetime customer value, and employee motivation, satisfaction, and retention.[27]

Neutral and negative relationships

Figure 5.1 also shows that there are as many areas on which corporate responsibility has a neutral or negative impact on business performance, as there are those on which there is a strong positive impact. Notably, the business case for engaging with business stakeholders appears weak and engaging with non-business stakeholders cannot be justified in terms of financial performance. Important dimensions of corporate responsibility, such as ethics and values, and protecting human rights, also have a neutral or negative relationship to financial performance measures, such as revenue, access to capital, and operational efficiency.

The weakness of this analysis (in addition to the comments made in the previous section) is that it does not differentiate between negative and neutral impact so that it is unclear, for example, if attention to social development has a neutral or negative effect on operational efficiency. (Indeed, in the narrower study of the business case in emerging economies, no mention is made at all of evidence of a negative case and the analysis is confined to no evidence, some evidence, and strong evidence.)[28] This is because many of the studies of the business case are not objective, and are inclined to emphasize the positive and discount the negative. Moreover, the data are dogged by problems in identifying causality, i.e. whether a particular business performance outcome can be attributed to a corporate responsibility action, how direct or indirect that relationship is, and whether corporate responsibility enhances business performance, or whether, as Waddock and Graves (1997) suggest, it may be the result of strong financial performance. These are common factors and features in studies of the business case,[29] and, combined with the aforementioned bias, may account for why there is so little information on the neutral and negative relationships.

Nonetheless, using the same weighting system applied in the previous section, the dimensions of corporate responsibility that least affect business performance are engagement with business stakeholders, principles and values, and social development (Box 5.3). The measures of business performance that are least affected by corporate responsibility are attracting customers, operational efficiency, and access to capital (Box 5.4). This does not mean that, for example, corporate responsibility is least relevant for operational efficiency or accessing capital; only that, at the present time, these are business performance measures for which there is the weakest evidence.

As Margolis and Walsh (2003) conclude, in their extensive study of corporate social performance, although there are serious methodological questions (see below), there is little evidence to suggest that paying attention to societal impact damages shareholder value.

Box 5.3 Dimensions of corporate responsibility for which there is least evidence of an impact on business performance (highest score = worst ranking)

Ranking	Dimension	Weighted score
1	Engaging business stakeholders	52
2	Ethics, principles, and values	49
2	Social development	49
4	Human rights	48
5	Engagement with non-business stakeholders	46

Box 5.4 Measures of business performance for which there is least evidence of an effect by corporate responsibility (highest score = worst ranking)

Ranking	Measure	Weighted score
1	Attracting customers	50
1	Operational efficiency	50
3	Access to capital	49
4	Innovation	47
5	Licence to operate	46

It is a weakness in current business case literature, however, that ways in which corporate responsibility might damage business performance are not properly explored. Corporate responsibility's critics like to make the case that it is anti-growth and that it therefore deprives people of the benefits of economic growth that, for example, have raised living standards in successful economies. There is no evidence that corporate responsibility is inherently anti-growth: on the contrary, some advocates of sustainable development say that serious economic growth is needed if we are to meet the needs of current and future generations, and some companies clearly see that addressing social and environmental issues in the future will provide growth opportunities.[30] But some companies, such as low-cost air carriers, would clearly suffer under tougher environmental norms, because air travel results in significantly higher greenhouse gas emissions than does travel by rail or sea.[31] Similarly, despite the instances of increased wages having been offset by productivity gains, it is counter-intuitive (and it therefore demands further examination) that increased labour costs due to corporate responsibility will never affect company growth.

As important, though, is that current studies are unidirectional, focusing on how corporate responsibility affects business performance and ignoring the ways in which business performance may impact on corporate responsibility. This leaves unanswered questions such as to what extent does successful pursuit of revenue growth have a positive or negative effect on human rights or environmental management? As is explored further later in the text, in relation to criticisms of corporate responsibility (see Chapter 13), the implicit primacy given to the benefits for business is one of the concerns of some observers.

How reliable is the evidence?

There are clearly reasons for questioning the evidence about the relationship between corporate responsibility and business performance, even if some broad trends are discernible. The studies involving SustainAbility are subject to criticism in academic circles, because the methodology employed is not as well set out as some would like and there is a suspicion that the research lacks academic rigour.[32] Concerns about the comprehensiveness and comparability of the data, about the direction of causation, and about how to make sense of the different variables mean that it is impossible to draw the kind of firm conclusions about the business case that would allow us to condone or condemn corporate responsibility. Salzmann et al. (2005) conclude that making the business case encounters two stumbling blocks:

1 the complex web of parameters (e.g. technology, regulatory regime, company visibility) and variables (e.g. location, industry, country, time) that can affect outcomes;

2 the difficulty of detecting the impact of corporate responsibility, because, except in a small number of areas—notably, eco-efficiency and brand reputation—it tends to be marginal to business practice for most companies and industries.

To this list we might add the veracity of the evidence. It is ironic, given that Sustain-Ability's 2001 report emphasizes the limited, and perhaps biased, nature of much of the evidence, that its report of a year later tucks any mention of methodological weaknesses away towards the end, while opening with the claim that: '*Many businesses . . . are gaining valuable business benefits from initiatives which help progress towards sustainable development.*'[33] Indeed, in launching a second phase of the research, a co-sponsor, the International Finance Corporation, declared that the 2002 study '*was a landmark: the first to make a compelling case as to why* [environmental, social, and governance] *factors are relevant for emerging-market corporate competitiveness*'.[34] This claim is made even though, as noted, the study only found seven areas of strong correlation between corporate responsibility and business performance, and although there were twenty-nine areas of some positive correlation, it was precisely this level of evidence that had been questioned in the 2001 report.

Such examples hint at the powerful forces that can push even objective researchers to propose an at best questionable basis for the business case. Some argue that, given how little evidence there is that corporate responsibility is damaging to profitability, we should not be asking '*Does corporate responsibility pay?*', but rather '*Under what conditions does corporate responsibility pay?*'[35] This might mean explaining the specific conditions within a company or industry, but, more broadly, it might mean asking under what market conditions companies will maximize total value by taking account of stakeholder expectations.[36] In relation to the former issue, there are very few studies of how the business case drives corporate responsibility management and most research concentrates on how corporate responsibility affects business success.[37] Regarding the latter, the relationship between corporate responsibility and the four conditions of perfect competition (i.e. a large number of buyers and sellers, complete information, homogeneity of products, and free entry and exit to and from the market), while alluded to by both advocates and critics of corporate responsibility,[38] has not been studied in any depth.

Consequently, the evidence that we have of the business benefits is almost exclusively to do with how corporate responsibility affects either legitimacy (the effect that social, economic, and environmental performance has on reputation, and relations with civil society and governments) or productivity (the direct benefits of cost savings, improved quality, employee morale, innovation, new markets, and better risk management).[39] From this, three types of business case emerge.

1 Corporate responsibility as a means of avoiding financial loss (e.g. by defending a company's reputation).

2 Corporate responsibility as a driver of tangible financial gains (e.g. by improving the quality of the workforce, by driving product innovation).

3 Corporate responsibility as an integral element of the company's strategic approach to long-term business performance (e.g. by prompting a move away from dependence on non-renewable natural resources).[40]

As we discuss later in this chapter ('A new kind of business case', p 150), some believe that a fourth type of business case is emerging, within which corporate responsibility is central to how companies learn, innovate, and manage risk in ever more dynamic and complex business environments. Most of the evidence available relates to preventing loss, or securing gains. There is, however, limited evidence of a direct correlation between corporate responsibility and financial performance. In one study, News International had the worst corporate responsibility performance, but the best share price, while The Body Shop's good corporate responsibility reputation did not protect its share price when it suffered from poor management and may even have made it more susceptible to public criticism when it was exposed for making false claims about helping developing country suppliers.[41] Nonetheless, some companies, such as Monsanto, have suffered financially partly because of corporate responsibility failings, while others, such as Shell, have used corporate responsibility to rebuild a damaged image.[42] Perhaps the difficulty again lies in how the problem is framed and, rather than trying to demonstrate that corporate responsibility is a predictor or guarantee of certain outcomes, we should view it, for example, as an approach to strategy and management practice.[43]

Additional facets of the business case

Regardless of the quality of the evidence, the kind of matrix discussed above suffers from two main deficiencies: its emphasis on unidirectional causality and its inability to consider the broader context within which companies operate. We have already mentioned the difficulty with unidirectionality in this chapter ('Neutral and negative relationships', p 142); it may be argued that to analyse the effect of shareholder value on corporate responsibility policies and strategies, for example, is to extend the utility of the matrix too far, but, inadvertently, the focus on unidirectional causality may serve to enforce the importance of the business case, even as the matrix exposes some of its limitations.

Second, as noted, if responsibility pays some of the time, but not all of the time, what is important is to understand what circumstances produce what outcomes. For example, what structural factors increase the likelihood that corporate responsibility will contribute to business success (e.g. increase in the importance of intangible assets, increase in the speed and volume of communications, growth in the role of the public sector as a provider of public goods, such as health care and education)? Similarly, what factors constrain the acceptance of corporate responsibility by companies (e.g. intensification of commercial competition, the short-term outlook of capital markets, a weak public policy environment)? Or what are the competitive dynamics that encourage companies to tackle societal issues (e.g. the early-mover advantage gained by Toyota in relation to hybrid vehicles)? And under what circumstances will a company, instead of using corporate responsibility to differentiate itself in the market, try to reshape market conditions by creating rules or norms that are intended to persuade competitors to emulate their behaviour (e.g. Rio Tinto's championing of the Global Mining Initiative, or Vattenfall's pioneering thinking on energy and climate change)?[44]

Amalric and Hauser (2005) distinguish between the business case for action by a single company and that for collective self-regulation by an industry, or other grouping of companies. Individual action on corporate responsibility, for example, can benefit the company by differentiating it as an employer (resulting in lower turnover costs, increased employee motivation, or allowing it to charge more for its products) and by helping it to maintain that difference as competitors try to emulate it. (The need to maintain differentiation is a lesson that early mover companies in corporate responsibility have sometimes failed to learn: for example, the difficulties that Levi Strauss has encountered in building on its early reputational advantage of establishing codes of labour and environmental conduct.)[45] Individual action is said to be a good way in which to tackle risk and reputation. It has also been shown to help companies to interact with regulators and to persuade governments to develop legislation that is in line with the company's interests.[46]

Collective self-regulation, by contrast, is beneficial in preventing new regulations that might reduce an industry's profitability (e.g. the establishment of the Hays Office in 1922, by the movie industry, to police the content of films; the launch of the Responsible Care programme by the Chemical Manufacturers' Association, following the Bhopal disaster). It can also help in defending the social acceptability of activities (e.g. the work of the World Dam Commission to define the conditions under which large dams contribute to sustainable development—see Case Study 5.4).

Whether collectively or individually, in some cases, companies that anticipate societal issues can enjoy a competitive advantage, both from being early movers in terms of technologies and strategies, and from being able to shape the overall direction of legislation and public debate. Measuring this latter type of benefit is difficult, although that, in itself, has not deterred industries from trying to influence public policy more generally, such as through political lobbying. Equally, companies may be reluctant to be too open about this aspect of the business case, for fear of adverse publicity about capturing or subverting the public policy process. Nonetheless, there is evidence that, on certain issues in relation to which business is seen as having an important and legitimate role to play, corporate responsibility does help companies to engage in public policy. A notable example is global climate change, in relation to which some companies have taken on a leadership role through their individual policies, their support for collective and multi-sector initiatives, and their innovations. The factors that determine what role a company or industry plays in relation to such major societal issues are only beginning to be understood in any depth. The nature of an industry, its social or ecological footprint, and its visibility are all likely contributors, as might be company ownership and whether the industry is dominated by numerator managers, who are focused on innovation, rather than denominator managers, who are primarily concerned with efficiency (see Chapter 4).[47]

CASE STUDY 5.3

Cap and trade—using markets to create a business case

Carbon emissions trading involves the trading of permits to emit carbon dioxide and other green-house gases. Countries cap their emissions at a certain level and then issue permits to companies, allowing them to emit a stated amount of CO_2 over a given time. Companies that produce fewer emissions than permitted can trade their surplus with those that fear they might exceeding their limit and want to avoid the hefty fines that they would consequently incur. Companies that can reduce their emissions for less than the cost of permits or fines will do so and, by steadily reducing the number of permits on the market, governments intend, over time, that it will be more profitable for companies to cut their emissions than to buy permits. Creating carbon-trading markets is part of the Kyoto Protocol, but, at present, the European Union's Emissions Trading Scheme is the only mandatory carbon trading programme.

(www.defra.gov.uk; www.unfccc.org)

Questions

The EU Emissions Trading Scheme was greeted by many in the environmental movement as a way of bringing the strength of the market to the problem of greenhouse gas emissions, and London has positioned itself as a centre for the anticipated boom in carbon trading.

1 Why did the scheme stumble early on, to the point at which the market had to be temporarily closed in late 2005?

2 Why do you think Chicago and New York have been less successful than London in establishing carbon trading?

3 Why did some pro-business bodies criticize Governor Arnold Schwarzenegger when he signed legislation that would lead to a carbon-trading scheme for California?

Another side of public policy in this context is that, through regulation and the wider policy environment, government can influence what constitutes the business case (see Case Studies 5.2 and 5.3). It can, for example, undermine the business case by providing perverse subsidies that encourage poor environmental practices; it can enact legislation that raises the bar on issues ranging from labour rights to corporate governance; it can stimulate initiatives, such as carbon trading, by setting national or regional policy frameworks. Jeroen van der Veer, Royal Dutch Shell CEO, has said that more regulation is needed to encourage both investment in new technologies and energy conservation,[48] and that work on the different types of economy required to achieve different levels of CO_2 emissions provides a clear example of how the business case alters, depending on the public policy framework within which business operates.[49] Governments such as those in El Salvador, some Brazilian states, and Cambodia have treated aspects of corporate responsibility as part of their own economic competitive advantage, although many more still believe that there is a fundamental dichotomy between high social and environmental standards, and the demands of economic growth.[50] Just as there is a debate within business about the contribution that corporate responsibility makes to business performance, so too, in government, there is a debate as to whether it is a driver of, or a drag on, national and regional competitiveness. One study for the European Union found a significant correlation between a country's competitiveness and its level of corporate responsibility.[51] But it is not possible to conclude from this either that competitiveness depends on a society's level of social or environmental responsibility, or that corporate responsibility can fuel competitiveness. But, as with other aspects of the business case discussed previously, perhaps the question is being framed incorrectly. There are inherent limits to the business case at both company and collective levels within the current market framework. To date, the business case for corporate responsibility has revolved around finding opportunities in relation to which companies can do well financially by doing good. But, as Zadek et al. argue, *'the challenge is not so much to "find" profitable opportunities in today's markets, as to create markets that systematically reward responsible practices'* (2003, p 1).

It is at this level, some claim, that the business case needs to become a political case in order for corporate responsibility to increase its contribution to society. We examine aspects of this further in Chapter 14 (e.g. government interventions to promote sustainable consumption and production), but there is still a strong sense that government (at least in developed economies) sees corporate responsibility as a way of reducing the need to intervene in the affairs of business. Certainly, there is a limited appetite for the kinds of intervention that may have the greatest impact, such as the role of European Union governments in creating a new market for carbon, yet it is exactly these kinds of intervention that some see as essential. For example, by putting a price on carbon, the carbon trading market allowed the investment community to understand the value of carbon emissions without going outside the constraints of portfolio theory, wherein price and value are inseparable.[52]

CASE STUDY 5.4

Dams and development—an industry-level business case

Throughout the 1990s, large dams became increasingly controversial in emerging economies. They promised significant gains, in terms of energy and water availability, but they could also have enormous damaging impacts for local communities and ecosystems. In 1997, the World Commission on Dams (WCD) was set up to look at the development effectiveness of large dams and to develop criteria, guidelines, and standards for all stages of dam construction, from planning, to operation, to decommissioning.

The WCD's commissioners were drawn from business, NGOs, government, international agencies, and academia. Companies involved in the Commission or its forums have included ABB, Enron, Hydro Quebec, and Siemens. The decision-making framework with which WCD came up is based on five core values: equity; sustainability; efficiency; involvement of local people in decision making; accountability. Among the issues with which it deals are: sharing the benefits of the dam among an array of stakeholders; how to allocate resources and benefits in ways that ensure peace, development, and security; how to gain public acceptance of dam projects. These were just some of the issues that had come to the fore during the various dam-related conflicts and protests that had previously taken place worldwide. Business and investment banks had long been keen to point out the economic advantages of large dams, which generate almost 20 per cent of electricity and provide water for up to 40 per cent of the world's irrigated lands. They can also aid regional development, exports, job creation, and the establishment of industry.

But large dams have negative social and environmental impacts: they can fragment and transform rivers, and reservoirs have led to up to eight million people being displaced around the world, with these communities often finding themselves more impoverished than before. There is evidence that a high percentage of malaria-related deaths occur in dam-irrigation regions. Dams can also result in debt burdens, and in the destruction of farmlands and fisheries, and the distribution of benefits has not always been equitable. As the WCD recognized early on, dams have made an important contribution to human development, but, in many cases, the benefits have come at an unacceptable and unnecessary price. It is the balance between the benefits and the price that the Commission has tried to address, not least by proposing a common framework that all sectors concerned with dams can adopt.

(Adapted from reports of the World Dam Commission, online at www.dams.org; Dubash et al., 2002)

Questions

The WCD is an example of an industry-backed, multi-stakeholder approach to identifying what constitutes the responsible dam and developing a framework for industry self-regulation.

1 Why is industry self-regulation more appropriate than separate company initiatives in this instance?

2 Does this kind of framework help companies to make a stronger business case internally?

3 Are there other industries or situations in which collective self-regulation is likely to be effective?

A new kind of business case

The above discussion shows that there are various limits to the business case, both in terms of theory and actual evidence. This has led some to argue for a different type of business case that essentially requires people to look at companies differently. Advocates of the liberal economic theory of the firm seize on this as proof that corporate responsibility is an attempt to undermine free enterprise, distracting company agents from their main purpose, i.e. shareholder value. Free markets, they claim, are essentially moral, allocating resources rationally, fairly, and efficiently. Interfering with those markets for specific social and environmental ends might even be considered immoral, because it might stifle economic growth, exacerbate poverty, and allocate capital to unsustainable, unviable activities. The 'doing well by doing good' logic of corporate responsibility's business case does little to stop such fears and criticisms, because as soon as something with positive social or environmental outcomes benefits the financial bottom line, it is dismissed by liberal economists as rational profit maximization and is therefore used as evidence that free markets, rather than corporate responsibility, address societal concerns.

We explore the liberal critique of corporate responsibility in more depth in Chapter 13, but much of the discussion about the business case does not refute the efficiency of free markets. Rather, corporate responsibility is presented as a way in which to address market imperfections and failures. As some liberal economists would agree, efficient resource allocation depends on markets yielding prices that reflect true social costs; when they fail to do so, such as when polluters do not have to pay the cost of pollution, then the invisible hand can lead one in the wrong direction.[53] Therefore, instead of seeing corporate responsibility as an assault on free markets, it can be argued that it will ultimately make markets, or at least companies, more efficient.

This argument takes three different, if sometimes overlapping, forms. One is that, although there may not be a causal relationship between corporate responsibility and business performance, there can be a correlation between the quality of a company's technical systems and processes, and its corporate responsibility practices, and good social and environmental performance can be achieved by companies that perform well financially.[54] If the most important factor with regards to profitability, growth, and future earnings is good management, then corporate responsibility may be an indicator of a well-managed company.

The second argument emerges, in part, from the above observation and, more generally, from a belief that there is a need for alternative measures of company performance. For example, some maintain that the current methods for assessing a company's value and performance are flawed because, among other reasons, they do not adequately value the kinds of intangible assets to which corporate responsibility adds value (e.g. reputation, licence to operate). Moreover, conventional methods are poor at predicting long-term business performance, because sell-side analysts, in particular, are primarily concerned with short-term financial performance. A repeated claim made about corporate responsibility is that its true value to business will become apparent once companies focus more on long-term performance, because responsible and sustainable products and strategies are those that are most profitable in the long run.[55] Indeed, according to Goldman Sachs, which has launched an Environmental and Social Index, 60 per cent of company value is determined by long-term returns and corporate responsibility issues will affect share prices if they come to be seen as affecting those returns.

For this to happen, however, proponents claim that there need to be significant changes in the way in which capital markets function, in the types of accounting system used (e.g. the adoption of full cost accounting of the kind developed at Glasgow University's Centre for Social and Environmental Accounting), and the other means by which business performance is measured. Yet, according to Charles Prince, Citigroup CEO, one of the harshest lessons of business is that few people outside the company really care about its long-term prosperity.[56] In some ways, then, arguing that the business case can only be made in the long run may serve to weaken the case for corporate responsibility by making it too contingent upon levels of transformation that are, at present, still at the margins of economic and political discourse.

Nonetheless, there are a number of corporate responsibility thinkers who argue that the strongest element of the business case is the important part that corporate responsibility will play in the successful companies of the future. The growth strategies of the past are portrayed as increasingly less effective, creating a need for new ways to grow. In this scenario, aspects of corporate responsibility are proposed as part of that change, requiring that corporate responsibility be accepted as part of core business strategy (see Chapter 4).[57] Thus, rather than asking how a dimension, such as human rights or eco-efficiency, affects access to capital, the business case hinges more on treating corporate responsibility as a critical link in innovation and learning, or as part of new, more sophisticated approaches to risk management.

This kind of thinking moves us a long way from trying to attach a monetary value to corporate responsibility activities and, if the original intention of emphasizing the business case was to legitimate corporate responsibility in the eyes of mainstream business, one can question whether wedding corporate responsibility to a new business paradigm will strengthen or weaken that legitimacy. The alternative business case is already being reflected in the ways in which some large companies are approaching, or at least talking about, corporate responsibility. For example, a group of companies within the World Business Council for Sustainable Development, an early pioneer of eco-efficiency, has tried (in their words) to reunite the interests of business and society by restating the purpose of business as follows: '[The] *fundamental purpose of business is to provide continually improving goods and services for increasing numbers of people at prices they can afford.*'[58] The group holds that tomorrow's leading companies will be those providing goods and services in ways that address major societal challenges, such as poverty, climate change, depletion of natural resources, globalization, and demographic shifts. This is not a major reinterpretation of the role of business and signatory companies claim most firms benefit society simply by doing business. But two distinctions separate the group's perspective from those who advocate that 'business is the only business of business'. First, the signatory companies state that, while substantial and sustainable action by business to address pressing societal needs has to be profitable, shareholder value is not an end in itself, but a measure of how successfully companies deliver value to society. Second, the group emphasizes the importance of taking a long-term perspective on company performance and thereby echoes what was noted earlier about the ways in which capital market short-termism undermines the business case. They stress that the purpose of any sustainable company has to be more than generating short-term value for shareholders; yet '*simply by adding the word long-term to shareholder value, we embrace everything necessary for the survival and success of the company*'.[59]

As already commented, any claim that the business case for corporate responsibility can only be made by changing the rules of the game may not strengthen the credibility of corporate responsibility, at least in the short run, because it clearly implies that, in order to make a business case, we first need to redefine the purpose of business. It can also be argued, however, that one of the contributions of corporate responsibility is to stimulate thinking about such fundamental issues. As Van Tulder (2006) notes, corporate responsibility will need to distance itself from simplistic debates about profit maximization if it is to be more than a fad. He holds that, whether it is Prahalad (2005) arguing for societal issues, such as poverty, to be integrated into company strategies, or Handy advocating for a new type of company scorecard that includes contributions to society and the environment, or de Geus and his belief that companies need to harmonize their values with those of society to survive societal turbulence, leading business theorists have consistently set out the rationale for a different kind of business case. But he also maintains that this is not a business case for corporate responsibility in the way that notion is typically conceptualized; rather, it is a business rationale for approaching the interface between business and society more efficiently, equitably, and effectively: what he terms '*societal interface management*'. Citing Mintzberg, he argues that companies are social institutions, the existence of which is justified only in so far as they succeed in serving society, in contrast with human beings, for example, who have an inherent right to be. This is a very different perspective to those that underpinned initial thinking about 'doing well by doing good' and the benefits of eco-efficiency, but building (or rebuilding) a societal case for business, rather than what can sometimes appear to be the business case for society, is, for some theorists and also executives, the kind of change that has to occur for the long-term prosperity of global society.[60] We examine this further in the context of the future of corporate responsibility in Chapter 14.

CASE STUDY 5.5

Factoring corporate responsibility into business decisions

Often, the decision facing managers is presented as being responsible, on the one hand, and profitable, on the other. But decisions can be less black and white than this. Consider, for example, the following hypothetical situation in which, in order to generate a profit, a company needs to source 100 bags of a commodity (e.g. sugar or tea). Imagine that wherever that company sources from, it will make a profit, but that the sourcing decision will affect the amount of profit it makes. The company therefore has a number of choices.

1. It can buy from the cheapest source able to meet quantity, quality and other conventional requirements, and this will generate the greatest profit (Option 1).

2. It can buy from a source that is more expensive, but which can promise to meet the buyer's needs both now and in the future (Option 2).

3. It can buy from two or more different sources, all meeting the same price, quality and other specifications, in order that the trade benefit a greater number of suppliers (Option 3).

4. It can use price, quality and conventional specification requirements to draw up an initial short-list of potential suppliers, and can then introduce a second level of screening that assesses those shortlisted suppliers on their social and environmental performance (Option 4).

5. It can choose to source from the supplier or suppliers with the best social and environmental performance (Option 5).

6. It can choose to source from suppliers working in poor areas or those areas in which the supplier will have the most positive impact on the environment (Option 6).

Questions

Each of these six options allows the company to make a profit and each promises some kind of benefit to others—but the balance between the financial benefits and the wider benefits is different in each scenario.

1. Are any of these options unacceptable from a business perspective?

2. Are any of these options unacceptable from a corporate responsibility perspective?

3. Which option strikes the best balance between financial performance and corporate responsibility considerations?

SUMMARY

The business case for corporate responsibility—which refers to the correlation between business performance and the actions taken to address specific dimensions of corporate responsibility—is one of the most talked-about areas of this field. Demonstrating that there are sound business reasons for taking corporate responsibility seriously has become increasingly important to maintaining the field's momentum and, for some, has come to be seen as synonymous with its legitimacy in the corporate world. While the case for making the business case has been made forcefully, however, the evidence of a business case remains fragmented, sporadic, and, with a few notable exceptions, weak.

The main areas in which attention to corporate responsibility has been recognized as contributing to business performance are eco-efficiency, protecting corporate reputation, and risk management. Eco-efficiency is the area in which there is the strongest correlation with financial performance, although there are a growing number of intriguing examples of both small and large companies developing products that address major societal (and particularly environmental) challenges. There are also numerous case studies that show how particular companies have used aspects of corporate responsibility to improve business performance. Overall, however, the available data are not sufficiently robust to draw conclusions about the conditions under which corporate responsibility assists business performance. The few attempts to analyse what is typically inconsistent and non-comparable data have concluded that actions under the broad umbrella of corporate responsibility have had neither a particularly harmful nor beneficial effect on business performance.

If corporate responsibility cannot be shown to harm a company's performance, it might be argued that the social and environmental benefits alone warrant some degree of investment. But there is still deep suspicion in some quarters that, despite the lack of evidence, corporate responsibility is damaging. Moreover, advocates of corporate responsibility are still keen to demonstrate the benefits to business in order to push ahead with what is seen as an increasingly ambitious agenda. One upshot of this is the tendency to argue that, in order to build a business case for corporate responsibility, we need first to revisit how we evaluate business performance, so that corporate responsibility is not seen as an add-on that needs to be justified by its impact on the bottom line, but rather as an integral part of business strategy.

DISCUSSION POINTS

1   A frequently heard reason for making the business case is that it helps to make corporate responsibility more comprehensible to senior executives and operational managers.
    • Choose a particular company or industry with which you are familiar. How would you go about making the business case to the executive team?
    • Is there a distinct financial performance case?
    • What do you think are the strongest and weakest areas of your case?
2   Eco-efficiency is the main area in which a strong business case has been made. There are, however, companies that are also developing and marketing new product lines, with the more ambitious goal of tackling major challenges, such as energy security, water shortages, and demographic change.
    • Why do you think it has proved easier to make a business case for eco-efficiency than for 'socio-efficiency'?
    • Can the success of eco-efficiency be attributed to corporate responsibility, or is it a case of rational profit maximization?

- Imagining yourself to be a venture capitalist, draw up a list of possible projects in which addressing social issues might be an attractive investment proposition.

3 Two important aspects of business performance that have been connected to corporate responsibility are brand reputation and risk management.
   - In which industries do you think these aspects are most important?
   - Choose one of those industries. How would you make the case that corporate responsibility promises benefits to reputation?
   - How would you make the case that corporate responsibility promises benefits to risk management?

4 Part of the difficulty associated with making the business case is that, for various reasons, the available data are considered inadequate.
   - Given the importance attached to making the business case, why are the data still weak?
   - Is there a business case for improving the quality of the data?
   - Outline a research programme (including themes and methodologies) that would strengthen our understanding of the business case and, especially, the conditions under which corporate responsibility assists business performance.

5 Some argue that the current emphasis on a company's financial performance obscures the importance of paying attention to non-financial performance measures and therefore makes it more difficult to justify corporate responsibility activities.
   - Is this a reasonable opinion?
   - Is it possible that financial analysts are ignoring important indicators of corporate performance because they are not paying attention to corporate responsibility?
   - What new experiments or initiatives for understanding corporate value do you think are most interesting?

FURTHER READING

VISIT THE
WEBSITE
for links to
useful sources
of further
information

- Holliday, CO, Schmidheiny, S, Watts, P, 2002, *Walking the Talk: The Business Case for Sustainable Development*, Sheffield: Greenleaf Publishing.
  Influential argument by European executives emphasizing the importance of sustainable development to business success.

- Preston, LE and O'Bannon, DP, 1997, 'The corporate social-financial performance relationship: a typology and analysis', *Business and Society*, 36(4), pp 419–28.
  First of a series of frameworks intended to help to identify the business case for considering non-financial performance.

- Steger, U, 2004, *The Business of Sustainability: Building Industry Cases for Corporate Sustainability*, Basingstoke: Palgrave Macmillan.
  Case studies from across Europe that show how the business case varies between industries.

- Willard, B, 2002, *The Sustainability Advantage: Seven Business Case Benefits of a Triple Bottom Line*, Gabriola Island, BC: New Society.
  An example of how corporate responsibility theorists conceptualize the business case.

- Zadek, S, 2000, *Doing Good and Doing Well: Making the Business Case for Corporate Citizenship*, New York, NY: Conference Board.
  Discussion of different models that companies can use to understand the business case.

ENDNOTES

[1] *Ethical Corporation* and Nima Hunter Inc, 2003.

[2] See, e.g., Hawkins, 2006.

[3] Vogel, 2005; www.ford.com/sustainability; Fitzpatrick, 2004; www.corporatewatch.org; ETI, undated; Porter and Van der Linde, 1995.

[4] Innovest and Environment Agency, 2004.

[5] www.bt.co.uk—accessed 25 August 2005.

[6] Willard, 2002.

[7] Steger, 2004.

[8] www.gemi.org—accessed 1 November 2006.

[9] Salzmann et al., 2005.

[10] Salzmann et al., 2005, offer a useful review of the literature.

[11] See, e.g., Margolis and Walsh, 2003; Salzmann et al., 2005; Schuler and Cording, 2006.

[12] Amalric and Hauser, 2005; see also, e.g., Griffin and Mahon, 1997; Margolis and Walsh, 2003.

[13] Based on categories in Zadek, 2000; SustainAbility and UNEP, 2001; Zadek et al., 2003.

[14] Adapted from SustainAbility and UNEP, 2001, with information from Zadek, 2000; Willard, 2002; Steger, 2004.

[15] Zadek, 2000.

[16] Willard, 2002.

[17] Zadek, 2000.

[18] Steger, 2004.

[19] Zadek, 2000.

[20] Salzmann et al., 2005.

[21] SustainAbility and UNEP, 2002. The 2002 study uses a somewhat simplified matrix, so that direct comparisons of categories with the 2001 study are not always possible. The term 'business measures' has been changed to 'business success factors', and the number examined reduced to six from ten. The areas of sustainability and corporate responsibility have been reduced from ten to seven, with 'Ethics, values, and principles', 'Human rights', and 'Working conditions' being removed. Some other areas have been reworded without appearing to change the meaning.

[22] See SustainAbility and UNEP, 2002, p 31.

[23] Porter and Van der Linde, 1995.

[24] www.mallenbaker.net—accessed 1 November 2006.

[25] Daum, 2003.

[26] The weighting is intended to attach more value to strong evidence than to weak evidence. It takes the original categories of 'Strong Positive', 'Moderate Positive', 'Weak Positive', and 'Negative/No' levels of impact, and weights the various source materials according to whether they were originally classified as 'Strong' or 'Weak' evidence. A higher rating is given to strong evidence than that given to weak evidence. Thus, e.g., source materials classified as providing strong evidence of 'Strong Positive' impact were rated 1; those providing strong evidence of 'Moderate Positive' impact were rated 2; those providing weak evidence of 'Strong Positive' impact were rated 3; those providing weak evidence of 'Moderate Positive' impact were rated 4. Strong evidence of 'Weak Positive' impact was then rated 5 and so on.

[27] *Ethical Corporation* and Nima Hunter Inc, 2003.

[28] SustainAbility and UNEP, 2002.

[29] Preston and O'Bannon, 1997; Salzmann et al., 2005.

[30] Holliday et al., 2002.

[31] Zadek et al., 2005.

[32] These criticisms have been raised when presenting the analysis in this chapter to academic audiences.

[33] SustainAbility and UNEP, 2002, p 4.

[34] Sustainability, undated.

[35] Zadek et al., 2005; Amalric and Hauser, 2005.

[36] Amalric and Hauser, 2005.

[37] Salzmann et al., 2005.

[38] See, e.g., Holliday et al., 2002; Henderson, 2001.

[39] Zadek et al., 2003.

[40] Zadek, 2000.

[41] Zadek, 2000; Hopkins, 2003.

[42] ABI, 2001.

[43] Zadek et al., 2005.

[44] Zadek et al., 2005.

[45] CCC, 2005a.

[46] Bernauer and Caduff, 2004.

[47] Holliday et al., 2002.

[48] Van der Veer, 2007.

[49] See the work of the Princeton Environmental Institute, in particular on stabilization wedges, online at www.princeton.edu/~cmi.

[50] Zadek et al., 2005.

[51] Zadek et al., 2003.

[52] Thanks to Steve Lydenberg for this observation.

[53] Bahgwati, cited in Holliday et al., 2002, p 17.

[54] Benjamin Heineman in *Wall Street Journal*, 2005; Weiser and Zadek, 2000.

[55] Forum for the Future, 2006.

[56] Blowfield and Googins, 2007.

[57] Holliday et al., 2002.

[58] WBCSD, 2006.

[59] WBCSD, 2006, p 9.

[60] See, e.g., Dyllick and Hockerts, 2002, on the need to move beyond eco-efficiency to 'socio-efficiency' and to factor not only efficiency, but also effectiveness, into social and environmental performance; see also the quotes from executives on the dangers to capitalism of not considering the role of business, cited in Blowfield and Googins, 2007.

6

Stakeholders, standards, and regional variations

Chapter overview

In this chapter, we take a deeper look at some of the most widely used methods for managing corporate responsibility and explore how they are used by companies, including how they are affected by differences in culture, region, and country. In particular, we will:

- discuss the role of stakeholder engagement in corporate responsibility management;

- examine the strengths and weaknesses of different approaches to stakeholder engagement;

- discuss the role of standards and similar instruments in managing corporate responsibility;

- explore the differences and similarities between standards;

- examine how standards are being implemented by companies;

- assess how local, national, and regional differences affect the management of corporate responsibility;

- examine how standards and stakeholder engagement differ in the context of developing countries.

Main topics

■ Key terms

Code of conduct

Developing country

Performance standard

Process standard

Stakeholder engagement

■ Online resources

- Case studies of the ways in which specific companies are using standards

- Exercises and discussion topics for students

- Additional materials on stakeholder management in practice

- Links to other web-based resources

Stakeholder engagement

There is an apparent contradiction at the heart of corporate responsibility management practice. On the one hand, corporate responsibility management is often depicted as managing what companies voluntarily accept as their responsibilities to society; on the other, to have credibility, there is an expectation that those responsibilities be well defined, consistent, and something for which the company is accountable. In other words, while the company can act of its own free will, once it has chosen to do so, limits are immediately placed on that freedom.

In this chapter, we explore two important areas of corporate responsibility management practice that are related to that contradiction. First, we examine stakeholder engagement, and how this is portrayed as defining and legitimizing the scope of corporate responsibility management. Second, we discuss the way in which standards (perhaps as a consequence of stakeholder engagement) are used to codify those responsibilities.

CASE STUDY 6.1

Chiquita and trade unions in stakeholder partnership

George Jaksch, director of corporate responsibility and public affairs at banana giant Chiquita, is convinced that involving unions in implementing the SA8000 labour standard, as well as its other corporate responsibility efforts, has provided benefits both for workers and the company. In the past, strikes and stoppages caused hardship, economic loss, and disruption. Now, dialogue and negotiation have become the preferred instruments for resolving problems, and for implementing solutions that benefit both employees and the company.

Says Jakcsh:

> While there is still room for improvement, we are well on our way from a situation of confrontation and conflict towards a culture of mutual respect and constructive dialogue. The strict requirements of SA8000 to comply with core conventions of the ILO, and to train all workers concerning their rights certainly provide a platform for improving working conditions. But in our company, where trade unions play an important role, their participation in this corporate responsibility effort is indispensable. Chiquita's framework agreement with the unions has opened the door for the participation of trade unions in a structured improvement process.

(ETI, 2005c)

Questions

Chiquita management has made collaboration with trade unions an important part of its stakeholder engagement strategy.

1   Do you think the company is right to consider the unions a stakeholder?

2   Are there other stakeholders with whom it should engage about workers' issues?

3   Is this an example of a company managing its stakeholders, or of stakeholder accountability?

Stakeholder theory

Stakeholder theory is increasingly regarded as one of the touchstones of good corporate responsibility management. It is also a highly contested area, in which similar terminology is used with reference to quite different, and often, opposing ideas. Dating back to the 1930s, business leaders have typically used the term 'stakeholders' as a way of distinguishing between the main groups towards which companies have different kinds of duty: in particular, shareholders, customers, consumers, and employees.[1] In 1984, however, Freeman's *Strategic Management: A Stakeholder Approach* presented stakeholders as something more extensive, complex, and nuanced than this. What is more, they were not simply to be viewed as a convenient taxonomic device: for Freeman, managing stakeholders effectively was essential to the very survival and prosperity of the enterprise. In what he calls '*radical externalism*', Freeman proposes that managers pay attention to stakeholders as a matter of course by adopting integrative strategic management processes.

In light of the very significant impact that Freeman's book has had on management theory, there are two points to note. First, as Walsh (2005) observes, Freeman wrote at a time when business was seen as weak and *'on the ropes'*. As discussed in Chapters 2 and 3, stagflation was undermining major capitalist economies; US business, in particular, was under threat from Japanese competitors; there were unprecedented levels of mergers and acquisitions; companies were increasingly targets of consumer and environmentalist advocacy. Ironically, given how stakeholder engagement is today portrayed by some as a way of harnessing or reducing the power of corporations, the business world that Freeman sought to help was something weak and troubled.

Second, in contrast with some later authors, Freeman is not positing stakeholder theory as an attack on the shareholder-centric theory of the firm that is central to liberal economics. On the contrary, he adopts a very instrumental approach to stakeholder theory, under which companies choose who their stakeholders are, based on the potential of those stakeholders to jeopardize the firm's survival. This is an important point to note because, subsequently, others have presented the shareholder and stakeholder theories of the firm as something distinct. But as Walsh notes, Freeman only raises this possibility right at the end of his book when he asks (and leaves unanswered):

> Can the notion that managers bear a fiduciary relationship to stockholders . . . be replaced by a concept of management whereby they must act in the interests of the stakeholders of the organization?
>
> (Freeman, 1984, cited in Walsh, 2005, p 249)

Freeman is not alone in subsuming stakeholder management to the purpose of wealth creation,[2] but his work is widely cited by those who have a quite different view of stakeholder engagement. Rather than sets of discrete, typically bilateral, relationships upon which the company chooses to embark with stakeholder groups, more recent stakeholder theory treats the firm as an organism that is embedded in a complex web of relationships, and requires the company to see these other organisms not as objects of managerial action, as was often the case hitherto, but as subjects with their own objectives and purposes. The stakeholder management model therefore involves the company being aware of, and responsive to, the demands of its constituents, including employees, customers, investors, suppliers, and local communities. In contrast with Freeman, an important consequence of this is that shareholders are no longer regarded as the most important constituents and shareholder value is not the sole criterion for assessing the company's performance.

This pluralist notion of the company's responsibilities clearly runs counter to the liberal economic model of the firm, which postulates that business contributes to the public good by pursuing its narrow economic goals and, hence, that managers should concentrate on maximizing the market value of their companies. It is predicated on the belief that, in real life, the distinction between economic and social ends is seldom as clear as liberal economists pretend, because economic decisions have social consequences and vice versa, and the very idea of separate social and economic worlds is seen by some as mistaken.[3] Although perhaps not what Freeman intended, the stakeholder model has become the dominant framework for seeing companies as integrated in, rather than separated from, the rest of society.

Management or engagement?

According to Andriof et al. (2002), today's stakeholder thinking concerns the interactive, mutually engaged, and responsive relationships that *'establish the very context of doing business, and create the groundwork for transparency and accountability'* (p 29). From this perspective, Freeman's stakeholder management is one that is too business-centric, but one reason that managers have accepted the stakeholder concept may be that it complements management thinking. In Chapters 1 and 2, we discuss the difficulty of defining what business' responsibilities are, and often managers are faced with sets of issues that beg the questions,' *What am I responsible for?'* and *'To whom am I responsible?'* For managers who have been trained to manage processes such as marketing, production, or finance, it can be easier to understand responsibility in the context of such functional disciplines and, therefore, responsibilities to defined constituencies may have more resonance than long, seemingly ad hoc, lists of normative social and environmental issues.[4]

In other words, for stakeholder theorists at least, the value of an issue for a manager derives from the fact that a stakeholder has legitimized it. As Rasche and Esser (2006) point out, this is in line with social theorist Habermas' notion of discourse ethics, wherein ethical norms are justified not by reference to a priori principles, but because all members of society can reach a consensus around them. In contrast with ethicists such as Mill, Kant, Nozick, or Rawls, who offer universal ethical principles (see Chapter 2), Habermas claims that ethical norms can vary according to differences in context. Thus, what is ethical in one situation can change, provided that it is tested and justified through a context-specific discourse involving members of society. Moreover, although the norms can change, what must remain constant and universal are the rules under which the discourse itself is carried out.

Corporate responsibility theory offers a great deal of advice on how to conduct a consistent, robust, and credible discourse with stakeholders (Box 6.1). The AA1000 Series, for

Box 6.1 Beliefs about good stakeholder engagement

Phases of managing stakeholder dialogue

1 Selection of stakeholders

2 Stakeholder dialogue

3 Interpretation of information from dialogue

4 Decisions about company actions

5 Response to the dialogue through activities

Key factors in acting on stakeholder dialogue

1 Awareness that an issue exists

2 Commitment to prioritize and resource an issue

3 Capacity/availability of resources to tackle an issue

4 Consensus amongst the company and its stakeholders over the issues and relevance of stakeholder dialogue in general

(Adapted from Pedersen, 2006; Andriof et al., 2002)

---

example, is, in some ways, an attempt to spell out the universal rules for reaching an ethical consensus through stakeholder participation (see Case Study 6.2).

CASE STUDY 6.2

Assuring the quality of corporate responsibility management—AA1000

AA1000 is a series of standards that aims to ensure the credibility of the corporate responsibility process. While most standards are performance standards that set out what constitutes good practice in terms of human rights, governance, environmental management, etc., AA1000 is about the way in which corporate responsibility gets managed. Its first document was the 1999 AA1000 Framework, intended as an overarching framework that can be used on its own or with other standards. It spells out five phases of corporate responsibility management.

1 Planning
   The company commits itself to social and ethical accounting, auditing, and reporting, with stakeholders playing a key role.

2 Accounting
   Through stakeholder consultation, the company identifies issues relating to social and ethical performance, the scope of the audit is defined, as are the indicators, and information is collected and analysed.

3 Auditing and reporting
   The company prepares its corporate responsibility report; it is audited by an external group; the information is then communicated and feedback received.

4 Embedding
   The company embeds its accountability systems.

5 Stakeholder engagement
   A principle that underpins the four other phases.

Recently, the AA1000 Assurance Standard was issued, intended as a way of assuring stakeholders of the quality of the company's reports, systems, processes, and competences. It is part of a system that provides core assurance principles, standards, and guidelines about practice and quality, implementation, and a qualification for assurance providers.

(Leipziger, 2003; AccountAbility, 2006)

Questions

The AA1000 Series seeks to build business and public confidence that what companies claim about their non-financial performance is accurate and relevant.

1 Why is this necessary if companies are already using performance standards?

2 Will this type of standard assure consumers and does this matter?

3 Why is the accounting industry, in particular, providing funding for the development of AA1000?

But there are a number of problems involved in applying stakeholder theory in everyday management. First, it can be difficult to identify who stakeholders are. At the broadest level, they are individuals, groups, or entities (including, some would argue, the natural environment) that claim rights or interests in a company and in its past, present, and future activities. To narrow this down, Freeman (1984) drew a distinction between 'primary' and 'secondary' stakeholders. Primary stakeholders are those without whose participation a company cannot survive (e.g. investors, employees, suppliers, customers, and the governments and communities that provide infrastructure and markets). Secondary stakeholders are those that influence the company or are affected by it, but who are not essential to its survival, although they may be able to help or harm the company (e.g. the media, terrorists). The manager's duty, therefore, is to create sufficient wealth, value, or satisfaction for primary stakeholders to ensure that they remain part of the stakeholder system. He may pay attention to secondary stakeholders as well, but there may often be circumstances under which the interests of primary stakeholders are pursued at the expense of those that are secondary (e.g. taking a money-losing product sold to poor communities off the market).

Stakeholders include groups with quite different expectations. One common distinction made is that between those who are influenced by the company's actions and those who have an interest in what the company does. In order to understand the nature of a particular stakeholder and to assess what priority to give its expectations, managers are often advised to make judgements about which have significant or insignificant degrees of interest, and about those with whom the company has high or low degrees of influence (see Figure 6.1). This type of approach, however, does little to help managers to make decisions based on a stakeholder's moral claim and has led to a situation in which companies are accused of responding to stakeholders with the loudest voices or most power, rather than to those with the greatest need or strongest entitlement. Phillips (2003) criticizes stakeholder theory for failing to distinguish between, and prioritize, stakeholders based on a moral rather than a business obligation. For Goodpaster (2002), stakeholder analysis is incomplete if it does not weigh the significance of the identified options for the

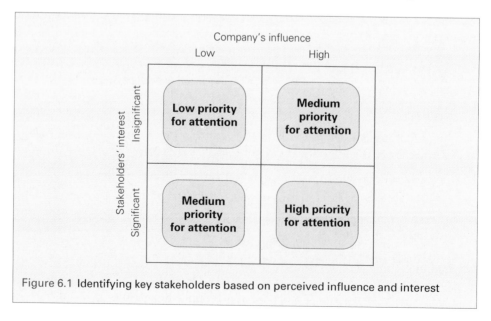

Figure 6.1 Identifying key stakeholders based on perceived influence and interest

different stakeholder groups and make a normative judgement that integrates this informa-tion into a decision. As Gibson (2000) argues, if we do not accept this ethical dimension to the notion of stakeholder, the term itself becomes meaningless, its use limited to a form of shorthand for referring to a, possibly ad hoc, group of individuals.

Partly because of this, Freeman abandoned the primary–secondary stakeholder distinc-tion, although it remains widely used by corporate responsibility practitioners. One out-come he saw was that stakeholders were being treated as the means to corporate ends, rather than as entities whose interests should be served by the company.[5] This is certainly evident in much of what is called 'stakeholder engagement' today, in which consultation and dialogue is carried out with the aim of gathering important input and ideas, anti-cipating and managing conflicts, improving decision making, building consensus among diverse views, and strengthening the company's relationships and reputation. As Case Study 6.3 highlights, there can be a strong business case for stakeholder engagement, including reduced costs, opening new markets, and protecting the company against activism. But this leaves companies open to criticism that they are picking and choosing who to call a stakeholder, and hence whom to listen to, and some managers feel that they are under pressure to respond to some stakeholders rather than others.[6]

We examine categories of stakeholder and their partnerships in detail in Chapter 10, but it needs to be recognized that there is an important distinction to be made between the promise of the stakeholder model, as described by some corporate responsibility the-orists, and the way in which it is actually being used by companies at the present time. In theory, stakeholder dialogue, engagement, and participation are at the heart of a more democratic form of corporate accountability. As a leading advocate of a stakeholder approach to corporate responsibility describes it:

> Corporate accountability, especially when based on stakeholder engagement . . . is all about learning and change: learning about the organization itself, about those who have a relation-ship with it, and learning about its place in the larger scheme of things.
>
> (AccountAbility, 2002, p 5)

In practice, the stakeholder model is more typically applied so that a company can man-age its stakeholders in the sense of influence and control. This is not to say that stake-holders are taken advantage of, or experience no benefit from this approach: at the very least, companies that have engaged in extensive stakeholder dialogue have become more sensitized and sensitive to stakeholder concerns. But it is also becoming clear that, if the stakeholder model is to become part of a new way of managing the business–society rela-tionship, companies will need to give up some of their power and influence in order to become accountable to, rather than simply in discussion with, the wider stakeholder community.[7]

CASE STUDY 6.3

Business advantage from stakeholder engagement

Unocal Oil Company experienced loud stakeholder criticism because of its alleged support of the military regime in Burma. Although the company consistently denied any wrongdoing, the experience made it more aware than many of the importance and value of having a good dialogue with one's stakeholders.

Now taken over by Chevron, Unocal learned many lessons about involving stakeholders in the planning, establishment, running, and eventual closing down of an oil or gas facility. Some of the basic lessons were:

1 to get started on stakeholder engagement as soon as possible;

2 that there are always more stakeholders than you imagine;

3 that communities will not necessarily have a single opinion;

4 to integrate stakeholder engagement into the project schedule;

5 that a company's behaviour and attitude can have at least as much impact as can structured programmes.

The company also believes that engaging with stakeholders brings business results. For example, a widespread, extensive stakeholder consultation about a new company code of conduct garnered useful advice, led to changes in the content, and eventually meant a critical shareholder resolution was withdrawn.

Likewise, when local and international NGOs put pressure on a financial institution to oppose a loan guarantee on social and environmental grounds, the results of stakeholder dialogue were used to demonstrate that Unocal was aware of the issues and the loan guarantee was approved. And when the company had bad news to report about an environmental problem, it broke the news early, brought stakeholders to see the affected site, and was able to demonstrate to local government, local communities, and the media that its response was credible and trustworthy, so that it was able to solve the problem without a backdrop of hostility.

(Adapted from a presentation on behalf of Chevron at Boston College's Center for Corporate Citizenship, 19 January 2006, online at www.bcccc.net; www.socialfunds.com— accessed 19 August 2006)

Questions

Unocal's interest in stakeholder engagement arose from negative experiences with civil society organizations, but it subsequently involved such organizations in stakeholder dialogues that, it claims, deliver business benefits.

1 What are the strengths and weaknesses of justifying stakeholder engagement using a business case?

2 Are there occasions on which stakeholder engagement is warranted even though there might be no clear business benefit?

3 Is the Unocal case study an example of stakeholder management or stakeholder accountability?

Corporate responsibility standards

Features of standards

Standards, guidelines, and codes of conduct or practice are largely synonymous terms for an important tool in the management of corporate responsibility. It may seem odd, given the emphasis often put on the voluntary nature of corporate responsibility, that standards —with their implications of compulsion—are part of corporate responsibility at all. This is especially so when they are employed to govern the behaviour of supposedly free and independent market actors (e.g. suppliers), a practice that is increasingly widespread. Irrespective of any doubts in principle, however, standards, codes, and similar instruments are a major feature of contemporary corporate responsibility management. The terms might be interchangeable, but there are many types and to say that a company has adopted a standard says little, in itself, about the performance, policies, or strategies of that company. Consider, for example, that over half of the 200 largest companies have business codes of some fashion, yet there are enormous differences between businesses in terms of what aspects of corporate behaviour are covered and the extent to which they influence what the company does.[8] Few companies want to admit to lacking a code, and, at their best, codes can provide a unitary purpose for diverse and dispersed organizations —but what exists, in practice, is often a lengthy and confusing menu of possibilities.

Paine et al. (2005) have tried to make sense of this by identifying eight principles that cover the statements, commitments, and requirements found in business codes (Box 6.2). These show that the codes go beyond much of what is included in corporate responsibility today. Many of contemporary corporate responsibility's issues fall under their principles of 'dignity' (e.g. labour rights, workplace health and safety), 'citizenship' (e.g. environmental management, community involvement), and 'responsiveness' (e.g. stakeholder engagement). As evident in the discussion of corporate responsibility in the value chain (see Chapter 4), there are some who would like corporate responsibility to do more to address the principles of transparency and fairness (e.g. treating suppliers fairly and ensuring fair competition). There are also those in the business community who argue

Box 6.2 Underlying principles of business codes

---

1 **Fiduciary principle**—aspects of a code that define the responsibilities of directors and management to the company and its investors.

2 **Property principle**—concerning respect for the property rights and assets of the company and its competitors.

3 **Reliability principle**—concerning the honouring of commitments.

4 **Transparency principle**—concerning the conduct of business in a truthful and open manner.

5 **Dignity principle**—concerning respect for people's dignity, including health and safety, human rights, freedom from coercion, and human development.

6 **Fairness principle**—aspects to do with engaging in free and fair competition.

7 **Citizenship principle**—aspects requiring the company to act as a responsible citizen of the community, including legal compliance, environmental responsibility, and non-involvement in politics.

8 **Responsiveness principle**—aspects requiring the company to be responsive to parties with legitimate claims and concerns about its activities.

(Adapted from Paine et al., 2005)

Box 6.3 Johnson and Johnson's credo

We believe our first responsibility is to the doctors, nurses and patients, to mothers and fathers and others who use our products and services. In meeting their needs everything we do must be of high quality. We must constantly strive to reduce our costs in order to maintain reasonable prices. Customers' orders must be serviced promptly and accurately. Our suppliers and distributors must have an opportunity to make a fair profit.

We are responsible to our employees, the men and women who work with us throughout the world. Everyone must be considered as an individual. We must respect their dignity and recognize their merit. They must have a sense of security in their jobs. Compensation must be fair and adequate, and working conditions clean, orderly and safe. We must be mindful of ways to help our employees fulfil their family responsibilities. Employees must feel free to make suggestions and complaints. There must be equal opportunity for employment, development and advancement for those qualified. We must provide competent management, and their actions must be just and ethical.

We are responsible to the communities in which we live and work and to the world community as well. We must be good citizens, support good works and charities and bear our fair share of taxes. We must encourage civic improvements and better health and education. We must maintain in good order the property we are privileged to use, protecting the environment and natural resources.

Our final responsibility is to our stockholders. Business must make a sound profit. We must experiment with new ideas. Research must be carried on, innovative programs developed and mistakes paid for. New equipment must be purchased, new facilities provided and new products launched. Reserves must be created to provide for adverse times. When we operate according to these principles, the stockholders should realize a fair return.

(www.jnj.com/our_company—accessed 7 August 2006)

that it is hypocritical for companies to talk about corporate responsibility if they disregard the principles of property and reliability.

Broad business codes can provide a context for managing corporate responsibility, as is the case, for example, with Johnson & Johnson's statement of principles (Box 6.3). For the most part, however, modern corporate responsibility has more narrowly defined concerns. In their compendium of codes, Cragg and McKague (2003) identify seven main issues covered by corporate responsibility standards:

1 the natural environment;

2 labour;

3 corporate governance;

4 money laundering;

5 bribery and corruption;

6 human rights;

7 corporate responsibility reporting principles (Box 6.4).

In some instances, these issues are addressed in individual standards, but they can also form part of comprehensive industry-specific or general business standards, such as the Forest Stewardship Council's principles of sustainable forest management and the Equator Principles for the financial industry. Moreover, in many cases, issues are addressed through individual company standards, which themselves can be far reaching, as in the Shell Business Principles, or focused on particular priorities, as with the Pentland Group's Code of Employment Standards for Suppliers.

Box 6.4 **Examples of corporate responsibility standards**

Issue covered	Examples of standards
Environmental	CERES principles ISO14000 environmental management series Kyoto Protocol
Labour	Fair Labor Association workplace code of conduct ETI base code International Confederation of Free Trade Unions basic code of labour conduct
Corporate governance	OECD principles of corporate governance Principles for corporate governance in the Commonwealth Toronto Stock Exchange guidelines for improved corporate governance
Money laundering	Wolfsberg anti-money laundering principles Basel Committee on banking supervision
Bribery and corruption	OECD convention combating bribery of foreign public officials in international business transactions International Chamber of Commerce rules of conduct to combat extortion and bribery Extractive Industry Transparency Initiative
Human rights	Amnesty International human rights principles for companies UN draft norms on the responsibilities of transnational corporations and other business enterprises with regard to human rights Voluntary principles on security and human rights
Corporate reporting	AA1000 series Global Reporting Initiative guidelines on social, economic and environmental reporting
Comprehensive	UN Global Compact principles OECD guidelines for multinational enterprises ISO 26000 corporate responsibility standard

The distinctions between standards have become important as interest has grown in assessing the effectiveness of so-called 'voluntary' standards. Particular attention has been paid to the way in which standards are developed, as a determinant of their robustness, effectiveness, and credibility, and the following types are common.

1 Company standards developed within a company for its own use, perhaps with some external consultation, and with reference to relevant international norms and standards (e.g. on human rights, emissions, or corruption).

2 Company standards built on consultation with relevant stakeholders and making explicit reference to international standards.

3 Industry standards developed by a peer group of companies, perhaps with external consultation, and with differing degrees of reference to international norms and standards.

4 Multi-stakeholder standards developed for an industry, or a wider range of companies, built on a consensus among business, non-government, and trade union organizations.

5 Independent standards made available to an industry, or wider range of companies, but developed by non-business groups, such as trade unions and NGOs.

6 Framework agreements between a company and trade unions.

Some argue that standards developed by companies, separately or with their peers, are more likely to reflect the concerns of Northern consumers than the full breadth of social or environmental issues relevant to a company, and that standards developed independently of business are more comprehensive.[9] Kolk et al. (1999) claim that certain types of standard are likely to have a greater impact than others: for example, that those developed by international organizations, such as the Organisation for Economic Co-operation and Development and the International Labour Organization, or those developed by civil society organizations, such as the Clean Clothes Campaign and Social Accountability International, will be more rigorous than those developed by individual companies or industries, such as Levi Strauss, Nike, and the Apparel Industry Partnership.

There is, however, less difference in content between company standards and independent ones today than there was a few years ago and Sethi (2003) argues that company standards can be more effective, provided that they are subject to external scrutiny (see below). Ranganathan (1998) says that a standard should meet the '3 Cs' used in financial auditing; that is, they must be:

1 *comprehensive*, or complete enough to cover the issues that are most pertinent or material to be the company;

2 *comparable*, to allow inter-company assessment of performance;

3 *credible* enough to allow business and other stakeholders to trust their integrity and to use them in making informed judgements.

This last requirement is also sometimes called 'materiality'.

Various additional characteristics of a credible standard have been identified, as follows.[10]

1 Content that is relevant to the industry, but not simply a reflection of the most publicized problems.

2 Clarity and conciseness in terms of language, style, and format.

3 Explicit reference made to relevant international standards and conventions.

4 Inclusivity, requiring the participation of all key stakeholders who have a legitimate interest in what the standard is measuring.

5 Continual improvement of the criteria against which performance is assessed.

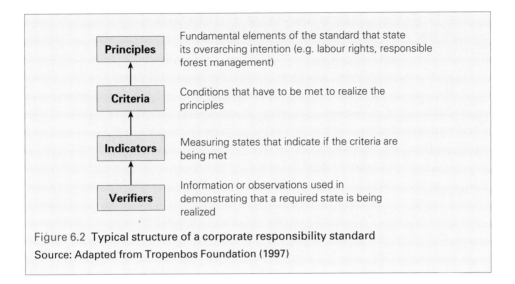

Figure 6.2 **Typical structure of a corporate responsibility standard**
Source: Adapted from Tropenbos Foundation (1997)

6 A commitment regarding to whom the results of any assessment will be disclosed.

7 Suitability of the standard for implementation, including setting out indicators that are measurable and trackable over time.

8 Availability of the standard in the main languages of the locations within which it will be used.

The actual structure and format varies, but, typically, a standard contains a hierarchy of principles, criteria, indicators, and verifiers, as set out in Figure 6.2. Some contemporary standards focus on the criteria and indicators, leaving the underpinning principles unstated, but these can often be inferred either from the owning organization's mission statement, or from its policies.

CASE STUDY 6.4

The Global Reporting Initiative guidelines

The Global Reporting Initiative (GRI) guidelines serve as a framework for reporting on social, economic, and environmental performance. Launched in 2000, they have now been through two extensive revisions based on input from thousands of people in many parts of the world. They are neither a performance standard nor a management system, although they can be useful to the development of both. Their primary purpose is to provide a common benchmark to encourage companies to communicate what actions they are taking to improve non-financial performance, the outcomes of these actions, and the future strategies for improving performance.

The guidelines, which are freely available at www.globalreporting.org, represent what GRI has identified as the most relevant reporting content. There are also supplements for industries, such as mining and banking, and technical protocols on specific indicators, such as child labour and energy. Companies can choose whether to produce reports '*in accordance with*' or more loosely '*with reference to*' the guidelines, and 90 per cent of those that cite the guidelines choose the latter. This figure may change as GRI introduces more levels of reporting, but questions about how many and how fast new levels should be introduced are indicative of a wider issue that GRI faces in balancing prescription and flexibility.

Despite any shortcomings, proponents say that the guidelines have provided the signposts that have led many companies away from producing reports consisting of, what critics call, photos of happy, smiling children and not much else, to those that at least begin to recognize the array of social, economic, and environmental issues with which the company is involved. Furthermore, by retaining the support of business and non-business constituencies while undertaking two major revisions, the guidelines have become a testing ground for global stakeholder engagement.

(GRI, 2002; Baker, 2002; Leipziger, 2003; www.globalreporting.org)

Questions

The GRI guidelines are intended to provide a common framework for company reporting on sustainability issues.

1 Why is this kind of common framework necessary?

2 Why has the GRI focused on guidelines rather than on a certifiable standard?

3 What are the strengths and weaknesses of this kind of approach?

Examples of standards

There are far too many standards to cover them all here, and a common complaint heard from managers is that they are required to comply with too many standards, many of which address the same issues. This is especially true among suppliers of Western retailers and brands, some of which have received up to forty audits in a month. The differences between certain types of standard are worth noting, however, and, in this section, we discuss examples of four types of common standard:

1 the company standard;

2 the industry standard;

3 the multi-stakeholder standard;

4 the independent standard.

Mattel—the company code[11]

As noted earlier, large companies are increasingly requiring suppliers to adopt 'voluntary' social and environmental standards as a condition of doing business. Mattel Inc, the multinational toy company, announced its global manufacturing principles in 1997. Alongside the principles was a commitment to developing a worldwide independent auditing and monitoring system—the first time such a commitment had been made in relation to a company standard. The manufacturing principles would apply to every facility manufacturing the company's products and, in line with labour standards such as SA8000, included provisions on wages, working hours, child labour, forced labour, discrimination, freedom of association, and working conditions. But the principles went beyond the concerns of labour standards to include legal and ethical business practices, product safety and quality, the environment, and import and export laws. They also required that suppliers take specific actions to ensure effective evaluation and monitoring of their facilities, and spelled out the consequences of non-compliance.

To make the principles effective, Mattel established the Mattel Independent Monitoring Council for Global Manufacturing Principles (MIMCO), a group of external monitors comprising three academics. MIMCO was responsible for regular audits, and had access to all facilities, workers, and supervisors, as well as to payroll and financial records, at plants of Mattel and its primary suppliers. After an initial pre-audit visit to all factories in Asia and Mexico, MIMCO established a three-year audit cycle, based on plant ownership and importance to Mattel's supply chain. An internal audit team now does the bulk of the auditing, but MIMCO (now integrated into the International Center for Corporate Accountability) conducts verification audits of a random sample of plants using its own audit protocols. The company has published findings in company-wide and country-specific vendor reports.

SA8000—the independent code[12]

In 1998, the Council on Economic Priorities (now Social Accountability International, or 'SAI') created SA8000, with advice from representatives of business, trade unions, and NGOs. It is a verifiable standard, focusing on labour rights and worker welfare, and intended to be applicable to any industry and in any country. It combines elements of ILO labour conventions with ISO management systems, and has been revised and extended, to include more detailed provisions for specific industries such as agriculture. SAI and its panel of companies, civil society organizations, and academics certify companies that comply with its provisions. This means that conditions in their facilities have been verified by independent, accredited SA8000 auditors, and that the auditors' findings have been ratified by SAI.

SA8000 is different from many standards in that it has both performance and process elements, prescribing not only the labour criteria with which a company must comply, but also acceptable systems for embedding the standard into daily management practice. Over 1,000 facilities in 55 countries have been certified to date. A bone of contention is that these facilities bear the cost of auditing, even though certification is typically a buyer's requirement. But this is not fundamentally different from other costs relating to management systems such as ISO certification.

Forest Stewardship Council—a multi-stakeholder standard[13]

The Forest Stewardship Council (FSC) was first mooted as an idea in 1990 in response to the failure of traditional approaches to arrest the decline of the world's forest resources. The organization, which is managed by a secretariat and overseen by a partnership comprising business, indigenous rights organizations, community groups, and environmental NGOs, acts as custodian to a certification standard that sets out key principles and criteria of forest stewardship. The standard provides a basis for assessing if a forest is being responsibly managed in relation to silviculture practices, environmental impact, working conditions, workers' and community rights, and indigenous people's rights. Certification of a forest involves a fairly extensive four-stage auditing process, including pre-assessments, field visits, peer review, and ratification. A certificate is valid for five years, although there may be interim inspections.

A feature of FSC is that it is not only a standard, but also a partnership. As an organization, it draws support from a wide membership base around the world. Moreover, its governance structure is designed to limit the influence of any single member, or category of member. The FSC board features representatives of those with a commercial interest, those with an environmental interest, and those with a social interest in forests, and these groups all have a say in major decisions at the general assembly. This structure is an interesting example of global democracy in action and, although it has been criticized for being slow and unwieldy, the FSC standard is widely regarded as the benchmark for forest certification.

The Equator Principles—an industry-wide code[14]

The Equator Principles stipulate how financial institutions should consider environmental and social issues in their project finance operations. The signatories are primarily European and North American banks, and the standard clearly reflects reputational concerns about their portfolios of lending to developing countries. These arise from the potentially high risk of adverse social and environmental impacts that are attached to the infrastructure, energy, extractive, and other projects financed in this way (e.g. relocation, ecological damage, impact on communities). The Principles commit banks to formulating environmental and social policies and processes against which individual projects can be assessed for compliance. Their provisions are based on the social and environmental policies and procedures of the International Finance Corporation, which, among other things, require banks to screen proposed projects according to their potential social and environmental impacts. The outcome of the screening process, in turn, triggers a range of follow-up activities, and the most dangerous projects are subjected to more rigorous assessment, public consultation, and information disclosure requirements.

While signatory banks agree to adopt these policies and procedures, implementation is left up to the individual bank and, in contrast with FSC or SA8000, there is no requirement that companies independently verify how they are implementing the standard. Indeed, the Principles explicitly state that they are a benchmark for use in the development of each member company's policies. There is, however, an implicit assumption that, by involving large project finance banks, the Principles will create an environment within which good social and environmental policies are the norm, and will encourage industry-wide improvements. The standard is too new to say whether this will happen and, at present, success is being measured in terms of the number and size of the signatory companies, with about forty banks signing up to the most recent revision of the Principles in 2006.

Implementing standards

Unless standards are implemented, they are a public relations exercise that, in an age of corporate scrutiny, are as likely to tarnish as to burnish a company's reputation. Sethi (2003) makes the case that *who* develops a standard is much less important in terms of its effectiveness than *how* it is used and that the critical part of implementation is the auditing, or verification, of company performance on a regular, systematic basis.

There are three types of auditing of corporate responsibility standards, as follows.

1 **First-party auditing**
   A company conducts internal auditing of performance against the criteria of its own standard.

2 **Second-party auditing**
   A company uses external parties to measure at least some aspects of performance against the criteria of the standard.

3 **Third-party auditing**
   A company uses accredited external auditors. Kolk et al. (1999) further distinguish between standards under which auditing is performed by an accredited professional and those under which civil society organizations are involved.

A variation on the above, found, for example, among industry associations in developing countries, is that under which an industry association or other body establishes the standards and then uses its own staff to audit companies against it. For reasons of objectivity, independent assessors then audit the management of the standards against auditing best practice and also verify company performance against the standards in a random sample of adopting companies.

Four types of organization are potentially relevant to the audit process, particularly those of the 'third party' kind:

1 the custodian body that develops and manages the standard;

2 the auditing organization that is accredited to verify a supplier's performance against the standard;

3 the company that is being audited against the standard;

4 the company that is not being audited itself, but which uses the standard to manage a supplier's performance.

Custodian bodies include Social Accountability International (SA8000) and the FSC. Several service providers now act as certification bodies, which verify performance against international standards (e.g. SGS, BVQI). The personnel are typically qualified in conventional auditing methodology. Auditors are often encouraged to consult with NGOs and others with specialist information, and some see such civil society organizations as competent verifiers themselves, not least in the evolving field of participatory auditing. There are also government agencies that can have a role in auditing (e.g. labour inspectorates).

Most auditing today is first or second party, but among external stakeholders, at least, there is a strong preference that companies use third parties. First- and second-party audits have been criticized for lacking transparency, and create the suspicion that the company is controlling the audit, or hiding unfavourable findings. But just as important can be the quality of the audit itself: how long it takes; who conducts it; with whom the auditors meet; the sources of information; consultation about the findings. Some third-party commercial providers promise to audit a facility in as little as a day, while some custodian bodies, such as the FSC, set a minimum acceptable time for the audit, and also specify requirements for company, supplier, and public consultation.

Other important aspects of implementation include what happens with the audit findings. Are they used as the basis for disciplinary action or commercial sanctions? Do they lead to remedial actions for workers, local communities, or others found to have been harmed? Are people who report violations protected? There have been highly publicized incidences in which auditors discovered under-age workers, who were subsequently dismissed, forcing them into even worse conditions. Nowadays, leading companies have policies on what to do in such cases, so that the worker is not harmed (e.g. company funding of worker's education and living costs).

Dealing with non-compliance of provisions is an important aspect of managing standards. A standard will often distinguish between criteria with which a company must comply to pass the audit and those with which immediate compliance is not required, provided that the company has a clear action plan for reaching compliance at a certain point. In either case, it is typically recommended that the indicators used to test criteria are those able to communicate performance to internal and external stakeholders, to inform management promptly of potential problems, to inform future management planning, and to recognize good performance.[15] Ultimately, however, the success of a standard may not depend on how well it is constructed or implemented, but rather on how acceptable these new non-governmental regulatory systems are to wider society. According to O'Rourke, they hold out both potential and peril:

> They offer the potential of opening up and strengthening regulatory systems and bringing in new voices and mechanisms for motivating improvements in global supply chains. They also harbor the peril of privatizing regulation, effectively closing off democratic forms of regulation and bypassing local governance.

(2003, p 3)

How national and regional variation influences corporate responsibility

So far, we have mostly presented corporate responsibility management as something uniform and standardized, little different, in essence, to quality or financial management, within which a company agrees upon, and implements, a particular policy and system. Effective stakeholder engagement can depend on cross-cultural understanding and the ability to accommodate diverse norms, values, and priorities. In our discussion of 'Corporate responsibility standards' (p 166), we suggested that universal definitions of good performance might prove problematic and this is certainly true in developing countries, which can have their own expectations of business behaviour. In this section, we explore how ideas of corporate responsibility, and hence its management challenges, differ from location to location.

We do not pretend that this is a comprehensive overview of geographical differences in corporate responsibility: rather, it is intended to give an idea of the types of variation that can occur and why. The 'Further reading' at the end of this chapter provides sources of more in-depth discussions of issues in particular regions. What is apparent from such sources is a growing sense that corporate responsibility needs to take into account geographical differences from region to region, from country to country, and within countries themselves. This is not surprising—the cultural dimension to management is, after all, a well-documented area of management theory—but it does present particular challenges in the corporate responsibility context, in which a significant part of many firms' strategies concerns communicating practices in one part of the world to audiences in other regions, who often judge the company's behaviour based on their own concerns, values, and expectations. Acknowledging geographical differences threatens to open the door to cultural relativism, at its extremes, leaving a multinational company in the unhappy position of defending locally acceptable practices that are abhorrent to Western consumers. Yet it can also be argued that to ignore diversity, or to try to impose one culture's values on another, is equally hazardous for the corporation, and runs the risk that corporate responsibility will not achieve anything truly meaningful either for local societies or for the environment.

Management in developing and emerging economies

Typically, discussions about geographical variants to corporate responsibility concentrate on national and regional differences, particularly in developing countries. Before we explore that aspect, however, it is important to note that, within any country, there will be local differences. For example, a dimension to the wealth divide that is a concern in China and India is the differences between the impacts of economic growth on rural and urban areas. Such differences are not unique to emerging economies and, for local operations managers especially, corporate responsibility priorities can be just as different depending on whether the managers are located in London and Glasgow, or in Texas and California.

An important factor is the local economic situation and Cannon (1994) identifies five types of community in which business might have a role to play to ameliorate the effect of economic downturns. The first is high-stress environments, in which the community has endured a long period of economic disadvantage, and has consequently suffered economically and psychologically. The second is structurally disadvantaged areas, such as remote islands or towns, that have lost their physical competitive advantage, as, for example, happened in Liverpool when UK trade shifted from having a transatlantic, to a more European, focus. Another type is the crisis zone, within which a dominant company or industry in a region collapses, as has happened with the automotive industry in the UK's Midlands. A different type of community is that of the transitional area, within which the important industries for the local economy are changing, as has happened in the German Ruhr. Finally, there are communities in which powerhouse industries that have been the catalyst for local growth (e.g. California's software industry) find themselves buffeted by competition from elsewhere and have to adjust accordingly.

From the managerial perspective, what matters here is that the type of situation in which the community finds itself affects perceptions of business' responsibilities and responses.[16] But these are not the only factors to take into consideration. Hamann et al. (2005) have pointed out, in the South African context, that corporate responsibility needs to take into account five realities. First, there is the historical legacy of poverty and inequality that is reflected today in the 55 per cent of the population living in poverty, in over 30 per cent unemployment, in chronic housing and sanitation shortages, and in high HIV prevalence. Second, corporate responsibility needs to recognize, and be rigorous enough to combat, the distrust of certain companies and industries arising from their complicity in exploitation and the apartheid regime. Third, there are established traditions of corporate responsibility in South Africa, particularly community social investment, and now black economic empowerment, through which black entrepreneurship is being encouraged. Fourth, the struggle against apartheid and the consequent emphasis put on legislation to ensure social justice, fundamental human rights, and democracy, mean that government has a crucial role to play in corporate responsibility. Finally, small and medium-sized companies in the formal and informal sectors make up 95 per cent of South African business and their role, capacity, and needs are all relevant for corporate responsibility.

These issues are not only pertinent to South Africa, or even Africa more widely. The particular issues that are high on the African corporate responsibility agenda may not be identical to those of other regions (Box 6.5), but, more significantly, they are often different to, or at least more nuanced than, the corporate responsibility agendas that many multinational companies think of as globally relevant. Often these agendas are built on what Western-based multinationals and other Western-based organizations think should be the priorities of Africa or elsewhere. Thus, for example, Western priorities for Africa might be to combat corruption, improve governance and transparency, and improve infrastructure, while local priorities might be to improve the terms of trading, create good jobs, and transfer technology. Such issues may not be mutually exclusive, but it can be questioned how far corporate responsibility can progress if both sets of priorities are not recognized.

Different perspectives on what corporate responsibility's priorities are have also been noted in Latin America, where advocates in the West may focus on rainforest conservation and biodiversity, while local people may be more concerned about poverty, poor education, bad housing, and scarce healthcare.[17] There is also a tendency to judge the success of corporate responsibility in terms of the number of companies publishing reports, adopting codes of conduct, and talking about stakeholders, rather than first examining the relevance and impact of what they are doing. According to Schmidheiny:

> the key [corporate responsibility] challenges for these regions . . . have to do not so much with the number of companies talking about [corporate responsibility], but with creating a homegrown, meaningful form of [corporate responsibility] that addresses local issues and improves society, while also strengthening government's capacity.
>
> (2006, p 22)

As Visser et al. (2006) point out, what makes corporate responsibility important in the context of any developing country is that it embodies many of the dilemmas that business faces in trying to be responsible, sustainable, and ethical. For example, it raises questions about when local traditions take precedence over international standards, about how far a company's responsibilities extend in providing public services, and about when business' involvement in local governance enhances a weak governance infrastructure

Box 6.5 Comparison of social and environmental issues across selected countries and regions

Country/region	Social and environmental issue
European Union	Decoupling growth from consumption Sustaining welfare, health, and labour standards in a global economy Clean air and emissions trading Marine environment and fisheries
USA	Energy security, including renewed calls for nuclear power Climate change policy Public health accessibility Social security Corporate governance
Latin America	Rich–poor divide Basic environmental management Good public governance and fighting corruption Infrastructure Competitiveness and security of small farmers
Africa	Good public governance and fighting corruption Terms of trading Infrastructure Conflict Managerial capacity
Japan	Nuclear power Air pollution Exploitation of offshore fisheries and foreign tropical forests Urban environment Foreign workers

(PWC, 2006; Ethical Corporation, 2006)

and when it constitutes an unhealthy intrusion into the political process. This last question reflects a wider theme that marks out discussions about corporate responsibility in developing economies, i.e. the role of government. While the European Union, for example, has chosen to emphasize corporate responsibility as a voluntary approach that places no extra legislative burden on business (see below), the role of government and the links between corporate responsibility and regulation are central to debates in developing nations. There are various explanations for this. For example, in China, the government has defined corporate responsibility in terms of its own priority of ensuring social stability and uses the term to mean government regulation.[18] In parts of Latin America, Asia, and Africa, an important element of the corporate responsibility agenda concerns fighting corruption and improving public governance, and therefore includes activities to build government capacity and the rule of law. Companies also do not want to be saddled with an unsustainable burden of providing public goods, and would therefore prefer to partner with government and others. In general, it seems to come down to the fact that the business community is reasonably satisfied that, in countries with developed economies and democracies, government is able to maintain social stability; it is more concerned that business will be over-regulated. In developing economies, however, especially those in which governments are either weak or dictatorial, the business community is more concerned about the rule of law, and the creation of social stability and a favourable business environment, and therefore under-, rather than over-, regulation is the issue.

None of this is to pretend that some companies have not, over the years, thrived in oppressive regimes, or that companies are not prepared to do business in countries, such as Burma and China, that are openly resistant to Western ideals of public governance. But there is evidence that companies operating in such countries at times use corporate responsibility not simply as a substitute for good public governance, but as a way of introducing good governance norms, in the hope that they will shape public institutions in the future.[19] This, in turn, reflects a belief that if ever there was a business case for taking advantage of unstable, oppressive political conditions, for multinational companies and industries in a global economy these conditions represent an undesirable risk—one that, if it cannot be avoided entirely (e.g. because of the physical location of natural resources, or the competitive advantage of low-waged labour), must be reduced, and corporate responsibility offers a means of achieving that end.

These are compelling arguments, especially if one believes that Western prosperity is a consequence of democracy as much as of capitalism. It is also worth noting that, in countries such as Morocco, governments have used corporate responsibility as a framework within which to promote a renewed commitment to better labour practices, controlling child labour, and new legislation to combat corruption, and to improve workplace rights of women and the disabled, and the rights of trade unions. Indeed, seeing this as a way of complying with trade agreements and attracting businesses in competition with lower waged competitors, the government has made corporate responsibility part of its strategy to win foreign investment.

Yet many still resent or resist corporate responsibility and see it as an outsiders' imposition. This is not simply a case of the status quo resisting reform. Developing countries can be victims of the subsidies and protections that the USA, European, and other countries give to industries such as agriculture and defence; policies that, in turn, are related to poverty and lack of economic opportunity. Moreover, poverty and exploitation are seen by some as the hallmark of colonial and post-war entrepreneurs, and this sudden conversion to responsibility is seen as hypocrisy, at best, and commercial gamesmanship, at worst.[20] In countries such as India, where some conglomerates date back to the nineteenth century, there is resentment of the implication that they are irresponsible, or have not built a relationship with the society. Tata, for example, has established various institutes that invest in social and environmental innovation, and has a long tradition of giving back to communities. In 1998, it formalized the Tata Code of Conduct, which includes areas such as involvement with communities, ethical conduct for company officers, and a commitment not to support any political party or political activity. This, in turn, is backed up with whistle-blower protections, and sanctions such as demotion and dismissal for anyone breaching the code.

One response to disquiet at the imposition of corporate responsibility from overseas has been the creation of local corporate responsibility organizations. While many individual companies have started to produce corporate responsibility reports, these are often aimed at overseas audiences, not least the US or European stock markets, on which some of these companies are now listed. Corporate responsibility organizations, however, have more flexibility in terms of developing a locally relevant corporate responsibility agenda, and they include the South-Africa-based African Institute for Corporate Citizenship, the EMPRESA network of corporate responsibility organizations in 16 Latin American countries, and the Chinese Association for Corporate Social Responsibility, which had been due to be established in 2006 by foreign and domestic companies, but which does not yet appear to be active.

Management in developed economies

Any attempt to explain corporate responsibility by geography alone is as doomed to fail as is the practice of treating geopolitical factors as irrelevant. The distinction between developed, developing, and emerging countries, at best, provides a framework for understanding certain variables and, while a country such as India may have much in common with China in terms of wrestling with economic growth, it is worlds apart in terms of its political institutions and the role of civil society. Moreover, one must be cautious that terms such as 'developing', 'developed', and 'emerging' are not used judgementally, reinforcing the stereotypes of 'good' and 'bad' that often inform one culture's views of another.

Nonetheless, while accepting that any categorization is flawed, there are aspects of being part of developed democratic economies, such as Western Europe, North America, Australia, New Zealand, Japan, and South Korea, that affect corporate responsibility management. As noted earlier, the role of government is given much more emphasis in discussions of corporate responsibility in developing and emerging economies. In contrast, after several years of debate over what role corporate responsibility would play in the European Union's strategy for growth and jobs in a competitive global environment, the European Commission announced, in 2006, that it would embrace corporate responsibility as a voluntary approach to help business to develop the skills for effective relationships with stakeholders, for mainstreaming corporate responsibility in the minds of business leaders and in business processes, and to provide companies with effective tools for internal analysis and evaluation (Case Study 6.5). In the words of Günter Verheugen, European Commissioner:

> There will be no monitoring, no benchmarking, no naming and shaming, no reporting requirements. [Corporate responsibility] is completely voluntary. We will never have a framework for [corporate responsibility] because it is a philosophy, a concept.[21]

Those who had wanted corporate responsibility regulation greeted this announcement with dismay; early corporate supporters, such as Volkswagen, welcomed it. It also does not mean that corporate responsibility will be voluntary across Europe. In France, for example, the 2001 *Loi relative aux nouvelles régulations économiques* (Law on New Economic Regulations) requires companies to report on social and environmental performance, while in Germany, the government's Sustainability Council has identified the stand-off between regulatory and voluntary approaches as an impasse that must be broken if bigger issues about the role of business in society, and the interplay between business strategies and public policy, are to be addressed. Equally, European norms are finding their way into international agreements such as the framework agreement between Peugeot–Citroën and 85 national unions that commits the company to global workplace and supply chain standards.

CASE STUDY 6.5

The European Alliance for Corporate Social Responsibility

In 2000, the European Commission launched its Lisbon Accords, a strategy for promoting jobs and growth as the European Union faces the challenges of threats to its competitiveness from abroad. At about the same time, a number of corporate responsibility initiatives were launched that would explore what corporate responsibility meant in a European context, promote corporate responsibility in business schools, build corporate capacity, and engage different sectors of society in a debate about the role of business in European society.

The involvement of the Commission was largely welcomed, because, depending on one's point of view, there was unease about what corporate responsibility meant and where its limits lay, and also about the lack of a government role in issues that hitherto had largely been the purview of elected parliaments. The 2001 Green Paper stirred up controversy, however, because it was seen to use corporate responsibility as a springboard for new regulations, rather than to create the conditions for the vigorous free market entrepreneurship that some saw as essential to Europe's prosperity.

The Green Paper was shelved, but in 2006, the Commission announced the European Alliance for Corporate Social Responsibility, which would help business to engage in corporate responsibility without putting any new regulatory burdens upon it. Vladimir Špilda, European Commissioner, declared corporate responsibility '*a business opportunity*'; Ethical Performance called the Alliance '*a ragbag of measures dressed up as strategy*' that effectively ended the EU dream of becoming a pole of corporate responsibility excellence. What it certainly left unresolved was whether corporate responsibility could fulfil what some saw as its most important role in the European context: to help to reconfigure the balance between institutions that, together, make up society.

(Habisch et al., 2005; *Ethical Performance*, 2006d; Špilda, 2006)

Questions

The European Commission has tried to carve out a European vision of corporate responsibility, based on the Union's historical values and the role that it sees business playing in a cohesive society in future.

1 Is government right to get involved in corporate responsibility in a facilitating, rather than a regulatory, way?

2 Would a regulatory approach do more to maintain European social values in the face of global competition?

3 Is it realistic for Europe to have its own vision of social welfare in the twenty-first century?

What the European Commission policy does highlight is the very different way in which corporate responsibility is being viewed in the West compared with the developing world. Similar government debates about corporate responsibility have taken place elsewhere. For example, in 2005, the Australian parliament commissioned a discussion paper to examine corporate responsibility in the light of that country's Corporations Act 2001. Its focus was on the duties that company directors have to stakeholders other than shareholders, and whether the Act needed to be revised for directors to consider those stakeholders and the wider notion of responsible business practices. The paper highlighted the importance of distinguishing between two approaches to corporate governance: the first, one under which other stakeholders interests are on a par with those of shareholders (a 'pluralist' approach); the second, one under which directors are given an explicit list of interests that need to be taken into account in advancing the well-being of shareholders (the 'elaborated shareholder benefit' approach). The pluralist approach is found in some state statutes in the USA, such as New York and Pennsylvania (although not in Delaware, where most US companies are incorporated), while the elaborated shareholder benefit approach was part of the UK Company Law Reform Bill 2005.

As we examine in the discussion of corporate governance (see Chapter 8), the purpose of the company and the fiduciary duty of directors is a major factor in considering how to manage corporate responsibility. Some in the corporate responsibility movement have hopes that increasing emphasis on stakeholder engagement will create a momentum in support of pluralist definitions of fiduciary duty, although this does not seem to have happened in the UK government's Operating and Financial Review. But what these alternative approaches reveal is that part of the debate about corporate responsibility in which companies are engaged concerns the nature and purpose of the company itself. Some of the hostility towards corporate responsibility described in Chapter 13 is also a reflection of this, with some arguing that corporate responsibility undermines the main purpose of private enterprise and others suggesting that it does not do enough to change that purpose.

Whatever side one takes, the fact is that, even in developed economies, there are different perceptions as to the role of business and, hence, its responsibilities. In Germany, for example, the corporate responsibility debate is strongly influenced by the wider social challenge of how to respond to globalization while maintaining high levels of social provision. In the UK, the emphasis on the business case (see Chapter 5) is partly due to the belief that markets serve the public good. In Finland, acceptance of a strong government role in labour markets has similarly shaped the direction of corporate responsibility. What stands out, therefore, is that companies are not simply managing standards or stakeholder relations, but that they are finding ways of navigating through variables that include culture and ideology, and the ways in which these are rubbing up against geopolitical events. For example, in much of Europe and Japan, corporate responsibility is situated at the nexus between cultural ideals of the common good and the challenges of economic globalization. In Russia, corporate responsibility is part of a wider ideal of reestablishing that country's international reputation. In the USA, it is increasingly about upholding widely held values of individualism and entrepreneurship, while maintaining a cohesive society.

Although much is made of the Anglo-Saxon model of free enterprise and its dominance over other models, it remains to be seen whether an Anglo-Saxon model of corporate responsibility will eclipse its alternatives, or even stand out as a discrete concept. In the meantime, many of the challenges of managing corporate responsibility will stem from the tension between unified and diversified visions of what responsibility entails.

SUMMARY

Two pillars of contemporary corporate responsibility are the standards that define what comprises good conduct in the area of non-financial performance and the concept of stakeholder engagement that views companies as parts of complex, interdependent webs, within which many groups claim a stake (i.e. a right) in the company by virtue of the impact that the company has on them, or their power to influence the company in some way. These two pillars interconnect in so far as standards gain legitimacy, in part, from being developed and used with stakeholder involvement of some kind, and one of the outputs of stakeholder dialogue can be a decision about what standards to adopt. There are, however, many examples of standards being designed and implemented without any real stakeholder engagement, and some advocates of stakeholder management, such as Phillips et al. (2003), believe that normative instruments such as standards run counter to the emphasis of stakeholder theory on continual dialogue and responsiveness.

There are many kinds of standard and a variety of institutional arrangements for developing them. It is in the area of implementation that stakeholder engagement is widely seen as good practice, although, in reality, many companies remain reluctant about how far to go in involving others in what are seen as management decisions. Nonetheless, the stakeholder model has clearly affected the way in which many companies see the world and their role within it, and there is widespread acceptance that, in addition to any responsibility to shareholders, there are also responsibilities to employees, consumers, customers and suppliers, and communities. How to create sufficient wealth, value, or satisfaction for all stakeholders is now being recognized as a defining challenge for some company managers, and failure to do so can be seen as a threat to the company's prosperity and survival.

But identifying stakeholders, prioritizing them, and working with them is not straightforward. Moreover, there is a world of difference between managing stakeholders, as many companies try to do, and the notion of stakeholder accountability, which some theorists see as the real goal of corporate responsibility.

The location from which a company is engaging with stakeholders or applying a standard has a significant effect on how these processes are managed. In fact, one of the features of corporate responsibility that distinguishes it from many other areas of management, such as quality control, is that good practice can vary by country or region. There have been particular problems in designing and implementing standards in developing countries, but expectations and values, and hence notions of good company performance, vary from place to place and over time, even in established capitalist economies. And herein lies the challenge of managing corporate responsibility:

not only the balancing of the expectations and values of diverse, often globally dispersed, stake-holders, and the demonstration of one's accomplishments in concrete terms, but also the accommodation of the fact that these expectations and values are subject to continual change.

DISCUSSION POINTS

1 One reason for the popularity of standards as a management device is that they create a level playing field, which can be applied to all companies regardless of country or company size. Yet some managers complain that there are too many standards managed in too many ways.
    • What are the advantages of having a relatively large number of standards at this stage in corporate responsibility's development?
    • How would you set about reducing the number of corporate responsibility standards?
    • As a company manager, how would you decide what standards your company should adopt?

2 There are both process standards and performance standards.
    • What are the strengths and weaknesses of process standards in a corporate responsibility context?
    • How do the process criteria incorporated into SA8000 strengthen its credibility as a performance standard?
    • Design a basic process standard for combating bribery and corruption in an international platinum-mining company.

3 Stakeholder has become a defining concept for modern corporate responsibility, even though stakeholder guru RE Freeman says that good stakeholder management negates the need for corporate responsibility.
    • Why does Freeman hold this view?
    • Is it possible for companies to manage corporate responsibility without stakeholder dialogue?
    • How can the natural environment participate in stakeholder dialogue?

4 Central to the stakeholder concept is that shareholders are one of several groups that have a claim on the company. In the USA, UK, Australia, and many other countries, however, investors have stronger rights, de facto and *de jure*, than others.
    • Should company boards of directors be structured to give representation to more stakeholders?
    • Given the legal structure of public companies, what can managers do to increase accountability to stakeholders?
    • How would you go about persuading sell-side analysts of the importance of stakeholder engagement?

5 The argument that corporate responsibility should be managed differently, according to the national or regional context, appears to run counter to the idea that companies need to adopt equally robust approaches to corporate responsibility wherever they are.
    • What are the risks for companies if they approach corporate responsibility differently, depending on the country in which they are based?
    • How do you think companies can balance diversity with consistency?
    • Is it feasible that Western companies will accommodate the priorities of countries in Africa or Latin America?

VISIT THE WEBSITE
for links to
useful sources
of further
information

FURTHER READING

- Andriof, J, Waddock, S, Husted, B and Rahman, SS, 2002, *Unfolding Stakeholder Thinking Vol 1: Theory, Responsibility and Engagement*, Sheffield: Greenleaf Publishing.
  Useful introduction to how stakeholder theory is used in corporate responsibility, including some criticisms.

- Freeman, RE, 1984, *Strategic Management: A Stakeholder Approach*, Boston, MA: Pitman.
  Influential early text on stakeholder management theory.

- Habisch, A, Jonker, J, Wegner, M and Schmidpeter, R (eds), 2005, *Corporate Social Responsibility Across Europe*, New York, NY: Springer.
  Detailed overview of differing perspectives on corporate responsibility in European countries.

- *Journal of Corporate Citizenship*, January 2004 (13), a special theme issue on corporate social responsibility in Asia.
  Journal of Corporate Citizenship, April 2005 (18), a special theme issue on corporate citizenship in Africa.
  Journal of Corporate Citizenship, January 2006 (21), a special theme issue on corporate citizenship in Latin America: new challenges for business.
  Journal of Corporate Citizenship, December 2006 (24), a special theme issue on corporate social responsibility in emerging economies.
  Four informative special editions of this academic journal, each exploring corporate responsibility from the perspective of different regions and emerging economies.

- Leipziger, D, 2003, *The Corporate Responsibility Code Book*, Sheffield: Greenleaf Publishing.
  Summarizes the key features of major corporate responsibility standards.

- Sethi, SP, 2003, *Setting Global Standards: Guidelines for Creating Codes of Conduct in Multinational Corporations*, Hoboken, NJ: John Wiley and Sons.
  Discussion of different options for implementing supply chain standards, based on the experience of Mattel.

ENDNOTES

1. Preston and Sapienza, 1990.
2. See, e.g., Post et al., 2002; Phillips, 2003.
3. See, e.g., the discussion of the work of Karl Polanyi in Chapter 3.
4. Clarkson, 1995.
5. Evan and Freeman, 1988.
6. CCC, 2005a.
7. CCC, 2005a; Rasche and Esser, 2006.
8. Kaptein, 2004.
9. See, e.g., Varley et al., 1998; Kolk et al., 1999; Seyfang, 1999; Ascoly et al., 2001.
10. See, e.g., MacGillivray and Zadek, 1995; ISEA, 1999; Leipziger, 2003; Mamic, 2004.
11. Sethi, 2003.
12. Leipziger, 2001.
13. Bartley, 2003.

14 Wright and Rwabizambuga, 2006.

15 Bennett et al., 1999.

16 Hopkins, 2007.

17 Schmidheiny, 2006.

18 Runping, 2006.

19 See, e.g., Moody-Stuart, 2005; Schmidheiny, 2006.

20 Saha, 2006.

21 Cited in Sewing, 2006, p 9.

7

Social accounting

Chapter overview

In this chapter, we look at how companies report their corporate responsibility activities to external stakeholder groups. We examine how the corporate responsibility reports of today have developed, considering the conventional financial reporting process and contrasting it with the approach of social accountants. In particular, we will:

- discuss the key role of accounting in understanding corporate responsibility;

- examine what is meant by 'social accounting';

- trace the emergence of corporate social reporting and social accounting research;

- examine the upsurge in social reporting that began in the 1990s;

- assess the relationship between conventional financial reporting and social reporting;

- examine the link between social reporting and sustainability/sustainable development;

- examine the role of 'third-party verification statements'.

Main topics

■ **Key terms**

Reporting awards

Social accounting

Social reporting

Third-party verification statements

■ **Online resources**

- Suggested additional information on social and environmental reporting
- Discussion topics for students
- Company and industry case studies
- Links to other web-based resources

The key role of accounting in understanding corporate responsibility

Corporate responsibility reporting is frequently treated as an emerging activity, born out of comparatively recent concerns for issues of environmental degradation, or social injustice. Though true to a degree, literature on corporate social reporting reveals that companies have been engaged in the reporting of their non-financial activities for a considerable time. Such reporting, however, was traditionally examined as part of the accounting, or financial reporting, function and, although overlooked by some, has been of interest to a minority of accounting researchers for some thirty or more years.

Many authors writing about corporate responsibility neglect to make the connection between their subject and the crucial role that accounting plays in the field. Whether it relates to the decision to adopt corporate responsibility strategies, or to how a company subsequently reports its activities, accounting plays a crucial role for a number of reasons and it might be useful to explain how this comes about.

It is important to bear in mind that conventional definitions of accounting stress that its purpose is to provide financial information that should be useful for decision makers. This is the starting point for most courses in accounting, and other conventions of accounting restrict the focus to 'the entity', typically a company. This means that accounting information tends to be built on data of relevance only to that entity, ignoring external events if they do not explicitly affect the entity. It is also worth remembering that the accounting function within a company has, essentially, two strands.

First, management accounting is accounting for internal use, i.e. the compilation of reports that are principally forward-looking and used to guide the company by providing information against which it can monitor progress. The company does use some historic information, but generally only as the basis for projections of future performance. Examples of this form of accounting might be the budget process or cash flow projections. Equally, however, in a strategic capacity, accounting techniques can be applied to decide whether or not a proposed strategy is adopted and these 'capital investment appraisal' projects apply specific formulae to proposals to establish if they are commercially sound. These techniques can establish the 'net present value (NPV)' of the project, or the 'internal', or 'accounting', rate of return, or simply the time period before a project delivers 'payback'. It is difficult to assess whether or not these techniques and controls are applied in the execution of corporate responsibility strategies, but it can be imagined that, if they are, they might produce hurdles against which a convincing argument would be needed to ensure progress. When we talk about the business case for adopting corporate responsibility strategies, we might assume that some of these techniques might be applied as assessment tools. This may create tensions between those proposing new projects and those keen to adopt only project that feature 'positive NPV', because of the difficulties of accommodating social and environmental factors into conventional approaches (see Chapter 6).

Second, financial accounting and reporting is, essentially, for external stakeholders. Reports of past activity and measures of historic performance are produced both as a legal obligation, and as an exercise of accountability to the owners of the business: the shareholders. They are produced using accounting conventions, policies, and standards that have developed over time and which are now enshrined in Generally Accepted Accounting Principles (GAAP). Recent developments in the internationalization of accounting standards are aimed at bringing consistency across national boundaries as companies adopt global perspectives in their operations. These are the results against which analysts' forecasts are measured, and against which anticipated company performance is compared and management competence assessed, in terms of market performance.

Traditionally, these measures of performance have focused exclusively on financial issues. Implicitly, as discussed elsewhere in the book, profit maximization is the goal against which performance is assessed and the only items that are applied to this equation are those to which, in the past, accountants have ascribed this privileged status. Thus, measures of profit omit to take account of by-products of commercial activity for which others have to pay, such as pollution, emissions, road use, etc.—issues that economists refer to as 'externalities' and issues that, in an effort to increase profitability, actually benefit from being maximized. In the past, it has been suggested that the reason why externalities have never been included in financial statements is to do with difficulties in measuring them, in financial terms, but if it is possible to assess the value of depreciation, intangible assets, and financial derivatives, this argument seems difficult to sustain. It is more that taking note of externalities is seen as an obstacle to commercial activity, affecting profits and competitiveness. We will return to discuss this issue further when we look at the meaning of 'social accounting'.

Although both management and financial accounting are relevant in discussions on corporate responsibility, it is the latter on which this chapter focuses. What we examine here is the external reporting function—a concept that is familiar to anyone who has researched corporate activity—and what we go on to look at now is how traditional financial accounting and reporting is contrasted with the approach taken in social accounting and reporting.

There are also two further aspects of accounting that deserve comment. First, accounting provides the accepted language of business, a language that even non-accountants are keen to adopt to instil elements of what are perceived as essential components of strategic arguments in a business framework. This language and the underlying notions that drive corporate activity, such as year-on-year growth and market positioning, shape the context of corporate activity and help to explain both the power of accounting within corporate activity, and how easily thereby it might act against longer term initiatives that have been designed to take account of sets of more responsible objectives.

Second, there is an implicit assumption about the nature of accounting that is shared by the public as well as by many accountants, i.e. that it is a 'neutral' or 'objective' activity. We have already explained that accounting is subject to GAAP, rules, and conventions that have been agreed by particular interest groups. Accountants thereafter apply their subjective judgements to the application of such principles—judgements that are values-based, and which often have social and environmental consequences that do not appear in subsequent financial statements. A number of studies have examined the complicity of accounting in such issues as environmental pollution and foreign exploitation,[1] plant closures,[2] and social conflict.[3] The perceived partisan nature of accounting informs a more critical approach that motivates much of the research output in such journals as *Critical Perspectives on Accounting*, *Accounting, Organizations and Society*, and the *Accounting, Auditing and Accountability Journal*. It can also be said that it is in this context that social accounting acts as a critique of conventional accounting practices.

CASE STUDY 7.1

Social accounting at Traidcraft plc

Traidcraft was established in 1979 as a 'Christian response to poverty', and is both a trading company and a development charity. It can also lay claim to being one of the pioneers of social accounting in the UK, having published its first independently audited report in 1993. Since that time, the methodological approach that Traidcraft developed with the New Economics Foundation has been adopted and adapted by many larger organizations.

The process is based on a step-by-step approach, as follows.

1 Define social objectives and ethical values of the organization.

2 Be clear about who are the stakeholders of the organization.

3 Establish indicators by which performance against the objectives and values can be measured.

4 Measure performance against the indicators.

5 Gather the views of stakeholders on the performance of the organization.

6 Report all of the above in as balanced a manner as possible.

7 Submit the report to an independent audit.

8 Publish the report.

9 Gather feedback from stakeholders on the report's findings.

(Adapted from www.traidcraft.co.uk)

Questions

Traidcraft was one of the first of the 'values-based' companies to embrace social accounts as a way of offering assurance to stakeholders about their activities.

1 Why is it important to be clear about who the stakeholders are?

2 Why is it essential to measure performance against indicators?

3 What is the benefit of an independent audit, given that compliance with standards is not compulsory?

The nature of social reporting

We have established that financial reporting is traditionally understood as the reporting of the financial results of a company's past activities to external stakeholders. The requirement for such reports is now part of company law in most countries, but, as in the UK and USA, the requirements almost invariably cover only the financial activities, and commonly call for the profit and loss account and balance sheet to be reported to the members of the company. These reports are often augmented by various other requirements of GAAP, but, with the exception of a few European countries, all of these requirements—either by law or quasi-law—relate to financial aspects of performance. Reporting of the non-financial aspects of a company's performance is largely voluntary.[4] It is the nature of this form of reporting that has attracted the interest of a growing number of accounting researchers since the genesis of social accounting, which can be traced back over thirty years. But before we look back at the emergence of social reporting, we should be clear about what it means. The social accounting project in the UK dates back to the mid-1980s and one of the earliest definitions of corporate social reporting, which still stands up today, states that it is:

> the process of communicating the social and environmental effects of the organisations' economic actions to particular interest groups within society, and society at large. As such, it involves extending the accountability of organisations (particularly companies) beyond the

traditional role of providing a financial account to the owners of capital, in particular, share-holders. Such an extension is predicated upon the assumption that companies do have wider responsibilities than to simply make money for their shareholders.

(Gray et al., 1987)[5]

Immediately, this definition challenges the taken-for-granted objectives of financial reporting. In this sense, it may be regarded as critical of mainstream accounting practice. Indeed, while some aspects of corporate responsibility can be interpreted as incorporating non-financial issues into conventional business practice, social accounting and corporate social reporting are, in many ways, a challenge to accounting and reporting conventions. This is because much of the discussion and debate within social accounting tends to challenge traditional accounting and reporting conventions, and that challenge begins to emerge when we further consider the above definition.

What is immediately obvious from the statement of Gray et al. and unavoidable in any subsequent discussion is the debate about what is meant by 'accountability'. We look again at this issue in the next chapter in the context of corporate governance, but it might be useful to consider, at this stage, how 'accountability' can be interpreted differently by different constituents, and how, within its meaning, there is an implicit relationship of unequal power between the person or body requiring an account and that which is giving the account. This unequal power relationship is evident in the use of phrases such as being *'called to account'*, or being asked to *'account for one's actions'*. Of course, the word 'account' is not always related to finance, but, in the corporate context, it invariably has this financial emphasis, and the power relationship here lies in the requirement laid down in law and in the custom for the directors of a company (the agents) to supply (financial) accounts to the owners (principals).[6] The same legal obligation to be called to account for responsibilities that go beyond the financial, however, is largely absent from the corporate sphere, and any such reporting is undertaken largely as a voluntary act and is the focus of much social accounting research. Social accounting theorists both challenge the primacy of the shareholder group and recognize an explicit obligation for companies to be accountable to wider society.

In the context of this book, the connection between a company's social performance and social reporting is obvious. In many ways, social reporting is the first insight into the social performance of the company, and, certainly, it is the easiest way in which a company can explain its approach and operationalization of its corporate responsibility strategy. Indeed, in research studies, social disclosures have frequently been used as a proxy for social performance.[7] But what a company reports will largely depend on how it defines its activities in terms of corporate responsibility and what it chooses *not* to report on is often as significant as the activities on which it does report. Indeed, many studies looking into the reporting activities of corporations comment on the way in which some companies appear to 'cherry pick' the activities on which they can report favourably, while ignoring those issues towards which criticism may be directed. Equally, many companies report on various issues that come within a broad corporate responsibility remit, while failing to address major issues at the core of the business activity. So, an energy company may stress how it promotes its staff development to improve leadership qualities in its employees, but may not detail how it aims to tackle the challenges of climate change.

The emergence of corporate social reporting

Before discussing these issues in further detail, it is useful to consider how social reporting developed and to understand that it is far from a recent phenomenon. For example, research in the 1980s demonstrates that some US and Australian companies were reporting on social issues before World War I.[8] Likewise, in the European context, a similar pattern was observed in the early days of Shell.[9] These studies suggest that company managers have always been concerned to some degree with considering non-financial issues that are relevant.

Hogner (1982) suggests that US Steel's disclosures were motivated by the need to respond to perceived societal pressures of the period. But it was, perhaps, as societal awareness of environmental issues grew in the 1960s, and as concerns over corporate behaviour were prompted by various company collapses and scandals in the 1970s, that companies responded by including more non-financial information in their annual reports. It was also in the 1970s that, in different countries, new laws required companies to report on aspects of performance relating to, inter alia, employment practices, pollution expenditure, and the like.[10]

There was also interest in the subject among the UK accounting profession and, in 1975, the publication of *The Corporate Report* represented a radical rethink of the role of reporting to external stakeholders.[11] It emphasized how the traditional role of the annual report could be made more relevant by the inclusion of social and environmental information. In the USA, the American Institute of Certified Public Accountants entered the debate, offering guidance on the measurement of social performance in a 1977 publication,[12] and the atmosphere was one of examining the role of reporting, in general, and the purpose of reports, in particular. The traditional reason that companies report an account of their activities is for the benefit of the 'users' of accounts. This would normally be thought to be the shareholders, but, in the case of social reporting, traditional theory (i.e. that this information is useful for the purpose of decision making) does not seem to stand up.

As interesting as its emergence in the 1970s might have been, however, so too was the decline in social reporting in the 1980s and its subsequent re-emergence in the 1990s. The decline is largely attributed to the political shifts in the USA and UK that came with the respective elections of Reagan and Thatcher, and the renewed focus on market economics. *The Corporate Report* largely failed to bring about any major changes and disappeared from the accounting agenda until memories of its recommendations were stirred, in the 1990s, with the initiatives pioneered by such organizations as the Institute of Social and Ethical Accountability, the Council on Economic Priorities, and the World Business Council for Sustainable Development.[13]

The upsurge in social reporting since the early 1990s

Programmes and initiatives

Despite the varying pattern of corporate reporting of social and environmental issues, a very clear upward trend in social reporting began to emerge in the 1990s and this can be readily observed from the triannual surveys conducted by the accountancy firm KPMG (see Case Study 7.2). Apart from minor changes in corporate governance recommendations, a number of factors began to influence change within companies. These included action at a number of levels, from initiatives within professions and industries, to UN and EU initiatives, all encouraging greater detail in the reporting of social and environmental issues.

For example, the UNEP/SustainAbility 'Engaging Stakeholders' programme was launched in 1994. It served to raise awareness among companies, initially, of environmental reporting and it continues to stress the business case for wider reporting. The programme has clearly encouraged participation by publicizing widely the results of the survey and the benefits of participation. The series of surveys continues to the present, and the latest report saw Standard & Poors join the research team and the report taking on even more of a market orientation.[14] The European Union Eco-Management and Audit Scheme also promoted the introduction and reporting of environmental management systems, following the introduction of BS 7750 in 1992 and, thereafter, the ISO 14000 series.

At a national level, the UK government's DEFRA/DTI Environmental Reporting Guidelines were published in 2001, and France has followed Denmark, Norway, Sweden, and Holland in introducing mandatory reporting requirements, although the focus here continues to display a financial emphasis. At a business-to-business level, the International Chamber of Commerce published its *Business Charter for Sustainable Development* in 1991, featuring a 16-point guide to environmental reporting. In 1995, the World Business Council for Sustainable Development (WBCSD) was established, through a merger of the Business Council for Sustainable Development and the World Industry Council for the Environment, the two organizations that responded on behalf of business to the challenges arising from the Rio Summit in 1992. The WBCSD maintains an influential voice for business and boasts a membership comprising major corporations worldwide.[15]

Around the same time, various industries began to look at how environmental issues affect the perceptions of activities within their sectors. A good example of this is the initiative by the European Chemical Industry Council (CEFIC). Founded in 1972, it has, over the years, expanded and developed its approaches to various aspects of concern within the industry. It is now closely allied to the International Council of Chemical Associations and, in 2006, the ICCA launched its Responsible Care Global Charter, a development of CEFIC's Responsible Care Programme's reporting guidelines.

At the level of the professions, the *Fédération des Experts Compatibles Européens* (FEE)— the coordinating organization for the European accounting professions—has been involved in developing reporting guidelines and making representation to the European

Parliament on connected issues. In the UK, the initiative taken by the ACCA in 1991 in establishing the Environmental Reporting Awards has done much to encourage and improve social reporting over the years (see below). The ACCA not only runs award schemes in the UK, but in several other countries around the world.[16]

Each of these initiatives, or a combination of more than one, served to increase the incidence and volume of environmental reporting. In the early stages of this development, the reports bore little resemblance to the best reports we see today. In general, reporting on environmental issues comprised a section in the annual report and was largely qualitative in nature. Even when the first standalone reports began to appear, they seemed to be, as Owen (2003) suggested, *rather crude exercises in public relations*.

Trends in social reporting

Two other trends emerged in the 1990s that, to some extent, still continue today. First, there was the separation of the 'environmental' from the 'social'. Whereas the reports in the 1970s had, in many ways, a shared focus, the trend in the 1990s was to separate the two and to place a greater emphasis on the environmental aspects of company performance. This is significant because corporate responsibility, as a field, is not concerned solely with issues of environmental management: indeed, at the core of the Brundtland definition of sustainability (see Chapter 9) is the notion of social justice. Second, criticism started to be levelled at companies for failing to embed social and environmental policies into the strategy and 'real' purpose of the business (see Chapter 5).

We can conjecture over the reasons for both trends. In the case of the environmental focus, it is worth remembering that there had been a spate of very significant environmental disasters in the mid- and late 1980s, including, for example, Bhopal in 1984, Chernobyl in 1986, Piper Alpha in 1988, and the *Exxon Valdez* disaster in 1989. For obvious reasons, media coverage of these events was heavy and prolonged, and the events themselves led to many changes in the way in which companies operated and reported. Indeed, each of these events had a lasting impact within their respective industries that is felt even today. Therefore, it is probably unsurprising that companies opted for more of an environmental focus in their activities and reports. In many ways, if this conclusion is correct, it also explains why the strategy may be easily criticized as an 'add-on', because, at least initially, that is what it was. It would have been a reaction, most likely of companies within the affected industry sectors, to how they perceived they should act. But the criticism remains today and is still an issue for some critics, as we see in Case Study 7.4 and later in the book (Chapter 13).

Research into social reporting

Although there is evidence of companies reporting non-financial aspects of their businesses going back over a hundred years, a genuine body of research only really began to emerge in the 1970s.[17] During the period 1970–1980, this mainly consisted of empirical (statistical) studies that, while focusing on some aspects of social and environmental information, still had a clear instrumental rationale aimed at discovering the usefulness of this information to investors.[18] Some discursive work began to appear towards the end of the 1970s,[19] however, and these works widened the debate to include more philosophical issues, with the phrase 'social responsibility' appearing in many studies.[20]

Research gained momentum from the mid-1980s, at which time a number of authors, principally in the UK and Australia, began to explore the social dimensions of corporate activity. Influential journals, sympathetic to this subject matter, were also founded in this period: the *Journal of Accounting and Public Policy* (established 1982), the *Accounting, Auditing and Accountability Journal* (1988), and *Critical Perspectives on Accounting* (1990) joined *Accounting, Organizations and Society* (1975) to provide a wide forum through which to engage academics and broaden the terms of the debate. Scholars from related disciplines became involved and the subject was given extra impetus with the debates that appeared in the first issue of *Advances in Public Interest Accounting* between Parker (1986) and Puxty (1986), and with the 1987 publication of Grey et al.'s *Corporate Social Reporting: Accounting and Accountability*.

These works presaged the increase in social reporting of the early 1990s, and heralded a social and environmental accounting project that has continued, and grown in strength, scope, and reach, ever since. Indeed, from modest beginnings, with only a handful of researchers worldwide, social and environmental accounting research is now conducted by hundreds of researchers in many countries and features in many international accounting conferences, as well as having a number of its own dedicated conferences, each year.[21]

Such evidence as there is from research studies looking at the value that investors place on such information is no more than suggestive of 'possible' relevance to investment decisions.[22] Indeed, despite the huge amount of research in the late 1970s and early 1980s into the link between social performance and financial performance, no clear theories emerged to explain the increasing incidence of social reporting. It prompted one author to suggest that the research was based on '*data in search of a theory*'.[23]

CASE STUDY 7.2

KPMG international survey of corporate sustainability reporting

Since 1993, KPMG has conducted a triennial survey of social, environmental, and sustainability reporting. An examination of the table below reveals that, initially, the survey looked at the top 100 companies in ten countries and actually included 810 companies, with a response rate to the survey of 85 per cent. This has grown over the years and now includes the top 100 companies in sixteen countries, plus the Global 250, and includes over 1,600 companies. The response rate is now 98 per cent.

The main findings of the 2005 report were as follows.

1 Corporate responsibility reporting has risen steadily since 1993 and substantially since 2002.

2 The nature of the reports has changed from purely environmental reporting up to 1999, to sustainability reporting.

3 Although 80 per cent of top 100 companies in most countries issue separate corporate responsibility reports, there has been an increase in the number of companies publishing corporate responsibility information in their annual reports.

4 Top reporting countries are Japan and UK, with high increases in Italy, Spain, Canada, and France.

5 Industrial sectors with relatively high environmental impact continue to lead in reporting. The financial sector (traditionally, a low reporting sector) shows a twofold increase.

Year of survey	Percentage of companies producing a corporate environmental report
For the top 100 companies	
1993	13%
1996	17%
1999	24%
2002	28%
2005	41%
For Global 250 companies	
1999	35%
2002	45%
2005	64%

(KPMG *International Survey of Corporate Responsibility Reporting* 2005)

Questions

An examination of the reporting trends since 1993 shows an increasing number of companies reporting on their social, environmental, and sustainability activities.

1 What do you think has prompted this increase across industrial sectors and countries?

2 What do you think has prompted such an increase in response rate from companies, from 85 per cent in 1993 to 98 per cent in 2005?

3 How do you see this trend developing in the future?

Researchers responded to Ullmann's (1985) call for new theories to be explored to explain the phenomena and a number of studies followed. Roberts (1992) discussed stakeholder theory in an empirical context and, subsequently, Gray et al. (1996), prompted also by evidence in increasing volumes of social disclosure, reviewed theories of disclosure that might explain the phenomena. Traditional theories of disclosure aimed at informing market participants were largely discounted and alternative theories focusing on political economy were considered. One of the most discussed of these was 'legitimacy theory'.

This theory suggests that company disclosures may be a reaction to the perception that companies have of how they are viewed by different stakeholder groups within society. The theory itself is based on the notion that companies have an implicit 'approval' from society that allows them to operate in return for performing actions beneficial to society. The company, therefore, needs to disclose details about its activities to achieve this objective and to reassure society about these activities. Until the late 1990s, this theory may have been thought likely to remain in the theoretical domain, but the events surrounding Enron and the collapse of Arthur Andersen, one of the world's largest and, at the time, most respected firms of accountants, demonstrated that it is, indeed, possible to lose the licence to operate if one's actions are seen to go beyond what society deems acceptable.

The substantive empirical study of the Gray et al. (1995a) paper was drawn from a database of social disclosure that was drawn up, and maintained, over many years.[24] It provides a database of categories of social and environmental disclosures that allow trends to be plotted and discussed with some authority, and has been the source of data for a number of studies that have added to the debate, and to the understanding of the practice of social and environmental disclosure.[25]

Research interest grew in response to this observed increase in disclosure, not least because of the voluntary nature of the activity, which goes against the conventional theories of the firm that suggest that companies expend resources in expectation of financial returns. Here is a voluntary activity, consuming resources, with a high degree of uncertainty about the financial return. Indeed, a huge amount of research time has been spent on trying to correlate social disclosure (as a proxy for social performance) with company financial performance.[26]

Researchers began to confirm the likely characteristics that explained why certain companies were predisposed to disclose more than others. A consensus began to emerge that, principally, large companies disclose more than small companies[27] and companies from environmentally sensitive industries disclose more than those from other sectors. This is, probably, unsurprising. First, large companies have greater resources and tend to have a more sophisticated reporting function within the structure of the company. Much of the information would have been collated for internal use and, therefore, is relatively simple to roll out for external consumption. Equally, it is probably intuitive that companies in the more environmentally sensitive industries tend to report more on their environmental impact. Companies from the extractive, and oil and gas, sectors have responded to adverse comment by increasing, over the years, emphasis within their annual reports on their environmental management practices. Third, in the UK, the privatized utilities have maintained a high level of social and environmental coverage of their activities, which was part of the remit on privatization.

Conventional financial reporting and social reporting

The major difference between conventional financial reporting and social reporting hinges on the approach taken to the use of the information reported upon. Traditionally, financial reports contain both aggregated data, which may conceal much of the underlying activity, and analyses that focus on very narrow performance measures. We can only imagine the range of activity that is represented by the income statements of a BP or Wal-Mart and, in looking at the earning per share figure or other performance ratios, no consideration is given to the wider implications of the range of activities that led to the derivation of that measure. Indeed, in the application of many accounting techniques, little concern is given to any factors outside the concern of the entity, and ratios of liquidity, profitability, and solvency, for example, are often used only to compare performance against historic or other data. The same figures are also often used to compare performance of one company against another (this type of comparison is frequently requested in degree and professional accounting courses dealing with 'financial statement analysis'). Equally, what Chua (1986) calls '*mainstream accounting research*' tends to have a similar narrow focus, and, regularly, research questions focus around issues of market efficiency and the usefulness of certain categories of information to investors. It is little wonder, therefore, that the bigger picture is often overlooked in an effort to examine the minutiae of procedure or practice.

On the other hand, social reporting, at a theoretical level, is concerned with how commercial activity links into other social systems and presents an alternative ontological approach to how one views the role of corporations. 'Systems theory', explained in more detail in Gray et al. (1996), is an approach that is '*designed to reverse the tendency in scientific thought towards reductionist reasoning*'. Systems theory has its origins in the natural sciences and can be explained as follows.

• An attempt to study a part without understanding the whole from which the part comes (reductionism) was bound to lead to misunderstandings. The part can only be understood in its context.

• Understanding tends to be directed by and limited to one's own discipline. Natural phenomena are complex and cannot be successfully studied by artificially bounded modes of thought.

(Gray et al., 1996 p 13)

The essence of systems thinking demands that we think about all of our activities in the context of how they affect other systems, with what Birkin (2000) calls an '*ontology of interconnected events*'. If the relevance to social reporting emerges from this logic then, in relation to sustainability issues, which are explained in detail in Chapter 9, it is highly persuasive.

Reporting issues for corporate management

From the management perspective, there are a number of problems. First, who is the intended audience? Traditionally, corporate reports are released for the benefit of the analyst/investor group. That constituency is relatively easy to define, and their needs have been the focus of investor relations departments and boardroom discussions for decades. The audience for reports on social, environmental, and sustainability issues is, however, much more diverse. These users may have widely diverging interests and their wish for information may not always be with the company's benefit in mind. Indeed, it is easy to make an argument that few investors take any interest in the non-financial aspects of corporate activity, except if it impinges on issues of risk or governance. Certainly, there is little evidence from research that investors are swayed by social and environmental disclosures. Thus, management must form an opinion on the purpose and scope of the report, and this may pose many challenges.

It is relatively straightforward to make statements along the lines of 'within this company we make every effort to maintain the highest standards of social and environmental practice'. Indeed, statements such as this peppered annual reports throughout the late 1990s. What is more difficult to do is to explain how any particular programme is to be rolled out and the effect that it might have on earning numbers. At that point, conflict will almost inevitably arise within organizations and one can see the kind of compromises that are reached by examining such reports, many of which fill the list of criticisms of awards judges (see Case Study 7.4).

If one looks at it from the outside the company, the picture is entirely different. As a member of society, concerned about aspects of corporate activity that affect you, you may view the issue as one of accountability. Companies often talk about 'transparency', yet, on close examination, it is sometimes difficult to uncover the level of detail that you require in order to be satisfied on any particular issue. On the other hand, how does the company know the level of detail that any single individual or group might want?

CASE STUDY 7.3

Problems with sustainability reporting

Of all of the reports that companies produce for external stakeholders, the sustainability report poses the greatest challenge. This is because sustainable development creates issues for business that, traditionally, it has not had to consider. At its simplest, sustainable development means passing along to future generations certain stocks of environmental capital. The issues highlighted here relate to eco-efficiency and eco-effectiveness. Other, equal challenges, supplied by the Brundtland Report in relation to sustainability, relate to notions of social justice among populations and, together, these issues challenge the roots of traditional corporate activity. (A fuller discussion takes place in Chapter 9.)

Such evidence as there is suggests that many large companies, 'despite being providers of essential products and services worldwide, are inherently unsustainable in the way they currently operate' (ACCA, 2006). Indeed, the inability of companies to address and report competently on such issues prompted the following comment by Rob Gray (2006a), who has been researching social reporting for over twenty years:

> Substantive social and environmental reporting and, especially, high quality reporting on (un)sustainability will demonstrate that modern international financial capitalism and the principle organs which support it are essentially designed to maximise environmental destruction and the erosion of any realistic notion of social justice.

(Schmidheiny and Zorraquin, 1996; WCED, 1987; ACCA, 2006)

Questions

There are strong arguments that ideals surrounding sustainable development should be at the heart of corporate responsibility strategies.

1 How can companies report activities in a convincing way that addresses the underlying priorities of sustainable development?

2 Is there a case for regulating the scope and detail of sustainability reports?

3 What assurances can shareholders take from sustainability reports that their investments are being competently handled?

The role of third-party verification statements

We have seen how research has found that increasing numbers of companies are now reporting on social and environmental performance. We will also note that, in judging the most recent ACCA awards for sustainability reporting, criticisms have been made of the quality of third-party assurance statements (see Case Study 7.4). Despite acknowledging that external assurance has become widespread, the judges were concerned about the language and tenor of many of the reports, which appeared to be:

> often written for the company's directors/senior management. Some assurance statements do not include or refer to any recommendation for improvement . . . and so offer no insight into how the assurance process is helping an organisation to improve its reporting and performance.
>
> (ACCA, 2006)

In view of the fact that these reports are designed to be targeted at external stakeholder groups, with the intention of giving assurance to that audience of the intentions and future actions of the company in order to build trust, it is useful to consider the reasons why companies might wish to consider using third parties to offer assurance.

CASE STUDY 7.4

Report of the Judges—ACCA UK Awards for Sustainability Reporting

The Association of Chartered Certified Accountants (ACCA) founded the Environmental Reporting Awards in 1991 to give recognition to the organizations that were reporting on environmental issues. Over the years, the criteria have expanded and the awards are now made for sustainability reporting, and are also replicated in several countries around the world.

Following the announcement of the winners, which now takes place in December of each year, the judges give feedback to participants, aimed at offering guidance for subsequent reports. While acknowledging the high standard of reporting by many companies, the following criticisms are taken from a much more comprehensive list contained in the report of the judges on the quality of the 2006 reports.

1 '. . . the quality of reporting had not improved significantly since last year.'

2 'Most reporters state in stand-alone sustainability reports that their contribution to sustainable development is at the forefront of the business. . . . These statements, however, are often not consistent with strategic statements in the Annual Report and Accounts.'

3 '. . . reports should also be transparent in specifying the dilemmas and challenges faced.'

4 'Boundary and scope of report needs to be clear.'

5 *'Reporting on economic impacts needs to be improved.'*

6 *'Value of assurance statements questionable in many reports.'*

7 *'Room for improvement: past recommendations still applicable today.'*

8 *'More disaggregated data required.'*

9 *'Quality of external assurance statements needs to improve.'*

(ACCA, 2006; www.accaglobal.com)

Questions

Despite a huge upsurge in the volume of reporting over the last few years, various aspects of reporting practice continue to invite criticism.

1 Is there a case for statutory standards to cover sustainability reporting, in the same way as there is for financial reporting?

2 If a voluntary approach is to continue, how might companies be persuaded to take notice of the criticisms levelled at them?

3 What is the value of such an award scheme?

The trend towards external verification

We know that the initial choice of whether or not to report at all is made by the company, as part of a strategy by the management and motivated for any number of reasons. It is a largely voluntary act and may have much to do with the activity of competitors, perceptions of stakeholder expectation, or other strategies to obtain *'managerial advantage'*.[28] As companies embrace a global perspective, many will view both the mandatory requirements of some countries and the recommendations under the Global Reporting Initiative sustainability reporting guidelines, which make specific reference to verification, as an opportunity to review and to implement external assurance practices. The trend has been observed to be growing steadily and, in its most recent international survey, KPMG (2005) found that the number of companies in the Global 250 with a formal assurance statement had increased to 30 per cent (from 29 per cent in 2002); for the top 100 national companies, it had increased to 33 per cent (from 27 per cent). The overriding motivation is probably to build trust between company management and external stakeholders over the implementation and maintenance of corporate responsibility strategies. In an ideal world, the verification process should achieve this and reassure the relevant audience, thereby adding value for the company.

This motivation is, however, easily contrasted with the theoretical purpose of such accounts—the idea that with transparency comes accountability. There is a real concern, expressed by a number of researchers, that the upsurge in reporting is part of a process whereby the accountability agenda is 'captured' by corporate management, who react to calls for greater accountability and transparency by artefacts, aimed at taking control of the agenda, and at taking equal control of the nature and extent of the information reported upon.[29] The idea that such reports only contain information that management wants released adds to criticisms that reports lack completeness and credibility.[30]

This notion continues to motivate social accounting researchers to examine the verification process, and to press for the imposition of strict and robust assurance processes.[31]

CASE STUDY 7.5

Leading-edge reporting practice

In a recent paper examining developments in reporting and auditing practices, Owen (2003) drew up a list of features that one should expect in a standalone social, environmental, or sustainability report.

1 **An organizational profile**
   To include size, markets served, and key environmental impacts.

2 **Evidence of board-level commitment**
   A statement from the organization's CEO, explaining the environmental management strategy being pursued.

3 **A (definitive) environmental policy statement**
   Committing the organization to pursue specific goals and objectives in terms of managing, measuring, and reporting. The policy statement is used as a basis for generating comprehensive and detailed targets against which performance may be measured.

4 **Targets and achievements**
   Addressing key issues concerning, for example, natural resource and energy usage, waste generation, and emissions to air and water.

5 **Performance and compliance data**
   Employing physical and financial measures in order to demonstrate progress towards achieving stated performance targets.

6 **Environmental management systems**
   Information on internal environmental audit procedures and progress towards certification standards, such as ISO or EMAS.

7 **An independent verification statement**
   Recent practice has addressed more complex issues, such as completeness of reporting and acceptability of performance, while also offering recommendations in terms of systems improvement, performance, and disclosure practice.

8 **Site-level data**
   Provided for organizations operating from multiple sites; transparency of local operations is often heightened by specifically naming a management contact on site.

(Adapted from Owen, 2003)

Questions

The content and format of environmental reports have developed considerably over the years.

1 Why do you think it is necessary for the CEO, rather than the environmental manager, to make a statement in the environmental report?

2 Why should targets be mentioned?

3 What is the purpose of reporting on activities in other countries?

SUMMARY

In this chapter, we have examined how companies report to audiences outside the company. This, we discovered, encompasses a complex series of issues that pose some serious challenges for management, especially if the process is designed to be more than an exercise in corporate communication or public relations. This process developed through extending the financial reporting function and, until relatively recently, the annual report was the usual medium through which such disclosures were made.

This posed a number of problems for companies as it became clear that stakeholder groups were scrutinizing the information contained in these social and environmental accounts with different intentions than those of the traditional audience of annual reports, i.e. the shareholder. Academics also began scrutinizing these social disclosures, offering varying levels of critique and, as the reporting medium moved to the internet, so pressure groups were now using the same medium to counter some of the claims made in corporate releases. Even when companies enter reporting award schemes, they rarely emerge without criticism.

There are various reasons for the dramatic increase in the incidence and volume of social reporting, and a large number of contributory factors, a combination of which is most likely to offer explanation. But with this increase has come criticism from certain quarters that the reports are more akin to public relations initiatives. Indeed, as the incidence and volume of corporate responsibility reports has increased, so criticism of corporate behaviour does not seem to have abated, not least because the material is accused of being incomplete or inadequate, as attested to by successive judging panels of environmental and similar awards.

Accounting plays an important part in this process of improving the credibility of corporate responsibility performance. Impacts and effects need to be measured in order to gauge accurately whether particular strategies are worthwhile and effective. The design and implementation of appropriate information systems and reporting structures play an essential part of this process. There are, therefore, strong arguments to be made that accountants become aware of the social, environmental, and sustainability issues that are challenging the 'business as usual' approach. These professionals will then be better placed to devise accounting systems that can capture non-financial activity in a more meaningful way. Equally, there are new forms of accounting that might be developed, looking to measure different things to those that are traditionally associated with accounting systems.

What this chapter sets out to demonstrate is that accounting plays a central role in the corporate responsibility process and has the potential to play an even greater role. Social, environmental, corporate responsibility, and sustainability reports have emerged from the financial reporting function within companies. But, whereas financial reporting procedures are highly regulated and controlled, there seems no appetite to impose such controls on non-financial reporting. If that situation continues, despite continued criticism over the format and content of such reports, then these reports will continue to require careful analysis and critical judgement.

DISCUSSION POINTS

1 Corporate reporting is traditionally associated with the accounting function.
   - Is it appropriate that accountants play any role in compiling corporate responsibility reports that, at face value, seem to have little to do with accounting?
   - Which other department within the structure of a company might take on this role?
   - What role does measurement play in compiling social reports?

2   In attempting to assess a company's commitment to a corporate responsibility, the volume and content of company disclosures play an important part.
  • To what extent can a company's social performance be judged from the various reports it publishes throughout the year?
  • What other sources of evidence may found?
  • How much notice should we take of those NGO reports that are often critical of company activity?

3   There is strong evidence from recent surveys that an increasing number of companies are reporting on social and environmental issues.
  • What theories can you suggest that might help to explain this trend?
  • What theories lie behind the notion that statements should be independently verified by third parties?
  • Given that there are no standards against which to base third-party verification statements, how is it possible to compare their value between companies?

4   Awards for producing high-quality social reports have attracted participation from some of the world's best-known companies.
  • Can you suggest reasons why companies should want to subject themselves to this level of scrutiny and so run the risk of criticism?
  • Why do so many criticisms from the judges recur year after year?
  • What makes it difficult for companies to address the judges' criticisms and what can be done about it?

5   One of the major criticisms by judges of the ACCA award is the failure to link strategies in sustainability reports with strategies in financial reports.
  • Why might the judges consider this to be important?
  • This criticism also suggests that financial reports are given more prominence. Why should this be?
  • What evidence should we look for of top-level board support for sustainable development initiatives?

VISIT THE WEBSITE for links to useful sources of further information

FURTHER READING

• Gray, RH, 2002a, 'Of messiness, systems and sustainability: towards a more social and environmental finance and accounting', *British Accounting Review*, 34(4), pp 357–86.
Arguments for rethinking accounting and making it more sensitive to environmental issues.

• Gray, RH, 2006b, 'Social, environmental and sustainability reporting and organisational value creation? Whose value? Whose creation?', *Accounting, Auditing and Accountability Journal*, 19(6), pp 793–819.
Revisiting and updating the debate on reporting on the social and environmental dimensions of business.

• Gray, RH, Owen, D and Adams, C, 1996, *Accounting and Accountability: Changes and Challenges in Corporate Social and Environmental Reporting*, London: Prentice Hall.
Making the case for social and environmental reporting.

• Mathews, MR, 1993, *Socially Responsible Accounting*, London: Chapman and Hall.
Early and innovative work on social accounting.

- Owen, DL, Swift, TA, Humphrey, C and Bowerman, M, 2000, 'The new social audits: accountability, managerial capture or the agenda of social champions?', *European Accounting Review*, 9(1), pp 81–98.

  Discussion about the contribution of corporate responsibility reporting to accountability.

- Owen, D, Swift, TA and Hunt, K, 2001, 'Questioning the role of stakeholder engagement in social and ethical accounting, auditing and reporting', *Accounting Forum*, 25(3), pp 264–82.

  Introducing stakeholder theory into alternative models of accounting.

ENDNOTES

[1] Tinker, 1985.

[2] Berry et al., 1985.

[3] Lehman, 1992.

[4] Changing corporate governance guidelines have increased the amount of recommended disclosure, categorized as social disclosure, relating to the remuneration of directors, following the Cadbury and Greenbury Reports in the mid-1990s. (See Chapter 8.)

[5] For a more recent discussion on the definition, see Gray et al., 1996.

[6] This 'agency' relationship lies at the heart of modern corporate activity and is further explored in Chapter 9.

[7] There are a number of examples in which disclosure is used when no other measure of performance is available: see, e.g., Belkaoui, 1976; Ingram, 1978; Mahapatra, 1984; Freedman and Ullman, 1986; Belkaoui and Karpic, 1989.

[8] Lewis et al.,1984; Hogner, 1982; Guthrie and Parker, 1989.

[9] Unerman, 2003.

[10] Gray, 2002b.

[11] ASSC, 1975.

[12] AICPA, 1977.

[13] Deegan, 2002.

[14] UNEP/SustainAbility/Standard&Poors, 2006.

[15] It also has an extensive website covering issues of climate change, international development, ecosystems, and the business role. There is a section on projects in progress and there are a large number of case studies for reference. See www.wbcsd.org.

[16] For a full list of awards schemes around the world, see www.enviroreporting.com.

[17] See Mathews, 1996, for a detailed discussion of the development of social accounting research in different time periods.

[18] See, e.g., Bowman, 1973; Bowman and Haire, 1976; Belkaoui, 1976.

[19] See, e.g., Estes, 1975; Estes, 1976a; Ramanathan, 1976.

[20] See, e.g., Jacoby, 1973; Browne and Haas, 1974; Feldberg, 1974; Beresford, 1975; Parket and Eilbert, 1975; Estes, 1976b.

[21] The Centre for Social and Environmental Accounting Research (CSEAR) at the University of St Andrews boast membership in excess of 300 people from over thirty countries and holds an annual conference for researchers each September; see www.st-andrews.ac.uk.

[22] Bowman, 1973; Chenall and Juchau, 1977; Ingram, 1978; Goodwin et al., 1996; Chan and Milne, 1999; Milne and Chan, 1999; Friedman and Miles, 2001.

[23] Ullmann, 1985.

[24] For a full explanation of the rationale and development of the database, see Gray et al., 1995b.

[25] See, e.g., Gray et al., 2001; Murray et al., 2006.

[26] For a detailed summary, see Margolis and Walsh, 2001.

[27] See Trotman and Bradley, 1981; Belkaoui and Karpic, 1989; Gray et al., 2001.

[28] Owen et al., 2000.

[29] See, e.g., Owen et al., 2000; O'Dwyer and Owen, 2005.

[30] Dando and Swift, 2003; Adams, 2004; Adams and Evans, 2004.

[31] O'Dwyer and Owen, 2005.

8

The place of corporate responsibility in the corporate governance framework

Chapter overview

In this chapter, we explain the meaning of 'corporate governance' and outline the development of corporate governance frameworks, which, in conventional terms, are always associated with the duties owed by the directors to the owners of the business. We examine this traditional model and consider thereafter how, and whether, it might be adapted to offer greater levels of accountability to a wider group of stakeholders. In particular, we will:

- examine what is meant by 'corporate governance';

- explore the 'drivers' of corporate governance;

- trace the development of the UK corporate governance framework;

- examine widening corporate accountability;

- discuss stakeholder accountability;

- envision corporate governance from a corporate responsibility perspective.

Main topics

■ **Key terms**

Accountability	Corporate governance framework
Auditing	Corporate malfeasance
Corporate governance	Stakeholder engagement

■ **Online resources**

* Suggested additional information on corporate governance worldwide

* Discussion topics for students

* Case studies and exercises on corporate governance

* Links to other web-based resources

What is 'corporate governance'?

In Chapter 2, we discussed the reasons for the move away from proprietor-run businesses to the company form of enterprise. One of the main reasons is to allow the issue of shares to raise capital, which makes it possible to reach a much wider investment community and therefore easier to raise larger amounts of money. In turn, the investor, whether an individual or an institution, such as a bank or a pension fund, will expect that their funds are handled with care and invested in such a way that, in due course, they will receive a return on their investment. But how do they know what managers are going to do with their cash? What structures are there in place to ensure that managers do not invest in risky projects, or simply squander the investors' money on a lavish expense-account lifestyle? Above all, in the context of corporate responsibility, how does corporate governance relate to the behaviour of companies and serve to encourage, restrict, or otherwise shape their relationship with wider society? In a corporate world in which optimum profit is the measure of success and reward, is there room for any notion of social responsibility?

In this chapter, corporate governance will be examined from the perspective of both investors and their agents (i.e. company managers). How frameworks of corporate governance have developed will be contrasted with the continuing scandal of corporate collapse and fraud. The role of the auditor will be examined, to see if there is more that the audit process can contribute to good corporate governance in the face of persistent criticism from some quarters. And the overarching shareholder focus will be questioned in relation to calls for more meaningful stakeholder engagement and higher levels of social responsibility.

Our primary focus is on governance as it applies to publicly held companies and we have especially highlighted the situation in the UK. We have made this choice because the Anglo-Saxon notion of the firm, with the primacy it grants to investors and the role of capital markets, while not universal, has come to epitomize the efficiency and hazard of the modern company. This is not to pretend that other models of corporate governance are unimportant in the corporate responsibility context (as reflected, for example, in the 'Further reading' suggested at the end of this chapter, and in case studies in Chapters 1 and 6), but it is the model of corporate governance in publicly held companies that has had, to date, the most significance for corporate responsibility.

Theories of corporate governance

It is probably fair to say that most large companies are not run by their legal owners; rather, they are run on behalf of the owners by a board of directors and by a management structure that is intended to best serve the interests of the owners. Definitions of corporate governance invariably reflect this owner–agent relationship, and focus on issues of control and accountability in this context. Before examining some of the definitions on offer, or considering whether these definitions are adequate to satisfy all of those interested in governance issues, however, it is useful to think about some of the theories and assumptions that lie beneath corporate activities in a liberal democracy.[1]

The most important of these is the assumption that underpins neoclassical economics, i.e. that individuals will act rationally to maximize their own utility. This means that they will organize their affairs to obtain the best they can to serve their own self-interest. This assumes that individuals will move their investments whenever necessary to obtain the highest possible returns. Firms will also act to maximize their profits and the theory is that the aggregate effect will be to maximize economic efficiency, which will ultimately bring benefits to all.[2] As touched on in Chapter 2, there are obvious defects to this argument, but the underlying principle of profit maximization lies at the heart of corporate activity. The equally strong assumption of self-interest, however, reveals a tension when we think of an agency relationship and has given rise to a refinement of these assumptions in what is now referred to as 'agency theory' (see also Chapter 1).[3]

Agency theory is based on the notion that companies operate by virtue of a *'nexus of contracts'*,[4] a coming together of the contractual requirements of manufacture, supply, and employment. It articulates some of the conflicts of interest that must exist between an agent and owner if agents are predisposed to act in a self-interested manner. It is easy to imagine how this might manifest itself in actual situations in which a manager might pursue policies that may not be in the best interest of the owners. Consider, for example, the manager who has the opportunity of taking on either of two projects. The first option is very safe and will bring a small return. The second option is more risky, but offers a much higher potential return if it is handled skilfully. It might be argued that the manager should undertake the second option, because it offers the owner the best chance of maximizing the return on investment. But the manager may not see things in the same way, preferring instead to play it safe, recognizing that the first option probably requires less effort and achieves enough to keep him in the job—an option that is known as 'satisficing'. The manager may well argue that his decision is the best, because of the privileged information that he holds surrounding all the issues involved in the decision. This problem, known as 'information asymmetry', is of recurring concern to shareholders and one to which we shall return below. What, then, can shareholders do to ensure that managers return some of the profits and manage their investments carefully? How can corporations be governed effectively?

In fact, one oft-quoted definition of corporate governance states simply that it '*deals with the ways in which suppliers of finance to corporations assure themselves of getting a return on their investment*'.[5] This very narrow definition predicates a huge volume of research in the field of accounting and finance, and is vigorously defended when criticism is made that, for example, it omits the interests of all other stakeholder groups.[6] Leaving that particular debate aside for the moment, however, this shareholder emphasis is shared in many other influential definitions and discussions. The OECD, for example, broadens the scope slightly, but still maintains a strong shareholder focus:

> A good corporate governance regime helps to assure that corporations use their capital efficiently. Good corporate governance helps, too, to ensure that corporations take into account the interests of a wide range of constituencies, as well as of the communities within which they operate, and that their boards are accountable to the company and the shareholders. This, in turn, helps to assure that corporations operate for the benefit of society as a whole. It helps to maintain the confidence of investors—both foreign and domestic—and to attract more 'patient', long-term capital.
>
> (OECD, 1999)

While there is reference to other stakeholders, in both this report and the updated version published in 2004, there remains a strong shareholder focus, which has been endorsed by other organizations with an interest in promoting this version of corporate governance. For example, the International Corporate Governance Network, in commenting on the OECD guidelines, reaffirms that '*the board is accountable to shareholders and responsible for managing successful and productive relationships with . . . stakeholders*'.[7]

This view of the purpose of corporate governance reflects the broader idea that the social responsibility of the firm is to create shareholder value (see Chapter 2). It dominates the thinking of many business leaders, and is central to the legal definition of corporate purpose and fiduciary duty in the UK and much of the USA. As touched on in Chapter 6, however, in recent years, there has been a resurgence of the idea that companies have responsibilities to a wider group of stakeholders than only shareholders. Furthermore, although some theorists argue that it is enough to recognize and manage stakeholder groups, others believe that companies need to be accountable to them even though they may have no financial interest in the firm. Stakeholder accountability is highly contentious and its position in corporate responsibility is contested, as we discuss in Chapter 10, but to understand how it has won a place in the development of governance structures, we need to consider the events that have brought calls for changes in corporate governance during the last two decades.

The 'drivers' of corporate governance reform

Over the last twenty years, a number of interconnecting events have combined to keep up pressure for change in the way in which corporations are managed and regulated. To understand how some of these changes have come about, it is useful, first, to consider the changing nature of corporate activity in the last few decades—in particular, corporate ownership and the seeming rise in malfeasance.

Changing ownership structure

The size and scope of companies has obviously increased over this period, often by merger and acquisition, but, additionally, the mix of ownership has altered. Clearly, as companies increase in size and as the number of their subsidiaries also increases, so there are implications for the way in which such conglomerates are regulated. But equally, as classes of ownership change, so mechanisms of corporate governance have to adapt to reflect the altering landscape of corporate activity. The Office for National Statistics (ONS) has released a detailed analysis of classes of owners of equity in UK-listed companies. The results for the first year and the last year in the survey are summarized in Box 8.1. If we examine the trends over that period, we can see clearly the shift from individual to institutional and overseas' investors. In the same period, as individual shareholding declined to almost a quarter of the 1963 level, so bank and institutional investment rose from 30.3 per cent to 51.5 per cent, and foreign investment rose from 7 per cent to 32.6 per cent.

Corporate collapse and malfeasance

While it is true to say that there is a long history of corporate failure going back at least as far as the South Sea Bubble of 1718, the events in the latter part of the twentieth century brought sustained calls for increased regulation of companies to protect investors. If we consider, for example, the UK in the 1980s, there were a number of high-profile collapses, ending with the scandals involving media tycoon Robert Maxwell (see Case Study 8.1), and the Bank of Credit and Commerce International (BCCI; see Case Study 8.2). Other corporate failures involving well-known listed companies added to the calls for changes in the regulatory framework. What was particularly significant in the worst examples was

Box 8.1 Summary of share ownership in the UK 1963–2004

Category of investor	1963 (%)	2004 (%)
Rest of the world	7.0	32.6
Insurance companies	10.0	17.2
Pension funds	6.4	15.7
Individuals	54.0	14.1
Unit trusts	1.3	1.9
Investment trusts	0.0	3.3
Financial institutions	11.3	10.7
Charities	2.1	1.1
Non-financial institutions	5.1	0.6
Public sector	1.5	0.1
Banks	1.3	2.7

(The Office for National Statistics; http://www.statistics.gov.uk/statbase/tsdtables1.asp?vlink=srs)

that, in the year before the collapse, they had all been given unqualified audit reports by reputable firms of chartered accountants, with an opinion that their accounts represented a 'true and fair view' of the financial affairs of the company, giving no hint to investors, or other stakeholders, of its impending collapse.

In light of the issues raised by BCCI's collapse, the UK government set up a committee under the chairmanship of Sir Adrian Cadbury to look into the 'financial aspects of corporate governance', with the remit:

> to help raise the standards of corporate governance and the level of confidence in financial reporting and auditing by setting out clearly what it sees as the respective responsibilities of those involved and what it believes is expected of them.

Following the death of Robert Maxwell in November 1991, it soon became clear that similar issues were to be the focus of further damaging publicity for the financial regulators and the corporate governance framework.

CASE STUDY 8.1

The legacy of Robert Maxwell

Robert Maxwell's disappearance from the deck of his private yacht on 5 November 1991 initially drew affectionate eulogies from some who had known him throughout his eventful life. It was only in the weeks and months following his disappearance that the whole story of massive fraud and theft emerged: £900m was reputedly taken from pension funds to appease and pacify lenders, robbing some 30,000 people of their pension rights and presenting the UK government with a challenge to its corporate governance mechanisms on a scale that had never before been experienced.

After an eventful military career, Maxwell became involved in the business of scientific publishing and later founded Pergamon Press, starting an empire that had the Maxwell Communication Company (MCC) and Mirror Group Newspapers (MGN) as its flagships. By the time of his death, Maxwell had additionally built up a myriad of some 400 subsidiary companies and, under the banner of Headington Investments—owned by a Gibraltar trust company and the Maxwell Charitable Foundation registered in Lichtenstein—there were another 400 companies in existence. The flow of funds between these companies–what became known as the 'public' and the 'private' sides of the business—was at the heart of the governance issue.

From the 1950s, there were signs of malfeasance when Maxwell acquired a book wholesaler and ran it into the ground to fund the activities of several of his private companies. Then, when the sale of Pergamon Press to an American company fell through, a DTI enquiry concluded:

we regret . . . that, notwithstanding Mr Maxwell's acknowledged abilities and energy, he is not in our opinion a person who can be relied on to exercise proper stewardship of a publicly quoted company.

(HMSO, 1971)

Despite these warning signs, Maxwell continued to form companies and move assets (usually cash) between the public and private sides, depending on where it was needed most.

Following the purchase of MGN, he embarked on a series of business ventures that he hoped would make him a publishing billionaire to rival Rupert Murdoch, but which instead plunged him into such massive debt that, by 1991, it was beginning to attract the attentions of the financial press, and was being financed by massive movements of cash between companies and on day-to-day currency dealings.

It was only after his death that the full story began to unravel and the recriminations began. Failures were identified in the abilities of the existing regulatory bodies to draw connections between all of Maxwell's various companies and in the abilities of the regulators to instigate investigations. Non-executive directors were also accused of failing to inform the boards of those cash transfers about which they knew. The pension fund trustees were blamed for inaction, the stock exchange was blamed for failing to supervise the conduct of his listed companies, and the Serious Fraud Office was blamed for failing to start an investigation until pressured by a Swiss bank. In addition, each company had received a clean audit report from its auditors.

(Bower, 1988; 1996; Clarke, 1993; HMSO, 1971)

Questions

The collapse of Maxwell's companies sent shock waves through the financial world.

1 What steps have been taken since 1991 to try to prevent similar situations arising?

2 What difference would an audit committee have made to the outcome?

3 What is the role of the institutional investor in corporate governance?

The development of the UK corporate governance framework

The Cadbury Committee was, in fact, the first of a series of committees that examined and reported on aspects of corporate governance, and it was part of an ongoing process that has not yet run its course. What follows is a summary of the steps taken on the initiative of a variety of agencies, each with a sometimes specific, and at other times overlapping, interest in particular aspects of governance. The early initiatives were responses to specific 'shocks' to the financial systems, but later on in the process, there appears to have been a much more coordinated approach to the codes of conduct that were developed over the period.

The Cadbury Report (1992)

In response to the grave concerns about the general sinking confidence in financial reporting, auditing, and corporate governance, the Financial Reporting Council (FRC), the London Stock Exchange (LSE), and the Consultative Committee of Accountancy Bodies (CCAB) convened a committee to consider *'the financial aspects of corporate governance'*. The committee met under the chairmanship of Sir Adrian Cadbury, past chairman of Cadbury Schweppes and, at that time, director of the Bank of England. It met for the first time in May 1991 and was charged to consider:

> aspects of corporate governance . . . the way in which boards set financial policy and oversee its implementation, including the use of financial controls, and the processes whereby they report on the activities and progress of the company to the shareholders.
>
> (Cadbury, 1992, p 13)

The committee sat for over 18 months and, when the Cadbury Report was actually published, it was in the form of a 'code of conduct' for companies. It recommended that company boardrooms be constituted in such a way that they would feature appropriate sub-committees dealing with matters of remuneration, audit, and nomination, with independent non-executive directors, and, more crucially, a separation in the roles and functions of the CEO and the chairman. At the time, there was some debate about whether to make the recommendations compulsory, but, in a trend that continues today, companies were eventually asked to comply with the recommendations in a voluntary way. Indeed, the Cadbury Report is widely regarded as the pioneer of the voluntary approach that has become the model for other internationally recognized governance codes.[8]

The Greenbury Report (1995)

Despite the recommendations of Cadbury, there continued to be discontent with some aspects of corporate behaviour. Specifically, the pay and benefits awarded by boards of directors to themselves brought disapprobation from many quarters. Singled out for particular attention were the bosses of the utility companies that had been privatized by the Thatcher government of the 1980s. Especially galling for some was the fact that these increases were accompanied by staff cuts and price increases. 'Fat cat' scandals were the ready fodder of the tabloid press, with some individuals coming in for particular vilification.[9] In a move that was designed to restore confidence, the Confederation of British Industry (CBI) convened a committee under the chairmanship of Sir Richard Greenbury, then chairman of Marks and Spencer. It met with the remit:

> to respond to public and shareholder concerns about Directors' remuneration. The key themes are accountability, responsibility, full disclosure, alignment of Director and shareholder interests, and improved company performance.
>
> (Greenbury, 1995)

In terms of '*accountability*', there was a focus on disclosure. Equally, there was an implicit agenda to link remuneration with performance. The recommendation, again voluntary, was that the remuneration committee should comprise non-executive directors, who would report annually on policy and disclose full details of the remuneration packages of the directors. It was also seen that, if rewards could be linked to performance, then there would be greater congruence between the wishes of shareholders and the interests of directors. Since Greenbury, a feature of the company annual report has been the detailed level of disclosure on all aspects of directors' remuneration, with valuation of such items as stock options and pension contributions.

The Hampel Report (1998)

As Greenbury was publishing his report, so another committee was convened to look at how such voluntary codes were being implemented. A number of companies had decided not to implement the Cadbury recommendations for various reasons and, once again, the behaviour of corporate boards choosing this course of action came in for criticism. The new committee's remit was agreed with the sponsor organizations: the LSE, the CBI, the CCAB, the Institute of Directors, the National Association of Pension Funds, and the Association of British Insurers. Sir Ronnie Hampel, then the chairman of ICI, chaired the Committee. Of particular interest in the context of this book is that, in his report, mention is made of interested parties who are not shareholders for the first time:

> Good governance ensures that constituencies (stakeholders) with a relevant interest in the company's business are fully taken into account. In addition, good governance can make a significant contribution to the prevention of malpractice and fraud, although it cannot prevent them absolutely.
>
> (Hampel, 1998, p 17)

This theme is discussed further below, when all of the codes of governance are analysed through the lens of corporate responsibility, but other recommendations that had far-reaching implications were that, first, there should be increased dialogue between companies and their institutional investors, and, second, that institutional investors should consider using their votes to influence company policy wherever possible.

The Combined Code (1998)

At the same time as Hampel was reporting, an initiative of the LSE aiming to consolidate the three previous codes was published. The Combined Code, as its name suggests, tabulates the recommendations of the three previous committees in terms of the responsibilities of companies, on the one hand, and institutional investors, on the other. All of the issues of remuneration, audit, shareholder relations, etc., are covered. It is appended to the Listing Rules of the LSE—now the Listing Rules of the Financial Services Authority (FSA).[10] The 'comply or explain' principle of reporting, first mentioned by Cadbury, was reinforced in the Combined Code, which laid down, in unusually prescriptive form, the requirement to report any deviation from the code.[11]

The Turnbull Report (1999)

The Turnbull Committee was convened by the Institute of Chartered Accountants of England and Wales to give guidance specifically on issues of internal control that were highlighted in the Combined Code as being of particular importance. The subsequent report first outlined existing procedures, then made recommendations for improving internal control systems. It represented the first initiative, worldwide, to focus on this specific aspect of corporate governance, going much further than the Treadway Commission did in the USA in 1987. While not being overtly prescriptive, it nevertheless sought to give guidance on how to establish and maintain robust systems of internal control.[12]

All of this activity led the 1990s to be referred to by commentators, such as Charkham (2005), as '*the decade of corporate governance*'. Yet despite this concerted effort on the part of interested parties, from the stock exchanges to the accountancy profession, to improve systems and thus avoid further criticism, corporate scandals continued. The fall of Barings Bank in 1995 had sent further shock waves through the financial world, but it was the collapse of Enron and Worldcom in the USA that, again, led to calls for further attention. The once-dormant proposal of two US legislators became the most far-reaching (and hastily passed) piece of governance legislation—the Sarbanes–Oxley Act 2002. Ironically, the requirements of 'SarbOx' have been blamed for driving companies to seek listings outside the USA, not least on the London exchanges within which, after the various initiatives described earlier, most listed companies had implemented the voluntary recommendations. Nonetheless, it was felt that that the role being played by non-executive directors was not robust enough in terms of ensuring good practice and governance. Additionally, further criticism was levelled at the accountancy profession for what appeared to be a continuing inability to uncover, through the audit process, signals of underlying corporate distress or malfeasance. This led to a flurry of activity and the establishment of yet more committees to try, once again, to develop systems of governance that would be sufficient to prevent further scandals.

CASE STUDY 8.2

The BCCI scandal—lessons learnt?

The collapse of the Bank of Credit and Commerce International (BCCI) is probably one of the worst examples of corporate fraud and audit failure in recent times. Long-standing critics of the audit profession observed the ramifications with dismay and frustration; with losses of more than

$10bn, critics such as Austin Mitchell MP have called it the biggest banking fraud of the twentieth century. The Bank of England belatedly closed BCCI down in July 1991, having chosen to rely on audits by major accountancy firms rather than on government auditors with which to regulate banks. Such firms have been criticized for not owing a 'duty of care' either to the Bank of England or to bank depositors.

Instead of mounting an open and independent inquiry into the real, or alleged, audit failures at BCCI, successive governments have continued to support the auditing industry. They have passed responsibility to accountancy trade associations, expecting them to mount an investigation. Yet, these associations have no independence from the auditing industry: they are financed and controlled by the auditing industry, and are in no position to call multinational members to account. The outcomes not surprisingly, therefore, may satisfy the auditing industry, but leave the costs to be borne by savers, investors, employees, and other stakeholders who lost their savings, homes, investments, and jobs.

Audit stakeholders have no way of checking the efficiency and standards of audit work. Some claim that audit work is falsified by trainees who find the work boring and uninteresting, and who are encouraged to cut corners,[13] and that regulatory oversight is weak. The auditing industry is regulated by accountancy trade associations rather than by an independent regulator. There is no independent complaint investigation system and no ombudsman to adjudicate on complaints of poor audit work. Rather than developing policies to advance and protect the interest of stakeholders, the accountancy trade associations have mobilized their financial and political resources to protect auditing firms from lawsuits issued by injured stakeholders. The audit regulators have proved adept at covering up auditor non-compliance with legislation and accountancy firm involvement in money laundering.

(Mitchell et al., 1998; Cousins et al., 1998; Dunn and Sikka, 1999; Willet and Page, 1996)

Questions

Audits are time-consuming and expensive, and are supposed to give assurance on the financial reports produced.

1 To what extent can audit be kept separate from corporate governance?

2 Why do you think it is so difficult to call audit firms to account in cases of corporate collapse?

3 Should it be the responsibility of audit firms to detect fraud?

The Higgs Report (2003)

The first of these committees was the result of the UK government wishing to extend the remit of its Company Law Review and an acknowledgement of the globalization of financial markets. It was probably the first time that the collapse of a company in one country precipitated such a wide-ranging enquiry in another. The subsequent report of the Higgs Committee dealt with the responsibilities of non-executive directors, with recommendations that '*at least half the board*' should be made up of non-executive directors and that they should be paid at a rate commensurate with the additional responsibility. There was also a recommendation that non-executive directors should forge closer links with the 'principal' shareholders and that statements should be made in the annual report about the steps taken to implement this recommendation.

The Smith Report (2003)

At the same time as the Higgs Committee was sitting, the government asked the Financial Reporting Council to consider the particular role of audit committees within the governance framework and the relationship that they should have with the company's external auditor. In the case of Enron, as with Maxwell's companies a decade earlier, the company had received a clear, or 'unqualified', audit in the financial year before the collapse and it was clear that the audit committee had failed by some degree (despite the fact that the chair of the audit committee was a chartered accountant).[14]

The committee, under Sir Robert Smith, chairman of the Weir Group, reported in January 2003 and had a number of specific points to address, mostly to do with the role of the audit committee within the overall board structure. It was also charged with safeguarding the interest of shareholders.[15] The Smith Report reinforced the belief that accounting firms needed to be careful in deciding which services to offer to a company if they were also conducting its audit. For many, this recommendation did not go far enough, because pressure for more fundamental reforms to the audit industry was resisted.

The Revised Combined Code 2003

In light of the reports of Higgs and Smith, the 1998 Combined Code was revised, to take account of the various recommendations, and published in July 2003. Companies were expected to implement its recommendations for financial years beginning after November 2003. The principle recommendations include the following.

1 There should be a clear division of responsibilities at the head of the company between chairing the board and running of the company's business. No one individual should have unfettered powers of decision.

2 The chair should be independent at appointment.

3 At least half of the board should comprise non-executive directors.

4 One of the non-executive directors should be appointed senior independent director, to be the point of contact for concerned shareholders.

5 The appointment process of new directors should be *formal, rigorous and transparent*.

6 There should be time limits on non-executive appointments.

7 A director of a FTSE 100 company should be a non-executive director on no more than one other board.[16]

In addition to the provisions of these codes of practice, various bodies added guidance for specific professions or financial sectors, such as pensions or investment trusts,[17] leading to a hope that systems of governance can be put in place to ensure that boards of companies may become aware, at the earliest opportunity, that things are not proceeding as they should be. It is also worth noting that, during this time, these developments in the UK were being observed closely in other countries and that most of the main points are now incorporated in the codes in other countries.[18]

The Hermes principles of corporate governance

Hermes is a fund manager that is independent of any broader financial services group. It invests funds on behalf of around 200 clients, including pension funds, insurance companies, government entities, and financial institutions, as well as charities and endowments. Hermes' largest client is the BT Pension Scheme, which, as owner of Hermes, gives its investment management perspective a unique insight and close alignment to the needs of other long-term investors, and especially pension funds. With over twenty years' experience of managing money for its initial sponsors, British Telecom and the Post Office, Hermes was created in 1995, when it became wholly owned by the BT Pension Scheme.

Hermes' corporate governance programme is founded on a notion that companies with interested and involved shareholders are more likely to achieve superior long-term financial performance than are those without. For example, Hermes undertook an extensive engagement with Premier Oil, an international exploration and production company with operations focused on UK oil and Asia gas, after it became clear that its share price was languishing and it appeared unable to deliver on its stated strategy.

Hermes had been in communication with Premier Oil for a number of years over concerns about its board structure, in particular, the shortage of independent directors on the board as a result of the two major shareholders, Petronas and Amerada Hess, having significant board representation. In mid-2000, Hermes accelerated its engagement, because these apparent failures in governance seemed to be preventing the company from addressing its strategic problems. Through a series of meetings with members of the executive team and non-executive board members, Hermes explained its concerns about the company's situation and learned what the company was doing to address its problems. In response to the initiatives recommended by Hermes, the reaction from the market was very positive and, over the 18 months of Hermes' engagement with the company, the share price doubled relative to that of the oil and gas sector.

(Adapted from **www.hermes.co.uk**)

Questions

Hermes seeks to improve company performance by asking companies to address corporate governance matters effectively; Hermes helped Premier Oil to improve its share price by engaging with it on corporate governance issues.

1 How does this reflect the corporate responsibility stance of the company?

2 What more can institutions do to improve the corporate responsibility approach within companies?

3 What more can companies do to integrate responsibility into governance agendas?

Commentary on governance codes from a corporate responsibility perspective

It is clear that corporate collapses are not only of concern to government, professional bodies, investors, and the public at large, but that various agencies have worked in a coordinated way to try to refine mechanisms of governance and to try to minimize the probability of future crises. The language of governance has changed, as is evident, for example, in the Hampel Report's acknowledgement of stakeholder interests. At the same time, the language of governance has been adopted by corporate responsibility, notably the widespread use of terms such as 'accountability' and 'transparency' in corporate responsibility reports, as guiding features of the required procedures. There is a long and wide literature on the subject of accountability, and we now review some of this.

Accountability

At the root of accountability is the notion of the giving and the receiving of 'an account'—and not necessarily a financial account (see Chapter 7). With this notion comes the idea that there is often an element of 'duty' attached to the giving, and some form of privilege in the receiving, of an account. In discussions on accountability, Tricker (1983) argues that accountability only exists in this state, when the right to account is enforceable. As discussed in Chapter 7, within the concept so defined, there is a clear asymmetry of power between the person or body calling for an account and those charged with giving one. We see it, for example, in courtrooms, within which individuals are 'held to account' for their actions. This theme is developed by Roberts and Scapens (1985), and by Roberts (1991), who suggest that the act of being required to 'give an account' strengthens these power relationships.

Company law gives strength to this approach by setting out clearly the duties of directors in the discharge of accountability to shareholders. For example, they are required to prepare financial statements and to present them to shareholders, and these commercial relationships and responsibilities are the focus of the agency theorists mentioned earlier.[19]

CASE STUDY 8.4

Stakeholder accountability—challenging the primacy of shareholders?

We have discussed elsewhere in the book the contested nature of stakeholder theory: first, the managerialist viewpoint, involving looking at the problem from the organizational perspective under which stakeholder groups have to be prioritized and managed in line with the objectives of the organization; second, from the societal viewpoint, under which stakeholders see themselves as having a right to hold organizations, especially corporations, accountable for their actions.

Most writing on the subject concentrates on the managerialist stance—something that is hardly surprising in light of the frameworks that we have explored already. But this presents business with another challenge, because for stakeholder engagement to be 'meaningful', companies must look beyond their own carefully defined goals to see how far these goals coincide with societal goals, even as they may appear to the corporation. One way of overcoming this is the kind of voluntary approach found in the AA1000 Series, which puts stakeholder engagement at the heart of accountability through such tools as a framework on how to establish a systematic stakeholder engagement process to ensure transparency and responsiveness to different elements of society (see Chapter 6).

Another way is to make it mandatory for companies to take stakeholder interests into account. In 2000, arising from its Company Law Review, the UK government began developing the Operating and Financial Review (OFR), which, among other things, would require companies to disclose more details of their social and environmental risks and opportunities. The OFR was greeted by some as a major step in encouraging companies to report more fully on such issues, and interested groups from business, government, and civil society became engaged in an extensive dialogue. It was therefore unexpected when, in November 2005, the UK Chancellor announced the OFR was to be scrapped, despite the apparent support of many major companies.

Civil society groups and ethical investors launched a chorus of criticism and began court proceedings that led to new consultations on an alternative to the OFR called the 'Business Review'. Although the Business Review still requires companies to report against non-financial performance indicators, companies do not need to verify statements and it provides less guidance regarding on what companies should report. It is, however, part of the Companies Act 2006, which requires directors to have regard *so far as reasonably practicable* for the interests of employees, communities, and the environment, and to make it easier for shareholders to sue directors for failing to take social and environmental risks into consideration. This Act is the first to put into UK statutory law that directors have secondary duties to stakeholders other than shareholders, but it fails to give stakeholders the right to enforce those duties through legal action.

(Adapted from information available from the UK Department for Trade and Industry, online at www.dti.gov.uk/bbf)

Questions

A central thrust of modern corporate governance thinking is the notion of 'meaningful stakeholder engagement'.

1 What is the distinction between meaningful engagement and stakeholder management?

2 What are the advantages and disadvantages of mandatory and voluntary approaches to encourage stakeholder engagement in terms of effecting change in corporate governance?

3 Does the Companies Act 2006 adequately address the problem of directors having pluralist responsibilities to shareholder and stakeholders?

This is a very limited and functionalist way in which to view accountability. Although it is the basis on which the codes outlined above are based and also the underlying assumption that drives most research in the field of corporate governance, in terms of social responsibility, 'accountability' has been given a much wider meaning that goes beyond the agency notion of directors discharging accountability to shareholders. At the heart of this alternative analysis is the notion that company boards are accountable for the impact of their actions to society in general, as what might be termed the 'universal investor'.

The concept of accountability can be taken even further than that, to include the inequalities of power between groups in the democratic political system.[20] As discussed in Chapter 2, a feature of the modern corporation is how it is often treated as a citizen—but in a democracy, companies do not have a vote. A much-debated way of surmounting this difficulty is the way in which companies influence the political process (e.g. through lobbying and political donations). Yet this influence is not normally readily apparent to voters who may, therefore, vote for a political party without fully understanding how its policies have been reached. This raises questions as to whether a voter's choice is truly 'democratic' if he or she lacks access to all of the information necessary to reach an informed decision.[21] To make informed choices requires all participants to have the same information. It is the hope of many that corporate responsibility reports will provide that information, but, as we have discussed in Chapter 7, these reports have so far been regularly criticized for being partial, incomplete, and lacking a number of features that are necessary if they are to be considered truly 'transparent' and if the companies can be said truly to have discharged their duty of accountability.

CASE STUDY 8.5

Thames Water—corporate governance policy on stakeholder engagement

In common with most utilities companies, Thames Water is mindful of the need to engage with its customers. Already heavily regulated, water companies in the UK are under increased scrutiny as climate change enters the consciousness of consumers, especially when publicity centres on banning the use of hosepipes, on the one hand, and leakage from water pipes on the other.[22]

On its website, under the section on corporate governance, Thames Water explains its policy on stakeholder engagement in these terms:

> We engage with stakeholders in many ways, ranging from one to one meetings with regulators to open days for the public and surveys to measure customer and employee satisfaction. What we learn is used to assess risks to the company, to shape policies and processes, and to inspire new ways of doing business.

The company cites various examples of this:

1 its price review, based on stakeholder consultation and embedded into its five-year business plan;

2 its employee survey to measure employees' opinions, motivation, and satisfaction levels;

3 its annual stakeholder review meeting;

4 its community engagement meetings;

5 its water resource planning workshops, to discuss the company's approach relating to water resource management, and the difficulties and issues that it faces.

(Adapted from Thames Water Plc, www.thameswater.co.uk—accessed 8 May 2007)

Questions

Stakeholder engagement is supposed to improve governance mechanisms.

1 How can companies justify stakeholder engagement in terms other than pure public relations?

2 What steps should companies take to ensure that all relevant stakeholders participate in engagement exercises?

3 How do the specific steps taken by Thames Water impact on its systems of corporate governance?

'Meaningful stakeholder engagement'

As discussion of stakeholder management and partnerships in Chapters 6 and 10 show, engaging with stakeholders is an important part of how corporate responsibility is managed—but there is an enormous difference between taking the views of shareholders into consideration and being accountable to them in any meaningful way (see Case Study 8.4). Writers on the subject of corporate governance, who are prepared to acknowledge the challenges that corporate responsibility poses to the traditional view of corporate governance, still fall short, in most cases, from suggesting that the corporate governance agenda should change, or that corporate responsibility should become the leading driver for change in either the legal or quasi-legal framework for company regulation. Hampel (1998) makes it clear that, while *the directors as a board are responsible for relations with stakeholders; they are accountable to the shareholders* (p 12). Charkham (2005) talks about being accountable to shareholders and *taking into account* the views of stakeholders. Even Kiernan (2005), when calling for *dramatic changes in the thought process and actions of company directors, executives, and institutional investors* (p 216), focuses on the *business case* for altering course, based on assessments of balance sheet, operational, capital cost, and other *risks*.

Companies and corporate governance advisors, such as Hermes, talk of 'meaningful stakeholder engagement' as a way of either making companies aware of, or aware of how to live up to, their social and environmental obligations. We have seen in Case Study 8.3 how Hermes 'engaged' with Premier Oil to bring about a different approach to corporate governance issues, and we are aware of the calls for investors, especially institutions, to exercise their voting rights at general meetings. Before becoming too embroiled in an argument about the effectiveness, or otherwise, of shareholder groups, however, it is wise to consider the issues upon which shareholders are allowed a vote at a general meeting.

Far from being able to influence policy in any meaningful way, especially from a corporate responsibility perspective, holders of shares have very limited rights under the regulations governing company administration in most countries with a liberal economy. Therefore, calls for shareholders to become more active in controlling the policies of a company tend to miss the point. Resolutions on which votes can be cast at general meetings tend to be restricted to rather functional, administrative issues. For example, if we examine the 'Notice of meeting and resolutions to be proposed' at the AGM of BP for 2006, we see that, of the 22 resolutions proposed, none relate to anything to do with the company's brand activities, but instead to things such as adopting the accounts, agreeing directors' remuneration, agreeing the appointment of auditors, re-electing directors, and a couple of resolutions concerning the allotment and buy-back of shares.[23]

From time to time, shareholders call for particular directors to be removed and, in theory, this is possible. But this is not a straightforward thing, and requires close attention to the legal details. In the UK, there are requirements to give notice of such intentions, allowing the company time to develop strategies to thwart any such move. In practice, the appointment and removal of directors is very much a decision of the incumbent board, and the wishes of institutional investors are accommodated within that framework. Certainly, there is a feeling that institutional investors should play a bigger role in this area and few company boards would act against the desires of such organizations, but as far as private shareholders are concerned, their powers to influence corporate behaviour are limited and to be effective would require a level of concerted action that is beyond the will of most investors. These hurdles to changing corporate behaviour are important, given the emphasis that some in the socially responsible investment community attach to proxy voting as an instrument of change (see Chapter 11), and the growing debate over the role of business in society as an evolution of corporate responsibility experience and theory (see Chapter 14). Companies with strong corporate responsibility reputations are by no means immune to charges of abusing governance processes,[24] and, while organizations such as CERES and Corporation 2020 have demonstrated the link between corporate governance and corporate responsibility, for the most part, the gaps between what many stakeholders would consider good governance and the priorities of mainstream corporate responsibility practice ultimately pose a threat to the credibility of corporate responsibility as a concept.

SUMMARY

Increasingly, corporate governance is being linked with concepts of corporate responsibility. In this chapter, we have seen how a framework of corporate governance has developed in the wake of some spectacular corporate failures, which have focused attention on the way in which companies are run both internally and in relation to external auditors. We have noted how, in the discharge of 'accountability', the relationship between the board and the shareholder is enshrined within corporate governance codes, and how writers on the subject support this, almost without question.

This has caused those who see corporate responsibility as the ethical driver of corporate governance mechanisms to call for more rigorous control of the audit firms, which seem easily to escape accountability in cases of corporate collapse. The case studies highlight both these issues and the initiatives that have been made by various organizations on a voluntary basis to improve the way in which companies approach governance issues. As time goes on, it seems likely that more questions will be posed in the arena of corporate governance around ethically based issues that, at present, continue to remain unresolved by the conventional approaches to the subject.

DISCUSSION POINTS

1 Directors of companies owe certain fiduciary duties to the owners of the companies.
  • How far should a 'duty of care' include social and environmental responsibilities?
  • What steps can directors take to demonstrate that they are taking their fiduciary duties seriously in respect of ethical issues?
  • Referring to such work as that of Kent Greenfield (2006) and Corporation 2020, what key features would you want to see in an alternative governance framework?

2 Codes of corporate governance have developed to include supervision of audit procedures.
  • How effective can an audit committee be in supervising the audit procedure within a major corporation?
  • Can part-time non-executive directors ever be adequately effective?
  • Using the example of a FTSE 100 company, how would you modify the workings of the audit committee to incorporate corporate responsibility issues?

3 Most codes of corporate governance stress the importance of shareholders over other stakeholders.

- What groups of stakeholders might have particular interests in issues of corporate governance?
- What is the difference between stakeholder engagement and stakeholder management?
- Imagining that you are an activist shareholder: how would you argue for greater stakeholder representation in the company's governance structures?

4 A number of governance initiatives offer companies the opportunity to adopt voluntarily certain standards of conduct.
   - Can voluntary codes ever be effective?
   - Can a case be made for regulation?
   - From the perspective of a financial journalist ten years from now, write an article about the effect that the EU Accounts Modernization Directive or the UK Companies Act will have had on the way in which companies are governed.

5 Corporate governance frameworks are not drawn up with corporate responsibility as a guiding structure.
   - How would they differ if corporate responsibility were to become a major consideration?
   - What changes would need to be made to the legal framework to incorporate corporate responsibility issues?
   - What examples can you find from around the world (historical and contemporary) of legislative attempts to incorporate corporate responsibility into governance frameworks?

FURTHER READING

VISIT THE WEBSITE for links to useful sources of further information

- Charkham, J, 2005, *Keeping Better Company*, Oxford: Oxford University Press.
  Comparison of governance strategies in five different countries.

- Dallas, G (ed), 2005, *Governance and Risk: An Analytical Handbook for Investors, Managers, Directors and Stakeholders*, New York, NY: McGraw Hill.
  Analysis of the problems of governance from multiple perspectives.

- Mallin, CA, 2004, *Corporate Governance*, New York, NY: Oxford University Press.
  Internationally focused textbook on corporate governance.

- Solomon, J, 2007, *Corporate Governance and Accountability*, Chichester: John Wiley and Son.
  Latest edition of an overview of governance and accountability issues.

ENDNOTES

[1] Most societies, certainly in the developed world, operate under some form of liberal economic democracy. It is so called because, in such societies, citizens are free to pursue their interests without political interference (liberal freedom), able to combine or trade in markets (economic freedom), and free to elect their political leaders (democratic freedom): see, e.g., Held, 1996. An interesting discussion on the fundamental differences between liberal democracy and totalitarian democracy can be found in Talmon, 1985. For a discussion about the failings of liberal economic democracies, see Gray et al., 1996.

[2] This idea that, if we look after returns to shareholders, we are ultimately going to benefit society is explained by what is known, in free-market economic thinking, as the 'trickle-down effect'. The logic is that if our capital markets are information efficient, we should achieve the highest degree

of allocative efficiency, which should ensure optimal economic growth and, therefore, maximum economic well-being and social welfare: Gray, 1996.

[3] This theory is primarily associated with Jensen and Meckling's (1976) exposition of the inter-relationship among owners, agents, and ownership structure.

[4] Jensen and Meckling, 1976.

[5] Shleifer and Vishney, 1997.

[6] See, e.g., Jensen, 2001.

[7] www.icgn.org.

[8] Jones and Pollitt, 2004.

[9] For example, despite the furore following the Maxwell and BCCI scandals, criticism of company boards continued, as directors played 'follow my leader' in awarding themselves pay increases far greater than the levels awarded to their staff. The governor of the Bank of England was awarded a pay rise of 17 per cent; the CEO of British Telecom received 43 per cent; the CEO of National Power received 58 per cent; the boss of British Gas received 66 per cent: *Hansard*, 27 June 1991.

[10] This change took effect on 1 May 2000, because criticism had also been levelled at the system of supervision within the financial services sector.

[11] Combined Code, 1998.

[12] Turnbull, 1999.

[13] Willett and Page, 1996.

[14] Lord Wakeham, former UK Energy Minister and who was party to the decision to allow Enron to build England's largest power plant in Teesside, was chair of the audit committee. He received fees as a consultant and as a non-executive director at the same time: *The Guardian*, 14 February 2003.

[15] Smith, 2003b, p 46.

[16] Combined Code, 2003.

[17] See www.ecgi.org/codes.

[18] For a full list of corporate governance codes by nationality, see www.ecgi.org/**codes**.

[19] See, e.g., Jensen and Meckling, 1976; Fama, 1980.

[20] 'Pluralism' suggests a society made up of different groups of people, with sometimes complementary and sometimes competing interests, but with equal power to influence opinion. 'Neo-pluralism' recognizes that power is not equally shared and that some groups, and individuals, exert undue influence on policy. For further discussion of this topic, see Gray et al., 1996.

[21] An emerging example of this is how global climate change is interacting with government towards the adoption of policies designed to deal with the threat. Already, we see nuclear energy entering the electricity-generating debate in the UK and senior government ministers beginning to suggest it as an option to meet emissions targets under the Kyoto Protocol: see *The Guardian*, 14 June 2006.

[22] For full reports regarding leakage targets and performance, see www.ofwat.gov.uk.

[23] See www.bp.com.

[24] See, e.g., the experience of companies such as Enron and Home Depot under CEO Bob Nardelli.

9

Sustainable development

Chapter overview

In this chapter, we grapple with the concept of 'sustainable development', tracking its rising importance in the business context, as global warming and climate change are recognized as business issues. In particular, we will:

- consider what is meant by the term 'sustainable development';

- examine the background to the various initiatives that resulted in the Brundtland Commission Report in 1987;

- assess the evidence provided by scientific reports into issues of climate change;

- identify the challenges that sustainable development poses for 'business as usual';

- review research into new models of sustainable business;

- examine the capital market implications of sustainable development.

Main topics

■ Key terms

Brundtland Commission

Climate change

Financing sustainability

Global warming

Sustainable development

■ Online resources

- Suggested additional materials on sustainability-related issues

- Exercises and discussion topics for students

- Emerging sustainability initiatives

- Links to other web-based resources

Meanings of 'sustainability' and 'sustainable development'

A brief examination of how these terms are defined by various entities offers a bewildering series of options to researchers and students of the subject. For example, for BP, sustainability means *'the capacity to endure as a group'*;[1] for United Utilities, *'development that conserves natural resources, protects and enhances the environment, supports the communities we serve, and maintains economic growth'*;[2] for AMEC, *'a commitment to acting responsibly in all that we do, whilst taking into account the concerns of our stakeholders'*.[3] Indeed, it is more than likely that each corporation will have its own way of interpreting what these terms mean in relation to its own commercial activities. As such, each company can identify particular challenges and explain how they are being met effectively, to give assurance to stakeholders and investors alike.

The questions that we wish to address in this chapter, however, relate to how effectively corporations are actually addressing the challenges of sustainable development and to answer these, we must first establish for ourselves what the term means. To that end, we look at the background to the emergence of 'sustainable development' as an idea and the imperatives that led to the definition that was initially ascribed to it. This is because, for many, issues of sustainability lie at the theoretical heart of corporate responsibility: if we ruin our biosphere, as scientific evidence suggests, then all other corporate responsibility initiatives become irrelevant.

The UN World Commission on Economic Development

It is now some twenty years since the World Commission on Economic Development (WCED, more commonly known as the 'Brundtland Commission') deliberated on, inter alia, *'environmental strategies for achieving sustainable development by the year 2000 and beyond'*. Having sat for almost three years, the Commission finally agreed a definition of 'sustainable development', which, although intended more as a challenge to governments, is widely referred to in debates about the role of business (see 'The WCED definition of sustainable development', p 235). This definition requires companies to act in *'three time zones'*:

1 dealing with liabilities arising from a time at which it was acceptable to externalize part of a company's costs onto the environment, people, or future generations;

2 meeting the increased expectations of today's citizens and consumers that the company will be a responsible citizen;

3 taking account of the interests and rights of future generations.[4]

How effective and sufficient has been the progress that has been made since the Brundtland Report was published is a matter of debate. The authors may well have been alarmed had they been able to foresee the escalation of the threat to the environment posed by the effect of industrial activity on climate change. Yet in order to appreciate fully the difficulty of linking corporate activity to notions of sustainable development, it is useful to review the processes that led up to the Report's publication.

The Commission was established by the United Nations in 1983, as the result of a process that can be traced back to the 1960s, at which time environmental concerns became the focus of various pressure groups. Carson's *Silent Spring* (1962) had raised popular consciousness about the dangers of excessive pesticide use, and some progress had been made in improving air and water quality in industrialized areas through 'Clean Air' Acts and similar laws. By the early 1970s, non-government organizations (NGOs), such as Friends of the Earth and Greenpeace, had been established in response to the perceived dangers posed to the planet by such phenomena as nuclear testing and the flooding of vast areas caused by dam building.

The calls for a UN conference on the environment originated from the Swedish ambassador to the UN, however, who was particularly concerned with the effects of 'acid rain' and the general acidification of the water systems in Scandinavia. By the time the conference took place in Stockholm in 1972, the issue of pollution had been widened to include the problems being experienced by developing countries. In 1971, a UN-sponsored meeting of experts in pollution in Founex, Switzerland, had, for the first time, made the explicit connection between industrial development—a perceived desire of developing nations—and environmental degradation, which was seen as the price the nation had to pay. Indeed, environmental protection was seen as one of the limiting factors to development.[5] But, in what some saw as a rather contradictory compromise, this meeting concluded that *'there is no inherent contradiction between environment and development, and that these two concerns should be mutually supportive'*.[6]

This conundrum of whether environmental issues can be tackled without jeopardizing economic growth remains central to sustainable development debates today. For example, the 2007 Stern Review for the UK government argued that not only was there not a contradiction, but that tackling climate change was a prerequisite for long-term prosperity. Certainly, the debate was not settled at Stockholm, but, in many ways, the conference was of greater international significance than is often reported. It involved the participation of not only more than a hundred countries, but of over 400 inter-governmental and NGOs. It ended with the *Stockholm Declaration on Human Environment* and the *Action Plan for the Human Environment*.[7] In sum, it not only raised the environment to national consciousness, but also placed it firmly on the international agenda.[8] Indeed, within twenty years of the end of the conference, over a hundred countries had a government department dealing with the environment. Also, the principles of the sovereign right to exploit national resources and the responsibility for transboundary pollution became explicit, and were subsequently ratified in international agreements such as the UN Framework Convention on Climate Change (see 'Climate change and global warming', p 237). It also led to the establishment of the United Nations Environment Program (UNEP) a year later.[9]

In addition, throughout the 1970s, there was continuing concern about a number of issues that impacted on notions of justice and fairness. The oil supply crisis in 1973 caused oil prices to rise to their highest ever levels (after inflation adjustment). While the debt of developing countries was already rising, this enormous rise in oil prices brought debt to crisis levels, not only because of the increased costs of oil (from which some developing nations benefited), but because lending institutions awash with oil money encouraged such countries to take on more debt than they could afford—something that has only started to be resolved in recent years, with debt relief programmes. Equally, a number of projects designed to aid prosperity in the developing world, particularly huge hydroelectric schemes involving dam building and population relocation, were criticized for their adverse social and environmental ramifications.

In 1982, a special session of UNEP's governing council was convened to discuss Stockholm, *'ten years on'*. It was here that it was decided that something far more radical and wide-ranging was needed to look much further forward. It was felt that, while the world economy had grown considerably, the least developed countries had made little ground and that, in fact, many had seen a fall in per-capita production during the 1980s.[10] It was at this point that the UN convened the World Commission on Environment and Development under Gro Harlem Brundtland,[11] *'at a time of unprecedented growth in pressures on the global environment, with grave predictions about the human future becoming commonplace'*. Its aim was to build a future that would be *'more prosperous, more just, and more secure'*, resting on ecologically sound policies and practices. Even at the outset, however, there was an overwhelming conviction that, in order to attain this goal, *'significant changes in current approaches'*, would have to be confronted, which would involve changes in individual attitudes and lifestyles, and, more crucially, *'changes in certain critical policies . . . and the nature of co-operation between governments, business, science and people'.*[12]

The significantly different approach that this Commission took was to try to conceptualize the relationship between the environment and development, in light of the continuing disparity between levels of prosperity in the Northern and Southern Hemispheres, and the sentiments expressed at Founex in 1971. During its sitting, which lasted two and a half years, a number of unprecedented events occurred: the famine in Ethiopia, which led to the death of over a million people, was broadcast to the West in graphic detail. It led to the 'Band Aid' concerts in London and Philadelphia, transmitted on television non-stop for over 16 hours. The role of the government of Ethiopia, in terms of its willingness and ability to help it own peoples, was questioned amid accusations of corruption and ineptitude.[13]

Additionally, Joe Farman discovered the 'hole' in the ozone layer over Antarctica. The importance of this discovery was not fully understood at the time and was met with some scepticism, because US monitoring satellites did it not immediately corroborate the discovery. Once the monitoring parameters were adjusted to access the data, however, and the phenomena was confirmed, the implications began to impact on policymakers.

As these events unfolded, another tragedy struck: this time, in Bhopal, India, in 1984. In what has become an iconic study of corporate responsibility or irresponsibility, Union Carbide, which had established a site in Bhopal in 1969 to manufacture pesticides, initially imported one of the key ingredients, methyl isocyanate (MIC), before developing its onsite manufacturing facility in 1979. It seems clear from subsequent investigations that the level of maintenance was seriously short of the required standards. In November 1984, a leak of MIC caused the deaths of some 20,000 people. The health of over 120,000 remains affected by the effects of the gas and the site is still not considered safe.[14]

In late April 1986, a nuclear reactor at Chernobyl in the USSR (now Ukraine) exploded and thirty people were killed at the scene. Again, lack of maintenance was cited as the main cause and, like Bhopal, the legacy remains.[15] The developed world did not escape either: in November 1986, agricultural chemicals and solvents leaked into the River Rhine following a chemical spill that was the result of a fire at a factory operated by Sandoz, a pharmaceutical conglomerate, in Basel, Switzerland. The Swiss government failed to act quickly enough to contain the spill, and, as a result, the drinking water of millions of people was affected and countless fish died.

CASE STUDY 9.1

Business and ecosystems

Over the past 50 years human activity has altered ecosystems faster and more extensively than ever before in human history.

This is the main finding of the Millennium Ecosystem Assessment (MA), a four-year, international, scientific appraisal of the condition and trends in the Earth's ecosystems. The MA classified ecosystem services (i.e. the benefits that people and businesses obtain from ecosystems) into four categories, as follows.

1 **Provisioning**
Goods such as food, water, and fibre.

2 **Regulating**
Biophysical processes controlling natural processes.

3 **Cultural**
Those providing recreational, aesthetic, or spiritual values.

4 **Supporting**
Underlying processes, such as soil formation, photosynthesis, and nutrient cycling.

The MA assessed 24 ecosystem services and found the majority to be degraded. The MA also identified six interconnected challenges that are of particular concern for business, because they further affect the integrity of ecosystems and their capacity to provide services:

1 water scarcity;

2 climate change;

3 habitat change;

4 biodiversity loss and invasive species;

5 overexploitation of oceans;

6 nutrient overloading.

The business case

Business and ecosystem services are inextricably linked. Corporations not only affect ecosystem services, but also *rely* upon them. For example, the pharmaceutical industry benefits from nature's provision of genetic resources; agribusiness depends on nature's pollination, pest control, and erosion regulation services; tourism builds on cultural services and the insurance industry benefits from the natural hazard protections that some ecosystems provide. Because of these interrelationships, the trends and six challenges identified by the MA pose significant risks to companies (as well as to their suppliers, customers, and investors) including those of the following types.

1 **Operational**
The increased scarcity and costs of raw materials, such as fresh water.

2 **Disruptions to business operations**
Those caused by natural hazards and higher insurance costs for disasters, such as flooding.

3 **Regulatory**
The emergence of new government policies, such as taxes and moratoria on extractive activities.

4 **Reputational**
Damage to corporate reputation from media and NGO campaigns, shareholder resolutions, and changing customer preferences.

5 **Access to capital**
Restrictions as the financial community adopts more rigorous investment and lending policies.

(www.millenniumassessment.org; Earthwatch et al., 2006)

Questions

The notion of 'risk' is becoming increasingly associated with environmental factors, as policymakers and business leaders alike increasingly recognize the implications of unchecked economic growth.

1 How 'real' do you assess these risks to be?

2 What steps can businesses take to deal with these risks?

3 How can the costs associated with these risks be minimized?

The WCED definition of sustainable development

Some of these events are acknowledged as having had an impact on the Commission,[16] and what emerged was a vision for a sustainable future that was dependent on some fundamental changes to what, in the West, had become an accepted way of life, with standards of living measured in terms of capital accumulation, levels of technological application, travel options, etc. In this vision, the environment was to be placed at the centre of strategic decision making. Rather than being seen as a limiting factor in the cause of continued development, the environment was to be seen as an *'aspect of policy'* if growth was to be sustained.[17] It also articulated notions of justice and fairness to the peoples of the developing world, in terms of fair shares of the world's resources and redistribution of wealth to improve the standards of living of the world's worst off.

> Humanity has the ability to make development sustainable—to ensure that it meets the needs of the present generation without compromising the ability of future generations to meet their own needs. The concept of sustainable development does imply limits—not absolute limits, but limitations imposed by the present state of technology and social organization on environmental resources and by the ability of the biosphere to absorb the effect of human activities.
>
> (WCED, 1987, p 8)

This definition of sustainable development—'*meeting the needs of the present generation without compromising the ability of future generations to meet their own needs*', as it is commonly paraphrased—carries with it a number of implications and, equally, a number of challenges to the business world. In the next sections, we look at this definition, which may, at first glance, seem relatively straightforward, and consider the implications within each part of it. First, we look at the implications of the needs of this generation ('intra-generational' equity) and the needs of this generation, together with those of the next generation ('inter-generational' equity).

Intra-generational equity and inter-generational equity

If we break down the definition and look at its component parts, we begin to unravel the complexity of the idea and to understand why it poses such a potential challenge to present commercial activity. '*Development that meets the needs of the present generation*' suggests fair distributions across the present population of the world, in terms of quality of life, measured, perhaps, by comparative standards of living or benefits from sharing the resources of the planet. There is some evidence that this is not happening at the present time. If we reflect on living standards in terms of Western developed societies and think of the comforts that the majority of the population enjoy, we can still observe that there are levels of inequality many find unacceptable and which, in extreme cases, have resulted in civil unrest.[18] If we then reflect on the developing world, we need little reminding that poverty and famine still blight many peoples of the world. For example, few of over 50 per cent of Africa's 812 million people have access to safe drinking water.[19] It can be argued, therefore, that we are not achieving the first of the tenets of sustainable development and, if that is the case and we are not meeting the needs of the present generation, it is logical to ask if the next generation will fare any better.[20]

The challenge that this offers business is how commercial activity can be organized to address the needs of the peoples of the world, when the theory of the firm suggests that the overriding imperative is to maximize shareholder wealth.[21] We have already discussed the business case for adopting some of the strategies for sustainability (see Chapter 5), but most of that case involves identifying opportunities for business, whether in terms of market niche, efficiencies, or in terms of tackling issues of risk and reputation. Putting environmental or social issues at the heart of business strategy is a more challenging proposition and, if these strategies seriously seek to address social justice issues, then the challenges become even more profound.

Eco-justice and eco-efficiency

Wrapped up in this definition are notions of 'eco-justice' and 'eco-efficiency'. By 'eco-justice', we mean that there is some fairness applied to the distribution of benefits that accrue from the development of the world's resources. To read the history of various European nations' colonial past, for example, is to read how single countries sought to exploit the resources of many other countries without considering the needs of the indigenous peoples. Robins (2006) draws parallels between the companies that led the colonial charge and today's multinationals. He is not alone in believing that commercial exploitation continues to ignore the needs of local communities, and that, often, the profits from such activities are expatriated from the host country, to benefit shareholders and investors who are far removed from the theatres of activity.

Eco-justice is often interpreted as laying the blame at business' door for impacts that may not have been anticipated at the time, or which may not even be substantiated by the evidence. Even when legal decisions, such as those against GE over the Hudson River or those in the case of the *Exxon Valdez*, show that companies are culpable, pointing fingers of blame may not motivate companies to be environmentally responsible. 'Eco-efficiency', on the other hand, is a concept that has an appeal to the commercially minded. The idea that one should 'get more from less' is the sort of challenge to which a company can rise and there is ample evidence that industrial processes are becoming more efficient. As noted in Chapter 5, in discussion of the business case, it is in this area that we see most innovation. There are good commercial reasons for this, but there are also drivers from outside the economic sphere. Most of these stem from an increasing recognition that industrial activity poses specific threats to the world's environmental health.

It is, however, important not to conflate notions of eco-efficiency with those of sustainable development. Eco-efficiency may well become the goal of each commercial entity, but, in itself, this might not prevent overall world resources from becoming depleted. So far, we have reviewed the development and challenges of sustainable development in terms of the Brundtland Commission's remit; we now move on to look at what has now been identified as the greatest threat to modern society—climate change.

Climate change and global warming

The notion that the planet has a finite capability to absorb or to process the results of human activity is the underlying theory of sustainable development, yet, even in the mid-1980s, the scientific basis for concern was only just emerging. Indeed, between 1940 and 1970, as the mean worldwide temperature cooled by 0.2°C, so interest in the phenomena of 'greenhouse' effects waned from what had previously been a passing interest. Following the first World Climate Conference in Geneva in 1979—a predominantly scientific gathering, sponsored by the World Meteorological Organization (WMO)—a call was put out to governments to *'foresee and prevent potential man-made changes in climate'*.[22] The first serious concerns were raised in 1985, when UNEP and WMO jointly organized a scientific conference in Villach, Austria. Here, predictions were made of the possibility of global temperature rises that would be greater than those in all history and of consequent sea level rises of over 1 metre by 2050.[23] In addition, two years later, UNEP published a further report, *Environmental Perspectives to the Year 2000 and Beyond*, which provided a framework within which to operationalize the findings of the Brundtland Commission, and which led the UN General Assembly to convene its Conference on Environment and Development (UNCED), widely known as the 'Earth Summit', held in Rio in June 1992.

Before the Earth Summit, the UN had begun to frame a document for ratification at Rio. The UN Framework Convention on Climate Change (UNFCCC) was adopted by the UN in 1992 and became open for member-country signature at Rio. By June 1993, it had received 166 signatures. It has since been ratified by 189 states and by the European Union as a bloc.[24] But the scepticism held in some quarters on the science of climate change is clear in the wording of the original document, under which a precautionary approach is urged *'in the absence of scientific certainty'*. A tension was developing within governments between appearing to support calls for a cut in emissions, on the one hand, and the political imperative of doing nothing to threaten economic growth within their own economies.

In response to this political impasse, in 1997, the UNFCCC held a summit in Kyoto to try to bind countries into a legally binding Protocol aimed at reducing greenhouse gas emissions. The Kyoto Protocol, as it became known, which came into force in 2005, was to be remembered as much for those who refused to ratify the agreement as for the measures that were proposed. Notably, the USA would not sign, for fear of harming its own economic growth prospects, and this stance was also adopted by Australia, Japan, China, South Korea, and India.[25] This position became entrenched by these countries with the formation of the Asia–Pacific Partnership on Clean Development and Climate, also known as 'AP6'. This non-treaty pact is designed to allow foreign, environment and energy ministers from partner countries to collaborate to develop technology designed to reduce emissions. Unlike the Kyoto Protocol, which imposes limits on emissions, this agreement allows the member countries to set their own goals.[26]

Yet, while all of this political activity was going on, more and more conclusive evidence was emerging about the inevitability and immediacy of the threats from global warming and climate change. Throughout 2005 and into 2006, there appeared to be news, on an almost daily basis, of new evidence of the science, or of the likely effects of climate change. Centres of research, such as the Hadley Centre operated by the UK Meteorological Office and the Tyndall Centre for Climate Change, have each published numerous reports on the subject and countless articles have been published in scientific journals such as *Science* and *Nature*. In 2007, scientists on the UN Intergovernmental Panel on Climate Change (IPCC) gave their strongest statement yet that not only is global warming happening, but that it is primarily as a result of human activity.[27] What stands out from the IPCC's fourth assessment is the growing sophistication of the science behind our understanding of climate change. While some in business have long taken climate change seriously, some industries (notably, coal, oil, and gas companies associated with high carbon dioxide emissions), have backed climate change sceptics, not least with funding. Since BP broke ranks with the Global Climate Coalition (an oil-industry group that had sought to discredit climate change science) in 1997, however, the business community as a whole has become split: sometimes castigated, as in ExxonMobil's backing of the American Enterprise Institute's offer of prize money to scientists able to refute the IPCC's findings, and sometimes lauded, as in Wal-Mart's commitment to taking non-renewable energy off its shelves.[28]

Scientific enquiry has taken many forms, from the examination of ice cores and ancient coral, to thermal photography and the mapping of flood levels. Most of these studies require some form of interpretation, which is often contested by the 'climate change deniers', but the fact that the three warmest years on record have occurred since 1998—and that 19 of the warmest 20 on record have occurred since 1980—should be compelling for most.

CASE STUDY 9.2

The Stern Review

In October 2006, Sir Nicholas Stern, head of the UK government Economics Service and adviser to the UK government on the economics of climate change and development, presented his report to the Prime Minister and the Chancellor of the Exchequer on the *Economics of Climate Change*. His findings include the following.

1 The scientific evidence is now overwhelming: climate change presents very serious global risks and it demands an urgent global response.

2 The scientific evidence points to increasing risks of serious, irreversible impacts from climate change associated with business-as-usual (BAU) paths for emissions.

3 Climate change threatens the basic elements of life for people around the world: access to water, food production, health, and use of land and the environment.

4 The damages from climate change will accelerate as the world gets warmer.

5 The impacts of climate change are not evenly distributed—the poorest countries and people will suffer earliest and most—and if, and when, the damages appear, it will be too late to reverse the process. Thus we are forced to look a long way ahead.

6 Climate change may initially have small positive effects for a few developed countries, but the much higher temperature increases that are expected by the mid- to late twenty-first century under BAU scenarios are likely to be very damaging.

7 Emissions have been, and continue to be, driven by economic growth; yet stabilization of greenhouse gas concentrations in the atmosphere is feasible and consistent with continued growth.

8 Establishing a carbon price—through tax, trading, or regulation—is an essential foundation for climate change policy.

(Adapted from Stern, 2007)

Questions

The Stern Review's findings suggest that developed countries will not suffer as much as developing countries.

1 Why might this be and what are the responsibilities of the developed world in relation to the developing world?

2 What difference can taxation make to climate change?

3 What are the challenges in turning the recommendations of the Stern Report into reality?

The challenge to business

We opened this chapter with examples of how three businesses approached the challenges of sustainability. To our knowledge, no business has ever announced that it is unsustainable; conversely, there is little evidence that any major corporation is truly sustainable. Investors require returns on their investment and returns are obtained by growing the profits of the business. The challenge is that growth of the business has invariably meant increasing resource usage, which both depletes the earth's stock of resources and leads to increased emissions.

Traditionally, the government might have controlled growth through regulation, but in today's climate of neoliberal capitalism, command-and-control regulation has gone out of favour. Governments might consider initiatives such as insuring risk, taxation, or schemes of emissions trading, but business is, largely, left to manage these challenges itself—something to which some companies have started to draw politicians' attention, through initiatives such as the European Corporate Leaders Group on Climate Change. Furthermore, it can be argued that business has been proactive in initiatives aimed at avoiding regulation, by either demonstrating that it is behaving responsibly,[29] or sponsoring activities that attempt to play down some of the perceived threats of climate change and other environmental issues.[30]

As with the business case for adopting a corporate responsibility agenda (see Chapter 5), however, many perceive that these challenges are bound together with opportunities to engage with new technologies, and with new approaches to deliver alternative products and processes. To the fore in this endeavour is the World Business Council for Sustainable Development (WBCSD), stressing that the opportunities to open new markets, develop new businesses, and access new revenue streams mean that companies should not shirk the challenges that sustainable development presents. New initiatives, involving business leaders, are encouraging those most closely involved in the business debate to offer solutions to these challenges. Indeed, in the recent publication by the Tomorrow's Leaders Group of the WBCSD, when considering the *'role of business in tomorrow's society'*, there are a number of objectives for business going forward. These include developing new businesses and new technologies, setting global benchmarks and new strategies, and offering greater opportunity to larger sections of world communities.[31]

The Tomorrow's Leaders Group accepts what, for some, remains a contentious idea: that sustainability can be achieved without compromising economic growth. As noted earlier, the Stern Review goes further and argues that stabilizing climate change is actually essential for economic growth. There are attractive features to sustainability-led growth (e.g. the opportunities for technological innovation and new markets), but, as Stern also recognizes, government may well have to steer business in new directions and towards adopting new business models.

CASE STUDY 9.3

The aviation industry and climate change

Householders, motorists, and businesses will have to reduce their carbon dioxide emissions to zero in order to accommodate the growth in the aviation industry if government climate change targets for 2050 are to be achieved. Even if the growth were to be halved, the rest of the economy would need to achieve cuts beyond the targets set for 2050, according to the Tyndall Centre for Climate Change Research, requiring the rest of the economy to cut carbon dioxide far beyond government targets. Kevin Anderson, who led the research, says:

> If the UK government does not curb aviation growth, all other sectors of the economy will eventually be forced to become carbon neutral. It will undermine the international competitiveness of UK industry.

Aviation is especially polluting, because planes burn vast amounts of kerosene fuel at high altitudes. The rapid growth of the industry stems from falling ticket prices and increasing passenger demand, and some predict that UK passenger numbers alone will more than double, from 180 million to 475 million, over the next 25 years.

(Tyndall Centre for Climate Change, 2005; news.bbc.co.uk—accessed 19 February 2007)

Questions

Inexpensive air travel has been a growing trend over the last few years.

1 How do you think the airline industry might respond to its responsibilities as far as global warming is concerned?

2 What role should government play in mediating this process?

3 What are the likely implications for cheap airline travel?

New models of sustainable business

In light of the challenges that sustainable development poses for business, researchers have been working to develop enterprise models that take account of the parameters of sustainable development. Some have looked at the capitalist business model to see if it can be adapted to meet these challenges; others have sought to develop new models. Writing on the theory behind such new models, Birkin (2000) calls for managers to adopt a different ontology,[32] recognizing the '*inter-connectedness*' of corporate decision making. This may be seen as a development of, or an alternative to, the '*systems thinking*', offered by Gray (2002a) as his explanation of a similar phenomena: that of reductionism, under which the focus is on a specific aspect of a system, rather than on the system itself.[33]

What both authors call for is a recognition that concentration on specific issues may not be helpful if sustainability is the goal and that wider consequences of specific actions need a much more considered response. Birkin developed his thesis by arguing for the consideration of '*relationships*' within models of business and, in particular, of the relationships among resource flows, resource flow impacts, stakeholder analysis, and carrying capacity assessments.[34] In developing this model of sustainable business, Birkin suggests that only by examining the interaction among these elements will managers fully appreciate the impacts of their actions and the necessary changes that have to be faced to become sustainable.

This idea of embedding sustainability into business strategy is discussed further in Chapter 14. Others have suggested a fundamentally different approach to this form of modelling, by thinking outside the conventional financial model. Traditionally, the 'bottom line' refers to the profit that a company makes in financial terms; 'capital' means financial capital to most people. But if we think of capital in wider terms that encompass the different aspects of resource application, then we can develop different business models (see Case Study 9.4).

CASE STUDY 9.4

The 'five capitals' model

Forum for the Future, the sustainable development NGO, believes that a sustainable future can be achieved, but that:

> We are facing a sustainability crisis because we're consuming our stocks of natural, human and social capital faster than they are being produced. Unless we control the rate of this consumption, we can't sustain these vital stocks in the long-term . . . but for this to happen, it is the responsibility of every organization, business or otherwise, to manage these capital assets sustainably.

Building on models from the field of international development, Forum suggests that there are five types of sustainable capital from which we derive the goods and services that we need to improve the quality of our lives:

1 Natural capital

Any stock or flow of energy and material that produces goods and services. It includes:

(a) *resources*—i.e. renewable and non-renewable materials;

(b) *sinks*—that absorb, neutralize, or recycle wastes;

(c) *processes*—i.e.climate regulation.

Natural capital is the basis not only of production, but also of life itself.

2 Human capital

This consists of people's health, knowledge, skills, and motivation. All of these things are needed for productive work. Enhancing human capital through education and training is central to a flourishing economy.

3 Social capital

This concerns the institutions that help us to maintain and develop human capital in partnership with others: for example, families, communities, businesses, trade unions, schools, and voluntary organizations.

4 Manufactured capital

This comprises material goods or fixed assets, which contribute to the production process rather than being the output itself: for example, tools, machines, and buildings.

5 Financial capital

This type of capital plays an important role in our economy, enabling the other types of capital to be owned and traded. But, unlike the other types, it has no real value in itself and is representative only of natural, human, social, or manufactured capital: for example, shares, bonds, or banknotes.

According to Forum for the Future:

> Sustainable development is the best way to manage these capital assets in the long-term. It is a dynamic process through which organizations can begin to achieve a balance between their environmental, social and economic activities.

> (www.forumforthefuture.org.uk; BEP, undated; Scoones, 1998)

Questions

Concepts of different forms of capital allow businesses to consider new ways of appraising their activities and developing their activities in a more responsible way.

1 How likely is it that these models will be adapted to mainstream corporate life?

2 Is there any merit in further developing these concepts?

3 As an alternative, how might the traditional business model be adapted?

Taking this idea of different kinds of capital, some researchers have constructed new models of business that they employ to decide, *ex ante*, whether or not a business is sustainable. Pioneering work in this field has been conducted with BP, and by Bebbington (2001a) and Baxter et al. (2004), who, in developing a sustainability assessment model, have advanced the notions of 'full cost accounting' and offer additional possibilities in terms of investment appraisal.[35] Briefly, a sustainability assessment model is applied to assess the social, economic, resource, and environmental impacts of a project over its life cycle, and then to reduce these impacts into a cash–value measurement. These data are then used in the project investment appraisal. This model tracks the internal and external effects of the proposed investment, and allows a much more rounded appraisal to be made than that of traditional accounting techniques such as net present value or internal rate of return, which focus purely on financial issues.

Capital markets and sustainable development

Despite these initiatives to find new models of sustainable business, there are those who believe that the most fundamental challenge to sustainable practices is that posed by the way in which capital markets reward and punish participants. Although the tension between sustainability and the capital market has been acknowledged for some time, the debate was widened in the 1990s with the work of Stephan Schmidheiny, *Changing Course* (1992), and Schmidheiny with Federico Zorraquin, *Financing Change* (1996). Both of these authors are industrialists who depend upon the capital market system for their business success, yet have tackled problematic questions regarding the role that capital market activity might play in either helping or hindering the development of sustainable practices.

Elsewhere in this book, we have looked at some of the mechanisms that govern the ways in which companies operate (see Chapters 7 and 8), but it might be useful to review briefly the mechanisms of the capital market system, to illustrate the dilemmas that they reveal.

First and foremost, capital markets transfer funds from those who save to those who wish to apply these funds to means of producing goods or services. In this process is achieved a separation of ownership from control (see Chapter 8). In traditional business models, this equation is not seen as problematic: savers expect a return on their savings by way of an annual dividend, or by a capital gain when they sell the shares, or both. Businesses aim to operate at a level that gives a return in excess of this 'cost of capital' and which allows them to invest in new projects, as well as giving a return to shareholders. The problem, in relation to the connection between capital market investment practices and sustainable development, arises in the way in which companies are rewarded, or punished, by the market and the way in which financial intermediaries are rewarded for their expertise in investment.

Signals to the market

It is acknowledged in the finance literature that markets respond to 'signals'. These signals are interpreted from information about company activity that is obtained from diverse sources. For example, if a company is thought to be underperforming, a good signal to the market might be an announcement of a change in top management; reducing declared dividends is seen as a bad signal. These signals are interpreted by financial analysts in terms of potential future cash flows and are reflected in patterns of investment, or disinvestment. They contribute to some of the changes that we witness in share price movements over time. Traditionally, the information that tends to move share prices is normally financial, relating to earnings forecasts, dividend policy, investment policy, etc. Indeed, the nature of the investments that a company makes in the course of its operations is central to the way in which the future performance of a company may be assessed.

These strategies are disclosed in the course of both formal and informal discussions with analysts, and the concern here is that the fear of communicating the wrong signal may act to inhibit companies from undertaking innovative or experimental investments, which may be necessary if a sustainable development agenda is to be adopted.[36]

Schmidheiny and Zorraquin (1996) list several 'worrying' assumptions about sustainable development that might convey the wrong signal to markets. They include the facts that:

- there is a common perception that sustainability requires longer-term investments, where pay-back times might not fall in the 'good signal' time span;
- a concerted effort to innovate may reduce present earnings;
- for global companies, investment in sustainable development initiatives in developing countries bring with it additional high risk premiums; and
- accounting and reporting systems do not adequately reflect risks and opportunities.

(p 8)

Another issue that companies try to avoid signalling to the market is the threat of regulation. The idea that governments are about to intervene in a particular sector creates uncertainty, which is interpreted as a bad signal. This helps to explain why companies combine to form strong associations aimed at helping to persuade governments that there is no need to regulate. If they can demonstrate that they are handling thorny issues, the hope is that governments will accept that industry is capable of regulating itself. The World Business Council for Sustainable Development is one such organization, boasting a large number of major corporations worldwide within its membership. The Global Reporting Initiative is another example and adoption of its guidelines (see Chapter 6) has been used to demonstrate that serious efforts are being made to address previously perceived reporting imperfections. These examples and countless others, at professional, industry, national, or supranational levels, are all designed to counter the possibility of the adverse market effect of announcements of regulation.

Those in favour of a more regulated approach, however, are somewhat dismayed at the behaviour of the market in this respect, because regulation only represents a level of activity beyond which behaviour is so unacceptable that it has to be stopped. It is not necessarily as good as we might want it to be, but, ironically, operating to the minimum standards allowed by law might be seen by the market as a positive signal. It also gives rise to the acronyms that are taken as a guide to much commercial activity in the area of environmental management systems, such as 'BATNEEC' and 'CATNIP'.[37]

The question is, what will it take for the market to reward behaviour that goes beyond regulation, even if that involves expenditure that might have an adverse impact on short-term earnings? At what stage, for example, might markets see initiatives such as switching away from biomass back to coal in the production of electricity as a bad signal?[38]

Rewarding financial intermediaries

Linked to the above discussion is the nature of the reward structure to financial market participants. Those involved in the investment process as financial intermediaries work within a bonus system, which can represent a large percentage of an individual's salary and which, collectively in the City of London in 2006, amounted to some £8bn,[39] a sum of money that almost equates to the GDP of Uruguay.[40] One can speculate whether these intermediaries disregard longer-term investment opportunities in favour of the short-term returns on which their remuneration depends. Although climate change is grabbing investors' attention, overall, there is limited evidence for concluding that capital market activity will change in response to what some see as the demands of sustainable development. As Chuck Prince, Citigroup CEO, has put it: *'The investment community has no sense of social responsibility. And when I say "no sense," I can't use smaller words than that.'*[41]

In Joel Barkan's documentary film (2004), *The Corporation*, a Wall Street trader, Carlton Brown, enthuses over the profits made from trading in gold on 11 September 2001, as the twin towers turned to dust. When discussing the possibility of disease affecting the population numbers of pigs, Brown talks of the opportunities that the news presents: *'It's almost ludicrous not to jump on board.'* Other interviewees talk of the market as *'amoral'*, suggesting that issues of morality and ethics should have been negotiated before the trading process began—that is, that it is not the trader's job to think about morality. These are important questions that are not fully acknowledged by market participants. There is nothing in corporate governance guidelines that gives companies any direction or reassurance should they consider any such strategy and shareholder return remains the main driver of market activity.

There are, however, attempts to engage analysts in considering social and environmental impacts. A 2006 survey of analysts found no innate hostility to sustainability, but a dearth of tools with which to incorporate the issue into assessments.[42] The CFA has recently included governance in its exams for the first time and some approaches pioneered by the socially responsible investment community are starting to be noticed by the investment mainstream (see Chapter 11). The Enhanced Analytics Initiative, the UN Principles for Responsible Investment, the London Accord, and the Marathon Club, which all have the backing of major financial institutions, are working in different ways to get financial intermediaries to take sustainability seriously (see Case Study 9.5). These emergent trends are discussed further in Chapter 14.

CASE STUDY 9.5

Engaging the investment community in sustainability

Sections of the investment community have been experimenting with different initiatives to raise the profile of sustainability among investors and analysts. The Marathon Club is a group of institutional investors looking at ways in which to encourage investment for the long term. The London Accord is intended to study how climate change can be brought into financial decision-making analysis. The Enhanced Analytics Initiative (EAI) puts the focus on brokers incorporating non-financial issues into their research. The members of EAI—including BNP Paribas, USS, Investec, and Hermes—have agreed to spend 5 per cent of their brokerage fees with firms that focus on extra-financial indicators. The United Nations' Principles for Responsible Investing (PRI) seek to have sustainable development included in conventional investment. The PRI's backers are investors that are responsible for 10 per cent of global capital or more than $4,000bn of assets, including Dresdner, Citigroup, Goldman Sachs, and UBS. By signing up to the PRI, they commit to integrating environmental, social, and governance issues into conventional investment analysis, to being active, responsible owners by promoting good corporate practice in these areas, and to reporting transparently on what actions have been taken in this area.

(www.enhancedanalytics.com; www.unpri.org; www.marathonclub.co.uk—
all accessed 2 February 2007)

Questions

Engaging with the capital markets has become an increasingly important part of sustainable development.

1 What is the significance of the initiatives outlined in this case study?

2 Is any one of these initiatives especially important?

3 Why have analysts, in particular, been singled out as needing to understand sustainable development?

SUMMARY

This chapter began and ended with looking at how companies portray their activities in terms of sustainability. In between, we examined how concepts of sustainable development emerged and were defined, how that definition conceals subtle notions of equity and fairness, and how these notions present challenges to the 'business as usual' model of corporate behaviour. Although there are broadly accepted definitions of sustainable development, individual companies still choose to define the concept in their own ways. As will be discussed in relation to the impact of corporate responsibility (see Chapter 12), companies are, at best, only starting to understand that they must take responsibility for some of their most significant sustainability consequences. This is evident in the sustainability reports that many companies are producing and, as we have illustrated, some companies approach this task by redefining sustainable development in ways that can be addressed while leaving out the issues that present the greatest challenges. This also relates to the accountability framework within which reporting sits (see Chapter 7).

If, initially, such reports were dismissed as a public relations exercise, the seriousness with which issues such as climate change and sustainable energy are being taken by both governments and the private sector strongly suggests that sustainability will become an increasingly important part of the business agenda. In some ways, this makes getting the management and reporting frameworks right even more important. As Fred Pearce wrote in the *New Scientist*: '*Climate change is the most crucial scientific question of the twenty-first century. The winning side will shape economic, political and technological development for years, even centuries.*'[43] This and other aspects of sustainable development, such as demographic change, may also be among the most crucial business questions and with equally significant prizes at stake. Although questions remain about the exact science of climate change (as they do in relation to most areas of scientific enquiry), there is an overwhelming consensus—and one that is increasingly endorsed by business—that it poses a real risk and is related to human activity.[44] As the different dimensions of sustainable development become more apparent in everyday life, so people will turn to major institutions to take a lead in controlling harmful emissions. Business is clearly one such institution and its role is likely to become more prominent, not least because the conventional command-and-control regulatory model of government is being tested by the social and political realities of globalization.

DISCUSSION POINTS

1   Some believe that business can only go so far in addressing sustainable development without the support of other members of society.
    - Do markets incentivize short-term and continued-cost externalization of the kind cited as a threat to sustainable development?
    - Are consumers motivated as much by encouraging good performance in sustainability as they are by punishing poor performance?
    - Would NGOs be likely to criticize a company more or less if it were to take on sustainable development issues?

2   One of the most controversial areas is whether economic growth and sustainable development are compatible.
    - Is the Stern Review right to say that sustainable development is essential for economic growth?
    - Is it possible to run a business that will grow within the limits of the earth's ecosystem?
    - Is it possible to grow a business while shrinking its environmental footprint?

3   The accountancy profession is seen by some as an essential element in encouraging companies to tackle sustainable development.
    - What can the accountancy profession bring to sustainable development that will help companies to change their business models, enabling them to operate with less of an environmental impact?
    - To what extent does the accountancy profession lock companies into outdated business models?
    - What can it do to remove the barriers to client change?

4   In the 1970s and 1980s, there were many dire predictions of ecological collapse that did not materialize, and many natural systems have proved to be less fragile and faster to mend than once thought.
    - What ecosystem services was it feared were being irresolvably degraded in that era?
    - Does the fact some predictions were not borne out undermine or strengthen current arguments about climate change and other aspects of sustainable development?
    - Which industries have most to win, or lose, from adopting a 'business as usual' attitude to sustainable development?

5   Climate change is a very important and high-profile aspect of sustainable development, but it is not the only one.
    - About which other aspects of sustainable development is it important for business to be thinking?
    - Are there contradictions and dichotomies between some of these various aspects?
    - Which of these aspects are beyond the concerns of corporate responsibility at the present time?

VISIT THE WEBSITE
for links to useful sources of further information

FURTHER READING

- Elkington, J, 1998, *Cannibals With Forks: The Triple Bottom Line of 21st Century Business*, Gabriola Island, BC/Stony Creek, CT: New Society Publishers.
  Influential introduction to the case for considering social, economic, and environmental added value.

- Gore, A, 2006, *An Inconvenient Truth*, London: Bloomsbury Publishing.
  The book accompanying the Oscar-winning film about the importance of climate change.

- Hawken, P, 1993, *The Ecology of Commerce: A Declaration of Sustainability*, New York, NY: Harper Business.
  Arguments for the importance of sustainability to business.

- Henriques, A and Richardson, JA, 2004, *The Triple Bottom Line: Does It All Add Up? Assessing the Sustainability of Business and CSR*, London: Earthscan.
  Critical analysis of triple bottom-line theory and practice.

- Schmidheiny, S and Zorraquin, F, 1996, *Financing Change: The Financial Community, Eco-Efficiency, and Sustainable Development*, Cambridge, MA: MIT Press.
  Influential early book by two business leaders on the role of the finance industry in sustainability.

- Welford, R, 1995, *Environmental Strategy and Sustainable Development: The Corporate Challenge for the 21st Century*, London: Routledge.
  Theoretical analysis of the significance of environmental management and sustainability to corporations.

ENDNOTES

1 www.bp.com.

2 United Utilities Sustainable Development Policy, 2006, online at www.unitedutilities.com.

3 www.amec.com.

4 BEP, undated.

5 Grubb et al., 1993.

6 Tobin, 1997; Engfeldt, 2002.

7 www.unep.org

8 It also signified a triumph for the efforts of an individual who was to rise to considerable prominence in the UN environmental initiatives. Maurice Strong was appointed Secretary-General of the Stockholm Conference, because it was felt that he had the necessary connections to get both the developing and developed nations to cooperate. There is also evidence that it was Strong's personal intervention that led to China's participation.

9 The headquarters of UNEP is in Nairobi and its first Executive Director was Strong.

10 Tolba and El-Kholy, 1992.

11 Again, Strong was one of the Commissioners.

12 WCED, 1987, p 356.

13 Since then and despite massive amounts of aid raised in the West for the starving of Africa, famines still occur and continuing allegations of malpractice are laid at the feet of host governments.

[14] There are many websites that chronicle the sad tale of Bhopal and the tragedy surrounding those affected.

[15] Incidences of thyroid cancer in children of up to 15 years old increased tenfold between 1986 and 1997, and it is feared that about 2,500 people have died as the direct consequence of the radiation leak.

[16] Tolba and El-Kholy, 1992.

[17] Grubb et al., 1993.

[18] *The Times*, 4 November 2005, reported that: '*The poor suburbs of Paris were set ablaze in the worst of eight consecutive nights of rioting, with 500 cars torched and a gym and primary school razed.*' The report continued: '*Unemployment among French men aged 15 to 24 has risen from 15 per cent four years ago to more than 22 per cent. It is thought to be as high as 30–40 per cent among young second- and third-generation immigrants in poorer high-rise suburbs.*'

[19] UNEP, see **www.unep.org**.

[20] See, e.g., Gray, 1992; Hawken, 1993; Welford, 1995; Daly, 1996; Tobin, 1997; Elkington, 1998; Birkin, 2000; Gray and Bebbington, 2000; Suranyi, 2000; Bebbington, 2001b; Epstein and Roy, 2001; Gray, 2002b; Gray and Collison, 2003; Bebbington et al.; 2004; Gray, 2006b.

[21] See; e.g. Jensen and Meckling, 1976.

[22] WMO, 1979.

[23] UNEP, 1987.

[24] See **unfccc.int/kyoto_protocol**.

[25] The alignment in policy between the government of a country and the economic desires of its most significant corporations is nothing new, but, because the size of some commercial enterprises now dwarfs the GDP of many small nations, the issue has attracted widespread popular interest in the last few years.

[26] At the time of writing, a new US stance on climate change has just been announced at the 2007 G8 government meeting.

[27] IPCC, 2007.

[28] See **www.walmartfacts.com**.

[29] See, e.g., **www.csr.org**.

[30] See, e.g., **www.exxonsecrets.org**.

[31] See, e.g., Vigar, 2006.

[32] 'Ontology' refers to our perception of reality, the way in which we 'view the world'. Instead of seeing the world as a myriad of discrete issues, each to be managed on its own, Birkin, 2000, calls for managers to adopt an '*ontology of interconnected events*', within which the consequence of one action will have an effect on others.

[33] This concept is discussed in more detail in Chapter 8, along with the roots of social and environmental accounting.

[34] Birkin, 2000, pp 303–4.

[35] For further information on full cost accounting, see Bebbington, 2001b.

[36] See, e.g., Murray et al., 2006.

[37] BATNEEC: 'Best Available Technology Not Entailing Excessive Cost'; CATNIP: 'Currently Available Technology Not Involving Prosecution'.

[38] See *The Guardian*, 13 September 2006.

[39] *The Guardian*, 20 November 2006.

[40] www.worldbank.org

[41] Blowfield and Googins, 2007, p 23.

[42] Hummels, GJA and Wood, D. 2005, *Knowing the Price, but also the Value? Financial Analysts on Social, Ethical and Environmental Information*. Neyenrode Business Universiteit and Boston College.

[43] environment.newscientist.com—accessed 7 February 2007.

[44] For those who remain sceptical, a very accessible summary of the latest science and predictions is available in Al Gore's book and film, *An Inconvenient Truth*, 2006, in addition to the sources already cited in this chapter.

10

Stakeholder partnerships

Chapter overview

In this chapter, we explore the significance of stakeholders and partnerships, and how they relate to the way in which corporate responsibility is perceived and managed by different sectors of society. In particular, we will:

- identify the different types of stakeholder and discuss difficulties with the 'stakeholder' concept;

- explore the notion of stakeholder partnerships and their popularity;

- examine the aims, motivations, and limitations of partnerships;

- identify the different types of partnership;

- review experiences of managing partnerships;

- assess the UN Global Compact as an example of an international, multi-stakeholder partnership.

Main topics

■ **Key terms**

Civil society

Government

Partnership

Stakeholder

State

UN Global Compact

■ **Online resources**

• Suggested additional case studies of real-life partnerships

• Exercises and discussion topics for students

• Further discussion and materials on the challenges of implementing partnerships

• Links to other web-based resources

Stakeholders

The theme of this chapter is partnerships, as one way in which to implement corporate responsibility. Such partnerships occur between stakeholders, a conceptual framework for understanding society that has been touched on in various sections of this book. In fact, for some, the relationship between companies and their stakeholders establishes the very context of doing business in the modern world. One of the challenges in stakeholder engagement as management practice (see Chapter 6) is to understand the differing value propositions of the various stakeholders. Certainly, to understand corporate responsibility partnerships, we need to know something of the nature of the different stakeholder groups. In the past, discussions of stakeholder categorization focused on the distinct duties or obligations that companies have to their shareholders, employees, business customers, consumers, and local communities. These groups have not lost their importance, but, over time (and especially in the context of partnerships), they have been replaced as an analytical framework by a sectoral categorization of stakeholders. Preston and Post (1975) were the first to make the case for thinking in terms of sectors and, nowadays, discussions about stakeholders typically take for granted that there are three broad constituencies—business, government, and civil society—each with discernible interests. In the following sections, we use this tri-sector categorization to discuss who the different stakeholders are and their aims for corporate responsibility. But we will additionally question not only the usefulness, but also the consequences of this method of categorization itself.

Business as stakeholder

The expectations and intentions of business in relation to corporate responsibility are discussed at length throughout this book, and are varied and complex. For some, there is the desire to realize the value proposition that free enterprise can be managed to maximize societal, rather than only financial, good. Equally, there is the belief that corporate responsibility will help business to maintain and strengthen its licence to operate in a global economy, or will contribute to the creation of a system for governing corporations in that economy that, as far as possible, relies on self-regulation. At a less visionary level, corporate responsibility is also seen by business as a way in which to protect its reputation, reduce risk, identify new opportunities, and all of the other facets of the business case for corporate responsibility.

All of these interpretations of corporate responsibility affect what companies do, but they also highlight the impossibility of defining business as one particular thing. As discussed in Chapter 4, a company's approach to corporate responsibility depends on factors such as its industry, size, and location. On top of this, the purpose of the company is influenced by the place of incorporation and its actions are affected by investors' expectations. Publicly listed companies operate under very different constraints than those of privately held ones.[1] Certainly, the nature of ownership (including the role of hedge funds and private equity firms) seems, intuitively, to be an influence on business' intentions as a stakeholder, even if this has yet to be properly studied from a corporate responsibility perspective.

Managers are often frustrated, because non-business stakeholders do not understand business operations. For example, a non-government organization (NGO) may not understand the structure of the supply chain or the ownership of companies within it, leading it to think that certain companies have more influence than they actually do. From a stakeholder perspective, the position that companies occupy in relation to each other, as a result of contracts, business goals, and peer group interaction, is crucial.

A further dimension to understanding what we mean by 'business as a stakeholder' is understanding the internal dynamics of the firm. For a long time, in the tri-sector model of stakeholders, business tended to be treated as homogenous, not only in the sense that all companies were alike, but also in that everyone within the company was assumed to have common interests. One only needs a passing knowledge of industrial disputes to realize that this is profoundly wrong. To address this, some began to include employees as stakeholders and employee concerns are now found in some corporate responsibility reports. The exact position of employees in the stakeholder framework is, however, still unclear: are they a subset of business, or are they a distinct category? The history of worker organization and worker–management conflict would suggest that employees' interests are best understood as something separate from those of the company, especially if the company's interests are treated as synonymous either with those of its investors or those of its senior executives. Yet there is a real reluctance in corporate responsibility literature to take this step. This might well be because identifying conflicting interests in this way stirs up controversy, given that much of people management theory in recent years has focused on common goals, teamwork, and shared interests. It might also be because there are established channels for dealing with employee–management issues and that, as a management approach, corporate responsibility is seen as unwelcome or unnecessary in this regard.

Whatever is the practical reasoning, a theory of corporate responsibility that ignores the interests of employees except when they are the employees of other companies (i.e. as with labour rights in supply chains) is odd, at best, and fundamentally flawed, at worst. According to McDermott (1991), the company is precisely the locus of conflicting interests in the modern world. For example, investors and executives often have opposing interests, as the corporate scandals of the early 2000s revealed. The highly trained employees of the knowledge economy, who have transferable skills, are able to take advantage of flexible labour markets and not only feel little loyalty towards their employer, but may even feel obliged to keep moving jobs to demonstrate their worth. It is this group to which managers refer when they argue that corporate responsibility is important to attract and retain personnel; such employees are in a quite different position to that of the traditional blue-collar worker, whose job depends on whether a company invests or disinvests in a particular location.

The differences in interest that arise from such distinctions show how misleading it can be to talk of business as if it were a homogenous stakeholder, or even to use language such as something being '*in the interests of the company and its employees*'. The implication of such phrases is that a company is something different to its employees, begging the question, what then do we mean by 'company'? There is a well-developed literature focusing on what the company is and, while not wanting to revisit that here, it is important to be aware of the tension between seeing the company as a discernible entity and as a legal fiction that brings together different entities, each with their own interests and agendas. To an extent, it is up to senior management to balance these diverse claims, but, in the Anglo-Saxon model of the corporation, it is very clear that shareholders have the greatest entitlement. This may not be significant by itself, but some cite a combination of global competition for capital and an increasingly short-term, high-return attitude to investment as causing the very dilemmas in the relationship of business with society that corporate responsibility attempts to resolve (see Chapter 14).

CASE STUDY 10.1

Who is the right partner?

Imagine the situation: ACME Wheels, a bus and tram company that operates in several urban areas, has drafted a company-wide set of business principles, aimed at establishing it as a leading corporate citizen in its industry. The principles will set an example in what is typically a highly regulated industry, but ACME Wheels' CEO has gone on record that he does not simply want to stave off regulation: he wants to create a vision of the well-run public service company of the future.

Having drafted the principles, the company wants to gather stakeholder opinions. Moreover, in the longer term, ACME Wheels wants stakeholder representatives to oversee how the principles are implemented. So far, it has had letters of interest from local authorities in several of the main metropolitan areas in which it operates, a NGO representing elderly citizens, the National Union of Students, and an international environmental NGO. A major bus manufacturer has declined to participate and the company is deciding who else to invite.

Questions

1 Given what the company is trying to achieve, who are the main stakeholder groups that it should invite to discuss the principles?

2 Why might some of these groups be reluctant to participate?

3 How can the company ensure optimum participation?

Government as stakeholder

An interesting development is that, in contrast with early definitions of the stakeholder, government is now recognized as a category in its own right. This is not because government was unimportant in the past: on the contrary, it is because of the subsequent perceived shifts in the nature of public governance, related to globalization, that it needs to be re-emphasized that government has an interest and an obligation regarding business. The facts that, in some ways, power has shifted away from nation states and that there is a trend towards global institutions help to reveal something about government's agenda vis à vis corporate responsibility (see Chapter 3). Alongside this, however, is the post-war trend for national governments to uphold human rights across international frontiers and, in recent years, to see business (rather than only government and the international agencies of the United Nations) as a means by which to achieve this aim.

None of the above means, however, that government readily embraced corporate responsibility, or vice versa—at least early on. The perceived failure of government-convened events, such as the Rio Earth Summit, to come up with legally binding agreements provided the impetus for some business–NGO partnerships (e.g. the Forest Stewardship Council), even as the events themselves proved a catalyst for business-driven initiatives such as the World Business Council for Sustainable Development. As government reports, such as that by the UK House of Commons (1999), acknowledge, those involved in corporate responsibility tended to dismiss government as a useful partner, while government itself variously resented corporate responsibility's intrusion into its traditional territory, was suspicious of the idea of self-regulation, and simply did not recognize its potential or implications. This changed, partly, as NGOs began to see corporate responsibility's limitations in serving their own interests (and hence began revisiting government's role) and, partly, because governments started to see its possibilities in serving theirs. Kofi Annan, seventh UN Secretary-General, for example, recognized the potential of corporate responsibility when, at the World Economic Forum in 1999, he invited business to partner government in upholding international human rights. Not only did this lead to the creation of the UN Global Compact, which we discuss later in this chapter ('The United Nations Global Compact', p 271), but it also implicitly recognized the limits of trying to uphold international human rights conventions without the willing participation of companies.

Some make too much of corporate responsibility as a new approach to governance, or of how much government has ceded power because of globalization. Most aspects of business' relationship with society still fall under government's mandate and, as Sklair (2002) observes, even if governments have not acted, there is a fundamental difference between what a government cannot do and what it *will not* do. Moreover, the role of government in the development of corporate responsibility is often overlooked. Not only have government departments, such as the UK Department for International Development, the US State Department, and the Swedish International Development Agency, all funded corporate responsibility in various ways, local governments—particularly in the wake of the Rio Earth Summit—have been among the most aggressive champions of voluntary approaches to improving environmental management. Equally, companies praised for their corporate responsibility policies, such as United Utilities and Lloyds TSB Scotland, acknowledge that their programmes have often been a response to meeting government requirements, such as providing services for poor consumers.

The difficulty with discussing government as a stakeholder is that, as with business, the term 'government' is shorthand for something of enormous complexity. First of all, government is often used interchangeably with the term 'state', yet these are quite different concepts. The nation state is an impersonal, corporate entity to which society attributes responsibilities and burdens that cannot be borne by others.[2] The state acts through representatives that, in democracies, are elected governments, but might also be monarchs, dictators, and others. Governments are a changing cast of characters who control the state's assets. They can wield enormous power, but they do so as agents of the state. It is the state, not its representatives, that assumes moral burdens—often burdens that individuals would neither want nor be able to justify (e.g. inflicting violence on individuals and groups). This is a crucial point in any understanding of the government as a stakeholder: governments exist to serve the interests of the state, and to mediate between the interests of the state and its people; governments are not stakeholders in their own right, in the sense of having interests separate from those of the state. The confusion arises because politicians may well have separate interests and may want to develop these, with the intention of influencing how the state is run. But when government officials engage in corporate responsibility, they do so to further the state's interests, because to do anything other than this would be to abuse their authority.

The state comprises various institutions that carry out its functions, both in terms of government and distributing its resources. There are different functions and areas of expertise that need to be taken into consideration; there are also different levels of government and, while most publicity is given to national and international corporate responsibility initiatives, local-level partnerships are an important and lively area of activity. There are also differences of interest between elected officials and civil servants, or public employees, as well as between those in authority and those in opposition.

Although there are signs, especially in parts of Latin America, of a resurgent government hostility to business, in recent decades, politicians have largely praised the leadership of the private sector, and have sought ways in which to introduce its benefits and values into the public sector. The privatization of public agencies and the growth in public–private partnerships to fund, and manage, public services have made the links between government and business more apparent. Governments have also invited business to be more directly involved in the formulation of public policy itself,[3] and the lines between the public and private sectors are blurred, not only because of the long tradition of politicians pursuing business interests, but also because of lobbying, the secondment of private sector managers to government departments, and the election of business leaders into public office. The money required to run for public office in some countries also drives politicians to build close ties with the private sector and with business leaders.

All of this influences what government hopes to achieve through corporate responsibility. Indeed, when governments struggle to maintain public services without increasing direct taxation, or find themselves reliant as much on the support of professional interest groups (e.g. NGOs, academics, the media, or business leaders) as on popular support,[4] it is fair to say that government looks to corporate responsibility as a way in which to address its own challenges, such as distrust or disinterest among the electorate in advanced economies, a sense of ineffectiveness in dealing with global issues, and the need to have the support of business to remain in power and to continue fulfilling its obligations to the public.

Civil society as stakeholder

CASE STUDY 10.2

The rationale of a NGO partnership

WWF, the international environmental NGO, has long been an advocate of partnerships involving business (e.g. the Forest Stewardship Council, the Marine Stewardship Council, and the Roundtable on Sustainable Palm Oil). It also has as a goal of its International Living Waters programme the reduction of the impact of 'thirsty crops' on fresh water and, in particular, that of those that are internationally traded, such as sugar. It has therefore chosen to utilize international markets to help to catalyse change for the benefit of the environment.

But is a partnership the best approach to this international-level intervention? On the one hand, WWF recognizes that it would have little impact if acting alone; on the other, there have been a proliferation of initiatives, with the result that any one partnership can lack the critical mass to bring change. Furthermore, while large partnerships can be cumbersome, they need to be big enough to include the relevant skills and experience, and the prime movers need to be aware that organizations excluded from the partnership may set up competing initiatives.

In considering a partnership, WWF also needs to think about whether to work with companies directly or through an industry association, how to link into other partnerships with which WWF is already involved (e.g. WWF America's collaboration with the International Finance Corporation on better agribusiness management), and who outside the industry should be involved (e.g. irrigation equipment manufacturers). Last, but not least, before deciding about any partnership, WWF needs to reach internal agreement about the process for setting adequate performance standards for sugar cultivation.

(Adapted from Perkins, 2004)

Questions

Much of the literature on partnerships as a corporate responsibility approach focuses on the company perspective.

1 Using the WWF example, what are some of the differences in what NGOs ask when assessing a partnership compared with companies?

2 What are the similarities?

3 Do you think WWF would be right to adopt a partnership approach in this instance?

Contemporary corporate responsibility has eagerly embraced civil society, although it can be difficult to identify precisely what this concept means. 'Civil society' has historically referred to private interests that are distinct from those of the state. Today, even if the exact meaning is ambiguous, the term refers to uncoerced collective action, based on shared interests, purposes, and values, by institutions that are distinct from those of the state and the market.[5]

In corporate responsibility, 'civil society organization' is often used as a synonym for non-government organization (which is itself normally called 'non-governmental', despite the fact that many are active in the realm of modern-day public governance). An NGO is, however, only one type of civil society organization—a category that also includes charities, community groups, identity-based and faith-based organizations, professional associations, trade unions, self-help groups, social movements, business associations, coalitions, and advocacy groups. This is important from a corporate responsibility perspective, in which engagement with civil society stakeholders, on the one hand, refers to a relatively narrow selection of organizations and, on the other, assumes that civil society is found everywhere, although, by definition, it can only exist if people enjoy the rights of citizens (i.e. the enfranchised inhabitant of a country) and is therefore absent from many countries.

Where civil society does exist, it is an error to treat all organizations within this sector as the same, or even as similar. Some companies are eager to engage with NGOs not only because of their expertise, but also because they occupy the moral high ground in many important areas of the corporate responsibility agenda. The results are, at times, frustrating, because some NGOs have proved to be unaccountable, lacking grass-roots support, and ineffective at providing services.[6] But, more importantly, even in the many cases in which the organizations are credible, there are significant differences that affect their position as stakeholder. Some organizations focus on advocacy and policy, some on service delivery, and others on a mixture of the two. Strictly speaking, service delivery organizations are not civil society organizations, because they are not pursuing private interests that are separate from those of the state. Uphoff (1996) says that legitimate civil society organizations are characterized by active memberships that support the undertaking of collective action and points out that many NGOs should be considered as a subset of the private sector, because donors or governments fund them with the aim of delivering particular services to customers.

In corporate responsibility, this distinction is seldom made and, depending on the circumstances, companies are as willing to partner with non-profit service providers, as they are to do so with advocacy groups. Yet even among the genuine civil society organizations, there are differences that will affect the nature and suitability of any partnership. For example, there is a world of difference between the mission of an organization such as Oxfam (*'creating lasting solutions to global poverty, hunger, and social injustice'*) and that of the National Rifle Association (committed to defending citizens' rights to bear arms and educating citizens in how to use guns), and companies may get credibility from engaging with one, while they may attract opprobrium for engaging with the other. Some even advise companies to stay away from all NGOs, for fear that the companies will become *'pawns of environmentalists, social activists and backroom Marxists'*.[7]

As Korten (1990) makes clear in his typology of development NGOs, an organization can evolve from being a humanitarian agency, such as the Red Cross, to one that concentrates more on sustainable development (e.g. World Vision), to one that is an advocate of systemic change to address major issues such as poverty and the environment (e.g. War on Want). An organization such as Save the Children has, over time, come to be active in all three areas.

It is possible to argue that confusion about civil society works to companies' advantage, because it allows them to pick and choose with whom to engage. But to do so would probably undermine the credibility of corporate responsibility as a whole. For example, the term 'non-government organization' does not normally include free trade unions, even though the latter are democratic membership organizations, but through repetition, not least in corporate responsibility texts, NGOs are presented as legitimate representatives of worker interests, while unions risk being marginalized.[8] This is also dangerous for NGOs because, rather than being the radical voices that fill the gaps in domestic and global democracy, they might become what Meiksins Wood (1995) calls *'alibis of capitalism'*. There are already calls to subject NGOs to the same kind of scrutiny and accountability that is demanded of companies in the context of corporate responsibility. As Parkin (2001) points out in her celebration of NGOs in the democratic process, NGOs worldwide have a GDP of $1.1 trillion—that is, larger than that of all but seven of the world's national economies—but the consequences of having to protect their financial interests and their frequent dependency on governments for funding are not well known.[9] A sceptic might argue, therefore, that, when NGOs engage with companies, they are not doing so solely to represent a position, but also to demonstrate to private and public funders that they can persuade corporations to adopt shared goals. As Rowley and Moldoveanu (2003) observe, company managers may make the mistake of thinking that what motivates civil society organizations to act is their interest in an issue; in reality, organizations mobilize based not only on the issue itself, but also on how important it is for their identity and the extent to which other organizations are prepared to act.

Partnerships

Reasons for partnership

'Partnership' has become a very popular word in Western democracies, reflecting the belief that different sectors of society share responsibility for delivering societal goods. For example, public–private sector partnerships (PPPs) have gained traction in some countries as a way in which to deliver public services, from schooling, to incarceration. In theory, any arrangement between separate organizations to achieve defined ends qualifies as a partnership, but those such as PPPs—justified largely on financial grounds—are well outside what the term means in a corporate responsibility context. Many corporate responsibility partnerships involve a company and another entity, but some are more complex than this, involving multiple organizations from different sectors. There are now organizations offering training and brokering services to address the demand for expertise in partnership building.[10] There is no single reason for this trend in favour of partnerships. Various claims are made: that they are crucial to competitiveness in a global economy; that they define the rules and boundaries of that economy; that they offer new ways of holding companies to account; that they provide companies with access to new markets and ideas; that they lead to the creation of win–win situations, in which all stakeholders see added value.[11] From a business perspective, partnerships provide managers with unconventional mechanisms for seeing their situation anew, and for rediagnosing situations and opportunities in ways that challenge preconceived ideas and habits.[12] Depending on the industry and type of company involved, they can help companies to secure their licence to operate, to maintain relations with local and global communities, to prevent and resolve disputes, and to manage the impacts of investment and disinvestment in particular locations.[13] As is evident from the earlier discussion of stakeholders, however, others have their own ambitions for such partnerships and assess them based on how this type of relationship adds value to their own work.

The aims of partnerships range from the broad and grand, to the narrow and specific. For example, the 2002 World Summit on Sustainable Development, which is attributed with stimulating various partnerships between government and civil society, placed business at the centre of international efforts to reduce poverty. In contrast, a partnership might be formed between airport authorities, local government, local community groups, and environmental NGOs, with the specific purpose of negotiating a runway extension. Equally, as we shall discuss further, partnerships involve different levels of participation and involvement, ranging from a company promising to report on social and environmental performance to stakeholders, or to fund a specific project, to civil society, business, and government groups collaborating together to achieve certain ends. It is not that one type of partnership is necessarily better than another—the question is what is fit for purpose—but it must be recognized that there are different types, each with implications for goals, design, and implementation.

From a company perspective, partnerships are motivated by one of three things. First, they provide an alternative way of implementing the kind of company-led community relations and development programmes that have long been part of how business manages its relationship with wider society. Second, there can be a compelling business rationale, such as access to new markets, avoidance of litigation, or the chance to burnish brand image. Third, partnerships are a response to the trend towards civil regulation. In discussions about the advantages of partnerships, this last motivation is often described in terms of providing an alternative to formal regulation by government and is part of debates we describe in other chapters about corporate responsibility as a form of voluntary regulation. This is, however, only part of the story. It is not that anyone can choose between civil regulation and state regulation: civil regulation refers to the process by means of which business and others in society are compelled to take action, not because of the law, but because civil society demands it.[14] Partnerships can therefore be seen as a way in which to comply with civil regulation and, in this sense, it is a mistake to suggest that they are voluntary. Rather, they are voluntary only in so far as an organization can decide whether or not to comply: non-compliance with civil regulation entails risks no less than does failure to abide by the law.

Whatever the motivation, discussions about partnership in a corporate responsibility context tend to be built on certain assumptions. When Freeman (1984) originally wrote of business engaging with stakeholders, he was largely talking about bilateral partnerships between a company and another organization, but today's partnerships often mean working with multiple organizations, which can come from different sectors, and much of the literature deals with business–NGO engagement. There is a risk that the term can be overused, however, and partnership in a corporate responsibility sense is something different to the type of public–private partnership that governments promote to finance and deliver public services.

Another assumption is that partnerships are a better way of working—one that is built on mutual benefit, lessening of conflict, and complementarity. They often involve some sharing of responsibility between the three sectors we talked about earlier. As Warner and Sullivan describe it, in the context of the mining, oil, and gas industry:

> Tri-sector partnerships are, in essence, a new form of strategic alliance . . . [A] voluntary collaboration to promote sustainable development based on the most efficient allocation of complementary resources across business, civil society and government.
>
> (2003, p 17)

Box 10.1 lists some of the complementary competencies and resources that different stakeholders bring to a project partnership.

Types of partnership

Partnerships can operate at different levels of society (e.g. local, regional, national, and international), and can evolve over time to meet changing needs and expectations. For example, a mining company may convene a partnership comprising local communities, international development and environmental NGOs, and national government agencies when it begins exploration, but as the project progresses through construction, operation, and, eventually, closure, the partnership may well change to include local NGOs and government representatives. It may even spawn different partnerships to address particular aspects of the mine's presence. Each of those stakeholders stands to benefit from the partnership, but in its own way (Box 10.2).

Warner and Sullivan (2003) describe a wide range of partnership experiences in the mining, oil, and gas industries, and conclude that there are six types of partnership.

1 **Knowledge sharing**
   Long-term voluntary agreements between stakeholders to share information about the company's activities (e.g. feasibility studies, proposals, and evaluations).

Box 10.1 Stakeholders' complementary contributions to partnerships

Government contribution	Business contribution	Civil society contribution
Strategic coordination through local development plans	Job creation	Local knowledge
Access to budgets for public services	Knowledge of procurement and supply chain management	Mobilization of community participation
Regulatory provisions	Building local infrastructure	Independent monitoring
Brokering or capacity-building roles	Capital equipment, technical skills, and logistics	Local and international credibility
	Performance-led work ethic and access to international best practices	

(Adapted from Warner and Sullivan, 2003; UNEP et al., 2005)

2 **Dialogue**
Medium-term voluntary agreement that key stakeholders will consult with each other on specified activities, such as preparing regional plans, developing environmental standards, and deciding on reporting requirements.

3 **Informed consent**
Voluntary agreement by each party not to take action without the prior consent of others.

4 **Contractual**
Medium-term agreement between certain stakeholders to provide specified services to others in the partnership.

5 **Shared work plans**
Medium-term voluntary agreement between stakeholders to carry out separate, defined tasks in pursuit of common goals.

6 **Shared responsibility**
Long-term agreement between stakeholders to share responsibility for implementing tasks and to be responsible to each other for their delivery.

This typology emphasizes the voluntary nature of most partnerships, even though there may be contractual and other legally enforceable elements within them. This is in contrast with most business relationships, within which agreements are typically legally binding. As Davy (2003a) notes, however, there are different types of obligation between partners, some of which is formal and some of which is informal. For example, the company can have legal (formal) obligations to meet requirements pertaining to

Box 10.2 Partnership outcomes for different stakeholders—examples from mining

Outcomes for business

Enhanced licence to operate, because communities affected by operations will be satisfied that the business unit is responsive to their concerns	Availability of new social capital for the business
Reduced community dependency on the business unit (e.g. owing to empowerment of communities to manage their own development)	Becoming 'company of choice' in the eyes of governmental authorizing agencies and removing political objections to future ventures
Basis for resolving local disputes that might delay financial approval or operations	Reduced risk to marketing, sales, and share price associated with negative image of social and environmental performance

Outcomes for local communities

Additional resources for community development	Ensuring that those impacted by operations have an equal or greater level of welfare, income, subsistence, and security
Fairer settlement/compensation for community assets	Access to the technology, finance, and markets that are necessary for new assets, and skill sets that can be transformed into sustainable livelihoods
Improved infrastructure and capacity to manage it	

Outcomes for the public sector

Agreed revenue distribution mechanisms before commencing operations	Increased legitimacy with local populations
More equitable distribution of revenues across government, and between government and communities	Exposure to new ways of working and international good practice
Enhanced tax and skills base	Empowerment of local communities

(Adapted from Warner and Sullivan, 2003)

environmental impact assessments or employment law and informal obligations, under a partnership agreement, to provide infrastructure, to transfer skills, and to report to external stakeholders. Moreover, companies can face informal sanctions if they breach the partnership agreement, and more important than complying with specific agreements can be the way in which the partnership builds and maintains trust. For example, since 1999, Tesco, the supermarket chain, has initiated 12 UK-wide regeneration partnerships in low- to moderate-income urban areas. Its aim is to develop new stores in underserved areas and, as well as creating employment, these account for a quarter of the company's new investments in the UK.[15] Therefore, the partnerships that the company creates with community groups, and with the public and private sectors, to build a workforce with skills that the stores need, are essential for strategic business development, but are something that depend not on compulsion, but a shared belief that the outcomes will be beneficial.

The above typology can be applied to different industries and is not only relevant to geographically specific activities. For example, the Ethical Trading Initiative, a multi-stakeholder partnership aimed at improving the monitoring of labour standards in supply chains, is a shared responsibility partnership, while the informal agreements between business and civil society that have led to social reporting are a well-established form of knowledge-sharing partnership. As mentioned earlier, in corporate responsibility, the term 'partnership' usually refers to one between sectors—but this need not always be the case. IBM's corporate community relations unit, for example, has created internal partnerships (e.g. with its research laboratories) so that corporate knowledge can be applied to social and education problems.[16] Likewise, having committed itself to using organic cotton for environmental reasons, Nike found that it could not buy sufficient quantities. Unable to change this situation on its own, the company partnered with 55 other businesses to create the Organic Cotton Exchange, a non-profit organization committed to building a global organic cotton industry.[17]

Davy (2003b) highlights that partnerships in conflict situations have unique characteristics. Recognizing that some industries not only operate in conflict-affected regions, but can exacerbate, or be the cause of, that conflict, he stresses the role that partnerships can play in such situations. For example, the partnership between ExxonMobil, the World Bank, civil society organizations, and the governments of Chad and Cameroon promised a model for how companies could be transparent about royalties and taxes, could encourage governments to be accountable for how they spend oil revenues, and could make social and environmental investments. Partnerships can provide a way of bypassing the conflict, as was attempted with the business–civil society partnerships in South Africa involving BP and Rio Tinto during the apartheid era. They can also be a way in which companies can uphold their own policies regarding areas such as international human rights and environmental management when government is unwilling, or unable, to do so.

In this type of situation, a partnership may not be a means to an end, but an end in itself, in so far as they foster trust and mutual understanding between disparate groups. There are, however, limitations to partnerships in conflict situations, not least in the delivery of humanitarian aid, for which the need to obtain stakeholder consent might stand in the way of the International Commission of the Red Cross' principles that aid providers have unimpeded access to affected populations, and that aid be provided regardless of ethnic origin and political, or religious, beliefs. Partnerships may also be inappropriate where conflicts have left a legacy of grievances that will need to be resolved before any genuine cooperation between the relevant parties is possible (see Case Study 10.3).

Finally, partnerships can be classified according to their purpose. Svendesen and Laberge (2005) argue that most partnerships are formed because companies have to engage with stakeholders in order to comply with regulations, to solve operational problems, or to respond to public pressure for greater accountability. They claim that companies tend to approach these partnerships as if they were closed systems and seek to control stakeholder relationships in order to meet organizational goals. As already noted, Freeman's seminal work on stakeholder management put the company at the hub of numerous bilateral relationships, the purposes of which are, typically, to reduce risks, to enhance reputation, to improve the bottom line, or to develop new business opportunities. In contrast, there are a number of partnerships that are best thought of as stakeholder networks. These are convened by a company to tackle challenges that it cannot address on its own, but, once the network is formed, it has a life of its own that cannot be controlled by a single organization and is inherently dynamic, unpredictable, and evolving. In conventional partnerships, company managers manage stakeholders, and behave as gatekeepers and benefactors; in networks, they must create the space in which the network can grow—and must then relinquish control.

CASE STUDY 10.3

Project partnerships—examples from Azerbaijan and Indonesia

Extractive industries are often at the heart of conflict for a variety of reasons. In Azerbaijan, one of the growth areas for oil and gas exploration, the issue has been how to prevent oil investment acting as a trigger for conflict. In the area around the Kelian gold mine in Indonesia, the issue is how to resolve conflicts that have arisen as the mine closes down.

International Alert, a conflict protection NGO, approached BP, Statoil, Exxon, and the state-owned Socar Company, to develop a partnership that also involved farmers' organizations, human rights groups, women's groups, and two foreign embassies. The organizations focused on building mutual understanding and a platform for joint analysis that led to the identification of six themes seen as critical for peaceful development in the country. These included developing local businesses, meeting the needs of the displaced, strengthening civil society, and building regional political stability. This ambitious agenda has spawned more narrowly focused initiatives, such as the Business Development Alliance aiming to foster local enterprise. Indeed, one of the lessons learned, according to International Alert, is that, in conflict prevention situations, the initial partnership is not a means, but an end in itself, intended to build trust and understanding between parties.

At the Kelian mine (90 per cent owned by Rio Tinto), the challenge is not the future, but the legacy of the past. Local communities felt that they had not benefited from the mine and, in particular, accused the company of failing to pay adequate compensation for land, of human rights abuses, including sexual misconduct, of broken promises regarding development projects, and of inadequate retrenchment packages for mine workers. A Mine Closure Steering Committee (MCSC) was established, and anyone affected by, or able to affect, the closure of the mine was eligible to join. The MCSC established working groups that were responsible for consulting with stakeholders on four key aspects of the closure. It put in place various measures to ensure accountability and transparency, and committed the company to a consensus-based decision-making process. This has resulted in agreement on handing over infrastructure to local communities (e.g. health clinics, schools), construction of new infrastructure, investment in community development projects, ensuring the mine infrastructure is safe, and that neighbouring lands are not degraded.

(Hamann, 2003; Killick, 2003)

Questions

Partnerships promise new ways of resolving conflict.

1 Under what circumstances are partnerships likely to be more effective than other approaches to dealing with conflict?

2 Should companies take the lead in conflict resolution?

3 How are partnerships likely to differ, depending on whether they are about conflict prevention or resolving grievances?

The value of partnerships

Examples in the previous section are reminders that partnerships are not appropriate in all circumstances and need to be tailored to specific ends. But the issue is not only that partnerships may be inappropriate: they may not be as efficient as other alternatives on offer. Mitchell et al. (2003) claim that the value added by a partnership can be assessed by calculating the value of outcomes attributable to the partnership, and then subtracting that attributable to external factors and that of those outcomes that might have been achieved using alternative partnership or non-partnership approaches. This type of cost–benefit approach to valuing partnerships may be unhelpful, however, not least because, as some managers have pointed out, the value of partnerships can lie in the prevention of something such as a lawsuit or a shutdown, which is often intangible.[18]

Three simple questions can be asked by any party of any partnership concern.

1 What is its effectiveness in achieving the stakeholders' common aims?

2 Does it provide benefits for all involved?

3 Is it the best way of realizing the different organizations' goals?

The last question points to the importance of assessing the various alternatives. All stakeholders are likely to do this, although most of what we know about the process comes from a company perspective. For example, the company may have the option of subcontracting its social or other commitments to a development organization, or it may feel that involving partners adds little value to what it can achieve by directly managing a community development programme. It may consider building the infrastructure in areas such as health care and education itself, but may involve government in the project with a view to eventually handing it over for public ownership. It may also consider establishing an independent organization, such as a trust or foundation, that might appear to be more credible to external stakeholders than a company-managed initiative and may prove more sustainable than either the shared work plan or shared responsibility models of partnership described in the previous section.

As to whether partnerships provide benefits for those involved, it is worth summarizing what we have discussed about the types of partnership and their qualities. Five different cases can be made for stakeholder partnership:

1 it is a better way of doing business;

2 it is a new way of regulating business;

3 it is an alternative way of harnessing the power and resources of business, and of redistributing benefits;

4 it is a more effective way of dealing with the realities of global governance;

5 it is an entirely new way of thinking about business.

Ultimately, the value of a partnership for any stakeholder is how well suited it is to serving these quite diverse purposes.

Implementing partnerships

There are numerous sources of advice on implementation (see the 'Further reading' at the end of this chapter) and this section presents only a broad overview. The UN Environmental Programme has published a stakeholder engagement manual that is based on practitioner experiences from around the world. Aimed at company managers, it concentrates on the value-added potential of partnerships and identifies a five-stage process of engagement with stakeholders (Box 10.3).

Warner (2003) adds to this the needs to:

1 assess what internal and external resources are required and available;

2 build consensus and construct mechanisms for managing the partnership.

He emphasizes the importance of assessing the partnership option internally before making any commitment to others and sets out a number of considerations. For example, the company needs to know what are the stakeholders' priorities, what investments and programmes the company already has in place, the alternatives to a partnership approach, the resources that are available (or that can be leveraged) within the company, any legal obstacles to forming a partnership, and what the risks are of working through a partnership. Stacey (2003) describes a matrix used by Rio Tinto as a strategic framework for identifying and rating partnerships.

Box 10.3 Five stages of stakeholder engagement

1 Identifying the company's business objectives and how they relate to stakeholders.

2 Analysing existing relationships.

3 Deciding what kind of relationship the company wants with different stakeholder groups.

4 Assessing the competencies, and capacities, of stakeholder groups to engage with the company and the appropriate forms of engagement (e.g. meetings with the company, public meetings, joint projects).

5 Following up on the outputs from engagement, and monitoring and maintaining the partnership over time.

(Adapted from UNEP et al., 2005)

The implementation process is often described as a 'virtuous circle' building on the 'think–plan–do–check' model of quality management. For example, a partnership intended to help the company to innovate might have six phases: stakeholder engagement; understanding stakeholder perspectives and needs; distilling business-relevant knowledge; identifying new risks and opportunities; product and process innovation; codification of new approaches, leading to further engagement.[19] This broadly mirrors the five elements of engagement underlying the AA1000 Series on stakeholder accountability (see Chapter 6): planning; accounting; auditing and reporting; embedding; engagement. But as the various AA1000 documents recognize, any element or phase of partnership management needs to be unravelled. For example, there are different principles that apply depending on what stage the partnership is at (Box 10.4). Furthermore, management practice will vary according to the type of partnership. There are obvious differences in management requirements between a contractual model of partnership and one that is based on shared responsibilities. There are also significant differences between those partnerships within which the company is a participant and those within which it is the convenor of a network of other organizations.[20]

Much of the guidance on implementing and assessing partnerships reflects common beliefs about the nature and value of the partnership approach. Caplan (2003) claims that the literature on partnerships too often promotes the idea that they are, by their very nature, harmonious and built on trust, common vision, and voluntary commitment. He argues that there are various myths and half-truths behind this belief. First, multi-sector partnerships, in his first-hand experience, are rarely built on a common vision, because stakeholders have different reference points and, if they focus too much on what they have in common, their aspirations get diluted or masked. The partnership then ends up with a mission statement of which nobody feels ownership. He points out that stakeholders can appear to share values when what is actually happening is that they are using the same words to mean different things. For example, for a company, 'sustainability' has some relationship to cost recovery; for the public sector, it means something that is technically sound that can sustain itself in the future; for a development NGO, it is to do with empowerment and giving communities a voice.

Second, while trust is a much-vaunted element of partnerships, it might be more accurate to say that individuals within the partnership build a mutual respect for that which people and organizations can offer. Trust is most likely when organizations can choose with whom to partner, but this rarely happens and most partners are thrust upon each other. Consequently, more important than trust can be creating an understanding of what the various partners can and cannot do. Indeed, more significant than genuine trust can be knowing partners well enough to predict how they will behave within the partnership.

Third, as noted earlier, a perceived strength of partnerships is that they leverage the core competencies of the partners. In reality, however, organizations may compete for what they want to contribute, so that, for example, both companies and NGOs may feel that they have relevant outreach skills and local knowledge, or government agencies and NGOs may both want to play a monitoring or watchdog role.

As seen earlier in the discussion of civil regulation, many partnerships are not truly optional and are therefore voluntary only in the sense that they are not a legal requirement.

Box 10.4 Principles for managing partnerships

Partnership exploration stage

Find the most practicable strategy	Involve stakeholders in design
Be purpose-driven	Set realistic expectations
Be willing to negotiate	Be prepared to say 'No'
Consult	

Partnership building stage

Appreciate the importance of perceptions	Accept that differences of interest will arise
Integrate cultural values and priorities	Encourage joint problem solving
Build trust, confidence, and respect	Identify the important voices, rather than the loudest
Be willing to negotiate	

Partnership maintenance stage

Recognize reciprocal obligations	Adapt to internal and external events
Have clear work plans	Measure added value
Maintain internal and external communications	Do not be a slave to business value
Be willing to negotiate	Instigate continual learning

(Adapted from Warner and Sullivan, 2003; CCC, 2005c)

Caplan (2003) reinforces the point made previously that partnerships are not always the best way in which to deliver the intended outputs, but he also stresses that focusing on tangible deliverables can distract organizations from understanding the real value of partnerships. For example, in assessing an African water partnership, it is easy to argue that the end result is the number of new standpipes and that contractors might have installed these. The true value, however, is how many female children no longer have to walk four miles to collect water and can, as a consequence, now go to school, and this is only achievable by involving community stakeholders directly in the project.[21]

Increasingly, the lessons of partnership seems to be that it is not a panacea to corporate responsibility challenges, and that organizations need to enter into them with their eyes open to both the strengths and the weaknesses. There are many views on why partnerships are important and how to engage in them, and perhaps insufficient information on what is appropriate in different situations. But, overall, there is little argument about the importance attached to partnerships as part of corporate responsibility's arsenal.

CASE STUDY 10.4

From boycott to agreement at Mitsubishi

In 1993, Tachi Kiuchi, CEO of Mitsubishi Electric America, was told by junior school children that his firm was destroying the world's rainforests. Other parts of the conglomerate were similarly targeted in a campaign coordinated by the NGO, Rainforest Action Network (RAN). RAN, which seeks change by discrediting corporate reputations, chose Mitsubishi because it had the highest profile of the companies with an interest in logging. Not surprisingly, nobody at Mitsubishi wanted to sit at the table with RAN's activists and preferred to seek out more moderate environmental groups. But while Kiuchi might have disliked the RAN message, he recognized their skill in mobilizing the public and saw the potential of that power being used to his company's benefit. After a visit to the rainforests to see the situation at first hand, he felt able to address RAN's complaints armed with knowledge of Mitsubishi's role in deforestation. He gave presentations at important environmental events and his willingness to field questions, plus his knowledge of the issues, won some environmentalist support. Using a professional partnership-brokering organization, the company also sounded out willingness within RAN to have direct engagement.

At the same time, the company began working with a renowned environmental institute, the Rocky Mountain Institute, to understand better and to resolve the deforestation problem—leading to the creation of a new organization, the Systems Group on Forestry. That initiative failed when two key non-business partners fell out, but, in the process, senior figures at Mitsubishi US and RAN came to admire and respect each other. Mitsubishi Corporation in Tokyo was, however, less enthusiastic and refused to pursue any partnership, leaving only two parts of the US operation on board.

Yet getting rid of those who were unwilling to partner proved to be no bad thing, allowing the eventual partnership to be more focused. After a period of shuttle diplomacy between Mitsubishi US and RAN, a ten-point agreement was reached that required the company to change its purchasing policies and to lobby the government on carbon reductions, and which required the NGO to end its support for a boycott of the company's products. Not all of the agreement was implemented, but some parts of it had demonstrable impacts (e.g. 75 per cent reductions in paper use) and the NGO–corporate partnership maintained its credibility, becoming a model for both civil society and business initiatives.

(Asmus, 2007; www.commondreams.org; www.ethicalconsumer.org—both accessed 18 May 2007)

Questions

The RAN–Mitsubishi agreement is an early example of how confrontation turned to partnership.

1 What type of partnership would you classify this as?

2 What are the arguments for and against other companies responding in the way in which Mitsubishi US did?

3 What are the key lessons for managers from this case?

The United Nations Global Compact

Partnerships aimed at helping business to meet the challenges of upholding their responsibilities in developing countries have come to the fore in recent years.[22] The most prominent of these is the United Nations Global Compact, established in 2000 as a direct result of the call of the then UN Secretary-General, Kofi Annan, for business leaders to partner with UN agencies, and for civil society to support universal environmental and social principles. The partnership is a response to the neglect of social and environmental protections in the promotion of economic globalization, and is based on the premise that the longevity of globalization and the international economic order depends as much on such protections as it does on free markets and economic inclusivity (see Chapter 3). It is also a recognition that previous UN efforts to require business to uphold such protections had failed, in part, because of political pressure from the economically powerful member States. Therefore, the Compact marks a new approach, appealing directly to business for its voluntary endorsement of the UN's goals.[23]

As Kell and Levin (2003) point out, the Compact was never intended to resolve all of global capitalism's deficiencies, but rather to lay a foundation of shared values, as embodied in various UN conventions and declarations, and to attempt to harness the skills and resources of the private sector to uphold those values.

> The ultimate measure of success for the initiative is the degree to which it promotes concrete and sustained action by its varied participants, especially the private sector, in alignment with broad UN objectives, the [Compact's] principles, and the international Millennium Development Goals. It does not substitute for effective action by governments, nor does it present a regulatory framework or code of conduct for companies. Rather the Global Compact is conceived as a value-based platform designed to promote institutional learning with few formalities and no rigid bureaucratic structures.
>
> (Kell and Levin, 2003, p 152)

The above description clarifies some points of confusion about this partnership. First, it is not a standard in the sense of those codes and guidelines discussed in Chapter 6. Second, it is not an alternative to government regulation. Third, the partnership is voluntary and consensual, built on what are held to be universal values. Fourth, it is, in part, a partnership for fostering and sharing learning. But learning is only part of its mission, as its three stated goals make clear.

1 To build consensus and inspire recognition of social and environmental concerns in the global marketplace, especially around problematic areas (Goal 1).

2 To develop a learning bank of corporate best practices, and to integrate the Compact's ten principles into business strategies and operations (Goal 2).

3 To generate concrete, sustained implementation of the Millennium Development Goals (Goal 3).

There are four main areas of activity that are intended to achieve these goals:

1 learning forums to analyse case studies and examples of good practice;

2 global policy dialogues on the challenges of globalization;

3 multi-stakeholder collaborative development projects to further the Millennium Development Goals;

4 support for new national networks.

The international development perspective is further stressed in the Global Sustainable Business initiative that has emerged from the Compact. The goals and activity areas show that, as well as a learning network, the Compact is a public policy network. It comprises both wide networks of different sectors, which come together for annual learning forums and semi-annual policy dialogues, and also strategic networks, within which specific stakeholders collaborate in collective actions such as the aforementioned development projects.

An increasingly important part of the Compact is the local networks that serve as forums within which companies can exchange experiences in a particular region. The Compact sees these as a shift towards decentralization and a dispersal of network ownership, although, so far, civil society organizations have been hesitant about becoming involved in them.[24] The growth in these networks has meant changes in the role of the Global Compact's Office, which sits in the office of the UN Secretary-General. Its main roles are to provide financial and political support, to offer a global platform for Compact members, to encourage participants to use the outputs from local networks, to develop its own products, and to provide legitimacy to local initiatives. In addition to the Office and the local networks, there is a 20-person advisory board, comprising mostly business leaders, although with some NGO and trade union representatives.

Central to the Compact's work are its ten Principles (Box 10.5), which reflect the commitments of UN member States under the Universal Declaration of Human Rights, the 1992 Rio Declaration on the Environment and Development, the 1998 ILO Fundamental Principles and Rights at Work, and the 2003 Convention against Corruption. Companies that sign up to the Compact make a clear statement of support for the Principles, signed by the CEO and endorsed by the board. They must include some reference to the progress they are making towards this commitment in their annual report or other public documents, including how they are internalizing the Principles in their operations.[25]

In 2005, following criticism that the Compact lacked teeth, it introduced a review procedure for dealing with complaints concerning signatory companies. There is now a formal process whereby the Compact Office receives and assesses the merits of complaints, and can then suggest remedial action or, if necessary, remove the company from the signatory list.

The pressure to introduce a review procedure is indicative of some of the tensions surrounding the Compact. In order to win business support, it needs to be inclusive and avert suspicions that it is regulation by the back door. But to be credible in the eyes of

Box 10.5 The ten Principles of the Global Compact

1 Businesses should support and respect the protection of internationally proclaimed human rights within their sphere of influence.

2 Businesses should ensure that their own operations are not complicit in human rights abuses.

3 Businesses should uphold the freedom of association and the effective recognition of the right to collective bargaining.

4 Businesses should uphold the elimination of all forms of forced and compulsory labour.

5 Businesses should uphold the effective abolition of child labour.

6 Businesses should eliminate discrimination in respect of employment and occupation.

7 Businesses should support a precautionary approach to environmental challenges.

8 Businesses should undertake initiatives to promote greater environmental responsibility.

9 Businesses should encourage the development and diffusion of environmentally friendly technologies.

10 Businesses should work against corruption in all its forms, including extortion and bribery.

(www.unglobalcompact.org)

government or civil society it needs to demonstrate that it can influence business behaviour and that it is willing to hold signatory companies to account. To date, the Compact has had mixed success in influencing business. Although over 2,500 companies (including 20 per cent of the world's 500 largest companies) have signed up, US companies, in particular, have been reluctant to join, partly because they fear litigation based on any alleged failure to comply with the Principles and partly because they see limited value in being associated with a UN initiative.[26] Furthermore, nearly 40 per cent of signatories are not communicating progress against the Principles.[27]

The impact of the Compact is hard to assess. In 2004, it announced it was undertaking an in-depth study of the impact on business, but the results have not been published and the website section titled 'Impact and progress of the Global Compact's 106 largest companies' provides only data on the companies' economic performance, rather than on how this relates to the Millenium Development Goals, or on how the Compact has influenced their behaviour. An independent study of how the Compact's Principles have been embedded into Novartis Pharmaceuticals is available and shows, among other things, how they were used to give proper consideration to human rights in business decisions. The Compact itself highlights how it has fostered dialogue on globalization, strengthened business awareness of the UN conventions, stimulated innovative thinking within the UN, and led to the creation of multi-stakeholder projects, such as the partnership in Venezuela between Amnesty International, Statoil, and the UN Development Programme aimed at strengthening national human rights awareness. The Compact admits, however, that there has been limited progress in getting companies to integrate the ten Principles into core business strategies and operations.[28]

There have been criticisms from NGOs both outside and within the Compact, and from certain UN agencies.[29] The introduction of a review procedure, after the Compact long denied that this was its role, shows that it can respond to criticisms. But it seems likely that it will always be a target, not only because it endorses aspects of globalization that some find abhorrent (see Chapter 3), but also because, in order to grow, it needs the support of business and is consequently always open to the charge that it is being co-opted by corporate interests. For example, after long proclaiming that it did not take funding from companies, in 2005, it established the Global Compact Foundation to raise money from non-government sources for the Compact's work. As important to responding to specific criticisms will be the Compact's success in meeting the measures of its effectiveness (see Case Study 10.5), because, as with many complex and important partnerships, success does not that mean criticisms and alternative viewpoints will fade away; rather, a cessation of dialogue and debate may, in many instances, be a sign of failure.

CASE STUDY 10.5

Measures of the Global Compact's effectiveness

Georg Kell, executive head of the Compact, has spelled out four measures for assessing the Compact's effectiveness.

1 The Compact's ability to communicate information transparently and accessibly within the network by, for example, making company reports and case studies available.
   NB The Compact had to drop an earlier requirement that companies submit examples of how they enact the ten Principles, although all are still expected to report on overall progress.

2 The effectiveness of the Compact's rules of engagement in offering open and equitable access to all stakeholders.
   NB Some NGOs have refused to participate, because they see the Compact as promoting an unacceptable model of liberal economic globalization.

3 The willingness of companies to share information.
   NB Some companies have refused to share information, either because of commercial confidentiality, or because the current structure allows signatories to freeride.

4 The ability to balance the achievement of the Compact's goals relating to impact and the need to protect the partnership's integrity.
   NB Although the Compact is strict about not letting companies use its name as an endorsement, it has had difficulty keeping out freeriders and preventing false reporting.

(Kell and Levin, 2003; McIntosh et al., 2004)

Questions

For the Compact to be successful, it needs to have credibility with stakeholders from different sectors.

1 How appropriate are the above measures of effectiveness in ensuring that the partnership addresses all stakeholders' expectations and concerns?

2 How should the Compact respond to those who criticize it?

3 What can the Compact do to encourage more active involvement from companies?

SUMMARY

Stakeholder partnerships have become a major component of corporate responsibility. They involve more than simply engagement by the company with those it influences or by whom it is affected. They require, instead, that stakeholders work together with particular aims in mind and, while they take different forms, partnerships share in common the idea that different stakeholders can come together to achieve outcomes that no single one could deliver on its own.

It is common to divide stakeholders into three sectors: business, government, and civil society. This is useful in understanding broad objectives and limitations, but can also mask significant differences in terms of intentions, motivation, and likely behaviour. Both business and non-business groups require a more sophisticated understanding of stakeholders than is sometimes implied. It must also be recognized that 'partnership' refers to a wide range of relationships and that there is no 'one size fits all' approach. Different types of partnership require different degrees of commitment, involvement, and resourcing. They can also send different messages about what a company wants to achieve. Many partnerships follow a command-and-control approach, under which stakeholders are viewed as something to be managed and the partnership is justified in strict business ends. Others see partnerships as evidence of a new way of approaching the business–society relationship, within which companies co-exist rather than seek to dominate. Indeed, partnerships are seen by some as a way in which to hold companies to account to society as a whole.

The view that a company takes of partnerships and the ends that it wants to achieve ultimately affect what partnerships it engages in and its management strategy. There is divided sentiment, both in business and beyond, about the value and risk of partnerships, and it is clear that partnerships are not an easy option either for company managers or for other stakeholders. Nonetheless, they have generated considerable enthusiasm and some of the more innovative corporate responsibility initiatives are the result of a partnership approach.

DISCUSSION POINTS

1 Corporate responsibility partnerships are typically voluntary, even though there may be contractual elements to them. This distinguishes them from the many business relationships that are legally binding.
    • What does the non-binding nature of partnerships say about corporate responsibility?
    • Can stakeholders be made accountable to each other without formal contracts?
    • What criteria would you propose in order that both companies and their stakeholders might evaluate the value of a particular partnership?

2 Different types of stakeholder participate in partnerships.
    • Is the distinction between business, government, and civil society useful in the partnership context?
    • What distinguishes a 'partnership' from an 'interaction'?
    • How would you go about establishing a credible partnership in China?

3 There are a growing number of international partnerships within which geographical proximity is less important than shared interests.
    • What are some of the partnerships that fall into this category?
    • What do they have in common?
    • How do they differ from geographically defined partnerships?

4   Managers often want to see the financial value of partnerships.
  • Is it possible to demonstrate how a partnership contributes to the bottom line?
  • What are the most convincing non-financial arguments for partnerships?
  • As the director of a NGO, how would you demonstrate the financial added value of a partnership to a South African mineral company?

5   Throughout this book, we give examples of partnerships that have been set up for various reasons. There are many more examples we have not mentioned.
  • Which partnerships do you think are the most important and why?
  • Can you identify examples for each of the six types of partnership?
  • Is 'partnership' an overused or underused word in corporate responsibility?

VISIT THE
WEBSITE
for links to
useful sources
of further
information

FURTHER READING

• Fussler, C, Cramer, A and Van Der Vegt, S (eds), 2004, *Raising the Bar: Creating Value with the United Nations Global Compact*, Sheffield: Greenleaf Publishing.
  Detailed presentation of the potential benefits of engagement with the UNGC.

• United Nations Environment Programme, Accountability and Stakeholder Research Associates, 2005, *Stakeholder Engagement Manual —From Words to Action: Vol 1—The Guide to Practitioners' Perspectives on Stakeholder Engagement*, New York, NY: United Nations Environmental Programme, Accountability and Stakeholder Research Associates.
  Comprehensive (if uncritical) manager-oriented handbook on stakeholder engagement.

• Utting, P and Zammit, A, 2006, *Beyond Pragmatism: Appraising UN-Business Partnerships*, Market, Business and Regulation paper no 1. Geneva: United Nations Research Institute for Social Development.
  Useful introduction to the theory of partnerships, backed up with lessons from the UN's experiences.

• Warner, M and Sullivan, R (eds), 2003, *Putting Partnerships to Work*, Sheffield: Greenleaf Publishing.
  Informative introduction to the various aspects of implementing partnerships, with a particular focus on oil, gas, and mining.

ENDNOTES

[1] Blowfield and Googins, 2007.

[2] Runciman, 2003.

[3] MacLean, 1999; Grinspun and Cameron, 1993.

[4] Crenson and Ginsberg, 2002; Putnam, 2000; Phillips, 2003; Ellsworth, 2002.

[5] A variety of definitions of 'civil society' can be found online using any search engine.

[6] Walker, 1994; Edwards and Hulme, 1996.

[7] Corcoran, 2006.

[8] See e.g. Peters, 1999; Rayner and Raven, 2002. In Holliday et al., 2002, NGOs are mentioned 20 times in the index, whereas trade unions are referred to only once.

[9] Edwards and Hulme, 1996.

[10] For example, the International Business Leaders' Forum and Cambridge University's Programme for Industry.

[11] See, e.g., articles in the journal, *Partnership Matters*, issues 1–3.

[12] Sabapathy et al., undated.

[13] Warner and Sullivan, 2003.

[14] Murphy and Bendell, 1999.

[15] Tesco *Corporate Responsibility Report* 2007, online at **www.tescocorporate.com**.

[16] Sabapathy et al., undated.

[17] Svendsen and Laberge, 2005.

[18] CCC, 2005c. Mitchell et al., 2003, seem to agree with this: out of six benefits that they cite in their case study, four are given as intangible, i.e. with no assigned monetary value.

[19] Sabapathy et al., undated.

[20] Svendsen and Laberge, 2005.

[21] For other lessons from organizations' experiences in implementing partnerships, see the case studies in Warner and Sullivan, 2003; UNEP et al., 2005; the materials available at **www.thepartneringinitiative.org**.

[22] See, e.g., Nelson, 1996; Pedersen, 2005; Fox and Prescott, 2004.

[23] Bendell, 2004b.

[24] Kell and Levin, 2003.

[25] Williams, 2004.

[26] Williams, 2004.

[27] Of 2,500 companies listed, 928 are listed as non-communicating, according to the UN Global Compact website—accessed 31 August 2006.

[28] Kell and Levin, 2003.

[29] Bendell, 2004b.

11

Socially responsible investment[1]

Chapter overview

In this chapter, we examine socially responsible investment (SRI), or the integration of social, environmental, and governance issues into shareholder decisions. We outline the origins and development of SRI, and address the impact that these investment strategies can, and do, have on individuals, companies, and wider society across the globe. In particular, we will:

- review the history and development of socially responsible investment;
- examine criteria used to screen socially responsible investments and the screening processes;
- look at the financial performance of SRI funds, compared with traditional funds;
- discuss engagement and present alternative socially responsible investment strategies, such as social and environmental venture capital;
- provide an overview of the international market for SRI and its development in different regional contexts;
- examine emerging trends in SRI.

Main topics

■ **Key terms**

Engagement

Negative screening

Positive screening

Socially responsible investment (SRI)

Triple bottom line

Venture philanthropy

■ **Online resources**

- Additional SRI-related case studies
- Exercises and discussion topics for students
- Additional materials on SRI
- Links to other web-based resources

The origins and development of socially responsible investment

In Chapter 8, we addressed the place of corporate responsibility in the corporate governance framework and how companies shape their relationships with a wider society. That discussion included consideration of the structures that are in place to ensure that managers do not invest in risky projects. This chapter looks at the structures in place to ensure that investors—individual investors, institutional investors, and fund managers—consider carefully the social, environmental, and ethical consequences of their investments. This approach to investment, with the intention of maximizing financial return (the 'bottom line') while valuing the social and/or environmental impact is known as 'socially responsible investment' (SRI). Other terms used include 'ethical investment', 'values-based investing', 'mission-based investing', 'socially aware investing', and simply 'responsible investing'.

Box 11.1 The SRI perspective on performance

According to Xavier de Bayser of Integral Development Asset Management (IDEAM):

Performance is a major aspect of an investment decision. But what is the real meaning of performance? The word 'performance' comes from the English 'to perform' which itself comes from the French '*par-former*'. The real meaning of performance is, therefore, achievement. And the achievement of an investment cannot only depend on return and risk. This would be a very limited approach. The investor has to think about a third dimension: the meaning.

(Bellagio Forum for Sustainable Development and Eurosif, 2006, p 11)

In this chapter, we ask why SRI is appealing to investors. What are the expectations of socially responsible investors, beyond those of financial performance? What are they trying to achieve in relation to risk and reward?

We begin by setting out the historical development of SRI and the evolving interests of investors. Strategies for investing in publicly traded companies and funds are addressed, including the screening methods that are used in assessing a company's products, services, or business practices. We examine how investors are contributing to social and environmental impact through their investment activities (Box 11.1) and, subsequently, how the role of fund managers is evolving. The provision of alternative investment opportunities is also discussed, including social and environmental venture capital. We look at different geographies and, in relation to the international SRI marketplace, at the investment options that address the unique social, environmental, and economic factors of those regions.

The origins of ethical investment

The principles of socially responsible investing are rooted in the Judaeo-Christian and Islamic traditions, which embrace peace and avoid business practices designed to harm fellow human beings. In the USA, the Religious Society of Friends (also know as the 'Quakers') is credited with planting the seeds of modern SRI as early as the seventeenth century, by following strategies that adhered to their principles of non-violence and human equality. Early Methodist stock market investment strategies purposely avoided companies that were involved with alcohol or gambling and this, in essence, created some of the first 'screens' or frameworks under which investors could evaluate business practices.

Some churches and charities with sufficient capital were able to persuade individual financial institutions to establish ethical funds, eliminating those companies that were engaging in business practices they perceived as unethical. It was, however, not until the mid-1960s that retail funds were available to private investors: the first such fund was established in Sweden in 1965. The Vietnam War marked another milestone in SRI, when certain investors started screening their investments to identify companies that supported the war: in 1971, the Pax World Fund was launched in the USA, which responded to the demand for investment options that excluded companies benefiting from that war.

In the 1980s, concerns arose among investors about supporting businesses with operations in South Africa, thereby supporting apartheid and the poor treatment of employees. Stocks were removed from portfolios, based mainly on ethical or non-financial reasons, and a divestiture movement in South Africa by US corporations emerged. While the public statement was significant, there is some evidence that institutional shareholdings increased when companies divested.[2] Attention also shifted to domestic business practices, including the use of child labour.

As discussed in Chapter 8, awareness of corporate conduct and responsibility grew during the 1980s and 1990s. In 1983, the Ethical Investment Research Service (EIRIS) was established, providing research on company activities and, subsequently, informing the development and analysis of more investment vehicles for both institutional and private investors. The first UK ethical fund—the Friends Provident Stewardship Unit Trust—was set up in 1984, while the US Social Investment Forum conducted the first industry-wide survey and identified $40bn of assets in social investing. Funds addressing concerns about the environment were also established, including the Merlin Ecology Fund (renamed the Jupiter Ecology Fund). In 2001, FTSE launched the FTSE4Good family of social indices, which will be discussed later in this chapter ('Fund indices', p 284). This sent a strong signal to investors that SRI was indeed becoming mainstream.

Since 2003, SRI funds and other offerings have emerged to meet the needs and interests of most investors with offerings in large-cap funds, US domestic equity index funds, international funds, and small-cap offerings. In 2005, the first socially screened Exchange-Traded Funds (ETFs) were launched. Catholic, Protestant, and Islamic faith-based investors all have options, and newer funds have been developed that focus specifically on labour and equal employment issues, as well as on the environment. New funds are being developed continually and in 2004, having seen the success of Islamic banks in the Middle East and Indonesia, HSBC launched its Amanah Pension Fund, a fund that was designed to comply with Shari'ah law, obeying special rules according to, and avoiding certain investments that are contrary to, Islamic teaching.

At the political level, the year 2000 signalled the mainstreaming of SRI in Europe, and the beginning of a more international and coordinated approach towards the disclosure of social, environmental, and ethical practices. The EU heads of state agreed to the Lisbon Agenda, in which corporate social responsibility and measures promoting sustainability were core to achieving the goal put forward: 3 per cent average economic growth and the creation of 20 million jobs by 2010. The first Global Reporting Initiative (GRI) Sustainability Guidelines were also released, setting out a framework for reporting (see Chapter 7).

In 2001, the European Sustainable and Responsible Investment Forum (Eurosif) was launched with the support of national European social investment forums and the European Commission. Also in the UK, the Myners Review of Institutional Investment published its final report, a short list of non-mandatory principles for investment decision making that applied to all pension funds and institutional investors. In the same way as the Cadbury Code addressed corporate governance (see Chapter 8), the Myners Review addressed investment, helping to set a new standard advocating shareholder activism.[3] In 2002, at the World Summit on Sustainable Development in Johannesburg, the 'London Principles' were announced to address how the financial sector, specifically,

Box 11.2 The 'London Principles'

Economic prosperity

Principle 1   Provide access to finance and risk management products for investment, innovation, and the most efficient use of existing assets.

Principle 2   Promote transparency and high standards of corporate governance in themselves, and in the activities being financed.

Environmental protection

Principle 3   Reflect the cost of environmental and social risks in the pricing of financial and risk management products.

Principle 4   Exercise equity ownership to promote efficient and sustainable asset use, and risk management.

Principle 5   Provide access to finance for the development of environmentally beneficial technologies.

Social development

Principle 6   Exercise equity ownership to promote high standards of corporate social responsibility by the activities being financed.

Principle 7   Provide access to market finance and risk management products to businesses in disadvantaged communities and developing economies.

(Adapted from www.environmental-finance.com)

could contribute to sustainable development (Box 11.2). Also that year, a second version of the GRI Guidelines was published.

Large-scale global SRI initiatives have continued. In 2004, Kofi Annan, then Secretary-General of the United Nations, issued *Who Cares Wins*, drafted in conjunction with several leading international financial institutions, outlining roles and responsibilities for different groups, including cooperation, working towards the goals of better investment markets, and working towards more sustainable societies. The document envisages a coordinated initiative by analysts and brokers, investors and asset managers, pension trustees, governments, multinational agencies, regulators, stock exchanges, non-government organizations, consultants, accountants, and educators.

In 2006, the UN Global Compact and United Nations Environment Programme's Finance Initiative (UNEP-FI) coordinated the creation of the Principles for Responsible Investment (Box 11.3). Initially, twenty mainstream investors worth $2 trillion signed on to the agreement. Within one year, as of June 2007, assets quadrupled to $8 trillion and the number of signatories grew to 183 (see Chapter 14).[4]

The G8 declaration from the 2007 meeting in Germany highlighted investment decisions, transparency, and sustainable development.[5] The latest iteration of the GRI—called the G3—has become the de facto standard. It must, however, be remembered that all of these initiatives, including GRI and the Global Compact, are non-binding and voluntary. And while there has arguably been significant progress made in the last decade, it can be argued that more is needed—raising further questions about what it would take, or if

Box 11.3 UN Principles for Responsible Investment

1 We will incorporate ESG (environmental, social, and corporate governance) issues into invest-ment analysis and decision-making processes.

2 We will be active owners and incorporate ESG issues into our ownership policies and practices.

3 We will seek appropriate disclosure on ESG issues by the entities in which we invest.

4 We will promote acceptance and implementation of the Principles within the investment industry.

5 We will work together to enhance our effectiveness in implementing the Principles.

6 We will each report on our activities and progress towards implementing the Principles.

(www.unpri.org)

indeed it is possible, for SRI to become the investment norm. The answer to these questions will be taken up in later sections of the chapter.

Criteria for socially responsible investment and screening processes

For all socially responsible investors, there is a fundamental question that needs answering at the pre-investment stage when researching publicly traded companies and investment funds: is the company to be included in the fund engaging in business practices that go against social, ethical, or environmental principles? Individual and institutional investors take different approaches to answering this question, and to determining which companies are therefore 'socially responsible'. This section reviews one of the core SRI strategies applied before investment to address this question: 'screening', or the evaluation of investment portfolios and funds based on environmental, ethical and/or social criteria. Here, we review the different types of screen that are used, and introduce some of the funds and fund indices that employ screens.

Negative screening

'Negative' screening eliminates companies that are engaging in what are perceived to be negative business or environmental practices. In a survey of 201 socially screened funds in the USA, the Social Investment Forum (SIF) found that tobacco is the most commonly applied social screen, affecting more than 88 per cent of the total assets in the socially screened fund universe. Alcohol affects 75 per cent and gambling affects roughly 23 per cent.[6] Other negative screens include weapons, pornography, nuclear energy, poor employment practices, the manufacture of hazardous or ozone-depleting substances, genetic engineering, and animal testing. The potential risk associated with negative screening is the possibility of altering the geographic or sector allocation of the investment portfolio.

'Norms-based' screening requires monitoring corporate compliance with internationally accepted norms, such as the Millennium Development Goals, the International Labour Organization core conventions, or the UN Global Compact.[7] This is usually grouped together with negative screening, used to eliminate specific risks to the portfolio, and to communicate with the general public and corporate members on the ethics of the organization. Because the screen itself makes an ethical statement, it might also be used to guard the reputation of the investor.

Positive screening

'Positive' screening is the selection of investments that perform best against corporate governance, social, environmental, or ethical criteria, and which support sustainability. Positive screening is associated with a 'triple bottom line' investment approach, ensuring that a company performs well according to economic, social, and environmental criteria. 'Best-in-class' screening is one such strategy, which selects the best within a given sector of investments, while 'pioneer' screening chooses the best-performing company against one specific criterion.

Examples of positive screens might include: improvement of health and safety conditions; integration of environmental criteria into the purchasing process; prevention of corruption; elimination of child labour; promotion of social and economic development.[8]

Fund indices

While investors might choose individual stocks or investment funds, fund indices have also been developed. Each of the indices uses a different weighting system for financial and non-financial performance. Three of the major socially responsible investing indices discussed in this chapter are KLD's Domini 400, the Dow Jones Sustainability Group Indexes, and the FTSE4Good Index, which is produced jointly by the *Financial Times* and the London Stock Exchange.

In May 1990, the Domini 400 Social Index (DSI) was launched by Amy Domini, Peter Kinder, Steve Lydenberg, and Lloyd Kurtz. The index removed 200 of the 500 stocks in the Standard and Poor's 500 (S&P 500)[9] through the application of social screens and then added in another hundred stocks to balance out the new index by sector. The goal of the index was to set a benchmark for SRI fund managers, similar to the S&P 500, which was subject to social and environmental screens. Today, approximately 250 DSI companies are S&P 500 companies, a hundred are non-S&P 500, and fifty others are chosen for their 'exemplary' records of environmental, social, and corporate governance practices.

The Dow Jones Sustainability Indexes (DJSI) were established in 1999 as the first indices to track sustainability-driven companies on a global basis. They were launched together by the Dow Jones Indexes, STOXX Limited (a European index provider) and SAM Group (a pioneer in SRI). There are over $5bn assets in DJSI-based investment vehicles. The DJSI uses a rules-based methodology and focuses on best-in-class companies. Assessment criteria include corporate governance, risk and crisis management, codes of conduct (including anti-corruption), labour practices, human capital development, sustainability and project finance (for banks), climate strategy (including eco-efficiency and protection of biodiversity), and emerging markets strategy.[10]

The FTSE4Good Index was launched in July 2001 and is derived from the FTSE Global Equity Index Series as an initiative of FTSE, in association with EIRIS and the United Nations Children's Fund (UNICEF). Today, there are two series: a benchmark index and a tradable index. The initial screening process looks at the starting universe—FTSE All-Share Index; FTSE Developed Europe Index; FTSE US Index; FTSE Developed Index—and screens against tobacco producers, companies providing parts, services, or manufacturing for whole nuclear weapon systems, weapons manufacturers, and owners or operators of nuclear power stations that mine or produce uranium. Positive screens are applied on the subsets of companies, corresponding with each of the original indices, to include companies that are working towards environmental sustainability, have positive relations with stakeholders, and uphold and support universal human rights. The inclusion criteria *'originate from globally recognized codes of conduct such as the UN Global Compact and the Universal Declaration of Human Rights'*.[11] In 2004, FTSE4Good launched a Japan index to add to the series. New climate change criteria were introduced in 2007.

New indices and initiatives

While the KLD's Domini 400, Dow Jones Sustainability Indexes, and FTSE4Good remain the flagship indices, other initiatives have emerged to address newer dimensions of the SRI market. In 2003, Dutch asset management company Kempen Capital Management and SNS Asset Management launched Europe's first SRI smaller companies index. USA-based Kenmar announced a new SRI hedge fund of funds, which was to be made available in mid-2007. SRI indices are also spreading to emerging markets, with the JSE SRI Index, based in South Africa, and the OWW Responsibility Malaysia SRI Index, which applies criteria to the FTSE Bursa 100 Index to determine if the companies are deemed socially responsible. One of the six groups of criteria in the Malaysian index is community, including Rakyat policies (based on Islamic banking principles, see Case Study 11.5) and Halal accreditation.

Brazil's Stock Exchange, BOVESPA, took the concept one step further by creating a a 'social stock exchange' (SSE), replicating the stock market environment for non-profit organizations. In this exchange, investors meet NGOs rather than corporations.[12] The current focus is on educational projects that benefit children between the ages of 7 and 25 who live in poor communities.[13] Education specialists recommend the best NGO projects to the board of BOVESPA, which then approves a list to become the portfolio of projects presented to investors by BOVESPA and its 120 brokerage firms. Individuals or organizations can buy 'social shares' in the projects, which are transferred entirely to the listed organizations without commissions, fees, or deductions. As of 2007, almost $2.3m has been raised for 43 NGOs listed on the SSE.[14] In June 2006, an SSE was launched in South Africa called SASIX (South African Social Investment Exchange), with the support of the Johannesburg Stock Exchange.

The concept of a 'social stock exchange' is, however, arguably too alien for most investors. When the idea of SSE was presented to other exchanges in Latin America and

Europe, it was met with resistance. As Celso Grecco, president of Attitude Marketing Social, was told by a representative of a European stock exchange:

> I just don't understand what we have to do with social matters. Let's leave it to our government, because we pay taxes and this is their business. Let's leave it to the Red Cross, to Oxfam, to the foundations. I don't believe my mother would understand seeing a stock exchange involved in social issues; imagine what my shareholders would think. Our business is to do business.
>
> (Grecco, 2007, p 132)

This reflects the sentiment of those who are generally sceptical of socially responsible investment, believing that the 'business of doing business' and addressing social issues are not compatible, or that SRI means compromising the end goal of doing business. But are SRI investments underperforming and giving financial reasons for investors to put their money elsewhere? The next section examines this issue, comparing the financial performance of SRI funds to that of other funds and indices.

CASE STUDY 11.1

SRI as a concern for pension funds—TIAA-CREF

TIAA-CREF provides retirement savings products for academic, research, medical, and cultural workers in the USA. Formed by the Carnegie Foundation in New York in 1918 as the Teachers Insurance and Annuity Association of America, it is now one of the world's largest financial services organizations, with more than $406bn in assets, 3.2 million retirement system participants, and 15,000 participating institutions. Since the 1970s, it has been an active social investor, and was one of the first investors to engage with corporate boards and management to advocate for change on the issue of South African apartheid.

> TIAA-CREF recognizes that it operates in a society not simply a marketplace and that its fiduciary responsibility is necessarily linked to its social responsibility. TIAA-CREF therefore takes positions on social issues that it believes will positively impact shareholder value.
>
> (UNEP et al., 2007, p 67)

Recognizing that some of its members have strong views on particular social issues, in 1990, it set up the CREF Social Choice Account (SCA) to provide an option that gives consideration to special social criteria. It is the largest comprehensive socially screened fund, featuring 430,000 investors and $9bn in assets. The account is managed by a partnership between KLD Research Analytics and TIAA-CREF's internal investment managers. Results of a 2006 study conducted by TIAA-CREF found that:

> an overwhelming majority, or 91 per cent, of participants who are not invested in SCA, and 85 per cent who are invested in it, agree or strongly agree with the statement that financial return is most important when making investment decisions.
>
> (Lacy, 2006)

Its engagement policy is that of 'quiet diplomacy', involving confidential discussions with board members and executives to voice any concerns. Every year, one or two topics of importance are selected for systematic engagement across the TIAA-CREF portfolio.

(UNEP et al., 2007; www.tiaa-cref.org; Lacy, 2006)

Questions

1 How can taking positions on social issues positively impact shareholder value?

2 Are you surprised by the findings of the TIAA-CREF 2006 study? Why or why not?

3 Considering the membership of TIAA-CREF, what type of screen do you think they would want to see as socially responsible investors? (NB TIAA-CREF's website will also provide ideas.)

Ethical fund performance compared with traditional funds

While SRI investors take a 'triple bottom line' approach, the economic or financial return on investment still remains an important part of the investment decision. While a company may engage in socially, ethically, and environmentally sound business practice, the financial performance, or potential for return on investment, is undoubtedly an important factor driving the investment decision. As Statman (2000) found, socially responsible investors do not sacrifice return for social responsibility.

SRI index performance

In an analysis of 29 SRI indices (not investment funds), Schröder (2005) found that they did not exhibit a different risk-adjusted return to that of conventional benchmarks. In other words, there was no significant difference in SRI and conventional index performance. Schröder did note, however, that many SRI indices have a higher risk relative to the benchmarks. A closer look at the performance of the KLD DS400, DJSE, and the FTSE4Good indices provides a clearer picture of the overall performance of the SRI industry in comparison with overall market performance.[15]

Comparing the performance of the KLD's DS400 Index to the S&P 500 (as of May 2007), the former has outperformed the latter since its inception in 1990 (12.28 per cent compared with 11.71 per cent). Annualized returns over a ten-year period are equal, with 7.78 per cent returns. Looking at the five-year, three-year, and one-year periods, however, the picture looks slightly different, showing an underperforming DS400 Index. Equally, analyses of the FTSE4Good indices, conducted over different time periods, found that investors would not necessarily be worse off by investing in a fund that tracks the FTSE4Good index.[16] An important factor to consider is the risk of the market sectors and individual stocks that are included in the index.

SRI fund performance

Several academic studies that have compared the performance of ethical and non-ethical funds have found no difference in financial performance.[17] Looking at the performance of SRI funds, there have been periods during which SRI funds have outperformed non-SRI funds. In 2002, SRI World Group found that the returns of thirty-two of sixty-two SRI funds beat more than half of their peer non-SRI mutual funds. Regarding three-year performance results, thirty of fifty-two SRI funds topped more than half of their peer non-SRI mutual funds. According to Standard and Poor's, the best performing SRI fund in 2004 was the £583m F&C Stewardship Growth Fund, which returned 21.8 per cent compared with the mean UK equity fund return of 12.2 per cent.

According to the Social Investment Forum (SIF):

> Socially and environmentally responsible investing in the United States [proved] remarkably robust during 2001 and 2002, despite sluggish market conditions that . . . resulted in a downturn in assets in the wider investment universe. Most notably, socially screened portfolios . . . grew 7 per cent, while the broader universe of professionally managed portfolios fell 4 per cent.
>
> (SIF, 2003, p i)

Assets in socially screened portfolios climbed to $2.15 trillion in 2003, an increase from the $2.01 trillion counted in 2001. Screened portfolios grew 7 per cent from 2001, while the broader universe of all professionally managed portfolios fell 4 per cent during the same period.

Accompanying the success stories, however, is notable criticism of SRI funds. While there are some funds with five-year returns of 50 or 60 per cent, the shorter term returns for one year might only be 3 per cent or lower.[18] Another consideration is the inherent bias in some SRI funds towards technology stocks and the overall volatility of such stocks since the late 1990s. But with any traditional or SRI investment decision, the portfolio, and the reputation and experience of the fund manager, must all be carefully considered.

Relative size is another problem when looking at the figures used to portray SRI's success. Although growth rates in percentage terms can be large, the actual amount invested in SRI funds is small when compared, for example, to that invested in hedge funds.[19] Additionally, SRI screening of some kind is being applied beyond the relatively small universe of SRI retail funds, making it increasingly difficult to calculate the exact size of the SRI market.

Engagement

While one fundamental question posed by SRI investors arises at the pre-investment stage, another arises at the post-investment stage: is the company *continuing* to engage in socially responsible business practices? Engagement is the process by means of which investors become involved with the business to influence its activities, behaviours, and operations. This section discusses some of these engagement strategies, including shareholder activism, proxy voting, policy statements, and engaging at different levels.

Traditionally, engagement occurs in response to the company's approach to corporate responsibility, or to a change in ethical and social practices. Other issues that might be cause for concern include the company's overall performance, internal controls, compliance, or general business practices, and responsible investors may raise these matters. Both private and institutional investors may raise the issues, although, typically, it is fund managers that play the largest role in the process. Chatterji and Levine (2006) argue that fund managers are in a position to play an important role in reforming performance metrics of socially responsible funds, enabling firms better to monitor social responsibility and manage shareholder value.

Shareholder activism

Shareholder activism includes activities that are undertaken in the belief that investors and shareholders can work together with management to change course and to improve financial performance over time. These activities can be conducted privately or publicly. Private methods might include letters to other shareholders, or to company management, to raise concerns. Institutional investors might raise issues during their routine meetings with company managers, or communicate their concerns to other investors to build pressure on the company; they might even join forces with other like-minded investors to take subsequent public actions. Public mechanisms for shareholder advocacy include raising questions during annual general meetings, or calling an extraordinary general meeting to propose shareholder resolutions. Investors might also issue press statements, or arrange briefings to make their reservations known to the wider international community of investors.

Proxy voting

At a company's annual general meeting, shareholders are given the opportunity to vote on a number of issues on the agenda. Following major corporate scandals such as Enron, Parmalat, and WorldCom, more shareholders are beginning to understand the importance and relevance of their voting and active participation. Usually, proxy voting applies to issues of corporate governance and, by voting against the mandatory approval of annual accounts and reports, shareholders and investors register their protest against company practices. Leading social issues that are likely to be the focus of attention include climate change, environmental reporting, sustainability, global labour standards, the HIV/AIDS pandemic, corporate political contributions (particularly in conjunction with election cycles), and equal employment opportunity. Voting practices vary from country to country, and Box 11.4 highlights some of the international resources and guidelines available. A study by Shearman and Sterling (2005) of the largest 100 US publicly traded companies found that nearly one third did not include any shareholder proposals in their proxy statements during the 2005 proxy season. The study did find, however, an increase in shareholder proposals supporting the removal of supermajority voting provisions in its proxy statement and for majority voting in director elections.

The Institutional Shareholders' Committee (ISC) Statement of Principles recommends that 'Institutional shareholders and/or agents should vote all shares held directly on behalf of clients wherever practicable to do so'. It further recommends that institutional shareholders should:

> not automatically support the Board; if they have been unable to reach a satisfactory outcome through active dialogue then they will register an abstention or vote against the resolution. In both instances it is good practice to inform the company in advance of their intention and the reasons why.
>
> (IMA, 2005, p 20)

Box 11.4 Resources on voting guidelines

Organization	Code
Commissie Tabaksblat (Tabaksblat Commission—The Netherlands)	Concept Code on Corporate Governance (*Concept-Code voor Corporate Governance*)
International Corporate Governance Network (ICGN)	Global Share Voting Principles
Mouvement des Entreprises de France (MEDEF—France)	Bouton Report (*Rapport Bouton*), *Promoting Better Governance in Listed Companies*
National Association of Pensions Funds (NAPF—UK)	Corporate Governance Policy and Voting Guidelines for Investment Companies
Organisation for Economic Co-operation and Development (OECD)	Guide for Multinational Enterprises
Swiss Stock Exchange (SWX—Switzerland)	SWX Code

Quarterly reporting to clients is standard; at which point the fund managers could also report how they voted and any shareholder resolutions. More and more, voting details are made available on fund websites, which could list resolutions, issues, and companies for any given period.

CASE STUDY 11.2

CalPERS in Japan

CalPERS, or the California Public Employees' Retirements System, provides pensions to nearly 1.5 million active and retired teachers in California. Its fund managers are cited as having revolutionized corporate governance in the USA in the 1980s and 1990s. It was one of the first foreign pension funds to invest in Japan and, in 1992, owned $3.7bn in Japanese equities. As Jacoby (2007) explains, there were three stages to CalPERS' activities in Japan:

1 pursuing activities on its own, voting proxies, using the media, and meeting with company officials;

2 working together with other institutional investors and domestic groups that also wanted to change Japanese corporate governance;

3 withdrawing from large-scale activism and moving towards '*firm-specific efforts based on relational investing*' (p 6).

Between 1988 and 1990, CalPERS voted proxies in ways similar to other foreign investors and then wanted to replicate its US proxy voting practices in Japan. CalPERS was particularly concerned with barriers to takeovers and the absence of independent directors, each of which CalPERS had grappled with in the USA. Dividend levels were also an issue of concern and CalPERS wanted so see more cash go to shareholders. Not wanting to be accused of greed or insensitivity to Japanese norms, however, the company was careful to vote against inadequate dividends as well as against excessive dividends.

But proxy voting proved to be an ineffectual way of inducing governance change in Japan and, beginning in the mid-1990s, CalPERS instead applied more 'general principles' of corporate governance. It also engaged in a public relations campaign, championing the virtues of foreign investors. By 1996, it had $5.6bn invested in Japanese equities. It also found allies, who shared the CalPERS vision, to engage in its second phase of activism, including local partners, and a small group of Japanese businessmen and academics that added legitimacy.

(Jacoby, 2007; www.calpers.com; Sterngold, 1993)

Questions

1 How do financial institutions diffuse the US model of corporate governance?

2 What was it about the local Japanese context that brought about a change in strategy?

3 What are the advantages and disadvantages of adopting a partnership strategy to foster change?

Policies statements, structures, and resources

Policy statements are commonly made by fund managers and are usually posted on the institution's website. The majority of fund managers employ dedicated staff to handle engagement, corporate governance, and SRI issues. Additional assistance might be provided by outside agencies. Policy statements might address monitoring the company, communication procedures with executive management, intervention strategies, and voting policies. The ISC Statement of Principles of engagement recommends that investors:

1 publish a policy statement on engagement;

2 monitor and maintain a dialogue with companies;

3 intervene where necessary;

4 evaluate the impact of their policies;

5 report to clients.[20]

The structure of engagement addresses how teams are organized within the fund to deal with corporate governance and SRI: a specialist team might cover only one, or both, dimensions of engagement. It is standard practice for fund managers to use external resources to provide research into the voting decision and to review internal resources that are dedicated to engagement. The central point of contact at the company is usually the head of corporate governance or SRI, but might also be a member of the senior management team. Another consideration is the process within the investment institution, such as the coordination of views among portfolio managers and analysts, and the participation of engagement specialists in company meetings with portfolio managers and analysts.

Levels of engagement

At the highest level, engagement is integrated into the investment process. Final decisions on controversial issues might be taken by senior management. It is also common for engagement specialists to work closely with portfolio managers. Most fund managers attend company meetings once a year and those who are more active will attend more meetings, often with independent company directors. This can be escalated by setting up additional meetings with management, expressing concerns to the company's advisers, meeting the chairman and the directors, or joining with other institutions on particular issues.[21]

Other SRI approaches

This section provides an overview of other SRI investment options that are not publicly traded.

Since 2001, various strategies have been developed, including venture philanthropy, social and environmental venture capital, community investment, and microcredit.

Venture philanthropy

'Venture philanthropy' refers to the application of the venture capital model, principles of entrepreneurial business, and the deployment of private equity to the social and environmental sectors. On the heels of the technology boom over the last two decades and the economic success of innovative technology entrepreneurs, we are now seeing a broad range of initiatives apply the strategies of venture capital—a recognized driver of innovation—within the social sector. Rather than expect a financial return, venture philanthropists are looking for 'social returns', or 'high impact' in the constituency that is addressed by the social project in receipt of the investment.

The term 'venture philanthropy' is not new and was used by John D Rockefeller III as early as 1969, at hearings on the subject of tax reform, before the US Committee on Ways and Means.

> Private foundations often are established to engage in what has been described as 'venture philanthropy', or the imaginative pursuit of less conventional charitable purposes than those normally undertaken by established public charitable organizations.
>
> (Council on Foundations, 2001)

In 1984, Bill Somerville, then executive of the Peninsula Community Foundation, used the term to explain the foundation's work. However, while the term is not new, its use and its definition are evolving and spreading internationally, embodying the following:

1 a long-term investment in organizations;

2 a partnership between the donor and the recipient (usually a charitable or non-profit organization);

3 provision of finance;

4 provision of expertise, skills, and/or resources that add value to the development of the organization and/or entrepreneur (which often includes access to the venture philanthropist's network of partners, who might be able to provide services such as accounting, marketing, or strategic consulting);

5 a view towards maximizing a 'social return on investment', or the bottom-line learning, towards outcome-based solutions to the underlying problem;

6 a focus on accountability, because venture philanthropists hope to understand the cause of the social problem in order to develop effective solutions;

7 an exit strategy, making the organization self-sustaining and financially independent after a few years of support.

Much has been written about the pioneering venture philanthropy organizations, largely based in the USA, which embraced these principles to support local, social innovation (e.g. Venture Philanthropy Partners, REDF—creator of the 'Social Return on Investment' Index—Accumen Fund, and Social Venture Partners to name a few). In the last five years, these principles have been embraced by philanthropists throughout the world to drive social innovation in both industrialized and developing countries, including traditional foundations (e.g. Rockefeller), newer foundations (e.g. Bill and Melinda Gates, Google.org), and individuals charting their own course in the social sector (e.g. the USA's Pierre Omidyar and South Africa's Mark Shuttleworth). This and other forms of what is commonly called 'social entrepreneurship' are discussed further in Chapter 14.

Environmental venture capital

'Environmental venture capital', or 'cleantech', looks at investment opportunities of private funds in entrepreneurial, environmental projects and companies that will reap financial, social, and environmental rewards for the investors. Opportunities for these investments include sustainable energy technologies, such as renewable energy, solar power, transportation, and distributed generation of power. In North America, $933m was invested in cleantech deals in the third quarter (July–September) of 2006.[22] Given the funding required for research and development, infrastructure, and other start-up costs, the typical investment size and scale of a cleantech project is large. For example, California-based Cilion raised $200m in just two funding rounds with its promise *'to supply America with 500 million gallons of environmentally friendly ethanol fuel per year'*.[23]

It is expected that fossil fuel-dependent nations, such as China and India, will need to take actions to safeguard a reliable stream of fossil fuels, to identify alternative sources of energy, and to pursue greater energy efficiency through technology and innovation. Renewable energy technology is seen as a way in which to reduce dependence on fossil fuels. In early 2007, Cleantech China™ was launched as a joint venture between Tsinghua Holdings Venture Capital (THVC), based in Beijing, and the Cleantech Venture Network, based in the USA.

There are a multitude of renewable projects presently active in the USA and in Europe. Germany has taken the lead in developing wind power, with some German states sourcing more than more than 1,800 megawatts of their power from wind. To date, solar and wind power have attracted the most investment dollars, while other experimental technologies are being tested, such as biomass—producing electrical power from agricultural crops—and photovoltaics—producing electricity from sunlight.

Cleantech investors expect both a high environmental and financial return. Fluctuations in oil prices, global concerns about water supplies, and an attention to fossil-fuel dependency have inspired both technological innovation and entrepreneurs looking build enterprises to address the environmental challenges. Cleantech investors are supporting this new wave of innovation. There is, however, also evidence of caution, because investment dollars deployed in cleantech have fluctuated and decreased at times, owing to the high risk involved with the development of new technology.

CASE STUDY 11.3

CANOPUS Foundation, Germany

The CANOPUS Foundation, based in Freiburg, Germany:

> promotes private *social investment* and *social enterprise* in order to fight poverty and environmental degradation, and provides business development assistance for social entrepreneurs in developing countries working in the field of clean energy technologies.

It invests only in non-profit organizations that operate in the field of clean energy technologies.

CANOPUS, like many other European venture philanthropy funds, provides several non-financial services in addition to its giving of grants. A recent study from the Skoll Centre of Entrepreneurship[24] found that many such funds deliver support through both their board members and through partnerships. At CANOPUS, business development is built into every project activity. In-house project managers (which are not all fully-paid staff) undertake site visits, field trips, and conduct reports. In addition to its in-house resources, CANOPUS works with people within its network of cities and local governments to identify those active in sustainable development who are on site, willing, and able to act as consultants. Specific services are provided through CANOPUS partners who have provided pro bono services to the foundation, including business plan evaluation, accounting, and writing year-end balance sheets for the portfolio organizations. Fundraising support is also provided to the entrepreneurs. The Foundation is prepared to receive calls, or to go a step further and take part in a meeting with the entrepreneur to speak in support of the project. CANOPUS is also said to be a useful partner in helping the entrepreneur to understand clean energy markets, supply and demand, and to get margins at the lowest price.

(Author's interview with CANOPUS Foundation; John, 2007)

Questions

1 Which aspects of the partnership do you feel are most beneficial to the social and/or environmental entrepreneur—funding, business services, strategic advice, etc.?

2 Why does the CANOPUS Foundation refer to itself as a venture philanthropy organization rather than as an environmental venture capitalist or cleantech investor?

3 How might the needs of a social entrepreneur differ from those of a business entrepreneur?

Community development investment funds

Community investing is defined by the Social Investment Forum as:

> financing that generates resources and opportunities for economically disadvantaged people in urban and rural communities in the U.S. and abroad that are under-served by traditional financial institutions.

(SIF, 2001, p 6)

Community development investment funds deploy equity and equity-like investments into small businesses in geographic areas that are traditionally overlooked by traditional venture capital and private equity funds. Typically, the businesses are located in disadvantaged communities, which will increase the entrepreneurial capacity of the area and create jobs, and results in what is termed 'high social impact'. Other development investment funds pool together investors, such as banks, corporations, insurers, foundations, and public pension funds, to provide support that can enable to provision of affordable housing, education, community centres, and small businesses.

Microcredit

'Microcredit' is the lending of very small loans (or 'microloans') to individuals. The concept emerged out of initiatives in the 1970s by organizations, such as Accion International and the Muhammad Yunus' Grameen Bank, which wanted to provide economic opportunity to poor people looking to start small businesses. Traditional banks were not interesting in making small loans, so a system of community banking was set up (called 'solidarity groups' within the Grameen Bank), under which small informal groups were formed to conduct business with the banks. The fundamental idea was to make money available to the poor, based on terms and conditions that were appropriate and reasonable.

While microcredit has helped in the alleviation of poverty for millions—particularly for women in Bangladesh—there are critics of the concept. A little money can support the development of a one-person business or the beginnings of a small shop, for example, but scaling up the business to the next level is not always easy when further financial support is needed. Other critics argue that savings need to be encouraged as well and so, for example, as Kenya's Equity Bank rolls out the microfinance concept to Africa, it is developing both loan and savings products.

CASE STUDY 11.4

Climate change, SRI, and emissions trading

According to the European Commission, the potential costs of all cumulative global damage due to climate change and global warming will be €74 trillion if effective action is not taken. The Association of British Insurers estimates that costs from typhoons, windstorms, and hurricanes will increase to an average of $27bn (€22.4bn) per year by 2080, from an estimated $16bn (€13.3bn) per year in 2005. The International Energy Agency reports that $16 trillion of investment in energy infrastructure will be needed over the next 25 years, which will also need to include the development of new technologies.

Emissions trading is one policy that has been developed within the EU as a strategy through which to achieve the Kyoto Protocol target of reducing emissions within the fifteen Member States (at the time of signing in 1998) by an average of 8 per cent over the period 2008–2012 from a baseline rate of emissions in 1990. The EU Emissions Trading Scheme affects over 6,000 European companies, forcing them to consider the price of carbon in business decision making. The Carbon Disclosure Project (CDP) was launched in 2000 to provide a secretariat to support collaboration from the largest institutional investors on the business implications of climate change. The investors collectively sign a single global request for the disclosure of information on greenhouse gas emissions. More than 1,000 large international corporations report their emissions through CDProject.net. On 1 February 2007, the fifth CDP request was signed by more than 280 institutional investors with assets of more than $42 trillion and was sent to over 2,400 companies.

(UK Government and European Commission, 2005; **www.cdproject.net**; Allianz and WWF, 2005)

Questions

1 Do you think that emissions trading will promote disclosure of information on greenhouse gas emissions?

2 Can emissions trading be an exclusively European operation, or does it have to be global (involving countries such as the US, China, and India) in order to be successful?

3 In the CDP, what assumptions are made about the organization of the fund manager and engagement strategies within the financial institution?

Markets and ethics

If the news of SRI's success is to be believed, efficient markets should be responding by normalizing SRI strategies into the investment mainstream. We can see how far this is actually happening by exploring SRI markets by geographical region.

North America

The SRI community itself frequently demonstrates its success by referring to its growth. The Social Investment Organization estimates total SRI assets in Canada in 2006 at $503.6bn, an increase from $65.5bn in 2004. SRI assets in the USA rose more than 258 per cent from $639bn in 1995 to $2.29 trillion in 2005, in comparison to the broader universe of assets under professional management, which increased less than 249 per cent from $7 trillion to $24.4 trillion over the same period.[25] Over 9 per cent of the $24.4 trillion in 2005, tracked in Nelson's Information's Directory of Investment Managers, is involved in socially responsible investing, equivalent to nearly one out of every ten dollars under professional management in the USA. Of the $2.29 trillion assets in 2005, $179bn were in socially screened investments, including mutual funds and separate accounts.

Mutual funds have been the fastest growing segment of SRI. Between 1995 and 2005, there has been a 15-fold increase in assets in SRI mutual funds: $1.5 trillion in assets were in socially screened separate accounts, managed for individual clients ($17.3bn) and institutional client accounts ($1.49 trillion). This represents 3 per cent of the $5,716.1bn that is held in separately managed accounts (SMAs), identified by Money Management Institute.[26] Shareholder advocacy has also become increasingly important. In 2005, institutional investors that filed, or co-filed, resolutions on environmental or social issues controlled nearly $703bn in assets. Assets in community investing institutions, managed on behalf of institutions and individuals, accounted for $19.6bn.

SRI-oriented institutional investors include pension funds, foundation endowments, university and college endowments, corporations, governments, hospitals, religious organizations, and other institutions that integrate social, environmental, and ethical issues into their investment strategies and practices. As of 2005, $1.49 trillion was held in socially screened investment assets. The largest segment of institutional investors is public pensions, including public retirement plans, educational savings plans, and local investment pools. Pension funds commonly screen against tobacco and against companies with operations in countries with repressive regimes (e.g. Sudan). The Investor Network on Climate Risk, started by the Coalition for Environmentally Responsible Economies (CERES), brings together institutional investors, who are concerned about climate change and who might conduct screens on environmental factors, to engage in shareholder activism.

Foundations and endowments form another large group of institutional investors who are looking to align the guidelines set in their programmes with their investment strategies. Typically, 95 per cent of a foundation's resources are used to generate income: this is called the asset 'corpus' and normally leaves 5 per cent to support payouts, administration costs, and grant-making activities. But if the asset corpus is invested only to maximize financial return (sometimes without any consideration to the make-up of the portfolio), only 5 per cent of the resources are driving 100 per cent of the social mission of the foundation. An idea put forward by some scholars and foundations is that, if the 95 per cent of the foundation's resources could be used to maximize the financial, social, and environmental impacts—taking a 'blended value' approach—the benefits generated by the investments could be exponentially greater than the impact of grants alone.[27]

Europe

There is often confusion and disagreement about what assets are managed according to SRI principles. According to EIRIS, £6.1bn is managed by SRI funds, but, according to 2006 research by Eurosif, there are €1,033 trillion assets invested in 'broad' SRI, as of 31 December 2005.[28] 'Broad' SRI includes positive and negative screens, engagement by fund managers, and the inclusion by asset managers of corporate governance and social, ethical, or environmental risk into financial analysis. This figure does not include Scandinavian data, such as Sweden's AP funds and the Norwegian Pension Fund Global, with its approximate €175bn of assets. Eurosif estimates that the broad SRI market might be as high as 10–15 per cent of the European funds under management. This might appear a high number, but it raises the question of how broad is 'broad'? If, for example, companies are screened for little more than pornography or eco-efficiency (one that is largely an illegal activity; the other, a proven business efficiency—see Chapter 5), SRI may be nothing more than efficient fund management, spurring doubts about the extent to which some of the figures on SRI are useful.

We can make some sense of this by looking at institutional investors. These account for 94 per cent of the European SRI market, with the remaining 6 per cent reserved for the retail market. Looking more closely at 'core' SRI practices, defined as screening, Eurosif discovered a different balance of investors among the different countries. In Italy, for example, core SRI is carried out almost entirely by the retail market. The drivers for SRI in Europe are also somewhat different to those in the USA. What might be called the 'business case' for SRI is becoming more obvious in Europe, particularly with increased awareness about climate change, the emergence of carbon emission quotas, and carbon trading. In addition, there is more European legislation, at both the national and supranational levels. The REACH Directive is one example that is intended to establish an integrated system for registering, evaluating, and authorizing chemicals, and doing away with a complex web of laws. The establishment of the Statement of Investment Principles for pension funds in the UK set the stage for similar reforms in Germany, Austria, and Italy.

Asia and the Pacific Rim

The membership of the Association for Sustainable and Responsible Investment in Asia (ASrIA), founded in 2001, includes institutions managing over \$4 trillion in assets. In 2007, ABN AMRO launched the first Indian SRI mutual fund, working with CRISIL, an Indian research and ratings company, as well as with KLD. Vyvyan et al. (2007) speak of a gap between SRI investment behaviour and attitudes in Australia. SRI funds comprise less than 0.5 per cent of funds under management in Australia, although several studies have reported that more than 50 per cent of respondents would consider SRI as a portion of their portfolio. Vyvyan et al. found that, ultimately, financial performance is the most influential factor in deciding whether or not to make an investment, even among environmentalists, whom they found '*were not significantly influenced by their beliefs*' (2007, p 380).

Yet the apparent unresponsiveness of the Australian investment community again raises a critical question: if socially responsible investment is so compelling, why are more people not doing it? Is it still perceived as being too risky, or as less profitable than other investment alternatives? Research has suggested that some investors may not know of the alternatives available to them. A study of foundations, conducted by the Bellagio Forum for Sustainable Investment and Eurosif (2006), revealed that 43 per cent of respondents believed that using SRI criteria in their asset management strategies would reduce returns, compared with the 15 per cent who thought that SRI strategies made no difference, and only 1 per cent who that thought that they would increase returns. This same perception crosses into the business world. A meta-analysis of social and financial performance by Orlitzky et al. (2003, p 427) argues against the traditional dichotomy and '*and/either/or trade-off*' between corporate financial performance and corporate social or environmental performance, which they claim is not justified given the positive correlation between the two and their bidirectional relationship.

What might appear to be a war of statistics about the utility or otherwise of SRI strategies may well escalate in the coming years, but this could have the opposite effect to that which some might wish. The more convincing the evidence becomes of a positive correlation between environment, society and governance, and financial performance, the less likely the need for a discrete field called socially responsible investment, because SRI strategies will be seen as nothing more than sound investment. This might be exacerbated by the fact that, at present, the definition of responsible investment is so broad that it verges, at times, on being meaningless. But, more importantly, there are still insufficient analytical tools for evaluating responsibility and hence how companies are to be valued. We look at trends in this area in Chapter 14 and also at how the behaviour of the investment community may affect corporate responsibility. In the final section of this chapter, we focus on trends within the SRI community itself.

CASE STUDY 11.5

Islamic ethics and SRI

There are an estimated 1.5 billion Muslims in the world, making up nearly a quarter of the world's population. The market for Islamic asset management is positioned to grow exponentially. According to a study by Merrill Lynch and Cap Gemini (2006), the Middle East region has the highest concentration of high net worth individuals, with an estimated wealth of over $1.2 trillion. Hakim and Rashidan (2002) reported that assets in Islamic institutions have grown 40-fold since 1982 to reach over $230bn.

As Segrado summarizes:

Islamic banking presents a holistic approach, based on Islamic principles on behalf of the individual and at the same time of the society he/she belongs to giving serious consideration to the global development constraints of the society.

(2005, p 9)

The principles of Islamic investing are outlined as follows.

(a) *Al Zakat* (the fourth pillar of Islam): One of the most important principles of Islam is that all things belong to God, and that wealth is therefore held by human beings in trust. The word *zakat* means both 'purification' and 'growth'. Our possessions are purified by setting aside a proportion for those in need.

(b) *Al Riba*: The prohibition of taking interest rates. Amongst Islamic scholars, there are two interpretations of what *Riba* means:
   i) a modernist view, according to which reasonable interest rates are allowed; and
   ii) a conservative view which states that any kind of fixed interest is wrong.

(c) The prohibition of unproductive speculation or unearned income (*Al Maysir*) as well as gambling (*Al Quimar*).

(d) Freedom from excessive uncertainty.

(e) The prohibition of debt arrangements—most Islamic economic institutions advise participatory arrangements between capital and labour.

(Segrado, 2005, pp 7–8)

Some brought up in the Christian-rationalist tradition of the West view Islamic traditions as radically different, but in comparing Islamic SRI mutual funds and indices with other types of SRI, there is a lot of common ground. A few of these Islamic funds include the Dow Jones Islamic Index Fund (IMANX), which passively tracks the Dow Jones Islamic Market US Index (IMUS), the Amana Income Fund (AMANX), and the Amana Growth Fund (AMAGX). The IMANX screens against alcohol, tobacco, pork-related products, conventional financial services (banking, insurance), weapons and defence, and entertainment. The fund also does not invest in the interest-paying instruments that are used traditionally by mutual funds. A distinguishing feature is, however, the lack of environmental screens in Islamic funds.

(Hakim and Rashidan, 2002; Segrado, 2005; Maali et al., 2006)

Questions

1 Compare one of the SRI indices mentioned earlier with one of the Islamic SRI indices. What similarities and differences do you see in the companies and screening processes?

2 What are some ways of addressing the lack of environmental screens on the fund—i.e. what other initiatives might be taken by investors or fund managers to raise any concerns?

3 How does the average performance of the AMANX or AMAGX compare to that of the Dow Jones over the last five years?

Trends in SRI

We conclude this chapter with a look at trends in SRI, the expansion of its definition, and new SRI initiatives. First, however, it is important to revisit some of the global trends that underscore growth in both developed and emerging markets. Climate change topped the agenda of the 2007 G8 Summit, signalling global, regional, and domestic regulatory pressure. Changing consumer and investor demographics signal trends towards 'greener' consumers, aware of their carbon footprint and seeking more environmentally friendly alternatives (see Chapter 9). In other words, some of the long-established concerns of SRI are now higher on political and business agendas than ever before. As discussed in Chapter 14, the consequences of this will be varied and far reaching, but it is certain to make the gap between SRI and mainstream investment interests narrower than has so far been the case.

The growth of screened funds

A study by Mercer Investment Consulting[29] predicts that environmental and social factors will become a common component of mainstream investment management over the next ten years. A broader and more diverse range of offerings is expected to emerge.

SRI products are now developing for emerging markets. BankInvest Global Emerging Markets SRI, an emerging market equity fund, is one of the pioneers. The negative screen excludes companies that have continuing violations of human rights, the environment, and labour rights, and those that derive more than 10 per cent of turnover from war material, alcoholic beverages, gambling, tobacco, or 3 per cent from pornography. The positive screen rewards the best and fast movers, and companies that have a high score in supporting human rights, labour standards, the environment, and corporate governance. The first investor in this fund was Mistra, the foundation for strategic environmental research, that is based in Sweden and which manages its assets in a socially responsible way. Some 80 per cent of its capital of SEK3.6bn is invested on the basis of environmental and ethical criteria.

Socially responsible bonds or bond funds provide another investment vehicle. These bonds offer a comparatively low-risk alternative, particularly to endowments and institutional investors looking for safe investment strategies with guarantees.

Reconceptualizing the social return on investment

Quantifying the link between social, environmental, and financial performance remains a challenge for companies trying to implement their sustainability strategy.[30] There exists today a proliferation of surveys and non-financial performance metrics, emerging out of lists developed by ISO (14000), CERES, and the Global Reporting Initiative. The Dow Jones Sustainability Indices use corporate board size as a measure of good corporate governance, but metrics that are easy to report are not necessarily the best for comparative purposes, nor most informative.[31] Already we see how different international standards for labour, safety, and the environment result in different cost structures for operations and measuring social returns seems likely to become more complex, not less. As Chatterji and Levine point out:

> Validity [of the measure] can also depend on context. Many non-financial performance metrics measure water in terms of meters cubed (e.g., the Dow Jones Sustainability Index . . .), but in regions where water is renewable and priced at its social value, water conservation is not an important social goal. Society is not better off if this 'environmental' metric induces firms to spend $100 to save water that is only worth $50 to society. At the same time, in most of the world water is not priced near its social value, especially when water is being pumped out of an aquifer that is slow to refill. In that case, it makes sense to encourage firms to spend $100 to save water worth $200 to society. Unfortunately, none of the existing metrics distinguish whether water is initially misallocated.
>
> (2006, p 6)

SUMMARY

In this chapter, we have looked at the development of socially responsible investment, and at its appeal to investors as a way in which to maximize financial, social, and environmental returns in the long term. We have looked at both pre-investment and post-investment strategies used to identify SRI opportunities—namely, screening and engagement. In reviewing the comparative performance of SRI investments to traditional investment routes, we learned that, on the whole, there is no significant difference in the performance of the SRI indices or funds, but that performance also needs to be reviewed in conjunction with risk and the different expectations of the investor.

While there are those who think that SRI and traditional investment are diametrically opposed, it can be argued that we are in the midst of a convergence. Cleantech, for example, is at the intersection—appealing to both traditional investors and to traditional SRI investors. This convergence may continue as reporting mechanisms become more transparent, analytical methods become more sophisticated, established SRI issues become of increasing concern to companies and investors, and SRI offerings continue to grow. But this is not to predict that SRI will radically transform the investment world, and the importance of SRI needs to be considered in the context of the other business, governance, and investment trends that are discussed elsewhere in this book.

DISCUSSION POINTS

1 SRI strategies require consideration of ethical, moral, environmental, social, and governance issues.
   - How would you go about identifying SRI investment opportunities?
   - What are some initiatives that try to ensure that companies are disclosing their social or environmental business practices, so that investors can make an accurate assessment?
   - What do investors expect from their SRI investments and how might their expectations differ from those of traditional investments?

2 This chapter reviewed the chronology and spread of SRI initiatives throughout the world, particularly since the 1980s.
   - What has driven consumer demand for responsible investment offerings and what are likely drivers for the next decade?
   - What are some of the various pre-investment and post-investment SRI strategies?
   - What are some of the initiatives that have helped to encourage the international expansion of SRI?

3 Most screening techniques are not limited to one screen (e.g. the exclusion of tobacco industries), but consider a variety of factors.
   - Pick one of the SRI indices discussed in this chapter and explain its selection criteria.
   - If you were to apply an Islamic screen to this SRI index, what companies would you remove and why?
   - Pick one of the companies on your screened list and look at recent proxies and/or shareholder resolutions filed. Discuss reasons why corporate governance actions might have been taken.

4 Revisit the section on 'The origins of ethical investment' (p 280).
   - What new initiatives are likely to emerge or develop between now and 2015?
   - Please describe and comment on the Global Reporting Initiative. What are its merits and limitations?
   - Which leading social issues are likely to gain attention in your country in relation to corporate governance and why?

5 Please review the section on 'Engagement' (p 288).
   - As a private investor, what are some of the ways in which you might make others aware of your concerns about a company's SRI practices?
   - As a fund manager, how might you communicate to the company your concerns about its business practices?
   - What are some of the ways in which you think international investors might better coordinate on their engagement efforts, either as institutional members or as members of organizations such as the UN Global Compact?

FURTHER READING

VISIT THE
WEBSITE
for links to
useful sources
of further
information

- Chatterji, A and Levine, D, 2006, 'Breaking down the wall of codes: evaluating non-financial performance measurement', *California Management Review*, 48(2), pp 29–51.
  Informative discussion of approaches to measuring non-financial performance and the current state of play.

- Epstein, M and Roy, MJ, 2003, 'Making the business case for sustainability: linking social and environmental actions to financial performance', *Journal of Corporate Citizenship*, January (9), pp 79–96.
  Arguments in favour of the efficacy of SRI.

- European Social Investment Forum, 2006, *European SRI Study 2006*, Paris: Eurosif.
  Overview of the current state of the SRI industry by one of its main industry bodies.

- Investment Management Association, 2005, *Survey of Fund Managers' Engagement with Companies*, online at www.investmentuk.org.
  Insights into the experiences of fund managers when engaging companies on SRI issues.

- Social Investment Forum, 2006, *2005 Report on Socially Responsible Investing Trends in the United States*, Washington, DC: Social Investment Forum.
  Overview of SRI in the USA.

ENDNOTES

1 This chapter was written by Kimberly Ochs.

2 Teoh et al., 1995.

3 More detailed information can be found online at www.hm-treasury.gov.uk.

4 Odell, 2007.

5 GRI, 2007.

6 SIF, 2006, pp 6–7.

7 More information can be found about the Millennium Development Goals online at www.un.org/millenniumgoals and the ILO core conventions at www.labourstart.org/rights.

8 See extensive lists available at www.eufosif.org.

9 The Standard and Poor's 500 is an index of 500 large-cap companies and is often used as a baseline for comparison. Stocks are chosen using S&P's methodology. Detailed guidelines can be found at www.indices.standardandpoors.com.

10 See www.sustainability-index.com for a summary of indices and screening criteria.

11 www.ftse4good.com.

12 See www.bovespasocial.org.br.

13 Grecco, 2007, p 131.

14 Grecco, 2007, p 132.

15 See www.kld.com/indexes.

16 Cobb et al., 2005; Collison et al., 2007.

17 See, e.g., Kreander et al., 2002; 2005; Gregory et al., 1997; Bauer et al., 2002.

18 See historical data on Ave Maria Catholic Values fund, or Calvert Large Cap Growth, as examples of this.

[19] Total money in SRI Funds 2005 = £6.1bn; total money in hedge funds 2006 = $1.786 trillion. Based on figures from EIRIS and HedgeFund.net.

[20] IMA, 2005, p 5.

[21] IMA, 2005.

[22] Kho, 2007.

[23] See www.cilion.com—accessed 6 June 2007.

[24] John, 2007.

[25] SIF, 2006, p iv.

[26] SIF, 2006, p 11.

[27] Emerson, 2002.

[28] Eurosif, 2006.

[29] Ambachtsheer, 2005.

[30] Epstein and Roy, 2003.

[31] Chatterji and Levine, 2006.

Part 3

The impact, critics, and future of corporate responsibility

12

The impact of corporate responsibility

Chapter overview

In this chapter, we examine the impact that corporate responsibility has had. In particular, we will:

- consider why understanding 'impact' is important;

- look at the different ways in which impact is assessed and the ways in which we learn about impact;

- establish a framework for understanding the different dimensions to impact;

- provide an overview of the impact of corporate responsibility to date;

- discuss the challenges of assessing impact;

- examine how our current understanding of impact might affect the future development of corporate responsibility.

Main topics

■ **Key terms**

Corporate reporting

Corporate social performance

Environmental, social, governance
(ESG)

Non-financial performance

Social and environmental ratings

■ **Online resources**

- Additional examples of corporate responsibility's impact

- Exercises and discussion topics for students

- Suggested questions to encourage analysis of corporate responsibility reports

- Links to other web-based resources

Understanding impact

What does corporate responsibility do? Does it help to make the earth more sustainable? Does it restore trust in corporations? Does it reduce poverty? Uphold international human rights? Reduce corporate malfeasance? Increase business profitability? Lessen corruption and improve public governance? End illegal activity such as smuggling and human trafficking?

  These are some of the areas in which, as we have already seen, corporate responsibility is intended to have an impact. In this chapter, we look at the evidence to support these claims. In business or any area of life, understanding the impact is essential for making decisions, justifying courses of action, and recognizing the point at which we stand on particular journeys. In the corporate responsibility context, impact is essential if corporate responsibility is to defy its critics and move from being a 'feel-good thing' to being recognized as a 'good thing'. Whether one looks at the theoretical work on corporate social performance in the 1970s and 1980s, or at that on social accountability since the 1990s, the importance of measurement is apparent. Yet, given the emphasis put on '*if you want it to count, count it*', or the rooting of important corporate responsibility tools and methods in financial accounting, it is surprising how patchy attempts to measure corporate responsibility have been and that we do not know more about corporate responsibility's overall impact.

Corporate responsibility has big goals, such as contributing to sustainable economic development, improving the quality of life for workers and their communities, and accelerating progress towards the Millennium Development Goals. Moreover, these contributions are often linked to conventional ones of corporate growth and profitability. Part of this chapter is concerned with finding out what evidence there is to show how far corporate responsibility has met these goals and, as importantly, the extent to which the evidence itself is being gathered. As we will see, the information is fragmented and, to make sense of it, we offer a framework that clarifies the different types of impact about which we do know something ('A framework for understanding impact', p 314). We use this framework in an overview of the current state of play in 'Different dimensions of the impact of corporate responsibility' (p 315), and conclude the chapter with a section discussing 'The challenges of determining impact' (p 330) and what might happen in the future.

The meaning of 'impact'

In its most general sense, 'impact' refers to the outcomes associated with particular actions. Although this is too simple a definition, it draws attention, first, to the importance of outcomes (cf. outputs) and, second, to the significance of causality. As examples in this chapter reveal, discussion of impact often confuses 'outputs' for 'outcomes'. But although the two words overlap in some contexts, the former is narrower in meaning, referring to the specific actions that are needed to achieve a larger result, whereas the latter is the larger result itself. (For example, degrees are an *output* of university that have the *outcome* of creating a better educated population.) Thus, in the corporate responsibility context, a corporate responsibility report is an output, not an outcome, if our aim is to enable business to manage its relationship with society better.

Demonstrating a causal relationship between inputs, outputs, and outcomes is, however, far from straightforward. A company might be clear about what it wants to achieve (e.g. to remove child labour from its supply chain), but even if this happens, can it be sure that the outcome was the result of its own actions rather than, for example, a concerted enforcement effort by the police? Roche (1999) argues that one should not place too much emphasis on causality, defining impact assessment as '*the systematic analysis of lasting or significant changes—positive or negative, intended or unintended—in people's lives brought about by an action or series of actions*' (emphasis added). This definition also highlights how, for many, impact refers to the outcomes for people, although as we shall see, the beneficiary of corporate responsibility may also be a company or a particular stakeholder group.

How we learn about impact and the limits of our knowledge

There are three readily available sources of information relating to the impact of corporate responsibility: corporate responsibility reports (including social, environmental, and sustainability reports); ratings of companies such as FTSE4Good, the Ethibel Sustainability

Index, the KLD Indexes, ARESE social ratings, and the Dow Jones Sustainability Indexes; case studies of companies undertaken by companies, corporate responsibility organizations, and others.

There are also case studies of companies and industries that are undertaken by a variety of organizations monitoring corporate behaviour (e.g. CorpWatch, Christian Aid, *Stichting Onderzoek Multinationale Ondernemingen*, or 'SOMO'—the Centre for Research on Multinational Corporations). These have been very influential in the overall development of corporate responsibility and, in important ways, have set out benchmarks against which the corporate responsibility practices of firms can be assessed. There are reports documenting the progress of companies within particular partnerships, such as the annual reports on compliance with labour standards by the Ethical Trading Initiative or the Fair Labor Association. There are also publicly available reports about the certification of particular resources in accordance with the criteria of bodies such as the Marine Stewardship Council, or, in some cases, of facilities such as those adopting the ISO 14000 series (although often the information most pertinent for assessing the impact of these is considered proprietary and not in the public domain).

In addition, there are what can be called 'trend-tracking' reports, focused on particular aspects of corporate responsibility (Box 12.1). There has been a well-documented rise in the number of corporate responsibility reports and, according to the KPMG 2005 *Corporate Responsibility Survey*, 52 per cent of the 250 largest public companies in the world were issuing reports; 68 per cent of these contained economic, as well as social and environmental, information. The framework of the report, and how that is used over a number of years, is an important factor in showing impact. Forty per cent of the companies in the KPMG survey used the Global Reporting Initiative Sustainability Reporting Guidelines described in Chapter 9, and the Association of Chartered Certified Accountants reporting awards refer both to the GRI and AccountAbility reporting frameworks.

Box 12.1 Surveys and reports on corporate responsibility performance

- *State of Corporate Citizenship* (USA)—an annual report highlighting trends and corporate attitudes to corporate responsibility among US companies.
- *Business Ethics*' 100 Best Corporate Citizens list.
- Covalence's Ethical Ranking—a reputation index of the largest market capitalizations in the Dow Jones Index, based on their contributions to human development.
- *Business Week*/Climate Group's Climate Change Rankings—multinational companies by their total reduction of greenhouse gases.
- *Sustainability Reporting Survey* (Germany)—an overview of company reporting.
- Fortune 100 Accountability Rating—scoring Global 100 companies on how seriously their future decisions will consider non-financial matters.
- GMI's Corporate Governance Ratings—3,200 global companies.
- KPMG produces an annual corporate responsibility survey focused on reporting trends.
- Transparency International's Global Corruption Barometer—public opinion of corporations.
- World Economic Forum's biannual *Trust Poll*.

Various company reports also refer to the UN Global Compact, the International Labour Organization's core labour standards, the UN Declaration on Human Rights, the Kyoto Protocol, and other agreements that, while not binding on business, are often used in defining corporate responsibility performance. As we shall discuss later, a significant area of impact is how corporate responsibility's success has impacted its own behaviour ('The impact of corporate responsibility on itself', p 328) and the adoption of common standards that facilitate comparison between companies is an important aspect of this.

The limitations of the information

Before we look at the types of impact that the above sources of information reveal, it is worth noting some of the comments that have been made, particularly about reports, ratings, and case studies. The 2005 KPMG survey of corporate responsibility reporting noted that industries with the greatest environmental impact have the highest levels of reporting (e.g. 80 per cent of electronics and computers, utilities, automotive, and oil and gas companies produce reports), although there has been a rapid rise in the financial sector, which is not considered to be an industry with a heavy environmental footprint. The range of topics is increasing so that, now, about two-thirds of reports have sections on corporate governance and 85 per cent mention climate change. Nonetheless, certain issues are seldom reported upon, such as economic impacts (25 per cent of reports), and, in general, environmental impacts are better reported on than social ones. Furthermore, while 40 per cent of reports base their content on GRI guidelines, only 21 per cent employ stakeholder consultation to identify the issues that the reporting company should be addressing.

The use of particular standards—even if well regarded—tells us only so much about impact. As Clark (2005) shows, corporate responsibility is being undermined by such practices as the falsification of records and the training of workers in how to respond to auditor questioning. The UK consultancy firm, Impactt Ltd, says that 95 per cent of factories it visits in China probably falsify records and that managers can buy software to help with this. In response, some have called for stronger independent assurance and, in 2005, 30 per cent of reports were independently assured in some way, mostly by the large accounting firms. As the 2002 *Trust Us* report[1] points out, however, there are big questions about how far such companies have restored public trust in their own integrity, although there is evidence that competition between firms and the need for credibility has improved the market for standards.[2]

As discussed in Chapter 7, the Association of Chartered Certified Accountants, which runs sustainbility reporting award programmes in different parts of the world, has identified recurring weaknesses in company reports. These are summarized in Box 12.2, but those that particularly stand out are the lack of systemic ecological footprint analysis of the company's impact, the lack of comprehensive maps of stakeholders, and the lack of information on the key impacts that the company's operations and products, or services, have on society and the natural environment.[3]

Ratings, in as much as they derive data from corporate reports, will reflect the above limitations to some degree. The situation is also confused by the heterogeneous methods

Box 12.2 **Areas in which corporate responsibility reports show weakness**

- Few companies define what they mean by sustainability and, even if they do, it is not reflected in the main body of the report.
- There is insufficient information on the key issues for the organization and how these were decided upon.
- Few companies define the issue on which they are reporting and its implications for their business.
- Reports list different social, economic, and environmental imperatives, but they do not show how the organization resolves conflict between imperatives.
- Little consideration is given to the impact that being a truly 'sustainable business' would have on the organization's operations. The reports do not offer information by which to assess whether the organization is capable of, or understands, what it would require to make this transformation.
- There is a tendency to aggregate and summarize performance information without making available information from specific locations.

(Summarized from ACCA, 2005)

they use. Schafer (2005) distinguishes between ratings systems that are economically oriented (i.e. those that focus on the economic impact of ethical, environmental, and social criteria on the company) and those that are normatively oriented, within which evaluation criteria are dominated by what he calls 'ethical' motivations. Among the economically oriented systems (which he says are dominant), there are four groups:

1 risk assessment approaches (how the company deals with its social or environmental risks);

2 efficiency models (how management strategies relate to sustainability, on the assumption that sustainability offers competitive advantage);

3 industries of the future (identifying the above-average growth companies inside what are considered to be the hot sectors of tomorrow);

4 best-practice corporate responsibility management (identifying companies with the best approaches to corporate responsibility management).

For Margolis and Walsh (2003), this focus on the economic consequences for the company is a basic weakness in our understanding. Echoing some of what we have discussed regarding the business case (see Chapter 5), they say '*if corporate responses to social misery are evaluated only in terms of their instrumental benefits for the firm and its shareholders, we never learn about their impact on society*'.[4] Indeed, they argue that the emphasis on instrumental benefits is so great that there is little attempt to examine when it is permissible or necessary to act on other stakeholders' interests if they are not consistent with those of shareholders.

This is not a widely shared view. Environmentalist Jonathan Porritt applauded Unilever's award-winning 2005 environmental report for relating the company's approach to its business success and the 2004 European Sustainability Reporting Awards praised other reports, such as those of Kesko in Finland or of BT in the UK, for setting out the business rationale for corporate responsibility. Even fairtrade companies, such as Traidcraft, often talk about their success, to some degree, in terms of instrumental benefits (e.g. revenue, sales, staff turnover).[5] Nevertheless, the consequences of an economic orientation in reporting and ratings will become apparent when we look, in the next section, at what we do and do not know about the actual impact of corporate responsibility. Moreover, we should not be surprised at this orientation, given the degree to which corporate responsibility has sought legitimacy by rooting important elements of its methods and approaches in the norms and instruments of financial management, accounting, and managerial efficiency.

Finally, we need to note the limitations of case studies as a way in which to assess impact. These have proved important in terms of drawing attention to particular issues and examples of company behaviour. The most well known are probably those of civil society organizations, such as the Clean Clothes Campaign's case study of an Indonesian factory producing for Fila, or SOMO's 2005 investigation of labour rights violations in computer factories. There are also interesting examples commissioned by companies, such as Impactt Ltd's (2005) study of overtime in Chinese factories. But by their very nature, case studies tend to use differing methodologies and it is difficult to aggregate findings. Moreover, as Elliott and Freeman (2003) note, the organizations that produce many of the case studies typically only need to understand the situation on the ground in order to start a campaign; from that point on, the main dynamics happen away from the site of the problem, i.e. through the media, company responses, consumer reaction, and government action. Equally, the organizations are reluctant to say which companies are strong performers, because they do not want to jeopardize their own credibility. This makes sense from the NGO or trade union perspective, but means that it is difficult to use case studies to draw conclusions about the impact of corporate responsibility.

CASE STUDY 12.1

Who do we trust?

We know surprisingly little about the impact of corporate responsibility, especially when it comes to understanding corporate responsibility's contribution to major world issues, such as poverty alleviation, global warming, and sustainability. In the absence of hard information about outcomes, Mitnick (2000) says that we need to know what companies want, how they are achieving their goals, and whether we should have confidence in what they claim.

With that in mind, consider a press release by a major public relations firm, headlined, *The Cocoa Trade is a European Success Story*. Describing a study by the confectionery industry, the press release says that major companies buy cocoa from developing countries and shows how large the chocolate market is in Europe. It concludes, '*Cocoa trading is an efficient tool to overcome poverty and to reach the United Nation's Millennium Development Goals*'.

Yet a glance inside the full report reveals that the industry does not collect comprehensive data about cocoa producers and the authors acknowledge that the industry has no clear methodology to quantify its impact.

Now, consider the fact that the same claims and statements did not actually come from the mainstream confectionery industry, but from fairtrade organizations. The claims about contributing to poverty alleviation were made in a press release by Traidcraft and the admissions about the lack of data or consistent methodology are in a related report by the International Federation of Alternative Trade.

(IFAT, 2006; www.traidcraft.co.uk—accessed 30 March 2006)

Questions

The fairtrade movement's success depends on its credibility and reputation for delivering greater benefits to poor and small farmers than those of conventional trade.

1 Do you think that its claim to be an efficient tool for achieving the Millennium Development Goals is credible, given the data it collects about its impact?

2 Do you think the levels of public trust are different for fairtrade organizations compared with multinational companies?

3 What might be the consequences for corporate responsibility in the future if levels of trust do not reflect our knowledge of companies' performance?

A framework for understanding impact

If we think about the possible answers to the question posed at the start of this chapter— *'What does corporate responsibility do?'*—it is readily apparent that 'impact' has a different meaning if we are talking, for example, about helping to make the earth more sustainable than if we are referring to reducing corporate malfeasance, or to improving business profitability. What is recognized as impact also differs if one is looking at instrumental or normative dimensions of performance.

To help to make sense of these different dimensions, we offer a framework that captures the different ways in which impact is being interpreted. It is based on what others have written about the impact of corporate responsibility and measuring corporate social performance,[6] and also the different aspects of impact included in a selection of award-winning corporate responsibility reports.[7] What emerges are five dimensions on which corporate responsibility seeks to have an impact.

1 **The 'big picture'**
This refers to large social and environmental issues, including global warming, human rights, economic growth, and poverty reduction.

2 **Instrumental benefits**
This covers the connection between financial performance, and social and environmental performance, including the impact of making the business case for corporate responsibility.

3 **Business attitudes, awareness, and practices**
These refer to the impact that corporate responsibility is having on the way in which companies think about non-financial aspects of business operations and the way that they operate.

4 **Non-business stakeholders**
This refers to the impact of corporate responsibility on other stakeholders, including the critics who advocate for greater social and environmental responsibility.

5 **The impact of corporate responsibility on itself**

This area covers the way in which corporate responsibility's evolution and growth has affected how we think about and practise corporate responsibility today.

We use this framework throughout the following section.

Different dimensions of the impact of corporate responsibility

The impact of corporate responsibility on the 'big picture'

In various chapters, we have seen that corporate responsibility is being linked to many of the biggest challenges around the world. These include how we:

1 respond to climate change;

2 address the consequences of globalization;

3 uphold international human rights;

4 increase justice and equity, especially in the poorest countries;

5 fight corruption and poor governance;

6 achieve stable and sustainable economic growth.

Although some corporate responsibility initiatives have been framed in terms of these big picture issues, it is impossible to show attributable impact at this level. Instead, we can only understand pieces of the mosaic. The GRI Guidelines and various internationally used standards are attempts to break these overarching goals down into addressable pieces.

In this section, we examine what is known about the impact of corporate responsibility on some of these issues. Areas such as corruption or governance are inherently unsuited to measurement of external outcomes, at least in the short term, and have largely been viewed in terms of changes in business attitudes and practices (see 'Impact and the business case', p 321). Therefore, we will look at the broad areas of environmental, social, and economic impact.

Environmental impact

Environmental management has been central to corporate responsibility since the 1980s and it is not surprising that we know more about the impact of corporate responsibility in this area compared with others. The term embraces such aspects as natural resource management, waste management, recycling, marketing of green products, and pollution prevention and control. There are a number of well-developed initiatives that can demonstrate their impact over a period of several years. For example, in 1995, the Forest Stewardship Council had certified less than 5 million hectares of responsibly managed forest, but that figure had grown to over 68 million by 2006.[8] This means that 775 forests in 66 countries are being managed, largely by companies, according to the responsible forest management criteria promoted by FSC. Even though relatively few tropical moist forests have been certified (2.4 per cent of the total certified forests) and over 8 per cent of the forests are in Europe or North America,[9] this is a significant impact, and, moreover, FSC's persistence in using relatively demanding social and environmental criteria has made it more difficult for competing standards to introduce less challenging targets.

Many companies, such as Diageo, Procter and Gamble, and Unilever, have successfully reduced their water use. For example, Unilever has lowered its own worldwide usage by 54 per cent over ten years and has extended this by working with its suppliers so that, for example, tomato growers have reduced their consumption by half.[10] Although Unilever is often cited as a leader in terms of environmental reporting, other areas of impact are also worth noting. In 2005, the company estimated that, by the following year, it would source 60 per cent of the fish it sold within Europe from sustainably managed fish stocks; it has increased its paper-based packaging to 83 per cent in Europe; it has reduced diesel fuel usage for transportation; it has lowered carbon dioxide emissions from its manufacturing operations by 25 per cent since 1995. It demonstrates year-on-year reductions in units per tonne of production in what it recognizes as seven key areas of eco-efficiency, including energy, hazardous waste, and improvements in the management of ozone-depleting gases.

In some instances, Unilever is managing the environment in compliance with national laws. This is common to many companies, especially in developed economies, where it can be difficult to conclude what is an impact of corporate responsibility and what is the result of government regulation. In fact, unlike social impacts, most environmental information seems to concern developed, rather than developing, economies, even though government regulation in the latter seems likely to be weaker.[11] In the USA, however, where federal government has not been at the forefront on environmental issues such as global warming, companies, such as DuPont, Procter and Gamble, and Coke, have adopted targets for reducing greenhouse gas emissions that broadly reflect the spirit of the Kyoto Protocol, although, as the 2005 FTSE4Good report highlights, US firms overall are much less likely than European firms to address environmental criteria.

BP, the second largest oil and gas sector company, has remained at the forefront of thinking about how business can contribute to sustainability since, in 1996, becoming the first energy firm to withdraw from the Global Climate Change Coalition, which challenged scientific arguments for climate change. It said it would reduce its greenhouse gas emissions at twice the rate specified in the Kyoto Protocol and met those targets nine years ahead of schedule, reducing emissions by the equivalent of 9.6 million tonnes and bringing operational savings of $250m.[12]

Figures on individual company performance in important areas of environmental management are available for most major companies in oil and gas, automotive, utilities, and other industries with high levels of environmental impact. But commentaries on ratings and reporting continue to emphasize that too many companies have not identified what their key sustainability issues are, or how they most affect the environment.[13] The information available is synthesized by ratings organizations, but there has been little attempt to assess the overall impact of corporate responsibility on key areas of environmental management. Furthermore, the data highlight trends (e.g. the year-on-year percentage change in a particular performance area), but does little to show what is the 'right' number, such as the level of carbon dioxide emissions that is ultimately acceptable, or the amount of water usage needed to maintain a certain ecosystem. Indeed, companies have tended to shy away from this type of claim. For example, at the launch of the European Retailers' Group's Guidelines on Good Agricultural Practice in November 2000, the organization's chair said that the initiative was not intended to measure or report the overall environmental impact of implementing the guidelines.[14] Failure to gauge systemic impact will become a more important issue as certain approaches are accepted as best practice, something that is already evident in the questions being posed about carbon trading.[15]

Social impact

Social impact includes such issues as human rights, working conditions, labour rights, the impact on indigenous peoples, and the impact on local communities. As already noted, this is a more recent development than that of environmental management and, not surprisingly, there are fewer data on impact, although companies such as Reebok provide comprehensive human rights data. Adopting labour standards in supply chains has become a significant component of corporate responsibility. Vogel's (2005) comprehensive review of the literature concluded that there had been little systematic analysis of the impact on workers and their families, but a study of 800 suppliers in 51 countries concluded that, if monitoring of labour conditions were to be accompanied by other interventions (e.g. improved factory management), there would be significant improvements for workers.[16] A comprehensive multi-country empirical study of the impact of monitoring a labour standard showed that conditions in some places had improved (especially with regards to health and safety, and child labour), but that this had little effect on wages or freedom of association, and some improvements had even left workers worse off (e.g. a decline in take-home pay due to reduced working hours).[17] The apparel industry, in particular, has made significant advances in driving out child labour and the ILO says that child labour fell by 11 per cent during 2000–2004. There is also evidence, however, that removing children from an export-oriented factory can be a mixed benefit if other opportunities are worse, or if opportunities for education decrease. In fact, the net impact can be that Western consumers have their demand for goods produced by adult labour fulfilled, but that there is no change in the numbers of working children.[18]

Exploring labour conditions in Indonesia, Harrison and Scorse (2004) conclude that codes of labour conduct, together with anti-sweatshop campaigns, were responsible for increasing wages in export-oriented factories during the 1990s and, moreover, that this was achieved without lessening employment opportunities. This finding is interesting, because of the large dataset with which they had to work, but smaller studies can also be insightful. For example, data from 142 southern Chinese factories audited by Verité in 2002–2003 revealed excessive overtime in 93 per cent of cases. This seems to support the findings of Impactt Ltd that compliance-focused auditing of labour conditions has had little impact on improving working hours. As ETI remarked in its 2003–2004 report, improved compliance with codes is not necessarily a sign of sustained improvements in labour practice and may only mean that suppliers are becoming better at passing audits.

This is probably truer for some aspects of social performance than it is for others. For example, although there may be little sign that workers are getting true living wages because of corporate responsibility, Vogel (2005) concludes that there are attributable signs of improvements in working conditions, and ETI's annual reports consistently show that the majority of non-compliances detected and addressed relate to workplace health and safety. Although this has been derided for being a simple target in terms of the greater corporate responsibility challenge, when one considers that, in 2005 in China, based only on official figures, there were a quarter of a million workplace accidents and over 126,000 deaths,[19] advances in working conditions are a significant achievement.

But companies are frequently not making data about social impact available. According to Ruggie et al. (2006), only one company—BP—has made public the findings of a human rights impact assessment. Likewise, companies may admit to the need for public reporting on all material aspects of their performance, but this does not mean that they are consistently reporting on the benefits of programmes with potentially significant social impact, such as those in the pharmaceutical industry to combat HIV/AIDS in poor countries.[20] This reinforces the impression noted earlier that many companies are not systematically identifying key issues.

The picture is not necessarily clearer when one examines niche areas of corporate responsibility with explicit social objectives. For example, Vogel (2005) describes the impact of Rugmark, the anti-child labour label, in terms of its expansion as a segment of its industry rather than in terms of its ability to provide a better life for the more than 3,000 children in its rehabilitation and educational programmes.[21] A series of case studies comparing the social impact of fairtrade, organic farming, and forest certification projects found that they increased livelihood opportunities and income levels for many participants, and provided access to new markets, and the opportunity to develop human and social capital.[22] The studies also showed, however, that certain groups of people can be excluded, projects can have negative impacts on those not participating in them, and, ultimately, that the most significant long-term determinants of success are factors that are not normally considered to be part of corporate responsibility, such as building the capacity to run a business, overcoming trade barriers, and lowering entry barriers to new markets.

Markopoulos' (1998; 1999) case studies show some of the social impacts of forest certification, although he points out that, in the small schemes in poor communities that are his focus, it can be difficult to discern the direct impacts because of the amount of other development activity taking place. He shows that increased commercial opportunities are a positive outcome, not least for indigenous people, but that these can only be realized if accompanied by improved management: certification alone does not relate to existing market requirements for quality, price, volume, etc. Thornber (2000), in a separate case study within which forest certification had ultimately been withdrawn, shows that there were relatively few social impacts and that the most important changes were the relatively basic technical, organizational, and management information improvements to local institutions.

There are also many case studies of fairtrade initiatives. For example, the three presented in Traidcraft's 2005 social report claim that, in addition to increasing farmers' incomes by 15 per cent, this company's approach to corporate responsibility has reduced migration from rural areas, improved working conditions, and encouraged better environmental management. But as Ronchi (2002) points out, the Fairtrade Labelling

Organization International (FLO International) does not look at producer-level impact and hence little is known about impacts such as those that fairtrade has on women. What it does focus on is the economic impact, which we discuss below.

The insights offered by case studies, such as those available on Rio Tinto's website, suggest that individual company programmes are having positive impacts for local communities, but we cannot know for sure what this tells us about the overall impact of corporate responsibility. In areas such as human rights and security, the consequences for local communities of voluntary principles and other corporate responsibility approaches will always be difficult to measure, while the outcomes of actions such as investing or disinvesting, which may even be a consequence of corporate responsibility policies, are not normally being addressed.

Economic impact

Economic impact has only recently appeared on the corporate responsibility agenda and, as yet, few corporate responsibility reports communicate direct or indirect economic impacts.[23] There are some case studies that largely seek to test models for defining the meaning of economic impact,[24] and mining companies such as Anglo American and Rio Tinto have only now begun to examine the economic impacts of their investments in local communities.[25] Fairtrade, however, offers some of the clearest indications of the kind of economic impact that corporate responsibility has brought so far, particularly relating to the economic condition of producers in poor countries.

In assessments of the impact of fairtrade, a number of proxies for economic benefit for producers are often used. These include the growth in the volume of fairtrade produce, the increase in the number of producer groups, sales outlets, and importing organizations, and the ability of fairtrade to maintain a floor price that is equivalent to the cost of production.[26] For example, the fairtrade price for coffee in 2003 was $1.26 per pound compared with $0.82 per pound on the world market. As the fairtrade company, Traidcraft, recognizes, however, sales volume and market growth are not necessarily synonymous with the benefit brought to poor producers, and, in its award-winning social accounts, it looks at the value of purchases, the sales of goods from developing countries, and the percentage of cost of sales spent in developing countries' volume of sales, revealing, for example, that not only have sales of products from developing countries increased, but that the money spent there has risen from £2m in 2001 to £3.4m in 2005.

Case studies of producer groups around the world show that the fairtrade price for farmers can be significantly higher than that available on conventional markets. For example, a study of seven cooperatives found that the price to farmers was twice the world price and three times that which was paid by local traders, while in Ethiopia, fairtrade producers get 70 per cent of the export price compared with 30 per cent for coffee sold on conventional markets.[27] As Vogel (2005) remarks, although fairtrade may only result in modest increases in per capita incomes, this can be the difference between destitution and survival. Case studies show, however, that the benefits are not necessarily shared across communities, and for popular fairtrade commodities, notably coffee, the fundamental problem may be overproduction and the lack of alternative income sources, rather than market access.[28]

As Ronchi (2002) acknowledges, overall information on the actual impact that fairtrade has on individual producers is scarce and the International Federation of Alternative Trade admits that there is neither a comprehensive collection of data about fairtrade producers, nor a clear methodology about how to quantify the impact of fairtrade.[29] Filling this kind of information gap will be a challenge for corporate responsibility more widely in the coming years.

CASE STUDY 12.2

Anglo American demonstrates multiple impacts

Anglo American plc is one of the world's largest mining companies and has produced a sustainability report since 2000. According to its Business Principles, its aim in being a good corporate citizen is to show that it uses resources and its influence in society to the good. To demonstrate impact, it reports on five areas: governance and ethics; economics; human capital; social capital; the environment. Each year, it reports on the current year's performance against targets set at the start of the year and sets targets for the coming year. For example, under social capital, the company promised to involve its African employees in HIV/AIDS counselling, to increase its community engagement plans, and to adopt principles on security and human rights for its mining sites.

Like many companies, Anglo American's reporting on environmental performance is more detailed than that on other areas. Among other actions, the company is committed to:

1 monitoring and participating in international processes to consider ways of meeting the challenges of climate change;

2 understanding stakeholder concerns about climate change;

3 collaborating in research and development programmes to address the challenges of climate change;

4 the efficient use of energy and reduction of greenhouse gas emission intensities at its operations;

5 incorporating climate change considerations in its business planning;

6 exploring opportunities for the use of the market-based emissions reduction mechanisms that are proposed in the Kyoto Protocol.

It reports performance and sets goals for management systems, energy and carbon dioxide emissions, air quality, water use, biodiversity, and land use. In many instances, the company is still establishing baselines and systems for measuring performance, and, in 2004, it reported that 83 per cent of its operations had been ISO 14001 certified. It is open about the areas in which it has yet to meet targets, as was the case, for example, with its 2004 energy efficiency and carbon dioxide emissions targets, or areas in which it missed targets, as happened with the goal of eliminating all work-related fatalities.

(www.angloamerican.co.uk/corporateresponsibility—accessed 31 May 2006;
www.bitc.org.uk/resources—accessed 31 May 2006)

Questions

1 Using 'A framework for understanding impact' (p 314), what are the areas in which Anglo American appears best able to demonstrate the impact of corporate responsibility?

2 What are the strengths and weaknesses of the five-dimension approach to reporting that has been adopted by the company?

3 Do you think that, over time, the company will be able to report in as much detail about non-environmental dimensions of operations as it does about environmental ones?

Impact and the business case

As Margolis and Walsh (2003) pointed out, the majority of impact studies since the 1970s have concentrated on the relationship between social (or environmental) performance and financial performance. They concur with McWilliams and Siegel (2000) that there is not a strong correlation between doing well financially and doing good for society.

But making the business case for corporate responsibility remains important (see Chapter 5), and is highlighted as an important aspect of corporate responsibility reporting by the ACCA and other European bodies involved in social accounting. The emphasis on the business case sets corporate responsibility apart from other areas of management[30] and the rationale for expecting investments in corporate responsibility to create shareholder value when other business investments are not held to the same standard is certainly questionable.

This has come about, in part, because socially responsible investment, in order to distinguish itself from the conventional investment world, seeks to establish a link between wealth creation and the way in which companies address social and environmental issues. Vogel (2005) says that over a hundred studies of social investment funds agree that share prices are neither harmed nor helped by including social criteria in stock selection. Moreover, SRI fund managers have not so far demonstrated a superior track record of predicting long-term value (see Chapter 11). He concludes that *'remarkably few firms have been rewarded or punished by the financial markets for their social performance'*.[31]

There are other ways of examining corporate responsibility's outcomes from a business case perspective, as we explore in Chapter 5. There is a fair amount of anecdotal evidence that employees and prospective applicants value corporate responsibility and a company's overall image, although there has not yet been a definitive analysis of this. At times, it gets personal and there is some evidence that employees of companies such as Nike and Dow found that they had to respond to taunts about their company's reputation made over the barbeque grill.[32]

The financial return on corporate responsibility can also be seen, to some degree, in its impact on consumer behaviour. Smith (2003a) argues that corporate responsibility has helped companies to avert boycotts of brands and has increased consumer loyalty. We have already mentioned the emergence of corporate responsibility labelling, such as FSC, Rugmark, and Fairtrade, although companies can be reluctant to publicize their performance in this way. For example, Dunkin' Donuts uses Fairtrade-certified coffee in its franchised outlets, but this has not been included in the company's marketing. Indeed, with notable exceptions, such as organic food produce, corporate responsibility has largely been used to prevent harm being done to a brand (e.g. through naming and shaming), rather than to promote a positive image of the brand.

As described in Chapter 5, the strongest link between financial and non-financial performance is probably the impact of corporate responsibility on environmental management. The often-significant improvements in environmental management that we cited earlier are largely attributed to their neutral or positive impact on the financial bottom line. Company reports provide a wealth of case study material in this area, although, as noted earlier, many companies are not rigorous when it comes to identifying the most material issues for their business and it can therefore be hard to conclude if they are addressing genuine priorities, or simply those that are the most financially advantageous.

There is a question as to whether this same kind of positive financial link can be made for areas of social performance. There are numerous individual cases in which companies have stressed that there is money to be made from tackling social needs (e.g. from Vodafone/Citigroup's targeting of the migrant remittance market, valued at \$270bn, to Innocent's growth to become a £80m business in ethical smoothies).[33] Collinson has developed and tested a methodology for assessing the business costs of ethical supply chain management, and some consultancy firms, such as Cost Benefit Systems, have product offerings that claim to demonstrate the return on investment of corporate responsibility activities.[34] In general, however, this remains an unexplored area.

While most companies emphasize the financial–ethical win–win outcomes brought by corporate responsibility, Cooperative Financial Services in the UK is exceptional in that it reports on the business opportunities foregone as a result of applying its ethical principles. Although this is widely admired, it might also only be possible because of the organization's cooperative status, and a publicly held company might face legal action if it appeared to be breaking its fiduciary obligations by disclosing this type of business decision.

CASE STUDY 12.3

Wal-Mart's conversion

Wal-Mart, the world's largest retailer, built its business model around low prices, supply chain innovation, and the ability to source more cheaply than its competitors. It came under repeated criticism for everything, from the minimum-wage jobs at its shops, the impact that its megastores had on the local environment, to its encouragement of poor labour practices by its suppliers, especially in China. For years, it took the criticisms, pointing to its share price and booming sales to vindicate its business model.

But in 2005, CEO Lee Scott admitted that the broadsides had taken their toll. While criticisms and lawsuits continued unabated, the share price no longer seemed so strong. The company took steps to strengthen its worldwide labour inspection programme, hired Business for Social Responsibility to help it to engage with other organizations, and set up consultation groups with its major suppliers to look at how to make its supply chains more sustainable. Scott is enthusiastic that Wal-Mart can have a big impact and, at the same time, reduce costs by, for example, reducing its packaging, improving the efficiency of its transportation fleet, and making its stores consume less energy.

Says Scott, explaining why he was now prepared to talk to Wal-Mart's critics: '*When growth was easier, this idea of simply ignoring critics was okay.* [But] *as the share price slows, you have to get to this point.*' Asked why Wal-Mart still stood accused of paying rock-bottom wages with few benefits, however, he answered that no company could forget what industry they were in and low wages were a fact of life in retail. He also said he saw 'no benefit' in reaching out to unions and cautioned that Wal-Mart would need to be careful about taking actions that did not eventually lower its costs.

(*Business Week*, 2005; *FinancialWire*, 2006; Tucker, 2006)

Questions

The business case has been an important contributing factor in encouraging new thinking at Wal-Mart.

1 Based on the evidence in this case study, on what aspects of social, economic, and environmental performance is Wal-Mart likely to focus as it develops its corporate responsibility strategy?

2 Are there other aspects on which Wal-Mart might also have a significant impact?

3 Do you think that, ultimately, focusing on the business case will appease the company's critics and establish its reputation as a sincere proponent of corporate responsibility?

Impact on business attitudes, awareness, and practices

A very important part of the impact of corporate responsibility in recent years has been the way in which it has affected business thinking and practice. Wood (2000) commented that the business world had rapidly caught up with the position at which business and society scholars thought it should be in the distant future, absorbing and making its own the lessons of environmental awareness, stakeholder management, community relations, codes of conduct, and public affairs. The fact that 52 per cent of the Global Fortune 250 list of companies produced corporate responsibility reports in 2005 (up from 42 per cent in 2002) is one indicator of this change. The number of companies producing non-financial reports has risen from fewer than a hundred in 1993 to over 2,000 today. Japan and the UK have the highest reporting rates (80 and 71 per cent of the top hundred firms in each country, respectively), and there have been rapid rises in Italy, Spain, Canada, and France.[35] In the USA, small, medium, and large companies increasingly believe that corporate responsibility needs to be a priority for companies[36] and, while validation from the top of the company is ultimately essential, in some instances it is changes in behaviour at middle management levels that drive internal reform.[37]

As we see throughout this book, this is not only rhetoric. Although there may be many companies that have still to commit to corporate responsibility, and the uptake is stronger in certain sectors and types of firm (e.g. export-oriented companies, or those with a high public profile),[38] there has been a significant change in awareness and behaviour. It was hard to imagine, as short as five years ago, a company declaring a five-year plan addressing health, working conditions, climate change, waste, and sustainable raw materials, yet this is what UK-based retailer Marks and Spencer did, in 2007, in its Plan A programme. Few major multinational companies with extensive supply chains would now deny that they have a responsibility for the social and environmental performance within those chains—a marked change to the situation in the early 1990s. Not only have they introduced standards for their vendors in areas as diverse as resource management, good agricultural practice, bribery and corruption, human rights, and labour practices, but these have also evolved over time, both in terms of their content and overall implementation. For example, despite predictions that a large number of labour standards might lead to contentious issues being omitted,[39] in reality, competition has largely mitigated against weak standards and to a degree disingenuous monitoring.[40] A similar trend has been observed in the field of forest management standards. But there is evidence that companies pick and choose which standard to join, based on how stringent or lax it is perceived to be.[41]

The successful use of particular corporate responsibility approaches in one industry appears to encourage other industries to become engaged. For example, one can trace the uptake of labour standards in the European horticulture industry to the earlier success of food safety and good agricultural practice guidelines,[42] and their acceptance in industries such as apparel and agriculture ultimately made it easier for other industries, such as electronics, to adopt similar models. Likewise, industries and individual companies have looked at previous examples of partnerships between stakeholder groups and concluded that this is something that can be beneficial. Early thinking that corporate responsibility would somehow be part of individual firms' comparative advantage has largely been displaced by a belief in the greater potential of shared learning and joint initiatives. Thus, for example, leading organizations behind international labour codes of conduct—such as the Workers' Rights Consortium, Social Accountability International, the Fair Wear Foundation, and the Clean Clothes Campaign—are running part of the Joint Initiative on Corporate Accountability and Workers' Rights to develop common guidelines on aspects of monitoring and implementing the provisions of voluntary codes of labour practice. The Equator Principles for managing social and environmental dimensions of project financing in developing countries are the result of a partnership between a range of major financial institutions. There are also a growing number of examples of global framework agreements between international unions and multinational companies.

It is not only that the number of corporate responsibility initiatives has grown; there are also clear signs of learning, both in terms of how to implement corporate responsibility and what issues can, or should, be considered. Sometimes, this can be as elementary as recognizing the size of the challenge, such as the enormity of supply chains and the different tiers of production.[43] It might also be about understanding the limitations of a particular approach, such as that, ideally, voluntary codes should not be an alternative to governments enacting and enforcing appropriate legislation.[44] Or it might involve learning more about effective monitoring, and the importance of involving overseas workers and supplier management in implementing standards.[45]

The Ethical Trading Initiative is an interesting example of how a corporate responsibility initiative can influence companies and change their practices in different ways. We have seen that ETI's impact on workers is not straightforward, but, based on its annual reports, ETI can claim to have had the following types of impact on company behaviour:

1 improving the knowledge of its member organizations and others about how to monitor labour conditions among suppliers;

2 improving knowledge about what to monitor and what the elements are of the chains (e.g. that there are homeworkers and smallholder farmers, as well as large factories and commercial farms, who are parts of the supply chain);

3 raising member companies' awareness of labour rights issues;

4 influencing legislation (e.g. ETI played an important role in the UK Gangmasters (Licensing) Act 2004);

5 increasing the overall level of monitoring of overseas' suppliers;

6 building the capacity of companies and others to implement voluntary labour standards.

Furthermore, there are measurable outcomes in support of some of the above claims, such as changes in buyer behaviour as they integrate labour rights into their business practices, examples of terminating business relations with persistently non-compliant suppliers, increased ability to identify non-compliance in factories, and the integration of labour standards into supplier contracts.

Examples of how corporate responsibility has affected attitudes and behaviour are to be found throughout this book. What we want to emphasize here is that this is an important element of corporate responsibility's impact. Overall, corporate responsibility has increased awareness of, and has spawned initiatives to address, issues as diverse as corruption, international development, labour rights, global warming, human rights, environmental management, and sustainable resourcing. It has raised the profile of long-established concerns, such as workplace health and safety, diversity, and discrimination, especially in suppliers' facilities. It has turned these issues into ones of legitimate business interest, even if it has not always found effective ways of addressing them (or, as importantly, has not yet been able to demonstrate its effectiveness). Its impact has been recognized in countries such as China, where corporate responsibility has become something of a buzzword.[46] In recent years, the appearance in corporate responsibility discussions of corporate taxation, company valuation, responsibilities to women, the role of small producers, the place of local suppliers and small retailers, the terms of trading, and other topics has shown that new issues continue to be recognized, even if it is less clear if and how they can be addressed from within a corporate responsibility framework.

It is important, however, to also acknowledge the limits of this impact. Some companies are clearly very responsive; others are less so and some, hardly at all. While 52 per cent of large companies issue corporate responsibility reports, this figure means that 48 per cent still do not and the rate of growth in reporting is slowing;[47] as noted, FTSE4Good has expressed concern about the lack of uptake in the USA, other than by its leading multinational companies. Equally, most social and environmental standards apply to export-oriented production and the impact of corporate responsibility on the behaviour of producers for domestic markets (the majority) is unknown. Moreover, it might remain difficult to implement standards effectively, even in export sectors, because auditing capacity is not keeping up with demand[48] and its quality has been criticized, not least by companies.[49]

Companies, such as Nike and Gap, have undergone significant change in terms of their social and environmental outlook and practices, but many companies do not make available the information that would help others to assess the degree and effectiveness of their commitment. Similarly, belonging to a partnership means very little if the quality and nature of that partnership is unclear. For example, membership of ETI, Instituto Ethos, FSC, or the UN Global Compact all have different implications in terms of what companies hope to achieve and agree to commit to, ranging from agreeing to uphold a set of principles, to committing to embedding particular principles into key areas of business operations and to being held to account for doing, or not doing, so. There is some evidence that partnerships with members from different sectors of society are associated with stronger corporate responsibility performance, compared with those that only involve business, although the latter are still more effective than when companies work on their own.[50] As Chapter 10 explores in more detail, however, it is still uncertain what constitutes a successful partnership and how this can be evaluated. A standard such as the AA1000 Stakeholder Engagement Standard goes some way towards assessing the process of effectively implementing corporate responsibility, in the same way that the GRI Guidelines attempt to define sustainability, although it has been criticized for not taking power relations seriously.[51] Methodologies used by some of the ratings indices also seek to value the degree to which corporate responsibility is embedded into companies, but we are a long way from understanding, or being able to compare, the relative effectiveness of companies' different approaches.

CASE STUDY 12.4

Changing awareness

Many companies insist that their suppliers adopt codes of labour practice that protect workers' rights. Monitoring these standards, and using them to engage with NGOs and trade unions, has increased the awareness of company managers about the conditions under which their products are made. For some, it has also raised awareness about how decisions at the buyer's end can affect the lives of workers (e.g. rush orders can lead to excessive overtime).

A major impact that buying companies can have is when they decide to shift production from one place to another. A few companies are starting to ask whether it is acceptable for them always to chase the lowest production costs and whether they have a responsibility to help the countries from which they source to move up the ladder of production, thereby stopping the perceived race to the bottom. There are a few small steps that such companies have identified, as follows:

1 They should reward suppliers with good labour practices by continuing to do business with them.

2 They should collaborate with other sectors of society in the producing country to find alternatives to relocation. In deciding whether or not to relocate, they should consider what would be the consequences for the country and workers.

3 They should build mitigation measures into their entry and exit strategies for each country.

4 Likewise, they should build mitigation measures into their contracts with suppliers.

(Adapted from ETI, 2005a; Barrientos and Smith, 2007)

Questions

Considering the consequences of relocation and factoring these into business decisions is an example of how corporate responsibility has increased companies' awareness of how they interact with societies.

1 What other examples are there in which companies have started to be aware of issues that were not previously on their radar screens?

2 Can changes in awareness and attitude be demonstrated and communicated as outcomes of corporate responsibility?

3 Do you think that raising managers' awareness of this type of issue will ultimately affect company behaviour?

Impact on other stakeholders

A further way to look at the impact of corporate responsibility is to look at its outcomes for others in society. For example, we mentioned earlier the growing number of framework agreements between international trade unions and multinational companies that, at least indirectly, seem to relate to a rising awareness of corporate responsibility. Furthermore, after years of declining union strength, particularly in developed economies, union recognition agreements are part of the criteria used in ratings indices such as FTSE4Good, and freedom of association and collective bargaining are often included in corporate responsibility standards.

There is mixed evidence about the impact that corporate responsibility has had on consumers, with some citing evidence of consumers' willingness to pay higher prices for improved working conditions, while others suggest that attributes unrelated to corporate responsibility, such as customer satisfaction and financial performance, ultimately have more influence on a company's reputation.[52] Environmental and health issues have affected branding, even if there are differences of opinion about what an 'ethical brand' is. A positive relationship between corporate responsibility and purchasing decisions might be expected, but measuring the related benefits seems difficult and a company's reputation can vary greatly from country to country (Box 12.3).

There is evidence that corporate responsibility policies impact consumers only indirectly by creating a general context within which decisions are made, while some studies point to the layers of factors that get taken into account in any ethically motivated consumer decision.[53] Corporate responsibility has had a relatively small, but nonetheless significant, impact on the investment community, as evidenced by the growth in socially responsible investment (see Chapter 11). It has also had some success in persuading students to think more critically about the role of business, rather than simply to criticize companies. For example, NetImpact is a 10,000 member-strong network of, primarily, MBAs and graduate students seeking to use the power of business to improve the world. Although mostly based in the USA, it has started to establish chapters in Europe and it will be interesting to see if this less aggressive approach will prove more sustainable than, for example, the Workers Rights Consortium, which, despite having used college campuses

Box 12.3 Country variations in ratings of brand reputation

France	UK
1 Danone	1 Co-op
2 adidas	2 Body Shop
3 Nike	3 Marks and Spencer
4 Nestlé	4 Traidcraft
5 Renault	5 Cafedirect and Ecover
Germany	**USA**
1 adidas	1 Nike
2 Nike	2 PepsiCo
3 Puma	3 Procter and Gamble
4 BMW	4 Prudential Insurance
5 Demeter	5 Sony Playstation
Spain	
1 Nestlé	
2 Body Shop	
3 Coca Cola	
4 Danone	
5 El Corte Inglés	

(Grande, 2007; Werther and Chandler, 2006)

to affect corporate behaviour, has struggled to maintain more than a handful of its 140 college chapters.[54] Less structured, web-based networks, such as the CSR Chicks listserv, have also become a way in which corporate responsibility both influences people and is sustained.

The impact of corporate responsibility can also be seen in various aspects of government. Although few countries have gone as far as the UK in creating a minister for corporate responsibility, corporate responsibility has been recognized in legislation in both France and the UK. Corporate responsibility reporting is likely to increase as a result of the EU Accounts Modernization Directive, which requires that directors' reports contain a business review including information that is material to the well-being of the environment, communities, and employees, although this is somewhat weaker than had once been proposed in the UK in 2005, before the termination of the Operating and Financial Review.

The impact of corporate responsibility on itself

Over the past few years, there have been significant changes in how we conceive of, and conduct, corporate responsibility and, in any discussion of impact, we should not ignore how the experience of addressing corporate responsibility has affected the evolution of corporate responsibility itself. Earlier, we mentioned an expansion in the range of issues that fall within the, at least theoretical, purview of corporate responsibility. By comparing the initial GRI Guidelines with its two subsequent iterations in 2002 and 2006, we can see how the range of criteria for reporting on sustainability has been extended, the indicators used in measurement have become more sophisticated, and the advice on using the guidelines has expanded (e.g. the guidance on sustainability reporting for small and medium-sized enterprises). Similarly, the AA1000 series relating to stakeholder engagement has been through several modifications since its launch in 1999, incorporating the experiences of its users and others. In 2004, the UN Global Compact extended its principles to include anti-corruption, in part, because this had already become part of corporate responsibility's pantheon of issues.

Moreover, the experience of one initiative affects others. For example, national social and environment standards, such as those of the Wine Industry Ethical Trade Association in South Africa or of the Agricultural Ethics Assurance Association of Zimbabwe, have been strongly influenced by European initiatives. It is interesting to note how what were once contentious issues have been adopted, even to the point of being considered corporate responsibility best practice. There were concerns that codes of labour practice would be more likely to address issues that damaged a company's reputation (e.g. child labour, health and safety) than those that were opposed by management (e.g. freedom of association, collective bargaining), but while some rights have proved easier to address than others, in general, the most credible and influential initiatives have proved to be those that set the bar relatively high. The same is true in areas such as forest certification and good agricultural practice, in which criteria and indicators have tended to become more rigorous over time, and is also evident, to some degree, in the ongoing negotiations around the nascent ISO 26000 Social Responsibility standard. Even issues that were once regarded at least as pushing the edge of the envelope, if not contentious, have started to filter into the mainstream. For example, advocates of more local involvement and capacity building in implementing social and environmental standards have seen some of their demands begin to be accommodated.

This is not to say that there is a virtuous race to the top. Some projects seeking to extend the boundaries of corporate responsibility have failed despite their close links to other corporate responsibility actors and initiatives. The Sigma Project, involving Forum for the Future, Accountability, and the British Standards Institution, sought to provide guidelines on meeting social, environmental, and economic challenges, but, despite business and government support, its future is unclear, although BSI has launched a sustainability standard (BS 8900). The Race to the Top project, coordinated by the International Institute for Environment and Development, brought together NGOs, trade unions, and UK retailers to track what supermarkets are doing to promote a greener and fairer food system, but ended in 2003.[55] Beyond the UK, the Global Alliance for Workers and Communities, established by major US companies and NGOs to help empower workers, also withered away after failing to win long-term support. Furthermore, while some governments are eager to promote corporate responsibility as an alternative to mandatory regulation, some companies believe impact on big issues such as climate change can only be achieved through government intervention. As Jeroen van der Veer, Royal Dutch Shell CEO, says: '*In order for market forces to work we (paradoxically) need more regulations . . . [No] single company or industry can effectively address the challenge of global climate change.*'[56]

CASE STUDY 12.5

Predicting the responsible companies of tomorrow

The Accountability Rating by AccountAbility and csrnetwork reviews published reports from Fortune Global 100 companies, and measures how seriously they consider non-financial factors in running their businesses and in making future decisions. It rewards companies for stakeholder engagement, governance, and business strategy, as well as for performance management, non-financial reporting (e.g. on human rights, labour, and environmental standards), and independent assurance of reports.

The rating is not intended to be a moral evaluation, but an indicator of which companies are thinking about how to turn today's social and environmental challenges into tomorrow's business value. It strongly reflects the values of the AA1000 Series, which links sustainability to stakeholder partnerships, but has been criticized for ignoring power relations within corporate responsibility partnerships (see Chapter 10). In 2005, European companies maintained a significant lead over US companies, with the former scoring an average 40 compared with the latter's 24, and with European firms occupying seven of the top ten positions overall. Asia was also ahead of the USA, with an average score of 28.

BP was the top company for the second year in a row with a 78 score, followed by Shell, Vodafone, HSBC, Carrefour, Ford, Tokyo Electric Power, Electricité de France, Peugeot, and Chevron Texaco. But while the top ten companies had an average score of 63, the average overall was just 32 points, leaving most companies falling short of the rating's 40-point 'pass mark.' HSBC was probably the biggest winner, rising from 45th to fourth place in a year, thanks largely to its adoption of the Equator Principles for project financing and its adoption of AccountAbility's AA1000 standard to assess its governance structures.

(Adapted from www.bcccc.net—accessed 14 November 2005; Newton, 2005)

Questions

1 How do ratings or surveys such as the AccountAbility Rating help to improve our understanding of the impact of corporate responsibility?

2 Is it valid to say that there is a correlation between the performance of companies and the region in which they are headquartered?

3 What does the AccountAbility Rating tell us about how corporate responsibility is impacting on itself?

The challenges of determining impact

The picture that emerges is that measuring corporate responsibility's impact is as difficult today as it was in the past. There are three main reasons for this, each of which we examine in this section:

1 the practical challenges of assessing impact;

2 the problem of what to measure;

3 the question of in whose interests it is to understand impact.

There are three main sources for information on impact: ratings indices; corporate reports; case studies of individual companies, industries, or locations. These are self-referential to a large degree in that, for example, in compiling ratings, researchers will use corporate reports and case studies, in addition to other sources of information, while the report may allude to the company's rating as a performance indicator. A fundamental difficulty is that the basic data needed to assess impact are often lacking, because, for example, the company has not properly identified its key issues, or has not reported on them in a clear and consistent fashion. But ratings indices can exacerbate this problem by the a priori assumption that they make about outcomes and causal relations. For example, they assume that the outcome of a blend of stakeholder participation and rigorous social or environmental standards will be better working conditions, sustainable fisheries, etc. Consequently, what is measured is more likely to be the criteria of the standard and indicators for the partnership, rather than an attempt to examine the contribution that such a combination makes towards those bigger goals.

Mattingly and Berman (2006) argue that some ratings indices make incorrect assumptions about associations between different types of social action and that, because they do not properly recognize the context within which actions take place, they end up rewarding actions that appear to be proactive, but which are not especially laudable (e.g. those that are easily solved problems or easily achieved targets). In doing so, they overlook those that may appear weak or reactive, but which are actually impressive if the context is understood (e.g. becoming a pioneer in tackling hazardous waste in an otherwise unresponsive industry). In other words, Mattingly and Berman claim that a company that is a strong performer in an industry that is predicted to deliver beneficial products in the future tends to get a better rating than that of a company in an industry that is facing serious social and environmental challenges, yet there is not any evidence (and, at present, no means for assessing) if the impact of the former is really greater than that of the latter.

Ratings indices continue to evolve and some of the above limitations may be overcome. For example, the Enhanced Analytics Initiative seeks to redress some of the current information gaps by encouraging quality, long-term research, which considers material extra-financial issues that can be used by sell-side analysts. In 2006, the Center for Sustainable Innovation in Vermont, USA, launched Social Footprint to assess the degree to which corporate responsibility contributes to true sustainability. Trucost Ltd, a London financial research firm, has also launched TrueVa (True Valuation) to measure companies' overall value added by subtracting from the firm's operating surplus not only its costs of capital, but also the environmental damages that it imposes elsewhere in the economy.

Ratings indices and other attempts to synthesize company performance are nonetheless hampered by a strong dependency on case studies, including those from companies, in media stories, and in academic or other reports. There is a tendency for organizations to choose the case study that best tells the story they want to communicate, but even in instances in which that is not true, taken together, case studies do not have the consistency of approach to constitute a systematic body of evidence, or, if taken individually, may not have the necessary depth from which to draw wider conclusions. This is starting to change as impact assessments about particular corporate responsibility approaches and initiatives being to appear. Two early assessments by business and academics observed that increased incomes alone did not prove that people were better off because of corporate responsibility initiatives and that other, harder to measure, factors, such as terms of trade and building strong local institutions, were important. Equally, standards did not adequately capture local people's concerns and priorities.[57] Moreover, even if researchers know what information to gather, there are challenges in obtaining it, either because of the risk of false documents and of respondents who are reluctant to talk honestly or openly, or because of the sheer size of company operations.[58] And when the data are reliable, it can still be difficult to demonstrate whether an action or outcome is the result of corporate responsibility, or of some other event, such as changes in local laws or improved enforcement.[59]

One challenge is how to measure and assess the effectiveness of initiatives that are intended to encourage learning about how to tackle large issues, rather than to have a direct, demonstrable impact on those issues themselves. For example, the UN Global Compact highlights how about half of its signatory companies have changed their policies to reflect the Compact's principles and the high level of managers' recognition of the Compact's role as a catalyst for change (see Chapter 10). But relatively few companies have participated in the Compact's learning forums, raising questions about whether participation in the network is responsible for these outcomes.[60]

Various corporate responsibility theorists have questioned what we are trying to measure when we talk of the impact of corporate responsibility, corporate social performance, and corporate social action. As noted earlier, Margolis and Walsh (2003) believe that there has been too much focus on the relationship with financial performance, with the result that what matters most to corporate responsibility's stated beneficiaries is being ignored. Freeman (1984) argues that it is the level within a company at which action is taken that ultimately determines effectiveness and his view that the effectiveness of stakeholder engagement is perhaps the most crucial indicator of the impact of corporate responsibility has become widespread (see Chapter 6).

Mitnick (2000) separates out three broad areas of performance, based on his notion that what we want to be assured of is:

1 what companies want to achieve through managing their relationship with society (what he terms their '*commitment*');

2 what they are doing to realize those ends (the '*relevance*' of their activities);

3 whether we can believe what they claim ('*belief*').

The five types of impact discussed in the framework earlier can be fitted within these categories: for example, our knowledge of the 'big picture' relates to the company's 'commitment', while the impact of corporate responsibility on business behaviour and practices is part of understanding the 'relevance' of companies' actions. Our overview of what we know about impact shows that we know more about activities that seek to demonstrate relevance than we do about those that demonstrate commitment. But Mitnick stresses that what matters to companies' stakeholders is demonstrating outcomes—and most of the information we have about corporate responsibility relates to outputs or activities.[61] In other words, the data available today are not providing stakeholders with the information that they want.

The accuracy of that observation depends, however, on knowing who is really interested in corporate responsibility's impact. It is quite possible to argue that it is not in the self-interest of certain stakeholder groups, with a significant influence on corporate responsibility, to gain a more sophisticated understanding of the impact of corporate responsibility. As noted, groups such as worker or environmental activists have particular aims when collecting data and may not be motivated to monitor a particular company over the longer term. Professional monitors, on the other hand, have an interest in building a long-term relationship with a company, but are subject to confidentiality agreements and other restraints on how their data are used. Companies, in turn, may have an interest in selecting what they disclose and to whom, especially when reporting is voluntary. Even without this, the resource implications of proving a company's impact on societal issues may be too great.[62] Whether from companies or multi-stakeholder partnerships, what is disclosed to the public is often a synthesis of a larger, more complex, picture that, according to some, too often requires the public to trust the reporters without providing adequate justification for this trust.[63] Arguably, unless there is a change in how investors value companies, real impact in the sense that is intended by Margolis and Walsh (2003) is not in the interests of the most influential groups that are engaged in corporate responsibility. That kind of impact may only matter to corporate responsibility's stated beneficiaries, whether these are the poor, the natural environment, the victims of human rights abuses, or future generations. Yet the outcomes of corporate responsibility for this type of stakeholder have still not been thoroughly demonstrated and it remains an open question whether others are prepared to invest in providing this type of information.

SUMMARY

Many claims are made about how corporate responsibility can help business to have a positive impact through its social, environmental, and economic performance. The reality is, however, that the data to demonstrate such impact are lacking, and, moreover, that collecting and collating such data does not appear to be a priority, even for companies, such as those engaged in fairtrade, that have built a business model around the contribution that they make to society. This is not to deny the numerous case studies of companies addressing important issues, or the efforts of ratings, surveys, and company reports to demonstrate the efficacy of what companies are doing.

Moreover, the various approaches to measuring impact reveal that there are many levels and categories of outcome. Most of what we know about impact relates to the instrumental benefits of corporate responsibility, i.e. how it affects the financial bottom line. This can be considered a sign of progress, in that it creates a link between good business management and corporate responsibility, but it can also be a cause for concern if it precludes companies from considering actions for which the business case is weak.

Also, much of what we know relates more to actions than it does to outcomes. For example, companies may have environmental policies in place, or may be committed to international standards on corruption, but the actual outcome of these actions is often not known This is less true of environmental issues than it is of those that are social or economic, and the growing sophistication of some companies' environmental management and reporting is a possible harbinger of the future of corporate responsibility more broadly. Even here, however, there is no clear consensus about what acceptable levels of performance look like, or about how to measure impact beyond the level of the individual company.

It remains an open question how the current partial understanding of impact will affect corporate responsibility in the future. Critics are using the lack of information to conclude that corporate responsibility is an inadequate response to tackling the social and environmental consequences of modern business. There is pressure within corporate responsibility for companies to become more rigorous in terms of what they manage and the targets they set themselves. Ultimately, what we know about impact will depend on the demand for information and the current situation suggests that the various stakeholders are only beginning to understand what it is they need to know.

DISCUSSION POINTS

1   Some people claim that, when we talk about corporate responsibility's 'impact', what we are actually referring to are its 'actions' or 'outputs'.
   • What are examples of the distinction between 'actions' and 'outputs', and 'outcomes' and 'impacts'?
   • What is the significance of thinking in terms of actions rather than outcomes?
   • Taking a real company's corporate responsibility report as the basis, how would you modify it to focus on outcomes?

2   Margolis and Walsh (2003) say that, because companies are so focused on understanding the instrumental benefits, they may never tackle some of the key impacts they have on society.
   • Do you think this argument is valid?
   • Give examples in which society in general might want a company to have an impact, although there may not be a clear business case.
   • Under what conditions do you think companies will take action if there is not a business case?

3   One area of corporate responsibility in which there appears to have been significant changes is in terms of management awareness and attitude.
   • Is it valid to regard these changes as indicators that corporate responsibility is bringing about wider changes?
   • Is it more important to understand this type of change in the context of some companies than that of others?
   • How would you set about measuring and communicating this type of change to external stakeholders?

4 Companies seem to have made most progress in demonstrating their environmental impact.
   • How far do you think the experience with environmental impact is a forerunner for what we will see with social and economic impact? What do you think are the possible differences?
   • What are the weaknesses in our understanding of environmental impact at present?
   • What is the most important thing that a company can do to have a positive impact on public trust in its environmental performance?

5 Economic impact is something that has started to appear in some corporate responsibility reports.
   • What distinguishes 'economic impact' from financial performance?
   • What are the ways in which a company has an economic impact?
   • Using the Unilever–Oxfam study of impact in Indonesia as a basis (Clay, 2005), how would you develop this into a framework for understanding economic impact in another industry?

FURTHER READING

• Association of Chartered Certified Accountants, 2005, *ACCA UK Awards for Sustainability Reporting 2005: Report of the Judges*, London: ACCA.
  Interesting insights into the strengths and weaknesses of corporate responsibility reports (especially if compared with those of previous years).

• Margolis, JD and Walsh, JP, 2003, 'Misery loves companies: rethinking social initiatives by business', *Administrative Science Quarterly*, 48(2), pp 268–305.
  Widely cited study of impact from a corporate social performance perspective.

• McWilliams, A and Siegel, D, 2000, 'Corporate social responsibility and financial performance: correlation or misspecification?', *Strategic Management Journal*, 21(5), pp 603–9.
  Useful discussion of approaches to understanding the impact of corporate responsibility.

• Mitnick, BM, 2000, 'Commitment, revelation, and the testaments of belief: the metrics of measurement of corporate social performance', *Business and Society*, 39(4), pp 419–65.
  A management theorist's framework for understanding social outcomes.

• Nicholls, A and Opal, C, 2005, *Fair Trade: Market-Driven Ethical Consumption*, London: Sage.
  Comprehensive (if largely uncritical) overview of fairtrade, largely from a consumer and entrepreneurial perspective.

• Sustainability and United Nations Environment Programme, 2002, *Trust Us: The Global Reporters 2002 Survey of Corporate Sustainability Reporting*, London: SustainAbility/United Nations Environment Programme.
  One of the first analyses of corporate responsibility reporting, with findings that remain relevant today.

• Vogel, D, 2005, *The Market for Virtue: The Potential and Limits of Corporate Social Responsibility*, Washington, DC: Brookings Institution Press.
  Detailed critique of corporate responsibility's effectiveness as a response to social and environmental challenges.

VISIT THE WEBSITE for links to useful sources of further information

ENDNOTES

[1] SustainAbility and UNEP, 2002.

[2] See, e.g., Elliott and Freeman, 2003, on improved labour standards and monitoring.

[3] See also Chapter 7. The 2007 ACCA awards, released after the publication deadline for this book, also reflect these broad criticisms. Information can be obtained from www.accaglobal.com.

[4] Margolis and Walsh, 2003, p 282.

[5] See, e.g., Traidcraft, 2005; IFAT, 2006.

[6] There is a distinction to be drawn between corporate social performance and corporate responsibility. CSP is an *ex post* measurement of past performance (e.g. assessing if there is a relationship between social impact and corporate reputation), whereas corporate responsibility can be *ex ante*.

[7] The main sources for understanding the impact and measurement of corporate responsibility and corporate social performance were Sethi, 1975; Anshen, 1980; Wartick and Cochran, 1985; Margolis and Walsh, 2003; the discussion in Birch, 2003. The company corporate responsibility reports used included the Anglo American 2005 Report, Unilever 2005 Environmental Report, Cooperative Financial Services Report 2005, and Traidcraft Report 2005.

[8] Forest Stewardship Council statistics published at www.certified-forests.org—accessed 10 March 2006.

[9] Vogel, 2005.

[10] Unilever, 2005.

[11] Vogel, 2005, pp 110–11.

[12] Vogel, 2005, p 126.

[13] FTSE4Good, 2005; ACCA, 2005.

[14] Michael Blowfield, personal observation, 15 November 2000.

[15] See, e.g., the BBC news broadcast 13 March 2007 headlined 'BA green scheme fails to take off'.

[16] Locke et al., 2006.

[17] Barrientos and Smith, 2007.

[18] Elliott and Freeman, 2003.

[19] Phylmar Group, 2006.

[20] Abbott Laboratories, 2005; www.gsk.com—accessed 15 May 2006.

[21] Vogel, 2005, p 102.

[22] NRET, 1999.

[23] See BSR, 2005; KPMG, 2005.

[24] www.economicfootprint.org offers economic impact reports for the agriculture, mining, pharmaceutical, and financial services sectors.

[25] Rio Tinto case studies, and its framework for understanding linkages between its investment in communities and their development, can be found at www.riotinto.com.

[26] See, e.g., Raynolds et al., 2004; IFAT, 2006; Nicholls and Opal, 2005.

[27] Raynolds et al., 2004; Vogel, 2005.

[28] See Collinson and Leon, 2000; Nelson and Galvez, 2000; Vogel, 2005.

[29] IFAT, 2006, p 6.

[30] Vogel, 2005.

[31] Vogel, 2005, p 73.

[32] Vogel, 2005, p 59.

[33] UK government data at www.financialdeepening.org—accessed 5 June 2007; www.innocentdrinks.co.uk—accessed 5 June 2007.

[34] Collinson, 2001; Collinson and Leon, 2000.

[35] KPMG, 2005.

[36] CCC, 2005c.

[37] Manga et al., 2005.

[38] Vogel, 2005.

[39] Varley et al., 1998.

[40] Eliott and Freeman, 2003, p 63.

[41] Lenox and Nash, 2003.

[42] Blowfield, 2000a.

[43] ETI, 2004.

[44] ETI, 2004; Vogel, 2005.

[45] O'Rourke, 2003; ETI, 2005b.

[46] McGregor, 2007.

[47] Presentation to launch Global Reporters Survey 2006, online at www.sustainability.com—accessed 7 May 2007.

[48] Ascoly and Zeldenrust, 2003.

[49] ETI, 2006.

[50] Jenkins, 2001; Kolk and Tulder, 2002.

[51] Newton, 2005.

[52] Compare, e.g., Brown, 2004; Elliott and Freeman, 2003, with Vogel, 2005.

[53] Brown and Dacin, 1997; Bhattacharya and Sen, 2004.

[54] Kauffman and Chedekel, 2004.

[55] Information on Sigma is accessible at www.projectsigma.com—accessed 21 March 2006. Information on Race to the Top, including an analysis of why it failed, is accessible at www.racetothetop.org—accessed 21 March 2006.

[56] Van der Veer, 2007.

[57] DFID, 2002.

[58] DFID, 2002; ETI, 2004.

[59] ETI, 2004; Vogel, 2005; Barrientos and Smith, 2007.

[60] Vogel, 2005, pp 157–8.

[61] Mattingly and Berman, 2006.

[62] Weiser and Rochlin, 2004.

[63] Sustainability and UNEP, 2002.

13

Criticisms of corporate responsibility

Chapter overview

In this chapter, we focus on the critics of corporate responsibility, especially those outside the field. In particular, we will:

- review the criticisms of corporate responsibility that have been made in previous chapters;

- discuss why some see corporate responsibility as being anti-business or anti-free markets;

- examine how some regard corporate responsibility as being too pro-business;

- explore why corporate responsibility has been criticized for failing to deal with major areas of the interaction of business with society;

- discuss why some feel that corporate responsibility needs to become more rigorous and tougher in its approach.

Main topics

■ **Key terms**

Civil society organizations

Corporate accountability

Liberal economics

Self-regulation

■ **Online resources**

- Suggested material on the theoretical critiques of corporate responsibility

- Exercises and discussion topics for students

- Examples of company-specific criticisms

- Links to other web-based resources

Introducing critiques of corporate responsibility

If corporate responsibility came to prominence as a criticism of business behaviour, in recent years, it has itself become the object of criticism. To a degree, this reflects the extent to which ideas of corporate responsibility have influenced business thinking, public debate, and public policy in some parts of the world: after all, nobody criticizes what is irrelevant. We raise some of those criticisms in other chapters (e.g. in Chapter 1, difficulties in defining corporate responsibility; in Chapters 6 and 7, the many challenges of implementing corporate responsibility).

These criticisms are part of an often-lively debate within the field about how to carry out corporate responsibility in ways that are efficient, effective, and best able to satisfy the needs of business while recognizing the concerns of other stakeholders. They are largely technical or instrumental in nature, focusing more on 'how to do it' than on 'what it means' and 'why to do it'. For a few, this focus in itself has been the subject of criticism, because it turns corporate responsibility into a pursuit of technical excellence and ignores (or stifles discussion of) more fundamental questions about what the responsibilities of business to twenty-first-century society are.[1] This situation is changing and a scan through mainstream corporate responsibility media such as *Ethical Corporation*, *CSRWire*, and *Ethical Performance* shows that such topics are becoming more widely discussed. But it is debatable how effective new discussions of what constitutes responsibility will be and how desirable they are.

Corporate responsibility theorists and practitioners have raised each of these two questions over the past few years. Doubts about effectiveness stem from a sense that the parameters of corporate responsibility have already been set, not least through the ways in which different issues and ideas are assessed and, ultimately, included or excluded. In Chapter 5, we discussed at length the importance of the business case and how this influences corporate responsibility. In Chapter 4, we showed how certain tools, techniques, and approaches have come to be regarded as best practice in the ways in which corporate responsibility is managed and implemented: new areas of responsibility are more likely to be accepted if they can be tackled using such established methods.

Doubts about the desirability of extending the realm of corporate responsibility to include a potentially endless array of new issues and expectations stem from a fear that companies will find the demands placed on them overwhelming, and will become more resistant to change. This itself derives from the experiences of academic corporate responsibility theory. As discussed in Chapter 2, there is a rich history of academic debate about what the nature of the corporation's responsibilities should be. But as we also saw, there was frustration, in the past, that academic debate was having little impact on the corporate world and, therefore, there is now a strong desire not to jeopardize the current enthusiasm among companies for addressing corporate responsibility concerns, even if these concerns are not as broad or their address as thorough as some might have liked.

The desire of some to want to 'protect' corporate responsibility for fear of stymieing progress ignores the fact that allegations regarding the negative effects of business behaviour continue to emerge from civil society organizations, academics, and legal actions. Most of the criticisms of corporate responsibility discussed so far emanate from within the loose community of corporate responsibility theorists and practitioners. In the rest of this chapter, we want to concentrate on voices that are external to that community: those who, for the most part, either reject corporate responsibility, or are waiting for a different approach before they condone it. We have divided their criticisms into four types of accusation.

1 *'Corporate responsibility stifles the primary purpose of business and, ultimately, hampers the functioning of free markets.'*

2 *'Corporate responsibility favours the interests of business over the legitimate concerns, demands, and expectations of wider society.'*

3 *'Corporate responsibility is too narrow in its focus and does nothing to address the key aspects of the business–society relationship today.'*

4 *'Corporate responsibility is failing to achieve its objectives and needs to adopt new approaches if it is to succeed.'*

Before exploring these, it is worth noting that each strand of criticism relates back to the theoretical perspectives outlined in Chapters 2 and 3. The argument that corporate responsibility stifles the primary purpose of business is rooted in liberal economics, whereas the view that it favours the interests of business is a development of the long-standing critique of free enterprise externalizing its costs onto wider society. Similarly, arguments that corporate responsibility is too narrow are part of a wider debate about the role of business in society and contrast with criticisms, rooted in management science, that new approaches are required if corporate responsibility is to succeed.

CASE STUDY 13.1

Mixed messages—critics on infant milk formula

In 1977, campaigners called for a boycott of Nestlé because of what they called its aggressive marketing of infant milk formula (powdered milk) to mothers in developing countries as a beneficial alternative to breast milk. In what became one of the longest running campaigns against a single company, a network of NGOs claimed that promoting infant milk formula (IMF) as an alternative to breast milk was having serious health consequences for babies.

The company retorts that the vehemence of the prolonged campaign is unwarranted and that it has long adopted a responsible approach to marketing what, in some situations, is a life-enhancing product. Yet, twenty years after the initial boycott, doctors' surgeries in countries such as Bangladesh are still lined with posters advertising IMF, often with photographs of white people and connotations of prosperity or health. Defenders of the company claim that it has done all it can to comply with World Health Organization codes and that continuing the campaign negates the efforts of many individuals within the company who have been trying to redeem its reputation. They point to the conclusions of an audit in Pakistan, which found nothing to incriminate the company on the charge of misselling, and to a prize-winning *Harvard Business Review* article,[2] which portrays the company as an exemplar of corporate responsibility.

But critics point out that, when the European Parliament examined the audit at a public hearing, the instructions from Nestlé were found to deviate from the standard World Health Assembly measures for auditing the marketing of baby milk. Additionally, the auditors were forbidden from talking with a well-known Nestlé critic in Pakistan and the company did not pass on documented evidence of malpractice from the NGO, Baby Milk Action. Moreover, a 2007 investigative report in *The Guardian* on IMF in Bangladesh found several violations of the WHO's 1981 code on marketing IMF. Indeed, according to NGO Baby Milk Action, Nestlé has violated the code more than any other company in the world.

(Adapted from **www.babymilk.nestle.com**; **www.babymilkaction.org**; Moorhead, 2007)

Questions

The example of infant milk formula raises a number of questions about the involvement of multinational companies in corporate responsibility.

1 Assuming that the accusations against Nestlé are true, do they undermine what Porter and Kramer (2006) see as the company's credibility as a responsible company in other areas of its operations, such as bottled water or coffee sourcing?

2 On the evidence available, does endorsement or criticism of Nestlé threaten to undermine the credibility of the academics or NGOs behind such claims?

3 Why have campaigners chosen to target Nestlé rather than its competitors on this issue?

'Corporate responsibility is anti-business'

On 20 January 2005, *The Economist* published a series of articles that presented corporate responsibility as a threat to the effective functioning of capitalism and free markets, and hence to global prosperity. On the one hand, the articles were a sign that corporate responsibility had come of age, and had entered mainstream business and economic debate; on the other, they offered a sharp rebuke to corporate executives, whom the magazine regarded as being too weak in the face of public criticism and as ignoring their fiduciary duty to shareholders by paying too much attention to the demands of others.

Reflecting a wider sense of anger and unease at the growth of corporate responsibility, the articles' core argument was as follows. The standard of living in Western industrial democracies is higher today than ever before and is at a level that would have been unimaginable 200 years ago: '*In the West today the poor live better lives than all but the nobility enjoyed throughout the course of modern history before capitalism.*'[3] This is largely due to the success of free enterprise, yet we have entered an age in which capitalism is deplored, suspected, and feared by a broad cross-section of society, even by some business leaders. This anti-capitalist sentiment stems from beliefs that profit has nothing to do with the public good, and that the pursuit of profit drives companies to put crippling burdens on society and the environment. These beliefs have given rise to corporate responsibility as a check on business behaviour. Yet they are ill founded, because they see profit as an unfortunate necessity that can be controlled and muzzled, whereas it is, in fact, the engine that allows business to make its phenomenal contributions to the public good and restrictions on profit or wealth creation—especially those that come from civil society rather than from governments—will be more harmful than anything else to society.

The articles repeatedly present corporate responsibility as a victory for the concerns of NGOs over the traditional priorities of business. But it is not simply that the public is failing to acknowledge the positive role that business plays that is *The Economist*'s concern: it is also that the uptake of corporate responsibility by mainstream companies might have a serious effect on business' ability to fulfil its role within the capitalist system. An example of this is that corporate responsibility distracts public company management from its primary purpose of serving the interests of shareholders. This echoes the views of Friedman (1962) and Jensen (1986), both of whom have argued that corporate responsibility negatively affects company agents' abilities to maximize profits for investors (see Chapter 8). *The Economist* fully accepts that managers must be ethical and that much needs to be done in this area. But it says that they should never lose sight of the fact they are employees, not owners, and that it is unethical to put the owners' assets to any use other than maximizing long-term value. Ideas such as the triple bottom line (see Chapter 1) distract management from this goal and, by making companies accountable on multiple fronts, threaten to make them accountable for nothing, because they offer no measurable test of business success.

Managers also get distracted if they pay attention to too many stakeholder groups. While it might be acceptable (and, indeed, good business practice) 'to take account of' multiple stakeholders (e.g. customers, workers, customers), this is quite different from 'being held accountable to' them, at least if that is not a policy decided by government. And even if, as in Germany, companies are legally required to have non-shareholders on the board, *The Economist* argues that owner interests should always be the primary concern.

The articles make clear that none of this is to argue in favour of corporate *irrespons-ibility*. On the contrary, there is need for governance reform and, *The Economist* says (although without offering any evidence), '*broken corporate governance and CSR are close relations. You often see them together*'.[4] In this, however, as in other areas of corporate reform, the articles stress that it is the role of government to regulate business and, in doing so, share much in common with quite different strands of corporate responsibility critic-ism that want to see government return to playing a stronger role in regulating business behaviour.[5] As one of the articles says, '*getting the most out of capitalism requires public intervention of various kinds, and a lot of it: taxes, public spending, regulation . . .*'.[6]

This focus on the role of government distinguishes these articles from the work of some other corporate responsibility critics, who see its threat in how it interferes with free mar-kets.[7] Certainly, a central tenet of the articles is that properly functioning markets are able to resolve many issues surrounding the allocation and valuation of resources, as per conventional liberal economic thinking, and one strand of their criticism is that, in many instances, corporate responsibility is simply unnecessary, or might better be called 'good management practice'. Moreover, it is needed neither by consumers, nor other stake-holders, because the marketplace provides them with a forum in which to express their opinions about companies (e.g. by not buying their goods, or by not working for them if they disagree with their policies).

The articles generated a lot of comment within the corporate responsibility commun-ity.[8] *Ethical Corporation* (2005) said that, along with the rehashing of old and frequently discredited arguments about markets' ability to price public goods, the articles began with a false premise, i.e. that the company's purpose is to make a profit, whereas profit should be seen as a right derived from fulfilling a social function, such as the production and dis-tribution of goods and services. Elsewhere, Geoffrey Chandler of Amnesty International also argued that *The Economist*'s basic premise was wrong: corporate responsibility does not begin from a belief that capitalism fails to serve the public interest, but rather from a belief that '*unprincipled capitalism inflicts collateral damage on all its stakeholders, including ultimately its shareholders*'.[9] It may well be that capitalism is the best mechanism for wealth creation, and for providing goods and services, but this is to ignore that it is today under threat from itself, because of a lack of underlying principle.

A recurring problem with criticisms of corporate responsibility is that people define the object of their critique in different ways. Nowhere is this more apparent than if we com-pare *The Economist*'s premise that it is contrary to the primary purpose of business with the views set out in the next section of those who see it as a *pro*-business agenda. Hostility towards corporate responsibility rooted in quite different starting points can be seen from the websites of CSRWatch—with the tag line '*Your eye on the anti-business movement*'—and the NGO coalition, Corporate Responsibility (CORE), which is a response to frustration around the failure of voluntary corporate responsibility approaches. Ironically or inev-itably, such sites often refer to the same articles and materials in support of their opposing arguments. Yet understanding the different assumptions that inform the various critiques is essential for making sense of how corporate responsibility is being perceived. While sharing much in common with the analysis of *The Economist* articles, others have emphasized different aspects of the damage done by corporate responsibility. Manheim (2004), for example, argues that corporate responsibility is part of an anti-corporate strategy, while CSRWatch consistently posts information criticizing a much wider set of initiatives (including those of government), such as the UN's Kyoto Protocol and the EU's Emissions Trading Scheme. At times, this has become more than a war of words, with lawsuits filed against prominent figures in the SRI movement and attacks launched on pension funds that are deemed too aggressive in enquiring about business behaviour.[10] Ironically, given that one of the criticisms of corporate responsibility is that it undermines the primacy of shareholders, some have argued that pro-corporate responsibility shareholders should be stifled.[11]

Some of the above smacks more of harnessing anti-corporate responsibility sentiment as part of a political agenda than of building a rational argument. But some have criticized corporate responsibility for being co-opted by politicians so that, in the UK, for example, the Labour Party has been blamed for using corporate responsibility as a way of avoiding tougher decisions about business regulation, while David Cameron, the Conservatives' leader, has developed close ties with Business in the Community and has spoken publicly about business needing to rethink its role. This stance has been attacked for emphasizing irresponsibility over the positive contributions that business makes and for appearing to put limits on market competition (e.g. by giving preferential treatment to small businesses). It has also been blamed for endangering economic competitiveness and for discouraging business from being '*proud and content*' about what it does.[12]

CASE STUDY 13.2

The Church and the Caterpillar—giving corporate responsibility muscle

The world's largest construction machinery company, Caterpillar, is a strong advocate of a values-based approach to corporate responsibility and has a worldwide code of business conduct that states that '*our success should also contribute to the quality of life and the prosperity of communities*'. This commitment was challenged in 2004, following claims by a UN Special Rapporteur that the company's equipment is being used to deny Palestinians the right to food by destroying their farmlands. Critics such as War on Want, a NGO, argue that the company sold equipment to the US government knowing that it would be sold on for use in military operations. Some NGOs and watchdog groups have denied this, and the company has retorted that it has neither the capacity, nor the legal right to determine how its equipment is used once it has been sold.

For both sides, this has become a test of the ability of corporate responsibility to guide companies in ethical decision making. The Synod of the Church of England voted to recommend selling the church's shares in the firm. This decision generated criticism of the Church of England itself: whether it was using a stance on corporate responsibility to attack Israeli national policy and whether disinvestment was more effective than using the church's holdings to engage with the company. The church's Ethical Investment Advisory Group advised against selling Caterpillar stock and instead began what it called a '*progressive dialogue*' with the company. The company, meanwhile, said it did not sell machinery to Israel, and found itself caught in the crossfire of a campaign targeting the policies of the US and Israeli governments.

The Caterpillar case remains controversial, with some arguing that it proves the effectiveness of corporate responsibility approaches, such as a voluntary code of conduct and stakeholder dialogue, and others saying that corporate responsibility has allowed the company to deny any culpability for human rights violations caused by its products. It is also possible to argue that the case is not ultimately about the role of the company, but shows how the public profile of multinational firms makes them a leveraging point in campaigning about wider geopolitical issues.

(War on Want, 2005; *Ethical Performance*, 2006a; UN Commission on Human Rights report on economic, social and cultural rights, January 2005, online at www.ohchr.org—accessed 30 June 2006; Caterpillar code of conduct, online at www.cat.com—accessed 18 July 2006)

Questions

The church's Ethical Investment Advisory Group says that disinvestment would be too strong at this stage, but that it is looking for change as a result of progressive engagement.

1 What changes do you think Caterpillar might make that would convince its critics that corporate responsibility can make a meaningful difference to company policies?

2 Is the company right to say that it cannot be held responsible for the end use of its products?

3 Is the company right to choose not to sell to the military in certain countries?

'Corporate responsibility is pro-business'

Justice, under capitalism, works not from a notion of obedience to moral law, or to conscience, or to compassion, but from the assumption of a duty to preserve a social order and the legal 'rights' that constitute that order, especially the right to property and the freedom to do with it what one wants.

(White, 2006, p 32)

What unites those who oppose corporate responsibility because it is anti-business and those who oppose it because it favours business interests is that it does not help business adequately to perform its role in society. What they disagree about, however, is what exactly that role is. Theorists such as Jensen (1986; 2002) make very clear that earning a profit by providing customers with goods and services at competitive costs is the central purpose of business. Yet those who question this view say that the purpose of business is to serve the public good—a vision that writers such as Kelly (2001) argue was evident in the early days of capitalism, but which has been lost because of changes in the legal definition and public perception of the corporation. In order to realign business with the values of society and to optimize its contribution, such writers claim that companies need to return to that original purpose, or, more accurately, that the legislative and economic environment surrounding publicly traded private companies needs to be reformed to allow them to change.

It is important to stress that what is held to be at fault is the system of public ownership rather than business itself. There is nothing inherent in the legal definition of a company that stops it from having a social purpose, and Kelly and others point to examples of privately held companies that have just that. But, it is argued, once a company is publicly owned, its purpose can only be to maximize profits. This means that no matter how well intentioned corporate responsibility might be, it ultimately will not serve the common good. Arguments such as those described earlier that business serves the common good by creating wealth and goods are refuted with examples of companies that have rigged prices, deceived regulators, caused environmental damage, produced harmful products, and otherwise acted in ways that were intended to create shareholder value (and management rewards) at the expense of public well-being. Moreover, some argue, the larger and more powerful some companies become owing to the opportunities of economic globalization, the greater the risk is that the public good will be jeopardized by what Bakan (2004) calls the 'pathological pursuit of profit'.

It is worth noting that some pro-business thinkers would agree that some of the corporate actions set out above are unethical, and that companies and the public would benefit from better governance, and from greater transparency and disclosure. They might also agree that what is required is better regulation of business, but what they mean by this is only regulations that improve market efficiency. This is in marked contrast to those who are sceptical of business' purpose, who tend to want to see regulation that limits both markets and companies. What both tacitly agree upon, however, is that corporate responsibility is not the best way in which to put right the wrongs of corporate behaviour.

One reason for this is that corporate responsibility is simply too weak for the task at hand. A company such as Unilever, for example, might put in place policies of social and environmental responsibility, but some blame its demand for palm oil for deforestation. Similarly, British Airways might have corporate responsibility policies, but it is part of an industry that is accused of externalizing its enormous environmental costs. This criticism focuses on corporate responsibility as a voluntary approach, something that is already tainted because self-regulation is seen as the corollary of diminished government capacity or unwillingness to regulate private enterprise, and becomes more damaged by examples of how companies have allegedly used voluntary initiatives to dilute their responsibilities to others. An oft-cited example of this is how companies have become signatories to the UN Global Compact—an action that requires them to uphold the Compact's ten responsibility Principles—and yet, according to critics, many such signatories continue to violate UN Principles, knowing that, until very recently, the Compact was without a disciplinary, or even a complaints, mechanism in relation to these transgressions (see Chapter 10). There are many other examples, such as the 2005 Amnesty International report on how the agreement about the Chad–Cameroon oil pipeline—held up as a model of corporate responsibility practice—actually created disincentives for the governments involved to protect human rights by making such rights the responsibility of the private sector, or a 2005 War on Want and GMB report, comparing the gaps between Asda's corporate responsibility commitments and its actual workplace practices.

As we will discuss later, such examples are, for some, evidence that corporate responsibility needs to be implemented more effectively; for others, they reveal the fallacy of trying to achieve justice without confronting power. Unless this is recognized, critics claim, then engagement with business through corporate responsibility or similar means leads to co-option by business and fosters an illusion that issues, such as global poverty, can be addressed while continuing to do business as usual.[13] An example of this is Africa, where critics point to how multinational companies, after years of being blamed for the continent's problems, have repositioned themselves as the solution. Thus, the political agenda for poor African nations is portrayed as one that increasingly strengthens the essential rights of business (e.g. market-based economies, free trade, private property rights), while offering little in return. Moreover, business partnerships have been given responsibility for government development programmes, such as the USAID-backed Corporate Council on Africa and the UK aid programme's financing of the Investment Climate Facility. Describing this situation, anti-corporate columnist, George Monbiot (2005) wrote:

> At the [2005] Make Poverty History march the speakers insisted that [anti-poverty activists] were dragging G8 leaders kicking and screaming towards [their] demands. It seems to me that the G8 leaders are dragging [their opponents] dancing and cheering towards theirs.

Again, there is an irony here: those who see corporate responsibility as anti-business regard it as an imposition of activist agendas onto corporations, while those who see it as pro-business regard it as a co-option and dilution of those agendas by corporate interests. Yet in both cases, corporate responsibility is being criticized for failing to meet competing expectations. As Broad (2002) and others describe, the array of expectations from those who oppose the behaviour of large corporations is diverse and more sophisticated than is typically portrayed in the media, and in articles such as those of *The Economist* discussed earlier. Consequently, the issues that corporate responsibility is accused of not addressing are equally diverse. For some, it is corporate responsibility's failure to tackle what are seen as aspects of corporate behaviour that pose a threat to the functioning of society and democracy that is at issue. This includes corporate lobbying of government, the avoidance of corporation taxation in developing countries and elsewhere, and the consequences for business and wider society of privatization and liberalization. Others highlight the behaviour of particular companies and industries, such as marketing and smuggling in the tobacco industry, the impact of supermarkets on small farmers, and the conditions of workers in computer manufacturing.[14]

There are a vast number of reports and briefings on these and similar issues, and as we will see in the next section not everyone sees corporate responsibility as being powerless to address them. In fact, a criticism of corporate responsibility sometimes heard from within the corporate responsibility community is that it has stimulated rather than appeased civil society organizations' demands. This is probably a misplaced sentiment, which assumes that there are a finite number of issues in which companies have a role in addressing, or that winning the support of such organizations will end their criticisms of corporate behaviour. Perhaps more significant is to note that, for some, the fact that corporate responsibility does not tackle certain issues is a sign of its inherent weakness, while, for others, it is part of the process of mapping out future challenges and directions.

Some who regard corporate responsibility as inherently weak are not opposed to business, per se, as is evident from their support for fairtrade and other alternative trading companies, and particularly for ethically oriented firms, such as nosweatapparel.com. Some also support the new agendas for engaging with companies. But none of this detracts from the repeated call for government intervention and legislative frameworks that prescribe business activity.

Mitchell (2001; 2005) says that corporate responsibility can only succeed if there is a well-developed conceptualization of corporate law that exposes human responsibility and accountability. Arguing that companies are nothing but their individual members, he suggests that the law, companies, and markets need to be structured so as to encourage responsible behaviour and to discourage the irresponsible. He highlights that corporate responsibility has come to the fore at the same time as executive pay has spiralled, corporate governance reforms have too often been about making it easier to conduct mergers and acquisitions, and shareholders—not least, institutional investors—have pressured companies into producing quicker and higher returns. Thus, we see two distinct trends happening: one called 'corporate responsibility', under which companies are reconsidering their duties to society, and the other wherein what critics see as irresponsible behaviour is increasingly considered to be acceptable business practice. Corporate responsibility is not only blamed for failing to mitigate the latter, but also for helping to foster it by putting a gloss on corporate reputations.

A frequently cited example of how corporate responsibility has been hijacked in this way is that of the tobacco industry (see Case Study 13.3). For some critics, there are industries, such as tobacco, arms, and gambling, that can never be responsible because of the very nature of their products and we have already seen how this principle has informed the responsible investment movement (see Chapter 11). There are also those who regard particular companies as egregiously irresponsible, and see it as proof positive of the coercion and co-option by business' interests of corporate responsibility when companies such as Nestlé—long-criticized for its marketing of IMF in poor countries (see Case Study 13.1)—are accepted into high-profile corporate responsibility initiatives such as the UN Global Compact.

A central question here is whether business is best influenced by engagement (e.g. through stakeholder partnerships) or by confrontation. We have discussed this at length in Chapter 10 and there are many civil society organizations, such as Oxfam and WWF, that engage with companies while keeping up a critique of business in society. For some observers, however, the crucial point is not who takes part in the process of engagement, but rather the norms and conventions that dictate that process, and thereby its possible outcomes. Hence, it is argued, the participation of some of business' harshest critics in a corporate responsibility partnership is not a sign of success, because the discourse (i.e. the language, mechanisms, tools, agendas, etc.) that governs it has already been settled and, moreover, is that which favours business' interests. Thus, for example, what can be dealt with or not in a corporate responsibility initiative, the priority given to an issue in terms of time, expertise and other resources, the array of possible solutions, and even the very language that is used to discuss the issues are all ultimately a reflection of what benefits or causes no harm to business. Moreover, this is something of which the participants themselves may be unaware, because, as Lukes (1974) has noted, '*the most effective and insidious use of power is to prevent . . . conflict arising in the first place*' (p 23).

The questions of power—who holds it, what form it takes, how it is exhibited, and what it allows or precludes—are an implicit underlying theme in many of the current critiques of corporate responsibility and those that are likely to occupy debates about the field in the coming years.[15]

In fact, the essential criticism set out in this section is that corporate responsibility (both theory and management practice) is not able to confront corporate power and that alternative approaches are therefore required. Thus, for example, while corporate responsibility has gone some way to challenging both management and neoliberal orthodoxy, it is ultimately an example of how business secures the conditions for the ongoing and long-term accumulation of wealth and power, albeit in more socially and environmentally sensitive ways.[16] The critiques outlined in the following sections, however, draw a different conclusion: one under which power can be addressed and dominant institutions reformed, even if this has not been achieved as yet.

CASE STUDY 13.3

Tobacco—can bad industries produce responsible companies?

For some corporate responsibility critics, nothing speaks more loudly to its pro-business agenda than the fact that some tobacco firms have positioned themselves as socially responsible. How, they ask, can companies that deliberately hid the addictive nature of nicotine from the public's knowledge be responsible? How can companies that have aggressively marketed their harmful products to the young be responsible? How can companies that knowingly produce something that will kill its consumers in any way claim to be responsible?

Since the 1950s, the industry has continuously been in the crosshairs of governments, consumers, and of course lawyers, but it was only in the 1990s, when state governments alleged that companies had long known about the addictive risk of nicotine and had not only lied about this in public enquiries, but had artificially boosted the nicotine content of cigarettes, that the industry finally agreed to multi-billion-dollar settlements. The settlements were held up as a victory for consumers—but to investors, at least, they were also seen as a victory for the industry and tobacco company stock prices rose.

They also prompted companies to think about corporate responsibility as an approach to managing their societal relations. BAT's endowment to the University of Nottingham to establish the International Centre for Corporate Responsibility prompted protests both on and off campus, and those who seem to embrace companies' commitment to behaving more responsibly, such as the Dow Jones Sustainability Group Index, have themselves been criticized.

Moreover, critics claim the way in which tobacco companies operate highlights the essential weaknesses of the corporate responsibility approach. For example, the World Health Organization has accused the industry of opportunism by making self-regulation on issues such as marketing to children part of their corporate responsibility programmes, thereby hoping to avoid legislation. Similarly, tobacco companies have been accused of working closely with PR firms simultaneously to promote corporate responsibility and to undermine scientific findings about the effects of smoking. But the industry points to the effectiveness of its anti-smoking campaigns on youth consumption. It highlights that smoking is a fact of life and that it is better to have a responsible industry, than the one dominated by organized crime that might emerge from prohibition. And they argue that the industry will make most progress when critics engage with it rather than when they attempt to isolate it.

(National Conference of State Legislatures, www.ncsl.orgs—accessed 4 July 2006; Palazzo and Richter; 2005)

Questions

Tobacco is one of a small group of industries the products of which knowingly cause human death or suffering.

1 What are other examples of such industries, and can they ever be considered responsible?

2 What do companies in these industries stand to gain from self-regulation?

3 Are the tobacco industry's critics right to refuse to engage as stakeholders with tobacco companies?

'The scope of corporate responsibility is too narrow'

CASE STUDY 13.4

The Principles for Global Corporate Responsibility

Developed in South Africa and supported by religious organizations around the world, the Principles for Global Corporate Responsibility are intended to be a benchmark against which others in society can measure the performance of business. Unlike many standards and guidelines, they do not pretend to be a tool for business, but rather a method by which civil society—and faith-based communities, in particular—can assess whether companies are behaving in ways that are consistent with the responsibility to sustain the human community and all of creation. They are explicitly intended for people of faith and belief, and regard business as a negative force in the polarization of rich and poor, undermining the integrity of human dignity, responsible for the destruction of the integrity of creation and for human greed, as evidenced in over-consumption and in the disproportionate wealth accumulation for the few.

The Principles cover the following aspects affecting corporate behaviour.

1 The relationship between corporations, communities, and ecosystems.

2 Support for a sustainable system of production and a more equitable system for the distribution of the economic benefits of capitalism.

3 Participation of stakeholders and those most affected by the activities of corporations in the decision-making processes of companies.

4 Preservation and protection of the environment for present and future generations.

5 Respect for the dignity of every person and for workers' rights in areas such as freedom of association.

6 Strong, independently monitored codes of conduct for corporations and suppliers.

7 Indigenous peoples' rights to full participation in the business decisions that pertain to their ancestral lands and their way of life.

8 Development of human rights policies based on the Universal Declaration of Human Rights.

9 The right of every worker to health care, and accessible and affordable medicines, including anti-retrovirals for the treatment of AIDS.

10 Corporate governance policies that balance the sometimes competing interests of managers, employees, shareholders, and communities, and that are based on ethical values, including inclusivity, integrity, honesty, justice, and transparency.

(www.bench-marks.org—accessed 25 August 2006)

Questions

These Principles have been promoted as an alternative approach to mainstream corporate responsibility standards and guidelines.

1 What do you think are the main differences between these and other standards mentioned in this book?

2 To what extent are the Principles a criticism of mainstream corporate responsibility?

3 Do faith-based organizations offer a distinct critique of corporate responsibility?

We have seen that corporate responsibility is criticized for not addressing what are seen as important areas of corporate behaviour and that, to a degree, those who are supportive of, and sceptical about, the role of business share this view. We have also seen that critics in both camps regard corporate responsibility as not being suited to addressing these larger issues and see government as the proper institution in many cases. This overlooks the fact that, for the time being at least, effective regulatory mechanisms do not exist in many areas of global business activity. Indeed, as pointed out in earlier chapters, corporate responsibility is, at least partly, a response to the limited power of national governments in a global economic system.

Consequently, there are some critics who regard corporate responsibility as desirable, but who feel that the range of issues it currently addresses is too narrow. We have already mentioned corporate lobbying, tax avoidance, and how practices in specific industries to do with marketing, smuggling, and sourcing are said to affect society adversely, especially in poor countries. Some point out that the CEO of Wal-Mart earns more in three hours than a US worker on minimum wage does in a year,[17] and that therefore not only fair wages, but also broader policies concerning wealth distribution should be part of the corporate responsibility agenda. Indeed, employment generally needs to be tackled more comprehensively than at present. For example, corporate responsibility does not typically require companies to address the social costs of moving their production to another location, even though the consequences of such actions can be highly beneficial for the company and potentially devastating for the communities left behind. Also, given the worldwide trend for more flexible labour arrangements that are said to aid company competitiveness, but make employment less secure than it has been in the past, corporate responsibility is challenged to address the nature of the employment contract by, for example, giving workers stronger protections. Flexibilization of the workforce is accused of having particular impacts on women, but gender issues are only starting to enter mainstream corporate responsibility.[18] Moreover, while corporate responsibility has had a significant impact on the way in which companies think about labour conditions in developing countries, issues that are central to labour relations in many developed economies, such as gay and disabled rights, have not been part of the mainstream corporate responsibility debate in places such as China, India, and Latin America.

Outside the workplace, there are expectations that corporate responsibility should do much more to ensure that a company's corporate responsibility policies are not at odds with its policies in other areas. Home Depot, the American DIY chain, has attracted praise from environmental groups because of its timber sourcing policies and, as well as being a major corporate philanthropist, it moved early to provide help to communities affected by the Katrina hurricane in 2005. Yet, in marked contrast to its response to civil society organizations, the company garnered a poor reputation for listening to shareholders, exemplified by then-CEO Robert Nardelli's refusal not only to answer questions properly at the company's annual meeting, but also his refusal even to allow the board to attend the meeting.[19]

Equally, companies that have established strong corporate responsibility credentials are criticized for abandoning, or for failing to build on, these when they face a crisis. Enron is a widely cited example of a company that had a strong corporate responsibility reputation that did not reveal, but rather masked, the corruption and malfeasance that eventually brought the company down. But tarring corporate responsibility with the Enron brush is probably unfair, given how that company's officers deceived so many institutions. A more illuminating example is Merck, the pharmaceutical company, which had long been held up to be a model of business ethics. That tradition appeared to help the company when, in September 2004, it responded to concerns about its pain reliever, Vioxx, by withdrawing it from sale—at least in the USA. It has since been alleged on numerous occasions, however, that, since 2000, the company had vigorously sought out researchers and physicians who would endorse the drug, and had tried to intimidate and stifle those who criticized it.[20]

Another area in which companies have been criticized for inconsistency between their corporate responsibility policies and their business practices is in their terms of trading and the way in which some companies use their power in the marketplace to drive out small businesses, or to force producers to adopt management practices that, ultimately, exploit workers, communities, and the natural environment. Just-in-time purchasing practices and promiscuous sourcing in search of low costs are examples from the apparel industry of how retailers and major brands are said to exploit their supply chains. These are issues that have started to register in mainstream corporate responsibility, but critics say that more needs to be achieved.

There are many more examples of aspects of business that critics say corporate responsibility could be addressing, but which it is not. Moreover, alternative agendas for business have also been proposed (see Case Study 13.4). But a list of issues does nothing to explain why some things have been included and others not. For some corporate responsibility theorists, as touched on in Chapter 1, this is a test of how the nature of business' role in society is defined and hence what we mean by 'corporate citizenship'.[21] A 2005 collection of critical essays from different academic disciplines reveals a number of ways of understanding this inclusion and exclusion.[22] At one level, companies are said to choose the limits of their actions. In some cases, they regard corporate responsibility as being fairly low down in terms of corporate objectives, allocated too few resources, and benefiting from little push to have the issues taken up by other agents (e.g. by government service agencies). In fact, it is claimed that corporate responsibility can be used to prevent alternative political, economic, and social solutions from being developed— something that has been observed in Nigeria, and also in South Africa, where, critics argue, corporate responsibility has had more to do with helping to erase memories of business' role in apartheid than in seriously tackling today's societal challenges.

Critics argue that corporate responsibility is more likely to include contentious issues if companies are under pressure from governments and civil society, and therefore that we should not view effective corporate responsibility as voluntary. But some take this further and argue that the limits of corporate responsibility may have already been reached. Not only may corporate responsibility be partially to blame for drawing attention away from certain traditional expectations about the role of business (e.g. payment of taxes to fund public policy initiatives), but many of the issues and conflicts that it is now being asked to address are, ultimately, the result of global economic and political systems that cannot be tackled at the company, industry, or other levels at which most corporate responsibility initiatives operate.

'Corporate responsibility fails to achieve its goals'

For those who see corporate responsibility as a whitewash, greenwash, or bluewash, the fact that corporate responsibility fails to deliver on its promises is no surprise. On numerous email listservs and blogs, corporate responsibility is dismissed as a kind of Faustian pact between business, NGOs, and government that weakens more effective policies. Such criticisms have been levelled at the UK's Business in the Community, which has spoken out against the need for government regulation of corporate responsibility.

It is often these types of organization, as much as companies, which are the focus of critics who claim that corporate responsibility has not lived up to people's expectations. They are blamed for focusing too much on corporate responsibility's successes and failing to consider its real impact. Bennett and Burley (2005) point out that only 3 per cent of multinational companies report on their social and environmental performance, and little over 2 per cent have signed up for the UN Global Compact: *In what realm of life other than the strange world of* [corporate responsibility] *would a 2–3 per cent take-up rate be considered to be a success?'*

Moreover, some say that being a signatory to the Global Compact has little effect on corporate behaviour. As already noted, the Compact only agreed a complaints procedure to deal with allegations that signatory companies were breaching its Principles in late 2005. Now, companies that do not respond to complaints can be removed from the signatory list, barred from Compact activities, and forbidden to use its logo. Almost immediately, Corpwatch, the NGO, lodged complaints against six firms, but the longer term question is how the Compact's small staff will make this system work among 2,500 participating companies, especially once the independently developed Global Compact Plus research tool begins to be used to assess and rank company performance.[23]

One criticism of the Global Compact is that the high profile granted to a voluntary initiative detracts from broader UN attempts to regulate business behaviour. For example, critics point to the way in which the Compact rose to prominence at the same time as the UN Commission on Human Rights was backtracking on its draft Norms on the Responsibilities of Transnational Companies and other Business Enterprises with regard to Human Rights, following pressure from business and the US government. Since then, John Ruggie, a respected Harvard academic with UN and corporate responsibility experience,

Box 13.1 The four myths of corporate responsibility

Myth	Reality
The market can deliver short-term financial returns and long-term societal benefits.	This assumes that shareholders are investors with an interest in the company's long-term success; today's investor is more accurately considered an 'extractor', i.e. driven by short-term profit seeking.
Ethical consumers will drive change.	In reality, consumers shop in their own narrow financial self-interest and are much more sensitive to price than they are to ethical considerations.
Companies will compete in a 'race to the top' over ethics.	Although companies may present themselves as socially responsible, there are many areas in which they deliberately pursue acts of social irresponsibility.
In the global economy, countries will compete to have the best ethical practices.	In reality, voluntary standards in developing nations have brought mixed results and competition for foreign investment has led such countries to weaken their insistence on strong labour or environmental standards.

(Adapted from Doane, 2005)

has been brought in to assess whether the UN should develop binding norms on human rights for multinational companies and made clear at the outset that he felt the current system of global rule making was imbalanced in favour of markets rather than human rights. His interim conclusion was that the norms so far were too difficult to monitor and enforce, and *'too engulfed by their doctrinal excesses'*.[24] But, in a subsequent report, he was optimistic that voluntary human rights initiatives would become the basis for binding standards and that it would be in business' interests to lobby government for stronger regulations.

Some find it bizarre that the UN sees business as the protector of civil rights, and such criticisms are indicative of wider concerns about the ability of corporate responsibility to achieve its goals. According to Doane (2005), what she refers to as 'CSR' is built on four myths (Box 13.1). These are a retort to some of the arguments put forward by corporate responsibility thinkers, such as Zadek's work on the competitive advantage of nations and the many people who have written about the business case. An alternative critique presented in an article in *The Economist* (2005d) builds on arguments that corporate responsibility is antithetical to business' core purpose and poses two tests that need to be passed.

1 Does corporate responsibility improve companies' long-term profitability?

2 Does it advance the broader public good?

It begins by distinguishing between policies that any well-run company should have in place (e.g. honesty, not paying bribes, taking the long-term view) and those that it claims are touted as corporate responsibility leadership (e.g. large expenditures of time and resources for charitable activities, spending more on environmental protection than required by law). It dismisses the former as simply being good management and, hence, not requiring a special term. The article goes on to identify three categories of the latter.

1 **Borrowed virtue**
   This refers to corporate responsibility that reduces profits, but raises social welfare.

2 **Pernicious corporate responsibility**
   These are actions that raise profits and reduce social welfare.

3 **Delusional corporate responsibility**
   These are actions that reduce both profits and welfare.

Corporate philanthropy is an example of '*borrowed virtue*' and is accused of amounting to '*charity with other people's money*'. Porter and Kramer (2002) dismiss this type of argument, arguing that philanthropy is acceptable if there is a clear business reason for it, primarily when it is related to competitiveness and skills building. But *The Economist* is more concerned with the remaining two types of corporate responsibility and claims that most corporate responsibility is of the 'delusional' variety: '*the kind . . . that merely goes through the motions, delivering no new resources to worthy causes, giving the firm's workers or customers no good reason to think more highly of it.*'

Although coming at the subject from quite different directions, both *The Economist* and Doane (2005) stress the importance of managing companies for the long term. In fact, a caveat applied throughout *The Economist*'s 2005 series of articles on corporate responsibility is that business serves the public good only when companies focus on '*long-term*' profitability. What is left unexplained is that, as discussed in Chapter 11, in recent years, there has been a strong trend in major capital markets towards short-term investment, even among institutional investors, and this is something that is well understood by corporate responsibility theorists. Although some of the challenges of corporate responsibility probably derive, in part, from investor short-termism, it is misleading either to argue that corporate responsibility disregards this problem, or to imply that executives feel free to manage companies with a long-term view.[25]

Similarly, it is disingenuous to claim that any worthwhile actions carried out under the banner of corporate responsibility are simply acts of good management. There are elements of good management practice today that were once unknown or unacceptable (e.g. systems for reducing water and energy usage, policies on bribery and corruption) and which might not have entered into the mainstream, but for corporate responsibility initiatives. Nonetheless, as we have seen in Chapter 12, there is surprisingly little information on the impact of corporate responsibility that can be used to defend it against criticisms that it is not achieving its goals.

Utting (2005b) makes clear that corporate responsibility has demonstrated progress, although in some areas more than others. For example, as mentioned in Chapter 12, it has had more effect on workplace health than on equal pay, job security, and abusive disciplinary practices. More importantly, however, while corporate responsibility has been successful in increasing the array of issues that companies agree it is legitimate for them to address, the procedures to implement standards often remain weak. He points to the examples of the Global Compact and the Global Reporting Initiative, which tend to rely on dialogue and shared learning between participating companies and other stakeholder groups, rather than on monitoring performance and compliance. He also criticizes current approaches for being too top-down, exclusionary, and technocratic, assigning a minimal role to local organizations. This situation is exacerbated, because corporate responsibility tends to categorize people and social formations in ways that are misleading, if not damaging, in certain societies and cultures.[26]

Certainly, some corporate responsibility initiatives reflect a belief that companies will improve their performance by learning from peers, and this has become the basis for the Global Leadership Network and the London Benchmarking Group. Whether this approach is more effective than others is unproven, but it is one that many companies find acceptable, even if, to outsiders, it raises questions about the degree to which business decides by itself what issues to tackle and what constitutes acceptable performance. Equally, it is criticized as a way in which companies can control the speed of progress, allowing them to put the emphasis on process rather than on measurable outcomes in relation to major social and environmental issues.

Frustration with the slow progress of corporate responsibility led a group of international NGOs, including WWF, Oxfam, Friends of the Earth, and Amnesty International, to refuse to participate in the UK government's 'draft international strategy for CSR'. They claimed that the strategy lacked direction and coherence, and that it inadequately analysed the mismatch between company behaviour and society's expectations.[27] As if to confirm the NGOs' scepticism, development of the strategy fizzled out—although this might be used as an argument against government involvement as much as it might be as evidence of the slowness of corporate responsibility (see Case Study 13.5).

SustainAbility, one of the organizations that also refused to participate, has more recently argued that a reason why corporate responsibility is not achieving its goals is that it has focused on the social and environmental aspects of the triple bottom line, largely overlooking the economic aspect. While fairtrade, fair pricing, and fair wages are addressed to some degree, critics argue that there is a need for a broader economic agenda that includes the accountability of companies, the affordability of products, diversity, and equity.[28]

BSR and AccountAbility, two other organizations that are closely associated with corporate responsibility, have developed a framework for including these kinds of economic responsibilities.[29] This is part of a wider trend, promoted from both inside and outside corporate responsibility, to expand its scope. Indeed, it is one of the achievements of contemporary corporate responsibility that it has reinvigorated thinking about what society should expect from companies, even if the irony is that it is now criticized for failing to answers some of the questions it has provoked.

For some critics, the answer to these questions is to be found in moving from corporate responsibility to what has been named 'corporate accountability'.[30] The often top-down, exclusionary nature of corporate responsibility noted earlier leaves it open to criticisms that it has been dominated by organizations with limited accountability to external agents, who have taken it upon themselves to set out how companies should balance the rights of business with its voluntary responsibilities. Corporate accountability offers the different promise of balancing companies' rights with a more robust set of obligations for which companies will be held to account. Thus, it is argued, the goals of corporate responsibility will only be delivered if, for example, officers of public companies are required to report on their social and environmental impacts, to consult with communities that will be affected by their companies' actions, and to take negative impacts into account in decision making. Equally, legal liability of company directors might be extended to include breaches of social and environmental laws, and the right of redress should be guaranteed for citizens and communities that have been affected by company activities.

Although the ideas of corporate accountability advocates are anathema to some who see the very promise of corporate responsibility as being a way of removing business' regulatory burden, it does highlight a dynamic that promises to inform the development of corporate responsibility over the coming years. This will be a debate, important to both private sector and public policy, over what aspects of the business–society relationship can be addressed by actions rooted in self-regulation, societal pressure, and business self-interest, and what aspects demand formal government intervention, whether through legislation or public sector management of social development. It is apparent from some of the views described in this chapter that some clearly favour one approach over the other, but, as is evident from our discussion of impact in Chapter 12, the information does not yet exist to decide what balance of approaches will be optimal.

CASE STUDY 13.5

Corporate responsibility is too slow—the draft international framework

In 2004, the UK government announced its draft international strategic framework on corporate social responsibility. The document stated that the government's vision for corporate responsibility was:

> To see UK businesses taking account of their economic, social and environmental impacts, and acting to address the key sustainable development challenges based on their core competencies wherever they operate—locally, regionally and internationally.

The strategy was particularly focused on the international dimension, on which it recognized that companies today have positive and negative impact that extends far beyond national borders.

The draft highlighted that there was a wide range of voluntary initiatives and processes, and that this had been a cause for concern, because of the confusion and dilution of effort it might cause. In response, some were calling for legal remedies, including a global instrument covering the whole ambit of corporate performance and behaviour. The document pointed out that, while regulation can be powerful, it is not always effective and is only one of the tools at government's disposal. It stated: '*We do not support the calls for development of a globally legally binding convention on CSR.*' It argued that such a convention would be counter-productive, taking the energy out of corporate responsibility and setting levels below those to which many major companies already adhered. Overall, the strategy recognized the complex set of issues that corporate responsibility encompasses, both within, and beyond, the factory gate or office door, and including responsibility for the behaviour of both the company and others. But to maintain momentum, it also called for the development of '*a flexible menu of practical and least burdensome approaches*'.

Intended to be a draft framework for discussion by stakeholders from government, business, and civil society, the document was no sooner issued than influential NGOs and corporate responsibility thinkers announced that they would refuse to participate. Their complaint was that the strategy, rather than using the government's power to drive forward the corporate responsibility agenda, amounted to support for a 'steady as she goes' policy that would be conducive to business, but which would fail to address corporate responsibility's increasingly evident shortcomings as a market-based solution.

(DTI, 2004; *Ethical Performance*, 2004)

Questions

The launch of the draft international framework proved to be the tipping point for some of corporate responsibility's supporters, who had found themselves taking a more critical stance as time wore on.

1 Aside from general disillusionment at slow progress, what do you think were the specific points in the strategy that evoked their anger?

2 Do you think that the approach of the UK government was justified?

3 What alternative roles can a national government play in making corporate responsibility more effective?

SUMMARY

Corporate responsibility has come in for increasing criticism, especially from outside the field, perhaps as a reflection of its growing influence on business life. The criticisms fall into four main areas: (a) that corporate responsibility is an agenda imposed on business by civil society organizations that damages profitability and, therefore, business' ability to generate wealth for society; (b) that corporate responsibility is now dominated by business, which is able to shape the agenda in its own narrow interests; (c) that the current concerns of corporate responsibility are too narrow and leave out many of the key issues for which the public expects business to take responsibility; and (d) that corporate responsibility, to date, has failed to achieve its goals, and needs to be more rigorous and innovative in the future.

The stance taken on these issues is often informed by individuals' responses to two questions: what is the purpose of business, and what kind of societal issues can corporate policies rooted in self-regulation, public pressure, and business self-interest adequately address? If one thinks that the primary purpose of business is to make a profit, then corporate responsibility will be criticized if it does not support that end. But if one thinks that the purpose is its social function (e.g. producing useful, affordable goods), then corporate responsibility will be assessed on a different set of criteria. Similarly, those who see legislation as a barrier to competitiveness will look at corporate responsibility in terms of its capacity to remove the regulatory burden, while those who are suspicious of market-based self-regulation will want to know whether corporate responsibility is as rigorous and effective as are government interventions.

In consequence, there is neither a dominant critique of corporate responsibility, nor even a common definition of what is meant by the term. But the points raised are often insightful, thought-provoking, and deserving of proper consideration, regardless of whether they are accepted or not.

DISCUSSION POINTS

1 The criticisms of corporate responsibility in this chapter are primarily external ones, i.e. those from outside the world of academics, practitioners, and companies that promote corporate responsibility as a legitimate area of business management. Yet we know from other chapters that there have been internal critiques of corporate responsibility.
   - What are the main differences between the internal and external critiques of corporate responsibility?
   - To which of the external criticisms should companies respond? Are these the same as those to which they are *likely* to respond?
   - Examine the external criticisms made of Berkshire Hathaway's investment in Chinese companies operating in Darfur, Sudan, and Warren Buffet's response, and explain which is strongest, and why.

2 A criticism made by liberal economists is that corporate responsibility hinders company financial performance and poses an obstacle to economic growth.
   - What evidence do such economists need to present to substantiate this claim?
   - In your experience, is there evidence to support *The Economist*'s claim that '*broken corporate governance and CSR are close relations*'?
   - What evidence can corporate responsibility advocates offer to show that it improves company management and makes companies more reliable engines of economic growth?

3 In the influential corporate responsibility book, *Walking the Talk*, Holliday et al. (2002) argue that sustainability is best achieved through open, competitive international markets that promote human progress by encouraging efficiency and innovation.
   - Does this claim support or counter the arguments of critics who regard corporate responsibility as being too favourable to business?
   - What alternatives to market-based solutions are these critics advocating?
   - Are such alternatives plausible in today's world?

4 A recurring criticism is that corporate responsibility has yet to deliver on its promises and therefore has not proved strong enough to deal with important aspects of the business–society relationship.
   - What are the most important areas in which corporate responsibility needs to demonstrate progress in order to win public support?
   - How would you structure an effective complaints procedure for use in relation to a voluntary set of principles?
   - Is imposing informal sanctions on business through actions such as 'naming and shaming' more likely to influence business behaviour than inter-company learning and peer pressure?

5 Among Doane's (2005) four myths of corporate responsibility are claims that companies and countries will compete to improve their ethical performance.
   - What do you think would dissuade companies from competing with each other on improving their social and environmental performance?
   - Are these reasons different to those that might dissuade countries from setting higher social and environmental standards?
   - Are corporate responsibility's critics right to argue that governments, rather than companies, must set these higher standards?

VISIT THE WEBSITE
for links to useful sources of further information

FURTHER READING

- Doane, D, 2005, 'The myth of CSR: the problem with assuming that companies can do well while also doing good is that markets don't really work that way', *Stanford Social Innovation Review*, Fall, pp 23–9.
  Examination of the shortcomings of corporate responsibility as a means of managing business' impacts on society.

- *The Economist*, 2005a, 'The ethics of business: good corporate citizens, and wise governments, should be wary of CSR', *The Economist*, 20 January, online at www.economist.com.
  The Economist, 2005b, 'The good company: the movement for corporate social responsibility has won the battle for ideas', *The Economist*, 20 January, online at www.economist.com.
  The Economist, 2005c, 'The world according to CSR', *The Economist*, 20 January, online at www.economist.com.
  The Economist, 2005d, 'The union of concerned executives: CSR as practised means many different things', *The Economist*, 20 January, online at www.economist.com.
  Collection of articles from a special edition of The Economist, critiquing corporate responsibility from a liberal economics perspective.

- Mitchell, LE, 2001, *Corporate Irresponsibility: America's Newest Export*, New Haven, CT: Yale University Press.
  Interesting discussion of why the nature of the modern corporation and its legal status make companies inherently irresponsible.

- Moon, J, Crane, A and Matten, D, 2005, 'Can corporations be citizens? Corporate citizenship as a metaphor for business participation in society', *Business Ethics Quarterly*, 15(3), pp 427–51.
  Article comparing differing notions of citizenship and what these reveal about the shortcomings of corporate responsibility.

- Utting, P, 2005, *Rethinking Business Regulation: From Self-Regulation to Social Control*, Technology, Business and Society programme paper no 3, Geneva: United Nations Research Institute for Social Development.
  Analysis of the role of modern business in changing models of governance.

ENDNOTES

1. See, e.g., Blowfield, 2005a; Levy and Newell, 2002; Strathern, 2000.
2. Porter and Kramer, 2006.
3. *The Economist*, 2005c.
4. *The Economist*, 2005a.
5. See, e.g., Vogel, 2005; Christian Aid, 2004.
6. *The Economist*, 2005b.
7. Henderson, 2001; 2004
8. A collection of responses can be found at **www.business-humanrights.org**.
9. **www.business-humanrights.org**—accessed 19 May 2007.
10. Rembert, 2005.
11. Woidtke et al., 2003.
12. *Financial Times*, 2006; Stern, 2006.

[13] Monbiot, 2005.

[14] Friends of the Earth, 2005, and WWF and SustainAbility, 2005, address lobbying; Christian Aid, 2005, examines corporate taxation; WDM et al., 2005, examines privatization and liberalization; Christian Aid et al., 2005, is a study of the tobacco company, BAT; Action Aid, 2005a; 2005b, are studies of the retail, food, and agriculture industries' impact on small farmers in developing countries; CAFOD, 2005, examines working conditions in the computer industry. An up-to-date source of similar reports is www.corporate-responsibility.org.

[15] Power in the corporate responsibility context is a central theme in Bendell, 2004a; Blowfield, 2005b; Newell, 2005.

[16] Utting, 2005b; Rajak, 2006.

[17] Data from www.issproxy.com—accessed 20 June 2006.

[18] Radin and Werhane, 2003, discuss changing employment contracts; Grosser and Moon, 2005, and Barrientos et al., 2001, discuss gender dimensions to corporate responsibility.

[19] Nocera, 2006.

[20] Ginsberg, 2005; Prakash, 2006.

[21] See, e.g., Moon et al., 2005; Wood et al., 2006.

[22] Frynas, 2005, and Fig, 2005, provide case studies of corporate responsibility in Africa; Nielsen, 2005, and Newell, 2005, provide insights into power in Bangladesh and India; Lund-Thomsen, 2005, and Jenkins, 2005, explore the wider context corporate responsibility operates within and its consequences.

[23] *Ethical Performance*, 2005a; 2005b.

[24] *Ethical Performance*, 2005d; 2006b.

[25] Blowfield and Googins, 2007.

[26] Dunn, 2004; Tharoor, 2001.

[27] *Ethical Performance*, 2004.

[28] Elkington and Lee, 2006.

[29] Available at www.economicfootprint.org.

[30] See Utting, 2005b; Bennett and Burley, 2005; Doane, 2005.

14

The future of corporate responsibility

Chapter overview

In this chapter, we focus on the current trends in corporate responsibility and consider in what directions the field is moving. In particular, we will:

- examine the mega-trends that will affect what is meant by 'corporate responsibility' over the coming years;

- explore aspects of contemporary corporate responsibility that may be refined or enhanced;

- discuss evolving types of approach to corporate responsibility;

- reflect on what corporate responsibility reveals about the changing role of business in twenty-first-century society.

Main topics

■ Key terms

Capital markets

Climate change

Corporate governance

Social entrepreneurship

Sustainable consumption and
production

■ Online resources

- Additional case studies of new trends in companies

- Exercises and discussion topics for students

- Links to other web-based resources

Where is corporate responsibility heading?

The world cries out for repair.

It is with this old Jewish saying that Margolis and Walsh open their 2003 overview of companies' social initiatives. The article recognizes the increasing pressure that companies are under to provide solutions to social and environmental problems, even as they pursue seemingly competing financial demands, not least because, despite their limitations, in the current era of economic globalization they may be the entities of last resort for achieving all manner of societal objectives.

The questions raised are at the heart of corporate responsibility today: is capitalism able to cure the ills of capitalism? Are social and environmental goals at odds with those that are financial, or is there a strong business case to be made for acting responsibly? Is business able to take responsibility for non-financial objectives and, if so, is this desirable? Does business have any choice but to consider its footprint on society, given that it has to comply not only with formal regulation, but the non-formal regulation that is imposed by civil society? Should business be held to account for areas of non-financial performance and, if so, how and by whom? These questions have all been raised in earlier chapters of this book, but they are not questions that are readily resolved. While part of the field of corporate responsibility is a vibrant, functionally oriented focus on crafting the tools with which companies can manage issues as diverse as human rights, eco-efficiency, and corruption, there is another part, within which the purpose and future direction of corporate responsibility are the main concerns.

Participants in the latter arena are posing such questions as: where is corporate responsibility heading? What will be its contribution to solving societal problems? Which parts of the corporate responsibility agenda should be allowed to wither and which nurtured? What new approaches and ways of thinking deserve investment?[1] After a decade or more during which corporate responsibility was seen as evidence of change, it is now common to hear that corporate responsibility itself is on the cusp of change. Some see a new confidence that is leading to grander transformations than previously imagined; some feel disillusionment; others view this moment as a turning point at which corporate responsibility might venture off into a number of quite different directions.[2]

White (2005) sets out three scenarios for corporate responsibility in the year 2015 that broadly reflect these differing viewpoints.

1 In Scenario 1, which he calls *'fad and fade'*, he imagines a severe economic downturn that causes companies and governments to concentrate on basic economic survival and recovery, and to discard any thoughts of making corporate responsibility integral to corporate strategy, management, and governance. Companies will still face corporate responsibility challenges, such as transparency, labour standards, human rights, and climate change, but government mandates and regulation, rather than business innovation, will drive their responses.

2 Under Scenario 2 (*'embed and integrate'*), calls for a business case for corporate responsibility have disappeared, because the benefits have already been persuasively demonstrated. Companies of all sizes and types of ownership accept corporate responsibility as the norm and not only adhere to international standards on good governance, labour practices, and environmental stewardship, but have melded their moral and ethical commitment to corporate responsibility into all facets of their business. In contrast with the fad-and-fade scenario, corporate responsibility is seen as an integral part of corporate management that will be resilient to economic conditions.

3 Scenario 3 (*'transition and transformation'*) describes a wholly different approach, under which frustration with the types of programme discussed in other chapters spurs the formation of a coalition of civil society, labour, and business, pushing for *'corporate redesign'*. For White, this transformation marks an ending of the narrow focus on short-term shareholder value and its replacement with a stakeholder model of the company, within which employees, communities, suppliers, and shareholders are all considered as 'investors' with the right to participate in the firm's governance and to benefit from its surplus.

These three scenarios are broad enough to accommodate the main ongoing discussions about the future of corporate responsibility. One strand of debate is how to enhance current approaches to corporate responsibility ('Enhancing corporate responsibility', p 372) and the fad-and-fade scenario questions whether this will ever be sufficient. But derailing corporate responsibility may not need anything as severe as a major economic downturn; already an anti-corporate responsibility movement has emerged, arguing that what is called the 'rhetoric of responsibility' is part of a left-wing agenda of government regulation and wealth redistribution.[3] From a very different perspective, some early advocates of corporate responsibility claim that the field is reaching its limits, and that it will fade if it does not concentrate on system-level change of the kind that would encourage companies to be consistent in their corporate responsibility actions and their public policy efforts.[4] Equally, it may turn out that corporate responsibility is made irrelevant because of economic prosperity rather than crisis (i.e. if the neoliberal vision is fulfilled).

Alternatively, it may prove that the strengths and weaknesses of current approaches to corporate responsibility are readily recognized, and are replaced by, or supplemented with, 'New types of approach' (p 378), such as social entrepreneurship, green innovation, and new models of philanthropy. But this is not necessarily proof of a deeper consciousness of the kind envisaged in White's second scenario; it might equally be the case that some are simply commercial responses to new opportunities (e.g. the demand for ways in which to mitigate climate change).

In understanding the future of corporate responsibility, therefore, it is important not only to examine the approaches that companies are adopting, but also the context (Figure 14.1). This is already apparent from existing corporate responsibility practice, which, as discussed in other chapters, has been affected by globalization, the growing influence of global market forces compared with government policy, and the interests and influences of global media and civil society. Other factors affecting the environment within which

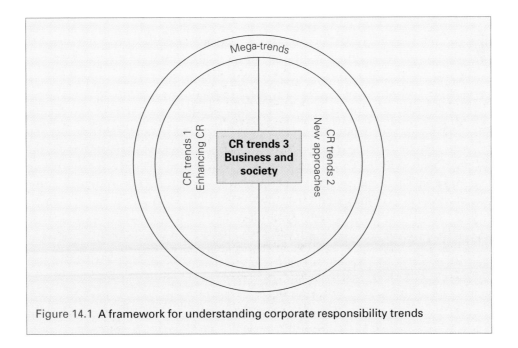

Figure 14.1 A framework for understanding corporate responsibility trends

business operates may have a similar effect in the future, including, for example, the inclusion of new scenarios, risk factors, and intangibles in the models that are used to set corporate strategy.[5] These are all very broad trends, however, that may go some way towards explaining the general environment within which business operates, but not necessarily the specific issues that corporate responsibility has to address. What, then, are some of the issues that are now appearing on corporate responsibility's radar screen?

Mega-trends affecting corporate responsibility

The global context—climate change, demographic change, and poverty

The consensus of the international science community is that greenhouse gas emissions will need to be reduced by 80–90 per cent by 2050 if we are to avert *'dangerous climate change'*.[6] Current emissions are the equivalent of more than 42 gigatonnes of carbon dioxide, and mainstream scientists say that this needs to drop to 5 gigatonnes by 2050 to avert extreme climate change. By that time, the world's population is likely to reach 9.1 billion, compared with 2.5 billion in 1950. Eight billion of these will be living in the poorest countries, within which illiteracy and malnutrition hamper human development. Climate change, demographic change, and poverty are, then, the three major trends that will set the context for corporate responsibility worldwide.

Climate change

Sizeable sections of today's business community believe that climate change is a phenomenon that has to be tackled. According to Stephen Schwarzman, head of private equity firm the Blackstone Group: *'Businesses have to do things to address* [climate change]. *It's not a green issue, it's not a red issue. It's the issue.'*[7] It is well beyond the scope of this book to discuss the science, or even the business implications, of climate change in any depth: there are all manner of questions relating to the types of response required, their cost, and their timing that have yet to be answered. But the future of corporate responsibility is likely to be greatly affected by the way in which business and government respond. For some, climate change is the most crucial scientific question of the twenty-first century, and the 'winning side' might shape economic, political, and technological development for years, even centuries, to come.[8] Although, like many aspects of corporate responsibility, responses to climate change have typically been treated as involving trade-offs in terms of profitability and competitiveness, some economists are now treating it as the pro-growth strategy of the future (Case Study 14.1).

CASE STUDY 14.1

The economics of climate change

Nicholas Stern, who led the UK government's review of climate change, conducted what amounts to an economic analysis of risk and tackled the elephant in the room, i.e. can we address climate change without derailing economic growth? Stern's conclusion was direct: *'Tackling climate change is the pro-growth strategy for the longer-term, and it can be done in a way that does not cap the aspirations for growth of rich or poor countries.'*

The costs of extreme weather, for example, could reach 0.5–1 per cent of GDP (compared with the 0.1 per cent cost of flooding in the UK today). Costs associated with climate change over this and the next century might reduce global per capita consumption by at least 5 per cent, and could be up to 20 per cent if environmental and health costs are factored in. Stern believes that climate change itself is anti-growth in the long run, and that correlations between emissions and GDP are outdated, because of the efficiencies and technological innovations that are associated with tackling climate change.

Economists such as Nordhaus and Dasgupta have queried Stern's findings, and argue that there are rational economic arguments for limiting up-front investment in climate change mitigation. Another group of economists has highlighted that Stern's choice of discount rate reflects an ethical belief that we should not value the cost of disaster to our grandchildren at less than the costs of the same disaster to ourselves and that a higher discount rate of the kind used in most economic analysis would make the costs of global warming in a hundred years' time appear small, or even negligible, in present-day terms. Such critics raise important questions, not only about methodology, but about how much and in what should we invest. Should the costs be evaluated as an investment or as insurance? Is adaptation a better option than mitigation? These are likely to be important questions affecting corporate responsibility in the coming years.

(Stern, 2006; Byatt et al., 2006; Rushe, 2007)

Questions

Stern's analysis of climate change has been criticized for presenting an unimpeachable moral argument, but a nonsensical rational economic one.

1 What is the rationale behind that criticism?

2 Is it valid?

3 Should companies only listen to rational economic reasoning?

Demographic change

The field of corporate responsibility may provide a framework within which business is able to help to resolve the challenges that climate change presents. But there is also a risk that climate change will swamp the corporate responsibility agenda and draw attention away from other major societal changes affecting business' relationship with society. Demographic change is an example of this that highlights some of the complexities of business' involvement in tackling sustainability.

The world's population has expanded enormously since 1950, but this growth has been unevenly spread in terms of age or location (Box 14.1). Although the total population is predicted to level off at 9.1 billion by 2050, 95 per cent of growth will be in poorer countries, while that of wealthier nations is expected to remain fairly stable at 1.2 billion. Demographic change will pose all sorts of challenges for companies, including migration (from poor countries to rich, and from rural to urban areas), wealth flows (transfer of remittances from migrant workers to families around the world), health care (as the number and proportion of elderly in developed economies and also in emerging ones, such as China and India, continue to grow), social welfare provision (due to the changing ratio of economically active and inactive people), competition for natural resources (from energy

Box 14.1 World demographics at a glance

- Total population has risen from 2.5 billion in 1950 to 6.5 billion today.
- Seventy-six million new inhabitants are added each year because births outnumber deaths by more than 2:1.
- Nearly half of the world's population is under the age of 25.
- Population in the least developed countries will triple by 2050 and will change little (it may even decline) in more developed regions.
- Emerging economies, such as China and India, have increasingly large proportions of elderly people (31 per cent and 21 per cent by 2050, respectively).

to land to water), and pressure on ecosystems (owing to increased demands for housing, waste disposal, food, etc.).

The upshot of these changes is not known for sure. Malthus' idea that population growth hinders development persists, but some argue that rapid population growth promotes economic prosperity by adding human capital and increasing market size. Perhaps the dominant view today is that population size and growth, in isolation from other factors, have little impact on economic performance. But this perspective ignores a critical variable: the way in which a population is distributed across different age groups and how this affects development. For example, a high proportion of young or old dependants can limit economic growth, because of the resources devoted to their care (especially by women). Countries with more working-age people can experience higher growth, because of the higher earnings and savings levels, and less spending on dependants, creating a 'demographic dividend' that developing countries might enjoy just as the US baby boomers did after World War II.[9]

Global poverty

Climate change and demographic change, although all within the broad ambit of corporate responsibility, require different, sometimes contradictory, solutions. Poverty—its consequences and its alleviation—is the third major issue affecting how corporate responsibility will develop and brings with it quite different problems. Around the world, people are living longer and are healthier than ever before. Overall, they are more literate and have higher incomes. But the picture is complex. About 1.2 billion people, or one-fifth of the world's population, still live in extreme poverty (i.e. on less than a dollar a day). Half of the world's people live on less than two dollars a day. If China is removed from the equation, the total number of extremely poor increased by 28 million during the 1990s and, in sub-Saharan Africa, GDP has fallen by 17 per cent since 1975. Poverty and the sense that the world's wealth is not fairly distributed is already a concern for some executives. Phil Marineau, Levi Straus CEO, has asked:

> Sixty-five percent of the world's wealth is in the United States. We're watching it being redistributed before our eyes. How [does a company] participate in that in a way that is consistent with [its] values and that earns people's trust?[10]

The consequences of poverty are already evident, to some degree, in terms of the terrorism that wealthier nations are experiencing. It is also something that business has been accused of exploiting by investing in places where wages are lower and where workers have least protections. Poverty can, however, also be regarded as a missed opportunity, in that the poor represent an underserved market—something that is at the centre of some of the 'New types of approach' to corporate responsibility discussed later in this chapter (p 378).

Furthermore, any discussion of poverty raises questions about the role that fast-growing economies, such as India, China, and Brazil, will play. Such countries have tended to be seen as risks in a corporate responsibility context, but the situation will become far more complex in coming years, because they serve not only as the producers of the world, but equally as important consumer markets, sources of financial capital, hosts of important ecosystems (e.g. tropical forests), and the sites of natural resource-based conflict (e.g. water access, land grabs, desertification). In many ways, these countries will become a testing ground for the role that business can play in creating a just and sustainable world. Moreover, as multinationals emerge from these countries, ideas of corporate responsibility that are rooted in quite different cultural, political, and philosophical traditions from those that have tended to dominate thinking thus far might influence developments in the field worldwide. Equally, these companies may find themselves wrestling with the consequences of a worsening divide between the rich and the poor, and with public pressure to resist global economic homogenization in favour of more localized, fragmented economies.

The power of multinationals

There is debate about whether corporate responsibility is something that all companies should address, or whether it only concerns the particular relationship that multinational firms have with the world (see Chapter 2). Some worry that attention to corporate responsibility will undermine small and medium-sized enterprises (SMEs), which are seen as essential to economic growth, not least in developing countries (see Chapter 4). The fear here is that corporate responsibility, in general, will put too onerous a burden on SMEs and that, in the developing country context, it might be used as a form of protectionism to limit access to wealthier markets.[11] This is not to say that SMEs should be 'unethical', but rather that there is a need to recognize that their approaches to responsibility may be different. Moreover, some imply that SMEs have an inherent value—something that is becoming evident, for example, in debates about the way in which supermarkets treat their small suppliers, or are forcing small businesses off of the high street.

The power of supermarkets reflects a wider concern about the power of large companies. Some critics of globalization have turned their attention away from trade legislation, and more towards anti-trust and anti-monopoly activism. For example, there is concern that we inhabit a world dominated by global oligopolies that not only have enormous purchasing power, but are also exercising great political power.[12] Consumers have benefited historically from anti-trust laws that present price gouging, but companies such as Wal-Mart and Tesco are today being accused of having such power, even over multinational suppliers such as Procter and Gamble, or Rubbermaid, that they can set prices almost at will. They are also suspected of using this muscle to intimidate local governments and to drive through planning applications for new stores, irrespective of local community sentiment.[13] And, of course, this same kind of power can be used against workers, as when McKinsey and Co helped Wal-Mart to prepare a memo on how to cut back employee benefits even though these were already among the lowest in the US retail industry.[14] Equally, there is excitement that such companies can use their power to tackle societal challenges.

The issue of corporate power applies to any industry, not only to that of retail. Suspicion is especially strong in relation to the lobbying of government on legislation, procurement, and spending.[15] Corporate responsibility itself has been a target for lobbyists. For example, the Confederation of British Industry lobbied to have sections of the Company Law Reform Bill altered to limit company accountability to stakeholders and has been accused, more generally, of influencing government sustainable development policies.[16] From a different perspective, WWF and SustainAbility (2005) compared corporate responsibility commitments and corporate lobbying activities, and found that, although many companies included discussion of lobbying in corporate responsibility reports, they were reluctant to lobby actively to improve social and environmental frameworks.

One area in which companies have been accused of using their power in ways that might harm the common good is taxation. Worldwide, there has been a trend to cut back corporate taxation, partly based on the argument that this will stimulate growth and generate more total revenues for government programmes. The Tax Justice Network and the Publish What You Pay Campaign are examples of civil society responses to the suspicion that companies are not paying their fair share, and even that corporate responsibility is window dressing that is intended to divert attention away from the tax evasion strategies of multinationals.[17] Greider (2006) proposes that corporate taxation could be refashioned, so that tax liabilities might be reduced for those that adhere to higher social or environmental standards. Parts of the accountancy profession argue, however, that there is insufficient understanding of the true scale of business' taxes and Pricewaterhouse-Coopers, for example, is proposing a new framework for reporting a company's total tax contribution, i.e. all of the direct and indirect tax that business pays into the economy.

Moreover, corporate power, per se, is only one facet of the business environment that will affect corporate responsibility in the future. Public companies have, for several years, been affected by the increasingly short-term perspective of the capital markets, with executives (whose own terms of office are increasingly short) focused on immediate returns rather than on building long-term shareholder value. Mainstream business groups, such as the Conference Board, the US Chamber of Commerce, and the Business Roundtable, have flagged investor short-termism as a problem, and some CEOs have gone on record saying that it is an important influence on how they address social and environmental issues.[18]

Short-termism has been linked by some to the trend for taking more companies to private investors. The rise in importance of private equity firms affects corporate responsibility in a number of ways. In so far as corporate responsibility is a response to public pressure, not least to that of parts of the investment community, it takes away a driver for change. It also makes elements of corporate behaviour less transparent. Private equity is also attracting high-calibre managers who may otherwise have been the innovators of corporate responsibility in public companies. But it may also be that, released from the pressure of meeting analysts' quarterly targets, these managers will be able to take a longer term perspective of the kind that many believe is essential to addressing the main social and environmental challenges.

Corporate governance

Business' interest in sustainable development has coincided with changing ideas about corporate governance and ethics, and there is a degree of overlap between the two agendas. The continuing trend towards greater transparency, for example, complements demands that environmental and social issues be incorporated into corporate governance. As noted in other chapters, aspects of sustainable development have also found their way (with mixed results) onto governance reform initiatives, such as the UK Company Law Review. In Europe, reporting on aspects of sustainability will increase as a result of the EU Accounts Modernization Directive, which requires that directors' reports contain a business review that includes information about environmental matters, employees, and social and community issues, including information on relevant policies and their effectiveness. This is reflected, for example, in the UK Companies Act 2006, which, for publicly listed companies, requires directors to report on non-financial issues to the extent that is necessary for an understanding of the business (see Chapter 8).

Central to such initiatives is a debate about the duties of corporate officers to those other than shareholders and the idea of enlightened shareholder value. Some legislation regarding directors' liabilities has been strengthened (e.g. the UK Corporate Manslaughter Bill), and recent decisions by the UK and EU courts mean that it is not only in the USA that companies can be held liable for their social and environmental actions abroad.[19] New regulations have also been introduced, relating to sustainability issues. For example, the EU's Pollution Prevention and Control Directive raises the bar on controlling industrial pollution across Europe, and its Waste Electrical and Electronic Equipment Directive deals with end-of-life issues for electronic products, which will influence the behaviour of both manufacturers and retailers.

The attention given to the responsibilities of business has increased further since the introduction of the 2007 UK Climate Change Bill, the first attempt to set legally binding targets on greenhouse gas emissions. But it is not legislation alone that is causing companies to act: codes of business practice that include aspects of corporate responsibility can serve to forestall legislation, but equally to meet requirements that companies demonstrate they have a strong control environment. Basel II (the revised international capital framework), for example, requires major financial institutions to show that they have key risk measuring and monitoring systems and controls in place.

Most large companies now have codes, or sets of principles, that span wide areas of non-financial performance and are underpinned by a framework of policies. Such codes can also help companies to deal with the ethical responsibilities and liabilities that stem from such legislation as the US Sarbanes–Oxley Act 2002, the UK bribery and corruption law, the US Foreign Corrupt Practices Act 1977, and the UK Enterprise Act 2002.

CASE STUDY 14.2

Tree-huggers at the gate

Kohlberg Kravis Roberts' 1989 acquisition of RJR Nabisco became infamous as an example of hard-headed, shareholder value-driven capitalism in Burrough and Helyar's *Barbarians at the Gate* (1990). Two decades on and KKR's record-breaking private equity deal to purchase the energy utility, TXU, has made headlines for different reasons.

TXU had been under attack from environmental groups because of its plans to build 11 old-technology, coal-fired power plants in Texas. The plans became bogged down in a swamp of public outcry, political manoeuvring, and litigation. In what some are holding up as a landmark collaboration between private equity and environmental activists, two environmental NGOs, the Natural Resources Defence Council and Environmental Defense, negotiated a deal whereby, in return for their backing the purchase, KKR agreed to suspend developments of eight of the power plants, pilot a 'clean coal' plant, cut greenhouse gas emissions, invest in alternative energy, and back government climate change legislation.

For the NGOs involved, it is another example of how to collaborate with business to achieve environmental objectives, although this, in turn, has led to criticism from other environmental groups that the KKR–NGO agreement contained too many loopholes. For KKR, the support of these multi-million-dollar NGOs reduces the risk that the purchase might otherwise represent and, it hopes, will strengthen TXU's licence to operate. It also signifies a new development in private equity strategy, under which firms bet on the profits to be made from social and political change.

(*The Economist*, 2007; Smith and Carlton, 2007)

Questions

The purchase of TXU is one of the first examples in which corporate responsibility issues and partnership with NGOs have overtly played a part in a private equity firm's investment decisions.

1 Although it is portrayed as a 'win–win agreement' between KKR and the NGOs, what do you think were the advantages for the former?

2 What do you think were the risks and potential disadvantages for the NGOs?

3 Do you think this will be a one-off example, or will it extend to other industries?

Enhancing corporate responsibility

What are likely to be the responses within corporate responsibility to the above mega-trends? Based on what is already happening and what is being talked about, there are two readily discernible types of change occurring. One is the emergence of 'New types of approach' to corporate responsibility (p 378); the other is the enhancement and refinement of some of the well-established responses, and it is to these that we first turn.

The professionalization of corporate responsibility

Perhaps the broadest refinement is likely to be the growing professionalization of corporate responsibility. Among other factors, this is an inevitable outcome of some of the wider trends in corporate governance that we have already noted. Internally, the increased focus on non-financial dimensions of governance generally means that boards want to know that non-financial risk is being managed effectively and that many companies are emphasizing the internal reporting of non-financial data. Cross-functional teams are being created to manage non-financial risk and compliance agendas, and, as noted in other chapters, new management and reporting systems are being developed to address corporate responsibility risks (e.g. the ethical and environmental management systems used in Nike and adidas' supply chains).

This is part of a trend for internal audit functions to extend their scope of work beyond the financial into areas such as health, safety and the environment, and responsible supply chain management. There are already many consultancy and certification businesses meeting the demand for outsourcing in these areas. To envisage how this will grow, one needs only to imagine the likely demand for metrics and reporting systems with which to track progress in companies with major commitments to corporate responsibility. For example, the UK's Marks and Spencer, which has introduced corporate responsibility criteria into product lines and sourcing decisions, and which is inviting public scrutiny into the conditions under which its products are made through its Behind the Label initiative, is a company the credibility of which will ultimately be closely linked to robust assurance mechanisms.

The more that these metrics become material to companies, the more impetus there will be for greater professionalization of corporate responsibility. This professionalization will happen in different areas of business. For example, corporate responsibility is likely to become a specific managerial competency, with prospective managers increasingly exposed to the field as an aspect of management practice; corporate responsibility professionals will undergo continual development; managers, in general, will need to be aware of the issues. Professionalization is also likely to lead professional service firms to build the capacity of accountants, lawyers, and others so that they can offer corporate responsibility services to companies. Equally, if corporate responsibility becomes of more importance to the investment community, analysts, fund managers, trustees, and others will need to meet new standards of professional competence (Box 14.2).

Box 14.2 **Initiatives aimed at professionalizing corporate responsibility—examples**

- Fifty FTSE100 companies have had their non-financial reports externally verified, ten of which verifications have been performed by one of the Big Four accountancy firms.
- The Prince of Wales's Accounting for Sustainability project is helping organizations to measure more effectively the environmental and social costs of their actions.
- PricewaterhouseCoopers and Ernst & Young are among the sponsors of the AA1000 sustainability assurance standard, which has a professional qualification element.
- The International Federation of Accountants (IFA) has issued standards on non-financial assurance engagements.
- The Institute of Chartered Accountants in England and Wales (ICAEW) has started to analyse sustainability from an accountancy perspective.

Beyond ethical sourcing

One driver of professionalization is concern that current services are of insufficient quality. For example, a 2006 report by the US National Labor Committee pointed to numerous labour rights abuses in audited factories and member companies of the Ethical Trading Initiative have been highly critical of the auditing of labour conditions.[20] Such auditing is a key feature of corporate responsibility management in global supply chains, and its poor quality has been cited as an indicator of the dysfunctional relationship between brand owners and their suppliers. In Chapter 6, we noted that companies such as Levi Strauss and Gap were keen to move away from a situation in which they felt they were policing suppliers through auditing, towards one that was intended to build the capacity of managers and workers. Moreover, even if the auditing were to be perfect, auditors alone would not improve social or environmental performance. As Utting (2005a) points out, there are about 70,000 multinational companies with 700,000 affiliates, served by innumerable millions of smaller companies. Yet no more than 5,000 companies produce corporate responsibility reports, about 700 firms use the Global Reporting Initiative's Guidelines, and a similar number have adopted SA8000. Even the most widely used certification scheme, ISO14001 on environmental management, has been applied in just over 90,000 facilities worldwide.

More ambitious still are efforts to think not only of single issues within the chain, but about what constitutes a sustainable supply chain as a whole, including social, economic, and environmental dimensions. The Sustainable Agriculture Initiative Platform, backed by companies such as Danone, Nestlé, and Unilever, is an example of this, although it is concerned primarily with the environmental aspects of agricultural production. Ongoing work by companies such Cadbury-Schweppes, as well as initiatives such as the Roundtable on Sustainable Palm Oil, are applying a larger lens that includes issues such as working conditions, land rights, and terms of trading.

Adopting international standards

The desire to use standards in supply chains more effectively is part of a wider debate in corporate responsibility about international standards. For example, in Boston in July 2006, at a meeting of representatives from corporate responsibility organizations such as the International Business Leaders Forum, AccountAbility, Business for Social Responsibility, and the Center for Corporate Citizenship, a United Nations representative proposed that the UN Global Compact and the Global Reporting Initiative's Guidelines be established as global frameworks around which corporate responsibility organizations might align their activities.[21] For some, this is seen as essential for corporate responsibility to reach critical mass and to obtain a broad political legitimacy: without it, it is feared that the corporate responsibility movement will disintegrate into specialized niches and an incoherent array of commercial applications.

A similar sentiment lies behind other collaborative initiatives, such as Jo-In, under which some of the most prominent ethical sourcing organizations are sharing learning on how to implement voluntary codes of labour practice. Although not made explicit, such collaboration is also an attempt to address complaints by companies that there are simply too many codes and that, if different standards were to be recognized as equivalent, this would reduce the cost of auditing and win more acceptance from suppliers.

There are legitimate concerns that, if those who support corporate responsibility cannot decide meaningful parameters with regards to the meaning and implementation of corporate responsibility, then the so-called movement will fragment. At the same time, it is equally appropriate to be concerned about who is most likely to influence any ultimate consensus and whether what emerges is a genuine agreement, or more the result of coercion. If we look again at the idea of using UNGC and GRI as the basis of a global framework, we see that the organizations involved in this discussion are corporate-funded in some way, whereas a major criticism of corporate responsibility discussed in Chapter 13 is that corporate influence is already undermining its legitimacy.[22] Hence, while alignment around particular definitions and approaches might be desirable, any trend in this direction will ultimately only be sustained if there is an accompanying consensus about what society expects from business (see 'The role of business in society', p 381).

Making corporate responsibility more inclusive

One of the challenges in creating a global vision of corporate responsibility is that norms and values are strongly influenced by cultural factors (see Chapter 2). Moreover, current corporate responsibility practices have been criticized for overlooking, or excluding, the priorities of particular social groups. For example, mirroring the male bias of which business is often accused, codes of labour practice have been criticized for favouring the interests of male workers and ignoring the needs of women.[23] Similarly, some argue that corporate responsibility practice can only be effective when it accommodates the cultural perspectives of the locations in which it is being implemented, while it has also been proposed that non-Western value systems, such as those practised in labour-intensive Indian organizations, are better suited to achieving positive outcomes.[24]

Awareness of the exclusiveness exhibited in some areas of corporate responsibility has been recognized for a number of years and is one of the insights provided by work in developing countries (see Chapter 6). But it is far from certain whether there will be a trend towards tackling the issue in any concerted way over the coming years. On the contrary, there may be a stronger trend towards seeing those who do not fit readily within the company's vision of what constitutes a legitimate stakeholder as hostile adversaries—something that may be inadvertently reinforced by the tools that companies use to manage corporate responsibility.[25]

Responsible consumers

One area of corporate responsibility that is already starting to receive more attention from companies is that of 'product' responsibility. There are different facets to this. In the area of corporate philanthropy, pharmaceutical companies and others are taking product donations more seriously in terms of ensuring that the products are useful and well used. Rather than designing a product and then ensuring that it is made responsibly, companies from Nike, to GE, to Boots, are using external inputs from the outset to think through the meaning of a responsible product—something that is being given a further push by legislation on product life cycle responsibilities (e.g. the EU Waste Electrical and Electronic Equipment Directive). Media and entertainment corporations, such as Time-Warner, are starting to put in place policies relating to how they portray others' products (e.g. the use of cigarettes in films) and, as discussed in 'Social entrepeneurship' (p 379), there is increasing thought going into the responsibility of companies to make products available to the poor.

Uniting each of these examples is a new sense of the company's responsibility towards consumers. This, in turn, reflects a renewed interest to engage the consumer in corporate responsibility and an awareness that one of the constraints faced by companies in advancing a corporate responsibility agenda is consumer ignorance, or indifference. January 2006 saw the high-profile launch of Product Red, a global 'brand' under which major companies, such as American Express, Motorola, and Giorgio Armani, launched product lines, some of the profits of which would go towards fighting HIV/AIDS in Africa (see Case Study 14.4).

Devinney et al. (2006), however, say that any belief that consumers are ready to make purchasing decisions based on ethical criteria is not borne out to any significant degree in practice. They point to a marked difference between consumer opinions and purchasing behaviour that suggests that morals stop at the wallet. If, as many corporate responsibility managers seem to believe, the adoption of corporate responsibility as an element of mainstream management practice depends on consumers making decisions based less on price and more on an awareness of what lies behind the price, then, over the coming years, we might see a variety of initiatives put in place.

Engaging financial institutions

The growth of socially responsible investment has been heralded as one of the successes of corporate responsibility (see Chapter 11), but to put that in perspective, the amount invested in SRI funds is less than 1 per cent of that invested in hedge funds.[26] It is not surprising, therefore, that many see the future development of corporate responsibility as closely linked to trends in the mainstream financial community.

Attention is already being paid to the environmental side of corporate responsibility. Green venture capital is well established, especially in the USA, where the amount invested in green technology companies rose by 35 per cent in 2005 to a total of $1.6bn.[27] Proven venture firms, such as Kleiner Perkins Caufield and Byers, which has created a $100m fund for green technology companies, are investing heavily in clean and green innovators. Attracted by trends such as rapid growth in renewable energy and green building materials, roughly 10 per cent of North American venture capital now goes into green technologies, while more than £660m has been invested in European clean technology since 2001.[28]

Corporate responsibility issues are highly unlikely to be addressed adequately without the engagement of financial markets—but markets only respond when a price is attached to an issue. This has happened with carbon trading, for which London has established itself as the global centre, while New York or Chicago might emerge as competitors should the USA commit to national emissions reduction targets.[29] Despite the European carbon market's problems in 2006, over 1 billion tonnes of carbon dioxide were traded in Europe alone, at a value of more than £12bn. Blue-chip investment houses have been major investors: Goldman Sachs took a 10 per cent stake in London-listed carbon trader Climate Exchange and Morgan Stanley has promised to invest $3bn in carbon trading by 2012.[30] But there is little sign that markets will be formed for other issues and limited debate about whether markets for other important issues, such as poverty, could ever be created.

Financial firms, such as Henderson Global Investment, have broadened the abbreviation 'SRI' (see Chapter 11) to mean 'sustainable and responsible investment' and focus on what they consider to be the technologies of the future. Along with initiatives that we have noted in other chapters, such as the emergence of specialist indices from within the conventional investment world (e.g. FTSE4Good and the Dow Jones Sustainability Indexes), these are examples of how corporate responsibility is starting to be integrated into mainstream analysis. In Germany, for example, investors and analysts are demanding increasingly sophisticated information on sector-specific sustainable development key performance indicators.[31] But overall, the investment community is ill equipped to judge the significance of sustainable development actions, because it remains focused on assessing financial data and management quality, and the sums of money saved through, for example, eco-efficiency, although large, may not be large enough to attract analysts' attention. Most investors see their role as based on price, rather than on the kind of adding value that some feel is achieved by relationship investing and other long-term relationships.[32]

To a degree, progress will depend on distinguishing what Lydenberg (2005) calls 'investable' issues that are material to a company, but not yet factored into the share price (i.e. mispricing) from those that are 'non-investable', for which engagement with investors is unlikely to have any effect. An important theme in future corporate responsibility debates will be how to tackle non-investable issues. Much will depend on the success of the initiatives noted elsewhere in this book in increasing the interest of mainstream analysts (e.g. the Marathon Club, the London Accord, the Enhanced Analytics Initiative, and the United Nations' Principles for Responsible Investing—see Chapters 9 and 11, and Case Study 14.3).

CASE STUDY 14.3

UN Principles for Responsible Investment

The United Nations' Principles for Responsible Investment (PRI) is one of several initiatives aiming to persuade investors to think of matters other than the financial bottom line when placing their money. Its backers are investors responsible for 10 per cent of global capital (or more than $4,000bn of assets), including Dresdner, Citigroup, Goldman Sachs, and USB. By signing up to the PRI, these investors commit to integrating environmental, social, and governance (ESG) issues into conventional investment analysis, to being active, responsible owners by promoting good corporate practice in these areas, and to reporting transparently on what actions have been taken in this area.

What marks out the PRI is that its supporters are major global institutions that are not known for putting their name to frivolous or marginal initiatives. The initiative's principles make explicit that ESG issues, or extra-financial risks, have an effect on the long-term performance of companies. They mark a step towards learning about measuring companies in ways that do not necessarily fit into the normal accounting framework and, ultimately, towards identifying long-term investment drivers.

(Scott, 2006; www.unpri.org—accessed 1 April 2007; www.greenbiz.com— accessed 1 April 2007)

Questions

The PRI has been welcomed as a step towards getting the international investment community to focus on long-term drivers of company value.

1 What is the significance of the PRI?

2 Are its principles genuine ones for responsible investment?

3 How will the PRI influence the development of corporate responsibility?

New types of approach

New philanthropy

There is a fine line between the enhancement of existing approaches to corporate responsibility and the emergence of new ones. Some of what is happening in the financial community, for example, is sufficiently innovative and far removed from the early endeavours of SRI as to warrant being called 'new'. The same is true of some of the pioneering work in corporate philanthropy. Earlier, we mentioned Product Red, the multi-company branding initiative aimed at raising funds for HIV/AIDS in Africa (see Case Study 14.4). This is one example of what might be called 'for-profit philanthropy', under which approach companies use commerce as a way of pursuing social goods. Google.org represents a different 'for-profit' approach, investing in start-up companies that address societal issues and forming partnerships with venture capitalists. It views profit as an opportunity, not as a primary goal, and supporters of this kind of approach insist that success will ultimately be measured against a social and environmental bottom line, not against one that is financial.[33]

CASE STUDY 14.4

Product Red

As first-world consumers, we have tremendous power. What we collectively choose to buy, or not to buy, can change the course of life and history on this planet.

So begins the manifesto of Planet Red, set up by Bobby Shriver and Bono to raise awareness and money for a charity, The Global Fund, which helps women and children affected by HIV/AIDS in Africa. Companies such as Motorola, American Express, and Apple have produced and marketed Product-Red-branded products, and a percentage of the sales of specially branded phones, credit cards, iPods, etc. goes to the fund.

Ad Age, an advertising trade magazine, has criticized this example of new philanthropy. It claims that, despite a marketing outlay by individual companies of $100m, the brand had raised just $18m by mid-2006. The figures have been contested and Product Red supporters say that $25m has been raised in six months on an investment of $40m. Perhaps more significantly, it has been pointed out that the sum paid to The Global Fund is five times higher than that which had been raised by corporate contributions over the previous five years. Indeed, an assumption that money spent on advertising is money that would otherwise have gone to charity does not reflect the way in which business operates. Moreover, the advertising spend was not intended simply to promote the products, but equally to raise awareness of the scale of the AIDS epidemic in Africa.

There are also criticisms that corporate spending on Product Red is masking cutbacks in other types of corporate philanthropy. Again, defenders of the initiative say that Product Red creates a regular stream of revenue for the charity, rather than leaving it dependent on annual donations from corporate philanthropy budgets. The aim is to create a sustainable source of funding for The Global Fund that will represent a new model for fundraising.

(Vallely, 2007; www.joinred.com—accessed 4 April 2007; www.adage.com—
accessed 4 April 2007)

Questions

Product Red is being presented as a new approach to corporate philanthropy—one that harnesses the power of consumer markets, branding, and marketing.

1 What are the features of Product Red that distinguish it from traditional forms of corporate philanthropy?

2 Would those with HIV/AIDS be better off if consumers were to give directly to charity rather than buying luxury items?

3 What would you propose as the measures of Product Red's long-term success?

Social entrepreneurship

New philanthropy shares much in common with the increasingly high-profile field of social entrepreneurship, not least in that social or environmental impact is a more important driver than wealth creation, even to the point at which some reject profit motivation in the social entrepreneurship context.[34] In reality, whatever the original meanings of the term, it now embraces a continuum of definitions including:

1 the application of sound business practice to non-profit management;

2 the use of entrepreneurial approaches to delivering social or environmental benefits;

3 the use of earned income strategies for social or environmental benefits (the 'double bottom line');

4 'complementary entrepreneurship', under which an enterprise uses income from commercial activities to invest in social and environmental activities;

5 partnerships between NGOs and for-profits;

6 'cause branding', such as Avon's campaigns around breast cancer, linking commercial activities to social or environmental issues.[35]

Indeed, social entrepreneurship may be becoming too broad a category to be meaningful. Even if one focuses solely on commercial activities, one finds a wide variety of enterprises. For example, the small and medium-sized enterprises delivering the kinds of goods and services that are aimed at poor segments of society described in Prahalad and Hart's 'bottom of the pyramid' model (2002) are a good example of social entrepreneurship (see Chapter 1). But, over time, some of the most successful models—notably, the microfinance initiative that was pioneered in Bangladesh and won a Nobel Prize for the Grameen Bank (see Chapter 11)—have been imitated by multinational companies, including Deutsche Bank and Citigroup.[36] Despite doubts about the role of big business in social entrepreneurship,[37] already companies such as Procter and Gamble, and Unilever, have targeted poor consumers as an area for growth and 'underserved markets', comprising a high percentage of low-income individuals and ethnic minorities, have been identified as a multi-trillion-dollar opportunity that is largely untapped.[38] Indeed, it might be said that companies such as Avon have built successful, international businesses around social entrepreneurs, not least women.

The various kinds of social entrepreneurship promise to become a major element in ideas about corporate responsibility in the coming years, not least because of the support of organizations such as the Skoll Foundation, with its mission to invest in social entrepreneurs, and the presence of laboratories such as Oxford University's Skoll Centre for Social Entrepreneurship. The 'bottom of the pyramid' has attracted a huge amount of attention as a new model for helping to lift developing nations out of poverty, and a growing number of private foundations are expressing interest in market-based solutions to social and environmental challenges. Yet, although using the power of business to address such challenges is attractive, experience to date makes clear that serving these markets requires a different approach to doing business (e.g. the business model, partnerships, and use of non-traditional sources of market information) and, as with corporate responsibility more widely, social entrepreneurs are accountable to multiple constituencies.[39]

Moreover, there is good reason to treat the potential of social entrepreneurship with caution. The tendency to view the poor and marginalized as consumers (perhaps to the detriment of creating opportunities for them to be entrepreneurs and skilled workers in their own right) is itself a new trend, the consequences of which are unknown. It is also questionable how far what happens under the social entrepreneurship banner truly grapples with the complexity of societal needs, and with the integration of social, economic, and environmental challenges.[40]

Sustainable consumption and production

Some critics fear that corporate responsibility stifles the growth that is the heartbeat of capitalism. Yet for sustainable development theorists, one of the key challenges of the coming decades is how to decouple certain types of growth—particularly those associated with harmful emissions and unsustainable energy use—from prosperity. This has especially come to the fore as the demands that fast-growing economies, such as India and China, will put on natural resources become apparent, and it has been estimated that for the consumption and production patterns of Canada or the UK to be adopted worldwide would require resources equivalent to those of three earths—to adopt those of the USA would require those of five.[41]

'Sustainable consumption and production' (SCP) embraces an array of approaches that are aimed at addressing this problem. It refers to the challenge of achieving continuous economic and social progress that respects the limits of the earth's ecosystems, and meets the needs and aspirations of everyone for a better quality of life, both now and for future generations. SCP requires better alignment between consumption, the natural resources needed for production, and the ecological sinks available to absorb waste.[42] Organisation for Economic Co-operation and Development (OECD) governments have been committed for decades to ensuring that the prices people pay reflect the full social and environmental costs involved, and European governments are committed to SCP through the 2000 Lisbon Agenda. Historically, however, governments have been weak and inconsistent in promoting SCP, for fear that consumers would have to pay higher prices. Moreover, concerns regarding relative national competitiveness have consistently trumped those about sustainable development.

Various principles have emerged for tackling SCP, but, as we have seen with other areas of corporate responsibility, the wider business environment does not always encourage companies to take sustainability-based decisions and may even create disincentives. Moreover, at present, the place of SCP initiatives in the context of corporate responsibility is still uncertain. On the one hand, the core issue—how growth can be achieved while realizing a drastic per capita reduction in the use of resources—is one that is central to corporate responsibility; on the other, much of the current interest has come from government and there is a sense that only government can break the kind of 'I will if you will' impasse that is preventing more business action in this area. But governments, too, are constrained by not wanting to take action unilaterally for fear that this would sacrifice competitive advantage, while those who view corporate responsibility as voluntary, rather than mandatory, may feel uncomfortable with government-driven SCP for ideological reasons.

The role of business in society

There is considerable opportunity for refining corporate responsibility approaches through, for example, improving management practices, enhancing technologies, and engaging a wider audience. There is, too, justification for extending the scope of corporate responsibility through new types of approach of the kind that is emerging in the fields of social entrepreneurship and sustainable consumption. The trends that we have described under both refinement and extension are significant, although not comprehensive. More importantly, however, they do not properly capture a potentially more far-reaching trend, which is for the discipline of corporate responsibility to become the crucible in which to reconsider the role of business in twenty-first-century society. We have already seen this in some of our earlier discussions about corporate responsibility. Some of the debate around the business case, accountability, or managing corporate responsibility touches on what is the purpose of business and whether or not this is in transition. It also brings us full circle, back to some of the earliest specific literature on corporate responsibility described in Chapter 2. That early thinking and much of what followed until the 1980s, while proving useful in terms of thinking about the responsibilities of business, has been criticized for failing to provide either the framework or the tools with which companies can incorporate corporate responsibility into management practice and there is a certain concern that reframing it now as 'business in society' will not help to build the bridges between theory and practice that, to an extent, mark the latest incarnation of the field out from those that preceded it. Given some of the criticisms in Chapter 13, however, that corporate responsibility, as currently practised, is not properly addressing major societal concerns, it can also be argued that the success or failure of contemporary approaches to corporate responsibility, first and foremost, depend on tackling the right issues and that these can only be identified through use of a business–society lens.

What is the role of business?

The trend towards expressly thinking about the role of business is already evident not only in academic work, such as that of Van Tulder (2006—see Chapter 4) and debates among members of the European Academy for Business in Society network, but also in the thinking of business leaders. Consider, for example, the following quote from Susan Rice, CEO of Lloyds TSB in Scotland:

> I think some people in business still say, as they would have done 20 or 40 years ago, "My job is to create value for my shareholders. . . . The rest will take care of itself. If I'm creating shareholder value, then I'm contributing to taxes. The government will do what the government does; it all just happens." Now, I think you've got more companies saying, "Well, actually, it's not enough. The government can't do it and actually is not very capable at doing it on its own . . . Therefore it's our place as a private-sector business to be involved".[43]

There is a strong libertarian school of political and economic thought that would celebrate the travails of government in serving societal needs and be appalled that this be interpreted as an invitation to business to take on social responsibilities. But there are prominent members of the business community who regard such as views as too ideological or unpragmatic. Michael Rake, former KPMG chairman (now chairman of BT), for example, has said:

> Failure to properly understand the need to take a longer-term view and other areas of responsibility toward communities and the environment will lead to real concern as to whether globalisation is aimed to benefit the few and not the many, and whether on this basis unbridled capitalism is sustainable.[44]

Or as Ralph Shrader, Booz Allen Hamilton CEO, sees it:

> the companies that are the most successful leaders are the ones that are living a full life. They're not just building a car, but rather considering the context in which that car gets built.[45]

It may be that most executives would rather that their companies did not have to take on such responsibilities, but that option may no longer exist. Business today has the competencies, resources, and infrastructure to help to meet societal challenges and, whether by its own devising or because of external events, finds itself having some responsibility to make these available for the public good. The question then becomes not so much what does business have to offer, but what should be the limits of what it does and how it acts. The answer to this lies in reconsidering what are the legitimate roles for business and other sectors in the context of twenty-first-century society.

As our earlier discussions of corporate responsibility's historical context demonstrated, this is not a historically unique notion (see Chapter 2). In 1940s' Europe, the perceived failure of business to distribute the benefits of capitalism equitably led to the nationalization of many industries, while 1950s' USA is typically portrayed as a virtuous circle in which the roles of business, government, and trade unions were complementary and clear. In the 1970s, the roles of business and government were altered as a new era of globalization was ushered in (see Chapter 3). Each time the legitimate roles of business and government have been redefined, it has been because this was seen as essential for society's prosperity. Now there is a situation in which, because of the major shifts that global society is undergoing, the roles assigned to business and government are widely held to be outdated.

The scepticism that has greeted politicians' proposals to incorporate corporate responsibility into political policy suggests, however, that there is a long way to go before there is a consensus about business' role in public governance. Robert Monks, corporate governance thinker, has said that, given the level of distrust about business' influence over government policy, the starting point should be: '*What is the responsibility of the "good company" with respect to government?*' His prescriptions that companies disclose relevant information, exercise restraint regarding trying to influence government, and obey the law are less ambitious than some would want from a comprehensive corporate responsibility agenda, but nonetheless are, in many respects, a significant departure from what is currently on offer.

The role of capital markets

In discussing the business case in Chapter 5, we saw that some corporate responsibility theorists believe that its greatest contribution is to long-term value—something also emphasized by parts of the SRI community (see Chapter 11). Governments have historically served as drivers of long-term changes in corporate practice (e.g. minimum wage, working hours, toxic emissions) and, despite a perceived weakening of government's role, in relation to issues such as greenhouse gases, governance, and sustainable production, it continues to be a powerful force in shaping business behaviour.

One area in which government intervention, or lack thereof, might significantly shape the future corporate responsibility agenda is the capital markets. We have already touched on some of the development and difficulties in this area, including the implications of the EU's Accounts Modernization Directive in pushing companies to focus on the materiality of corporate responsibility issues, but it is far from clear how a legal requirement for companies to report on how they are taking into consideration social and environmental issues will affect the investment community. As the global market for capital expands and the costs of trading tumble, investors—even institutional investors—are focused on increasingly shorter time horizons.[46]

Furthermore, the logic that owners of public companies are in a strong position to effect change has been challenged by the emergence of private equity firms as an alternative source of capital. Companies engaged in corporate responsibility, such as Georgia Pacific, Littlewoods, and Aramark, have all become privately held, removing them from many of the non-mandatory drivers associated with improved social and environmental performance (e.g. public reporting). This is not to say that publicly held companies are more likely to address corporate responsibility issues than are those that are privately held: Dunkin' Donuts, for example, is owned by a private equity firm, but has gone further than most in mainstreaming fairtrade coffee; Cargill, one of the largest family-owned companies in the world, is nonetheless under pressure from retailers to adopt ethical sourcing policies. Indeed, in some cases, it may be that, removed from the pressure to meet quarterly earnings targets, some privately held companies may be better placed to take a longer-term perspective than if they were publicly listed. Nonetheless, most large companies are publicly held and many large private companies, such as Levi Strauss, continue to look to the same capital markets to some degree.

Hence, there is a dichotomy that lies at the heart of corporate responsibility's future development: on the one hand, there are many corporate responsibility theorists and practitioners, both inside and outside the business community, who believe that companies that ignore the business–society perspective are putting their long-term prosperity in jeopardy; on the other hand, the short-term culture of the capital markets is affecting, and effectively putting damaging constraints on, how companies address societal issues. If the former viewpoint is true, then short-termism is damaging shareholder, as well as stakeholder, value, but this is going unnoticed. Whether this perspective is accurate or not is, at present, more a matter of supposition than demonstrable fact, but the reaction of the capital markets will have a major influence on future trends in corporate responsibility. This is true of the investment community's own decisions, as is already evident, for example, in the way in which climate change is starting to be factored into financial analysis. But it is also true in terms of the way in which the investment community affects the decisions of others. For example, it affects the advice that executives follow so that even a company with a strong corporate responsibility track record might find itself under pressure to make decisions that would undermine its reputation, in the name of optimization and efficiency (see Case Study 14.5).

CASE STUDY 14.5

CEOs on the struggle with capital markets

Business performance today is viewed through a short-term lens and, although executive compensation packages at public companies are typically aligned with short-term shareholder interests, nonetheless, executives are highly aware that many of the societal issues with which they are concerned demand long-term solutions. This is echoed by John Brock, one-time CEO of InBev, who says:

> Wall Street is an important vector, but it's only one vector out of all the ones that you've got to consider. And if, as a business, that's the only one you consider, you're destined to fail; absolutely, categorically destined to fail.

Executives struggle, however, to communicate this to the capital markets, not least to sell-side analysts. As Charles Prince, Citigroup CEO, puts it:

> There is no reward for long-term growth. . . . Nobody cares at all about long-term, sustainable growth outside of the institution itself. It's one of the harshest lessons to learn about business. And why is that? Not

because people are bad. Investors get rewarded on how much profit they made, how much their port-folio grew. Not whether or not they're investing in something that lasts for 300 years.

Consequently, business today is approaching a situation in which management is finding it harder to communicate to investors what it feels are important dimensions to creating value in the long term. For some, balancing short- and long-term perspectives is simply one of the skills that CEOs need to have. Asks Ed Ludwig, Becton-Dickinson CEO:

You're the CEO of a public company. Do you manage for today or tomorrow? If I don't produce profits to my shareholders, then they'll find someone else who will. But on the other hand, if I don't plan for the future, then that's also limiting even though it takes longer to catch up with you.

These are early days in terms of persuading investors and analysts why new thinking about the business–society relationship matters. There is a legacy of investor mistrust following recent corporate scandals and a, perhaps understandable, concern that taking on societal issues will be the next vanity project of the 'imperial CEO'. There is also the fact that managing for long-term performance is hazardous, as is evident in the mixed success of ethical investors whose arguments that responsible companies perform better in the long run have been undermined, to some degree, by the collapse of companies such as Health South, WorldCom, and Enron. Indeed, mention of these collapses reminds us that boards can have significantly more influence than analysts or fund managers, and that the board might be a more fruitful place in which to tackle corporate responsibility issues.

(Adapted from Blowfield and Googins, 2007)

Questions

Many see the attitude of capital markets to social and environmental issues as a crucial determinant of future corporate responsibility trends.

1 What are the main reasons why the investment community is largely sceptical about CEOs' enthusiasm for corporate responsibility?

2 What events or changes might shift analysts' attitudes?

3 Is it the role of the CEO to change the opinions of the investment community?

Transforming the corporate purpose

In previous chapters, we have alluded to the ways in which consideration of corporate responsibility relates to debates about new forms of accountability and new ways of valuing the company, and how these, in turn, reflect a resurgence of interest in rethinking the purpose of business. This interest is manifesting itself in different arenas across the spectrum, from theory, to practice (Box 14.3).[47]

Activity in this area suggests that White's (2005) '*transition-and-transformation*' scenario (see 'Where is corporate responsibility heading?', p 363) may one day become a reality. It is as yet hard, however, to detect a widespread appetite for pushing through this kind of radical rethinking of business' purpose and a recurring question in this book is to what extent the ambitions of some regarding corporate responsibility can be realized without such reform. It would certainly seem to undermine claims that corporate responsibility is a pragmatic, practice-oriented response to the societal challenges that business faces if success were to prove ultimately dependent on new models of business that, in turn,

Box 14.3 Principles of the redesigned corporation

1 The purpose of the corporation is to harness private interests in the service of the public good.

2 Corporations shall accrue fair profits for shareholders, but not at the expense of the legitimate interests of other stakeholders.

3 Corporations shall operate sustainably to meet the needs of the present generation, without compromising the ability of future generations to meet theirs.

4 Corporations shall distribute their wealth equitably among those who contribute to its creation.

5 Corporations shall be governed in a manner that is participatory, transparent, ethical, and accountable.

6 Corporate rights shall not supersede or weaken the rights of natural persons to govern themselves.

(White, 2005)

would require revolutionary shifts in some of contemporary society's most embedded institutions.

Nonetheless, we should not ignore the possibility that society is at the threshold of major change. This is certainly the belief of some who see the future of business as closely intertwined with climate change and who hold that this will—in contrast with models of gradual, linear change in the past—precipitate dramatic, unpredictable, non-linear change. If non-linear theory is true, it could fundamentally affect the way in which we approach the world, causing policymakers and corporate managers to base their assumptions not on the expectations of gradual, predictable growth that justify a focus on efficiency and optimization, but rather on the new realities of unpredictability and vulnerability that, in turn, will make areas such as resilience, sufficiency, and complexity the new focuses of management. In such an environment of upheaval, the future directions within corporate responsibility would be hugely influenced by how useful the discipline proved itself to be, in relation to the innovative approaches to management practice, technology, and policy that would be required.

Among the criticisms of corporate responsibility is that it only tinkers at the edges of these major societal issues and trends, and has so far lacked the rigour (of theory and practice) to address the most important dimensions of the business–society relationship. With reference to climate change, for example, some of the most demonstrable changes in business practice in recent years relate to eco-efficiency, but these are minor variations to the established models of business that do little to tackle what some argue are the fundamental questions about capitalism's role in ensuring the sustainability of the earth's carrying capacity. Indeed, it can be argued that the question at the heart of corporate responsibility and its different forms that will surface over the coming years is whether capitalism itself is sustainable. For those who conclude that it is, corporate responsibility may be the discipline that allows them to consider if, and what, changes are needed to the capitalist model; for those who conclude that it is not, it remains to be seen if the frameworks and models within the corporate responsibility umbrella prove to be useful, obstructive, or irrelevant to the new paradigm.

SUMMARY

There are many elements to the corporate responsibility universe, as we have seen throughout this book. The indications are that this firmament will grow larger in the coming years for two reasons: first, there are pressing social and environmental issues that represent genuine challenges for both sustainability and global justice; second, there is an increasing expectation from different sectors of society that business will help to meet those challenges.

The future course of corporate responsibility will, to a large extent, be determined by how business' obligations to involve itself in major societal issues, such as climate change, demographic change, and global poverty, are defined and realized. No single institution will dictate how business responds: rather, as with other areas of corporate responsibility, the trends that emerge will be decided in various arenas of conflict, contestation, and collaboration. The growing power of multinational enterprise will be a significant factor, in terms of the resources and influence that major corporations possess, and the way in which they act as a pole star for both public protest and aspiration. Moreover, struggles within the corporate world—not least the rapid emergence of private equity funds as owners of what were hitherto publicly traded companies—will affect how ideas of corporate responsibility evolve.

Government responses both to the mega-trends affecting global society and to the changing form of the corporation will also significantly influence what happens in the name of corporate responsibility. In some areas, such as that of flexible labour markets, it would appear that many governments are comfortable encouraging voluntary approaches and relaxing regulations; in other areas, however, notably that of climate change, some governments appear reluctant to rely on non-mandatory solutions. Given this situation, defining corporate responsibility in terms of voluntary actions seems likely to be increasingly less useful. This does not mean that non-mandatory approaches will be unimportant, and there are various ways in which corporate responsibility as management practice may be refined and enhanced over the coming years. Equally, there are strong signs of new types of approach gaining prominence, some of which (e.g. social entrepreneurship) will constitute free market responses to societal needs and others (e.g. sustainable consumption and production) that are likely to require significant government intervention.

One of the major trends around corporate responsibility will, however, be less to do with management practice or government intervention, and more about the way in which we consider the role of business itself. Many of the current criticisms of corporate responsibility relate to how the prerogatives of the modern corporation determine its societal role. For some, this severely limits what business can do and, in important instances, causes business to act in ways that are counter to the overall societal good. This will remain the case, it is argued, until the corporate purpose is altered to reflect the rights, duties, and obligations of business as a citizen. There is by no means a consensus that such a radical shift should happen: some argue that this kind of philosophical reflection will divert attention away from the strength of current approaches as pragmatic management responses; others, that society should resist the notion of legal entities such as companies being thought of as citizens.

In terms of corporate responsibility as a discipline, there is no right or wrong answer to this type of debate. (Indeed, the weakness of recent corporate responsibility debates may be that thinkers have been too willing to champion either theory or practice as if they are mutually opposed, and their inability to consider reflexively what underlies this division.) Whether we are thinking about the chartered trading companies of the eighteenth and nineteenth centuries, the corporate philanthropists that emerged during the Industrial Revolution, the European cooperative movement, the place of international companies in twentieth-century banana republics, the sense of social obligation that is central to some of the most successful examples of business in Japan, South

Korea, and Germany, or the denial of responsibility to anyone other than shareholders that dictated much of corporate strategy in the 1980s and 1990s, we are constantly reminded that, regardless of what we choose to call it, the role of business in society is fundamental both to business and to the world at large. This will not change, regardless of what names we choose to assign to the pantheon of issues, practices, and hypotheses that have relevance to the business–society relationship. Future trends in corporate responsibility will not be determined by names, but by the discourse that evolves around the role of business and the relevance of corporate responsibility as a discipline, as a profession, as an antagonist, as a protagonist, or as a commentator in relation to that discourse.

DISCUSSION POINTS

1   White (2005) sets out six principles for a new type of company (see Box 14.3).
   - To what extent are these principles already embodied around the world in legal definitions of the company?
   - Are there principles on this list that you would alter or remove?
   - What principles would you add?

2   Demographic change is likely to be a significant influence on what is considered to be corporate responsibility in the coming years.
   - What are the ways in which demographic change might affect business in wealthy democracies?
   - What are the scenarios for business in 2050, resulting from demographic change in China, Brazil, or India?
   - What can business do to ensure that developing economies better enjoy their 'demographic dividend'?

3   Climate change has soared to the top of many companies' corporate responsibility agendas, and may well dominate both private and public sector thinking about sustainability for the foreseeable future.
   - What is the rational economic case for why companies should not consider climate change in their decision making at this time and how is it different to the moral case?
   - How will climate change shape company thinking about corporate responsibility?
   - What are the possible consequences of companies paying attention to climate change at the expense of other trends, such as demographic change, energy security, and global poverty?

4   Social entrepreneurship has been identified as an increasingly important approach to addressing corporate responsibility.
   - What are the weaknesses of the 'bottom of the pyramid' model?
   - What qualities will distinguish the 'corporate responsibility' entrepreneur from the conventional entrepreneur?
   - How, as an investor, would you appraise a request for start-up capital from a social enterprise?

5   Throughout this book, we have looked at the criticisms, strengths, and limitations of corporate responsibility.
   - Considering what has been discussed in earlier chapters, which of the trends in this chapter are likely to be most significant?
   - Which are those that are likely to be least significant?
   - Are there trends that have not been identified?

VISIT THE WEBSITE
for links to useful sources of further information

FURTHER READING

- Blowfield, ME and Googins, B, 2007, *Step Up: A Call for Business Leadership in Society—CEOs Examine Role Of Business In The 21st Century*, Chestnut Hill, MA: Center for Corporate Citizenship at Boston College.

  Leading CEOs and other senior executives go on the record about the changing role of business in society.

- Dees, JG, Emerson, J and Economy, P, 2002, *Strategic Tools for Social Entrepreneurs: Enhancing the Performance of your Enterprising Non-profit*, Chichester: John Wiley and Sons.

  Introduction to the practice of social entrepreneurship.

- Greenfield, K, 2006, *The Failure of Corporate Law: Fundamental Flaws and Progressive Possibilities*, Chicago, IL: University of Chicago Press.

  Arguments for a radical overhaul of company law.

- Henriques, A, 2007, *Corporate Truth: The Limits to Transparency*, London: Earthscan.

  An exploration of the limits of transparency in the contemporary corporate world and arguments about how far to push the boundaries.

- Wackernagel, M, Rees, WE and Testemale, P, 1996, *Our Ecological Footprint: Reducing Human Impact on the Earth*, Gabriola Island, BC: New Society Publishers.

  Influential attempt to measure the ecological impact of human activity.

- Weiser, J, Kahane, M, Rochlin, S and Landis, J, 2006, *Untapped: Creating Value in Underserved Markets*, San Francisco, CA: Berrett-Koehler.

  Wide range of North American case studies towards an understanding of the business potential of investing in poor communities.

ENDNOTES

1 These types of question have been posed, e.g., on corporate-responsibility-related listservs by people such as Jem Bendell and Seb Beloe.

2 See, variously, Bendell, 2005; Ward and Smith, 2006; Doane, 2005.

3 See, e.g., **www.cei.org** and **www.csrwatch.com**.

4 SustainAbility, 2004.

5 PwC, 2006.

6 International Panel on Climate Change fourth assessment, online at **www.ipcc.ch**.

7 *Financial Times*, 27 February 2007.

8 Pearce, 2005.

9 Bloom and Canning, 2006.

10 Blowfield and Googins, 2007, p 29.

11 Raynard and Forstater, 2002.

12 Lynn, 2006.

13 Darbyshire, 2007.

14 Greenhouse and Barbaro, 2005.

15 See, e.g., coverage of pharmaceutical lobbying: **www.bmj.com**; leahy.senate.gov/press—both accessed 13 March 2007.

16 **www.ethicalerformance.com**—accessed 7 March 2007; McRae, 2005.

[17] Riesco et al., 2005.

[18] Blowfield and Googins, 2007.

[19] SustainAbility, 2004.

[20] ETI, 2007.

[21] Bradley Googins, personal communication, 14 August 2006.

[22] Among the organizations receiving corporate funding to a significant degree are the International Business Leaders Forum, Accountability, Business for Social Responsibility, the Center for Corporate Citizenship, the Conference Board, the World Economic Forum, Harvard Kennedy School of Government, and Sustainability.

[23] Barrientos and Smith, 2007.

[24] Pio, 2005.

[25] See, e.g., Hughes and Demetrious, 2006; Blowfield, 2004.

[26] Total money in SRI funds 2005 = £6.1bn; total money in hedge funds 2006 = $1.786 trillion. Based on figures from www.eiris.org and HedgeFund.net—accessed 19 March 2007.

[27] McCarthy, 2006.

[28] McCarthy, 2006; Gascoigne, 2007.

[29] See also Chapter 12.

[30] www.altenergystocks.com—accessed 21 January 2007.

[31] Hesse, 2006.

[32] Lydenberg, 2005.

[33] Hafner, 2006.

[34] Dees, 1998; Leadbeater, 1997.

[35] Dees et al., 2002; Pomerantz, 2003; Fowler, 2000; Cone, 1996.

[36] Rangan et al., 2007.

[37] Low, 2001; Mort et al., 2003.

[38] Weiser et al., 2006.

[39] Weiser et al., 2006; Dees, 1998.

[40] Tilley and Parrish, 2006.

[41] Wackernagel et al., 1996.

[42] CPI, 2007.

[43] Blowfield and Googins, 2007, p 25.

[44] Blowfield and Googins, 2007, p 17.

[45] Blowfield and Googins, 2007, p 9.

[46] Bogle, 2005.

[47] See, e.g., contributions to *Business and Society*; alternative constructs of the corporation on the Corporation 2020 website; the work of authors such as Plender, 2003, and Greenfield, 2006.

APPENDIX

Corporate responsibility information resources

Here are some of the most well-known newsletters, magazines, and web resources offering regular news, analysis, and thinking on corporate responsibility. We have provided dedicated web links where these are available, but you should note that some of these online resources are available only by subscription.

Readers should also check the occasional coverage of corporate responsibility issues in management journals (such as the *Harvard Business Review*), development and economics journals (such as the *Third World Quarterly* and *International Affairs*), and the mainstream media (such as the *Financial Times* and *The Economist*).

Accountability Forum   Practitioner-oriented journal, focusing on accountability for sustainable development; published by Greenleaf Publishing.

Brooklyn Bridge-TBLI Group e-newsletter   Comprising articles and features on the triple bottom line and sustainability; online at www.tbli.org/index-newsletter.html.

Business and Human Rights Resource Center   Web-based resource with links to coverage of discrimination, environment, poverty and development, labour, access to medicines, health and safety, security, and trade; online at www.business-humanrights.org.

Business and Society   Academic journal, focusing on social issues and ethics, and their impact and influence on organizations; published by Sage and sponsored by the International Association for Business and Society; online at bas.sagepub.com.

Business Ethics   Quarterly academic journal debating issues of business ethics; published by Blackwell Publishing.

Business Ethics Magazine   Magazine of Corporate Responsibility Officers, a professional association; online at www.business-ethics.com.

Business Ethics Quarterly   Academic journal bringing different disciplinary perspectives to bear on the general subject of the application of ethics to the international business community; published by the Society for Business Ethics.

CasePlace   Collection of corporate responsibility-related case studies; online at www.caseplace.org.

The Chronicle of Philanthropy   Newspaper focusing on corporate philanthropy; online at www.philanthropy.com.

Chronos   E-learning tutorial on the business case for sustainable development; online at www.sdchronos2.org.

Corporate Citizenship Briefing   Magazine for corporate responsibility news and analysis; published by Corporate Citizenship Company; online at www.ccbriefing.co.uk.

Corporate Governance   Academic journal, focusing on international business and society; published by Emerald.

CorporateRegister.com   Online collection of corporate responsibility reports; online at www.corporateregister.com.

Corpwatch.com   Online information resource monitoring corporate behaviour and malfeasance; online at www.corpwatch.com.

Critical Perspectives on International Business   Academic journal, presenting social science perspectives on international business and society; published by Emerald.

CSR and government   British government website devoted to CSR information; online at www.societyandbusiness.gov.uk.

CSR Asia   Online resource offering information on corporate responsibility in Asia; online at www.csr-asia.com.

CSRWatch   Web-based media service offering criticisms of corporate responsibility; online at www.csrwatch.com.

CSRWire   Web-based resource featuring corporate responsibility news and press releases from publicly traded corporations; online at www.csrwire.com.

E-Business Ethics.com   Online resource offering information on business ethics, corporate citizenship, and organizational compliance; hosted by Colorado State University; online at www.e-businessethics.com.

Eldis   Information gateway to web-based resources on globalization and international development, including special section on corporate responsibility; online at www.eldis.org.

Ethical Corporation   Monthly magazine featuring corporate responsibility news and analysis in both print and online versions; free email newsletter also available; online at www.ethicalcorp.com.

Ethical Performance   Monthly newsletter on corporate responsibility and socially responsible investment; online at www.ethicalperformance.com.

ETHICOMP Journal   Journal on computer ethics and social responsibility, connected to the ETHICOMP conference series; online at www.ccsr.cse.dmu.ac.uk/journal/home.html.

Faith in Business Quarterly   Journal relating Christian faith and values to the business world; published by the Ridley Hall Foundation and Industrial Christian Fellowship; online at www.fibq.org.

Global Corruption Report   Annual report focusing on the consequences of corruption; published by Transparency International; online at www.transparency.org/publications/gcr.

Governancefocus.com   Web-based resource offering information on worldwide corporate and board governance issues; online at www.governancefocus.com.

GreenBiz.com   Free web-based resource for companies seeking information on environmental business practices; online at www.greenbiz.com.

Green Money Journal   Newsletter offering resources and contacts for environmentally and socially responsible investing; online at www.greenmoneyjournal.com.

Greener Management International   Management journal focusing on strategic environmental and sustainability issues; published by Greenleaf Publishing.

ID21   Online information service featuring links to research on globalization and international development, plus a series of issues Insights papers; online at www.id21.org.

Journal of Business Ethics   Academic journal, covering ethical issues related to business; published by Kluwer Academic Publishers.

Journal of Corporate Citizenship   Quarterly academic journal dedicated to corporate responsibility; published by Greenleaf Publishing.

New Academy Review   Now defunct quarterly journal that addressed strategic and policy issues related to corporate responsibility; online at www.new-academy-review.com.

Oneworld.net   Web-based community and resource focusing on globalization and development; online at www.oneworld.net.

Origo Cross-Sector News   News service focusing on the intersection between business and social innovation; online at www.origonews.com.

SD Gateway   Online resource offering information from members of the Sustainable Development Communications Network; online at www.sdgateway.net.

SocialFunds.com   Web-based resource for individual socially responsible investors; online at www.socialfunds.com.

Socially Responsible Investing Compass   Online resource featuring all existing green and ethical retail funds and indices in Europe; online at www.sricompass.org.

Society and Business Review   Practitioner-oriented journal, aiming to assist businesses in enhancing their commitment to societal purposes; published by Emerald.

Stanford Social Innovation Review   Journal focusing on strategies for non-profit organizations, foundations, and socially responsible businesses; online at www.ssireview.org.

SustainableBusiness.com   Online resource offering information and links for environmentally oriented businesses; hosted by Green Dream Jobs, a sustainable business jobs service; online at www.sustainablebusiness.com.

■ GLOSSARY

accountability   The obligation to render an account of one's actions.

auditing   The evaluation of an organization in order to establish the validity and reliability of information about that organization. Social auditing relates to the validity and reliability of information about a company's social performance (e.g. its impact on local communities, its relationship with stakeholders); environmental auditing relates to its performance in relation to the environment (e.g. emissions, waste management).

best-in-class screening   An approach to positive screening in socially responsible investment that involves selecting the best within a given sector of investments, based on certain criteria.

bottom of the pyramid (also known as base of the pyramid)   The potential commercial market provided by the six billion people who live on less than two US dollars a day. Developed by CK Prahalad and Stuart Hart, American business theorists, the concept regards poor people as a seriously underserved market that might be the engine of the next wave of global trade and economic prosperity. Examples include microfinance (the provision of innovative financial services to poor people in ways that help their development), Cemex's affordable housing programme, and Hindustan Lever's marketing of iodized salt to rural communities. Bottom of the pyramid is one of the most discussed areas of social entrepreneurship.

bribery   The giving of favour to influence another's action. (*See* corruption.)

Brundtland Commission (formally, the World Commission on Environment and Development) Convened in 1983 by the United Nations and widely known by the name of its chair, Gro Harlem Brundtland, the Commission proved to be a highly influential enquiry into environmental deterioration and the challenge of sustainable development. Its definition of sustainable development—development that meets the needs of the present without compromising the ability of future generations to meet their own needs—is frequently cited in discussions about the role of business in sustainability.

business and society   An area of academic enquiry (normally undertaken by social scientists), concerning the relationship between business and wider society. Long established, with its own journals and professional association, the themes of business and society have recently been more widely acknowledged by corporate responsibility scholars and practitioners. The consultancy firm McKinsey and Co is among those offering services that will help companies to understand business and society issues.

business ethics   Typically regarded as a strand of applied ethics, focusing on the ethical issues facing a company and its officers. The US branch of the field, in particular, is primarily concerned with helping individuals to navigate the ethical dilemmas that arise in a commercial context. There is, to a degree, an alternative European approach that is more concerned with the role of business in society, and with the ethical duties and obligations that arise from this. Some would argue that corporate responsibility is a subset of business ethics.

capitalism   An economic system under which the means of production are privately owned, and the price of inputs and outputs are determined by markets within which people engage on a free and voluntary basis, and within which goods and services are sold with a view to making a profit. Adam Smith, the eighteenth-century philosopher, was the first to describe comprehensively the free market capitalist system in his books *The Theory of Moral Sentiments* and *The Wealth of Nations*. He recognized that an economic system could not be treated as something separate from society, and hence had implications for the way we live. Issues relating to the moral dimensions of capitalism—such as the responsibilities, duties, and obligations of business—in many ways underlie corporate responsibility.

capital markets   The financial markets on which long-term debt and equity securities are traded. The role of these markets in influencing corporate behaviour is an area of debate within corporate responsibility.

change management (also known as transformation management)   A systematic approach to managing change within an organization that includes adapting to, controlling, and effecting change. Within management practice, corporate responsibility is often described from a change management perspective.

civil regulation   A theory positing that companies are not only regulated by government, but increasingly by the norms and actions of civil society that control a business' licence to operate. This is most evident in the role that civil society organizations play in affecting company behaviour irrespective of legal requirements. In the 1990s, for example, trade unions and non-government organizations were able to pressurize Nike into paying attention to working conditions in its supply chain, despite there having been no government pressure to do so.

civil society   Historically, the term has meant private interests that are distinct from those of the state, but in the corporate responsibility context, it tends to refer more specifically to the uncoerced collective action around shared interests, purposes, and values of institutions that are distinct from those of the state and the market (e.g. civil society organizations).

civil society organizations (CSOs)   Non-government, non-business organizations with a social function. CSOs include non-government organizations and free trade unions, and are an important constituency both in influencing corporate behaviour (civil regulation) and in conducting partnerships.

climate change   Significant change in measures of climate, such as temperature, or precipitation, that last for an extended period (i.e. decades or longer). These changes can be the result of natural factors and processes, such as alterations in ocean circulation, or of human activity, such as deforestation and burning fossil fuels. (*See also* global warming.)

code of conduct/practice   A set of principles, typically with accompanying criteria, that set out a company's commitment to maintaining a standard in a specific area of its operations. Corporate responsibility codes set standards regarding the natural environment, labour, corporate governance, money laundering, bribery and corruption, human rights, and corporate responsibility reporting principles. While codes may make mention of legal requirements (e.g. minimum wage, toxic emissions), they are themselves voluntary in nature.

corporate accountability   A company's moral or legal obligation to account for its actions and performance to its stakeholders. In the corporate responsibility context, it is also often discussed in terms of the capacity of those stakeholders to influence company actions.

corporate citizenship   At times used synonymously with corporate responsibility, CSR, etc., but (in the USA, in particular) can specifically refer to discretionary initiatives undertaken by a company, such as employee volunteering and corporate philanthropy.

corporate governance   Conventionally refers to the system by which companies are directed and controlled for the benefit of shareholders. In some jurisdictions, the scope of benefit includes multiple stakeholders, and, in recent years, there has been renewed interest in the balance between economic and social goals, and between individual and communal goals as the object of governance, as per the 2002 Cadbury Report.

corporate governance framework   The regulatory structure, designed to safeguard investors' assets, within which the rules for the running of companies are outlined.

corporate malfeasance   Misconduct by a company or by an officer of a company.

corporate philanthropy   Proportion of corporate revenues donated for philanthropic purposes. (In the USA, the amount is typically one per cent.) Once associated with somewhat arbitrary donations to worthy causes, there is increasing focus on strategic philanthropy, under which donations are targeted towards areas that are synergistic with the company's interests or competencies.

corporate reporting   The act of public reporting on a company's performance. In the corporate responsibility context, emphasis has been placed on the publishing of social, environmental, and sustainability reports that, in some cases, form part of the company's annual report to shareholders.

corporate responsibility   An umbrella term embracing theories and practices relating to how business manages its relationship with society.

corporate social performance   The way in, and degree to, which a business organization's principles of social responsibility and related processes motivate actions on behalf of a company and deliver outcomes of societal benefit.

corporate social responsiveness   The response of companies to the demands that they address their social responsibilities. The term was introduced by scholars in the mid-1970s to denote a greater focus on corporate responsibility as an area of management practice, in contrast to more theoretical debates about the meaning of responsibility that had previously dominated academic thinking.

corruption   The misuse of power associated with a public or corporate office for the purpose of personal gain. It includes bribery, which is the giving of favour to influence another's action.

defensive corporate responsibility   Actions taken by a company or industry to protect its reputation and to reduce its risk in relation to aspects of its non-financial responsibility.

deterritorialization   The detachment of social practices from a specific place, so that the relationship between culture and geographical location is no longer paramount. The phenomenon is a consequence of the social and political processes associated with globalization.

developing country   A country with low per capita income relative to the world average. In many developing countries, incomes can be less than two US dollars a day. (*Compare* emerging economy.)

eco-efficiency   Achieving efficiencies through the reduced use of natural resources and energy, fewer harmful emissions, greater recycling and reuse, increased lifespan, and the increased use of renewable resources in the design, manufacture, and consumption/use of products.

economic globalization (also referred to as liberal economic globalization)   Increased world integration as a result of free trade, and financial, technology, and labour flows. The terms is sometimes treated as synonymous with globalization, but, strictly speaking, refers to only one feature of that phenomenon.

embedded economy   Stemming from Polanyi's argument (1944) that a feature of capitalism is the way in which the economy is treated as something separate from society ('*disembedded*'), whereas the interests of justice and prosperity are best served when the economy is interrelated with social, political, and religious institutions ('*embedded*'). Corporate responsibility (theory and practice) can be interpreted as concerned with re-embedding business so that it is more than simply an economic actor.

emerging economy   A country that, based on GDP and indicators of human development, is considered to be on a path towards being included among the wealthy/developed nations in the foreseeable future. (*Compare* developing country.)

engagement   An approach, used in responsible investment, by which investors become involved with the companies in which they invest in order to influence the activities, behaviours, and operations of those companies.

environmental auditing   The evaluation of an organization to ascertain the validity and reliability of information about that organization's claims concerning its performance in relation to the environment (e.g. emissions, waste management).

environmental ethics   Enquiry into the ethical relationship of human beings to the environment and non-human entities, and into the value and moral status of these.

environmental impact assessment   Assessment of a company or facility's environmental consequences, normally focusing on inputs and outputs within a particular geographical location.

environmental, social, governance (ESG)   Commonly used term that captures the areas of non-financial performance with which corporate responsibility management practice is often concerned.

ethical sourcing   A company's recognition of its responsibilities for the social and environmental conditions under which products are manufactured/grown within its supply chain. Typically, this involves the application of a code of practice as a condition of doing business with suppliers, although it may also involve engaging with suppliers to improve their capacity to meet that standard.

ethical theory   Theories of what is right and wrong, based on reason. (*Compare* moral theory.)

ethical trade   An umbrella term for a variety of approaches under which companies take responsibility for the conditions under which products are manufactured/grown within their supply chains. Includes ethical sourcing, fairtrade, and sourcing from sustainably managed forests and fisheries.

fairtrade   A trading partnership established as a contribution to achieving greater equity in international trade through, for example, ensuring a price paid to the producer that is greater than the cost of production, a surplus paid to the producer group (not the individual) for investing in social development activities, and a long-term relationship between producer and buyer. Originally intended to help small producers in developing countries, larger producers are now included, and, for these, the emphasis is on worker rights. Fairtrade takes different forms, but is most widely associated with the Fairtrade label, which certifies that an item has been produced and traded according to the principles set out by the Fairtrade Labelling Organizations International (FLO International).

fair wage (also called a living wage)   A wage sufficient to provide the basic needs (food, shelter, education, health care), with some discretionary income, for a worker and his or her immediate dependents within a reasonable working week (typically, not more than forty hours). It is often a provision in codes of labour practice and workers rights, although it is sometimes replaced with a minimum wage, which is a legally defined wage that should reflect a fair wage (although, in practice, it may not).

financing sustainability   An emerging facet of corporate responsibility, dealing with the interrelationship between companies' corporate responsibility objectives and the behaviour of the finance community (investors, analysts, fund managers, etc.). At its core is the perceived mismatch between the long-term nature of sustainability and the short-term orientation of much investment activity.

free trade union   A type of trade union that is able to operate without interference from employers and government.

global commons   Natural assets important to human well-being that are outside national jurisdiction (e.g. the oceans; outer space; the atmosphere).

global governance   Historically, governance has referred to the exercise of political, economic, and administrative authority in the management of the affairs of a country or other locality. Globalization and accompanying phenomena, such as deterritorialization, present particular challenges for governance, because important areas of life cannot be managed by the nation state alone. Hence, increasing concern is paid to global governance, including the governing of global commons, such as the atmosphere, and the behaviour of multinational companies. The institutions for addressing such issues are, however, still weak and incomplete for the most part, giving rise to what some see as a governance deficit. The emergence of corporate responsibility as an area of business practice can be seen as a contribution to filling that deficit by making companies pay attention to their global social and environmental performance.

globalization   A term used to refer to the increasing global connectivity, integration, and interdependence in the economic, social, technological, cultural, and political dimensions of existence. It is often used to focus on particular aspects of the phenomenon (e.g. global cultural homogenization, economic globalization, the spread of particular ideas such as democracy and free markets), but what marks it out as historically unique is the interplay of its different facets, which presents all manner of challenges for global governance, justice, and sustainability.

Global Reporting Initiative   The custodian body behind an international effort to create a common framework for the voluntary reporting of the economic, environmental, and social impact of business' and other organizations' activities. This framework is set out in the GRI Guidelines.

global warming   The average increase in atmospheric temperature near the earth's surface and in the troposphere, which can contribute to changes in global climate patterns (*see also* climate change).

government   A particular group of legitimate representatives of the state.

health and safety (also known as occupational health and safety; workplace health and safety) The dimension of corporate responsibility relating to the health and safety of people at work. Some of the most measurable outcomes of corporate responsibility programmes have been in this area.

human rights   Basic entitlements accorded to all human beings. There are significant differences of opinion as to what these rights should be, although the most commonly mentioned ones in a corporate responsibility context concern legal, civil, and political rights, especially those set out in the Universal Declaration of Human Rights.

human rights impact assessment   An assessment of the human rights dimensions of a company's operations, including, for example, issues of the rights of indigenous peoples, intimidation of local communities by company security forces, and the fundamental rights of workers in the workplace.

Industrial Revolution   The historical period, lasting throughout most of the nineteenth century, during which the economies of the USA and many European nations shifted from an agricultural to a manufacturing base, with an accompanying strengthening of the capitalist economic system.

integrated business strategy   In a corporate responsibility context, 'integration' refers to the embedding of corporate responsibility issues into mainstream business practice. The consequence of this is that corporate responsibility becomes a business driver that creates value for the company at the same time as the company creates value for wider society. (*Compare* corporate philanthropy.)

international development   The policies and programmes undertaken by government and non-government agencies in developed and developing economies, with the intention of alleviating poverty and creating sustainable livelihoods for people in developing countries.

liberal economic globalization   See economic globalization.

liberal economics   A theory of economics that is rooted in the belief that individuals' economic actions based largely on self-interest ultimately make the greatest contribution to the common good. Some see globalization as synonymous with economic liberalism, particularly its free flow of capital, goods, services, and (more contentiously) labour with minimal government or other non-market interference.

licence to operate   The right granted to a company (or other organization) to carry out its business. In the corporate responsibility context, licence to operate usually refers to the licence granted by a community or other stakeholder group, rather than by a formal regulatory authority.

limited liability   Form of incorporation under which the liability of a partner or investor is limited to the value of his or her shares in the company. The introduction of this legal concept in the nineteenth century greatly affected the role of business, the nature of investment, and the notion of risk.

living wage   See fair wage.

microfinance   Financial model that involves making small loans available to help poor people who are denied access through conventional lending channels, typically towards their starting, or expanding, a small business.

Millennium Development Goals (MDGs)   A set of eight targets (including eradicating extreme poverty and hunger, improving maternal health, and ensuring environmental sustainability) that were adopted by all countries represented in the UN General Assembly, and which are to be achieved by 2015. The targets commit countries to a particular vision of international development and are widely used as a framework for measuring development progress.

minimum wage   A legally defined wage that should reflect a fair wage (although, in practice, it may not). (*See also* fair wage.)

moral theory   Theories of right and wrong, based on norms and custom. (*Compare* ethical theory.)

the Natural Step   An approach to sustainability that is based on four systematic principles, relating to people's capacity to meet their needs, and aspects of the interaction between humanity and the earth. Karl-Henrik Robèrt first proposed the approach in 1989, following the publication of the Report of the Brundtland Commission.

negative screening   An approach to socially responsible investment that involves the excluding of certain companies based on their poor performance against corporate governance, social, environmental, or ethical criteria. (*Compare* positive screening.)

New Deal   The legislative and administrative programme, established under FD Roosevelt's administration during the 1930s, which was intended to promote economic recovery and social reform following the Great Depression. It marked the end of a period during which the theories of liberal economics had gone largely unquestioned, particularly in the USA.

non-financial performance   Aspects of business performance not normally addressed in financial reporting and auditing, including wider environmental, social, and governance indicators.

non-government organization (NGO)   A loose term distinguishing a range of organizations that are concerned with particular social and environmental objectives from profit-making organizations and government agencies. Commonly called 'non-governmental organizations', some actually perform a governmental function by way of their role in influencing the process of governing (*see also* civil regulation).

occupational health and safety   See health and safety.

offensive corporate responsibility   Policies, strategies, and programmes undertaken with the specific intention of addressing societal needs in order to gain commercial advantage. (*Compare* defensive corporate responsibility.)

partnership   A collaboration between two or more parties conducted with the intention of realizing mutually acceptable or beneficial outcomes that are greater than those which any single party could achieve. Stakeholder partnership has become an important area of corporate responsibility management practice.

performance standard   A code of conduct or similar instrument by means of which achievement is largely measured in terms of specific outcomes, such as workers being paid a fair wage, the eradication of workplace discrimination, etc. Codes of labour practice, organic standards, and good agricultural practice guidelines are examples of this type of standard. (*Compare* process standard.)

pioneer screening   An approach to positive screening in socially responsible investment that involves choosing the best-performing company against one specific criterion.

positive screening   An approach to socially responsible investment, under which companies are chosen based on their performance against corporate governance, social, environmental, or ethical criteria. Positive screening can be subdivided into best-in-class screening and pioneer screening. Conversely, SRI investors can use negative screening.

process standard   A code of conduct or similar instrument by means of which achievement is largely measured in terms of the process that an organization undergoes rather than fixed outcomes. The ISO 14000 series on environmental management and the AA1000 series are examples of this type of standard. (*Compare* performance standard.)

proxy voting   A method of voting at a company's annual general meeting on environmental, social, and governance issues.

reporting awards   Schemes offering awards for the quality of corporate reports.

reputation management   The aspect of management practice that is concerned with understanding perceptions of an organization's reputation, and the actions necessary to protect or enhance it. Reputation management has been identified as a significant driver of defensive corporate responsibility.

rights   Powers, privileges, or other entitlements that are assured by custom or law.

Rio Earth Summit   A meeting, in Rio de Janeiro in June 1992, of over a hundred heads of state, plus representatives of non-government organizations, business, and local government, which was the summit of an international discussion of environmental and development issues of the kind raised by the Brundtland Commission. It was the first time that a multi-sectoral dialogue had been conducted to address these issues, and resulted in leaders signing a number of important agreements, including the United Nations Framework Conventions on Climate Change (UNFCCC) and the Convention on Biological Diversity (CBD), the Rio Declaration on Environment and Development, and Agenda 21 (an international plan of action for achieving a more sustainable pattern of development in the twenty-first century). The meeting is highly significant in the history of contemporary corporate responsibility, because it recognized the importance of business–government–civil society cooperation in achieving sustainable development goals—something that was developed further at the 2002 World Summit on Sustainable Development.

risk management   The aspect of management practice that is concerned with understanding and acting upon the degree of risk presented to an organization by political, social, environmental, and economic factors. Risk is often seen as a driver of defensive corporate responsibility and is evident, for example, in the support of food companies for sustainable agriculture and fisheries.

screening   A strategy used in socially responsible investment. (*See also* positive screening.)

self-regulation   This refers to the practice of a company or other organization voluntarily putting constraints on what it does—e.g. through the adoption of a code of practice or adherence to voluntary guidelines—even though the constrained policy or action might be legal. Some see voluntary self-regulation as a defining feature of corporate responsibility.

shareholder activism   Actions taken by shareholders with the intention of improving corporate governance.

small and medium-sized enterprises (SMEs)   A classification of company that is normally based on number of employees (or, occasionally, on turnover). In the EU, a small enterprise employs less than 50 people and a medium one, less than 250; in the USA, the figures are higher, but still not more than 100 and 500 respectively. SMEs comprise the vast majority of businesses in the world (99 per cent in the EU) and account for the bulk of private sector employment generation.

social accounting   Accounting for the non-financial aspects of corporate reporting.

social and environmental ratings   The rating of companies for investment purposes, according to defined criteria for their social and/or environmental performance. Examples include the Domini 400 Social Index, the KLD Climate Change Index, the FTSE4Good Index series, and the Dow Jones Sustainability Indices.

social auditing   The evaluation of an organization to ascertain the validity and reliability of information about that organization's claims concerning its social performance.

social contract   The implied agreement between members of a society that defines and puts limits on the duties, responsibilities, and obligations of each member. Social contract theory is associated with the ethical theory of John Locke and underpins ideas about the company's licence to operate.

social entrepreneurship   An imprecise term used to refer to a wide range of organizations—both profit-making and non-profit—for which the primary purpose is to deliver social and/or environmental value in contrast with financial value.

social impact assessment   Assessment of the social consequences of a company or facility, normally focusing on inputs and outputs within a particular geographical location. (*Compare* environmental impact assessment and human rights impact assessment.)

socially responsible investment (SRI)   An approach to investing that considers the social, environmental, and ethical consequences of investments within the context of financial analysis.

social reporting   The reporting of the social and environmental aspects of corporate activity.

stakeholder   An entity with a stake in another organization, by virtue of the fact he, she or it is affected by, or has influence over, that organization. In corporate responsibility terms, 'stakeholder' usually refers to the stake that an individual or organization has in a company, and includes employees, local communities, shareholders, customers, and clients.

stakeholder dialogue   The convening of a discussion between a company and (all, or some of) its stakeholders.

stakeholder engagement   The managed process of interaction between a company and its stakeholders.

stakeholder management   The application of stakeholder theory to management practice. It includes stakeholder engagement, stakeholder dialogue, and stakeholder partnership.

stakeholder partnership   A partnership between a company and its stakeholders, intended to capitalize on their combined capabilities in pursuit of a particular purpose.

state   An organized political community, occupying a definite territory and governed by a sovereign government. In some corporate responsibility literature, the term 'state' is used interchangeably with government—but the terms are distinct.

strategic philanthropy   A form of corporate philanthropy, under which donations are targeted towards areas that are synergistic with the company's interests or competencies.

sustainability   Referring to those forms of human economic and cultural activity that can be conducted without long-term degradation of the resources that used. The term is often used interchangeably with sustainable development.

sustainable consumption and production   Continuous economic and social progress that respects the limits of the earth's ecosystems, and meets the needs and aspirations of everyone for a better quality of life—now, and for future generations.

sustainable development   According to the Brundtland Commission, which is the most widely known definition, this is human development to meet the needs of the present generation without compromising the ability of future generations to meet their own needs.

third-party verification statements   Statements made by third parties, verifying the content of corporate reports.

trade union   An association of workers in any trade, or allied trades, for the protection and furtherance of their interests in regard to wages, hours, and conditions of labour, and for the provision, from their common funds, of pecuniary assistance to the members during strikes, sickness, unemployment, old age, etc. There is an important distinction between free trade unions and yellow unions. (*Compare* workers' committee.)

transformation management   See change management.

triple bottom line   A framework for measuring company performance and added value, in terms of economic, social, and environmental parameters. Triple bottom line accounting is an extension of the conventional financial accounting framework to measure these additional areas of performance.

United Nations   A supranational organization founded in 1945, with the purposes of:
(a) maintaining international peace and security; (b) developing friendly relations among nations;
(c) cooperating in solving international economic, social, cultural, and humanitarian problems, and in promoting respect for human rights and fundamental freedoms; (d) acting as a centre through which nations can work jointly to attain those ends. It comprises member States, as well as bodies such as the General Assembly, Security Council, and the International Court of Justice, and it administers programmes to achieve its purpose through agencies such as the UN Development Programme, UN Environment Programme, and the International Labour Organization.

Universal Declaration of Human Rights   A 1948 UN Declaration—signed and ratified by most of the world's countries—that sets out a basic definition of universal human rights. The Declaration is often referred to in human rights and worker rights codes of conduct.

United Nations Global Compact   A United Nations-convened initiative to promote concrete and sustained action by business participants, to align their actions with broad UN social and environmental objectives, the Compact's ten principles, and the international Millennium Development Goals (MDGs). It aims to achieve this through: (a) learning forums to analyse case studies and examples of good practice; (b) global policy dialogues on the challenges of globalization; (c) multi-stakeholder collaborative development projects to further the MDGs; (d) support for new national networks, such as those in India and South Africa.

venture philanthropy   Application of the venture capital model of investment and the deployment of private equity to achieve social and environmental outcomes.

Washington Consensus   The set of policies that, during the 1980s and 1990s, became a condition of loans to countries from the World Bank. Countries were required to open their domestic markets to foreign competition, to limit state intervention (including income redistribution, public education, and welfare provision), and to establish policies that would promote a favourable business environment. The Consensus encouraged private foreign direct investment and encouraged countries—such as Indonesia and Mexico—to focus on export markets. Some saw it as responsible for creating the exploitive social and environmental conditions that, in turn, led to calls for greater corporate responsibility, especially in relation to multinational corporations.

welfare state   A system under which government seeks to provide an economic safety net for the general population (e.g. through unemployment, child, and disability benefits), and the opportunity for individual improvement (e.g. through health care and education). A feature of Communist Bloc countries, it also became widespread in Western Europe (especially after World War II), was mirrored in the US New Deal, and was a feature of many newly independent governments in Africa and Asia. It put a greater tax burden on business, in return for reducing the pressures on companies to take on social responsibilities. Dismantling of the welfare state was typically a condition of the Washington Consensus policies adopted by developing countries in the 1980s and 1990s.

World Commission on Environment and Development   See Brundtland Commission.

workers' committee   Sometimes treated as the equivalent of a trade union, but different, in that it brings together employees within a single company (rather than a trade). Some workers' committees are similar to yellow unions.

workplace health and safety   See health and safety.

yellow union   A type of trade union that is tightly controlled by parties other than union members.

■ BIBLIOGRAPHY

Abbott Laboratories, 2005, *2004 Corporate Citizenship Report,* Chicago, IL: Abbott Laboratories.

Abrami, R, 2003, *Worker Rights and Global Trade: The US–Cambodia Bilateral Textile Trade Agreement*, Harvard Business School Case Study, Cambridge, MA: Harvard Business School.

Accountability, 2002, *AA1000 Conversations: Lessons from the Early Years—1999–2001*, London: AccountAbility.

Accountability, 2006, *What Assures?*, London: Accountability.

Accounting Standard Steering Committee, 1975, *The Corporate Report*, London: ICAEW.

Ackerman, RW and Bauer, RA, 1976, *Corporate Social Responsiveness : The Modern Dilemma*, Reston, VA: Reston Publishing.

Action Aid, 2005a, *Power Hungry: Six Reasons to Regulate Global Food Corporations*, London: Action Aid.

Action Aid, 2005b, *Rotten Fruit*, London: Action Aid.

Adams, C, 2004, 'The ethical, social and environmental reporting–performance portrayal gap', *Accounting, Auditing and Accountability Journal*, 17(5), pp 731–57.

Adams, C and Evans, R, 2004, 'Accountability, completeness, credibility and the audit expectations gap', *Journal of Corporate Citizenship*, April (14), pp 97–115.

Adler, J, 2006, 'Going green', *Newsweek*, 17 July, online at www.msnbc.msn.com.

Allen, T and Thomas, A (eds), 2000, *Poverty and Development into the 21st Century*, rev'd edn, Oxford: Open University in association with Oxford University Press.

Allianz and World Wildlife Foundation, 2005, *Climate Change and the Financial Sector: An Agenda for Action*, London: Allianz/WWF.

Amalric, F and Hauser, J, 2005, 'Economic drivers of corporate responsibility activities', *Journal of Corporate Citizenship*, Winter (20), pp 27–38.

Ambachtsheer, J, 2005, *SRI: What Do Investment Managers Think?*, Toronto, ON: Mercer Investment Consulting, online at www.merceric.com.

American Institute Of Certified Public Accountants, 1977, *The Measurement of Corporate Social Performance: Determining the Impact of Business Actions on Areas of Social Concern*, New York, NY: AICPA.

Anderson, R, 2003, 'Ethics ain't rocket science', *Seattle Weekly*, 6 August, online at www.seattleweekly.com.

Anderson, R, 2005, 'From CEO to cipher', *Seattle Weekly*, 9 March, online at www.seattleweekly.com.

Andrews, K, 1973, 'Can the best corporations be made moral?', *Harvard Business Review*, May–June (51), pp 57–64.

Andriof, G and McIntosh, M (eds), 2001, *Perspectives on Corporate Citizenship*, London: Greenleaf Publishing.

Andriof, J, Waddock, S, Husted, B and Rahman, SS, 2002, *Unfolding Stakeholder Thinking Vol 1: Theory, Responsibility and Engagement*, Sheffield: Greenleaf Publishing.

Anshen, M, 1980, *Corporate Strategies for Social Performance*, New York, NY: Macmillan.

Arnold, DG and Hartman, LP, 2003, 'Moral imagination and the future of sweatshops', *Business and Society Review*, 108(4), pp 425–61.

Ascoly, N, Oldenziel, J and Zeldenrust, I, 2001, *Overview of Recent Developments on Monitoring and Verification in the Garment and Sportswear Industry in Europe*, Amsterdam: Centre for Research on Multinational Companies.

Ascoly, N and Zeldenrust, I, 2003, *Considering Complaints Mechanisms*, Amsterdam: Centre for Research on Multinational Companies.

Ashridge Centre For Business And Society, 2005, *A Catalogue of CSR Activities*, Berkhamsted: Ashridge Centre for Business and Society.

Asmus, P, 2007, 'NGO engagement', *Ethical Corporation*, 5 April, online at www.ethicalcorp.com.

Association of British Insurers, 2001, *Investing in Social Responsibility: Risks and Opportunities*, London: Association of British Insurers.

Association of Chartered Certified Accountants, 2005, *ACCA UK Awards for Sustainability Reporting 2005: Report of the Judges*, London: ACCA.

Association of Chartered Certified Accountants, 2006, *ACCA UK Awards for Sustainability Reporting 2006: Report of the Judges*, London: ACCA.

Attfield, R, 1999, *The Ethics of the Global Environment*, West Lafayette, IN: Purdue University Press.

Bagehot, W and Marshall, A, 1885, *The Postulates of English Political Economy*, New York, NY/London: GP Putnam.

Bakan, J, 2004, *The Corporation: The Pathological Pursuit of Profit and Power*, New York, NY: Free Press.

Bakan, J, Crooks, H and Achbar, M (writers), Achbar, M and Abbott, J (dirs), 2004, *The Corporation*, Vancouver, BC: Big Picture Media Corp.

Baker, M, 2002, 'The GRI: the will to succeed is not enough', *Business Respect*, 6 April (27), online at www.mallenbaker.net.

Baker, RW, 2005, *Capitalism's Achilles Heel: Dirty Money and How to Renew the Free-Market System*, Chichester: John Wiley and Sons.

Bales, K, 2004, *Disposable People: New Slavery in the Global Economy*, rev'd edn, Berkeley, CA: University of California Press.

Ballinger, J, 1992, 'The new free trade heel: Nike's profits jump on the backs of Asian workers', *Harper's Magazine*, August (285), pp 46–7.

Ballinger, J and Olsson, C, 1997, *Behind the Swoosh: The Struggle of Indonesians Making Nike Shoes*, Uppsala/Brussels: Global Publications Foundation/ICDA.

Barmann, TC, 2006, 'Glaxo settles Paxil complaint with 46 states', *The Providence Journal*, 29 March, p E1.

Barrett, R, 1998, *Liberating the Corporate Soul: Building a Visionary Organization*, Boston: Butterworth-Heinemann.

Barrientos, S, Dolan, C and Tallontire, A, 2001, *Gender and Ethical Trade: A Mapping of the Issues in African Horticulture*, Chatham: Natural Resources Institute.

Barrientos, S and Smith, S, 2007, *The ETI Code of Labour Practice: Do Workers Really Benefit?*, Falmer: Institute of Development Studies, University of Sussex.

Bartley, T, 2003, 'Certifying forests and factories: states, social movements, and the rise of private regulation in the apparel and forest products fields', *Politics and Society*, 31(3), pp 433–64.

Basu, K and Palazzo, G, 2005, *An Inductive Typology of Corporate Social Responsibility*, Best paper proceedings of the annual meeting of the Academy of Management Conference, Hawaii.

Bauer, R, Kees, K and Otten, R, 2002, *International Evidence on Ethical Mutual Fund Performance and Investment Style*, Maastricht University, Limburg Institute of Financial Economics, November.

Bauman, Z, 1998, *Globalization: The Human Consequences*, New York, NY: Columbia University Press.

Baxter, T, Bebbington, J and Cutteridge, D, 2004, 'Sustainability assessment model: modelling economic, resource, environmental and social flows of a project', in A Henriques and J Richardson (eds), *The Triple Bottom Line: Does It All Add Up?*, London: Earthscan, pp 113–20.

Beauchamp, TL and Bowie, N (eds), 1988, *Ethical Theory and Business*, 3rd edn, Englewood Cliffs, NJ: Prentice-Hall.

Bebbington, J, 2001a, *Sustainability Assessment Modelling at BP: Advances in Environmental Accounting*, London: ACCA.

Bebbington, J, 2001b, 'Sustainable development: a review of the international development, business and accounting literature', *Accounting Forum*, 25(2), pp 128–57.

Bebbington, J, Larrinaga, C and Moneva, JM, 2004, *An Evaluation of the Role of Social, Environmental and Sustainable Development Reporting in Reputation Risk Management*, Communication to the 27th Annual Congress of the European Accounting Association, Prague.

Beck, U, Giddens, A and Lash, S, 1994, *Reflexive Modernization: Politics, Tradition and Aesthetics in the Modern Social Order*, Cambridge: Polity Press.

Belkaoui, A, 1976, 'The impact of the disclosure of the environmental effects of organizational behaviour on the market', *Financial Management*, Winter, pp 26–31.

Belkaoui, A and Karpic, PG, 1989, 'Determinants of the corporate decision to disclose social information', *Accounting, Auditing, and Accountability Journal*, 2(1), pp 36–51.

Bellagio Forum For Sustainable Development and Eurosif, 2006, *PRIME Toolkit Primer for Responsible Investment Management of Endowments*, Osnabrueck: Bellagio Forum for Sustainable Development.

Bendell, J, 2004a, *Barricades and Boardrooms: A Contemporary History of the Corporate Accountability Movement*, Programme paper 13, Geneva: United Nations Research Institute for Social Development.

Bendell, J, 2004b, *Flags of Inconvenience? The Global Compact and the Future of the United Nations*, Nottingham: International Centre for Corporate Social Responsibility.

Bendell, J, 2005, *Lifeworth Annual Review of Corporate Responsibility 2005*, Lifeworth.

Bennett, C and Burley, H, 2005, 'Corporate accountability: an NGO perspective', in: S Tully (ed), *Research Handbook on Corporate Legal Responsibility*, Cheltenham: Edward Elgar, pp 372–94.

Bennett, M, James, P, Klinkers, L, James, P and Klinkers, L, 1999, *Sustainable Measures : Evaluation and Reporting of Environmental and Social Performance*, Sheffield: Greenleaf Publishing.

Bentham, J, 1789, *An Introduction to the Principles of Morals and Legislation, etc.*, London: T Payne and Son.

Beresford, DR, 1975, *Social Responsibility Disclosure in 1974 Fortune 500 Annual Reports*, Ernst and Ernst.

Berle, AA and Means, GC, 1932, *Modern Corporation and Private Property*, Chicago, IL: Commerce Clearing House.

Bernauer, T and Caduff, L, 2004, 'In whose interest? Pressure group politics, economic competition and environmental regulation', *Journal of Public Policy*, 24(1), pp 99–126.

Berry, A, Capps, T, Cooper, DJ, Hopper, TM and Lowe, EA, 1985, 'NCB accounts: a mine of disinformation?', *Accountancy*, January, pp 10–12.

Bhagwati, JN, 2004, *In Defense of Globalization*, Oxford: Oxford University Press.

Bhattacharya, CB and Sen, S, 2004, 'Doing better at doing good: when, why, and how consumers respond to corporate social initiatives', *California Management Review*, 47(1), pp 9–24.

Birch, D, 2001, 'Corporate citizenship: rethinking business beyond corporate social responsibility', in G Andriof and M McIntosh (eds), *Perspectives on Corporate Citizenship*, London: Greenleaf Publishing, pp 53–65.

Birch, D, 2003, 'Corporate social responsibility: some key theoretical issues and concepts for new ways of doing business', *Journal of New Business Ideas and Trends*, 1(1), pp 1–19.

Birkin, F, 2000, 'The art of accounting for science: a prerequisite for sustainable development?', *Critical Perspectives on Accounting*, 11(3), pp 289–309.

Block, W and Barnett, W, 2005, 'A positive programme for laissez-faire capitalism', *Journal of Corporate Citizenship*, Autumn (19), pp 31–42.

Bloom, DE and Canning, D, 2006, 'Booms, busts, and echoes', *Finance and Development*, 43(3), pp 8–15.

Blowfield, ME, 2000a, *A Guide to Developing Agricultural Markets and Agro-Enterprises; Fundamentals of Ethical Trading/Sourcing in Poorer Countries*, Washington DC: World Bank.

Blowfield, ME, 2000b, 'Ethical sourcing: a contribution to sustainability or a diversion?', *Sustainable Development*, November (8), pp 191–200.

Blowfield, ME, 2004, 'Implementation deficits of ethical trade systems: lessons from the Indonesian cocoa and timber industries', *Journal of Corporate Citizenship*, January (13), pp 77–90.

Blowfield, ME, 2005a, 'Corporate social responsibility: the failing discipline and why it matters for international relations', *International Relations*, 19(2), pp 173–91.

Blowfield, ME, 2005b, 'Corporate social responsibility: reinventing the meaning of development?', *International Affairs*, 81(3), pp 515–24.

Blowfield, ME, 2005c, *Does Society Want Business Leadership? An Overview of Attitudes and Thinking*, Chestnut Hill, MA: Center for Corporate Citizenship at Boston College.

Blowfield, ME and Frynas, JG, 2005, 'Setting new agendas: critical perspectives on corporate social responsibility in the developing world', *International Affairs*, 81(3), p 499.

Blowfield, ME and Googins, B, 2007, *Step Up: A Call for Business Leadership in Society—CEOs Examine Role Of Business In The 21st Century*, Chestnut Hill, MA: Center for Corporate Citizenship at Boston College.

Bogle, JC, 2005, *The Battle for the Soul of Capitalism*, New Haven, CT: Yale University Press.

Bouckaert, B and De Geest, G (eds), 1998, *Encyclopedia of Law and Economics*, Cheltenham: Edward Elgar.

Boulton, L and Lamont, J, 2007, 'Private wealth "can eclipse G8 infighting poverty"', *Financial Times*, 9 April, p 6.

Bower, T, 1988, *Maxwell: The Outsider*, London: Aurum Press.

Bower, T, 1996, *Maxwell: The Final Verdict*, London: HarperCollins.

Bowman, EH, 1973, 'Corporate social responsibility and the investor', *Journal of Contemporary Business*, Winter, pp 21–43.

Bowman, EH and Haire, M, 1976, 'Social impact disclosure and corporate annual reports', *Accounting, Organizations and Society*, 1(1), pp 11–21.

Braithwaite, J and Drahos, P, 2000, *Global Business Regulation*, Cambridge: Cambridge University Press.

British Telecom, 2005, *BT Social and Environmental Report 2005*, BT Group.

Broad, R (ed), 2002, *Global Backlash: Citizen Initiatives for a Just World Economy*, Oxford: Rowman and Littlefield.

Bromwich, M and Hopwood, AG (eds), 1983, *Accounting Standards Setting: An International Perspective*, London: Pitman.

Bronte, C, 1849, *Shirley*, London: Smith, Elder.

Brown, DK, 2004, *Improving Working Conditions: What Works and What Doesn't—Existing Empirical Evidence and Historical Experience*, Paper for presentation at Globalization and Labor in Developing Countries conference, Brown University edn.

Brown, TJ and Dacin, PA, 1997, 'The company and the product: corporate associations and consumer product responses', *Journal of Marketing*, 61(1), pp 68–84.

Browne, J, 2004, 'Beyond Kyoto', *Foreign Affairs*, 83(4), pp 20–32.

Browne, MN and Haas, PF, 1974, 'Social responsibility: the uncertain hypothesis', *MSU Business Topics*, 22(3), pp 47–51.

Buchanan, JM and Yoon, YJ, 2002, 'Globalization as framed by the two logics of trade', *The Independent Review*, 6(3), pp 399–405.

Buckley, PJ and Ghauri, PN (eds), 1999, *Multinational Enterprises and Emerging Markets: Managing Increasing Interdependence*, Oxford: Pergamon.

Bunting, M, 2005, 'Africa's flash moment', *Guardian Weekly*, 24–30 June, p 5.

Burrough, B and Helyar, J, 1990, *Barbarians at the Gate: The Fall of RJR Nabisco*, New York, NY: Harper and Row.

Business and The Environment Programme, undated, *The World in Context: Beyond the Business Case for Sustainable Development*, Cambridge: Business and the Environment Programme, Cambridge University.

Business for Social Responsibility, 2002, *Designing a CSR Structure: A Step-By-Step Guide Including Leadership Examples and Decision-Making Tools*, San Francisco, CA: Business for Social Responsibility.

Business for Social Responsibility, 2005, *Reporting on Economic Impacts*, San Francisco, CA: Business for Social Responsibility.

Business Week, 2005, 'Social issues retailing: can Wal-Mart fit into a white hat?', *Business Week*, 3 October, pp 94–6.

Butler, E, 1985, *Hayek: His Contribution to the Political and Economic Thought of Our Time*, New York, NY: Universe Books.

Byatt, I, Castles, I, Henderson, D, Lawson, N, McKitrick, R, Morris, J, Peacock, A, Robinson, C and Skidelsky, R, 2006, 'The Stern Review 'Oxonia Papers': a critique', *World Economics*, 7(2), pp 145–51.

Cadbury, Sir Adrian, 1992, *Report of the Committee on the Financial Aspects of Corporate Governance*, London: Gee and Co Ltd.

Cambridge Programme For Industry, 2007, *Sustainable Consumption and Production*, Cambridge: Cambridge Programme for Industry.

Cannon, T, 1994, *Corporate Responsibility: A Textbook on Business Ethics, Governance, Environment—Roles and Responsibilities*, London: Pitman.

Caplan, K, 2003, 'The purist's partnership: debunking the terminology of partnerships', *Partnership Matters*, (1), pp 31–5.

Carey, J, 2006, 'Business on a warmer planet', *Business Week*, 17 July, online at **www.businessweek.com**.

Carney, D (ed), 1999, *Sustainable Rural Livelihoods: What Contribution Can We Make?*, London: Department for International Development.

Carney, WJ, 1998, 'Limited liability', in B Bouckaert and G De Geest (eds), *Encyclopedia of Law and Economics*, Cheltenham: Edward Elgar, pp 659–91.

Carroll, AB, 1979, 'A three-dimensional conceptual model of corporate performance', *Academy of Management Journal*, 4(4), pp 589–99.

Carroll, AB, 1999, 'Corporate social responsibility: evolution of a definitional construct', *Business and Society*, 38(3), pp 268–95.

Carroll, AB, 2000, 'A commentary and an overview of key questions on corporate social performance measurement', *Business and Society*, 39(4), pp 466–78.

Carson, R, 1962, *Silent Spring*, Boston, MA/Cambridge, MA: Houghton Mifflin/Riverside Press.

Catholic Agency for Overseas Development, 2005, *Clean Up Your Computer' Progress Report*, London: CAFOD.

Caufield, C, 1996, *Masters of Illusion: The World Bank and the Poverty of Nations*, New York, NY: Henry Holt.

Center For Corporate Citizenship, 2005a, *Going Global: How US-Based Multinationals are Operationalizing Corporate Citizenship on a Global Platform*, Chestnut Hill, MA: Center for Corporate Citizenship at Boston College.

Center For Corporate Citizenship, 2005b, *Integration: Critical Link for Corporate Citizenship*, Boston, MA: Center for Corporate Citizenship at Boston College.

Center For Corporate Citizenship, 2005c, *State of Corporate Citizenship in the US: Business Perspectives in 2005*, Boston, MA: Center for Corporate Citizenship at Boston College/US Chambers of Commerce.

Chan, CCC and Milne, MJ, 1999, 'Investor reactions to corporate environmental saints and sinners: an experimental analysis', *Accounting and Business Research*, 29(4), pp 265–79.

Chandler, AD and Mazlish, B (eds), 2005, *Leviathans: Multinational Corporations and the New Global History*, Cambridge: Cambridge University Press.

Charkham, J, 2005, *Keeping Better Company*, Oxford: Oxford University Press.

Chatterji, A and Levine, D, 2006, 'Breaking down the wall of codes: evaluating non-financial performance measurement', *California Management Review*, 48(2), pp 29–51.

Chenall, RH and Juchau, R, 1977, 'Investor information needs: an Australian study', *Accounting and Business Research*, 7(26), pp 111–19.

Christian Aid, 2004, *Behind the Mask: The Real Face of Corporate Social Responsibility*, London: Christian Aid.

Christian Aid, 2005, *The Shirts off their Backs : How Tax Policies Fleece the Poor*, Briefing paper, September, London: Christian Aid.

Christian Aid, Action on Smoking and Health and Friends of The Earth, 2005, *BAT in its Own Words*, London: Christian Aid/ASH/Friends of the Earth.

Chryssides, GD and Kaler, JH, 1993, *An Introduction to Business Ethics*, London: Chapman and Hall.

Chua, WF, 1986, 'Radical developments in accounting thought', *The Accounting Review*, LXI(4), pp 601–32.

Clark, E, 2005, 'Manufacturing the evidence', *Supply Management*, 26 May, online at **www.supplymanagement.co.uk**.

Clarke, T, 1993, 'Case study: Robert Maxwell—master of corporate malfeasance', *Corporate Governance: An International Review*, 1(3), pp 141–51.

Clarkson, MBE, 1995, 'A stakeholder framework for analyzing and evaluating corporate social performance', *Academy of Management Review*, 20(1), pp 92–117.

Clay, J, 2005, *Exploring the Links Between International Business and Poverty Reduction: A Case Study of Unilever in Indonesia*, Oxford: Oxfam.

Coase, R, 1937, 'The nature of the firm', *Economica*, 4(16), pp 386–405.

Cobb, G, Collison, DJ, Power, DM and Stevenson, LA, 2005, *FTSE4Good: Perceptions and Performance*, London: Certified Accountants Educational Trust.

Cody, E, 2004, 'Unrest stirs among Chinese factory workers', *Boston Sunday Globe*, 28 November, p A10.

Coffee, JC, 2000, *The Rise of Dispersed Ownership: The Role of in the Separation of Ownership and Control*, Columbia Law and Economics working paper 182, New York, NY, Columbia Law School.

Coleman, G, 2002, 'Gender, power and post-structuralism in corporate citizenship', *Journal of Corporate Citizenship*, Spring (5), pp 17–25.

Collinson, C, 2001, *The Business Costs of Ethical Supply Chain Management: Kenya Flower Industry Case Study*, Chatham: Natural Resources Institute.

Collinson, C and Leon, M, 2000, *Economic Viability of Ethical Cocoa Trading in Ecuador*, Chatham: Natural Resources Institute.

Collison, DJ, Cobb, G, Power, DM and Stevenson, LA, 2007, 'The financial performance of the FTSE4Good indices', *Corporate Social Responsibility and Environmental Management*, 14(5), forthcoming.

Combined Code, 1998, *The Combined Code: Principles of Corporate Governance*, London: Gee and Co Ltd.

Combined Code, 2003, *The Combined Code on Corporate Governance*, London: Financial Reporting Council.

Committee to Encourage Corporate Philanthropy, 2006, *Leading Survey Shows Corporate Philanthropy Up 14%: Results in from 91 Companies Who Gave $10 Billion in 2005*, Press release, 5 June, online at www.corporate philanthropy.org.

Cone, CL, 1996, 'Doing well by doing good', *Association Management*, 48(4), pp 103–8.

Cooper, CL (ed), 2005, *Leadership and Management in the Twenty-First Century*, Oxford: Oxford University Press.

Cooperative Financial Services and Cooperative Insurance, 2005, *Sustainability Report 2004*, Cooperative Financial Services.

Corcoran, T, 2006, 'Just say no to NGOs', *National Post*, 1 April, online at www.canada.com/ nationalpost.

Cornell, B and Shapiro, AC, 1987, 'Corporate stakeholders and corporate finance', *Financial Management*, 16(1), pp 5–14.

Council of Public Relations Firms, 2003, *Statement from Council of Public Relations Firms' President Kathy Cripps Regarding the* Nike v Kasky *Case*, Press release, 26 June, online at www.prfirms.org.

Council on Foundations, 2001, *Venture Philanthropy: A Model of Innovation vs a Model of Intrusion*, Board briefing, February, Washington DC: Council on Foundations.

Cousins, J, Mitchell, A, Sikka, P and Wimott, H, 1998, *Auditors: Holding the Public to Ransom*, Basildon: Association for Accountancy and Business Affairs.

Cragg, W and McKague, K, 2003, *Compendium of Ethics Codes and Instruments of Corporate Responsibility*, Toronto, ON: York University.

Crane, A and Matten, D, 2004, *Business Ethics*, Oxford: Oxford University Press.

Crenson, MA and Ginsberg, B, 2002, *Downsizing Democracy: How America Sidelined its Citizens and Privatized its Public*, Baltimore, MD: Johns Hopkins University Press.

Dallas, G (ed), 2005, *Governance and Risk: An Analytical Handbook for Investors, Managers, Directors and Stakeholders*, New York, NY: McGraw Hill.

Daly, HE, 1996, *Beyond Growth: The Economics of Sustainable Development*, Boston, MA: Beacon Press.

Dando, N and Swift, T, 2003, 'Transparency and assurance: minding the credibility gap', *Journal of Business Ethics*, 44(2), pp 195–200.

Daum, JH, 2003, *Intangible Assets and Value Creation*, Chichester: John Wiley and Sons.

Davies, PWF, 1997, *Current Issues in Business Ethics*, London: Routledge.

Davis, I, 2005, 'Ian Davis on business and society', *The Economist*, 26 May, online at www.economist.com.

Davis, K, 1973, 'The case for and against business assumption of social responsibilities', *Academy of Management Review*, 16(2), pp 312–22.

Davy, A, 2003a, 'Companies in conflict situations: a role for partnerships?', in M Warner and R Sullivan (eds), *Putting Partnerships to Work*, Sheffield: Greenleaf Publishing, pp 220–9.

Davy, A, 2003b, 'Ownership and control of outcomes', in M Warner and R Sullivan (eds), *Putting Partnerships to Work*, Sheffield: Greenleaf Publishing, pp 210–19.

Deegan, C, 2002, 'The legitimising effect of social and environmental disclosures: a theoretical foundation', *Accounting , Auditing and Accountability Journal*, 15(3), pp 282–311.

Dees, JG, 1998, *The Meaning of 'Social Entrepreneurship'*, Draft report for the Kauffman Center for Entrepreneurial Leadership, Stanford, CA: Kauffman Center for Entrepeneurial Leadership.

Dees, JG, Emerson, J and Economy, P, 2002, *Strategic Tools for Social Entrepreneurs: Enhancing the Performance of your Enterprising Non-profit*, Chichester: John Wiley and Sons.

Deloitte, undated, *Partnerships for Small Enterprise Development*, New York, NY: UNIDO, UN Global Compact, and UNDP.

Demirag, I, 2005, *Corporate Social Responsibility, Accountability and Governance*, Sheffield: Greenleaf Publishing.

Department for International Development, 2002, *The Challenges of Assessing the Poverty Impact of Ethical Trading: What Can Be Learnt From Fair Trade Initiatives and the Sustainable Livelihoods Approach*, London: Department for International Development.

Department For Trade And Industry, 2004, *DTI International CSR Strategy Consultation*, London: British Department for Trade and Industry.

Derbyshire, D, 2007, 'How Tesco bypasses opposition to stores', *Daily Telegraph*, 27 January, p 6.

Devinney, TM, Auger, P, Eckhardt, G and Birtchnell, T, 2006, 'The other CSR', *Stanford Social Innovation Review*, Fall, pp 30–7.

Dilorenzo, TJ, 2004, *How Capitalism Saved America: The Untold History of Our Country, from the Pilgrims to the Present*, New York, NY: Crown Forum.

Dion, M, 2001, 'Corporate citizenship as an ethic of care, corporate values, codes of ethics and global governance', in J Andriof and M McIntosh (eds), *Perspectives on Corporate Citizenship*, Sheffield: Greenleaf Publishing, pp 118–38.

Doane, D, 2005, 'The myth of CSR: the problem with assuming that companies can do well while also doing good is that markets don't really work that way', *Stanford Social Innovation Review*, Fall, pp 23–9.

Dolan, C and Humphrey, J, 2004, 'Changing governance patterns in the trade in fresh vegetables between Africa and the United Kingdom', *Environment and Planning A*, 36(3), pp 491–509.

Dolan, CS and Opondo, M, 2005, 'Seeking common ground', *Journal of Corporate Citizenship*, Summer (18), pp 87–98.

Donaldson, T and Dunfee, TW, 1999, *Ties That Bind: A Social Contracts Approach to Business Ethics*, Boston, MA: Harvard Business School Press.

Drucker, PF, 1946, *Concept of the Corporation*, New York, NY: The John Day Company.

Dubash, NK, Dupar, M, Kothari, S and Lissu, T, 2002, 'A watershed in global governance: executive summary', *Politics and the Life Sciences*, 21(1), pp 42–62.

Du Cann, R, 1993, *The Art of the Advocate*, Harmondsworth: Penguin Books.

Dunn, E, 2004, 'Standards and person-making in East Central Europe', in A Ong and S Collier (eds), *Global Assemblages: Technology, Politics and Ethics as Anthropological Problems*, Malden, MA: Blackwell, pp 173–93.

Dunn, J and Sikka, P, 1999, *Auditors: Keeping the Public in the Dark*, Basildon: Association for Accountancy and Business Affairs.

Dyllick, T and Hockerts, K, 2002, 'Beyond the business case for corporate sustainability', *Business Strategy and the Environment*, 11(2), pp 130–41.

Earthwatch, International Union For The Conservation Of Nature And Natural Resources, World Business Council For Sustainable Development and World Resources Institute, 2006, *Business and Ecosystems*, London: Earthwatch/IUCN/WBCSD/WRI.

The Economist, 2005a, 'The ethics of business: good corporate citizens, and wise governments, should be wary of CSR', *The Economist*, 20 January, online at www.economist.com.

The Economist, 2005b, 'The good company: the movement for corporate social responsibility has won the battle for ideas', *The Economist*, 20 January, online at www.economist.com.

The Economist, 2005c, 'The world according to CSR', *The Economist*, 20 January, online at www.economist.com.

The Economist, 2005d, 'The union of concerned executives: CSR as practised means many different things', *The Economist*, 20 January, online at www.economist.com.

The Economist, 2007, 'Eco-warriors at the gate', *The Economist*, 3 March, online at www.economist.com.

Edwards, M and Hulme, D, 1995, *Non-Governmental Organisations: Performance and Accountability—Beyond the Magic Bullet*, London: Earthscan.

Elkington, J, 1998, *Cannibals With Forks: The Triple Bottom Line of 21st Century Business*, Gabriola Island, BC/Stony Creek, CT: New Society Publishers.

Elkington, J and Lee, M, 2006, 'It's the economics stupid: has the corporate responsibility movement lost sight of the big picture?', *Grist Magazine*, 9 May, online at www.grist.org.

Elliott, KA and Freeman, RB, 2003, *Can Labor Standards Improve Under Globalization?*, Washington, DC: Institute for International Economics.

Ellsworth, RR, 2002, *Leading With Purpose: The New Corporate Realities*, Stanford, CA: Stanford Business Books.

Emerson, J, 2002, 'Horse manure and grantmaking', *Foundation News and Commentary*, May–June, pp 22–3.

Engfeldt, L-J, 2002, 'The road from Stockholm to Johannesburg', *UN Chronicle*, (3), online at www.un.org/Pubs/chronicle.

Englander, E and Kaufman, A, 2004, 'The end of managerial ideology: from corporate social responsibility to corporate social indifference', *Enterprise and Society*, 5(3), pp 404–50.

Epstein, MJ and Roy, MJ, 2001, 'Sustainability in action: identifying and measuring the key performance drivers', *Long Range Planning*, 34(5), pp 585–604.

Epstein, M and Roy, MJ, 2003, 'Making the business case for sustainability: linking social and environmental actions to financial performance', *Journal of Corporate Citizenship*, January (9), pp 79–96.

Estes, J, 1976a, *Social Responsibility Disclosure*, New York, NY: John Wiley and Sons.

Estes, RW, 1975, 'A comprehensive social reporting model', in LJ Seidler and LL Seidler (eds), *Social Accounting: Theory, Issues and Cases*, Los Angeles, CA: Melville Publishing, pp 185–204.

Estes, RW, 1976b, *Corporate Social Accounting*, New York, NY: John Wiley and Sons.

Ethical Corporation, 2005, 'Why *The Economist* is wrong about CSR', *Ethical Corporation*, January, pp 6–7.

Ethical Corporation, 2006, 'Multi-fibre agreement forum in Bangladesh', *Ethical Corporation*, April, p 37.

Ethical Corporation and Nima Hunter Inc, 2003, *The Business of Business: Managing Corporate Social Responsibility—What Business Leaders are Saying and Doing 2002–2007*, London: Nima Hunter Inc.

Ethical Performance, 2004, 'Angry critics run boycott over "slow" CSR progress', *Ethical Performance*, July, p 3.

Ethical Performance, 2005a, 'Firms put on notice as UN Compact gets teeth', *Ethical Performance*, October, p 1.

Ethical Performance, 2005b, 'The United Nations deserves some credit', *Ethical Performance*, October, online at **www.ethicalperformance.com**.

Ethical Performance, 2005c, 'Ruggie takes on delicate task of considering UN norms', *Ethical Performance*, October, p 7.

Ethical Performance, 2006a, 'Caterpillar gets reprieve', *Ethical Performance*, 7(11), online at **www.ethicalperformance.com**.

Ethical Performance, 2006b, 'Criticisms augur end of "flawed" human rights norms', *Ethical Performance*, 7(11), online at **www.ethicalperformance.com**.

Ethical Performance, 2006c, 'Explorers discover at least 147 different species of CSR', *Ethical Performance*, January, online at **www.ethicalperformance.com**.

Ethical Performance, 2006d, 'Sliding ingloriously down the pole of excellence', *Ethical Performance*, 7(11), online at **www.ethicalperformance.com**.

Ethical Trading Initiative, 2003, *Raising the Stakes: Annual Report 2003*, London: Ethical Trading Initiative.

Ethical Trading Initiative, 2004, *Putting Ethics to Work: Annual Report 2003/2004*, London: Ethical Trading Initiative.

Ethical Trading Initiative, 2005a, *Annual Report 2004/2005: Driving Change*, London: Ethical Trading Initiative.

Ethical Trading Initiative, 2005b, *ETI Smallholder Guidelines*, London: Ethical Trading Initiative.

Ethical Trading Initiative, 2005c, *Moving Production: Stalling the Race to the Bottom*, Shaping a new agenda briefing paper 4, London: Ethical Trading Initiative.

Ethical Trading Initiative, 2006, *Ethical Trade: A Comprehensive Guide for Companies*, 2nd edn, London: Ethical Trading Initiative.

Ethical Trading Initiative, 2007, *Getting Smarter at Auditing: Tackling the Growing Crisis in Ethical Trade Auditing*, Report from ETI members' meeting 16 November, London: Ethical Trading Initiative.

Ethical Trading Initiative, undated, *Bridging the Gap Between Commercial and Ethical Agendas*, London: Ethical Trading Initiative.

European Commission, 2002, *Social Agenda: Companies Face Their Social Responsibilities in Europe and Abroad*, October (3).

European Social Investment Forum, 2006, *European SRI Study 2006*, Paris: Eurosif.

Evan, WM and Freeman, RE, 1988, 'A stakeholder theory of the modern corporation: Kantian capitalism', in TL Beauchamp and N Bowie (eds), *Ethical Theory and Business*, 3rd edn, Englewood Cliffs, NJ: Prentice-Hall, pp 97–106.

Evans, EJ, 1983, *The Forging of the Modern State: Early Industrial Britain 1783–1870*, London: Longman.

Evers, H and Schrader, H, 1994, *The Moral Economy of Trade: Ethnicity and Developing Markets*, New York, NY: Routledge.

Fama, E, 1980, 'Agency problems and the theory of the firm', *Journal of Political Economy*, 88(2), pp 288–307.

Feldberg, M, 1974, 'Defining social responsibility', *Long Range Planning*, 7(4), pp 39–44.

Felix, D, 1995, *Biography of an Idea: John Maynard Keynes and the General Theory of Employment, Interest and Money*, New Brunswick, NJ: Transaction Publishers.

Ferguson, N, 2003, *Empire: How Britain Made the Modern World*, London: Allen Lane.

Fig, D, 2005, 'Manufacturing amnesia: corporate social responsibility in South Africa', *International Affairs*, 81(3), pp 599–618.

Financial Times, 2006, 'Mind your business: Conservatives should not pander to anti-corporate prejudice', *Financial Times*, 11 May, online at www.ft.com.

Financial Times, 2007, 'Super returns have bankers flying high', *Financial Times*, 27, February, online at www.ft.com.

Financialwire, 2006, 'Faith-based institutional investors file shareholder-sponsored resolutions aimed at reforming Wal-Mart', *FinancialWire*, 6 January, online at www.financialwire.net.

Fitzpatrick, M, 2004, *Business Case for Sustainability: Finding a New State of Equilibrium*, Keynote address presented at the Green Chemistry and Engineering Conference, 29 June, Washington DC.

Food and Agriculture Organization, 2003, *Agriculture, Food and Water*, Rome: Food and Agriculture Organization.

Forum for the Future, 2006, *Clean Capital: Financing Clean Technology Firms in the UK*, London: Forum for the Future.

Fourie, A and Eloff, T, 2005, 'The case for collective business action to achieve systems change: exploring the contributions made by the private sector to the social, economic and political transformation process in South Africa', *Journal of Corporate Citizenship*, April (18), pp 39–48.

Fowler, A, 2000, 'NGDOs as a moment in history: beyond aid to social entrepreneurship or civic innovation?', *Third World Quarterly*, 21(4), pp 637–54.

Fox, T and Prescott, D, 2004, *Exploring the Role of Development Cooperation Agencies in Corporate Responsibility*, Paper presented to the Conference on Development Cooperation and Corporate Social Responsibility, 22–23 March, Stockholm.

Frederick, WC, 1960, 'The growing concern over business responsibility', *California Management Review*, 2(4), pp 54–61.

Frederick, WC, 2006, *Corporation Be Good!: The Story of Corporate Social Responsibility*, Indianapolis, IN: Dog Ear Publishing.

Freedman, M and Jaggi, B (eds), 2000, *Advances in Environmental Accounting and Management Vol 1*, London: Elsevier.

Freedman, M and Ullmann, A, 1986, *Social Disclosure and Economic Performance*, Paper presented to BAA Conference, Aberystwyth.

Freeman, D, 2003, 'Homeworkers in global supply chains', *Greener Management International*, Autumn (43), pp 107–18.

Freeman, RE, 1984, *Strategic Management: A Stakeholder Approach*, Boston, MA: Pitman.

Freeman, RE, Pierce, J and Dodd, R, 2000, *Environmentalism and the New Logic of Business: How Firms Can Be Profitable and Leave Our Children a Living Planet*, Oxford: Oxford University Press.

Freeman, RE and Venkataraman, S (eds), 2002, *Ethics and Entrepreneurship*, Charlottesville, VA: Society for Business Ethics.

Friedman, AL and Miles, S, 2001, 'Socially responsible investment and corporate social and environmental reporting in the UK: an exploratory study', *British Accounting Review*, 33(4), pp 523–48.

Friedman, M, 1962, *Capitalism and Freedom*, Chicago, IL: University of Chicago Press.

Friedman, TL, 2005, *The World is Flat: A Brief History of the Globalized World in the Twenty-First Century*, London: Allen Lane.

Friends of the Earth, 2005, *Hidden Voices: The CBI, Corporate Lobbying and Sustainability*, London: Friends of the Earth.

Frynas, JG, 2005, 'False promises: evidence from multinational oil companies', *International Affairs*, 81(3), pp 581–98.

FTSE4Good, 2005, *Impact of New Criteria and Future Direction: 2004–2005 Report*, London: FTSE.

Fukuyama, F, 1989, 'The end of history?', *National Interest*, Summer (16), pp 3–18.

Fussler, C, Cramer, A and Van Der Vegt, S (eds), 2004, *Raising the Bar: Creating Value with the United Nations Global Compact*, Sheffield: Greenleaf Publishing.

Galbraith, JK, 1952, *American Capitalism: The Concept of Countervailing Power*, Boston, MA: Houghton Mifflin.

Gascoigne, C, 2007, 'Good for the planet, good for profits', *Sunday Times,* 28 January, online at **business.timesonline.co.uk.**

General Electric, 2005, *Solving Big Needs: GE Corporate Citizenship Report 2005,* Fairfield, CT: General Electric.

Germain, RD, 1999, *Globalization and its Critics: Perspectives from Political Economy,* Basingstoke: Macmillan/St Martin's Press.

Gibson, K, 2000, 'The moral basis of stakeholder theory', *Journal of Business Ethics,* 26(3), pp 245–57.

Giddens, A, 1990, *The Consequences of Modernity,* Stanford, CA: Stanford University Press.

Gilpin, R and Gilpin, JM, 1987, *The Political Economy of International Relations,* Princeton, NJ: Princeton University Press.

Ginsberg, T, 2005, 'Threats to critics of Vioxx alleged', *Philadelphia Inquirer,* 5 June, accessed 10 June online at **www.lexis.nexis.com.**

Gleick, PH, 1999, *The World's Water: The Biennial Report on Freshwater Resources,* Washington DC: Island Press for the Pacific Institute for Studies in Development, Environment and Security.

Global Environmental Management Initiative, undated, *The Business Case for Pursuing Water Sustainability: New Opportunities, New Risks,* online at **www.gemi.org.**

Global Reporting Initiative, 2002, *Sustainability Reporting Guidelines,* Boston, MA: GRI.

Global Reporting Initiative, 2007, *The G8 Encourage GRI Reporting To Promote Development And Support Investors,* press release, 8 June, Amsterdam.

Goodpaster, KE, 2002, 'Stakeholder thinking: beyond paradox to practicality', in J Andriof, SA Waddock, B Husted and SS Rahman (eds), *Unfolding Stakeholder Thinking Vol 1: Theory, Responsibility And Engagement,* Sheffield: Greenleaf Publishing, pp 43–64.

Goodwin, D, Goodwin, J and Konieczny, K, 1996, 'The voluntary disclosure of environmental information: a comparison of investor and company perceptions', *Accounting Research Journal,* 9(1), pp 29–39.

Gore, A, 2006, *An Inconvenient Truth,* London: Bloomsbury Publishing.

Grande, C, 2007, 'Ethical consumption makes mark on branding', *Financial Times,* 20 February, p 24.

Gray, RH, 1992, 'Accounting and environmentalism: an exploration of the challenge of gently accounting for accountability, transparency, and sustainability', *Accounting, Organizations and Society,* 17(5), pp 399–425.

Gray, RH, 1996, 'The interesting relationship between accounting research and accounting practice: a personal reply to Professor Whittington', *Journal of Applied Accounting Research,* 3(1), pp 5–34.

Gray, RH, 2002a, 'Of messiness, systems and sustainability: towards a more social and environmental finance and accounting', *British Accounting Review,* 34(4), pp 357–86.

Gray, RH, 2002b, 'The social accounting project and accounting organizations and society. privileging engagement, imaginings, new accountings and pragmatism over critique?', *Accounting, Organizations and Society,* 27(7), pp 687–708.

Gray, RH, 2006a, *Does Sustainability Reporting Improve Corporate Behaviour? Wrong Question? Right Time?,* Presented at the ICEAW–Information for Better Markets Conference, London.

Gray, RH, 2006b, 'Social, environmental and sustainability reporting and organisational value creation? Whose value? Whose creation?', *Accounting, Auditing and Accountability Journal,* 19(6), pp 793–819.

Gray, RH and Bebbington, KJ, 2000, 'Environmental accounting, managerialism and sustainability: Is the planet safe in the hands of business and accounting?', in M Freedman and B Jaggi (eds), *Advances in Environmental Accounting and Management Vol 1,* London: Elsevier, pp 1–44.

Gray, RH and Collison, D, 2003, 'Can't see the wood for the trees, can't see the trees for the numbers? Accounting education, sustainability and the public interest', *Critical Perspectives on Accounting,* 13(5/6), pp 797–836.

Gray, RH, Javad, M, Power, D and Sinclair, D, 2001, 'Social and environmental disclosure and corporate characteristics: a research note and extension', *Journal of Business Finance and Accounting,* 28(3/4), pp 327–56.

Gray, RH, Kouhy, R and Lavers, S, 1995a, 'Corporate social and environmental reporting: a review of the literature and a longitudinal study of UK disclosure', *Accounting Auditing and Accountability Journal,* 8(2), pp 47–77.

Gray, RH, Kouhy, R and Lavers, S, 1995b, 'Constructing a research database of social and environmental reporting by UK companies: a methodological note', *Accounting, Auditing and Accountability Journal*, 8(2), pp 78–101.

Gray, RH, Owen, D and Adams, C, 1996, *Accounting and Accountability: Changes and Challenges in Corporate Social and Environmental Reporting*, London: Prentice Hall.

Gray, RH, Owen, D and Maunders, KT, 1987, *Corporate Social Reporting: Accounting and Accountability*, Hemel Hempstead: Prentice Hall.

Grayson, D and Hodges, A, 2004, *Corporate Social Opportunity: Seven Steps to Make Corporate Social Responsibility Work for Your Business*, Sheffield: Greenleaf Publishing.

Grecco, C, 2007, 'The Bovespa Social Stock Exchange', in M Koch-Weser and W Jacobs (eds), *Financing the Future: Innovative Funding Mechanisms at Work*, Berlin: Terra Media Verlag, forthcoming.

Greenbury, Sir Richard, 1995, *Directors' Remuneration: Report of a Study Group Chaired by Sir Richard Greenbury*, London: Gee and Co Ltd.

Greenfield, K, 2006, *The Failure of Corporate Law: Fundamental Flaws and Progressive Possibilities*, Chicago, IL: University of Chicago Press.

Greenhouse, S and Barbaro, M, 2005, 'Wal-Mart memo suggests ways to cut employee benefit costs', *New York Times*, 26 October, online at www.nytimes.com.

Gregory, A, Matatko, J and Luther, R, 1997, 'Ethical unit trust financial performance: small company effects and fund size effects', *Journal of Business Finance and Accounting*, 24(5), pp 705–25.

Gregory, CA, 1982, *Gifts and Commodities*, London: Academic Press.

Greider, W, 2006, 'The future is now', *The Nation*, 26 June, pp 23–6.

Griffin, JJ and Mahon, JF, 1997, 'The corporate social performance and corporate financial performance debate: twenty-five years of incomparable research', *Business and Society*, 36(1), pp 5–31.

Grinspun, R and Cameron, MA, 1993, *The Political Economy of North American Free Trade*, New York, NY: St Martin's Press.

Grosser, K and Moon, J, 2005, 'Gender mainstreaming and corporate social responsibility: reporting workplace issues', *Journal of Business Ethics*, 62(4), pp 327–40.

Grubb, M, Koch, M, Munson, A, Sullivan, F and Thomson, K, 1993, *The Earth Summit Agreements: A Guide and Assessment*, London: Earthscan.

Guthrie, J and Parker, LD, 1989, 'Corporate social reporting: a rebuttal of legitimacy theory', *Accounting and Business Research*, 19(76), pp 343–52.

Habisch, A, Jonker, J, Wegner, M and Schmidpeter, R (eds), 2005, *Corporate Social Responsibility Across Europe*, New York, NY: Springer.

Hafner, K, 2006, 'Google founders start for-profit philanthropy', *New York Times*, 14 September, online at www.nytimes.com.

Hakim, S and Rashidan, M, 2002, *Risk and Return of Islamic Stock Market Indexes*, Working paper for Invested Interests, online at www.investedinterests.com.

Hale, A and Shaw, LM, 2001, 'Women workers and the promise of ethical trade in the globalised garment industry: a serious beginning?', *Antipode*, 33(3), pp 510–30.

Hamann, R, 2003, 'Kelian Equatorial Mining: mine closure', in M Warner and R Sullivan (eds), *Putting Partnerships to Work*, Sheffield: Greenleaf Publishing, pp 138–50.

Hamann, R, Agbazue, T, Kapelus, P and Hein, A, 2005, 'Universalizing corporate social responsibility? South African challenges to the international organization for standardization's new social responsibility standard', *Business and Society Review*, 110(1), pp 1–19.

Hampel, Sir Ronald, 1998, *Committee on Corporate Governance: Final Report*, London: Gee and Co Ltd.

Hardt, M and Negri, A, 2000, *Empire*, Cambridge, MA: Harvard University Press.

Harrison, A and Scorse, J, 2004, *Moving Up or Moving Out? Anti-Sweatshop Activists and Labor Market Outcomes*, NBER working paper no 10492, Cambridge, MA: National Bureau of Economic Research.

Harrison, R, 1964, *Animal Machines*, London: Vincent Stuart.

Hart, SL, 2005, *Capitalism at the Crossroads: The Unlimited Business Opportunities in Solving the World's Most Difficult Problems*, Upper Saddle River, NJ: Great Britain and Wharton School.

Hawken, P, 1993, *The Ecology of Commerce: A Declaration of Sustainability*, New York, NY: Harper Business.

Hawken, P, Lovins, AB and Lovins, LH, 1999, *Natural Capitalism: Creating the Next Industrial Revolution*, Boston, MA: Little, Brown and Co.

Hawkins, D, 2006, *Corporate Social Responsibility: Balancing Tomorrow's Sustainability and Today's Profitability*, London: Palgrave Macmillan.

Hayek, Von, FA, 1944, *The Road to Serfdom*, London: Routledge and Sons.

Hayek, Von, FA, 1960, *The Constitution of Liberty*, Chicago, IL: University of Chicago Press.

Hebrew Union College–Jewish Institute Of Religion, 1980, *Ethics and Corporate Responsibility*, Cincinnati, OH: Hebrew Union College–Jewish Institute of Religion.

Held, D, 1996, *Models of Democracy*, Cambridge: Polity Press.

Held, D and Koenig-Archibugi, M (eds), 2003, *Taming Globalization: Frontiers of Governance*, Cambridge: Polity Press.

Hemingway, CA and Maclagan, PW, 2004, 'Managers' personal values as drivers of corporate social responsibility', *Journal of Business Ethics*, 50(1), pp 33–44.

Hemp, P and Stewart, T, 2004, 'Leading change when business is good', *Harvard Business Review*, 82(12), pp 61–70.

Henderson, D, 2001, *Misguided Virtue: False Notions of Corporate Social Responsibility*, London: Institute of Economic Affairs.

Henderson, D, 2004, *The Role of Business in the Modern World*, London: Institute of Economic Affairs.

Hennigfeld, J, Pohl, M and Tolhurst, N (eds), 2006, *The ICCA Handbook on Corporate Social Responsibility*, Chichester: John Wiley and Sons.

Henriques, A, 2007, *Corporate Truth: The Limits to Transparency*, London: Earthscan.

Henriques, A and Richardson, JA, 2004, *The Triple Bottom Line: Does It All Add Up? Assessing the Sustainability of Business and CSR*, London: Earthscan.

Her Majesty's Stationery Office, 1971, *Report on the Affairs of International Learning Systems Corporation Ltd and Interim Report on the Affairs of Pergammon Press Ltd*, London: HMSO.

Hesse, A, 2006, *Sustained Added Value*, Bonn: Deloitte and the German Federal Ministry of the Environment.

Higgs, D, 2003, *Review of the Role and Effectiveness of Non-Executive Directors*, London: DTI.

Hill, P, 1970, *Studies in Rural Capitalism in West Africa*, Cambridge: Cambridge University Press.

Hogner, RH, 1982, 'Corporate social reporting: eight decades of development at US Steel', *Research in Corporate Social Performance and Policy*, 4, pp 243–50.

Holliday, CO, Schmidheiny, S, Watts, P, 2002, *Walking the Talk: The Business Case for Sustainable Development*, Sheffield: Greenleaf Publishing.

Hoogvelt, AMM, 2001, *Globalization and the Postcolonial World: The New Political Economy of Development*, Baltimore, MD: Johns Hopkins University Press.

Hopkins, M, 2003, *The Planetary Bargain: Corporate Social Responsibility Matters*, London: Earthscan.

Hopkins, MJ, 2007, *Corporate Social Responsibility and International Development: Is Business the Solution?*, London: Earthscan.

House Of Commons Select Committee On Trade And Industry, 1999, *Sixth Report: Ethical Trading*, London: House of Commons.

Hughes, P and Demetrious, K, 2006, 'Engaging with stakeholders or constructing them?', *Journal of Corporate Citizenship*, Autumn (23), pp 93–101.

Hummels, GJA and Wood, D, 2005, *Knowing the Price, but also the Value? Financial Analysts on Social, Ethical and Environmental Information*. Boston, MA: Nyenrode Business Universiteit and Boston College.

Hutton, W, 1995, *The State We're In*, London: J Cape.

Impactt Ltd, 2005, *Changing Over Time: Tackling Supply Chain Labour Issues Through Business Practice*, London: Impactt Ltd.

Ingi, 1991a, 'Button up, button down: women workers and overtime in Indonesia's garment and textile industry', *Inside Indonesia*, June, pp 5–6.

Ingi, 1991b, 'Unjust but doing it! Nike's operations in Indonesia', *Inside Indonesia*, June, pp 7–9.

Ingram, RW, 1978, 'The investigation of the information content of (certain) social responsibility disclosures', *Journal of Accounting Research*, 16(2), pp 270–85.

Innovest, 2005, *Intangible Value Assessment: Swiss Reinsurance Company*, London: Innovest Strategic Value Advisors.

Innovest and Environment Agency, 2004, *Corporate Environmental Governance: A Study into the Influence of Environmental Governance on Financial Performance*, London: Environment Agency.

Institute of Social and Ethical Accountability, 1999, *Accountability 1000: Overview of Standard and its Applications*, London: Institute of Social and Ethical Accountability.

Intergovernmental Panel on Climate Change, 2007, *Fourth Assessment Report*, Geneva: WMO/IPCC.

International Council for Science, United Nations Environment Programme and World Meteorological Organization, 1986, *Report of the International Conference on the Assessment of the Role of Carbon Dioxide and Other Greenhouse Gases in Climate Variations and Assorted Impacts*, WMO document no 661, 9–15 October, Villach.

International Fair Trade Association, 2006, *Fair Trade in Europe 2005: Facts and Figures on Fair Trade in 25 European Countries*, Culemborg: International Fair Trade Association.

Investment Management Association, 2005, *Survey of Fund Managers' Engagement with Companies*, online at www.investmentuk.org.

Jackson, IA and Nelson, J, 2004, *Profits with Principles: Seven Strategies for Delivering Value with Values*, New York, NY: Currency/Doubleday.

Jacoby, NH, 1973, *Corporate Power and Social Responsibility: A Blueprint for the Future*, New York, NY: Macmillan.

Jacoby, S, 2007, 'Principles and agents: CalPERS and corporate governance in Japan', *Principles and Agents*, 15(1), pp 5–15.

Jamison, L and Murdoch, H, 2004, *Taking the Temperature: Ethical Supply Chain Management*, London: Institute of Business Ethics.

Jenkins, RO, 1999, 'The changing relationship between emerging markets and multinational enterprises', in PJ Buckley and PN Ghauri (eds), *Multinational Enterprises and Emerging Markets: Managing Increasing Interdependence*, Oxford: Pergamon.

Jenkins, RO, 2001, *Corporate Codes of Conduct: Self-Regulation in a Global Economy*, Geneva: UNRISD.

Jenkins, RO, 2005, 'Globalization, corporate social responsibility and poverty', *International Affairs*, 81(3), pp 525–40.

Jenkins, RO, Pearson, R and Seyfang, G (eds), 2002, *Corporate Responsibility and Labour Rights: Codes of Conduct in the Global Economy*, London: Earthscan.

Jensen, MC, 1986, 'Agency costs of free cash flow, corporate finance, and takeovers', *American Economic Review*, 76(2), pp 323–9.

Jensen, MC, 2001, 'Value maximisation, stakeholder theory, and the corporate objective function', *European Financial Management*, 7(3), pp 297–317.

Jensen, MC, 2002, 'Value maximization, stakeholder theory, and the corporate objective function', *Business Ethics Quarterly*, 12(2), pp 235–56.

Jensen, MC and Meckling, WH, 1976, 'Theory of the firm: managerial behavior, agency costs and ownership structure', *Journal of Financial Economics*, 3(4), pp 305–60.

John, R, 2007, *Beyond the Cheque: How Venture Philanthropists Add Value*, Interim report for Finance for Change, Skoll World Forum, 29 March, Oxford.

Johnson, J, 2004, *Global Trends in Employment, Productivity and Poverty*, Paper presented at the conference on Globalization and Labor in Developing Countries, Watson Institute for International Studies, 10–11 December, Brown University.

Johnston, DC, 2003, *Perfectly Legal: The Covert Campaign to Rig Our Tax System to Benefit the Super Rich—and Cheat Everybody Else*, New York, NY: Portfolio.

Jones, I and Pollitt, M, 2004, 'Understanding how issues in corporate governance develop: Cadbury Report to Higgs Review', *Corporate Governance: An International Review*, 12(2), pp 162–71.

Jones, LB, 1995, *Jesus, CEO: Using Ancient Wisdom for Visionary Leadership*, New York, NY: Hyperion.

Jonkers, J, 2005, 'CSR wonderland: navigating between movement, community and organisation', *Journal of Corporate Citizenship*, October (20), pp 19–22.

Journal of Corporate Citizenship, January 2004 (13), a special theme issue on corporate social responsibility in Asia.

Journal of Corporate Citizenship, April 2005 (18), a special theme issue on corporate citizenship in Africa.

Journal of Corporate Citizenship, January 2006 (21), a special theme issue on corporate citizenship in Latin America: new challenges for business.

Journal of Corporate Citizenship, December 2006 (24), a special theme issue on corporate social responsibility in emerging economies.

Kabeer, N, 2000, *The Power to Choose: Bangladeshi Women and Labour Market Decisions in London and Dhaka*, London and New York, NY: Verso.

Kaminsky, JS, 1995, *Corporate Responsibility in the Hebrew Bible*, Sheffield: Sheffield Academic Press.

Kaptein, M, 2004, 'Business codes of multinational firms: what do they say?', *Journal of Business Ethics*, 50(1), pp 13–31.

Kauffman, M and Chedekel, L, 2004, 'As colleges profit, sweatshops worsen', *Hartford Courant*, 12 December, online at www.courant.com.

Kell, G and Levin, D, 2003, 'The Global Compact network: an historic experiment in learning and action', *Business and Society Review*, 108(2), pp 151–81.

Kelly, M, 2001, *The Divine Right of Capital: Dethroning the Corporate Aristocracy*, San Francisco, CA: Berrett-Koehler.

Kennedy, PM, 1987, *The Rise and Fall of the Great Powers: Economic Change and Military Conflict from 1500 to 2000*, 1st edn, New York, NY: Random House.

Kho, J, 2007, Cleantech VC Investment Falls 34% in 4Q, *Red Herring*, 17 January, online at www.redherring.com.

Kiernan, M, 2005, 'Sustainable development', in G Dallas (ed), *Governance and Risk*, New York, NY: McGraw Hill, pp 216–32.

Killick, N, 2003, 'BP and others, Azerbaijan: conflict prevention', in M Warner and R Sullivan (eds), *Putting Partnerships to Work*, Sheffield: Greenleaf Publishing, pp 98–107.

Klein, N, 1999, *No Logo: Taking Aim at the Brand Bullies*, New York, NY: Picador USA.

Koch, K, 1974, *War and Peace in Jalémó: The Management of Conflict in Highland New Guinea*, Cambridge, MA: Harvard University Press.

Koch-Weser, M and Jacobs, W (eds), 2007, *Financing the Future: Innovative Funding Mechanisms at Work*, Berlin: Terra Media Verlag.

Kolk, A and Tulder, RV, 2002, 'Child labor and multinational conduct: a comparison of international business and stakeholder codes', *Journal of Business Ethics*, 36(3), pp 91–301.

Kolk, A, Tulder, RV and Welters, C, 1999, 'International codes of conduct and corporate social responsibility: can transnational corporations regulate themselves?', *Transnational Corporations*, 8(1), pp 143–80.

Korten, DC, 1990, *Getting to the 21st Century: Voluntary Action and the Global Agenda*, West Hartford, CT: Kumarian Press.

Korten, DC, 1995, *When Corporations Rule the World*, West Hartford, CT and San Francisco, CA: Kumarian Press/Berrett-Koehler.

KPMG, 2005, *KPMG International Survey of Corporate Responsibility Reporting 2005*, Amsterdam: KPMG.

Kramer, M and Kania, J, 2006, 'Changing the game: leading corporations switch from defense to offense in solving global problems', *Stanford Social Innovation Review*, Spring, pp 20–7.

Kreander, N, Gray, R, Power, D and Sinclair, D, 2002, 'The financial performance of European ethical funds 1996–1998', *Journal of Accounting and Finance*, 1, pp 3–22.

Kreander, N, Gray, R, Power, D and Sinclair, D, 2005, 'Evaluating the performance of ethical and non-ethical funds: a matched pair analysis', *Journal of Business Finance and Accounting*, 32(7/8), pp 1465–93.

Krugman, P, undated, *Why Aren't We All Keynesians Yet?*, online at web.mit.edu.

Kurtenbach, E, 2005, 'Chinese sofa factory workers go on strike', *Associated Press*, 3 November, online at www.ap.org.

Lacy, L, 2006, *Socially Responsible Niche Untapped: TIAA-Cref*, 25 July, online at www.firstaffirmative.com.

Ladkin, D, 2006, 'When deontology and utilitarianism aren't enough: how Heidegger's notion of "dwelling" might help organisational leaders resolve ethical issues', *Journal of Business Ethics*, 65(1), pp 87–98.

Laffer, AB and Miles, MA, 1982, *International Economics in an Integrated World*, Glenview, IL: Scott/Foresman.

Leadbeater, C, 1997, *The Rise of the Social Entrepreneur*, London: Demos.

Lehman, C, 1992, *Accounting's Changing Roles in Social Conflict*, London: Paul Chapman.

Leipziger, D, 2001, *SA8000: The Definitive Guide to the New Social Standard*, London: FT/Prentice Hall.

Leipziger, D, 2003, *The Corporate Responsibility Code Book*, Sheffield: Greenleaf Publishing.

Lenox, MJ and Nash, J, 2003, 'Industry self-regulation and adverse selection: a comparison across four trade association programs', *Business Strategy and the Environment*, 12(6), pp 343–56.

Levy, DL and Newell, P, 2002, 'Business strategy and international environmental governance: toward a neo-Gramscian synthesis', *Global Environmental Politics*, 2(4), pp 84–101.

Levy, DL and Newell, P, 2005, *The Business of Global Environmental Governance*, Cambridge, MA: MIT Press.

Lewis, N, Parker, L and Sutcliffe, P, 1984, 'Financial reporting to employees: the pattern of development 1919–1979', *Accounting Organizations and Society*, 9(3/4), pp 275–90.

Light, A and Smith, JM, 1997, *Space, Place, and Environmental Ethics*, Lanham, MD: Roman and Litterfield.

Lindblom, CK, 1994, *The Implications of Organizational Legitimacy for Corporate Social Performance and Disclosure*, paper presented at the Critical Perspectives on Accounting Conference, New York.

Lindsey, B, 2002, *Against the Dead Hand: The Uncertain Struggle for Global Capitalism*, New York, NY: John Wiley and Sons.

Locke, R, Fei, Q and Brause, A, 2006, *Does Monitoring Improve Labor Standards? Lessons from Nike*, MIT Sloan School of Management working paper 4612–06, Cambridge, MA: MIT.

Lort-Phillips, L, 2006, 'China: one country, two systems', *Corporate Citizenship Briefing*, December/January (85), online at www.ccbriefing.co.uk.

Low, MB, 2001, 'The adolescence of entrepreneurship research: specification of purpose', *Entrepreneurship: Theory and Practice*, 25(4), pp 17–26.

Lukes, S, 1974, *Power: A Radical View*, London: Macmillan.

Lund-Thomsen, P, 2005, 'Corporate accountability in South Africa: the role of community mobilizing in environmental governance', *International Affairs*, 81(3), pp 619–34.

Lydenberg, SD, 2005, *Corporations and the Public Interest: Guiding the Invisible Hand*, San Francisco, CA: Berrett-Koehler.

Lynn, BC, 2006, 'Breaking the chain: the antitrust case against Wal-Mart', *Harper's Magazine*, July, pp 29–36.

Maali, B, Casson, P and Napier, C, 2006, 'Social reporting by Islamic banks'. *Abacus*, 42(2), p 266.

Macgillivray, A and Zadek, S, 1995, *Accounting for Change: Indicators for Sustainable Development*, London: New Economics Foundation.

Maclean, J, 1999, 'Towards a political economy of agency in contemporary international relations', in M Shaw (ed) *Politics and Globalisation: Knowledge, Ethics and Agency*, London: Routledge.

Mahapatra, S, 1984, 'Investor reaction to corporate social accounting', *Journal of Business Finance and Accounting*, 11(1), pp 29–40.

Maitland, A, 2005, 'Big business starts to scratch the surface', *Financial Times*, 14 September, online at www.ft.com.

Maitland, A, 2006, 'A responsible balancing act', *Financial Times*, 1 June, online at www.ft.com.

Mallin, CA, 2004, *Corporate Governance*, New York, NY: Oxford University Press.

Mamic, I, 2004, *Implementing Codes of Conduct: How Businesses Manage Social Performance in Global Supply Chains*, Sheffield: Greenleaf Publishing/International Labour Office.

Manga, JE, Mirvis, P, Rochlin, SA and Zecchi, K, 2005, *Integration: Critical Link for Corporate Citizenship; Strategies and Stories from Eight Companies*, Chestnut Hill, MA: Center for Corporate Citizenship at Boston College.

Manheim, JB, 2004, *Biz-War and the Out-Of-Power Elite : The Progressive-Left Attack on the Corporation*, Mahwah, NJ and London: Lawrence Erlbaum Associates.

Manne, H and Wallich, HC, 1972, *The Modern Corporation and Social Responsibility*, Washington DC: American Enterprise Institute for Public Policy Research.

Margolis, JD and Walsh, JP, 2001, *People and Profits: The Search for a Link Between a Company's Social and Financial Performance*, Mahwah, NJ and London: Lawrence Erlbaum.

Margolis, JD and Walsh, JP, 2003, 'Misery loves companies: rethinking social initiatives by business', *Administrative Science Quarterly*, 48(2), pp 268–305.

Markopoulos, M, 1998, *Impacts Of Certification On Community Forest Enterprises: A Case Study Of The Lomerio Community Forest Management Project, Bolivia*, London: IIED.

Markopoulos, M, 1999, *Community Forest Enterprise and Certification in Mexico: A Review of Experience*, Oxford: Oxford Forestry Institute.

Marland, G, Boden, TA and Andres, RJ, 2003, 'Global, regional, and national CO_2 emissions', in *Trends: A Compendium of Data on Global Change*, Carbon Dioxide Information Analysis Center, Oak Ridge, TN: Oak Ridge National Laboratory, US Department of Energy.

Martin, RL, 2002, 'The virtue matrix: calculating the return on corporate responsibility', *Harvard Business Review*, 80(3), p 68.

Marx, K, 1865, *Value, Price, and Profit: An Introduction to the Theory of Capitalism*, abridged by P Zarembka, 2000, Amsterdam and New York, NY: JAI/Elsevier Science, online at ourworld.compuserve.com.

Mathews, MR, 1993, *Socially Responsible Accounting*, London: Chapman and Hall.

Mathews, MR, 1996, 'Twenty-five years of social and environmental accounting research. Is there a silver jubilee to celebrate?', *Accounting , Auditing and Accountability Journal*, 10(4), pp 481–531.

Mattar, H, 2001, 'Ethical portals as inducers of corporate social responsibility', in S Zadek, N Hojensgard and P Raynard (eds), *Perspectives on the New Economy of Corporate Citizenship*, Copenhagen: The Copenhagen Centre, pp 113–21.

Matten, D and Crane, A, 2005, 'Corporate citizenship: toward an extended theoretical conceptualization', *Academy of Management Review*, 30(1), pp 166–80.

Mattingly, JE and Berman, SL, 2006, 'Measurement of corporate social action: discovering taxonomy in the Kinder Lydenberg Domini ratings data', *Business and Society*, 45(1), pp 20–46.

Maxwell, S, 2005, *The Washington Consensus Is Dead! Long Live The Meta-Narrative*, London: Overseas Development Institute.

May, SK, Cheney, G and Roper, J (eds), 2007, *The Debate Over Corporate Social Responsibility*, New York, NY: Oxford University Press.

McCarthy, RJ, 2006, Venture capitalists flock to green stocks. *Inc.com,* (March 28 2006),.

McDermott, J, 1991, *Corporate Society: Class, Property, and Contemporary Capitalism*, Boulder, CO: Westview Press.

McDonough, W and Braungart, M, 2002, *Cradle to Cradle: Remaking the Way We Make Things*, New York, NY: North Point Press.

McGregor, R, 2007, 'China's good corporate citizens find their voice', *Financial Times*, 25 February, online at www.ft.com.

McIntosh, M, Waddock, SA and Kell, G (eds), 2004, *Learning to Talk : Corporate Citizenship and the Development of the UN Global Compact*, Sheffield: Greenleaf Publishing.

McMichael, P, 2004, *Development and Social Change: A Global Perspective*, 3rd edn, Thousand Oaks, CA: Pine Forge Press.

McMurtry, J, 2002, *Value Wars: The Global Market Versus The Life Economy*, London and Sterling, VA: Pluto Press.

McQuaid, K, 1977, 'Young, Swope and General Electric's new capitalism: a study in corporate liberalism 1920–33', *American Journal of Economics and Sociology*, 36(3), pp 323–34.

McRae, S, 2005, *Hidden Voices: The CBI, Corporate Lobbying and Sustainability*, London: Friends of the Earth.

McWilliams, A and Siegel, D, 2000, 'Corporate social responsibility and financial performance: correlation or misspecification?', *Strategic Management Journal*, 21(5), pp 603–9.

Meiskins Wood, E, 1995, *Democracy Against Capitalism: Renewing Historical Materialism*, Cambridge: Cambridge University Press.

Melcrum, 2005, *How to Structure the Corporate Responsibility Function*, London: Melcrum Publishing.

Merrill Lynch and Cap Gemini, 2006, *World Wealth Report 2006*, online at www.capgemini.com.

Milne, MJ and Chan, CCC, 1999, 'Narrative corporate social disclosures: how much of a difference do they make to investment decision-making?', *British Accounting Review*, 31(4), pp 439–57.

Mirvis, PH, 2000, 'Transformation at Shell: commerce and citizenship', *Business and Society Review*, 105(1), p 63.

Mirvis, PH and Googins, BK, 2006, *Stages of Corporate Citizenship: A Developmental Framework*, Chestnut Hill, MA: Center for Corporate Citizenship at Boston College.

Mitchell, A, Sikka, P, Arnold, P, Cooper, C and Willmott, H, 2001, *The BCCI Cover Up*, Basildon: Association for Accountancy and Business Affairs.

Mitchell, J, Shankleman, J and Warner, M, 2003, 'Measuring the added value of partnerships', in M Warner and R Sullivan (eds), *Putting Partnerships to Work*, Sheffield: Greenleaf Publishing, pp 191–200.

Mitchell, LE, 2001, *Corporate Irresponsibility: America's Newest Export*, New Haven, CT: Yale University Press.

Mitchell, LE, 2005, 'Roles and incentives: the core problems of corporate social responsibility', *Ethical Corporation*, October, pp 46–50.

Mitnick, BM, 2000, 'Commitment, revelation, and the testaments of belief: the metrics of measurement of corporate social performance', *Business and Society*, 39(4), pp 419–65.

Monbiot, G, 2005, 'Africa's new best friends', *Guardian Weekly*, 5 July, p 4.

Moody-Stuart, SM, 2005, 'The role of business in developing countries', *Business Ethics: A European Review*, 13(1), pp 41–9.

Moon, J, Crane, A and Matten, D, 2005, 'Can corporations be citizens? Corporate citizenship as a metaphor for business participation in society', *Business Ethics Quarterly*, 15(3), pp 427–51.

Moorhead, J, 2007, 'Milking it', *The Guardian*, 15 May, pp 7–11.

Mort, GS, Weerawardena, J and Carnegie, K, 2003, 'Social entrepreneurship: towards conceptualisation', *International Journal of Nonprofit and Voluntary Sector Marketing*, 8(1), pp 76–88.

Murphy, DY and Bendell, J, 1999, *Partners in Time? Business, NGOs and Sustainable Development*, Geneva: UNRISD.

Murray, A, Sinclair, D, Power, D and Gray, RH, 2006, 'Do financial markets care about social and environmental disclosure? Further evidence and exploration from the UK', *Accounting, Auditing and Accountability Journal*, 19(2), pp 228–55.

Nace, T, 2003, *Gangs of America: The Rise of Corporate Power and the Disabling of Democracy*, San Francisco, CA: Berrett-Koehler.

Narlikar, A, 2005, *The World Trade Organization: A Very Short Introduction*, Oxford: Oxford University Press.

Natural Resources and Ethical Trade, 1999, 'Ethical trade and sustainable rural livelihoods', in D Carney (ed) *Sustainable Rural Livelihoods: What Contribution Can We Make?*, London: Department for International Development, pp 107–29.

Nelson, J, 1996, *Business as Partners in Development: Creating Wealth for Countries, Companies and Communities*, London: Prince of Wales Business Leaders' Forum.

Nelson, J and Zadek, S, 2000, *Partnership Alchemy: New Social Partnerships in Europe*, Copenhagen: The Copenhagen Centre.

Nelson, V and Galvez, M, 2000, *Social Impact of Ethical and Conventional Brazil Nut Trading on Forest-Dependent People in Peru*, Chatham: Natural Resources Institute.

Nelson, V and Tallontire, A, 2002, 'Assessing the benefits of ethical trade schemes in cocoa (Ecuador) and Brazil nuts (Peru) for forest-dependent people and their livelihoods', *International Forestry Review*, 4(2), pp 99–109.

Newell, P, 2005, 'Citizenship, accountability and community: the limitations of the CSR agenda', *International Affairs*, 81(3), pp 541–58.

Newton, A, 2005, 'Defining the art of conversation', *Ethical Corporation*, November, pp 46–7.

Nicholls, A and OPAL, C, 2005, *Fair Trade: Market-Driven Ethical Consumption*, London: Sage.

Nielsen, ME, 2005, 'Child labour in the Bangladeshi garment industry', *International Affairs*, 81(3), pp 559–80.

Nocera, J, 2006, 'The board wore chicken suits', *New York Times*, 27 May, pp B1–B2.

Nozick, R, 1974, *Anarchy, State, and Utopia*, New York, NY: Basic Books.

Nussbaum, MC and Sen, AK, 1993, *The Quality of Life*, Oxford: Clarendon Press/Oxford University Press.

Odell, AM, 2007, 'Principles for responsible investment quadruples assets in first year', *Social Funds*, 1 June, online at **www.socialfunds.com**.

O'Dwyer, B and Owen, DL, 2005, 'Assurance statement practice in environmental, social and sustainability reporting: a critical evaluation', *British Accounting Review*, 37(2), pp 205–29.

Okali, C, 1983, *Cocoa and Kinship in Ghana: The Matrilineal Akan of Ghana*, London and Boston, MA: Kegan Paul International for the International African Institute.

Olsen, L, 2004, *Making Corporate Responsibility Work: Lessons from Real Business*, Ashridge: Ashridge Centre for Business and Society and the British Quality Forum.

O'Reilly, M, 2005, *Costing the Earth: The Kenya Flower Trade*, BBC Radio 4, 28 July, online at **www.bbc.co.uk**.

Organisation for Economic Co-operation and Development, 1999, *Principles of Corporate Governance*, Paris: OECD.

Orlitzky, M, Schmidt, FL and Rynes, SL, 2003, 'Corporate social and financial performance: a meta-analysis', *Organization Studies*, 24(3), pp 403–41.

O'Rourke, D, 2003, 'Outsourcing regulation: non-governmental systems of labor standards and monitoring', *Policy Studies Journal*, 31(1), pp 1–29.

O'Rourke, KH and Williamson, JG, 1999, *Globalization and History: The Evolution of a Nineteenth-Century Atlantic Economy*, Cambridge, MA: MIT Press.

Orr, D, 2005, ' "The triumph of neo-liberalism" but will it really make poverty history? What the campaign shows is how the political landscape has altered', *Independent (London)*, 25 June, p 14.

Owen, D, 2003, *Recent Developments in European Social and Environmental Reporting and Auditing Practice: A Critical Evaluation and Tentative Prognosis*, ICCSR Research Paper Series, Nottingham: University of Nottingham.

Owen, DL, Swift, TA, Humphrey, C and Bowerman, M, 2000, 'The new social audits: accountability, managerial capture or the agenda of social champions?', *European Accounting Review*, 9(1), pp 81–98.

Owen, D, Swift, TA and Hunt, K, 2001, 'Questioning the role of stakeholder engagement in social and ethical accounting, auditing and reporting', *Accounting Forum*, 25(3), pp 264–82.

Oxfam, 2005, *Rigged Rules and Double Standards: Trade, Globalisation and Poverty*, Oxford: Oxfam.

Paine, L, Deshpande, R, Margolis, JD and Bettcher, KE, 2005, 'Up to code: does your company's conduct meet world-class standards?', *Harvard Business Review*, 83(12), pp 122–33, 154.

Palazzo, G and Richter, U, 2005, 'CSR business as usual? The case of the tobacco industry', *Journal of Business Ethics*, 61(4), pp 387–401.

Parker, LD, 1986, 'Polemical themes in social accounting: a scenario for standard setting', *Advances in Public Interest Accounting*, 1, pp 67–93.

Parket, R and Eilbirt, H, 1975, 'Social responsibility: the underlying factors', *Business Horizons*, 18(4), pp 5–10.

Parkin, S, 2001, 'Thirst for justice', *The Guardian*, 11 July, p 8.

Pearce, F, 2005, 'Climate change: menace or myth?', *New Scientist*, 12 February, online at www.newscientist.com.

Pedersen, ER, 2005, 'Guiding the invisible hand: the role of development agencies in driving corporate citizenship', *Journal of Corporate Citizenship*, Winter (12), pp 43–57.

Pedersen, ER, 2006, 'Making corporate social responsibility (CSR) operable: how companies translate stakeholder dialogue into practice', *Business and Society Review*, 111(2), pp 137–63.

Pedersen, ER and Huniche, M (eds), 2006, *Corporate Citizenship in Developing Countries: New Partnership Perspectives*, Copenhagen: Copenhagen Business School Press.

Perkins, R, 2004, 'Sweeter partnerships? An NGO's engagement with the sugar sector', *Partnership Matters*, 2, pp 33–5.

Peters, G, 1999, *Waltzing with the Raptors: A Practical Roadmap to Protecting Your Company's Reputation*, New York, NY: John Wiley and Sons.

Phillips, R, 2003, *Stakeholder Theory and Organizational Ethics*, San Francisco, CA: Berrett-Koehler.

Phillips, R and Caldwell, CB, 2005, 'Value chain responsibility: a farewell to arm's length', *Business and Society Review*, 110(4), pp 345–70.

Phillips, R, Freeman, RE and Wicks, AC, 2003, 'What stakeholder theory is not', *Business Ethics Quarterly*, 13(4), pp 479–502.

Phylmar Group, 2006, *Phylmar eNews*, February, online at www.phlymar.com.

Pio, E, 2005, 'Eastern karma: perspectives on corporate citizenship', *Journal of Corporate Citizenship*, July (19), pp 65–78.

Plender, J, 2003, *Going Off the Rails: Global Capital and the Crisis of Legitimacy*, Chichester: John Wiley and Sons.

Polanyi, K, 1944, *The Great Transformation*, New York, NY: Farrar and Rinehart.

Pomerantz, M, 2003, 'The business of social entrepreneurship in a "down economy"', *Business Emmaus*, 25(2), p 25.

Porritt, J, 2005, *Capitalism: As If the World Matters*, London: Earthscan.

Porter, ME and Kramer, MR, 2002, 'The competitive advantage of corporate philanthropy', *Harvard Business Review*, 80(12), pp 56–68.

Porter, ME and Kramer, MR, 2006, 'Strategy and society: the link between competitive advantage and corporate social responsibility', *Harvard Business Review*, 84(12), pp 78–92.

Porter, ME and Van Der Linde, C, 1995, 'Green and competitive: ending the stalemate', *Harvard Business Review*, 73(5), pp 120, 134.

Post, JE and Altman, BW, 1992, 'Models of corporate greening: how corporate social policy and organizational learning inform leading-edge environmental management', *Research in Corporate Social Performance and Policy*, 13, pp 3–29.

Post, JE, Preston, LE and Sauter-Sachs, S, 2002, *Redefining the Corporation : Stakeholder Management and Organizational Wealth*, Stanford, CA: Stanford Business Books.

Prahalad, CK, 2005, *The Fortune at the Bottom of the Pyramid*, Upper Saddle River, NJ: Wharton School Publishing.

Prahalad, CK and Hart, SL, 2002, 'The fortune at the bottom of the pyramid', *Strategy and Business*, 26(1), pp 2–14.

Prakash, S, 2006, *Conflicted Safety Panel Let Vioxx Study Continue*, Washington DC: National Public Radio.

Preston, LE and O'Bannon, DP, 1997, 'The corporate social-financial performance relationship: a typology and analysis', *Business and Society*, 36(4), pp 419–28.

Preston, LE and Post, JE, 1975, *Private Management and Public Policy: The Principle of Public Responsibility*, Englewood Cliffs, NJ: Prentice Hall.

Preston, LE and Sapienza, HJ, 1990, 'Stakeholder management and corporate performance', *Journal of Behavioral Economics*, 19(4), pp 361–75.

PricewaterhouseCoopers, 2006, *Corporate Responsibility: Strategy, Management and Value*, London and New York, NY: PricewaterhouseCoopers.

Pr News, 2006, *Guide to Best Practices in Corporate Social Responsibility*, London: PR News.

Putnam, RD, 2000, *Bowling Alone: The Collapse and Revival of American Community*, New York, NY: Simon and Schuster.

Puxty, AG, 1986, 'Social accounting as immanent legitimation: a critique of a technicist ideology', *Advances in Public Interest Accounting*, V(1), pp 95–111.

Quinn, TK, 1962, *Unconscious Public Enemies*, New York, NY: Citadel Press.

Radin, TJ and Werhane, PH, 2003, 'Employment-at-will, employee rights, and future directions for employment', *Business Ethics Quarterly*, 13(2), pp 113–30.

Rajak, D, 2006, 'The gift of CSR: power and the pursuit of responsibility in the mining industry', in W Visser, M McIntosh and C Middleton (eds), *Corporate Citizenship in Africa: Lessons from the Past, Paths to the Future*, Sheffield: Greenleaf Publishing, ch 15.

Ramanathan, KV, 1976, 'Towards a theory of corporate social accounting', *The Accounting Review*, LI(3), pp 516–28.

Rangan, VK, Quelch, JA and Herrero, G, 2007, *Business Solutions for the Social Poor: Creating Social and Economic Value*, San Francisco, CA: Jossey-Bass.

Ranganathan, J, 1998, *Sustainability Rulers: Measuring Corporate, Social, Environmental and Social Performance*, Washington DC: World Resources Institute.

Rasche, A and Esser, DE, 2006, 'From stakeholder management to stakeholder accountability: applying Habermasian discourse ethics to accountability research', *Journal of Business Ethics*, 65(3), pp 251–67.

Rawls, J, 1971, *A Theory of Justice*, Cambridge, MA: Belknap Press.

Raynard, P and Forstater, M, 2002, *Corporate Social Responsibility: Implications for Small and Medium Sized Enterprises*, Vienna: United Nations Industrial Development Organization.

Rayner, J and Raven, W (eds), 2002, *Corporate Social Responsibility Monitor*, London: Gee and Co Ltd.

Raynolds, LT, Murray, D and Leigh Taylor, P, 2004, 'Fair trade: building producer capacity via global networks', *Journal of International Development*, 16(8), pp 1109–21.

Rembert, TC, 2005, 'CSR in the crosshairs: a broad counter-attack against corporate reform is growing. (Could that be a sign of progress?)', *Business Ethics*, Spring, pp 30–5.

Ricardo, D, 1817, *On the Principles of Political Economy, and Taxation*, London: J Murray.

Riesco, M, Lagos, G and Lima, M, 2005, *The 'Pay Your Taxes' Debate: Perspectives on Corporate Taxation and Social Responsibility in the Chilean Mining Industry*, Geneva: United Nations Research Institute for Social Development.

Ring, PS, Bigley, GA, D'Aunoo, T and Khanna, T, 2005, 'Perspectives on how governments matter', *Academy of Management Review*, 30(2), pp 308–20.

Roberts, J, 1991, 'The possibilities of accountability', *Accounting, Organizations and Society*, 16(4), pp 355–68.

Roberts, J and Scapens, R, 1985, 'Accounting Systems and Systems of Accountability: Understanding Accounting Practices in their Organisational Contexts', *Accounting, Organizations and Society*, 10(4), pp 443–56.

Roberts, RW, 1992, 'Determinants of corporate social responsibility disclosure: an application of stakeholder theory', *Accounting, Organizations and Society*, 17(6), pp 595–612.

Robertson, R, 1992, *Globalization: Social Theory and Global Culture*, London: Sage Publications.

Robins, N, 2006, *The Corporation that Changed the World: How the East India Company Shaped the Modern Multinational*, London: Pluto Press.

Roche, C, 1999, *Impact Assessment for Development Agencies, Learning to Value Change*, Oxford: Oxfam Novib.

Roddick, A, 2000, *Business as Unusual*, London: Thorsons.

Ronchi, L, 2002, *Impact of Fair Trade on Producers and their Organisations: A Case Study with Coocafe in Costa Rica*, Falmer: Poverty Research Unit, University of Sussex.

Rosenberg, J, 2000, *The Follies of Globalisation Theory: Polemical Essays*, London: Verso.

Rowley, TJ and Moldoveanu, M, 2003, 'When will stakeholder groups act? An interest- and identity-based model of stakeholder group mobilization', *The Academy of Management Review*, 28(2), pp 204–19.

Ruggie, JG, 2003, 'Taking embedded liberalism global: the corporate connection', in D Held and M Koenig-Archibugi (eds), *Taming Globalization: Frontiers of Governance*, Cambridge: Polity Press, pp 1–38.

Ruggie, JG, Wright, M and Lehr, A, 2006, *Business Recognition of Human Rights: Global Patterns, Regional and Sectoral Variations*, Geneva: United Nations Human Rights Commission.

Runciman, D, 2003, 'Partnering the state', *Partnership Matters*, (1), pp 12–15.

Runping, Y, 2006, 'Business starts taking social responsibility seriously', *China View*, 17 May, online at news.xinhuanet.com.

Rushe, D, 2007, 'Stern takes the heat on cost of saving the world', *New York Times*, 25 February, p 11.

Sabapathy, J, Swift, T, Weiser, J and Polycarpe, M, undated, *Innovation Through Partnership*, London: Accountability and Brody-Weiser-Burns.

Saha, P, 2006, 'Doing ethics the Tata way', *Ethical Corporation*, June, pp 26–8.

Salzmann, O, Ionescu-Somers, A and Steger, U, 2005, 'The business case for corporate sustainability: literature review and research options', *European Management Journal*, 23(1), pp 27–36.

Schafer, H, 2005, 'International corporate social responsibility rating systems: conceptual outline and empirical results', *Journal of Corporate Citizenship*, October (20), pp 107–20.

Schaltegger, S, Burritt, R and Petersen, H (eds), 2003, *An Introduction to Corporate Environmental Management: Striving for Sustainability*, Sheffield: Greenleaf Publishing.

Schirato, T and Webb, J, 2003, *Understanding Globalization*, London: Sage Publications.

Schmidheiny, S, 1992, *Changing Course: A Global Business Perspective on Development and the Environment*, Cambridge, MA: MIT Press.

Schmidheiny, S, 2006, 'A view of corporate citizenship in Latin America', *Journal of Corporate Citizenship*, January (21), pp 21–4.

Schmidheiny, S and Zorraquin, F, 1996, *Financing Change: The Financial Community, Eco-Efficiency, and Sustainable Development*, Cambridge, MA: MIT Press.

Scholte, JA, 2000, *Globalization: A Critical Introduction*, New York, NY: St Martin's Press.

Schröder, M, 2005, *Is There a Difference? The Performance Characteristics of SRI Equity Indexes*, Working paper, Mannheim: Centre for European Economic Research (ZEW).

Schuler, DA and Cording, M, 2006, 'A corporate social performance–corporate financial performance behavioral model for consumers', *The Academy of Management Review*, 31(3), pp 540–58.

Schwartz, MS and Carroll, AB, 2003, 'Corporate social responsibility: a three domain approach', *Business Ethics Quarterly*, 13(4), pp 503–30.

Schwartz, P and Gibb, B, 1999, *When Good Companies Do Bad Things: Responsibility and Risk in an Age of Globalization*, New York, NY: John Wiley and Sons.

Scoones, I and University of Sussex Institute of Development Studies, 1998, *Sustainable Rural Livelihoods: A Framework for Analysis*, Brighton: Institute of Development Studies.

Scott, M, 2006, 'Bottom line is more than making a profit responsible investing', *Financial Times*, 9 October, p 8.

Segrado, C, 2005, *Islamic Microfinance and Socially Responsible Investments*, Microfinance at the University of Torino case study, MEDA Project.

Seidler, LJ and Seidler, LL (eds), 1975, *Social Accounting: Theory, Issues and Cases*, Los Angeles, CA: Melville Publishing.

Sethi, SP, 1975, 'Dimensions of corporate social performance: an analytical framework', *California Management Review*, 17(3), pp 58–65.

Sethi, SP, 2003, *Setting Global Standards: Guidelines for Creating Codes of Conduct in Multinational Corporations*, Hoboken, NJ: John Wiley and Sons.

Sewing, T, 2006, 'Mired in the regulation debate', *Ethical Corporation*, January, pp 13–14.

Seyfang, G, 1999, *Private Sector Self-Regulation for Social Responsibility: Mapping Codes of Conduct*, Norwich: University of East Anglia.

Shearman and Sterling, 2005, *Trends in the Corporate Governance Practices of the 100 Largest US Public Companies*, online at www.shearman.com.

Shleifer, A and Vishney, RW, 1997, 'A survey of corporate governance', *Journal of Finance*, 52(2), pp 737–83.

Sklair, L, 2002, *Globalization: Capitalism and its Alternatives*, Oxford: Oxford University Press.

Smith, A, 1759, *The Theory of Moral Sentiments*, London: A Millar.

Smith, A, 1776, *An Inquiry into the Nature and Causes of the Wealth of Nations*, Dublin: Whitestone.

Smith, C, 1994, 'The new corporate philanthropy', *Harvard Business Review*, 72(3), pp 105–116.

Smith, NC, 2003a, 'Corporate social responsibility: whether or how?', *California Management Review*, 45(14), pp. 52–76.

Smith, R and Carlton, J, 2007, 'Environmentalist groups feud over terms of the TXU buyout', *Wall Street Journal*, 3 March, p A1.

Smith, SR, 2003b, *Audit Committees Combined Code Guidance*, London: Financial Reporting Council.

Social Investment Forum, 2001, *2001 Report on Socially Responsible Investing Trends in the United States*, Washington, DC: Social Investment Forum.

Social Investment Forum, 2003, *Trends Report*, Press release, 4 December, online at www.socialinvest.org.

Social Investment Forum, 2006, *2005 Report on Socially Responsible Investing Trends in the United States*, Washington, DC: Social Investment Forum.

Solomon, J, 2007, *Corporate Governance and Accountability*, Chichester: John Wiley and Son.

Sorell, T and Hendry, J, 1994, *Business Ethics*, Oxford: Butterworth-Heinemann.

Soros, G, undated, *Towards a Global Society*, online at www.geocities.com/ecocorner, accessed 22 July 2005.

Špilda, V, 2006, 'Corporate social responsibility: the European perspective', *Ethical Corporation*, April, p 14.

Stacey, J, 2003, 'A global partnership with a mining multinational: exploring and realising the capacity for strategic biodiversity conservation', *Partnership Matters*, 1, pp 25–9.

Starbuck, WH, 2005, 'Four great conflicts of the twenty-first century', in CL Cooper (ed), *Leadership and Management in the Twenty-First Century*, Oxford: Oxford University Press, pp 21–55.

Statman, M, 2000, 'Socially responsible mutual fund', *Financial Analysts Journal*, 56(3), pp 30–9.

Steger, MB, 2003, *Globalization: A Very Short Introduction*, Oxford: Oxford University Press.

Steger, U, 2004, *The Business of Sustainability: Building Industry Cases for Corporate Sustainability*, Basingstoke: Palgrave Macmillan.

Stern, N, 2007, *Stern Review on the Economics of Climate Change*, London: HM Treasury.

Stern, S, 2006, 'Corporate responsibility and the curse of the three-letter acronym', *Financial Times*, 30 May, online at www.ft.com.

Sterngold, J, 1993, 'Japanese companies rebuff mighty US pension funds', *New York Times*, 30 June, p D1.

Stewart, TA and Immelt, J, 2006, 'Growth as a process', *Harvard Business Review*, June, pp 60–70.

Stiglitz, JE, 2002, *Globalization and its Discontents*, New York, NY: WW Norton.

Stiglitz, JE, 2005, *Fair Trade For All: How Trade Can Promote Development*, Oxford: Oxford University Press.

Stopford, JM, Strange, S and Henley, JS, 1991, *Rival States, Rival Firms: Competition For World Market Shares*, Cambridge: Cambridge University Press.

Strathern, M (ed), 2000, *Audit Cultures, Anthropological Studies in Accountability, Ethics and the Academy*, London: Routledge.

Sullivan, R, 2003, *Business and Human Rights: Dilemmas and Solutions*, Sheffield: Greenleaf Publishing.

Sumner, J (ed), 2005, *How to Structure the Corporate Responsibility Function*, London: Melcrum Publishing.

Suranyi, M, 2000, *Blind to Sustainability: Stock Markets and the Environment*, London: Forum for the Future.

Sustainability, 2004, *Gearing Up: From Corporate Responsibility to Good Governance and Scalable Solutions*, London: SustainAbility.

Sustainability, undated, *Developing Value 2: In Search of Emerging Markets Excellence*, Press release, online at www.sustainability.com, accessed 1 November 2006.

Sustainability and United Nations Environment Programme, 2001, *Buried Treasure: Uncovering the Business Case for Corporate Sustainability*, London: SustainAbility/United Nations Environment Programme.

Sustainability and United Nations Environment Programme, 2002, *Trust Us: The Global Reporters 2002 Survey of Corporate Sustainability Reporting*, London: SustainAbility/United Nations Environment Programme.

Sustainability, International Finance Corporation and Ethos Institute, 2002, *Developing Value: The Business Case for Sustainability in Emerging Markets*, London: SustainAbility/International Finance Corporation/Ethos.

Sutcliffe, H, 2005, 'Finding the CR structure that fits your organization', in J Sumner (ed) *How to Structure the Corporate Responsibility Function*, London: Melcrum Publishing, pp 6–10.

Svendsen, A and Laberge, M, 2005, 'Convening stakeholder networks: a new way of thinking, being and engaging', *Journal of Corporate Citizenship*, July (19), pp 91–104.

Talmon, JL, 1985, *The Origins of Totalitarian Democracy*, London: Harper Collins.

Teoh, SH, Welch, I and Wazzah, CP, 1995, *The Effect on Socially Activist Investment Policies on the Financial Markets: Evidence from South African Boycott*, Working paper 222, London: London Business School Institute of Finance and Accounting.

Tharoor, S, 2001, 'Are human rights universal?', *New Internationalist*, (332), pp 34–5.

Thompson, EP, 1963, *The Making of the English Working Class*, London: Victor Gollancz.

Thornber, K, 2000, *Impacts of Certification on Forests, Stakeholders and Markets: Case Study—Bainings Ecoforestry Project*, London: IIED.

Tilley, F and Parrish, BD, 2006, 'From poles to wholes: facilitating an integrated approach to sustainable entrepreneurship', *World Review of Entrepreneurship, Management and Sustainable Development*, 2(4), pp 281–94.

Tinker, T, 1985, *Paper Prophets: A Social Critique of Accounting*, New York, NY: Praeger.

Tobin, R, 1997, 'Encouraging signs: is the corporate world developing a social vision?', *Catholic Health Association of Canada Review*, 25(1), pp 19–21.

Tolba, M and El-Kholy, A, 1992, *The World Environment 1972–1992: Two Decades of Challenge*, London: Chapman and Hall.

Traidcraft, 2005, *Traidcraft Social Accounts 2004–2005*, Gateshead: Traidcraft.

Tricker, RI, 1983, 'Corporate responsibility, institutional governance and the role of accounting standards', in M Bromwich and AG Hopwood (eds), *Accounting Standards Setting: An International Perspective*, London: Pitman, pp 27–41.

Tropenbos Foundation, 1997, *Hierarchical Framework for the Formulation of Sustainable Forest Management Standards: Principles, Criteria and Indicators*, Leiden: Tropenbos Foundation.

Trotman, KT and Bradley, GW, 1981, 'Associations between social responsibility disclosure and characteristics of companies', *Accounting, Organizations and Society*, 6(4), pp 355–62.

Tucker, R, 2006, 'The next level of corporate responsibility', *Women's Wear Daily*, 16 May, online at www.wwd.com.

Tully, S (ed), 2005, *Research Handbook on Corporate Legal Responsibility*, Cheltenham: Edward Elgar.

Turnbull, N, 1999, *Internal Control: Guidance for Directors on the Combined Code*, London: ICAEW.

UK Government and European Commission, 2005, *Investing in the Future: A European Conference on Corporate Social Responsibility and the Finance Sector*, 1–2 December, reports online at www.csr.gov.uk.

Ullmann, AE, 1985, 'Data in search of a theory: a critical examination of the relationship among social performance, social disclosure and economic performance of US firms', *Academy of Management Review*, 10(3), pp 540–57.

Unerman, J, 2003, 'Enhancing organizational global hegemony with narrative accounting disclosures: an early example', *Accounting Forum*, 27(4), pp 425–48.

Unilever, 2005, *Environmental Report 2004*, London: Unilever.

United Nations, 2003, *Water for People, Water for Life: World Water Development Report*, New York, NY: United Nations.

United Nations, 2005, *Business UNusual*, New York, NY: United Nations.

United Nations Environment Programme, 1987, *Environmental Perspectives to the Year 2000 and Beyond*, Nairobi: UNEP.

United Nations Environment Programme, Accountability and Stakeholder Research Associates, 2005, *Stakeholder Engagement Manual—From Words to Action: Vol 1—The Guide to Practitioners' Perspectives on Stakeholder Engagement*, New York, NY: United Nations Environmental Programme, Accountability and Stakeholder Research Associates.

United Nations Environment Programme, Sustainability and Standard And Poors, 2006, *Tomorrow's Value: The Global Reporters 2006 Survey of Corporate Sustainability Reporting*, London: SustainAbility.

United Nations Environment Programme Finance Initiative, Asset Management Working Group and UK Social Investment Forum, 2007, *Responsible Investment in Focus: How Leading Public Pension Funds are Meeting the Challenge*, online at www.uksif.org.

Uphoff, NT, 1996, *Learning from Gal Oya: Possibilities for Participatory Development and Post-Newtonian Social Science*, London: IT Publications.

Utting, P, 2005a, *Beyond Social Auditing: Micro and Macro Perspectives*, Geneva: UNRISD.

Utting, P, 2005b, *Rethinking Business Regulation: From Self-Regulation to Social Control*, Technology, Business and Society programme paper no 3, Geneva: United Nations Research Institute for Social Development.

Utting, P and Zammit, A, 2006, *Beyond Pragmatism: Appraising UN-Business Partnerships*, Market, Business and Regulation paper no 1. Geneva: United Nations Research Institute for Social Development.

Vallely, P, 2007, 'Does the RED campaign help big Western brands more than Africa? The big question', *The Independent*, 9 March, p 50.

Van Der Veer, J, 2007, 'States should create a climate for change', *Financial Times*, 23 January, p 15.

Van Tulder, R, 2006, *International Business-Society Management: Linking Corporate Responsibility and Globalization*, London: Routledge.

Varley, P, Mathiasen, C and Voorhes, M, 1998, *The Sweatshop Quandary: Corporate Responsibility on the Global Frontier*, Washington, DC: Investor Responsibility Research Center.

Veblen, TB, 1904, *The Theory of Business Enterprise*, New York, NY: Charles Scribner's Sons.

Veitch, M, 2006, 'Going green will keep firms in the pink', *IT Week*, 12 July, online at www.itweek.co.uk.

Vigar, D, 2006, *From Challenge to Opportunity: The Role of Business in Tomorrow's Society*, Geneva: WBCSD.

Virilio, P, 2000, *The Information Bomb*, New York, NY: Verso.

Visser, W, 2006, 'Revisiting Carroll's pyramid: an African perspective', in ER Pedersen and M Huniche (eds), *Corporate Citizenship in Developing Countries*, Copenhagen: Copenhagen Centre, pp 29–56.

Visser, W, McIntosh, M and Middleton, C (eds), 2006, *Corporate Citizenship in Africa: Lessons from the Past; Paths to the Future*, Sheffield: Greenleaf Publishing.

Vogel, D, 2005, *The Market for Virtue: The Potential and Limits of Corporate Social Responsibility*, Washington, DC: Brookings Institution Press.

Vyvyan, V, NG, C and Brimble, M, 2007, 'Socially responsible investing: the green attitudes and grey choices of Australian investors'. *Corporate Governance*, 15(2), pp 370–81.

Wackernagel, M, Rees, WE and Testemale, P, 1996, *Our Ecological Footprint: Reducing Human Impact on the Earth*, Gabriola Island, BC: New Society Publishers.

Waddock, S, 2001, 'Integrity and mindfulness: foundations of corporate citizenship', *Journal of Corporate Citizenship*, January (1), pp 25–37.

Waddock, S, 2007, 'Corporate citizenship: the dark-side paradoxes of success', in SK May, G Cheney and J Roper (eds), *The Debate Over Corporate Responsibility*, New York, NY: Oxford University Press, forthcoming.

Waddock, SA and Graves, SB, 1997, 'The corporate social performance–financial performance link', *Strategic Management Journal*, 18(4), pp 303–19.

Walker, RBJ, 1994, 'Social movements/world politics', *Millennium: Journal of International Studies*, 23(3), pp 669–700.

Wall Street Journal, 2005, 'Corporate social concerns: are they good citizenship or a rip-off for investors' *Wall Street Journal*, 6 December, p R6.

Wallerstein, IM, 1978, *The Capitalist World-Economy: Essays*, Cambridge: Cambridge University Press.

Walsh, JP, 2005, 'Book review essay: taking stock of stakeholder management', *Academy of Management Review*, 30(2), pp 426–52.

Ward, H, 2003, *Legal Issues in Corporate Citizenship*, London: International Institute for Environment and Development.

Ward, H and Smith, C, 2006, 'Business as usual is not the answer to society's problems', *Financial Times*, 19 October, p 17.

Warner, M, 2003, 'Getting started', in M Warner and R Sullivan (eds), *Putting Partnerships to Work*, Sheffield: Greenleaf Publishing, pp 166–81.

Warner, M and Sullivan, R (eds), 2003, *Putting Partnerships to Work*, Sheffield: Greenleaf Publishing.

War on Want, 2005, *Caterpillar: The Alternative Report*, London: War on Want.

Wartick, SL and Cochran, PL, 1985, 'The evolution of the corporate social performance model', *Academy of Management Review*, 10(4), pp 758–69.

Waters, M, 2001, *Globalization*, 2nd edn. London and New York, NY: Routledge.

Weber, M, Parsons, T and Giddens, A, 1992, *The Protestant Ethic and the Spirit of Capitalism*, London and New York, NY: Routledge.

Weiser, J, Kahane, M, Rochlin, S and Landis, J, 2006, *Untapped: Creating Value in Underserved Markets*, San Francisco, CA: Berrett-Koehler.

Weiser, J and Rochlin, S, 2004, 'Walking in order to run: practical challenges in measuring community and economic development', *AccountAbility Forum*, 1(1), pp 26–32.

Weiser, J and Zadek, S, 2000, *Conversations With Disbelievers: Persuading Companies to Address Social Challenges*, New York, NY: BrodyWeiser.

Welford, R, 1995, *Environmental Strategy and Sustainable Development: The Corporate Challenge for the 21st Century*, London: Routledge.

Werther, WB and Chandler, D, 2006, *Strategic Corporate Social Responsibility: Stakeholders in a Global Environment*, Thousand Oaks, CA: Sage.

Wettstein, F, 2005, 'For causality to capability: toward a new understanding of the multinational corporation's enlarged social responsibilities', *Journal of Corporate Citizenship*, July (19), pp 105–17.

White, A, 2005, *Fade, Integrate or Transform? The Future of CSR*, San Francisco, CA: Business for Social Responsibility.

White, C, 2006, 'The spirit of disobedience', *Harpers Magazine*, April, pp 31–40.

Wiesmann, G and Simensen, I, 2007, 'German blue chips ponder switch to SE format', *Financial Times*, 12 April, p 24.

Wijnbeerg, N, 2000, 'Normative stakeholder theory and Aristotle: the link between ethics and politics', *Journal of Business Ethics*, 25(4), pp 329–42.

Willard, B, 2002, *The Sustainability Advantage: Seven Business Case Benefits of a Triple Bottom Line*, Gabriola Island, BC: New Society.

Willett, C and Page, M, 1996, 'A survey of time budget pressure and irregular auditing. practices among newly qualified UK chartered accountants', *The British Accounting Review*, 28(2), pp 101–20.

Williams, OF, 2004, 'The UN Global Compact: the challenge and the promise', *Business Ethics Quarterly*, 14(4), pp 755–74.

Windsor, D, 2001, 'Corporate citizenship: evolution and interpretation', in J Andriof and M McIntosh (eds), *Perspectives on Corporate Citizenship*, Sheffield: Greenleaf Publishing, pp 39–52.

Woidtke, T, Bierman, L and Tuggle, C, 2003, 'Reining in activist funds', *Harvard Business Review*, 81(3), pp 22–3.

Wolf, M, 2004, *Why Globalization Works*, New Haven, CT: Yale University Press.

Wood, D, 2000, 'Theory and integrity in business and society', *Business and Society*, 39(4), pp 359–78.

Wood, DJ and Logsdon, JM, 2001, 'Theorising business citizenship', in J Andriof and M McIntosh (eds), *Perspectives on Corporate Citizenship*, Sheffield: Greenleaf Publishing, pp 83–103.

Wood, DJ and Logsdon, JM, 2002, 'Business citizenship: from individuals to organizations', in RE Freeman and S Venkataraman (eds), *Ethics and Entrepreneurship*, Charlottesville, VA: Society for Business Ethics, pp 59–94.

Wood, DJ, Logsdon, JM, Lewellyn, PG and Davenport, PG, 2006, *Global Business Citizenship: A Transformative Framework for Ethics and Sustainable Capitalism*, Armonk, NY: ME Sharpe Inc.

World Bank, 2003, *Strengthening Implementation of Corporate Social Responsibility in Global Supply Chains*, Washington DC: World Bank Corporate Social Responsibility Practice.

World Bank, 2005, *World Development Report 2005: Better Investment Climate for Everyone*, Washington DC and Basingstoke: World Bank/Palgrave.

World Bank, 2006, *World Development Report 2006: Equity and Development*, Washington DC and Basingstoke: World Bank/Palgrave.

World Business Council for Sustainable Development, 2006, *From Challenge to Opportunity: The Role of Business in Tomorrow's Society*, Geneva: World Business Council for Sustainable Development.

World Commission on Environment and Development, 1987, *Our Common Future*, Oxford: Oxford University Press.

World Development Movement, War on Want, National Union of Students and Friends of the Earth, 2005, *2005 and Sustainable Development*,

WDM, War on Want, NUS and Friends of the Earth briefing, London: WDM/War on Want/NUS/Friends of the Earth.

World Economic Forum, 2006, *Harnessing Private Sector Capabilities to Meet Public Needs: The Potential of Partnerships to Advance Progress on Hunger, Malaria and Basic Education*, Geneva: World Economic Forum.

World Meteorological Organization, 1979, *Extended Summaries of Papers Presented at the World Climate Conference*, Geneva.

World Wildlife Fund and Sustainabillity, 2005, *Influencing Power: Reviewing the Conduct and Content of Corporate Lobbying*, London: WWF/Sustainability.

Wright, C and Rwabizambuga, A, 2006, 'Institutional pressures, corporate reputation, and voluntary codes of conduct: an examination of the Equator principles', *Business and Society Review*, 111(1), pp 89.

Zadek, S, 2000, *Doing Good and Doing Well: Making the Business Case for Corporate Citizenship*, New York, NY: Conference Board.

Zadek, S, 2004, 'The path to corporate responsibility (best practice)', *Harvard Business Review*, 82(12), pp 125–33.

Zadek, S, Hojensgard, N and Raynard, P (eds), 2001, *Perspectives on the New Economy of Corporate Citizenship*, Copenhagen: The Copenhagen Centre.

Zadek, S, Raynard, P and Oliveira, C, 2005, *Responsible Competitiveness : Reshaping Global Markets Through Responsible Business Practices*, London: AccountAbility.

Zadek, S, Sabapathy, J, Dossing, H and Swift, T, 2003, *Responsible Competitiveness: Corporate Responsibility Clusters in Action*, London: AccountAbility.

■ NAME INDEX

■ SUBJECT INDEX